THE BLACK PANTHER PARTY

[RECONSIDERED]

THE BLACK PANTHER PARTY

[RECONSIDERED]

Edited by Charles E. Jones

BLACK CLASSIC PRESS
BALTIMORE

The Black Panther Party Reconsidered
A DuForcelf Book
Published by Black Classic Press 1998
© Charles E. Jones
Panther Art © Emory Douglas
All Rights Reserved.
Library of Congress Card Catalog Number: 96–84818
ISBN 0–933121–96–2

Cover design by Laurie Williams/A Street Called Straight

Founded in 1978, Black Classic Press specializes in bringing to light obscure and significant works by and about people of African descent. If our books are not available in your area, ask your local bookseller to order them. Our current list of titles can be obtained by writing:

Black Classic Press
c/o List
P.O. Box 13414
Baltimore, MD 21203

Visit our website: www.blackclassic.com
A Young Press With Some Very Old Ideas

This book is dedicated to the spirit and legacy of
The Black Panther Party.

Acknowledgments

All anthologies are the products of the collective efforts of many people. This volume is certainly no exception. First and foremost, all of the contributors of this volume are especially grateful to the members of the Black Panther Party for sharing their experiences with us. This book is dedicated to the legacy of the Black Panther Party. Our intent is to offer a critical, yet balanced, assessment of a much maligned African American protest organization.

I wish to extend my appreciation to the contributors for their openness to suggested revisions and diligent attention to the completion of their respective chapters. I am especially grateful to Floyd W. Hayes III, Judson L. Jeffries, and Ollie A. Johnson III for reading and critiquing the entire manuscript.

During the course of the past four years, Eric Bridges, my graduate assistant, provided invaluable research support. I am also indebted to the student assistants of the Department of African-American Studies at Georgia State University. Terrance Williams and Cecily Walker generously lent their technical expertise to this project. The adroit administrative skills of Belinda Futrell permitted me, as a chair of a new department, to give greater attention to this project than normally would be expected.

I am indebted to W. Paul Coates, director of Black Classic Press, for his encouragement, valuable insight, and vision in publishing this volume. I am also grateful to former Panther Minister of Culture, Emory Douglas for the Panther art which distinguishes this volume. I thank Apryl Motley, for her professionalism and dedication, which ensured the production of a quality manuscript, and Sarah Trembath, for providing invaluable production assistance. Jean Currie Church made valuable contributions while proofing, and did an excellent job creating our index. The fine copyediting of Ruby Essien also enhanced the manuscript in its early stages.

An African-American Research and Development grant sponsored by the Office of the Provost at Georgia State provided me with vital release time from teaching duties. The financial support of Cleon Arrington, Vice President of Research and Sponsored Programs at Georgia State is also greatly appreciated.

A special debt is owed to the members of the National Conference of Black Political Scientists and the Association for the Study of Afro-American Life and History for the intellectual exchange that undoubtedly improved many of the interpretations of this volume. I also wish to thank Anita Fellman for alerting me to the work of several contributors of this anthology. The critical eye of Gerald Bradley vastly improved several chapters in this volume.

Special thanks are extended to my parents, retired Sgt. Major Charles D. and Helen Jones for the values they instilled in me, which have guided my academic career. My heartfelt gratitude is reserved for Kimberly whose thoughtful feedback, critical assistance, and loving encouragement have sustained me throughout the completion of the manuscript.

Contents

Part III:
ORGANIZATIONAL DYNAMICS

Part IV:
GENDER DYNAMICS

Introduction

Reconsidering Panther History: The Untold Story

Charles E. Jones

During the late 1960s, the Black Panther Party (BPP) dominated public consciousness. In many cities across the nation, members of the BPP, in their uniform of a black beret, black pants, powder blue shirt, black shoes, and black leather jackets, organized the Black community for revolutionary change in America. The popular Party slogans "Power to the People" and "Off the Pigs" reverberated during the politically vibrant days of the turbulent sixties. On the street corners of the nation's major cities, a common fixture was the Party member hawking *The Black Panther*, the organization's newspaper. In the heart of Black communities with BPP affiliates, Panthers implemented numerous survival programs that fed, clothed, and provided medical services to community residents.

The Party's commitment to armed self-defense and revolutionary politics made it an inevitable target of government attention. Police–Panther gun battles became a defining feature of the early Panther experience. Indeed, in 1969, six Party members were killed by local police officers while another four Panthers died during organizational conflict between the BPP and Us, a southern California-based cultural Black nationalist organization.[1] Panther political rallies and legal mobilization campaigns were the order of the day. The Huey Newton trial (which led to the Free Huey movement) and the New Haven 14 and Panther 21 trials, as well as numerous other legal battles, captivated both the American and international public.

As a result of these and other highly charged events, the BPP was a mainstay of the national media and a frequent headline maker of both the mainstream and dissident press: "17 'Panthers' Arraigned in Sacramento Court: Invasion Cases Continued" (*San Francisco Examiner*); "Black Panthers Controlled by Communists, Senate Unit Says" (*Los Angeles Times*); "U.S. Troops Flown in for Panther Rally; New Haven Braces for Protest by 20,000" (*New York Times*); "Baltimore Police Raid Panther Headquarters" (*Guardian*).[2] After sixteen years of political activism in which the BPP endured pervasive political repression, crippling internal conflicts, the resignation of key leaders, and a battle-fatigued membership, the organization faded out of existence during the early 1980s. Thirty years after the founding of the BPP on October 15, 1966, the Panthers remain the subject of immense public attention.

Recent news events, cultural productions, memoirs, and the emergence of Pantheresque groups have rekindled interest in the BPP. One contributing factor to the continued interest in the BPP was the inglorious death of Huey P. Newton, the organization's cofounder and symbol. On August 12, 1989 on the streets of West Oakland, California, Newton was shot to death by Tyronne Robinson, a twenty-five-year-old street-level drug dealer. The murder of Newton attracted press coverage from the nation's leading newspapers, which featured news stories and obituaries on Newton's life, his leadership of the BPP, and his downward spiral of self-destructive behavior. The untimely death of the cofounder of the BPP provided the impetus for former Panthers to establish two newspapers that highlighted the history and writings of the organization. The Commemoration Committee for the Black Panther Party published the first edition of *The Commemorator* in November 1990. A monthly publication, the newspaper reprints key Party documents and provides a forum for progressive politics in the Oakland Bay area. In 1991, another ad hoc group of former Panthers published *The Black Panther: Black Community Service*, a quarterly paper distributed nationally by four regional committees. This newspaper also reprints important Party writings and provides analysis of contemporary political events primarily by former BPP members.[3]

Popular cultural productions referencing the BPP have also helped to rekindle interest in the organization, especially in the younger generation. In particular, the musical genre of rap/hip-hop "has become a conduit for African-American culture to [a] greater extent than even jazz."[4] This musical format, rap/hip-hop, serves as a nexus "between a relatively apolitical generation of the 1970's and 1980's with the staunch Black Nationalist African American subculture of the 1960's."[5] Cultural transmission of images about the BPP through the lyrics and music videos of rap artists offers an alternative and readily accessible source of knowledge for members of "Generation X." As early as 1988, the rap group Public Enemy made reference to the Black Panther Party in their lyrics. On two of their compact discs, *It Takes A Nation of Millions to Hold Us Back* and *Fear of a Black Planet*, several selections referenced the Black Panthers. For example, the song "Party For Your Right to Fight" describes the government's efforts to neutralize the Panthers:

> J. Edgar Hoover
> Coulda' prove to ya
> He had King and X
> Set up; also the Party with Newton
> Cleaver and Seale
> He ended.[6]

Moreover, a popular Panther Party slogan—"Power to the People"—served as the title of one of the tracks on *Fear of a Black Planet*. Tupac Shakur's particularly poignant music video "Dear Mama" includes flashes of the *New York Times* headlines of the arrest of his mother, Afeni Shakur, a member of the New York 21. Paris, the self-proclaimed "Black Panther of Rap," frequently incorporates symbols of the BPP in his recordings and included short biographies of Bobby Seale, Huey Newton, and Eldridge Cleaver on the liner notes of his *Devil Made Me Do It* compact disc. Hip-hop music magazines have also featured stories on the BPP. For example, in 1993, *Rap Pages* published a two-part series on the BPP and its imagery in the music genre. In 1995, Avatar Records capitalized on the popularity of the Panthers with the release "Pump Ya Fist: Hip Hop Inspired by the Black Panthers," a recording that featured several hip-hop artists.[7]

The recent wave of Panther memoirs has also increased public awareness of the BPP. Since 1989, four Party members have written autobiographies highlighting their respective experiences in the organization. The first of these was Earl Anthony's *Spitting in the Wind: The True Story Behind the Violent Legacy of the Black Panther Party*. Anthony, who joined the BPP in 1967 and later turned FBI informant, offered a largely uncorroborated exposé of alleged criminal activities committed by the organization. He writes that "over three hundred others [Panthers] were suspected of being police informants and killed by Panthers themselves" without providing any evidence to substantiate this allegation.[8]

Three other memoirs were authored by leaders of the BPP. Elaine Brown, who chaired the BPP from 1974 to 1977, recounts her life in *A Taste of Power: A Black Woman's Story,* while the former Chief of Staff, David Hilliard chronicled his life story in *This Side of Glory: The Autobiography of David Hilliard and the Story of the Black Panther Party*. In a candid assessment of Party dynamics, Brown offers insights into the gender issues and the undercurrent of violence pervading the organization, particularly during its later years. David Hilliard wrote an equally frank retrospective account of his participation in the BPP and his fight against drug and alcohol dependency. He describes the Party's role in the Panther–police shoot-out that led to the death of Bobby Hutton on April 6, 1968 in great detail. He also provides a poignant insight into the erratic and often punitive behavior of Huey Newton. William Brent, an early Panther recruit who held the rank of captain, documents his BPP experience in his autobiography *Long Time Gone: A Black Panther's True-Life Story of his Hijacking and Twenty-five Years in Cuba*. Although Brent shed important light on the relationship between Panther expatriates and the Castro-led Cuban government, his memoir reveals less about the BPP than do other biographies because of his relatively short stint (less than one year) in the organization.[9]

In the midst of this veritable explosion of Panther memoirs, several out-of-print books on the BPP have been reissued. In 1991, the Holloway House

Publishing Company reissued *Bitter Grain: The Story of the Black Panther Party*. Author Michael Newton (no relation to Huey Newton) gave one of the few, albeit limited, treatments of the BPP as a national organization in his investigation by moving beyond the singular focus on Oakland or government repression to explain the Panther phenomenon. While the author describes the Party activities outside of California, his examination is often cursory and superficial. For instance, in his analysis of Panther affiliates in southern states, Michael Newton relies on a single incident to assess BPP mobilization efforts. As a result, he fails to capture many important regional Party developments such as the Winston-Salem, North Carolina chapter's Joseph Waddell People's Free Ambulance Service.

Other reissued works include Gilbert Moore's *Rage,* which chronicles the 1968 murder trial of Huey P. Newton, who was accused of killing Officer John Frey. Writers and Readers Publishing, Inc. has reissued two important books by Huey Newton, his autobiography *Revolutionary Suicide* and his collection of Party writings *To Die For The People*. Finally, several classic works on the BPP have reappeared. Among these are Philip Foner's edited work *The Black Panthers Speak* and two Black Classic Press reissues, Bobby Seale's *Seize The Time: The Story of the Black Panther Party and Huey P. Newton,* which offers the most definitive treatment of the Party's early years (1966 to 1969), and George Jackson's revolutionary treatise *Blood In My Eye*.[10] Additional recent publications on the BPP include Hugh Pearson's ambitious, but flawed work *Shadow of the Panther,* which offers a biased journalistic account of the origins and demise of the BPP. Pearson's narrative details the corruption and erratic behavior of a drug dependent Newton, and he concludes that the Party was essentially an organization of street thugs. While the so-called dark side of the Party should not be dismissed or excused, unbalanced attention to this issue unfairly reduces the organization to a quasi-political underworld organization. Several mainstream African American popular magazines have also featured full-length stories on the Panthers. In its 1993 Black History Month issue, *Emerge* published a cover story article on the Panthers followed by a profile of the then-imprisoned Geronimo Pratt, a former leader of the southern California chapter of the BPP. The following year, *Essence,* a lifestyle magazine targeted at middle-class African American women, featured a story entitled "Panther Mania," which provides a historical synopsis of the organization.[11]

Theatrical productions and the feature-length movie Panther sparked renewed interest in the BPP. "Servant of the People: The Rise and Fall of Huey P. Newton and the Black Panther Party" by Oakland playwright Robert Alexander dramatized Newton's leadership and the eventual demise of the BPP. Staged by Atlanta-based Jomandi Productions and the St. Louis Black Repertory during the winter of 1995, this three-act play addressed the political repression of the Panthers, the organizational split, and Newton's unscrupulous behavior during the Party's later years. Although billed as a drama, the script was laced with gratuitous comedic one-liners and singing and dancing that seemed inappropriate for the subject matter. Kathleen Cleaver, the first woman to sit on the Party's Central Committee, wryly commented: "[It] makes fun of the way things were and exaggerates the level of confusion within the Party."[12] The one-man stage production "A Huey P. Newton Story" also debuted in 1995 at the Actor's Gang Theater in Los Angeles, California. Actor Roger Guenveur Smith wrote and performed in this production. His uncanny resemblance to Newton and his emulation of Newton's high vocal tonality and agitated mannerisms during the performance were haunting.

Panther, the movie, further broadened BPP sentiment among the African American mass public. Directed by Mario Van Peebles, the film's screenplay was adapted from a novel written by Mario's father, Melvin Van Peebles, who also wrote and directed "Sweet Sweetback's Baadasssss Song," a popular movie among Party leaders. *Panther* offers a partly fictionalized and uncritical account of the origins and the formative years of the BPP. African American public intellectual Michael Eric Dyson notes:

> Although *Panther* creatively joins fiction to fact, anyone familiar with the period can see the film is bold, revisionist history. The results are edifying and disturbing. The film accents some neglected truths while avoiding others, proving that cinematic imagination can be empowered or poorly served by selective memory.[13]

Despite glaring omission of the role of female Party members, internal organizational conflict, and the activism of Panther units outside of Oakland, the movie did stimulate a revival in public awareness of the BPP, particularly among the younger generation. However, the greatest liability of the film may have been its lack of commercial success, which could preclude several pending BPP movie projects from coming to fruition.[14]

The formation of Panther-like groups during the 1990s captured headlines and also triggered recollections about the political party founded by Huey Newton and Bobby Seale. Beginning in 1990 with the formation of the Black Panther Militia in Milwaukee, Wisconsin, the subsequent founding of the New Black Panther Party in Dallas, Texas, and the creation of the New African American Vanguard movement in Los Angeles, California, instantly provoked obvious comparisons between these Panther emulators and the Black Panther Party for Self-Defense. Black Panther Militia founder Michael McGee, a two-term council member and former BPP member, threatened violent reprisals against Milwaukee if economic development in the Black community did not occur by 1995. McGee declared that his militia offered a more radical form of the original Panthers. He drew his recruits from the city's gangs, "since," according to McGee, "they already know how to shoot, I'm going to give them a cause to die for."[15] Activities undertaken by the Black Panther Militia included community watch patrols, reminiscent of those implemented by the Nation of Islam, and an "Intercommunal Call to Arms Summit" held in Milwaukee during August 1991.

In 1991, Aaron Michaels, a talk show assistant, formed the New Black Panther Party in Dallas, Texas. The New Black Panther Party has sponsored breakfast programs at a city recreation center, donated food and furniture to community residents, and supported a membership of approximately 150 individuals. In addition, the group investigated African American church burnings in the state. During the summer of 1996, Michaels and two other members of the New Black Panther Party were arrested at a Dallas school board meeting. New Black Panther Party members threatened to attend the next board meeting armed, which caused an uproar in the city. An organizational news release, titled "Call For Black Men With Guns!" and published in the *Dallas Morning News* stated, "It was proven at the last board meeting that school security and the Dallas Police Department were not there to protect Black people. So Black people must be armed and ready to protect themselves."[16] However, unlike its predecessors, the New Black Panther Party failed to win the approval of Black community residents for this demonstration of armed self-defense.

In 1994, the New African American Vanguard Movement (NAAVM) appeared in Los Angeles, California. Three of the eight members of the Vanguard Leadership Council, the primary decision-making apparatus of the NAAVM, were members of the original Panther organization. Cofounder B. Kwaku Duren, attorney and former coordinator of the BPP southern California chapter, saw the NAAVM as a contemporary extension of the original Panther Party. Shareef Abdullah, the organization's Minister of Defense, stated that "because of the changes we viewed occurring over the past 30 years, we adopted a new revised Eight Point Platform and Program to address concrete conditions in our communities and to propose practical solutions to complex social problems."[17] Notwithstanding its revised platform, many of the activities of the NAAVM mirrored those previously implemented by the BPP some two decades earlier, including free food giveaways and the publication of an organizational newspaper.

In short, thirty years after the founding of the BPP, the organization still enjoys considerable popular attention. The passage of time has provided former Panthers an opportunity to benefit from a healing process to address the emotional toll of their participation in the BPP. Consequently, Party members are now more likely to share their organizational experiences. The renewed interest in the BPP has stimulated much needed and deserved attention to Panther politics. At a minimum the rediscovery of the Panthers has brought public awareness to an organization that Angela Davis maintains "radically transformed the Black liberation movement of the 1960's and early 1970's."[18] Ironically, the resurgence of interest in the Black Panther Party is in danger of contributing to a depreciation of the organization, since misconceptions about the Party remain largely unchallenged by the extant literature on the BPP. On the other hand, this new found attention directed toward the activities, dynamics, and legacy of the BPP provides an opportunity to begin the important process of reconsidering its history. This process is critically important in light of current interpretations that malign and minimize the role of the BPP in the African American liberation struggle.

BPP Literature: Vilified Revolutionaries

According to scholar–activist Manning Marable, "[B]y the late 1960's, the Black Panthers had become the most influential revolutionary nationalist organization in the U.S."[19] While its national influence began to subside after 1971, the organizational life span of the BPP lasted until 1982. Despite the Party's success as an African American organization committed to revolutionary change, the literature on the Panthers is beset with deficiencies. These shortcomings have resulted in the vilification of the BPP. Law enforcement officials, former White radicals, and Black social critics have all engaged in the demonization of the Black Panthers. At the forefront of the smear campaign against the BPP has been David Horowitz, a sixties student radical turned neoconservative in the 1980s. Through the auspices of the Center for the Study of Popular Culture, a right-wing California think tank, Horowitz vilifies the BPP. As coeditor (along with Peter Collier) of *Heterodoxy*, the Center's newsletter, Horowitz published a feature story on the Party titled "Black Murder Inc," which served as a response to the publication of Elaine Brown's autobiography *A Taste of Power*. Moreover, Horowitz also paid for a full-page ad in *Variety*, the trade magazine of the movie industry, condemning the film *Panther*. In their book *Destructive Generation: Second Thoughts About the Sixties*, Horowitz and Collier characterize the Panthers as a criminal gang. These negative assessments of the Panthers vastly undermine the historical significance of the BPP. Such efforts to denigrate the Panthers are part of a larger historiography that discredits leftist politics of the radical sixties. Nikhil Pal Singh critiques this antileftist bias in the emerging body of research on the sixties in chapter 2 of this volume.[20]

Furthermore, the BPP suffers from the dismissive attitude of scholars and activists. Its historical role in Black liberation activism in particular and leftist politics in general does not receive adequate attention. For example, the recently published *Encyclopedia of the American Left*, edited by Mari Jo Buhle et al., has only one entry on the Black Panther Party. None of the major Party leaders has biographical entries and the massive volume does not mention a single female member of the Party. The near invisibility of the Panthers also plagues several other scholarly accounts of the freedom struggle.[21]

Stanley Crouch, author and conservative African American social critic, refers to the BPP in the following manner:

> It is important to remember how this form of intimidation once worked for the so easily corrupted Black Panthers, a sixties' group of thugs with Marxist revolutionary pretensions who successfully cowed middle-class, well-educated North American Negroes like Angela Davis, who were caught up in the romance of Third World revolution and terrified of being prejudiced against their own kind.[22]

Kwame Ture (formerly known as Stokely Carmichael), veteran of the civil rights struggle and a former member of the BPP, argues that "many of them [Panthers] were not serious about struggling for the people. They were using the people's struggle to obtain positions of power."[23] Critics point to Eldridge Cleaver's retrogressive politics and Bobby Seale's promotion of his barbecue cookbook as examples of the political metamorphosis of the Panther leadership. In addition, the drug dependency of prominent leaders such as Newton, Hilliard, and Cleaver has been used by extension to denigrate the entire BPP organization. This disdain is also evident in a *New York Times* op-ed essay in which author Alice Walker alleges that the men in the Party were driven by the "charge of being a 'punk' that sends each and every one of these warriors into conniptions."[24] In actuality, what drove the men and the women in the BPP was a profound sense of commitment to improving the lives of Black and other oppressed people. It was this commitment that undergirded the activism for which some members ultimately lost their lives and others remain incarcerated.

Prior research on the BPP is often riddled with inaccuracies. Historian and scholar Sean Cashman comments in *African Americans and the Quest for Civil Rights, 1900–1990* that the BPP, "later led by Ron Karenga," comprised "a self-proclaimed revolutionary black nationalist movement dedicated to African American self-defense."[25] Similarly, another account of the Party, states:

> The Black Panther Party proved to be a conspirator in its death. There were too many cooks. There were the clashing philosophies of Newton, Seale, Eldridge Cleaver and Ron Karenga that roiled for years.[26]

Observers with even a minimal knowledge of Black Power Era politics know that Karenga headed Us, the southern California-based cultural Black nationalist organization and bitter rival of the Party.

Other accounts inaccurately identify Watts rather than Oakland, California, as the birthplace of the BPP. Similarly, literature written about the BPP frequently misidentifies Party leaders and their organizational positions. Eldridge Cleaver is identified as the Minister of Culture instead of the Minister of Information, while Emory Douglas, the renowned revolutionary artist and the Party's Minister of Culture, is referred to as Emory Dawson. One author cites Huey Newton, rather than Bobby Seale, as the Party's mayoral candidate in the 1974 Oakland municipal election, and another scholar mistakenly claims Denzil Dowell was the first BPP member killed by police, rather than Bobby Hutton, who was shot to death on April 6, 1968 in the aftermath of a Panther–police gun battle.[27] While these factual errors are minor, they nonetheless hinder the proper documentation of the Panther experience. Such glaring inaccuracies are symptomatic of the carelessness that characterizes much of the current literature on the BPP.

Previous Panther research is also hampered by a limited time frame. Most studies on the BPP only extend to 1971, which is well short of the 1982 date marking the official demise of the organization. Even many of the classic works on the BPP, for example Bobby Seale's *Seize the Time,* Gene Marine's *The Black Panthers,* and Reginald Major's *A Panther Is a Black Cat*—all originally published in the late sixties—do not examine Party activities beyond 1971. Contemporary research on the Party continues with this focus of analysis, as is evident in Kit Kim Holder's excellent dissertation on the history of the BPP. This time frame, 1966–71, receives greater attention because many observers maintain that by 1971 the "Panthers were finished as an effective or influential force."[28] During that year the BPP experienced major internal conflict resulting in an organizational split. The Party began to stress survival programs over its earlier military emphasis, which led many to conclude prematurely that the Black Panther Party ceased to exist. Consequently, the narrow time frame becomes problematic in that it ignores several important organizational developments, events, and activities that occurred after 1971; thereby limiting the public's knowledge and understanding of the history of the BPP. Post-1971 developments include the Party's strategic decision to reconsolidate the Party's influence in Oakland (1973), the Seale–Brown electoral campaigns (1973), the leadership of Elaine Brown (1974–77), and the destructive behavior of Huey Newton (1977–82).

Symptomatic of the paucity of longitudinal analyses of the Party are the many accounts that merely focus on a particular event usually stemming from an act of political repression. For example, five manuscripts have been published on the New York 21 incident, while Donald Freed's *Agony in New Haven: The Trial of Bobby Seale, Ericka Huggins and the Black Panther Party* documents the case of the New Haven 14, in which members of the New Haven branch along with Bobby Seale were charged with the murder of an alleged police informant named Alex Rackley. Similarly, Roy Wilkins, the former executive director of the NAACP, and Ramsey Clark, attorney general in the Johnson administration, in *Search and Destroy: A Report by the Commission of Inquiry into the Black Panthers and the Police,* investigated the death of Mark Clark and Fred Hampton during the infamous December 4, 1969 raid of the Chicago branch of the BPP.[29] Recent exceptions to this pattern of ignoring post-1971 developments include *A Taste of Power,* Elaine Brown's memoir, which describes Party affairs until her resignation in 1977, and *Panther: A Pictorial History of the Black Panthers and the Story Behind the Film.* The book *Panther*, coauthored by Mario Van

Peebles, Ula Y. Taylor, and J. Tarika Lewis, provides the only historical account of the BPP from its inception in 1966 to the demise of the organization in 1982.[30]

Until recently, a distinct bias toward the leadership of the BPP characterized much of the literature. Panther autobiographies and biographies disproportionately account for much of our knowledge about the Party. By contrast, little is known about the Party experience of rank-and-file members. Panther memoirs are primarily based on the lives and experiences of national Party leaders while the role and contributions of local Panther leaders are virtually unknown to the larger public. Memoirs by the leadership triumvirate of the BPP—Newton, Seale, and Cleaver—underscore this pattern. Newton's *Revolutionary Suicide*, Seale's *Seize the Time,* and Cleaver's *Soul on Ice* comprise part of the canon of BPP literature by Party members. Other works by BPP leaders include the two first-hand accounts by Earl Anthony, *Picking Up the Gun* and *Spitting in the Wind*. Three recently published autobiographies, *This Side of Glory* and *A Taste of Power,* written respectively by David Hilliard and Elaine Brown, along with William Brent's *A Long Time Gone* round off the current crop of autobiographical material by Panthers.[31]

Unquestionably, the experiences of Panther leaders offer vital insight into Party dynamics. However, the day-to-day activities, observations, and assessments of the multitude of rank-and-file members—the foot soldiers of the BPP—are overlooked. Exceptions to the preponderance of the voices of the Party leadership accounts include Chuck Moore's *I Was a Black Panther*, an account of a New York rank-and-file Party member who describes his guerrilla warfare training in Cuba and subsequent disillusionment with the BPP, and the autobiography of Assata Shakur, another New York rank-and-file member who now lives in exile in Cuba. Moreover, while the volume *Look For Me in the Whirlwind: The Collective Autobiography of the New York 21* primarily focuses on the New York Panther leadership, it does include biographical information on several rank-and-file members.[32]

Panther literature is further marred by the paucity of scholarly research. Heretofore, literature on the BPP has been dominated by personal memoirs and journalistic accounts of the organization. Autobiographies are invaluable resources in understanding Panther politics and reveal critical information about organizational affairs privy only to Party members. The revelation of the role of corporal punishment in Party discipline, discussed by both Brown and Hilliard, is but one example of such information.

Nevertheless, over reliance on memoirs limits our ability to reconstruct the history of the BPP. First, the nature of the genre is to focus primarily on the life of the author. As a result, limited attention is given to the organization as a whole. For example, Hilliard's recollections of the Party were drawn from his Oakland experience, and Elaine Brown readily admits that "I didn't want to write a chronicle of the Black Panther Party. I wanted to write a chronicle of a black woman's life."[33] Moreover, because memoirs are filtered through the perceptions of the writer, they sometimes become a forum for pursuing personal grudges and vendettas, which is less likely to occur in systematic, scholarly studies.

Journalistic accounts pose similar problems in developing an inclusive BPP history in that these works concentrate primarily on the more sensationalistic and melodramatic Party events and thus focus on but a small slice of Panther politics.[34] A grave consequence of the dearth of scholarly studies on the BPP has been the propagation of misconceptions, distortions, and blatant fabrications about the Party. The numerous allegations levied against the Panthers are seldom verified or substantiated. A case in point is Pearson's accusation that Newton confessed to William Payne, a fellow drug user, after an all-night session of smoking crack cocaine, that he killed Officer John Frey in 1967.[35] Pearson's account has never been corroborated by independent sources. Similarly, the statistics of Panther deaths provided by Earl Anthony in *Spitting in the Wind* perpetuates blatant falsehoods about the BPP. In addition to the 300 Panther informants he alleges were killed by Party members, Anthony claims,

> Another twenty-nine were killed by the police; three in the warfare between the Panthers and Karenga's Us group, and still another six were killed in 1971, in the struggle between the Newton and Cleaver factions for control of the group.[36]

Anthony's figures on the number of Party casualties are preposterous and were apparently taken out of thin air. While acknowledging that suspected police informers were killed at Panther facilities, (public records indicate that this occurred in Baltimore and New Haven), Anthony's figures grossly exaggerate the incidence of such deaths. These unsupported allegations undoubtedly contribute to the prevailing violent image of the BPP. [37]

Reginald Major, professor emeritus of Black Studies at San Francisco State University, describes this type of literature as "stealth history," which "has a distinctive political objective, to dampen, discredit and demonize the revolutionary potential of African Americans."[38] Major explains that stealth history deploys "the deliberate dismissal, manipulation or manufacture of important facts, in an attempt to slide a right wing point of view past an audience's falsity detectors."[39] Consequently, the challenge becomes that of counteracting the demonization of the BPP not by its glorification, but by properly documenting the Party's activism through a process of systematic scholarly research.

Reconsidering Panther History

This volume begins the process of reconstructing the history of the Black Panther Party, perhaps the most visible and controversial radical organization of the Black liberation struggle. It is a combined effort of former Panthers and scholars, and breaks new ground by uniting the two groups to tell the Panther story. Its aim is not to deify the Panthers, but rather to offer a critical and balanced analysis of their activities and politics. The BPP remains haunted by widespread scholarly dismissiveness undergirded by criminal-laden interpretations of the organization. Equally troublesome is the tendency to romanticize the Panthers uncritically as error-free super-Black revolutionaries. In this volume, contributors seek to challenge both caricatures of the BPP through systematic inquiry.

This collection of essays moves the discussion of the Panthers beyond the autobiographical and journalistic interpretations of the BPP. In contrast with much of the literature, which attempts to demonize the BPP, the interpretations and conclusions drawn by the authors are substantiated with documented evidence. The contributors to this volume employ multiple sources, including organizational records, interviews, COINTELPRO documents and other government publications, mainstream and dissident newspapers, including *The Black Panther*, and a multitude of secondary sources. As contributors they do not always agree. In fact the contributors provoke discussion from different vantage points. Agreement is not the purpose of this volume. The objective of this book is to begin the process of systematic scholarly investigation of the historical role of this African American revolutionary organization.

Following this introduction, the next section of the book lays out the contextual landscape for the analyses that follow. In chapter 1, Jones and Judson Jeffries examine the multifaceted legacy of the BPP, which they identify as the organization's commitment to armed self-defense, its tradition of community service, its support of self-determination for all people, and its serving as a model of political action for other oppressed groups. The authors also introduce the notion of "Panther mythology" to explain the vilification of the Panthers. Nikhil Pal Singh, in chapter 2, discusses the role of the Panthers in American political radicalism and the global anticolonial struggle. Singh explains the national and global prominence of the BPP and analyzes the Party's adaptation of Third World revolutionary thought to the confines of Black America.

Part II of the volume gives voice to rank-and-file members who performed the "grunt" work of the Party. Scores of foot soldiers in the organization were critical to the success of the BPP. They sold the Party's newspaper, fed children, implemented the organization's survival programs, and organized and defended the Black community. While these individuals were not widely known to the public, they had stellar reputations among their fellow comrades as servants of the people. Examples include Steve McCutchen of Baltimore, Jimmy Slater of Cleveland, and Cindy Smallwood of Oakland. This section begins with a poem by Melvin Lewis, a Party community worker from Chicago. Since poetry was a popular art form used by members of the BPP, their poems often appeared in *The Black Panther*. Memorable Party offerings include Alprentice "Bunchy" Carter's

"Niggertown," Newton's "Revolutionary Suicide," and Ericka Huggins' "Ericka's Poem." Huey Newton and Ericka Huggins also published the book of poetry *Insights and Poems.*[40] In his poem "Once I Was a Panther," Melvin Lewis reminisces about his days working with the organization in Chicago, one of the most effective Panther chapters. In chapter 4, the diary selections of Steve McCutchen, a ten-year veteran of the BPP, offer the reader a rare opportunity to experience the hopes, dedication, and emotional highs and lows of membership in the BPP from May 1969 to August 1970 through the eyes of a rank-and-file member. Panthers rarely maintained diaries. Given the atmosphere of police infiltration and expected betrayal, a diarist might be mistaken for an agent making notes for later use against the organization. McCutchen's diary entries are even more rare as they reflect his evolving state of mind and sometimes contradictory thoughts and actions. In chapter 5, Miriam Monges gives a retrospective account of her participation in the Party as a community worker in New York during the early 1970s. Her discussion of the consequences of challenging the government is particularly poignant. She discusses the difficulty of maintaining a family and raising children during the incarceration of her husband and Party comrade. In chapter 6, an interview with Jimmy Slater, a nine-year foot soldier of the Party, completes the rank-and-file section of the book. Slater shares his observations and critical insight of his membership in the BPP.

Part III of the volume examines the organizational dynamics of the Panthers. In chapter 7, Floyd Hayes and Frances Kiene trace the ideological development of the BPP. They analyze the Party's evolution from a Black nationalist organization to a proponent of intercommunalism. Hayes and Kiene illuminate the diverse set of political writings, ranging from the Declaration of Independence to Third World revolutionary treatises that were synthesized and adapted to Black America by Huey P. Newton, the Party's theoretician. Chapter 8, authored by JoNina Abron, a nine-year veteran of the BPP and the last editor of *The Black Panther*, provides an overview of the Party's many survival programs. After a discussion of the theoretical underpinnings of the survival programs, Abron documents the full array of community service projects implemented by BPP members. She shows that the Party's survival programs extended beyond the widely known free breakfast program to all significant areas of life. The BPP operated health clinics, liberation schools, pest and plumbing services, transportation to prisons, and an escort service for senior citizens free of charge to the public. These programs not only addressed the concrete needs of Black community residents, but also served as a consciousness raising device for the BPP to expose contradictions within the United States. Most importantly, Abron demonstrates that the survival programs were never intended to dilute the Party's commitment to revolutionary change. As Newton explains,

> We must not regard our survival programs as an answer to the whole problem of oppression. We don't even claim it to be a revolutionary program. Revolutions are made of sterner stuff. We do say that if the

people are not here revolution cannot be achieved, for the people and only the people make revolutions.[41]

In chapter 9, Christian Davenport conducts a content analysis of the organization's newspaper *The Black Panther Intercommunal News Service*. First published in April 1967, *The Black Panther* was a major organizational resource for the Panthers. The weekly publication ceased production in 1980. Davenport examined more than 225 issues of *The Black Panther* published between 1969 and 1973. The magnitude of his undertaking makes this study an impressive empirical analysis of the Party newspaper. He identifies several changes in the political message the BPP disseminated during the period of the study. These are attributed to internal factors (editorship turnover, organizational conflict, and a shift in organizational tactics) as well as external factors (government repression). Part III concludes with an essay on the international dimensions of the Black Panther Party authored by Kathleen Cleaver, a major Panther leader during the early years of the organization. In chapter 10, Cleaver examines the developments that led to the formation of the International Section of the Black Panther Party in Algiers, Algeria. She also highlights Party interaction with a host of socialist regimes ranging from North Korea to the Congo.

Similar to the rank and file, the voices of women in the Party have largely been absent from the literature on the BPP. At present, only two memoirs exist on the experience of female Panthers, Assata Shakur's *Assata: An Autobiography* and Elaine Brown's *A Taste of Power*. Additional rare exceptions to this omission of women from the literature on the Panthers are a pamphlet of an in-depth interview "My Life with the Black Panther Party," by Akua Njeri, a Chicago Panther, and a section titled "Black Panther Women Speak" found in the collection of BPP writings edited by Philip Foner. Part IV of this volume also helps to fill this glaring void in the literature on the Panthers. In chapter 11, Regina Jennings' recollective essay on her BPP membership focuses on Party gender dynamics. Jennings discusses how the Party transformed her life and instilled a sense of dedication to the freedom of African Americans and other oppressed people. Her reflections on the Party are also a reminder that revolutionary principles did not necessarily translate into a gender-neutral organization. In chapter 12, Tracye Matthews explores the interaction of race, class, and gender in her analysis of Panther politics from 1966 to 1971. Matthew's analysis illuminates the critical impact of gender dynamics on the organizational fortunes of the BPP. She also underscores the varied experience of Panther women, which makes an important contribution in light of the attempts to vilify the Panthers as virulent sexists. In chapter 13, Angela LeBlanc-Ernest extends the examination of Panther women to the demise of the organization in 1982. She describes the pivotal role assumed by women throughout the existence of the Panther Party, particularly the leadership of Elaine Brown.

Three explanations of the decline of the BPP constitute Part V of the volume, while the volume's final section explores the legacy of the organization. In chapter 14, Christopher Booker advances a popular interpretation of the demise of the BPP. He argues that Panther theoreticians erred in attempting to build a political organization based on the lumpen proletariat. He maintains that as a result of this recruiting emphasis, the Party was informed by a "lumpen mentality" that ultimately proved too costly. His provocative thesis is contested by several authors in this volume. In chapter 15, Winston Grady-Willis provides a historical discussion of the government's attempts to neutralize the African American freedom movement. He identifies the broad array of repressive tactics the government used to undermine the activism of the BPP. Moreover, he documents intergovernmental cooperation and participation to thwart the Panthers. Grady-Willis directs much needed attention to one of the lingering consequences of that repression, namely, the continuing incarceration of some members of the BPP. Government repression is a leading explanation for the demise of the BPP given by Party members and radical scholar–activists. The political repression contention was the central thesis of Huey P. Newton's doctoral dissertation, published posthumously in 1996. In *War Against the Panthers: A Study of Repression in America,* Newton broadens readers' understanding of state repression in a liberal democratic state. *Still Black, Still Strong: Survivors of the U.S. War Against Black Revolutionaries,* a collection of interviews with former Panthers, offers other insider accounts of the covert nature of government actions employed against the Party.[42] Ollie Johnson focuses on the internal factors that contributed to the downfall of the BPP. In chapter 16, he employs elite theory to inform our understanding of the authoritarianism and corruption that pervaded the Party during its later years. Unlike previous interpretations, Johnson documents and contextualizes the events of this period. His study avoids the simplistic tendency to attribute all Party woes to political repression. Rather, Johnson elucidates the combination of factors that led to the fall of the Panthers.

While many of the authors address the legacy of the BPP throughout the volume, Part VI offers a more focused discussion of this topic. In chapter 17, Akinyele Umoja focuses more attention on an important aspect of the earlier analysis of political repression by Grady-Willis, the issue of political prisoners. Umoja discusses the Party's role in the political-prisoner movement and identifies the largely forgotten Panther members who have been incarcerated over the past two decades. Umoja places Panther political prisoners in the context of a broader political movement comprising other African American protesters, as well as of Puerto Rican, Native American, and White radical activists. Chapter 18, by Clarence Lusane, addresses the relevance of Panther activism to contemporary Black politics. Lusane identifies the opportunities and the limitations gleaned from the activism of the BPP. He warns of the temptations to advocate armed struggle carelessly, as in the case of Mike McGee's Black Panther Militia. Nevertheless, Lusane does emphasize that there is much to be gained from the Panther experience. The Party's commitment to struggle, its solidarities with other oppressed groups, and its uncompromising leadership are examples of the elements that defined the BPP as one of the leading organizations of the Black Power Era.

NOTES

1. See Black Panther Party, *Fallen Comrades of the Black Panther Party*, pamphlet, n.d.; U.S. House Committee on Internal Security, Black Panther Party Part 1: *Investigation of Kansas City Chapter; National Organization Data,* 91st Cong., 2d sess., 1970. For further discussion of the acrimony between Us and the Black Panther Party, see Maulana Karenga, *The Roots of Us–Panther Conflict: The Perverse and Deadly Games Police Play* (San Diego: Kawaida Publications, 1976); Reginald Major, *A Panther is a Black Cat* (New York: William Morrow and Company, 1971), 105; Ward Churchill and Jim Vander Wall, *Agents of Repression: The FBI's Secret War Against The Black Panther Party and the American Indian Movement* (Boston: South End Press, 1988), 42.

2. "17 'Panthers' Arraigned In Sacramento Court: 'Invasion' Cases Continued," *San Francisco Examiner*, 4 Feb. 1967, 1; William Endicott "Black Panthers Controlled By Communists Senate Unit Says," *Los Angeles Times,* 4 August 1970, 1; Homer Bigart, "U.S. Troops Flown In For Panther Rally; New Haven Braces For Protest By 20,000," *New York Times,* 1 May 1970, 1; "Baltimore Police Raid Panther Headquarters," *Guardian*, 9 May 1970, 5.

3. For examples of the extensive media coverage of the murder of Dr. Huey P. Newton, see "Huey Newton Killed, Was a Co-Founder of Black Panthers," *New York Times,* 23 August 1989, A1; Dennis Hevesi, "Huey Newton Symbolized the Rising Black Anger of a Generation," *New York Times,* 23 August 1989, B7; Cynthia Gorney, "Huey Newton, Co-Founder of Black Panthers, Is Slain in Oakland," *Washington Post*, 23 August 1989, A6; Paul Clancy "Black Panther Co-Founder Slain," *USA Today,* 23 August 1989, A2; Jennifer McNulty, "Huey Newton Slain in Street," *Tampa Tribune,* 23 August 1989, A1; "Panther Co-Founder Shot to Death," *Richmond Times-Dispatch,* 23 August 1989, A2; Jennifer McNulty, "Newton, Co-Founder of Black Panthers, Shot to Death," *Virginia Pilot* (Norfolk, Va.) 23 August 1989, A1; Robin Clark "Bobby Seale Has Praise, No Tears for Huey Newton," *The Washington Post*, 24 August 1989, A3; DeWayne Wickham, "In Newton's World His Murder Was a Natural Death," *Rochester Democrat and Chronicle* (Rochester, N.Y.), 28 August 1989, A6. Additional information on *The Commemorator* and the *New Black Panther: Black Community Service* may be found in JoNina Abron, "'Raising the Consciousness of the People': The Black Panther Intercommunal News Service, 1967–1980" in *Voices from the Underground: Vol. 1, Insider Histories of the Vietnam Era Underground Press*, ed. Ken Wachsberger (Ann Arbor, Michigan: Mica Press, 1993), 357.

4. Errol A. Henderson, "Black Nationalism and Rap Music," *Journal of Black Studies* 26 (January 1996), 309; for a general overview of the discipline of Cultural Studies, see Lawrence Grossberg, Cary Nelson, and Paula Treichler, eds., *Cultural Studies* (New York: Routledge, 1992); Tricia Rose provides an excellent analysis of the impact of rap music on Black culture in *Black Noise: Rap Music and Black Culture in Contemporary America* (Hanover, New Hampshire: Weslyan University Press, 1994).

5. Henderson, "Black Nationalism and Rap Music," 311.

6. Public Enemy's *It Takes A Nation of Millions To Hold Us Back*, Columbia Records, 1988; see also *Fear of a Black Planet* (Columbia Records, 1988).

7. "Power to the People" is found on Public Enemy's *Fear Of A Black Planet*. Tupac Shakur's "Dear Mama" is on his *Me Against the World* (Interscope Records,

1995). See Paris' *Devil Made Me Do It* (Tommy Boy Records, 1989/90); also see Tonya Pendleton, "The Black Panthers: Party of the People: Part 1," *Rap Pages,* November 1993, 44–53; and "Pump Ya Fist: Hip Hop Inspired by the Black Panthers" (Avatar Records, 1995). Some of the contributing artists include KRS-One, Tupac, Chuck D., The Fugees, Kam, and Jeru the Damaja.

8. Earl Anthony, *Spitting in the Wind: The True Story Behind the Violent Legacy of the Black Panther Party* (Malibu, Calif.: Roundtable Publishing Co., 1990), 34.

9. Elaine Brown, *A Taste of Power: A Black Woman's Story* (New York: Pantheon Books, 1992); David Hilliard and Lewis Cole, *This Side of Glory: The Autobiography of David Hilliard and the Story of the Black Panther Party* (Boston, Mass.: Little, Brown and Company, 1993); William Lee Brent, *Long Time Gone: A Black Panther's True-Life Story of His Hijacking and Twenty-Five Years in Cuba* (New York: Times Books, 1996). See the following sources for reviews of these books: Kathleen Neal Cleaver, "Sister Act," *Transition* 60 (1993): 84–101; Angela Davis, "The Making of a Revolutionary," *Women's Review of Books* 10, 1: 3–4; Ellen DuBois, "Sisters and Brothers," *Nation* 235 (September 1993): 251–53; Mumia Abu-Jamal, "Another Side of Glory," *Black Panther, Black Community News Service*, Fall/Winter 1993, 7; Larry Rohter, "Black Panther, Long Exiled, Sums Up," *New York Times,* 9 April 1996, A–4.

10. See Michael Newton, *Bitter Grain: The Story of the Black Panther Party* (Los Angeles: Holloway Publishing Company, [1980] 1991); Gilbert Moore, *Rage* (New York: Carroll and Graf Publishers, 1993). This book was originally published as *A Special Rage* by Harper and Row in 1971; Huey P. Newton, *Revolutionary Suicide* (New York: Writers and Readers Publishers, 1995; Huey P. Newton, *To Die For the People* (New York: Writers and Readers Publishers, 1995); Philip S. Foner, ed., *The Black Panthers Speak* (New York: DaCapo Press, [1970] 1995); Bobby Seale, *Seize the Time: The Story of The Black Panther Party* (Baltimore, Md.: Black Classic Press, 1991); George Jackson, *Blood In My Eye* (Baltimore, Md.: Black Classic Press, 1991).

11. Hugh Pearson, *The Shadow of a Panther: Huey Newton and the Price of Black Power in America* (Reading, Mass.: Addison-Wesley Publishing Company, 1994). Pearson's study of the Black Panther Party has been the subject of debate and controversy. See the following reviews of *The Shadow of the Panther:* Bob Blauner, "The Outlaw Huey Newton: A Former Admirer Paints an Unromantic Portrait of the Black Panther Leader," *New York Times Book Review*, 10 July 1994, 1, 22; Reginald W. Major, "Lurking in the Shadows: *The Shadow of the Panther* Echoes Now Familiar Attacks on the Life and Times of the Black Panther Party," *San Francisco Bay Guardian*, 15 June 1994, 45–46; Christopher Lehmann-Haupt, "Recalling Huey Newton as a Hero and Villain," *New York Times*, 30 June 1994; Diane D. Turner, "In Defense of the Party For Self-Defense," *Brown Alumni Monthly Review* 27. BPP articles in popular periodicals include: Herb Boyd, "All Power To The People: As Militant Freedom Fighters the Black Panthers Left a Legacy That Is Distinctively African American," *Emerge*, February 1993, 40–44; Reginald W. Major and Marcia D. Davis, "Prisoner of War: Twenty-Four Years Ago The FBI and LAPD Did Battle with the Black Panthers and Geronimo Pratt Went to Jail. Today, Armed With New Evidence and Support, He May Win His Freedom," *Emerge*, June 1994, 30–35. Cheo Tyehimba, "Panther Mania," *Essence*, February 1995, 108–12; Kendra Lee, "Panther Power," *YSB: The Magazine for Young Sisters and Brothers*, May 1995, 32–40.

12. A. Scott Walton, "Veteran of Black Panthers Calls New Play 'A Travesty,'" *Atlanta Journal/Constitution,* 22 January 1995, C2; Robert Alexander, *Servant of the People: The Rise and Fall of Huey P. Newton and the Black Panther Party* (Atlanta, Ga.: Jomandi Productions, 20 January–12 February 1995); Roger Guenveur Smith, "A Huey P. Newton Story" in the National Black Arts Festival

Theater Program (Atlanta, Ga.: Atlanta Entertainment Media, 28 June–7 July 1996), 23–25.

13. Michael Eric Dyson, "Screening the Black Panthers," in *Between God and Gangsta Rap: Bearing Witness to Black Culture* (New York: Oxford University Press, 1996), 113–17. Also see *Panther* (Polygram Filmed Entertainment, 1995), and Mario Van Peebles, Ula Y. Taylor, and J. Tarika Lewis, *Panther: A Pictorial History of the Black Panthers and the Story Behind the Film* (New York: New Market Press, 1995).

14. See Nina J. Easton, "The-'60s-Aren't-Dead File: There Are Five Black Panther Movies in the Works," *Los Angeles Times,* 21 July 1991, 26. For an excellent discussion of the representation of the Black Panther Party in Black popular culture, see Tracye A. Matthews, "Myth, Meaning and Macho: Black Popular Culture and Remembrances of the Black Panther Party," paper presented at "The Black Panther Party Revisited: Reflections and Scholarship," 30th Anniversary Commemorative Conference of the Founding of the Black Panther Party, Department of African-American Studies, Georgia State University, Atlanta, Georgia, 24–25 October 1996. Other conferences commemorating the 30th anniversary of the founding of the Black Panther Party include "'It's About Time': The 30th Anniversary Celebration of the Founding of the Black Panther Party," October 11–13, 1996, Oakland California. This conference was sponsored by a national committee of former BPP members. Congressman Bobby Rush, a former leader of the Chicago Panthers, was the keynote speaker. The Carpenter Center for Visual Arts at Harvard University sponsored "The Black Panther Party 30th Anniversary Films Made; Re-made; To-Be-Made," October 10–12, 1996, Cambridge, Massachusetts. The three-day conference organized by Professor Gerald O'Grady showed several Panther films including the world premiere of *All Power To The People: The Black Panther Party and Beyond* by Lee Lew-Lee.

15. Isabel Wilkerson, "Call for Black Militia Stuns Milwaukee," *New York Times,* 6 April 1990, A2; Alex Kershaw, "The Return of the Black Panthers," *Weekend Guardian* (London, England), 22–23 August 1992, 10–11; *Donahue Show*, "Michael McGee and Black Rage in Milwaukee," 15 January 1991 (New York: Multimedia Entertainment, transcript 3121, 1991).

16. Nora López, "Black Panther Leaders Plan To Be Armed at School Board," *Dallas Morning News,* 12 June 1996, A38; Grace Bonds-Staples, "Drugs, Racism, Urban Neglect Lead To Black Panther Revival," *Fort Worth Star-Telegram*, 6 September 1991, 1, 13.

17. Malaika Brown, "Social Movement: Picking Up The Power," *Los Angeles Sentinel*, 6 July 1995, 1. B. Kwaku Duren, "We Demand Peace, Justice and Reparations," *Black Panther International Newspaper: The Official Newspaper of the New African American Vanguard Movement*, Summer 1996, 1.

18. Angela Davis, "The Making of a Revolutionary," *Women's Review of Books* (June 1993): 3.

19. Manning Marable, *Race, Reform and Rebellion: The Second Reconstruction in Black America* (Jackson, Miss.: University Press of Mississippi, 1991), 110.

20. David Horowitz, "Black Murder Inc.," *A Heterodoxy,* March 1993, 15; Peter Collier and David Horowitz, *Destructive Generation: Second Thoughts About the 60s* (New York: Summit Books, 1990); Todd Gitlin, *The Sixties: Years of Hope, Days of Rage* (New York: Bantam Books, 1987).

21. See Mari Jo Buhle, Paul Buhle, and Dan Georgakas, eds., *Encyclopedia of the Left* (Urbana, Ill.: University of Illinois Press, 1992); Sean D. Cashman, *African-Americans and the Quest For Civil Rights 1900–1990* (New York: New

York University Press, 1991); Robert Weisbrot, *Freedom Bound: A History of America's Civil Rights Movement* (New York: W.W. Norton, 1991).

22. Stanley Crouch, *The All-American Skin Game or The Decoy of Race: The Long and the Short of It, 1990–1994* (New York: Pantheon Books, 1995),180.

23. Roberto Santiago, "A Dialogue With Kwame Ture," *Emerge*, April 1991, 12.

24. Alice Walker, "Black Panthers or Black Punks?" *New York Times,* 5 May 1991, A23.

25. Sean Cashman, *African Americans and the Quest For Civil Rights, 1900–1990* (New York: New York University Press, 1991), 201.

26. Allegra Bennett, "Claws of the Panthers: Elaine Brown Surviving the 'Trauma' of Huey Newton and the Party," *Washington Times,* 22 March 1993, D2.

27. Alex Kershaw identifies Watts rather than Oakland as the birthplace of the BPP. See Alex Kershaw, "The Return of the Black Panthers," *Weekend Guardian* (London, England), 10; Peter Levy identifies Eldridge Cleaver as the Minister of Culture in *The New Left and Labor in the 1960's* (Urbana, Ill.: University of Illinois Press, 1994), 88; Robert H. Brisbane refers to Emory Douglas as Emory Dawson in *Black Activism: Racial Revolution in the United States, 1954–1970* (Valley Forge, Penn.: Judson Press, 1974), 207; James Jennings mistakenly identifies Huey Newton as the BPP's Oakland mayoral candidate in *The Politics of Black Empowerment: The Transformation of Black Activism in Urban America* (Detroit: Wayne State University Press, 1992), 19; and John A. Courtright cites Denzil Dowell as the first Panther to be killed by the police even though Dowell was never a member of the organization. See his "Rhetoric of the Gun: An Analysis of the Rhetorical Modification of the Black Panther Party," *Journal of Black Studies* 4 (1974): 255.

28. Robert Goldstein, *Political Repression in Modern America: 1870 to the Present* (New York: Schenkman, 1978), xvi.

29. See Donald Freed, *Agony in New Haven: The Trial of Bobby Seale and Ericka Huggins and the Black Panther Party* (New York: Simon and Schuster, 1973); Roy Wilkins and Ramsey Clark, *Search and Destroy: A Report By the Commission of Inquiry into the Black Panthers and the Police* (New York: Metro Applied Research Center, 1973).

30. Mario Van Peebles et al., *Panther: A Pictorial History of the Black Panthers and the Story Behind the Film* (New York: New Market Press, 1995).

31. See Bobby Seale, *A Lonely Rage: The Autobiography of Bobby Seale* (New York: New York Times Books, 1977); Eldridge Cleaver, *Soul on Fire* (Waco, Tx: Word Books, 1978); Eldridge Cleaver, *Soul on Ice* (New York: Dell Publishing Company, 1968); Earl Anthony, *Picking Up The Gun: A Report on the Black Panthers* (New York: Dial Press, 1970).

32. Kuwasi Balagoon et al., eds., *Look for Me in the Whirlwind: The Collective Autobiography of the New York 21* (New York: Random House, 1971); Chuck Moore, *I Was a Black Panther* (New York: Garden City, 1970).

33. Renee Graham, "She Still Believes in Panthers," *Boston Globe*, 22 February 1993, 32.

34. For example, see Michael J. Arlen, *An American Verdict* (New York: Anchor Books, 1974), which provides an account of the trial of the law enforcement officials who were involved in the December 4,1969 police raid in Chicago. Murray Kempton, *The Briar Patch: The People of the State of New York v. Lumumba Shakur et al.* (New York: Dell Publishing Company, 1973) examines

the New York 21 case, while Gail Sheehy, *Panthermania: The Clash of Black Against Black in One American City* (New York: Harper and Row, 1971) focuses on the New Haven 14 incident.

35. Pearson, *The Shadow of the Panther*, 6–8.

36. Earl Anthony, *Spitting in the Wind*, 34.

37. See Black Panther Party, *Fallen Comrades of the Black Panther Party*, pamphlet, n.d. While the actual number of Panther deaths is debated, the figures given by all of the contending sources have not exceeded twenty-eight. See Jay Epstein, "Reporter At Large: Charles R. Garry's List of Panthers Allegedly Killed by Police with Case Histories," *New Yorker*, February 13, 1971, 45–46.

38. Reginald Major, "Stealth History: A Political Process, A Review Essay of *The Shadow of the Panther* by Hugh Pearson and *The Rise and Fall of California's Radical Prison Movements* by Eric Crummins," *Black Scholar* 24 (Fall 1994): 39.

39. Major, "Stealth History," 39.

40. Alprentice "Bunchy" Carter's poem titled "Niggertown" is found in the Afro-American Liberation Army's *Humanity Freedom Peace* pamphlet n.d., 24; also see Huey P. Newton and Ericka Huggins, *Insights and Poems* (San Francisco: City Light Books, 1975).

41. Huey P. Newton, *To Die For The People*, 34.

42. Huey P. Newton, *War Against the Panthers: A Study of Repression in America* (New York: Harlem River Press, 1996); Jim Fletcher, Tanaquil Jones, and Sylvere Lotringer, eds., *Still Black, Still Strong: Survivors of the U.S. War Against Black Revolutionaries* (New York: Semiotext(e), 1993).

Part I

Contextual Landscape

Chapter One

"Don't Believe the Hype": Debunking the Panther Mythology

Charles E. Jones and Judson L. Jeffries

The summer of 1966 was marked by the rupture of the nonviolent integrationist-directed Civil Rights movement.[1] Although the movement's strategy proved successful in dismantling the vestiges of *de jure* segregation, the life chances of African American people nonetheless remained unchanged. Blatant acts of police brutality, inadequate housing, inferior social services, and rampant unemployment still plagued the African American community. By this stage it was clear that the traditional civil rights organizations were unable to alter the systemic forces that adversely impacted the lives of African American people, particularly in northern urban settings.

In the midst of this critical vortex, African Americans across the nation rebelled against the manifestations of institutional racism. The National Advisory Commission on Civil Disorders reported that forty-three racial riots occurred in the United States during 1966, a significant increase from fifteen reported racial revolts in 1964.[2] This surge in racial civil disorders coupled with the stalemate in the progress toward African American equality signaled that "the traditional southern-based nonviolent Civil Rights movement had largely ground to a halt and was in its death throes."[3]

The promotion of the Black power political strategy became the central response to this impasse. First articulated in June 1966 by Willie Ricks and Kwame Ture (Stokely Carmichael), two veterans of the Student Nonviolent Coordinating Committee, during the James Meredith-initiated "march against fear" in Mississippi, the concept resonated throughout Black America. Its nebulous nature spawned myriad manifestations that spanned the ideological spectrum of Black nationalism.[4]

Variations of the Black Power concept ranged from the Nixon presidential administration's inspired Black capitalism, adopted by the former director of CORE (Congress of Racial Equality) Floyd McKissick in his Soul City endeavor, to the working-class based variant offered by the League of Revolutionary Black Workers in Detroit. An example of the cultural nationalist's version of the Black power concept includes Us, led by Maulana Karenga in Los Angeles, while the Republic of New Africa offered the independent nation–state model. Finally, the application of Black power is evident in the formation of Black caucuses within political bodies and professional associations. It was in this context that the Black Panther Party for Self-Defense emerged in Oakland, California, on October 15, 1966.[5]

As a Black revolutionary cadre organization, the Black Panther Party (BPP) was committed to the self-defense and empowerment of African American people. It represented one of the rare instances of a successful blend of nationalism and socialist ideals by an independent African American political organization. One student of Black nationalism argues that "it is difficult to see how one could fail to acknowledge its [the BPP's] pre-eminence as the leading revolutionary Black nationalist group in the United States."[6] Political activist Sahu Barron concurs when he asserts that "the Black Panther Party revolutionary struggle represented not only a most genuine and thorough-going mass movement of that period, but remains the highest expression of Black liberation."[7]

Notwithstanding these lofty assessments of the BPP, its legacy has alternately been neglected, distorted, and discounted. For example, in one wide ranging account of the African American freedom struggle by historian Robert Weisbrot only one page out of 317 was devoted to the activities of the BPP.[8] In another study, William J. Grimshaw provides an in-depth examination of Black politics in Chicago (1931–91), but only makes a passing reference to the presence of the Party in the city.[9] This oversight is in striking contrast to the reality of the organizational effectiveness of the Chicago branch, one of the strongest affiliates of the BPP. More specifically, the role of Cook County State's Attorney Edward V. Hanrahan in the December 4, 1969 police raid, which resulted in the death of Panther leaders Mark Clark and Fred Hampton, was the catalyst for a major instance of split-ticket voting by the city's African American electorate. It was also a pivotal factor in the ultimate demise of the Daley political machine. African Americans in Chicago exacted political revenge in 1972 when Hanrahan was defeated for the state attorney's position. Dempsey J. Travis, an African American veteran of Chicago politics, recalls in his autobiography, "[O]n November 8, 1972 the voices of both Fred Hampton and Mark Clark were heard from the grave by the voters in voting booths on the south and west sides. The Black voters gave the Republican candidate, Bernard Carey, in their anti-Hanrahan campaign, sixty percent of their vote, thus defeating Hanrahan by a county-wide margin of 129,000."[10]

This chapter argues that the historical significance of the BPP has been distorted by a "Panther mythology"—defined as a set of falsehoods and misperceptions that minimize the historical significance of the Party. First, the study documents the legacy of the BPP. In the next section, the notion of Panther mythology is introduced to explain the depreciation of the Panthers. Finally, this mythology is critiqued in a manner that underscores the legacy of the Panthers.

Legacy of the Black Panther Party

Arguably the leading Black leftist organization in the African American liberation struggle, the BPP captured the imagination of oppressed people throughout the world. Its organizational life span lasted sixteen years from 1966 to 1982. Although not widely recognized, the Party produced a rich and multifaceted legacy that significantly impacted the Black liberation struggle. The legacy of the BPP consists of four components: (1) the saliency of armed resistance, (2) a tradition of community service, (3) a commitment to the self-determination of *all* people, and (4) a model of political action for oppressed people.

Armed Resistance. The Panthers represented the institutionalization of Malcolm X's notion of self-defense. Newton explained,

> [A]lthough Malcolm's program for the Organization of Afro-American Unity was never put into operation, he has made it clear that Blacks ought to arm. Malcolm's influence was ever present. We continue to believe that the Black Panther Party exists in the spirit of Malcolm...ever-present.[11]

Newton and Seale formalized the notion of self-defense in the original official title of the organization then named the *Black Panther Party for Self-Defense*. This emphasis on armed resistance was also incorporated into point seven of the Party's platform that stated, "[W]e therefore believe that all Black people should arm themselves for self-defense."[12] Several position papers written by Huey Newton further reenforced the paramilitary orientation of the organization. For example, in Executive Mandate Number One, issued on May 2, 1967 in Sacramento to protest the pending Mulford legislation, Newton encouraged Black citizens to arm themselves against police brutality and terror. In response to a surge in government repression in March 1968, the Party issued its third executive mandate, which declared "that all members [of the BPP] must acquire the technical equipment to defend their homes and their dependents."[13]

Organizational manifestations of the ideological imperative of "picking up the gun" abound. During its formative years (1966–68) the Party's commitment to armed self-defense was readily apparent. Panther police patrols, as well as armed Party members who served as bodyguards for Betty Shabazz at the Party's political rallies in Richmond, California, underscored its advocacy of armed resistance. And, of course, the May 1967 Sacramento incident in which an armed delegation of Panther lobbyists protested pending legislation highlighted the saliency of armed self-defense. Further evidence that demonstrated the BPP's paramilitary orientation include weapons-training classes, armed Panthers who openly engaged in close order drills with weapons in public parks, the guerrilla warfare propaganda printed in the Party's newspaper, and the highly publicized armed confrontations between Panthers and police officers throughout the nation.[14]

Scholar–activist Manning Marable reminds us that "remarkably few Black nationalists and Black Powerites had advocated violence against white-owned property, the subversion of authority, or the seizure of state power."[15] Perhaps the best known proponent of armed resistance among Black power groups, the BPP represented an exception to this tendency. Its success as an African American organization that explicitly mobilized on the basis of armed resistance remains unparalleled. According to Foner, "[N]ever before in the history of Black Americans has an admittedly revolutionary party won such support in the leading Black communities of this country."[16]

This is not to suggest that the BPP's advocacy of armed self-defense was unprecedented in the history of Black liberation struggle. Undoubtedly, the Panthers were inextricably linked to the tradition of African American radicalism. Well before the inception of the Black Panther Party for Self-Defense in 1966, African American activists such as Martin Delany and Maria W. Stewart were proponents of armed resistance. David Walker's *Appeal,* first published in 1830, is another example of an early precursor to the Panthers' advocacy of armed resistance. Black organizations that subscribed to armed self-defense and predated the formation of the BPP include the Universal African Legion, the militia component of the Marcus Garvey-led Universal Negro Improvement Association, and the African Blood Brotherhood of the 1920s. Examples of subsequent individuals and African American political formations that espoused armed resistance during the twentieth century include the late Robert Williams, leader of the local branch of the National Association for the Advancement of Colored People (NAACP) in Monroe, North Carolina, who in 1959 organized a rifle club to protect Black residents from the attacks of White vigilantes, and the Deacons for Defense and Justice, a southern Black armed-defense organization that provided protection for civil rights activists. Newton wrote in his autobiography that *"Negroes with Guns* by Robert Williams had a great influence on the kind of party we developed" and "[o]ne of their [Deacons for Defense and Justice] leaders had come through the Bay Area on a speaking and fund-raising tour, and we liked what he said."[17] Black power organizations, the Revolutionary Action Movement, and the Student Nonviolent Coordinating Committee offered additional models that affected the development of the BPP.

Significantly influencing Panther strategists also were the major Third World revolutionary luminaries of the period that included Frantz Fanon, Mao Tse-Tung, Fidel Castro, Che Guevara, and Ho Chi Minh. Consistent with Marxist revolutionary thought and practice, Panther theoreticians not only incorporated armed self-defense, but predicted the eventuality of all-out armed struggle in order to seize state power. An editorial on political violence in the Party's newspaper declared, "[T]he Black Panther Party recognizes, as do all Marxist revolutionaries, that the only response to the violence of the ruling class is the revolutionary violence of the people."[18]

Community Service. BPP members implemented a variety of "survival programs" designed to meet the material needs of community residents. Survival projects served as an organizing tool with which to expose inequities and contradictions within the United States. These community outreach projects embody the second feature of the legacy of the BPP. Feeding hungry school-age children, the Party's free breakfast program constituted the cornerstone of the BPP's survival programs.

Newton and other Party strategists adopted programs designed to satisfy the immediate needs of the people while simultaneously raising their level of consciousness. Publication of *The Black Panther,* the organization's newspaper, on April 27, 1967, is one such example. The newspaper disseminated news about the organization's activities and ideology. Stories on revolutionary movements abroad and the political struggles of African Americans and other racial groups in the United States were featured regularly in the newspaper. During its peak distribution period (1968–72), the Party sold an average of a hundred thousand copies per week.[19] Although the BPP was constantly under assault from government officials, the newspaper cadre of the Party ensured the weekly production of the newspaper by deadline for more than ten years. Moreover, Party members published a first-rate professional news product about which arch-conservative E. D. Hirsch, Jr., gave the following assessment in his highly acclaimed book *Cultural Literacy:*

> The writers for *The Black Panther* had clearly received a rigorous traditional education in American history, in the Declaration of Independence, the Pledge of Allegiance to the flag, the Gettysburg Address, and the Bible, to mention only some of the direct quotations and allusions in these passages. [And] they also received rigorous traditional instruction in reading, writing, and spelling. I have not found a single misspelled word in many pages of radical sentiment I have examined in that newspaper.[20]

Its overall effectiveness made the publication a likely target of government repression:

> The Black Panther Party newspaper is one of the most effective propaganda operations of the BPP. Distribution of this newspaper is increasing at a regular rate thereby influencing a greater number of individuals in the United States along the black extremist lines. Each recipient is requested to submit by 6/5/70 proposed counterintelligence measures that will hinder the vicious propaganda being spread by the BPP. The BPP newspaper has a circulation in excess of 139,000. It is the voice of the BPP and if it could be effectively hindered it would result in helping cripple the BPP.[21]

As the BPP grew from an Oakland Bay Area group into a national organization, many of the Party's local affiliates implemented programs to serve

**Selected Survival Programs
of the Black Panther Party, 1966–1982**

Program   Year Initiated

1. Intercommunal News Service (*Black Panther*)   1967

2. Free Breakfast for School Children   1968

3. Petition Campaign—Referendum for Decentralized
   Police Departments   1968

4. Liberation School/Intercommunal Youth Institute   1969

5. People's Free Medical Research Health Clinic   1970

6. Free Clothing Program   1970

7. Free Busing to Prisons Program   1970

8. Seniors Against Fearful Environment (S.A.F.E.)   1971

9. Sickle Cell Anemia Research Foundation   1971

10. Free Housing Cooperative Program   1971

11. Free Shoe Program   1971

12. Free Pest Control Program   1971

13. Free Plumbing and Maintenance Program   1971

14. Free Food Program   1972

15. Child Development Center   1972

16. Free Ambulance Program   1974

Sources: Black Panther Party, ed., *The Co-Evolution Quarterly* 3 (1974); G. Louis Heath, ed.,*Off the Pigs: The History and Literature of the Black Panther Party*; Kit Kim Holder, "The History of the Black Panther Party, 1966–1971: A Curriculum Tool for African-American Studies;" Daniel Joseph Willis, "A Critical Analysis of Mass Political Education and Community Organization as Utilized by the Black Panther Party As a Means for Effecting Social Change."

Table 1

the residents of their respective communities. For example, in May 1968 the Seattle branch of the BPP initiated a free breakfast program. In 1969, the Harlem branch started a housing advocacy program, the Kansas City, Missouri branch launched a community drug program, and its Richmond, California affiliate established a liberation school. By November 1969, the Party formalized these various community service activities into a nationwide "serve the people program." BPP affiliates were instructed by Chairman Bobby Seale to initiate a free breakfast program, institute free health clinics, develop Black liberation schools, and circulate petitions for a referendum vote on the decentralization of the police.[22] In subsequent years, the BPP launched additional community service projects, including an escort service for senior citizens, free food giveaways, and a pest-control service. In 1971,

Huey Newton eventually defined these community self-help projects as the survival programs of the BPP.

Notwithstanding criticisms that the Party's survival programs were reformist rather than revolutionary, at no time were these community service projects intended to displace the primary objective of the BPP, the social transformation of the United States. David Hilliard, the Chief of Staff, notes, "[W]e call the program a "survival" program—survival pending revolution—not something to replace revolution or challenge the power relations demanding radical action, but an activity that strengthens us for the coming fight, a lifeboat or raft leading us safely to shore."[23] Its survival programs operated as a vehicle for radical political socialization. Leslie McLemore, the noted student of African American politics, underscores the significance of this crucial endeavor:

> The transmission of radical militancy and cultural information through black secondary agents is one way to politicize and radicalize black people in order to bring about meaningful change in their social, political and economic status.[24]

Self-Determination of All People. Another critical facet of the legacy of the BPP is linked to the organization's commitment to the virtue and dignity of individuals regardless of race, gender, or sexual orientation. Unlike many of the Black power organizations of the period, the BPP demonstrated a willingness to enter into functional alliances with White leftist groups. Moreover, Panthers were early advocates of the rights of women and homosexuals during the embryonic stage of each of these liberation movements. In short, the BPP represented a model for genuine multiculturalism.

The first Panther biracial alliance occurred with the Peace and Freedom Party (PFP). On December 22, 1967, the BPP formed a coalition with the PFP. Under the terms of the alliance, the Panthers agreed to assist the PFP in collecting the necessary signatures to allow PFP candidates to be placed on the California ballot for the 1968 elections. In return, the Party gained the use of PFP's sound equipment, which was needed to mobilize support for the exoneration of Huey P. Newton. Other White organizations that enjoyed political relations with the BPP included the White Panther Party, a college-student-based radical organization with headquarters in Ann Arbor, Michigan and the Patriot Party, a revolutionary party of poor and working-class Whites based in Chicago.[25]

In contrast to cultural nationalist Black power organizations, the Panthers actively participated in White leftist politics. Party leaders spoke at the major antiwar rallies and leftist political gatherings. Bobby Seale addressed White student radicals in Chicago prior to the "Day of Rage" at the 1968 Democratic National Convention, and on November 15, 1969, David Hilliard, the Chief of Staff, delivered a speech at the San Francisco Moratorium Demonstration, one of the largest rallies of the antiwar movement. In turn, White radical activists frequently participated in major political events sponsored by the BPP. As early as 1967 Bob Avakian, an Oakland Bay Area White leftist, spoke at a rally sponsored by the Party to protest the death of Denzil Dowell in Richmond, California. Other examples of joint participation between the Panthers and White radicals included the 1969 United Front Against Fascism conference sponsored by the BPP in Oakland, California, and the 1970 Revolutionary People's Constitutional Conventions. Legal defense campaigns for Party members provided another avenue for White leftist participation in Panther activities. Several legal defense committees—Free Huey, New York 21, and New Haven 14—all received considerable support from White radicals. In addition, White radical lawyers provided invaluable legal assistance to members of the BPP.[26]

This commitment to revolutionary solidarity also extended to other racial ethnic groups. Over the course of its existence, the BPP worked with the Brown Berets, a Chicano leftist organization in southern California, and the Young Lords, a Puerto Rican group residing in Chicago and New York, as well as with the Red Guard Party, a Chinese revolutionary group located in the Oakland Bay Area. The BPP also enjoyed political relationships with several Black power organizations that included the Student Nonviolent Coordinating Committee, the League of Revolutionary Workers in Detroit, and the Republic of New Africa.[27]

Its revolutionary outlook also placed the BPP at the forefront of the women's liberation movement among its Black power and civil rights counterparts. The BPP was one of the few Black organizations to endorse and support Shirley Chisholm's presidential candidacy in 1972. Party members sponsored a fund-raising event for Chisholm's campaign, while her male colleagues in the Congressional Black Caucus questioned Chisholm's political judgment to seek the presidency.[28] Organizational policy within the BPP never officially prescribed a subordinate role for female members. Furthermore, female leaders in the BPP were not an anathema as was true of other organizations of the Black Power Era.

Revolutionary Black nationalism influenced the Party's position on gender relations. As such, Panther theoreticians viewed sexism as a by-product of class exploitation. Bobby Seale explained, "[I]n the Black Panther Party, we understand that male chauvinism is directly related to the class society."[29] He further notes that the organization sought

> to establish a system based on the goal of absolute equality, of all people, and this must be established on the principle of *from* each and every person, both male and female, according to their ability, and *to* each and every person, both male and female, according to their needs.[30]

Accordingly, the establishment of genuine gender equality in the Party entailed a developmental process. Newton readily admitted in 1970 that "we [Black Panthers] have not established a revolutionary value system; we are only in the process of establishing."[31] Ideological orientation, intraorganizational opposition, political maturation of the membership, organizational coalitions, and government repression all altered, redefined, and impacted gender dynamics in the BPP.

Undoubtedly, male Party members brought patriarchal norms with them to the organization. Moreover, female Panthers initially accepted truncated equality in a show of racial solidarity with their Black brothers. However, manifestations of gender bias were particularly evident during the formative years (1966–68) of the BPP. A gender-based organizational structure (Panther/Pantherette) and frequent male chauvinistic behavior are but two outcomes of early gender bias within the BPP.[32]

Far more pernicious was the Eldridge Cleaver inspired "pussy power" slogan. In an October 1968 speech delivered at Stanford University, Cleaver told the women in the audience that "you have the power to bring a squeaking halt to a lot of things that are going on, and we call that pussy power. We say that political power, revolutionary power grows out the lips of a pussy."[33] Unfortunately, this vulgar phrase was not that of a single male leader. Instead it enjoyed immense popularity among Panthers during the early era of the Party. Panther women were equally guilty of propagating the infamous pussy power slogan.[34] An apparent tendency of various male Party members to view female comrades as sexual objects also characterized early gender relations in the BPP. Some Party leaders attempted to exploit their rank to secure sexual favors from female subordinates. More than one woman left the Party because of incidents of sexual harassment, while others complained of a "macho cult" behavior which manifested in the reluctance of various male members to follow the orders of female superiors.[35]

Yet, the BPP did not remain frozen in a patriarchal state of existence. As one former female Panther, Safiya Bukhari-Alston, notes, "[T]he simple fact that the Black Panther Party had the courage to address the question [women's equality] in the first place was a monumental step forward."[36] Guided by its socialist ideology and challenged and inspired by its female comrades, the Party consciously and readily attempted to develop an antisexist organization.

Most notably, the Central Committee abolished the Panther–Pantherette structure when it reorganized the Party in late 1968. Newton later banned the pussy power slogan. Ironically, Eldridge Cleaver, the originator of the repulsive political phrase, wrote the Party's strongest condemnation of male chauvinism in the organization. In a published July 1969 letter in *The Black Panther* to Ericka Huggins, who was incarcerated on charges associated with the New Haven 14 case, Cleaver declared,

> that women are our other half, they're not our weaker half, they're not our stronger half, but they are our other half and that we sell ourselves out, we sell our children out, and we sell our women out when we treat them in any other manner.[37]

He concluded by issuing the following mandate to eradicate sexism in the BPP,

> It's mandatory, the Minister of Defense Huey P. Newton has said that it is mandatory that all manifestations of male chauvinism be excluded from our ranks and the sisters have a duty and the right to do whatever they want to do in order to see to it that they are not relegated to an inferior position, and that they're not treated as though they are not equal members of the Party and equal in all regards. And that they're not subjected to male practices.[38]

Clearly, this organizational directive reflected the increasing political maturation of the Panther leadership on the issue of gender equality. Male Panthers were alerted to and reprimanded for sexist behavior. In some cases, men in the Party who proved recalcitrant chauvinists were expelled from the organization. Jimmy Slater, a rank-and-file Panther, reported that such an expulsion occurred during his stint at the Cleveland branch of the Party. However, notwithstanding its new-found resolve to eradicate gender bias in the organization, the Party's enforcement of this valued objective was at times uneven and inconsistent. Burkhari-Alston recalled "[m]en who refused to take direction [orders] from women, and we had a framework established to deal with that but because of liberalism and cowardice, as well as fear, a lot of times the framework was not utilized."[39] Nonetheless, the imperfect state of gender relations should not be confused with recent assessments that paint the BPP as a virulent, sexist organization. Hugh Pearson, for example, describes an organization characterized by "wanton disrespect for women by many male Party members who just couldn't rid themselves of bad personal habits no matter how much they claimed allegiance to the 'revolution.'"[40]

Patricia Hill-Collins is generally correct when she writes in her groundbreaking Black feminist treatise that "even though Black women intellectuals have asserted their right to speak both as African Americans and as women, historically these women have not held top leadership positions in Black organizations."[41] However, Elaine Brown's assumption of the leadership mantle of the BPP in 1974 offered a rare exception to the male leadership bias so endemic to African American political organizations. Her tenure as chair of the Party (1974–77) can be partially attributed to the Party's reconceptualization of gender roles. Moving beyond gender-based distinctions in its leadership assignments and organizational duties, the BPP acted in accordance with its revolutionary framework. Consequently, the Party advanced the position that members of similar rank should carry out the same assignments. Men and women in the Party sold newspapers, fed children, and defended Panther offices together. Each member, male or female, received technical-equipment training, attended political education classes, and performed "Officer of the Day" duties. Moreover, women in the BPP held prominent leadership positions at national headquarters in Oakland and in various Panther chapters throughout the nation. Kathleen

Cleaver, Ericka Huggins, and Elaine Brown among others served on the Party's Central Committee. Panther women also held important leadership positions in local BPP affiliates: Audrea Jones led the Massachusetts chapter, while Hazel Mack provided key leadership in the North Carolina chapter; both are representative of the high degree of female leadership in the BPP.

The placement of gay rights on the agenda of the BPP in 1970 during workshops at the Party's Revolutionary People's Constitutional Convention also distinguishes the Panthers. Huey P. Newton's historic position paper on gay rights during the same year provides an explanation of the Party's support of gay liberation. He wrote,

> We have not said much about homosexuals at all, but we must relate to the homosexual movement because it is a real thing. And I know through reading, and through my life experience and observations that homosexuals are not given freedom and liberty by anyone in the society. They might be the most oppressed in the society.[42]

Newton concludes,

> We should be careful about using these terms that might turn our friends off. The terms "faggot" and "punk" should be deleted from our vocabulary, and especially we should not attach names normally designed for homosexuals to men who are enemies of the people, such as Nixon or Mitchell. Homosexuals are not enemies of the people. We should try to form a working coalition with the gay liberation and women's liberation groups. We must always handle social forces in the most appropriate manner.[43]

Demonstrably, the thinking of Newton and the Panthers predated that of other Black power and mainstream civil rights organizations. One observer, Alycee Lane, argues that "the historical significance of Newton's letter should not be underestimated"[44] :

> [I]t was the first time any non-gay black organization whether the mainstream, like the NAACP, or radical like Ron Karenga's Us—recognized the oppression of homophobia; connected that oppression to the plight of black people; and attempted—based on that connection—to build coalitions openly with lesbians and gay men.[45]

William B. Kelly, a long time gay activist in Chicago, adds that "the Black Panthers were one of the first radical groups to favor gay liberation."[46] Following the 1970 Revolutionary People's Constitutional Convention, the Gay Liberation Front proclaimed the BPP as the vanguard of the revolution, a proclamation that mirrored the earlier pronouncement of the Students for a Democratic Society.[47] The Party's commitment to the empowerment of all people, a derivative of its ideology, anchored its support for the self-determination of homosexuals.

Panther Model of Political Action. Panther politics offered a model adopted by oppressed groups both in the domestic and international arenas.

Its organizational influence on other oppressed groups constitutes the fourth and final component of the legacy of the BPP. In one assessment, Phillip Foner, the noted historian, concluded that the Panthers

> in a short time built one of the significant movements in the entire history of black Americans, as well as those of men and women of other races and colors—Puerto Ricans, Mexican-Americans, Chinese-Americans and Poor whites—who have been influenced by the Panthers to build a similar movement in their own communities.[48]

On the domestic front, the Panthers' influence on the Young Lords, originally a Chicago-based Puerto Rican gang that transformed itself into a revolutionary political organization under the leadership of Cha Cha Jiminez in 1969, is easily apparent. Parallels between the Young Lords and the BPP are remarkably striking. Both organizations advocated self-defense of their respective communities. The platform of the Young Lords included the following plank: "WE BELIEVE ARMED SELF DEFENSE AND ARMED STRUGGLE ARE THE ONLY MEANS TO LIBERATION"[49] Other similarities included organizational activities, such as the breakfast programs and health clinics sponsored by both the Young Lords and the Panthers.

Another Latino organization influenced by the BPP was the southern California-based "Brown Berets [which] became the largest non-student radical youth organization in the Mexican American community"[50] Although not fully in accord with the Party's Marxist orientation, the Brown Berets, nonetheless, shared the Panthers' commitment to armed self-defense. Chicano scholar and activist Carlos Munoz notes that "the Brown Berets became a paramilitary organization and, because of it, developed an image as the Chicano counterpart of the Black Panther Party."[51] At the 30th anniversary reunion of the founding of the BPP, Carlos Montes, the former Minister of Information of the Brown Berets, proclaimed that "the struggle and activity of the Black Panther Party inspired Chicano and all Third World communities in America in our fight for justice, equality and political empowerment."[52]

Panther influence also extended to organizations within the White community. The Patriot Party, for example, adopted the Panthers' revolutionary objective. Originally a splinter group from the Young Patriot Organization in uptown Chicago, the Patriot Party's members were poor and working-class Whites. In 1970, the organization claimed five national branches in Cleveland, Ohio; Eugene, Oregon; Chicago, Illinois; New Haven, Connecticut; and a headquarters in New York City. Similar to the Panthers, the Patriot Party operated a free breakfast program and other community service projects. Leadership structure in the Patriot Party also closely resembled that of the BPP. For example, Tom Doston held the rank of field marshal, a critical position in the Panthers' organizational hierarchy also. In addition, White radicals from Ann Arbor, Michigan went so far as to name their group the White Panther Party.[53]

The impact of the BPP transcended the borders of the United States. Panther activism served as a revolutionary exemplar for various oppressed indigenous groups in several foreign countries. Left-wing political formations in England (Black Panther Movement), Israel (Black Panther Party of Israel), Bermuda (Black Beret Cadre), Australia (Black Panther Party), and India (Dalit Panthers) drew from the organization founded by Huey P. Newton and Bobby Seale in the United States.[54] Members of the Black Beret Cadre formed in Bermuda in 1969 adopted the Panthers' signature black beret and sponsored liberation schools and political education classes. Similarly, the Black Panther Party of Israel created by Jews of Moroccan descent in 1971 implemented community services for the children in the slums of West Jerusalem.[55]

Debunking the "Panther Mythology"

Although the BPP produced an illustrious legacy, its historical significance is often minimized, thereby diminishing the role of the Party in African American radicalism. Given the rich multifaceted legacy of the BPP, how does one account for the under appreciation of the organization? This section introduces the notion of Panther mythology as an explanation for the depreciation of the BPP. It is then demonstrated that the portrayals emanating from this "mythology" are falsehoods, misconceptions, and distortions of Party dynamics. Panther mythology entails a set of misperceptions that combine to mute the legacy of the BPP. Depictions of the Party within the Panther mythology characterize the BPP as an anti-White, ultra leftist, lumpen-based, and media-created organization. When seen in this way, it becomes readily understandable why the contributions of the BPP are often diminished. However, the following analysis demonstrates that the mythology's depictions of the Party are inaccurate.

Myth 1: The BPP was an anti-White organization. As an African American, armed political organization, the Black Panther Party for Self-Defense instantly inspired allegations of Black supremacy. Within a year of the Party's creation, the media labeled the BPP a Black zealot group. The day after an armed delegation of Panthers interrupted the proceedings of the California General Assembly to protest the proposed Mulford legislation, the *Sacramento Bee* reported that the Party could "accurately be described as anti-white."[56] Images of the Panthers as Black hate mongers persisted long after the founding of the organization in 1966. For example, an editorial page story on the murder of Huey P. Newton in 1989, published in *The New York Times*, maintained "with black berets atop wide afros, leather jackets, shotguns and rifles, [the Panthers] looked like white America's worst nightmare come to life."[57] Similarly, Norman Hill, an author and journalist, described the Panthers as "the worst enemy the Black man has in America on a par with his implacable, ignorant, bigoted foes in the Southern United States and South Africa."[58]

Perhaps the most groundless portrayal of the BPP is its depiction as an anti-White racist organization. The depiction belied the Panthers' commitment to the principle of revolutionary solidarity and stands in stark contrast with the Party's prism of revolutionary Black nationalism. From the perspective of revolutionary Black nationalism, both race and class account for the oppression of African Americans. Newton notes that as

> a revolutionary nationalist group we see a major contradiction between capitalism in this country and our interest. We realize that this country became very rich upon slavery and that slavery is capitalism in the extreme. We have two evils to fight, capitalism and racism. We must destroy both racism and capitalism.[59]

From the Party's inception, the other cofounder of the BPP, Bobby Seale declared,

> [T]he Black Panther Party is not a Black racist organization, not a racist organization at all. We understand where racism comes from. Our Minister of Defense has taught us to understand that we have to oppose all kinds of racism.[60]

Consequently, during the Black Power Era, the BPP remained above the fray of blanket anti-White denunciations. Todd Gitlin, a prominent member of the Students for a Democratic Society recalls "at a time when most other black militants donned dashikis and glowered at whites, they [Panthers] welcomed white allies."[61] Under the Party's ideological doctrine, all White people were not defined as enemies of African Americans. Rather, the ruling class of the country, high ranking government officials, and the police were deemed the oppressors by Panther theoreticians. Newton remarked that "we don't hate white people; we hate the oppressor. And if the oppressor happens to be white then we hate him."[62]

Eldridge Cleaver attempted to operationalize the philosophical principle of revolutionary solidarity in a 1968 organizational directive entitled "Black Panthers and Black Racism." He appealed to his fellow comrades to

> be strong enough not to yield, not to be Uncle Toms, not to bootlick, not to sell out—but we must also be able to realize that there are white people, brown people, red people, yellow people in this world who are totally dedicated to the destruction of this system of oppression, and we welcome that. We will always be open to working with that. It is necessary for us to put forth the necessity for that. We realize that cultural nationalists in the black community are not our major enemies, they're not our major problem. White racism, ethnocentrism, the arrogance of people in power—these are the major enemies, and we will never confuse the two.[63]

Adherence to the principle of revolutionary solidarity by the BPP provided the impetus for alliances between the Panthers and various other White leftist organizations. Intraracial political cooperation, according to Kathleen Cleaver, "expanded the political base of the movement, and helped contradict the media's false portrayal of the Black Panthers as a group that hated whites."[64] Newton elaborates on the political imperative of Black–White alliances:

> The only way that we're going to be free is to wipe out once and for all the oppressive structure of America. We realize we can't do this without a popular struggle, without many alliances and coalitions, and this is the reason that we're moving in the direction that we are to get as many alliances as possible of people that are equally dissatisfied with the system.[65]

In short, the depiction of the Panthers as a Black racist organization contradicts the BPP's dedication to the empowerment of all people as reflected in the following popular Party slogan:

> We say All Power to the People—Black Power to Black people and Brown Power to Brown People, Red Power to Red People and Yellow Power to Yellow People. We say White Power to White People.[66]

Myth 2: The BPP was an "infantile leftist" organization. Similar to the anti-White portrayal of the Panthers, which minimizes the historical significance of the Party, the labeling of the Panthers as an "infantile-leftist" organization has also served to discount the role of the BPP in the African American freedom struggle. The Party's paramilitary orientation is the source of the ultraleftist depiction of the organization. Newton saw the gun as a major organizing tool for the BPP. The early recruiting success of this tactic was evident when the specter of armed uniformed Panthers at a rally in Richmond, California brought an influx of new members.[67]

Proponents of the ultraleftist interpretation saw the BPP as an adventurist organization that fostered revolutionary martyrdom by challenging people to "pick up the gun."[68] Henry Winston, the former national chairman of the Communist Party, U.S.A., for instance, argued that "the Party disdained the working class and glorified the super-revolutionary tactics of confrontation by an anarchistic élite."[69] Saul Alinsky, the Chicago activist and author of *Rules for Radicals,* was equally critical of the armed self-defense stance of the Panthers when he mockingly remarked that "a guy has to be a political idiot to say all power comes out of the barrel of a gun when the other side has the guns."[70]

In stark contrast to the proclivities of ultraleftist political organizations, the BPP assumed a defensive military posture. Indeed, the two cofounders adopted the name *Black Panther Party for Self-Defense* to emphasize the defensive nature of the organization. During the genesis of the Party, Seale explained to potential Panther recruits:

> We have to defend ourselves against them [the police] because they are breaking down our doors, shooting Black brothers on the streets, and brutalizing sisters on the head. They are wearing guns mostly to intimidate the people from forming organizations to really get our basic political desires and needs answered. The power structure uses

the fascist police against people moving for freedom and liberation. It keeps our people divided, but the program will be what we unite the people around and to teach our people self-defense.[71]

Opposition to spontaneous violence was an important principle of the Party's policy of armed resistance. Seale recalled, "[I]n 1966, numerous acts of police brutality had sparked a lot of spontaneous riots—something that Huey and I were against[—]these spontaneous riots."[72] Newton stressed that the Black Panther Party did not "think that the traditional riots, or insurrections that have taken place are the answer."[73] Panther leadership argued that indiscriminate political violence placed the people at a decided disadvantage and left them vulnerable to the military might of the state. Consequently, the Party opposed rioting. Instead, BPP strategists advocated systematic guerrilla military action as described in a 1968 position paper "The Correct Handling of a Revolution," written by Newton:

> When the Vanguard group destroys the machinery of the oppressor by dealing with him in small groups of three and four, and then escapes the might of the oppressor, the masses will be overjoyed and will adhere to this correct strategy.[74]

During the aftermath of the assassination of Martin Luther King, when many of the cities across the nation were plagued with racial unrest, Oakland remained peaceful. Observers, such as Jerome Skolnick, then director of the National Advisory Commission on Civil Disorders, attributed the absence of violence in Oakland to the work of the Panthers. Bobby Seale held a press conference at the Oakland police station to discourage the Black community from rioting. Similarly, the organizations's condemnation of the terrorist acts committed by the Symbionese Liberation Army (SLA) further attest to the BPP's opposition to wanton acts of political violence.[75]

However, the failure to adopt an offensive military strategy did create tensions within the BPP. Unanimity among Party members on the role of violence never existed. From its inception, there were members of the BPP who, according to Bobby Seale, "related only to the gun."[76] Moreover, the Party's newspaper, The Black Panther, regularly printed articles on weaponry and guerrilla warfare tactics. David Hilliard's candid autobiography revealed early signs of the tactical conflict that materialized in the so-called "Battle of 28th Street" that led to the death of Bobby Hutton, a teenage Panther and early recruit of the Party. Hilliard recounted how Eldridge Cleaver aggressively persuaded a group of Panthers to ambush Oakland police officers in retaliation for the assassination of Dr. Martin Luther King. Tactical differences over the role of political violence later erupted into intraparty strife in 1971. The Newton faction favored accelerating the Party's survival programs, while the Cleaver-led group advocated offensive military action. This organizational conflict would result in the deaths of Robert Webb and Samuel Napier.[77]

Notwithstanding the Party's advocacy of armed resistance, subsequent gun battles, and organizational conflict associated with this tactic, the singular focus on the paramilitary orientation of the BPP obscures the multitactical strategy of the Black Panthers. Unlike infantile-leftist groups, such as the SLA, the Panthers did not rely solely on the tactic of political violence. Instead, the BPP implemented a multifaceted strategy consistent with Lenin's revolutionary prescription that "Marxism does not tie the movement to any particular method. It recognizes the possibility that struggle may assume the most varied forms."[78] From the outset, members of the BPP engaged in nonmilitary organizing activities. These activities included petitioning for community control of the police, lobbying for the installation of traffic lights, teaching Black history classes, promoting tenant and welfare rights, and investigating incidents of police brutality. In 1969, the Party instituted its "serve the people" programs that were supplemented by a voter registration campaign in Cleveland and efforts to combat the narcotic trade in New York. In other words, the Panthers utilized a full panoply of tactics to achieve organizational objectives. Not only does the infantile-leftist interpretation discount the full extent of the Party's activism, it also reinforces a view that the BPP was essentially an artifact of the media.

Myth 3: The BPP was a media-created organization. Media fascination with the Party's rhetorical flair and Panther–police shoot-outs form the basis of the revolutionary phantom depiction of the BPP. According to this portrayal, the Party was merely a creation of the media with greatly exaggerated organizational capabilities and community support. BPP visibility and prominence are attributed to a sensationalist-driven media captivated by the revolutionary theatrics of the Panthers. *Esquire* magazine reports that "more than any other previous black image, the Panther has been created by television. The medium is a Panther lover."[79] Charles O'Brien, then deputy attorney general of California, explains: "[T]he media, particularly television, liked confrontation. They liked the angry rhetoric of the Panthers. They liked people waving around rifles. This made great news copy."[80] And Gail Sheehy, the noted journalist, asserts that "the Panther movement was created by and for the media."[81]

This characterization of the BPP as primarily a media-generated organization not only underestimates community support, it also depreciates the dedication of the organizational membership. The strong ties that the BPP chapters developed in their respective local communities are overlooked. For instance, African Americans throughout the country purchased the newspaper of the organization and provided critical assistance to the Party's various survival programs. Community churches hosted the free breakfast programs for which residents and local businesses often volunteered support and donated monies for the program.

Community citizens also displayed support by attending Panther programs. An estimated ten thousand people attended the 1968 birthday rally for the then-jailed Huey P. Newton. Crowds of two thousand or more people expressed their empathy and respect at the funerals of fallen members of the BPP. On other occasions, African American citizens alerted Party members to the surveillance activities of law enforcement officials. Renée Neblett of the Massachusetts chapter, for example, recounted an occasion when a phone employee warned her of FBI inquiries. Black community residents in New Orleans sheltered and provided medical assistance to a Panther organizer who was wounded during a police raid of the local Panther headquarters and the subject of a police manhunt. Paul Coates, a Panther leader in Baltimore, recalled community residents

> putting themselves in front of our building which was under the threat
> of being raided at any moment by the police. Here was a group of
> people, mostly who didn't know you personally, you know, [yet] have
> decided to place themselves outside [the Panther's office]. We're
> under siege for about two weeks as I remember it. Every day the line
> was refreshed for the time of the siege. The police backed down. They
> let it be known that they weren't going to raid the Panther
> headquarters.[82]

Panther allies could be found in unlikely quarters of the African American community. Notwithstanding the Party's often scathing criticism of mainstream civil rights organizations, both the NAACP and Southern Christian Leadership Conference (SCLC) lent support to the BPP. The NAACP contributed $50,000 to ensure the continuation of a commission created to investigate incidents between the Panthers and police. SCLC President Rev. Ralph Abernathy pledged to provide moral and material support to the New York Panther 21 at a January 24, 1970 press conference. Moreover, a Louis Harris survey conducted in 1970 found that twenty-five percent of African Americans agreed that the Black Panther Party represented their views. These examples offer compelling evidence of the extent and the degree to which the African American community supported the Black Panther Party.[83] To simply attribute the existence of the BPP to media coverage discounts the personal sacrifice, commitment, and activism exhibited by members of the Party. Party members who did not earn a salary endured a demanding, often fifteen-hour, daily regimen. Selling the Party's newspaper, staffing the organization's facilities, implementing survival programs, and mobilizing the community comprised the typical day of the rank-and-file Panther. As an organization targeted by the FBI's COINTELPRO program, membership could mean the forfeiture of one's freedom and in some cases the loss of one's life. The most glaring example of the latter was the December 4, 1969 raid in Chicago during which Fred Hampton and Mark Clark were shot to death by local police officers. Constant police surveillance and government harassment ensured the frequent arrest of Party members. Charles R. Garry, the chief legal counsel for the BPP reports that the organization paid over $200,000 in unrefundable bail-bond premiums for the release of arrested members during a critical two-year period (December

1967 to December 1969) in the Party's national growth.[84] Furthermore, the BPP was riddled with police informers and agent provocateurs who sought to disrupt organizational activities. Police agents, for example, were instrumental in the New York 21 case in which Panthers were arrested and later exonerated after a lengthy trial on charges of conspiracy to bomb New York City department stores, police stations, and subways.[85]

Myth 4: The BPP was a "lumpen-based" organization. The lumpen depiction of the BPP, advanced by governmental officials, scholars, and progressive activists, constitutes the final element of the Panther mythology. Proponents of the lumpen interpretation contend that the Party was primarily an organization of the Black criminal class, ex-prisoners, hustlers, and thugs. Jerry Leonard, former assistant attorney general under President Nixon, characterized the Black Panthers as "nothing but hoodlums," while Todd Gitlin, former student activist, refers to the Party as a "revolutionary gang."[86] Gitlin writes, "[T]hey called themselves a party, but the Panthers were closer to an outlaw political gang—precisely the unit which had exercised such a powerful hold on the dissident imagination since the beats and Brando and the Cuban *Barbados*."[87] Radical scholars Michael Omi and Howard Winant suggest that "the Black Panther Party sought to mobilize the lumpen proletariat," while other political groups organized students and union workers.[88] And Kwame Ture (Stokely Carmichael) declares that the Panthers "knowingly built a party on the lumpen proletariat when Marx and Engels said that they vacillate too much, have too much contact with the police, and can become spies. Stupid."[89] Thus, the consensus is that the lumpen proletariat sector of the African American community constituted the core of the BPP.

Observers further suggest that Party leaders committed an egregious tactical error by organizing the most volatile, untrustworthy, and undisciplined sector of the African American community. Amiri Baraka, poet and long-time political activist maintains that

> [u]nder the sinister influence of the Bakuninist-anarchist ideology spread by Elder Eldridge Cleaver, which masqueraded as Marxism, the Panthers pushed the incorrect line that the revolutionary class base that would lead socialist revolution was the lumpen, i.e., the pimps, hustlers, dope pushers, and prostitutes; thus romanticizing an inconsistent, sometimes dangerous, class already destroyed by capitalism.[90]

More specifically, Marx and Engels describe the composition of the lumpen proletariat class as "thieves and criminals of all kinds, living on the crumbs of society, people without [a] definite trade, vagabonds, people without a hearth or home."[91] Under the logic of Marxist analysis, individuals of the lumpen proletariat class "stand on the margins of the class system because they are not wholly integrated into the division of labor."[92] Furthermore, the undisciplined character and weak loyalties of this sector renders it incompatible with the rigors of revolutionary activity.

Contrary to Marxist doctrine, Newton and other Panther theoreticians viewed the lumpen proletariat as a potential leading revolutionary force. Panther strategists sought to harness the fearlessness exhibited by the so-called street brothers. Newton reasoned that "the brothers on the block" could play an invaluable role in the liberation struggle because of their courageousness. Party leaders were heavily influenced by the writings of Frantz Fanon on the critical role of the lumpen proletariat. Indeed, the lumpen was championed by Party comrades. Members of the Black Panther Party assumed a lumpen identity, despite possessing socioeconomic status contrary to that of the lumpen. [93]

Consequently, the lumpen portrayal of the organization appears understandable in light of the premium the Party placed on the lumpen class. Nonetheless, this depiction distorts the nature of the Panther membership. Several considerations cast doubt on the assertion that the primary social base of BPP was, in fact, the lumpen proletariat class of the African American community.

First, the initial conception of the "brothers on the block" notion was more inclusive than the traditional Marxist definition of the lumpen proletariat class. This is an important analytic distinction since the Party's version included the working poor as well as the criminal class identified by orthodox Marxists. Initially, the Panthers envisioned a lumpen more akin to a sub-proletariat class devoid of the parasitical lifestyle associated with the traditional lumpen sector. Seale explains,

> [W]e articulated and understood the lumpen proletariat as a potentially valuable force in developing a political revolutionary organization. Not the lumpen proletariat that the strict doctrinaire Marxists talk about. We were saying that our lumpen proletariat, even though they get into illegitimate activity, okay, it was also the Black mother who had to scrub Miss Anne's kitchen floors, right? [94]

However, the writings and leadership of Eldridge Cleaver promoted a narrow conception of the brother-on-the-block notion. While Cleaver does acknowledge a broader notion of the Black lumpen proletariat, he nonetheless emphasizes the criminal element of this class:

> those who live by their wits, existing off that which they rip off, who stick guns in the faces of businessmen and say 'stick' em up,' or 'give it up'! Those who don't even want a job, who hate to work and can't relate to punching some pig's time clock, who would rather punch a pig in the mouth and rob him than punch that same pig's time clock and work for him, those whom Huey P. Newton calls "the illegitimate capitalists." [95]

Cleaver's view of the lumpen mirrored that of his personal life. Prior to joining the BPP in 1967, Eldridge Cleaver spent much of his adult life in prison on an assortment of criminal charges. Under Cleaver's leadership (1967–71), the Party successfully recruited from the hustler/criminal element of the African American community, and Panther politics certainly resonated with the lumpen class as individuals with backgrounds similar to Cleaver's eagerly joined the Party. In fact, several early prominent West Coast Panthers, George Gaines, William Brent, and Alprentice "Bunchy" Carter, were former prison associates of Cleaver.

Nevertheless, the Party always drew members from a broad cross-section of the African American community. While the southern California chapter of the BPP may have been characterized by a distinctive lumpen character, affiliates like Boston possessed a strong student component.[96] From the Party's inception, African Americans from varied backgrounds joined the BPP. George Murray, the Party's first Minister of Education, was a college instructor. Earl Anthony, one of the first captains of the BPP and later FBI informant, was a law student and graduate of the University of Southern California, while Sidney F. Walton and John Williams were principals of elementary schools in Sausalito, California and Detroit, Michigan, respectively.[97] Furthermore, a host of Party members were high school or college students when they joined the BPP. Ericka Huggins, JoNina Abron, Walter Turner, Deborah Bremond, Yvonne Jenkins, and Charles Pinderhughes are all examples of the multitude of Party comrades who entered the organization as students. Indeed, the heterogeneous nature of the Party's membership became a recurring source of tension in the BPP. Renée Neblett spoke of such tensions in her interactions with members of the Detroit branch of the BPP, and Geronimo ji Jaga alludes to these differences in his discussion of Masai Hewitt, a former Minister of Education of the BPP:

> To make a long story short, he ends up being one of the best educators—he has a very deep resonant voice—and the more he teaches, the more I like him, because I'm learning. Because I've never had time to go deep into *Das Kapital*, or any of the other esoteric books. He's making sense of the economy, of fascism, of slavery, socialism—all this economic analysis.

> But he was still a nut. He was just so much like a kid! He was unable to relate to the "lumpen proletariat." He could relate to an Angela Davis, who was a *giant* in that same field, but to us regular folks he'd get very technical and very snotty-nosed. He would criticize the lumpen in a haughty, condescending way. He would get down on them and say, "Well, Marx wouldn't have liked that. That was the scum of society." And that would cause problems. [98]

This apparent diversity of the Panther membership underscores the importance of empirical verification of the lumpen assessment. A cursory glance of the social background of the members on the Party's first Central Committee, the primary decision-making organ of the BPP, indicates that of the eleven members, only one, Eldridge Cleaver, the Party's Minister of Information, possessed the traditional traits of the lumpen sector.

Original Central Committee of the Black Panther Party (April 1968)

Name	Position
Huey P. Newton	Minister of Defense
Bobby G. Seale	Chairman
Eldridge Cleaver	Minister of Information
David Hilliard	Chief of Staff
George Mason Murray	Minister of Education
Stokely Carmichael	Prime Minister
H. Rap Brown	Minister of Justice
James Forman	Minister of Foreign Affairs
Emory Douglas	Minister of Culture
Melvin Newton	Minister of Finance
Kathleen Cleaver	Communications Secretary

Source: G. Louis Heath, ed., *Off the Pigs: The History and Literature of the Black Panther Party* .

Table 2

Furthermore, neither one of the organization's cofounders, Newton nor Seale, fit the socioeconomic profile of the so-called lumpen proletariat. Newton, a college student, worked as a counselor with the city's antipoverty program, and Seale, a skilled worker of nine trades, also attended college and supervised an Oakland poverty center. Kathleen Cleaver, daughter of a United States ambassador and the only female member of the original Central Committee, dropped out of college to work full time in the movement. George Murray, the Party's first Minister of Education, taught English at San Francisco State University.

Interviews of former Panthers, along with additional data, suggest the socioeconomic profile of the rank-and-file Panthers contradicts the lumpen perception of the organization. A typical Panther was a young adolescent still in search of adulthood who was likely a high school or college student.[99] However, the diversity of the Party membership is often overlooked. For instance, one study suggests that the similarity of backgrounds helped to unify the Party and that the shared community of the Panthers was their "block boy" experience.[100]

Although the two cofounders of the BPP, Newton and Seale, did in fact champion the Black lumpen, they always attempted to develop an all-inclusive African American freedom organization. Bobby Seale explains,

> Huey understood that Oakland was a typical black community, so we took the ten-point platform and program—a thousand copies of it—and went to the black community with them. He didn't just pass out

the platform in people's hands. He stopped, talked, and discussed the points on the ten-point platform with all the black brothers and sisters on the block, and with mothers who had been scrubbing Miss Ann's kitchen. We talked to brothers and sisters in colleges, in high schools, who were on parole, on probation, who'd been in jails, who'd just gotten out of jail, and brothers and sisters who looked like they were on their way to jail.[101]

Newton and Seale sought to build an organization that omitted the social class bias of the mainstream civil rights groups and many of the Black nationalist formations of the sixties. In short, a reconsideration of the lumpen portrayal is in order.

Conclusion

This chapter has sought to enhance the understanding of the historical significance of the Black Panther Party. It offers an explanation—Panther mythology—for the depreciation of the Panthers. The analysis undertaken here should not be mistaken for idolatry of the BPP. Undoubtedly, the Party was guilty at times of dogmatism, unresolved conflicts (armed struggle vs. community programs; mass vs. cadre organization), and authoritarianism. Rather, this chapter is a reaffirmation of the legacy of the BPP that debunks the many misconceptions of the organization. Moreover, the study starts a process of documenting the history, accomplishments, and errors of the BPP. This is a crucial endeavor because "'the sixties' remain the site of intense ideological contestation more than twenty years after the decade's close."[102]

Scholarly research on the BPP is needed to counteract the demonization of the Panthers in particular and the Black power movement in general. Furthermore, the recent emergence of Panther-style organizations in Milwaukee, Wisconsin (Black Panther Militia); Dallas, Texas (New Black Panther Party); and Los Angeles, California (New African American Vanguard Movement) further stresses the crucial need for systematic scholarship on the BPP experience.[103] Former Panthers have complained that these contemporary Panther-like organizations are only captivated by the paramilitary stance of the organization, which makes them susceptible to replicating the errors of their predecessors. Lastly, scholarly analysis of the Panther experience would preclude one from either romanticizing or demonizing the BPP. Rather, a systematic examination should lead one to draw a more critical, yet balanced, appraisal of this noteworthy African American freedom organization.

NOTES

Acknowledgments: A version of this chapter was presented at the annual meeting of the National Conference of Black Political Scientists, March 12–15, 1992, in Oakland, California. The authors wish to thank Paula Dressel, Kimberly James, Joe McCormick, Robert C. Smith, and Akinyele Umoja for their helpful and insightful comments that strengthened this study. Charles E. Jones wishes to express appreciation to his graduate assistants Eric Bridges, Ellis Henderson, and Fred McKinney for their research assistance over the years. Most importantly, we express our gratitude to the members of the Black Panther Party for granting interviews and sharing their insights.

1. Robert L. Allen, *Black Awakening in Capitalist America: An Analytic History* (New York: Anchor Books, 1970), 23–28.

2. National Advisory Commission on Civil Disorders, *Report of the National Advisory Commission on Civil Disorders* (Washington, D.C.: U.S. Government Printing Office, 1968), 19–21.

3. Robert L. Allen, *Black Awakening in Capitalist America: An Analytic History* (New York: Anchor Books, 1970), 23.

4. See Robert C. Smith, "Black Power and the Transformation from Protest to Politics," *Political Science Quarterly* 96 (1981): 431–44; Clayborne Carson, *In Struggle: SNCC and the Black Awakening of the 1960's* (Cambridge: Harvard University Press, 1981), 215–28; and William L. Van Deburg, *New Day in Babylon: The Black Power Movement and American Culture, 1965–1975* (Chicago: University of Chicago Press, 1992).

5. See the following sources for additional information on the various applications of Black power: James T. Wooten, "Integrated City Rising on an Old Plantation," *New York Times*, 25 July 1972, 24. Soul City, North Carolina, initially conceived by Floyd McKissick in 1969, was located in a northern rural economically depressed area of the state between Warren and Vance counties. McKissick envisioned an integrated town of 55,000 people that would stimulate economic development in that region of the state. In 1972, the United States Department of Housing and Urban Development (HUD) guaranteed $14 million dollars in bonds issued by the city. However, HUD terminated funding in 1979 and liquidated all city assets in 1980. See A. O. Sullberger, "H.U.D. to Foreclose on Soul City, Troubled 'New Town' in Carolina," *New York Times*, 29 June 1979, A–12, and "Soul City and U.S. Agree on Plan to Liquidate Town," *New York Times*, 5 June 1980, A–16. The most comprehensive analysis of the League of Black Revolutionary Workers is James A. Geschwender, *Class, Race, and Worker Insurgency: The League of Revolutionary Black Workers* (Cambridge: Cambridge University Press, 1977). Also see Maulana Karenga, *Kawaida Theory: An Introductory Outline* (Inglewood, Calif.: Kawaida Publications, 1982); Maulana Karenga, "Society, Culture and the Problem of Self-Consciousness: A Kawaida Analysis," in *Philosophy Born of Struggle*, ed. Leonard Harris (Dubuque, Iowa: Kendall/Hunt, 1982). For additional information on the Republic of New Africa, see Milton Henry (Amiri Abubakari Obadele), "The Republic of New Africa: 'We Are the Government for the Non-Self-Governing Blacks Held Captive in the United States'" in *Black Nationalism in America*, eds. John H. Bracey, August Meier, and Elliot Rudwick (New York: Bobbs-Merrill Company, 1970), 518–22. Amiri Abubakari Obadele, "Free The Land: The True Story of the Trials of the RNA–11" in *Mississippi and the Continuing Struggle to Establish an*

Independent Black Nation in the States of the Deep South (Washington, D.C.: House of Songhay, 1984); a critique of this strategy is found in Matthew Holden, *The Politics of the Black "Nation"* (New York: Chandler, 1973), 68–70. John T. McCartney provides an in-depth discussion of the pluralist application of Black power in his *Black Power Ideologies: An Essay in African-American Political Thought* (Philadelphia: Temple University Press, 1992), ch. 9.

6. Alphonso Pinkney, *Red, Black and Green: Black Nationalism in the United States* (New York: Cambridge University Press, 1970), 98.

7. Sahu Barron, "A New Order in Babylon: The Revolutionary Legacy of the Black Panther Party," *Liberation!: Journal of Revolutionary Marxism* (December 1989): 3.

8. Robert Weisbrot, *Freedom Bound: A History of America's Civil Rights Movement* (New York: W.W. Norton, 1991).

9. William J. Grimshaw, *Bitter Fruit: Black Politics and the Chicago Machine 1931–1991* (Chicago: University of Chicago Press, 1992).

10. Dempsey J. Travis, *An Autobiography of Black Politics* (Chicago: Urban Research Press, 1987), 456. For additional information on the death of Mark Clark and Fred Hampton, see Wilkins and Clark, *Search and Destroy* and "The Black Panthers, 1968–1969 'How Serious and Deadly the Game'" in *Voices of Freedom: An Oral History of the Civil Rights Movement from 1950's through the 1980's,* eds. Henry Hampton and Steve Fauer (New York: Bantam Books, 1980), 511–38.

11. Huey P. Newton, *Revolutionary Suicide* (New York: Writers and Readers Publishing, 1995), 113.

12. Huey P. Newton, *To Die for the People* (New York: Writers and Readers Publishing, 1995), 5.

13. Newton, *To Die for the People,* 13.

14. See the various autobiographies of former Panthers for the importance of armed self-defense: Bobby Seale, *Seize the Time: The Story of the Black Panther Party* (Baltimore: Black Classic Press, 1991), 72–29, 134–55; Newton, *Revolutionary Suicide,* 101–27, 145–51; Newton, *To Die for the People,* 7–9, 11–19 and 82–91; William Lee Brent, *Long Time Gone: A Black Panther's True-Life Story of His Hijacking and Twenty-Five Years in Cuba* (New York: Times Books, 1996), 93–98; Elaine Brown, *A Taste of Power: A Black Woman's Story* (New York: Pantheon Books, 1992), 118–21; David Hilliard and Lewis Cole, *This Side of Glory: The Autobiography of David Hilliard and the Story of the Black Panther Party* (Boston, Mass.: Little, Brown and Company, 1993), 179–80; Earl Anthony, *Picking Up the Gun: A Report on the Black Panthers* (New York: Dial Press, 1970), 5–9; Earl Anthony, *Spitting in the Wind: The True Story Behind the Violent Legacy of the Black Panther Party* (Malibu, Calif.: Roundtable Publishing Co., 1990), 22–32. For information on the Seattle branch, see House Committee on Internal Security, *Black Panther Party: Part 2, Investigation of Seattle Chapter,* 91st Cong., 2d sess. (Washington, D.C.: GPO, 1970). See the following sources for a detailed discussion of Panther–police gun battles: Roy Wilkins and Ramsey Clark, *Search and Destroy: A Report by the Commission of Inquiry into the Black Panthers and the Police* (New York: Metropolitan Applied Research Center, 1973); Christopher Chandler, "The Black Panther Killings," *New Republic* 161 (10 January 1970), 41–49; Black Panther Party, *Fallen Comrades of the Black Panther Party* [pamphlet] (n.d.).

15. Manning Marable, *The Second Reconstruction in Black America, 1945–1990* (Jackson, Miss.: University Press of Mississippi, 1991), 110.

16. Philip S. Foner, introduction to *The Black Panthers Speak: The Manifesto of the Party: The First Complete Documentary Record of the Panther's Program*, ed. Philip S. Foner (New York: J. B. Lippincott Co., 1970), xxiv.

17. Examples of historical antecedents to the Black Panther Party's advocacy of armed self-defense include David Walker's *Appeal* (Baltimore: Black Classic Press, 1993); Martin R. Delany, *The Condition, Elevation, Emigration and Destiny of the Colored People of the United States* (1852; reprint, Baltimore: Black Classic Press, 1993); and Maria W. Stewart, *America's First Black Woman Political Writer* (Bloomington: Indiana University Press, 1987). Also, see the classic study on the leadership of Marcus Garvey by Tony Martin, *Race First: The Ideological and Organizational Struggles of Marcus Garvey and the Universal Negro Improvement Association* (Dover, Mass.: The Majority Press, 1976), 187, 194; the discussion of the African Blood Brotherhood in Mark Naison, *Communists in Harlem* (New York: Grove Press, 1983), 5–8, 17–18, and W. Burghardt Turner and Joyce Moore Turner, eds., *Richard B. Moore: Caribbean Militant in Harlem*(Bloomington, Ind.: Indiana University Press, 1992), 34–41. For examples of post-World War II proponents of Black armed resistance, see Robert Carl Cohen, *Black Crusader: A Biography of Robert Franklin Williams* (Secaucus, N.J.: Lyle Stuart, 1972); Robert F. Williams, *Negroes with Guns* (Chicago: Third World Press, 1973); and Charles R. Sims, "Armed Defense," in *Black Protest: History, Documents and Analyses, 1619 to the Present*, ed. Joanne Grant (Greenwich, Conn.: Fawcett Publications, 1968), 357–66; Maxwell C. Stanford, "Revolutionary Action Movement (RAM): A Case Study of an Urban Revolutionary Movement in Western Capitalist Society" (master's thesis, Clark Atlanta University, 1986); and Clayborne Carson, *In Struggle: SNCC and the Black Awakening of the 1960s* (Cambridge, MA: Harvard University Press, 1981), which examines the origins and demise of the Student Nonviolent Coordinating Committee.

18. The *Black Panther*, "On Violence," in *The Black Panthers Speak*, ed. Philip S. Foner (New York: J. B. Lippincott Co., 1970), 19–20.

19. Initially a monthly publication, *The Black Panther* became a weekly newspaper from January 1968 until 1978. Afterwards, the production of the newspaper was erratic, and it became a biweekly until it ceased publication. See JoNina Abron, "'Raising the Consciousness of the People': The Black Panther Intercommunal News Service, 1967–1980," in *Voices from the Underground: Volume I, Insider Histories of the Vietnam Era Underground Press*, ed. Ken Wachsberger (Ann Arbor, Mich.: Mica Press, 1993).

20. E. D. Hirsch, Jr., *Cultural Literacy* (New York: Vintage Books, 1988), 23.

21. Memorandum from the San Francisco field office to FBI Headquarters 5/15/70, U. S. Senate, *Final Report of the Select Committee to Study Government Operations with Respect to Intelligence Operations,* 94th Cong., 2d sess., 1976, S. Rept. 94, 755.

22. Jim Fletcher, Tanaquil Jones, and Sylvere Lotringer, eds., *Still Black, Still Strong: Survivors of the U.S. War Against Black Revolutionaries* (New York: Semiotext(e), 1993), 226; and G. Louis Heath, ed., *Off the Pigs!: The History and Literature of the Black Panther Party* (Metuchen, N.J.: Scarecrow Press, 1976), 84.

23. Hilliard and Cole, *This Side of Glory*, 211–12.

24. Leslie B. McLemore, "Black Political Socialization and Political Change: The Black Panther Platform as a Model of Radical Political Socialization," *Negro Educational Review* 26 (1975): 155.

25. For further information on the origins, nature, and activities of the coalition between BPP and Peace and Freedom Party, see Earl Anthony, *Picking up the Gun*, chap. 5; Gene Marine, *The Black Panthers* 106–22; Richard Major, *A Panther is a Black Cat* (New York: Morrow, 1971), 92–95; Bobby Seale, *Seize the Time*, 207-11; Ed Keating, *Free Huey: The True Story of the Trial of Huey P. Newton* (New York: Ramparts Press, 1971). For a discussion of the working relationship between the Patriot Party and the BPP, see "The Patriot Party Speaks to the Movement" in *The Black Panthers Speak*, ed. Phillip S. Foner, 239–42; G. Louis Heath, ed., *Off the Pigs!*, 96; Lawrence Lader, *Power of the Left: American Radical Movements Since 1946* (New York: W.W. Norton, 1979), 197, 269. See also Hugh Pearson, *The Shadow of a Panther*, 327; Todd Gitlin, *Sixties*, 372; and Lawrence Lader, *Power of the Left*, 330, for further discussion of the political ties between the BPP and the White Panther Party.

26. Julian Bond, Norman Dorsen, and Charles Rembar, *The Trial of Bobby Seale* (New York: Priam Books, 1970); Hilliard and Cole, *This Side of Glory*, 259–65; "Interview with Bob Avakian, The Black Panthers, The Early Years and What's Up Today," *Revolutionary Worker*, 14 May 1996, 6–7. White leftist participation in the two major BPP conferences is examined in G. Louis Heath, ed., *Off the Pigs!*, 186–87. Also see Donald Freed, *Agony in New Haven: The Trial of Bobby Seale, Ericka Huggins and The Black Panther Party* (New York: Simon and Schuster, 1973); Peter Zimroth, *Perversion of Justice: The Prosecution and Acquittal of the Panther 21* (New York: Viking Press, 1974); Marlise James, "Charles Garry, Chief Defense Counsel of the Black Panther Party," in *The People's Lawyer*, ed. Marlise James (New York: Holt, Reinhart and Winston, 1973).

27. See Kit Kim Holder, "The History of the Black Panther Party, 1966–1972: A Curriculum Tool for Afrikan American Studies" (Ph.D. diss., University of Massachusetts, 1990), 122–23; Philip S. Foner, "Alliances and Coalitions," in *The Black Panthers Speak*, ed. Philip S. Foner, 219. The most insightful discussion of the SNCC–BPP alliance is found in Clayborne Carson's *In Struggle*, 278–86; and James Forman, *The Making of Black Revolutionaries* (Seattle, Wash.: Open Hand Publishing, Inc., 1990), 522–43. For further discussion of the Party's relationship with the League of Black Revolutionary Workers see James Geschwender, *Class, Race and Worker Insurgency*, 140–42; and Michael Newton, *Bitter Grain: Huey Newton and the Black Panther Party* (Los Angeles, Calif.: Holloway House Publishing Company, 1991), 108.

28. See Shirley Chisholm, *The Good Fight* (New York: Bantam Books, 1974), 101–2; "Black Panther Party for Shirley Chisholm," *New York Times*, 28 April 1972, A4.; "Democrats Seek to Retain the Young," *New York Times*, 20 May 1972, A3.

29. Bobby Seale, *Seize the Time*, 393.

30. Ibid, 394.

31. Newton, *To Die for the People*, 153.

32. Angela D. Brown, "Servants of the People: A History of Women in the Black Panther Party" (senior thesis, Harvard University, 1992); and Seale, *Seize the Time*, 393–404.

33. Eldridge Cleaver, *Post-Prison Writings and Speeches* (New York: Vintage Books, 1969), 142–43.

34. For instance, Gail Sheehy in her book *Panthermania* purports that Elaine Brown was a major proponent of this slogan. See Gail Sheehy, *Panthermania: The Clash of Black Against Black in One American City* (New York: Harper Row Publishers, 1971), 19. However, what is often overlooked in the various critiques

of the "pussy power" slogan is the Party's revolutionary outlook which deemed that a person, male or female, used everything at their disposal to conquer the oppressor. Panthers pointed to the revolutionary role played by Vietnamese women who assumed the role of prostitutes to wage struggle against American soldiers. Similarly, Cora Presley's excellent study of the role of women in Kenya's Mau Mau movement notes that Mau Mau female leaders recruited female prostitutes who provided invaluable assistance to the struggle against colonialism in Kenya. See Cora Presley, *Kihuyu Women, The Mau Mua Rebellion and Social Change in Kenya* (Boulder, Co.: Westview Press, 1992). For a critique of the "pussy power" slogan see Jan Zahler Lebow, "From 'Pussy Power' to Political Power: The History of Women in the Black Panther Party," unpublished paper, Afro-American Studies seminar paper, UCLA, Fall 1986.

35. For example, Regina Jennings left the Black Panther Party because of sexual harassment. Also see Brown, *Servants of the People* for additional cases. Assata Shakur, among others, complained about macho behavior among male members. See Assata Shakur, (formerly Joanne Chesimard), *An Autobiography* (Westport, Conn.: Lawrence Hill & Company, 1987), 223–24.

36. Safiya Bukhari-Alston, "The Question of Sexism Within the Black Panther Party," *Black Panther Community News Service*, Fall/Winter 1993, 3.

37. Eldridge Cleaver, "Message to Sister Ericka Huggins of the Black Panther Party," in *The Black Panthers Speak*, ed. Phillip Foner, 99.

38. Ibid.

39. Safiya Bukhari-Alston, "The Question of Sexism Within the Black Panther Party," 3.

40. Hugh Pearson, *The Shadow of the Panther*, 176.

41. Patricia Hill-Collins, *Black Feminist Thought* (Boston: Urwin Human, 1990), 8.

42. Newton, *To Die for the People*, 153.

43. Ibid.

44. Alycee J. Lane, "Newton's Law," *BLK* (March 1991): 11.

45. Ibid.

46. Sarah Craig, "Panther Leader Slain: Early Gay-Rights Supporter Gunned Down," *Windy City Times (Chicago)*, 8 August 1989, 6.

47. Heath, ed., *Off the Pigs!*, 182.

48. Foner, ed., *The Black Panthers Speak*, xxxix.

49. Ibid., 237.

50. Carlos Munoz, Jr., *Youth Identity Power: Chicano Movement* (New York: Verso, 1989), 85.

51. Munoz, *Youth Identity Power*, 86.

52. Carlos Montes, "Letter of Solidarity: Brown Berets and the Black Panther Party," 9 October 1996; Author's personal collection. This letter was read at "It's About Time" the 30th anniversary celebration of the founding of the Black Panther Party, October 11–13, 1996, Oakland, California.

53. Pearson, *The Shadow of the Panther*, 327; and Foner, ed., *The Black Panthers Speak*, 239–43.

54. Citations on the Black Panther Movement in England include Philip S. Foner, ed., *The Black Panthers Speak*, xxxvii; "Black Panther Men Accused of Plot," *London Times*, 27 November 1968, 6; "National Conference on the Rights of Black People," May 22–23, 1971, flyer; the Black Panther Movement, April 23,

1971, The Archives of Labor History and Urban Affairs, Wayne State University, Detroit, Michigan; For the Black Panther Party of Israel, see Deborah Bernstein, "Conflict and Protest in Israeli Society: The Case of the Black Panthers of Israel," *Youth and Society* 14 (1984): 129–51; Arie Bober, ed., *The Other Israel: The Radical Case Against Zionism* (New York: Anchor Books, 1972), 24–31. For information on the Black Beret Cadre in Bermuda, see Holder, "The History of the Black Panther Party 1966–1972," 170, and "Revolutionary People's Communication Network: International News (Bermuda)," *Right On!* 1, 6 (1971): 13; "The Black Beret: Voice of the Black Community," *Right On!* 1, 10 (1971): 18. For the Black Panther Party in Australia, see "Black Panthers Form Party," *New York Times*, 19 January 1972, 6; John Collins, "Oodgeroo of the Tribe Nonnuccal," *Race and Class* 35 (1994): 80. On the Dalit Panthers in India, see Runoko Rashidi, "Dalits: The Black Untouchables of India," in *African Presence in Early Asia*, ed. Ivan Van Sertima and Runoko Rashidi (New Brunswick, N.J.: Transaction Books, 1988), 246; and V. T. Rajshekar, "The Black Untouchables of India: Reclaiming Our Cultural Heritage," in *African Presence in Early Asia*, 237.

55. See Deborah Bernstein, "Conflict and Protest in Israeli Society," 134.

56. Gene Marine, *The Black Panthers* (New York: New American Library, 1969), 67.

57. "The Black Panthers—Two Paths," *New York Times*, 24 August 1989, A24.

58. Norman Hill, ed., *The Black Panther Menace: America's Neo-Nazis* (New York: Popular Library, 1971), 10.

59. Huey Newton, "Huey Newton Talks to the Movement About the Black Panther Party, Cultural Nationalism, SNCC, Liberals and White Revolutionaries," in *The Black Panthers Speak*, ed. Phillip Foner, 51.

60. Seale, *Seize the Time*, 69–70.

61. Gitlin, *The Sixties*, 349.

62. Newton, "Huey Newton Talks to the Movement," 57.

63. Eldridge Cleaver, "Black Panther Black Racism," *Open City: Weekly Review of the L.A. Renaissance*, 27 December– 2 January 1968, 1. The Cleaver memo was originally prepared as an organizational directive and later published in the *Open City*.

64. Kathleen Cleaver, "How TV Wrecked the Black Panthers," *Channels* (November/December 1982): 99.

65. Huey P. Newton, "To the R. N. A." in *The Black Panthers Speak*, ed. Phillip Foner, 72.

66. Fred Hampton, "You Can Murder a Liberator but You Can't Murder Liberation," in *The Black Panthers Speak*, ed. Phillip Foner, 145.

67. Seale, *Seize the Time*, 139.

68. Spartacist League, "Rise and Fall of the Panthers: End of the Black Power Era?" *Marxist Bulletin* 5 (1978): 34–45.

69. Henry Winston, "Crisis of the Black Panther Party," in *Strategy for a Black Agenda*, ed. Henry Winston (New York: International Publishers, 1973), 213.

70. Israel Shenker, "For Alinsky, Organizers Clutch Key to the Future," *New York Times*, 6 January 1971, 39. Also see Saul D. Alinsky, *Rules for Radicals: A Practical Primer for Realistic Radicals* (New York: Vintage Books, 1971).

71. Seale, *Seize the Time*, 65.

72. Hampton and Fayer, eds., *Voices of Freedom*, 352.

73. Newton, "Huey Newton Talks to the Movement," in *The Black Panthers Speak*, ed. Phillip Foner, 62.

74. Huey P. Newton, "The Correct Handling of a Revolution," in *The Black Panthers Speak*, ed. Phillip Foner, 41.

75. See Jerome H. Skolnick, *The Politics of Protest: A Task Force Report Submitted to the National Commission on the Causes and Prevention of Violence* (New York: Simon and Schuster, 1969), 153; Holder, "The History of the Black Panther Party, 1966–1971," 219.

76. Seale, *Seize the Time*, 366.

77. Robert Webb, a Panther from San Francisco who aligned with the anti-Newton faction, was allegedly shot to death on March 8, 1971, in New York City by Newton supporters. In retaliation for the death of Webb, Samuel Napier, the Party's Circulation Manager of the Black Panther Intercommunal News Service was tortured and murdered on April 17, 1971, in New York City. See Kathleen Cleaver, "Sister Act," *Transition* 60 (1993): 98, and Hilliard and Cole, *This Side of Glory*, 325–26.

78. Geoffrey Fairbarn, *Revolutionary Guerrilla Warfare* (Baltimore, MD: Penguin Books, 1974), 73.

79. "Is It Too Late for the Panthers To Be Pals with You?" *Esquire* 74 (1970), 16.

80. Hampton and Fayer, eds., *Voices of Freedom*, 368.

81. Sheehy, *Panthermania*, 8.

82. Paul Coates, interview by Charles E. Jones, 21 April 1993, Baltimore, MD. Also see "Baltimore Police Raid Panther Headquarters," *Guardian*, 9 May 1970, 5, and Renée Neblett interview by Charles E. Jones, 10 May 1992, Boston, Mass.

83. Paul Delaney, "Blacks in New Orleans Say They Are Sheltering Panther Leader Wounded in Police Raid," *New York Times*, 20 September 1970, 60. Renée Neblett, interviewed by Charles E. Jones, 10 May 1992, Boston, Mass. See also Martin Arnold, "N.A.A.C.P. Will Give $50,000 to Aid Panther-Police Inquiry," *New York Times*, 14 May 1970, 34; "SCLC To Aid 21 Panthers," *Omaha World-Herald* (Omaha, Nebraska), 24 January 1970, 4; Louis Harris et al., *The Harris Survey Yearbook of Public Opinion 1970: A Compendium of Current American Attitudes* (New York: Louis Harris and Associates, 1971), 258.

84. Charles R. Garry, "The Persecution of the Black Panther Party" in *The Black Panthers Speak*, ed. Philip S. Foner, 257.

85. For additional information on the Panther 21, see Kuwasi Balagoon et al., eds., *Look For Me in the Whirlwind: The Collective Autobiography of the New York 21* (New York: Vintage Books, 1971); Paul Chevigny, *Cops and Rebels: A Study of Provocation* (New York: Random House, 1972); Peter Zimroth, *Perversion of Justice*.

86. Gitlin, *Sixties*, 34.

87. Ibid.

88. Michael Omi and Howard Winant, *Racial Formation in the United States from the 1960s to the 1980s* (New York: Routledge and Kegan Paul, 1986), 139.

89. Roberto Santiago, "A Dialogue with Kwame Ture" *Emerge* April 1991, 13.

90. Amiri Baraka (LeRoi Jones), "Black Liberation/Socialist Revolution," in *Daggers and Javelins: Essays of Amiri Baraka (LeRoi Jones)* (New York: Quill, 1984), 98.

91. Robert C. Tucker, ed., *The Marx–Engles Reader* (New York: W. W. Norton and Company, 1978), 601.

92. Anthony Giddens, *Capitalism and Modern Social Theory: An Analysis of the Writings of Marx, Durkheim and Max Weber* (New York: Cambridge University Press, 1971), 38.

93. The autobiographies of the two cofounders of the BPP shed insight on the revolutionary potential of the African American lumpen proletariat. See Huey P. Newton, *Revolutionary Suicide*, 73–77; Bobby Seale, *Seize the Time*, 64–65.

94. Bobby Seale, interview by Ronald Stephens, 4 May 1989, Philadelphia, Penn., 14.

95. See Eldridge Cleaver, *On the Ideology of the Black Panther Party, Part 1* [pamphlet] (San Francisco: Black Panther Party, 1970); Eldridge Cleaver, "On Lumpen Ideology," *Black Scholar* 3 (1972): 2–10, and Kathleen Cleaver, *On the Vanguard Role of the Black Urban Lumpen Proletariat* [pamphlet] (London: Grass Roots Publications, 1975).

96. See Brown, *A Taste of Power*, 137–41; and Charles "Cappy" Pinderhughes interview by Judson L. Jeffries, 12 August 1993, Boston, Mass.

97. Gene Marine, *The Black Panthers*, 2; Ed Montgomery, "Dismay Grows in Sausalito on Black Panther as Principal," *San Francisco Sunday Examiner and Chronicle,* 17 August 1969, A4; John Williams, interview by Charles E. Jones, 24 July 1993, Detroit, Mich.

98. Hilliard and Cole, *This Side of Glory*, 213–14; Renée Neblett interview by Charles E. Jones, Boston, MA, 10 May 1992.

99. Heath, ed., *Off the Pigs!*, 133.

100. Carolyn R. Calloway, "Group Cohesiveness in the Black Panther Party," *Journal of Black Studies* 8 (September 1977): 58.

101. Seale, *Seize the Time*, 64.

102. Alice Echols, "We Gotta Get Out of This Place: Notes Toward a Remapping of the Sixties," *Socialist Review* 92 (1992): 9.

103. For additional information on the Black Panther Militia in Milwaukee see James B. Nelson, "McGee Plans Panther Militia" *Milwaukee Sentinel*, 1 March 1990, 1; Norman Parish, "Black Panthers Co-Founder Critical of McGee's Plan," *Milwaukee Journal,* 6 March 1990, 1; B2. For information on the Dallas-based New Black Panther Party, see Grace Bonds Staples, "Drugs, Racism, Urban Neglect Lead to Black Panther Revival" *Fort Worth Star-Telegram* (Dallas-Fort Worth, Texas) 6 September 1991, 1 and 13; Peter Applebome, "Bitter Racial Rift in Dallas Board Reflects Ills in Many Other Cities" *New York Times,* 27 June 1976, A1–A8; "The New African American Vanguard Movement," *The Black Panther International News Service; The Official Newspaper of the New African American Vanguard Movement,* vol. 1 (1996); Malaika Brown, "Picking Up the Power," *Los Angeles Sentinel,* 6 July 1995, 1.

Chapter Two

The Black Panthers and the "Undeveloped Country"of the Left

Nikhil Pal Singh

I. America, the 1960s, and the Panthers

> *[T]he 1968–9 period represents a watershed: the whole fulcrum of society turns and the country enters, not a temporary and passing rupture, but a prolonged and continuous state of semi-siege. Its meaning and causes then, and its consequences since, have been neither fully reckoned with, nor liquidated. The political polarization which it precipitated fractured society into two camps: authority and its "enemies." This spectacle mesmerized the right, the center and the apolitical, precisely because it refused to assume the recognized forms of classical class conflict and the politics associated with it. But it also marked the left; and its legacies remain, active and unexorcised in the spectrum of radical and revolutionary politics to this day.*
> —Stuart Hall et al., *Policing the Crisis*

In discussions of the 1960s in the United States, the year 1968 figures prominently in defining the period and its consequences. The decade of the 1960s encompassed urban rebellions; the murders of Martin Luther King, Jr., and Robert Kennedy; Lyndon Johnson's abdication; the siege of Chicago in 1967–68; "festivals of the oppressed" (and not-so oppressed) at Woodstock and elsewhere in 1968–69; and ended with the largest student protests against the Vietnam war, killings at Kent State, and the Attica uprising and massacre in 1970–71. Nineteen Sixty-eight marks the culmination of this turbulent, if not revolutionary time. As the cultural and political flood tide of the 1960s, 1968 encapsulates the social anxiety and the political symbols of the decade. This is the moment, we are told, when the nation actually divided; these were the "days of rage" and "revolutionary suicide," a time of urban guerrillas, prison revolts, hippies and yippies, and, of course, the ever present specter of the repressive state—the FBI and its COINTELPRO program.[1]

Yet, the dizzying imagery and abundant metaphors can easily blind us to the ongoing struggle over the meaning of these increasingly distant social movements and political conflicts. In most accounts of the 1960s, 1968 actually has the proportions of myth and apotheosis, frequently in the form of a cautionary tale. Like other retrospective constructions, the story is necessarily ideological, a mobilizing of the resources of history and memory in political struggles for cultural authority and political legitimacy in the present. Thus, on the right, it is imagined that the politics of 1968 are ascendant in American culture, with tenured radicals leading an assault on the citadels of Western civilization and with countercultural preoccupations eroding the national character. The political center, meanwhile, pays homage to a hollow multiculturalism and rests assured that the political struggles and revolutionary hopes of the late 1960s were little more than the fads of youth with their enduring commodity value the surest alibi of measured retrospection. Finally, a putative left, ever in search of a "usable past" and a critical understanding of its failures, finds in 1968 the origins of its decline and bitterly debates the causes and consequences.

The historiography of the 1960s, of course, is significantly more complicated and contested than this brief summary admits. Nonetheless, at least on the left, a narrative of decline has become more dominant. As Alice Echols points out, this story tends to "dichotomize the decade into the 'good' and the 'bad' sixties," and in doing so places the preoccupations of White male New Leftists at the center as "representative of 'the sixties'" as a whole.[2] Echols and others have resisted subordination to a singular narrative of left emergence and decline[3] by mapping the different historical trajectories of the various "subaltern counter publics" that crystallized during the decade. For many of the self-declared founders of the New Left, the late or so-called bad sixties has been clearly repudiated as a series of deviations from the solid, participatory democratic—"in the American grain"—radicalism that flourished during the early years, particularly under the auspices of Students for a Democratic Society (SDS).[4]

Todd Gitlin and Tom Hayden, two influential New Left figures, for example, argue that the liberatory potential of the 1960s was foreclosed when SDS disintegrated in 1968–69, which they attribute to revolutionary posturing and sectarianism and to the divisions opened within the left by the Black power movement and radical feminism. Thus Hayden, while acknowledging his own political debts to the Southern civil rights struggles of the early period, suggests that the identity obsessions and political extremism of the late 1960s destroyed the more productive and practical (so-called good sixties) legacy of coalition politics rooted in a redemptive vision of the nation as a "beloved community."[5] More pointedly, Gitlin condemns what he calls "the bogey of race," claiming that the radical coalition was bullied into making misguided, unstrategic concessions to Black militants, in particular the Black Panthers, whose violent rhetoric and vanguardist politics in various ways hastened the implosion of the wider movement, what Gitlin, in another context, calls "the crack-up of the universalist New Left."[6]

Often what lurks beneath these glib, though characteristic, denunciations of the political excesses of the period is a more basic premise, namely, that meaningful social struggles must necessarily aspire to some form of hegemonic address. Following from this view, the specific argument is that broadly intelligible and effective political discourse in the United States, radical or otherwise, conforms, in one way or another, to the dictates of American universalism, populism, and patriotism. All three are said to have characterized the early New Left and Civil Rights movement, and, according to many New Left historians and critics, these elements have been central to every historically consequential example of American radicalism.[7] This claim is perversely bolstered by the success of Reaganism in the 1980s, which is seen to have effectively mobilized the resentments of the White working class (which somehow remains the benchmark of any "real" politics and the true subject of history). One implication of this argument is that the left itself should inhabit the political languages and traditions of American populism in order to fashion a hegemonic appeal and build mass support. Central to this position, finally, is a critique of minority discourses and radical, cultural politics, including forms of "ultra-left" internationalism and anti-imperialism. Minority discourses are deemed too narrow, particularistic, and subjective; and anti-imperialism and internationalism are said to have distracted from the difficult work of politics at home.[8]

Ironically, the desire to valorize a kind of Jeffersonian legacy of patriotic radicalism for the left is difficult to distinguish from a more conventional neoliberal or neoconservative position that combines wholesale criticism of the movements of the 1960s with an attack on the excesses of contemporary identity politics, especially on questions of race and racial difference. Fashioning itself again as a neopopulism, proponents of this view tend disingenuously to invoke class politics in order to cast aside any explicitly antiracist initiative. Here, as the story goes, the sixties took a fatal turn when White leftists and liberals went soft on race, that is, on the sunglass-wearing Black militants, and hard on class, that is, on the hard-hats and White ethnics (known more colloquially in our time as the "Reagan democrats"). Remarkably, commentators from a range of political positions have come to the same overarching conclusion: the heightening of antiracist militancy hastened the disintegration of fragile political coalitions, alienated a "silent majority" of Americans, initiated a justifiable "backlash" against civil rights reforms, and helped to undermine the urgent project of Black bootstrap self-discipline and progress.[9]

In sum, although the Civil Rights movement or the early New Left may be credited with significant, and even inspiring gains, the later movement is said to have failed because of its tendency to divide both the official and oppositional public spheres, which can be attributed to the word-mongering and separatist inclinations of Black militants, uncritical support for revolutionary movements around the world, and the masochism, even slavishness,

of White radicals and liberals in the face of militant Black demands. This
viewpoint has made strange bedfellows of rightist, centrist, and left-wing
commentators who see themselves as the defenders of a singular and unified
public sphere defined by codes of liberal civility against a late-1960s legacy
of flag-burning, bra-burning, and "burn-baby-burn" rhetoric. More important, despite their otherwise significant political differences, such critics are
united in the core belief that the American nation–state form is the necessary
horizon of social struggle, communal identification, and historical becoming. To paraphrase Benedict Anderson, perhaps more than anything else,
these commentators share in imagining that the nation is in fact *a community*, one that must be defended against those who would challenge or subvert its centrality as the primary arena of political affiliation, contestation,
and hope.[10]

Indeed, it is telling that even those who argue that American racial struggles were central to the rejuvenation, if not the wholesale reinvention of
American radicalism in the 1960s, reject the revolutionary instances of
Black power for similar reasons. Michael Omi and Howard Winant, for example, herald the emergence of Black power as a "great transformation" in
American politics, one that inaugurates a "new politics of social movements." Nevertheless, they criticize what they regard as its indulgences and
aberrations, in particular, that some Black radicals tried to adapt a political
analysis of colonial societies to American conditions and as a consequence
failed to grasp the "uniqueness and complexities of American racial ideology or politics."[11] This violation of the cardinal rule of America's racial/po-
litical exceptionalism is important because it is at the center of their version
of the generalized account of 1960s political failings, in which Black power
militants are viewed as the implicit or explicit cause of the disintegration of
an imagined potentially more promising, national popular struggle:

> Some organizations became romantically fascinated by Third World
> revolutionary movements whose lessons were largely *irrelevant to
> U.S. conditions*. This fragmentation resulted in the absence of a *unified
> politics* and in the inability to define a *coherent political subject*
> [emphasis added].[12]

Although Omi and Winant are either too polite or cautious to cite names,
more determined revisionists have not been as reluctant to identify the
source of their animus. In particular, the Black Panthers and the Black Panther Party have an odd centrality when it comes to filling the blank and definitively stating the wrong turn taken around 1968. Critics, scholars, and
former movement participants have joined together, taking their cues from
flippant conservatives like Tom Wolfe, in assailing the Panthers for crimes
ranging from racial intimidation to "radical chic."[13] Paradoxically, it is the
centrality and influence of the Panthers within the spectrum of oppositional
theories and practices of the late 1960s that is subject to the most derision,
even as the Panthers' actual role during the 1960s—yet to be the subject of

a comprehensive or rigorous historical account—is frequently rendered in an anecdotal, almost offhand manner. Nonetheless, more than any other 1960s actors, the Panthers seem to epitomize the irrationalist racial militancy and political extremism that are said to have hastened the left's disintegration and the onset of the so-called White backlash. It is in this sense that they have been consistently privileged figures in what I call the national allegory of 1968.[14]

To be sure, there remain a few stalwart dissenters who continue to portray the Black Panthers as they imagined themselves, namely, as the heroic vanguard of American youth and minority liberation movements, who were the primary targets and victims of a campaign of state repression and terror throughout the late 1960s and early 1970s. Invariably these accounts acknowledge the Panthers' social legacy, the justly famous survival programs—the free breakfast programs for children, *The Black Panther* newspaper, and political education classes—which then heightens the moral and emotional power of the story of their victimization at the hands of the state. Yet in many ways, accounts that cling to the image of the Black Panthers as the 1960s ultimate martyrs mirror those that vilify them. In the end, the single-minded emphasis on the state's violent campaign against the Party and its leaders rests on a similar reductionism, one that continues to inhibit historical investigation of the Panthers as a social movement or a critical reassessment of their cultural and political significance.[15]

In fact, in both instances, the case of the Panthers condenses many prevailing assumptions about the failures of liberation politics in America 1968. Ironically, this represents an extension of the way the (predominantly White) student left, along with the national media, superficially embraced and elevated the Party during the late 1960s. The views are structurally similar in that they accept at face value the idea that the Black Panthers are the privileged signifier of Black militancy writ large, along with all of its feared or longed for radical or subversive energies. Thus, the Black Panther becomes a kind of political "crossover" artist, mediating both official and oppositional relationships to the cultures of Black liberation, even as the more complex history and significance of Black radical traditions in the United States (and the Panthers' place within them) is left unwritten and unexplored. In this sense, the revolutionary synthesis that the Panthers embodied, though now the subject of resentful disappointment, ridicule, or lamentations about what might have been, remains caught in inflated, though essentially superficial terms, the taken-for-granted origin for a tale of decline, defeat, and woe.[16]

The paradox whereby the Panthers are symbolically central and yet historiographically underdeveloped may also be a function of the more general, ambivalent constitution of Black liberatory aspirations within the history of radical and reformist movements in the United States. In the late 1960s, in the context of colonial warfare and omnipresent and sustained racial oppression, the Panthers were the group who most definitively questioned who was best positioned to speak on behalf of radical, social transformation in America. To offer my own reading of the allegory, I suggest that the historical and personal memory that filters contemporary understandings of the 1960s is marked by what might be described as a "Panther effect," where the figure of the Black Panthers evokes the catastrophic sense of America's permanent racial chasm itself. Given that this historic blindspot on the old dream of Jeffersonian democracy and national popular politics has been so doggedly rationalized and concealed since the end of the 1960s in mystifying discussions of racial backlash, social and political fragmentation, and the so-called underclass, it is not surprising that the Panthers continue to haunt the radical and progressive imagination as a sign of the revolution betrayed, or defeated.

Generally, the evocation of trauma and failure is depicted as a question of who was the most violent during the 1960s, a discussion that proceeds as if violence is something transparent, rather than a concept in need of careful contextualization and theorization. Indeed, many accounts confirm this by regularly sliding between a condemnation of Panther gunplay and criticism of their militant or violent rhetoric, as if these are the same thing, or as if one automatically produces the other. This collapse of politics and poetics spurs obsessional efforts at adjudication, at sorting out the innocent from the guilty, the victims from the villains, and deciding where the Panthers finally fall. The irony of this is that while the Panthers' rhetoric is often dismissed as inflated, overheated, and out of touch, it invariably returns as the implicit cause and/or emblem of an all-too-real body count that effectively ends the discussion. What has resulted is a flattening and even erasure of the richness and ambiguity of the Panthers' racial and political self-fashioning, along with a more careful analysis and differentiation of the manifest and symbolic forms of violence that they both deployed and confronted.[17]

Since the 1989 drug-related murder of Huey P. Newton, cofounder of the Black Panther Party, there has been a spate of commentary, discussion, and writing that has again opened many troubling questions about the complex legacy of the Panthers. Recent memoirs by former Party leaders David Hilliard and Elaine Brown are self-conscious, critical portraits of the often brutal life in the Party, though as autobiography both works are sometimes skewed by an overt desire for personal exoneration and vindication.[18] This is hardly surprising given the overwhelming tendency of recent scholarship to indict the Panthers and everything they stand for. In fact, the most serious critics of the 1960s have been at the forefront of a veritable anti-Panther crusade. The best example of this is the work of David Horowitz and Peter Collier, Panther fellow-travelers during the 1960s, who now use the case of the Panthers as the occasion for their own second thoughts about their previous political commitments. For these conservative converts and many others, the Panthers were not only cynical ghetto hucksters who put one over on them, but were also the exemplars of Black nihilism, chauvinism, and law-lessness, and the progenitors of contemporary urban violence and crime.[19]

Yet the post-1960s reaction formations that now appear to dominate con-temporary U.S. political culture may not be the most reliable starting points for reconstructing our sense of the meaning of the Panthers' political experi-ment. Hailing from the other side of the post-war political divide bisected by the 1960s, Black journalist William Gardner-Smith held a diametrically opposite view. Returning to what he calls "Black America" in 1968 after twenty years of self-imposed exile in Europe and Africa, Smith was as-tounded by the intensification of political militancy around the country and the Black radicalism that was its center: "The '67 revolts marked the entry of the tough ghetto youths into the race battle, and the existing organiza-tions, led by intellectuals or the middle-class, could not cope with them—the Panthers had to be born."[20]

Indeed, with the important exception of the Nation of Islam, Smith be-lieved that the Panthers were doing something that was unprecedented within the Black movement of the day, namely, organizing the frustrated, undisciplined, and sometimes ingenious Black men trapped by rural out-mi-gration from the South into a state of permanent ghettoization and underem-ployment in the North. In the current conjuncture, what may be most worth reengaging in a discussion of the Panthers is the dramatic story of their at-tempts to politicize and reshape the frequently episodic and disjointed life-world of urban, Black subalterns by replacing the everyday violence and temporary fulfillments of hustling and surviving with a purposive frame-work for political action, motivation, and desire.[21]

Founded in Oakland in 1966, the Black Panther Party for Self-Defense was actually one of many Black nationalist groupings that sprang up in American cities during the latter half of the 1960s. Indeed, the Panthers must be viewed as a part of what Manning Marable calls the "fragmented nation-alist tradition" of Black America, "a social movement that retains deep roots within the cultural and social arena of Black life, yet acquires prominence only under certain historical conjunctures."[22] The intensification of the Southern freedom struggle, urban crisis, antiwar protest, and anticolonial revolution in the Third World was such a conjuncture, and very soon the Black Panthers were among those who stood at the forefront of efforts to in-vent a revolutionary politics for urban America.

In his revealing account of the Party's origins, Bobby Seale describes how he and Huey Newton first began raising money for the Panthers by hawking copies of Mao Tse-Tung's *Red Book* in nearby Berkeley. According to Seale, Newton came up with the plan to sell the books at the university, be-lieving that the idea of "Negroes with *Red Books*" would pique the curiosity of Berkeley's campus radicals and get them interested in supporting (and fi-nancing) the Panther Party.[23] The more important agenda, however, was to use the money to buy guns; for it was guns, Newton believed, that would give Panthers the necessary street credibility and allow them to capture the imagination of their primary audience: Black youth in the ghettos of Oakland and Richmond, California.[24] The symbolic formula of the book and the gun would be remarkably successful in authenticating all future claims by the Panthers to the status of revolutionaries.

As news of the first armed confrontations between Newton and the police started to spread by word-of-mouth networks in the local Black communities, the Panthers gained almost immediate recognition as a leading Black militant organization, and their local membership base was quickly established. Within three years there were thirty Panther chapters, one in every major city, and a membership numbering in the thousands.[25] More significant, almost every Black revolutionary figure of the time either had substantial contact or active membership in the Party, including the celebrated former convict-turned-writer Eldridge Cleaver, SNCC leaders Stokely Carmichael (now Kwame Ture), H. Rap Brown, James Forman, radical Black intellectual Angela Davis, and prison-movement icon George Jackson. In addition, the Panthers forged a series of tenuous (and frequently short-lived) alliances with like-minded organizations, such as the Dodge Revolutionary Union movement, Chicano nationalist Brown Berets, the American Indian Movement, the Puerto Rican Young Lords, Students for a Democratic Society, and women's and gay liberation organizations. Combining a flair for dramatic actions with a creative synthesis of many of the central radical ideas and revolutionary postures of the time, by 1968–69 the Panthers were considered by many to be the exemplary revolutionary organization in the country and the one most explicitly identified with anti-imperialism and internationalism.[26]

Few would have imagined that the Black Panther Party (as it was renamed) would exert such an enormous influence upon the history of the 1960s, or that the Panther leaders and Party members would travel to the ends of the earth as recognized agents of an American revolutionary struggle. Yet as I have suggested, there has actually been very little consideration of the political dynamics and cultural logic of the Panthers' local and global appeal. In fact, it may be impossible to understand the emergence of the Panthers and Black liberation politics in America 1968 apart from questions of translocal and transnational intercultural transfer and exchange. In other words, rather than defining the Panthers within the sutured confines of the national allegory of 1968, it may be more revealing to view them in terms of what Arjun Appadurai defines as the "mediascapes, ethnoscapes and ideoscapes" of a properly postcolonial "global cultural economy."[27] Indeed, the fact that policy elites and other official commentators noted with so much alarm that the 1960s "Black movement had as surprising a resonance abroad as at home" should point to obvious questions.[28] For the remarkable thing that remains to be considered is how a relatively small band of self-styled, revolutionary Black youth like the Panthers could assume national and global importance in the first place. What was the meaning of their attempt to adapt the rhetoric of national liberation and the anticolonial struggle to U.S. urban, Black minority populations and advanced capitalist conditions? And finally, why did their own most novel and resonant articulations so clearly betray the desire to disarticulate, if not dismember, the nation? The remainder of this essay is an attempt to offer extended, if at times provisional, answers to these questions.

II. Decolonizing America: Fanonism Reconsidered[29]

> *Decolonization never takes place unnoticed for it transforms individuals and modifies them fundamentally. It transforms spectators crushed with their inessentiality into privileged actors with the grandiose glare of history's floodlights upon them.* —Frantz Fanon, *The Wretched of the Earth*

Despite their initial rather narrow emphasis on policing and self-defense and the problem of Black communal autonomy, the Black Panther Party emerged in the midst of currents of revolutionary hope at home and abroad that led them to a more profound utopian purpose and mission. Significantly enough, this began with the Party leadership developing a thoroughgoing critique of the limits of nationalism—both the American nationalism of the mainstream Civil Rights movement and the forms of Black separatism and cultural nationalism espoused in different ways by their chief competitors for the allegiances of Black subalterns, the Nation of Islam, Maulana Karenga, and Amiri Baraka (LeRoi Jones).[30] The Panthers argued that the prevailing political and economic options presented to America's Black people were all inadequate. From a dead-end choice between low-wage work and crime, to the hollow and unrealistic promises of middle-class integration and uplift, to the fanciful or palliative notions of a separate Black economy or culture, the Panthers believed that no one had addressed the central problem, namely, the sustained imbrication and reproduction of racism within capitalist social and economic relations.[31] In this sense, the Panthers argued, Black nationalism and civil rights struggles each provided what were essentially "bourgeois" answers to the properly "revolutionary" needs of America's Black poor.[32]

Perhaps more than any other intellectual and political issue, the members of the Panther Party, like C. L. R. James before them, attempted to define what they considered to be "the Revolutionary Answer to the Negro Question in the United States."[33] In contrast to James, however, the Panthers, along with many other Black radicals during the 1960s, believed that racism was such a deep and defining contradiction in American life that the idea of Blacks and Whites united in class struggle toward a socialist revolution was simply out of the question. The problem, as the Panthers understood it, was to define Black political subjectivity and a revolutionary sense of Black peoplehood in the context of the failure of middle-class and working-class struggles for integration and the impossibility of Black nationalist schemes of separation. In the end, this dualism, which has structured Black American politics throughout the twentieth century, was one the Panthers straddled, albeit uneasily. They did so by blurring the two positions, by emphasizing separation and Black difference, not in terms of racially defined notions of Black nationhood, but as a question of highly localized, spatially defined demands for communal autonomy. They also emphasized integration and equality, not as a moment of entry into the American mainstream but as a commitment of solidarity with all those who defined America's margins and with all the victims of Americanism at home and around the world.

Like many other young Black power militants, the Panthers relentlessly criticized the older generation of integrationist elites for their accommodations to American nationalism and the state and for concealing intraracial class divisions among the agencies of the Black struggle.[34] Most important, the Panthers suggested that civil rights leaders had failed to grasp the main lesson of anti-imperialism, which was that the United States itself was not a nation into which Black people could be successfully integrated, but was an empire they needed to oppose—not a beloved community of shared traditions and aspirations—but a coercive state that needed to be overthrown. "We cannot be nationalists, when our country is not a nation, but an empire," Huey Newton writes. "We have the historical obligation to take the concept of internationalism to its final conclusion—the destruction of statehood itself."[35]

The Panthers reserved their most scathing criticism, however, for Black nationalists, especially those whom they derided as "pork-chop nationalists."[36] Although the Panthers recognized that Black nationalists had frequently opposed the United States government, they felt that nationalists made a different kind of error from the Civil Rights movement in choosing separatism over solidarity. Not only was this choice self-defeating, it was also a profound misreading of the political and historical interrelationships of racial and national oppression in the United States and around the world. Thus, while organizations like Maulana Karenga's Us correctly viewed Black people as domestic victims of the American empire, they had also demonstrated their interest in becoming at least partial beneficiaries of that empire. Indeed, as the Panthers pointed out, the nationalist emphasis on Black culture and Black business and the ease with which these ideas were taken up by integrationist elites demonstrated the degree to which Black nationalism was not fundamentally aimed at transforming the power relations of American capitalism and the American state. That someone as odious as Richard Nixon could blithely celebrate "Black Power" in terms of Black capitalism was cause for suspicion and alarm and indicated the need for a more rigorous political analysis and practice.[37]

In defining themselves as "revolutionary nationalists" and true internationalists, the Panthers attempted to formulate a distinction between the nationalism of liberation and the nationalism of oppression and, in Newton's words, "to reconcile support for revolutionary nationalism abroad, while disclaiming all forms of nationalism within the U.S. context as necessarily bound up with American oppression."[38] In making this distinction, the Panthers self-consciously redefined their own quasi-nationalist politics in terms of anticolonialism by fashioning themselves in the flamboyant image of anticolonial revolutionaries like Che Guevara and Ho Chi Minh and drawing upon a range of "resistance literature," from the *Red Book* to *The Autobiography of Malcolm X.*[39] Perhaps the best way to describe the Panthers is as "resolute counternationalists"—men and women who believed themselves to be "inoculated against all national anthems."[40] In this way, they embodied Black America's critical duality on questions of nationality and citizenship, looking simultaneously for a way into and a way out of the nation–state, as the latter was perceived both as a source of oppression, but also as the possibility of a subjecthood heretofore denied.[41]

Although the Panthers' adoption of a generalized Marxism and anticapitalism was important in this regard in legitimating them as revolutionaries, it was derivative of a more primary emphasis upon anti-imperialism and anti-Americanism. This is what produced the Party's extremely important, though troubled, alliance with the movement to stop the war in Vietnam, a stance that placed them at the center of a broad array of oppositional social forces. In fact, as one of the few Black radical groups willing to work closely with White radicals in the aftermath of the Civil Rights era, the Panthers became transmitters for struggles within the decolonizing world and for the appropriation and absorption of "third worldist politico-cultural models" across the spectrum of 1960s oppositional practices. It may actually be the case, as Frederic Jameson suggests, that the "entire progressive thrust of the '60s was predicated on precisely these kinds of political innovations: those that sought to bind support for "the great movements of decolonization in Asia, Africa and the Caribbean" with the demands of the "inner colonized" of the overdeveloped world.[42] In a similar vein, Stuart Hall points out that it was largely through groups like the Panthers that the metaphor of "the third world" was transformed into a broad, politically generative signifier—not of a strictly geographical relationship—but of "a set of characteristic economic, social and cultural exploitative relations."[43]

In developing their brand of "third worldism," the Panthers turned to what was by far their most important ideological resource, the writings of Frantz Fanon.[44] Although Fanon has undergone something of a revival in recent years, especially in literary studies,[45] his importance to the development of American Black radicalism during the late 1960s has never been properly charted. Works about the 1960s that actually mention Fanon often do so in passing, implying that his influence did not extend beyond supplying aphorisms for would-be revolutionaries. Writing in this vein, some critics have decried what they view as the sloppy application of ill-considered Fanonist ideas about violence and national liberation where they do not apply, namely, to the urban, metropolitan context.[46] Recently, and perhaps more acutely, Wilson Moses has resurrected a version of American exceptionalist argument, criticizing the popularity of Fanon among Black intellectuals and political radicals of the 1960s for overshadowing the more pertinent and meaningful work of American intellectuals like Harold Cruse.[47]

By pitting Cruse against Fanon, however, Moses himself obscures what may be a deeper relationship between their two projects. In the mid-1960s, it was Cruse himself, after all, who pointed to the popularity of Fanon among "the young Black generation of his day" in order to repudiate those who stressed "the fundamentally American outlook of the American Negro."[48] Cruse's own attempt to fashion an indigenous theory of Black liberation, moreover, began with an assumption that was also central to political experiments like the Panthers. "The racial crisis in America," Cruse writes, "is the internal reflection of this contemporary world-wide problem of the readjustment between ex-colonial masters and ex-colonial subjects."[49] Though Cruse's own exceptionalist sense of the American sociocultural situation may have prevented him from developing the theoretical and historical implications of this insight, he was clearly aware that the reinvention of Black nationalism in the American 1960s was in important ways related to the projects of decolonization.[50] Indeed, that the curmudgeonly Cruse so clearly recognized the political importance of Black Americans reading Fanon should give us pause. If nothing else, Cruse's work starts from a premise crucial for thinking about the history of Black political experiments and struggles, namely, that Black America's national question had never been fundamentally resolved and that attempts to do so cannot "hinge merely on pragmatic practicalities."[51]

Fanon's relevance was by no means immediately evident to the Panthers themselves. David Hilliard, for example, candidly recalls the feelings of self-loathing and futility brought on by his many frustrating attempts to make sense of Fanon's complex prose.[52] Yet Hilliard also tells of his perseverance and increasing excitement as he began to understand new concepts and ways of thinking about the Black experience in America in discussions of Fanon's writings in the Party's political education classes. Indeed, these programmatic efforts to understand the applicability of Fanon suggest that the Panthers may have been more careful students of his work than many of their erstwhile critics. In his last, and what was for America's Black militants his most important work *The Wretched of the Earth,*[53] Fanon himself had actually foreseen the extension of the anticolonial struggle in many of these unexpected directions.

Fanon's substantive references to the American context are prescient precisely in identifying the political examples out of which the Panthers would fashion themselves. Early on in the text, for instance, Fanon indicates just how significant he finds it that "minority groups" living within the borders of the world's superpower no longer "hesitate to preach violent methods for resolving their problems." "It is not by chance," he continues, "that in consequence Negro extremists in the United States organize a militia and arm themselves."[54] Although *The Wretched of the Earth* is sometimes cited for its arguments against the cultural conflation of the Black world into ideologies such as negritude,[55] I suggest that Fanon is actually identifying an important theoretical and historical basis for relating diverse regions of struggle. Fanon's brilliant text, as the Panthers recognized, was not addressed exclusively to the properly anticolonial Third World. In these passing comments about "the American Negro's new emphasis on violence" and the emergent problem of "minorities," Fanon is actually considering a series of questions concerning the global context of local conflicts, the implications of neocolonialism, and the possibility of internationalizing and thus extending struggles against empire.[56]

Further on in the text, Fanon suggests that despite the fact that anticolonial struggles had thus far only achieved partial victories, "the political logic of colonialism mandated that nations could be empires only over nonnations," a logic decisively weakened by the very first extension of the nation form to the rest of humanity.[57] What resulted from this process, however, was not simply the creation of new nations, but the constitution of a new political logic defining international relations—an empire without territories—what critics of American imperialism would refer to as "empire as a way of life."[58] In other words, although decolonization was not yet complete, the world had already been redefined in terms of the universalization of formal nationhood within a sphere of international commodity relations dominated by the United States. What this demonstrated, according to Fanon, was both the supersession of the political stakes defined by the Cold War and the foreclosing of the liberatory possibilities of decolonization itself as a simple question of nation-building.[59]

Thus, even as independent nationhood was being normalized, what Mossadegh in Iran, Arbenz in Guatemala, and the Cuban and Vietnamese revolutionaries discovered was that its organization was to be closely monitored, policed, and, if necessary, punished, depending upon whether a given nation–state was seen to be favorable or unfavorable to the expansion of American capitalism and the overall stabilization of the multilateral state system. Developing his own views along these general lines, Huey Newton actually came to the conclusion that nations–states were becoming things of the past as a result of the global hegemony of U.S.-sponsored capital. As Hilliard recounts,

> In prison Huey developed an analysis of the present political moment. . . . Nationalist struggles, even revolutionary ones, [he said] are beside the point. Capital dominates the world; ignoring borders, international finance has transformed the world into communities rather than nations. Some of these communities are under siege—like Vietnam—and others conduct the siege, like the United States government. The people of the world are united in their desire to run

their own communities: the Black people of Oakland and the
Vietnamese. We need to band together as communities, create a
revolutionary intercommunalism that will resist capital's reactionary
intercommunalism.[60]

Under the rubric of intercommunalism, Newton attempted to transcend
questions of nation–states and nationalism altogether by suggesting that
shifts in the spatial scales of capitalism had disrupted the organization of nations as integral territorial and ideological units.[61] More suggestively, by
avoiding the language of nation entirely, he sought to elide the American nation with the actions of an imperial state and link the intercommunal fates
of Vietnam and Oakland as equivalent local instances in a struggle with transnational dimensions.[62]

These formulations obviously beg many questions.[63] Nevertheless, by the
mid-1970s, the closure of the high era of decolonization with the end of the
bloody Vietnam war,[64] Nixon's formalization of detente, and the crisis of
the Bretton Woods system, would begin to bear out certain aspects of the
globalizing vision implicit in these projections. Since the mid-1970s, the
primary preoccupation of the world's dominant powers has revolved less
and less round the epochal struggle between capitalism and socialism and
turned instead to the problems of growth and uneven development within
the global economy.[65] The end of the Vietnam war, in this sense, may have
been the last, decisive battle of the ultra-imperial "American Century," pre-
saging the onset of a full-blown postimperial/postcolonial order. Yet far
from leading toward global equality via nationhood, the process of decolonization, as Fanon anticipated, has revealed "the impossibility of autarky"
within the context of the general extension and universalization of an
American model of imperialism, built from the outset on the premise of formal nationhood, free trade, open markets, and internal colonization. From
this point onward, primary struggles are "traversed by a constantly shifting
frontier—irreducible to the frontiers between states—between two humanities which seem incommensurable, namely, the humanity of destitution and
that of 'consumption,' the humanity of 'underdevelopment' and that of
overdevelopment."[66] This is the dynamic, in Fanon's prophetic view, that
now has the potential to "shake humanity to pieces."[67]

Rather than interpreting this transition in terms of a prophecy of endless
domination, in the 1960s, the generalization of colonization (rather than its
undoing) became the basis for a renewed vision of a universal struggle that
transmuted the Marxist opposition between the proletariat and the bourgeoisie into an opposition between the "revolutionary" and the "bourgeois," or
"the people" and the "power bloc."[68] The Panther's rhetorical signature, "all
power to the people," or their desire to equate themselves with the Vietnamese, functioned within this logic and cannot be dismissed merely as romantic
fascination or the products of faulty, analogical reasoning. In fact, the emergence of what Kwame Nkrumah formally labeled "neocolonialism"[69] and

what Henri Lefebvre called "neo-capitalism" was thought to have inaugurated a "vast displacement of contradictions," the most salient of which was the emergence of questions of colonization and struggles for liberation of an internal as well as external variety.[70] In this context, decolonization, in the "Fanonist" text, as appropriated by the Panthers and others, marked out a broad terrain of liberatory theory and practice, under the auspices of U.S. capitalism and the American state, that was responsive to a fundamental synchronization of the histories of internal and external colonization across the world. Rather than being the place where the 1960s ran aground, this ideological context may actually have been where it was first invented.[71]

It was in this complex sense, moreover, that Fanon himself referred to the arming of the Civil Rights movement in the U.S. South in the 1950s, in the figure of Robert Williams or Louisiana's Deacons for Defense, as the emergence of the violence of decolonization in the metropolitan center, which, up to that point, had been largely externalized and confined to the global periphery as a result of the Cold War.[72] Significantly enough, Malcolm X launched his later career about this time by making a similar observation, one that precipitated his break with the Nation of Islam and his rapid movement into a geopolitical imaginary redefined by Third World struggles. Responding to the assassination of President Kennedy in November 1963, Malcolm X suggested that it was simply a case of "the chickens coming home to roost."[73] When asked to elaborate upon a comment many considered tantamount to treason, he calmly recounted the bloody history of U.S. support of colonial and neocolonial regimes and specifically cited U.S. involvement in the assassination of Patrice Lumumba, the first premier of the former Congo. The death of Kennedy, Malcolm implied, was a sign that the U.S. was reaping the violence it had sown. By the late 1960s, after his own untimely death, Malcolm X would be the equivalent of America's Lumumba for those like the Panthers who claimed him as their own.[74]

In what may be a slightly more obscure case of anticolonial celebrityhood, Robert Williams began to fashion himself in much the same terms at the onset of the 1960s. A former U.S. Marine, Williams was an NAACP organizer in Monroe County, North Carolina, who in early 1959 challenged the national office by organizing local African Americans into rifle clubs for the purpose of self-defense. Later that year, in an event that would prove crucial to broadening the implications of his local efforts, Williams joined a well-publicized delegation that visited Cuba, in an effort to garner support for the new revolutionary government. After a series of confrontations with the NAACP leadership, the local Ku Klux Klan, and law enforcement agencies, Williams was forced to flee the county. He soon had the distinction of being the first Black radical of the 1960s to become the focal point of a nationwide FBI manhunt. Escaping first to Canada, Williams eventually made his way back to Cuba, where he was granted political asylum.[75]

Williams' Cuban exile quickly elevated him within the mediascapes and ideoscapes of decolonization, as he too joined an emerging pantheon of anticolonial heroes. In his newsletter, *The Crusader*, which he began publishing from Cuba, he even began to refer to the island as "liberated territory of the Americas."[76] Cognizant of the unique nature of his sudden celebrity, Williams remarked, "When the racists forced me into exile, they unwittingly led me onto a greater field of battle."[77] Williams's greater field of battle, of course, was the figure he cut in his own movement through space and across national borders that signified successful resistance to an American geography of apartheid and informal empire. Although his baldly titled book *Negroes with Guns* (comprising mostly press clippings and earlier speeches) is in large measure a reformist and pro-integrationist critique of principles of nonviolence[78] for young Black militants, Williams's confrontation with the American state was the prologue to their own brand of liberation politics.[79] Most importantly, what Williams's exile demonstrated was the incontrovertible power of what the Panthers later called "picking up the gun."

Although he faded somewhat from the American scene as he continued on in his travels from Cuba to China, Williams' experience was by no means exceptional. Indeed, within an international context dramatically reconfigured by the Cold War and decolonization, the most uncompromising and critical Black voices in the United States from the 1930s and 1940s—W. E. B. Du Bois, Paul Robeson, C. L. R. James and Richard Wright—had all been subject to some form of state harassment, internal detention, and even deportation. These figures were in different ways central to an earlier moment of antiracist radicalism that emerged under the auspices of the Popular Front and the left-wing of the New Deal. Indeed, these intellectuals believed that the incremental advances in the cause of racial democracy in America during the late 1930s and early 1940s (the success of the CIO, the March on Washington movement, Roosevelt's establishment of the Fair Employment Practices Commission, and the global defeat of fascism), had in fact created the context for completing America's "unfinished democratic revolution" at home and resolving what Du Bois in 1945 called the problem of "color and democracy" in the world arena.[80]

That James and Du Bois, as well as Wright and Robeson, spent the 1940s and 1950s locked in bitter conflict with various agencies of the American state and ended their lives either in some form of exile or ceaseless travel indicates the degree to which the substantive optimism of the racial liberalism of the 1940s was eviscerated by the Cold War. By the 1950s, solving Gunnar Myrdal's *American Dilemma* (1944) had been effectively sacrificed to securing the prerogatives of Henry Luce's American Century and a quasi-religious defense of what was called the "American way of life" in its death struggle with "demonic communism."[81] The surprising resurgence of American antiracism at the height of the Cold War, under the banner of civil rights and militant nonviolence, must be understood as a highly complex departure from this earlier tradition of antiracist radicalism as a result of the profound strictures placed upon progressive forces in the U.S. by polymorphous anti-Communism and Americocentric ultra-imperialism.

The renewal of antiracism in the 1950s is complex because its effectiveness was largely predicated on exploiting the tension between what Myrdal had called "America's claim to be humanity in miniature"—or the world's exemplary nation–state—and the continued irresolution of the Negro problem in the U.S. South.[82] Traditional civil rights forces in the United States, however, no longer articulated the moral and political significance of Black struggles in America in terms of the explicitly anti-imperialist aspirations of the earlier period. In contrast to Du Bois', Wright's and James' pre-Cold War invocations of the possibilities inherent within the American revolutionary democratic tradition, the Civil Rights movement of the 1950s was captive to the Cold War discourse on Democracy that accepted the necessity of an anti-Communist purge at home and upheld the prerogatives of the American national security state abroad. Indeed, the civil rights discourse itself, with its emphasis on Christian transcendence, consumer sovereignty, and national redemption, was successful, at least in part, because of the ways it was able to align itself with the principle markers of Cold War patriotism. The fact that Martin Luther King's late opposition to the Vietnam war could provoke wide condemnation and calls for his ostracism by other mainstream civil rights leaders indicates how far domestic antiracism had traveled from the internationalism of the 1930s and early 1940s.[83]

What is important about Robert Williams' and Malcolm X's respective journeys out of the old Southern Black belt and Black millennial sectarianism into the geopolitical ambit of decolonization is that both their careers signaled a profound return of the resurgent American antiracism of the 1950s to an earlier emphasis upon racialized geopolitics. Yet the still more important departure exemplified by a Williams or a Malcolm X was that they not only redrew the coordinates of the intranational struggles of Black Americans in light of events within the decolonizing world, they also began to draw on and popularize revolutionary practice and symbolism that stretched the borders of the American democratic imaginary. Thus, while the nonviolent Civil Rights movement linked the failure to enfranchise Black people in the U.S. South with forces that would mock the moral and political claims of American democracy and Judeo-Christianity in the international arena, Williams and Malcolm X joined in the mockery, ruthlessly criticizing America's democratic pretensions, and literally and figuratively severing their own "identificatory links" with the American nation–state.[84] In the context of the worldwide acceleration of struggles for decolonization, their uncompromising disaffiliation and disidentification opened up significant new routes for radical thinking at home by the latter half of the 1960s.[85]

The purpose of this extended discussion is to demonstrate that groups like the Panthers did not simply arise *ex nihilo* out of the supposed madness of 1968 and to suggest how they are a part of an admittedly discontinuous Black radical and revolutionary tradition. In the introduction to his biography of Huey Newton and the Panther Party, Bobby Seale suggests the complex of influences that created the Panthers in an allegory about the naming of his son. "The nigger's name is Malik Nkrumah Stagolee Seale," Seale writes; Malik for Malcolm X, Nkrumah to commemorate the first successful African revolutionary, and Stagolee for the folkloric Black hustler, badman and outsider.[86] To make sense of the Panthers, however, we must do more than invoke the characteristic markers of their militancy (that is, the relationship to Malcolm X, Fanon, the repudiation of nonviolence, etc.). Rather, we must situate these signs and invocations within a cultural and political history of African Americans' tortured negotiations for American nationality and citizenship. What significantly differentiates the Panthers is their significantly enhanced ability to bring their claims onto a world stage and their deep mistrust of attempts to domesticate their radicalism.[87]

The emergence of forty new nation–states between 1945 and 1960, most of them within the former colonial world, ushered in "a new world for America's Negroes."[88] In defining the Negro's "new mood" in 1960, James Baldwin put the issue more pointedly: "The American Negro can no longer, nor will he (*sic*) ever again be controlled by White America's image of him. This fact has everything to do with the rise of Africa in world affairs."[89] Baldwin, whose own political trajectory through the decade significantly led to increasing militancy, national disaffiliation, and a poetic identification with groups like the Panthers,[90] chose his words with characteristic care and precision. By the 1960s, both decolonization and the struggles against American racism were cast in terms of a geopolitics of images that would be decisive in shaping the specular-rhetorical appeal of groups like the Panthers. As the remarkable Black auto worker James Boggs recognized in 1965, "Revolutions have never depended upon sheer numbers, but rather upon the relationship of forces in the existing political arena. Today when the existing political arena is a world arena, the Negro's relationship is to the world."[91]

III. The Geopolitics of Pride and Shame

> Prophecy now involves a geographical rather than a historical projection; it is space not time that hides consequences from us.
> —John Berger, *The Look of Things*

> So where can these virtual martyrs prepare their revolt from?
> —Jean Genet, *Prisoner of Love*

The perception of a new, global, image-centered stage for insurgent politics can shed light on some of the continuities between traditions and formations of the Black struggle during the 1960s, especially around the problem of violence/nonviolence that governs the dominant conception of a break between the earlier and later parts of the decade. I would argue that the Panthers no less than the marchers and freedom riders of the early 1960s were engaged in a war of conscience aimed at the transfiguration of a historical system of Black shame into one of pride and empowerment. In terms of their specular logic then, the nonviolent protest strategy of the Civil Rights movement is not entirely opposite to the explicitly confrontational Panther strategy of picking up the gun and patrolling the police. Both attempted to expose racist violence upon Black bodies, and both were attuned to what I call the "geopolitics of pride and shame" governing televisual transmission, reception, and interpretation of their spectacular performances.

The Civil Rights movement, engaging the force and violence of the state under the international sign of militant pacifism and secured by the successes of Gandhian nonviolence in India, was not without its own global analogue and appeal. In this context, as Harold Isaacs suggested, Little Rock too entered a global vernacular and mediascape as the symbol of American racism and racial strife with "images of armed soldiers, screaming mobs and Negro children, circulat[ing] around the world."[92] Yet while the absorption of violence by civil rights protesters was predicated upon an appeal to the world's conscience, it primarily evoked the desire for national redemption and reconciliation through the shameful/shaming violence that was enacted across the martyr's body. Finally sending federal troops into Little Rock in 1957, the previously quiescent Eisenhower indicated that he realized just how potent this logic and imagery had become and justified his action as one that would reestablish the nation "in the eyes of the world . . . [and] restore the image of America, and all its parts as one nation indivisible."[93]

By contrast, Black liberationists of the late 1960s were buoyed by the fact that America's racial fissures had been opened for all the world to see. In the midst of the dramatic refiguring of an imaginary world system under the pressures of revolutionary nationalism emanating from Cuba, Algeria, China, and Vietnam, they seized every opportunity to demonstrate that America itself was neither united, nor secure. Thus, the Panthers not only repudiated the historical legacy of racist violence, but called for a reversal of its shameful/shaming effects. Refusing the premise of peace and reconciliation, the Panthers instead projected violence back upon the nation. In the emblematic, prison cell projections of George Jackson, they conjured another image of Black revolutionaries

> bringing the U.S.A. to its knees . . . . closing off of critical sections of the city with barbed wire, [with] armored pig carriers criss-crossing city streets, soldiers every-where, tommy guns pointed at stomach level, smoke curling Black against the daylight sky, the smell of cordite, house-to-house searches, doors being kicked down, [and] the commonness of death.[94]

Severing their own identificatory links with the nation–state, Panthers instead fashioned themselves as the avatars of Baldwin's doomsaying prophecy of *The Fire Next Time*.[95] Reversing the civil narrative of rights and redemption, they threatened to carve up the nation, defined the Black ghetto as a territory to be liberated, and in a final, brutal mockery, cast the most visible representatives of the American state—the police—as "pigs."[96]

The emphasis upon violence that Fanon thought so remarkable, in other words, was itself complex, expressive, and polyvalent and not, as some critics maintain, simply a descent into "psychopathic panegyrics."[97] What Williams, Malcolm X, and the Panthers all recognized, moreover, was that the relationship between violence and racism was inextricable. In Balibar's useful formulation, they understood that for the victims of racism there was "a permanent *excess* of actual violence and acts over [racist] discourses, theories and rationalizations," and it was these acts that needed to be met with a credible response.[98] By advocating organized counter-violence by Black people in the U.S., they suggested that the American state, as the holder of a monopoly on the legitimate uses of violence,[99] was either inadequate to, or complicit in the perpetuation of forms of racist violence that continued to be exercised over Black bodies. What this amounted to was a de facto repudiation of the state as the entity safeguarding a sphere of public civility and order. The call for violence, in other words, was a powerful assertion of the necessary autonomy of Black life in the United States, and regardless of the programmatic political vision to which it was attached, it constituted a challenge to the founding premise of the nation–state itself.

Although the arming of small pockets of the Civil Rights movement or the emergence of a figure like Malcolm X may have presaged the initial insertion of Fanonism into the U.S. context, it was the violent upheavals that took place in scores of American cities during the mid-1960s that confirmed its appeal. Of all the so-called race riots in American history—1863, 1919, 1943—the 1960s were a time when Black people were primarily on the offensive, attacking the representatives of the state (and private property). In all previous urban unrest of this sort, Black people had generally been the intended targets and primary victims. It is thus not surprising that supporters of Black aspirations described these riots as revolts or uprisings and that they became one of the rallying points for a Black power imaginary.[100] As Dan Watts of *Liberation* put it,

> [You're] going along thinking all the brothers in these riots are old winos. Nothing could be further from the truth. These cats are ready to die for something. And they know why. They all read. Read a lot. Not one of them hasn't read the Bible . . . Fanon . . . You'd better get this book. Every brother on the rooftop can quote Fanon.[101]

Astutely identifying the corresponding, radically localizing shift in the geopolitics of pride and shame, Eldridge Cleaver noticed that though "Watts [had been] a place of shame. . . an epithet," after the riot, "all the Blacks in

Folsom are saying, 'I'm from Watts baby'! . . . and proud of it."[102] Most significantly, as David Hilliard recalls, it was when the afterglow and "excitement of Watts was beginning to fade," that a few hundred miles to the north, the Panthers were founded.[103] Indeed, more than any other events, the Black riots that swept American cities in the mid-1960s occasioned the first programmatic understandings of Black liberation and full-fledged visions of a Black revolutionary struggle within the United States. In one of their most famous essays, two of the most original radical theorists of the 1960s, James and Grace Lee Boggs, declared "the city. . . the Black Man's Land."[104] Using urban population projections, the Boggs proposed what was actually a clever rewriting of a much older theory of Black liberation, the Communist Party's (CPUSA) Black belt thesis, which held that the contiguous counties holding a Black majority population within the Southern "Black belt" states really comprised an internal colony, an incipient Black nation with the right to self-determination. The CPUSA argued that Black outmigration from the South had nullified this position and abandoned it in 1958, embracing instead the NAACP's mainstream, integrationist slogan "Free by '63."[105] The Boggs, in effect, relocated the Black belt in light of Black urbanity.

Deploying the resonant historicization of the Civil War as America's "unfinished revolution," the Boggs argued that the Watts riots, like the Birmingham and Harlem riots the year before, was an initial skirmish in a "second civil war" that would be played out in America's cities. Vice President Humphrey seemed to confirm this view, when he claimed, "[T]he biggest battle we're fighting today is not in South Vietnam; the toughest battle is in our cities."[106] The use of national guardsmen alongside police to quell the riots, and the oft-repeated refrain that Vietnam itself was little more than a police action, sealed the association of intra- and international conflict and struggle. As Newton argued, "[T]he police are everywhere and use the same tools, and have the same purpose: the protection of the ruling circle here in North America."[107]

The Boggs', the Panthers', and other arguments and experiments that came on the heels of urban revolt embraced the Black ghetto as the basis of a renewed and very different kind of Black radical vision: the site of a radically dispersed Black nation and the model of the internal colonization of America's Black people.[108] Reappropriating ghettoized spaces from the pathologizing discourse of social science, Black liberation politics instead figured the ghetto as a place of "irredeemable *spatial* difference"[109] within the nation–state, irrecuperable to unifying temporal narratives of national belonging and citizenship.[110] The spontaneous violence of the ghetto revolts, in this sense, became the ultimate sign of the "vast displacement of contradictions" that Lefebvre and Fanon in their different ways understood as specific to the era of decolonization.[111] The Black Panther Party, though it never developed a comprehensive urban theory or strategy as did the Boggs', was nevertheless the product of this emergent understanding of the socio-spatial logic and politics of ghettoization. Once again seizing upon Fanon's work for appropriate concepts, the Panthers emphasized the colonizing, as opposed to the strictly national aspects of ghettoization, and identified Fanon's lumpen proletarian as a ghetto archetype and the most "spontaneously revolutionary" agent of the Black struggle in the overdeveloped world.[112]

Insofar as the Black revolution in America was understood to be an urban revolution, Fanon's work invited just these kinds of extrapolations (though only with a degree of license). According to Fanon, the peasantry and the lumpen proletariat were the only proven revolutionary groups in the struggles for decolonization in the underdeveloped world. Although he ultimately believed that the peasantry was the more stable and reliable of the two, he reserved some of his most moving and poetic insights for the lumpen, wresting this group from their residual and despised position within the Marxist revolutionary canon. Victims of the Third World's scourge of urbanization without industrialization, the lumpen, in Fanon's formulation, were rootless city dwellers, frequently less than a generation removed from the land, comprising the society's most degraded, least hopeful elements: "the pimps, the hooligans, the unemployed and the petty criminals." Yet it was "[t]hese workless less-than-men," Fanon writes, who in reality had the most to gain from a revolution, namely, the chance to be "rehabilitated in their own eyes, and in the eyes of humanity." "All the hopeless dregs of humanity, all who turn in circles between suicide and madness," Fanon exclaims, "will recover their balance."[113] It was in these images, David Hilliard remembers, that the Panthers found themselves.[114]

Specifically, the Panthers reasoned that police power exercised within the Black sections of the city (against the lumpen) operated in a manner similar to the uses of colonial power that Fanon had described. Policing within Black communities functioned as "a language of pure force" untempered by forms of ideological suasion or mediation in which the consent of the governed was sought out and gained without the use of violence.[115] In other words, in contrast to the forms of hegemonic power in which the modern state secures the terrains of civil society and its public spheres by the structuring of the population's moral reflexes, colonial power exercises control through violence and repression in the first instance. By staging confrontations with the police, Newton and Seale sought to dramatize how a form of colonial power was actually deployed against Black people in the urban areas of the U.S. under the auspices of policing. Flamboyantly displaying their own lawful and disciplined resistance to violent policing, the Panthers also showed how they were inured to the possibility of future hegemonic overtures by the state, because of their familiarity with the state as an instance of naked force and violence.

It was neither the simple fact of public disorder, nor the sheer power of allusion that allowed the urban presence of Black people to assume these new meanings. Once the Civil Rights movement moved northwards by the mid-1960s, it no longer encountered racism as a legally enshrined system of segregation and voting restrictions. In fact, even as the legal edifice of segregation was being dismantled by government decree, a much more enduring structure of "spatial apartheid" had been made visible by its inscription into the urban landscape.[116] In this sense, the vision of the ghetto as an internal colony, or perhaps better, a neocolony, was not simply an analogy. As James Blaut argues, although ghettos clearly lack the ability to press for self-determination as "politico-geographic units," like actual neocolonies, the formal problem of self-determination does not actually define the relations of exploitation and oppression that govern relations with dominant power.[117] These relations, moreover, are defined in rigid, socio-spatial terms, because ghettoized/colonized areas are excluded from sharing in social/global surpluses. They are instead sites of superexploitation, underemployment, underdevelopment, and of concentrated official and unofficial social violence.

In developing a strategy commensurate with this insight, the Panthers engaged in their own attempts to "hegemonize" the people of the ghetto, the Black youth gangs, former convicts, and the growing populations of prisoners.[118] The Panthers approached these groups armed with their own counter-nationalist pedagogy, "evoking and erasing national boundaries—both actual and conceptual—and openly disturbing the ideological maneuvers through which the nation is constituted as an imagined community."[119] Most overtly, the Panthers did this simply by appropriating anticolonial internationalism, geopoliticizing Black American struggles, and repudiating the exceptionalist framework of national(ist) becoming. Less obviously, the Panthers skillfully pursued a highly localized, spatial politics addressed directly to the denizens of a myriad of subnational, institutional spaces—the housing project, the school, the community organization, and the prison—whose physical repetition and functional organization are central to what Barbara Harlow has called the nation–state's own "discourse of boundaries,"[120] and to its apparent "sociological solidity" and substance.[121] The Panthers effectively tore these spaces out of the nation–state and claimed them as their own by organizing their own schools, asserting the de facto autonomy of community organizations, and most importantly, embracing the prison—already a place of effective anti-citizenship—as the exemplary site and source of counter-nationalist theory and practice.[122]

All over the United States, Panther chapters emerged, drawing together community organizers, students, former convicts, juvenile delinquents, and would-be organic intellectuals into a tenuous and volatile coalition. In Los Angeles, one of the leaders of the Slausons, one of the most feared of the L.A. street gangs, Alprentice "Bunchy" Carter, along with John Huggins, formed the most important Party chapter outside of Oakland. In Chicago, one of the Party's most innovative organizers, Fred Hampton, established the first ever "rainbow coalition," among the Blackstone Rangers, the Young Patriots, and the Young Lords, the city's largest Black, White, and Puerto Rican youth gangs.[123] In New York, a young former convict, Richard Moore (Dhoruba Bin Wahad), helped to build one of the most impressive Panther chapters, with well-organized breakfast programs, tenants rights projects, and other community-based organizations.[124] Finally, in Soledad, Attica, and several other major prisons, the Panthers developed a widespread following within existing prisoners' organizations and especially within prisoners' rights groups, attracting one of the most gifted and charismatic leaders of the prison movement, George Jackson.[125] As Mike Davis puts it, "For a time at least, it looked as if the Panthers might become the nation's largest revolutionary gang."[126]

It is not an accident that Los Angeles, Chicago, Soledad, and Attica were the scenes of the most infamous and bloody confrontations between Party members and sympathizers and the forces of the state. In Los Angeles, the FBI worked steadily to aggravate the already existing antagonism between the Panthers and Maulana Karenga's Us organization, which led to the shoot-out on the UCLA campus where "Bunchy" Carter and John Huggins were killed on January 17, 1969. In a more clear-cut case of state murder, Fred Hampton and Mark Clark were executed in their apartment by a squad of Chicago detectives on December 4, 1969, while responding to an informant's tip about a weapons cache on the premises. In New York City, the Panther 21 were framed on infamous conspiracy charges on April 12, 1969, and eventually acquitted after a costly series of trials. Meanwhile, Richard Moore (Dhoruba Bin Wahad), one of the initial 21, was rearrested on May 19, 1971, and later convicted for shooting two New York City police officers in a trial that eighteen years later was proved to have been built upon fabricated evidence. Finally, George Jackson was killed August 21, 1971, in Soledad prison, again under suspicious circumstances, a year after his brother Jonathan and two hostages died in a botched rescue attempt on August 7, 1970. Two weeks later forty-three men were massacred when Attica's prison rebellion (partly inspired by George Jackson's death) was crushed by state police forces sent in by Governor Nelson Rockerfeller.[127] When retold by Panther loyalists, these incidents have an almost folkloric quality to them now. Like the 1968 killing of "Lil" Bobby Hutton by the Oakland police, the deaths of these men have come to define the death of a movement and to provide the surest evidence of widespread state repression and terror against the Party.

While understanding the depth of state-sanctioned violence against the Party is essential, we must also consider the significant complicity of the Panthers themselves in hastening their own demise at the hands of police forces across the country. Throughout the brief history of the Party, the Panther leaders were engaged in a constant struggle to ensure the self-discipline and accountability of their members and to curtail what they referred to as their "jackanape" tendencies toward spontaneous, violent confrontation. Although the Panthers correctly understood criminality and violence as socially produced, even quasi-rebellious activities structured by conditions of oppression, in the end this insight became a rationalization for covert, market-driven, criminal activities in the name of politics and resistance. Finally, the Party was subject to enormous dissension and conflict within its own ranks that not only left it open to infiltration by police agents and provocateurs, but also destroyed the solidarity and cohesion that was absolutely necessary for survival. Perhaps most important of all, the Panthers failed utterly in the struggle to transform the criminal consciousness and workless, lumpen existence into a political organization capable of sustained struggle.[128] In the end, they lost even more than this in "saber rattling" brinksmanship and what Fred Hampton termed the "adventuristic, Custeristic" confrontations with the force and violence of the state.[129]

This, however, should not be the last word. The Panthers' trademark actions of picking up the gun and patrolling the police were not initially conceived as preludes to an armed revolt. Rather, they were actually strategic choices and carefully posed challenges to the so-called legitimate forms of state violence that had become all too regularly used within Black communities. In particular, Newton and Seale understood how the police had become the principal agents of official, state-sanctioned racism that had largely receded from public view only to be brutally reasserted at the margins in the policing of the Black ghettos. As Erik Erikson suggested in his provocative discussion with Huey Newton, by arming themselves with guns and law books and observing police behavior, the Panthers actually enacted a profound transvaluation of conventional racist imagery by exposing the most visible representatives of the law and the crucial transmission belt of state power as the symbols of uniformed and armed lawlessness. Asserting their own right to organized violence, the Panthers began to police the police, while emphasizing their own "disciplined adherence to existing law."[130] Invoking the United States Constitution, employing a logic of policing and the law against the police and the law, the Panthers thus posed a stunning challenge to the legitimacy of state power in Black communities.[131]

The violent demise of the Panthers, I would suggest, is still best understood when viewed within the context of these initial acts of subversion, namely, the threats they posed to the legitimate power of the state. Those who wield state power prefer unorganized "criminal" violence to the exemplary, potentially organized violence of political militants. In this sense, police hounding, infiltration, and provocation of the Panthers sought out and exposed their weakest tendency, namely, their familiarity with and expectation of violent confrontation with the force of law. As holders of the monopoly on the legitimate uses of violence, the state in effect set out to prove that the Panthers were nothing more than street thugs and criminals and that their politics was nothing more than sham and pretense. Although many contemporary scholars seem to take this for granted, J. Edgar Hoover himself knew better when he labeled the Party "the greatest threat to the internal security of the country" and directed his COINTELPRO agents to *"destroy what the BPP stands for."*[132] [Emphasis added] This would only be accomplished when the status quo was restored, in other words, when the "legitimate" violence of the state was once again pitted against the disorganized, opportunistic, and self-destructive violence of the street.

IV. Conclusion: Shadow States and Insurgent Visibility

After I came out in 1968 with "Say It Loud, I'm Black and I'm Proud," it was all over. The dark-skinned man had all of a sudden become cosmopolitan.
—James Brown, *James Brown: The Godfather of Soul*

The brief ascendancy of the Black Panther Party between 1968 and the early 1970s is consonant with the emergence of a broader set of social, cultural, and political transformations that historians and theorists have attempted to define under the rubric of postmodernism.[133] Despite their stridently anticapitalist pronouncements, revolutionary vanguardism, and consistent appeals for socialism, as I have already suggested, the primary determinations of Panther politics actually lay elsewhere. In the end, the Panther's style of political discursivity was neither Marxist, nor universalist, but was instead predicated on a dialectical projection of local/global liberation narrated in terms of a more primary antagonism toward the principles of American nationality and the state. It is in this sense that there is actually a more subtle dimension to the Panthers' challenge to state authority, one that may even explain why it engendered the massive retaliatory response it did from federal and local police authorities. Clearly, with only a few shotguns and a handful of members in many Party chapters across the country, the Panthers were no match and no "real" threat to the organized violence of the state. Yet, by the end of the decade up to twenty-eight Panthers had been killed by police, and hundreds were jailed in the nationwide campaign to destroy the Party.[134] I have already shown how Panther tactics worked to expose the ideological limits of state power. The language of exposure, however, does not go far enough in capturing what might be termed the postmodern dimensions of the Panthers' subversion. Similar to the "prefigurative" politics that Wini Breines suggests characterizes 1960s movements more generally, the Panthers' own political experiment was in many respects primarily performative.[135] Ultimately, their performance was one that did not simply challenge the legitimacy of the nation–state, but in effect, prophesied and enacted its dissolution.

As Jean Genet, one of the most astute observers of the Panthers during the 1960s puts it, "Wherever they went, the Americans were the masters, so the Panthers would do their best to terrorize the masters by the only means available to them. Spectacle."[136] For Genet, although the Panthers may have embraced the Maoist slogan "All political power comes from the barrel of a gun," they also knew that sometimes "power is at the end of the shadow or image of a gun."[137] The "shadow of the gun," moreover, was far more important for the Panthers than actual guns could ever be. This is nowhere better demonstrated than in their famous Sacramento action where a group of armed Panthers marched on the state legislature to protest the pending passage of a bill that would have outlawed the open carrying of firearms—a bill explicitly aimed at stopping the Panthers' armed patrols. This action, perhaps more than any other, put the Party in the national spotlight with headlines reading, "Armed Panthers in the State Capital." Yet, rather than fleeing in terror or running for cover, the reporters and spectators stopped, looked, and asked questions. The question on everyone's lips was, "Are those guns real? and If so, then are they loaded?"[138]

Rather than seeing the Panthers as the vanguard of a visible insurgency in the country, we should understand them as being the practitioners of an insurgent form of visibility, a literal-minded and deadly serious guerrilla theatre in which militant sloganeering, bodily display, and spectacular actions simultaneously signified their possession and real lack of power. The Panthers emphasis upon self-presentation, in this sense, provided a visual vocabulary that was a key component of their politics. The leather, the clothing, the celebration of Black skin and "natural" hair, and above all the obtrusively displayed guns were all part of a repertoire of styles, gestures, and rhetorical equations like "Black is Beautiful," and "Power to the People" that revealed Black visibility as the defining antithesis of national subjectivity in the United States. In the end, the Panther spectacle was one arrayed both against and within the realm of what Harold Cruse called "America's race psychosis," and it is here where it may have registered its deepest, most lasting, and most confusing effects. Given the fact that Black skin has historically demarcated and condensed all that lies outside the protection of the nation–state and its cultures of citizenship and civility, the Panther's ability to capture the imagination of a broad radical coalition during the late 1960s was crucially dependent upon the ways they at once resignified Blackness as a positivity, while at the same time drawing upon its threatening powers of nonidentity in the eyes of the state and the normative citizen–subject.

The immediate power of the Panthers' spectacle was that, for a time at least, it revealed the state's own spectacular and performative dimensions. Indeed, one way to understand the Panther's performance is to recognize how they literally made a spectacle of the state. Within the logic of this spectacle, the excess and escalation of the rhetoric and imagery that the Panthers invented or popularized ("Off the pig," "The sky's the limit," "Fuck Reagan," "Two, three, many Vietnams") worked to continually heighten the anxiety of those charged with the duty of securing the state. In this regard, the police agencies, once they had been verbally attacked and legally outmaneuvered, found as their only recourse the demonstration that their own power was backed by more than words and empty guns. The bind the Panthers presented to the forces of the state was that if their threats were to go unanswered, they would potentially be proved right. The emperor would be shown to have no clothes, and America would be revealed as little more than a mask of power—Mao's proverbial paper tiger.

It is precisely this point that New Left historians such as Maurice Isserman and Michael Kazin disclaim (implying their disdain for the Panthers), suggesting that the 1960s went awry when it became captive to "increasingly outrageous and opaque language . . . rhetoric, composed of equal parts Maoist jargon and Black street rap, that communicated little but the angry alienation of its practitioners."[139] The fact is, however, that the Panthers' "rhetoric" communicated a great deal more than this and was significantly more consequential. If the nation, as Benedict Anderson, Homi Bhabha, and others suggest, is secured through forms of representation, then the definitional struggle waged over its contours by Black militants was a deadly serious undertaking grounded in the historic sense of the separateness of Black life in America and a plausible reading of the contemporary world situation. Most importantly, by challenging the police and aligning themselves with the Vietnamese, the Panther's exercised what Pierre Bourdieu calls "symbolic violence" against the state itself, disrupting the state's own power to nominate and designate normative, national subjects, in other words, usurping the state's own "monopoly of legitimate symbolic violence."[140]

If we consider the more specific instances of the state—the police, border control agencies, diplomatic corps, the military, the public schools, and the other state agencies that in effect act as "proof" of the existence of the state, all depend in the first instance upon the fiction of the state in order to perform their functions.[141] The performativity of the state then is in no way contradicted by its supposedly material functions. On the contrary, the very sense that the state is something that actually exists requires the more or less continuous activity of heterogeneous institutions and discourses of state in order to assure us, in Gertrude Stein's words, that "there is a there."[142] This formulation also helps to explain why violence is at once liminal to the state and at the same time, its most important form of discourse. The constantly reiterated threat of violence—from within and from without—is ultimately what institutes the state as a social relation and form of social meaning we inhabit. Violence threatens to undo the state, but it is also its very condition of possibility.

The Panthers, then, were a threat to the state not simply because they were violent but because they abused the state's own reality principle, including its monopoly on the legitimate uses of violence. Patrolling the police armed with guns and law books was in this sense a form of mimicry in which Panthers undermined the very notion of policing itself by performing, and in effect deforming, it themselves. Here, we must grasp the fact that the police themselves are among the most important of the state's "actors." The continued, repeated performance of the police function is crucial to the institution of the everyday fantasy of being subject to a national, social state. By misrecognizing the status of policing as it operated within Black communities, the Panthers effectively nullified this fantasy and substituted a radical alternative. By policing the police, in other words, the Panthers signaled something far more dangerous than is generally acknowledged: the eruption of a nonstate identity into the everyday life of the state. That such a small and relatively poorly equipped band of urban Black youth could demand so much attention from federal and local police only attests to the tenuousness of the state itself and the degree to which it depends upon controlling and even silencing those who would take its name in vain.

Rather than preemptively repudiating the rhetorical and performative nature of the Panthers' politics then, it might be worth actually interrogating it further. How, for example, should we understand all the pseudo-titles (Chairman, Minister of Defense, Chief of Staff, etc.) of a government in waiting or the regalia (Black berets, leather jackets, boots and guns) of a standing army or paramilitary force? What I would suggest is that the Panthers were actually engaged in a broad series of acts that were aimed at subverting the state's official performance of itself, which went well beyond shadowing the police. Enabled by the multiplication of revolutionary centers around the world, the Panthers even pursued their own foreign relations, challenging the state in what is perhaps the most sacred of its constitutive monopolies. Thus, Minister of Defense Huey Newton boasted that the Panthers were the only Americans who actually had a foreign policy toward Vietnam and concluded his autobiography by describing how he visited China before Nixon (the world's master of affairs of state), managing thereby to rebuke the American President publicly in front of the Chinese.[143] Pursuing a political strategy made famous by Robert Williams and Malcolm X, the Panthers made journeys to China, Algeria, Mozambique, Guinèe-Bissau, Cuba, and North Korea, seeking the authenticity of revolutionaries with states through the internationalist rituals of delegation and diplomacy.

Black power in its revolutionary instance then was ultimately an oppositional discourse that exposed the hegemony of Americanism as incomplete, challenged its universality, and imagined carving up its spaces differently. This, finally, is where the use of the "analogy" of the internal colony becomes important (the precise sociological definition of "nation" notwithstanding),[144] not for its analytical accuracy, but for its figurative potential and contestatory power. The use of the idioms of nationalism and anticolonialism by Black power militants, in other words, must be understood more as practical and ideational deconstructions of the pretensions of nationality and state power (policing, waging war, schooling, diplomacy, etc.). Indeed, in their dramatic performance of their own noncitizenship and even anticitizenship, the Panthers necessarily implied a wholly different region of identification.

Most importantly, the Panthers were effective in projecting themselves as an outside force that was also inside the nation because they refused the terms of Black inclusion and citizenship in the American polity at precisely the point of African Americans' greatest augmentation and reform since the Civil War and Reconstruction as a result of the Civil Rights Act of 1964, the Voting Rights Act of 1965, and Johnson's War on Poverty programs. Indeed, it may be the case that it was the offer of state-aided integration and assimilation into civil society and the public sphere that gave such a powerful charge to the Panthers' refusals and contestations.[145] More than anything else, the Panthers resignified Blackness in all its geopolitical and intrapsychic density. Their much discussed and oft-repudiated emphasis on violence may actually have more to do with their repudiation of the "violence" that came with the imperative of Black assimilation itself, namely, the internalization of the frontiers of the nation and the "inhabiting of the space of the state" as a place where Black people "have always been—and will always be at home."[146] The Panthers saw assimilation posed in these terms as a ruse and a trap and repudiated its internally hegemonizing logic by remapping the frontiers of their own subjectivity in local and global terms.

Jean Genet, who spent several madcap weeks with the Panthers in 1970, was especially attuned to this dimension of Panther politics. Genet writes that in spite of their posture as the progressive vanguard in America, the Panthers' specular-rhetorical politics neither privileged strictly American political traditions nor drew primarily upon a common fund of American democratic imagery. As Genet puts it, the Panthers "built themselves upon a White America that was splitting."[147] Insofar as they invoked the American Constitution (for example, in support of their right to carry guns), they did so not as preservationists of American radical or legal traditions but as destroyers of the normative ties binding Black people and radical White youth to the American nation–state and its public cultures of liberal civility. The characteristic disdain that many intellectuals show for Panther-style politics, then, may have less to do with its outrageously "rhetorical" cast than with its specific rhetorical contents and imagined reality-effects. Seemingly progressive revisionist accounts of the 1960s are, in this sense, often more nationalist than left in their impetus. The anxieties about fragmentation and dispersion, identity politics, and excessive rhetoric that they express, I would suggest, are really anxieties about the nation–state itself and, in particular, about the status of (White, male) national subjectivity at the tail end of the bloody American century. In other words, exactly the kinds of anxieties the Panthers evoked. The glibness with which the Panthers are now invoked, for example, as a precedent for the White patriot and militia movements, or as an explanation for the violent turn in Black public culture exemplified in contemporary gangsta rap, only testifies to the lingering power of their performance. These spurious political connections, however, mystify much more than they reveal by ignoring the liberatory, radical, and other less semantically available aspects of the Panthers' experiment. Most damaging, this ersatz history blocks a more complete account of the historical trauma that the Panthers exemplified, namely, the legitimization anxiety and fragility of the postmodern nation–state.

Other sorts of revisions have been somewhat careless. The fact that an "avowed homosexual" like Genet would be, as he puts it, "invited in" by the Panthers should, for example, make us reconsider the characteristic indictments of their sexism and misogyny, from Michelle Wallace's celebrated critique of "Black Macho" in 1978 to Alice Walker's recent assertions that the Panthers were little more than psychologically damaged Black men afraid of being called "punks" and "sissies."[148] Although there is no question that there was sexism in the Panther Party, several of the Panthers also made what Edmund White describes as "an astonishing leap, given the period," by coming out and explicitly identifying gay liberation and women's liberation as causes that needed to be supported and embraced as a part of a broad revolutionary struggle.[149] At Genet's prompting, Newton himself undertook a self-critical appraisal of his own sexism and homophobia, producing a pamphlet in 1970 entitled "The Women's Liberation and Gay Liberation Movements," where he observed that homosexuals might actually be the most oppressed, and the most revolutionary participants in a coalition of oppressed peoples.[150]

This pamphlet was born out of an article in *The Black Panther* that was written on the occasion of the Panther-sponsored Revolutionary People's Constitutional Convention, which was attended by a diverse array of cultural and political radicals including radical women's groups, members of the Gay Liberation Front, representatives of the American Indian Movement, and others. Though Hilliard remembers the convention as a failure, the enactment of a Constitutional Convention under the auspices of the Panthers and in celebration of radical "minorities", excluded in the initial formulation of the great document, was an astonishing attempt to imagine alternative forms of kinship and community to the one organized around a conception of a unitary and universal, national subject. Ultimately, what this signaled was the existence of a spectrum of liberatory practices and "revolutionary peoples," all searching for a way in—and a way out. Liberation politics, as inaugurated and exemplified by the Panthers, in other words, was based less upon the defense of reified notions of identity than upon the desire to fracture a singular, hegemonic space by imagining the liberation of manifold symbolic spaces within the (national) territory, from the body, to the streets, a section of the city, the mind itself. Within the (im)possibly "heterotopian" impulses of this kind of politics, the multiplication of rhetorics of "liberation" and "autonomy" was uneasily met by a language of rights, inclusion, and participation—perhaps the necessary paradox of any liberatory practice that contends with the legacies of exclusion and marginalization within the ambit of a national security state.[151]

In terms of constructing a genealogy of the 1960s and its forms of identity politics in our own time, it is important that we understand how and why it was that the American Black movement in general, and the Panthers in particular, gained such centrality, especially when it came to supplying the ideological resources, the fund of metaphor, imagery, and symbolism that in crucial respects defined the radical potentialities of this moment. According to Kobena Mercer, "[T]he political positions of the Black Panthers had an empowering effect in extending the chain of radical democratic equivalences to more and more social groups precisely through their dramatic visibility in the public sphere."[152] Thus, in the imaginary constructs of the radical counterculture, for example—a "Woodstock Nation," a "youth colony," or a "White Panther Party"—the sign of "youth" reappropriated the sign of "race," and declared that "White middle-class kids are exploited and oppressed," that "long-hair is Black skin," and that "the student is a nigger."[153] Or as the gay liberationist delegation to the Revolutionary People's Constitutional Convention put it, "queer = chick = nigger," and imagined what it would take to transform San Francisco from "a ghetto policed by straights" to a "free territory."[154] In Mercer's terms, the Black struggles of 1968 exerted profound "metonymic leverage," acting as the "trigger struggle" and switch point for other minority and identity discourses, and serving as the central relay station for the absorption and appropriation of the liberatory impulses of decolonization from within the global media scape.[155]

Now it may be the case that the generalization and metaphorization of decolonization or, for that matter, racial oppression are what is most illegitimate about the recent history of liberation politics in America. The invocation of "decolonized sensibilities," "the inner colonized," or "the third world within" might not only be an example of sloppy analogical reasoning, it might also serve to erase the consequences of uneven development across the globe. It also may serve to efface and even trivialize the significant specificity of exceedingly different historic struggles.[156] Yet, rather than cavalierly dismissing any use of this language as illegitimate appropriation or as a product of romantic fascination and indulgence, it may be worth considering in more detail the profound relationship between 1960s social movements in the United States and the history of decolonization and neocolonialism. In the end, contemporary explorations of "the other question" and "cultural difference" are unthinkable apart from a consideration of this history and, in particular, of struggles against imperialism and racism that have "produced forms of politics that neither conform to traditional political categories, nor uphold their standards of coherence."[157]

Indeed, what may be most significant about 1968 was that it was marked by a series of attempts to break with or subvert the dominant staging of "race" within American culture which gave impetus to the broad reinvention of political radicalism in this country. The extension of the metaphorical valences of Black struggles beyond the United States, moreover, strained the nation–form, undermining normative, national self-identity. For a time at least, and this was certainly true of the Panthers, it seemed as though Black-people-in-struggle had seized control of "racial" assets, the fund of metaphor, symbolism, and imagery that have always been central to the construction of hegemonic "citizenship" in the United States by wrenching the self-perpetuating logic of America's "dilemma" and rupturing the self-assured dialectic of the "American Century." From James Brown's "Say it Loud, I'm Black and Proud" to the redolent phrase "Black is Beautiful," to the startling imagery of barefeet and Black fists raised in protest at the Mexico Olympic Games, to the oxymoronic saliency of the "Black Power" concept itself, the cultural politics of 1968 were centered on a series of dramatic and potentially liberatory transvaluations of the signifying content of Blackness. In the end, it is this uniquely subversive, insistently traumatizing legacy that has been least understood and most devalued in the official revisionist accounts. At the same time, this legacy remains to a greater and lesser degree most alive in the "racial" politics of cultural performance and in the critical reworking of antiracist theory and practice today.

Of course, the story of the Black Panthers is not without its own tortured ironies. If the logic of the "American Century" was in some sense predicated upon the promise of universal nationality for a decolonizing humanity and for Black people within the United States, its eclipse, as the Panthers understood it, had revealed the hollowness of the initial promise. In the wake of 1968, we have been subject to the explicit reconstruction of neocolonial and neoracist domination within the world-system and in the United States. Rigorously puncturing and exploding the historical basis and pretensions of American power, the Panthers more than any other group foresaw this. Indeed, this is the primary reason why they are now so readily blamed for the fact that the "dream" is still "deferred." Yet, in a sense, the Panthers, especially in their slide into drugs and crime in the 1970s, merely reflected a process by which neocolonialism and uneven development were being more ruthlessly internalized within the United States itself. Under the new regime, the state has increasingly stopped even attempting to secure its legitimation in the eyes of its Black people. Instead, what we have is the reconstitution of forms of repressive, racial alterity in the figures of contemporary, Black anticitizenry—criminals, drug users, wild youth, and welfare "queens"—all those for whom the Panthers held out such promise. Perhaps the greatest irony of the post-1968 period, now that the market appears as the global horizon of all human sociality, is that Black aesthetic commodities—"Black performativity," if you will—is that much more prominent within the public sphere, even as Black "citizenship" is increasingly devalued.[158]

To conclude, what C. L. R. James said of Marcus Garvey might also be said of the Panthers, "When you bear in mind the slenderness . . . [of his]

resources and the vast material forces and the pervading social conceptions which automatically sought to destroy him, his achievement remains one of the propagandistic miracles of this century."[159] Taking the Garvey movement somewhat as a precedent, it is perhaps not insignificant that so many anticolonial thinkers, including Fanon and Genet, and their American contemporaries like Harold Cruse and James Baldwin, took the "stage" and the "mirror" to be the metaphors that best explained the revolt of the colonized, and racialized subaltern. Indeed, it may be that the revolts of powerless people are always at first "theatrical," self-inflating, and bombastic. Lacking a significant purchase upon the "real," they inevitably appear unanchored, self-referential, and unintelligible to those who witness them for the first time. In retrospect, this may appear as weakness and even failure, though it is always impossible to fully calculate these effects, or what might happen within more favorable conjunctures. For the colonized and racial "other," who for so long stood holding up the mirror in which the "West" contemplated itself, the revolt against colonization briefly constituted its own referents and mirrors, shattering the calm, reflective surface of universal history into a thousand tiny fragments in which many began to see their own reflection for the first time. It is Fanon who best captured the ambiguities attendant on this moment, offering what might serve here as a final word on the Black Panthers:

> To tell the truth, there is a glaring divergence between what these men claim to be and what they have behind them. These countries without tramways, without troops, and without money have no justification for the bravado that they display in broad daylight. Undoubtedly they are impostors. . . . These men at the head of empty countries, who talk too loud are most irritating. You'd like to shut them up. But on the contrary, they are in great demand. They are given bouquets; they are invited to dinner. In fact, we quarrel over who shall have them. . . . They are 98% illiterate, but they are the subject of a huge body of literature. They travel a great deal. . . gold mines for airline companies. . . Perhaps we shall see that this, which caricatures itself often in facile internationalism is one of the most fundamental characteristics of underdeveloped countries.[160]

NOTES

Acknowledgments: I am indebted to many people who commented on this chapter, especially the participants in the 1992 American Studies Association Conference in Costa Mesa, Calif., and the 1993 Yale American Studies Graduate Conference in New Haven, Conn. I'd like to thank everyone who read an early version of this chapter, including Karam Singh, Michael Denning, David Waldstreicher, Carlo Rotella, Gunther Peck, Pamela Haag, Jean-Christophe Agnew, Lewis Gordon, David Scobey, Judith Smith, Eric Lott, Colleen Lye, and Rebecca McLennan. I am also grateful to Henry Abelove, Ashley Dawson, Matt Jacobson, Herman Lebovics, Tim Brennan, Nancy Cott, and Charles E. Jones for their comments on the final draft, and especially to Alys Weinbaum and Adam Green who helped me to see this through from start to finish.

1. This composite is drawn from several important historical works on the 1960s: Stuart Hall et al., *Policing the Crisis: Mugging, the State and Law and Order* (New York: Holmes and Meier, 1978); Todd Gitlin, *The Sixties: Years of Hope, Days of Rage* (New York: Bantam Books, 1987); George Katsiaficas, *The Imagination of the New Left: A Global Analysis* (Boston: South End Press,1987); Ronald Fraser et al., *1968: A Student Generation in Revolt* (New York: Pantheon Books, 1988); Ward Churchill and Jim Vander Wall, *Agents of Repression: The FBI's Secret Wars Against the Black Panther Party and the American Indian Movement* (Boston: South End Press, 1988); Alice Echols, *Daring to Be Bad: Radical Feminism in America, 1967–1975* (Minneapolis: University of Minnesota Press, 1989); Eric Cummins, *The Rise and Fall of California's Radical Prison Movement* (Stanford: University of California Press, 1994). The notion of "revolutionary suicide" is from Huey P. Newton's (recently reprinted), *Revolutionary Suicide* (New York: Writers and Readers Publishing, Inc., 1995 [1973]).

2. Alice Echols, "We Gotta Get Out of This Place: Notes Toward a Remapping of the Sixties," *Socialist Review* 92:2 (1992): 15.

3. For useful works that in very different ways complicate the dichotomizing narrative see Echols, *Daring to Be Bad,* and Van Gosse, *Where the Boys Are: Cuba, Cold War America, and the Making of a New Left* (New York: Verso, 1993). Gosse, in particular, affirms principles crucial to this chapter, namely, what he calls the "polycentric" nature of 1960s radicalism and, more importantly, the centrality of antiimperialism to the origins of a broad New Left (10–12).

4. The term "subaltern counterpublic" is coined by Nancy Fraser in her useful essay, "Rethinking the Public Sphere: A Contribution to the Critique of Actually Existing Democracy," *Social Text* 25/26 (1990): 56–80. The notion of subaltern counterpublics corrects the tendency to reify the bourgeois public sphere as unitary and universal (when it is in fact produced through a series of constitutive exclusions), and simultaneously recognizes the (civic-republican) "public sphere," as a realm of civil, communal discourse within the ambit of the nation–state and as a realm of "intrapublic" conflict in which "members of subordinated social groups invent and circulate counter-discourses, which in turn permit them to formulate oppositional interpretations of their identities, interests, and needs (67)." What remains unclarified in Fraser's essay is the specific historico-political relationship between the public sphere, as "a theater of political participation," "discursive relations" and conflicts (57), and the nation–state, which remains invested as the ultimate arbiter of the "common good" and the boundaries of the "we," and retains a monopoly on certain forms of public discourse, in particular

the discourse of "violence," something I will have occasion to discuss later in the chapter.

5. Tom Hayden, *Reunion: A Memoir* (New York: Random House, 1988), 419; Echols, "We Gotta Get Out of This Place," 14.

6. Gitlin, *The Sixties: Years of Hope, Days of Rage,* 348; Todd Gitlin, "From Universality to Difference: Notes on the Fragmentation of the Idea of the Left," *Contention* 2:2 (Winter 1993): 31.

7. By "American universalism," I mean the essential yoking together of Enlightenment notions of human universality and formal freedom with a vision of the American nation as a single great community. As I argue elsewhere this vision receives its most forceful articulation in the post-WWII period by Gunnar Myrdal in *The American Dilemma: The Negro Problem and Modern Democracy,* 2 vols. (New York: Pantheon Books, 1962 (1944)). Nikhil P. Singh, *Race and Reason,* vol. 3, Fall 1997: 62–70. According to John Higham, a contemporary proponent of this view, American universalism is "*our* egalitarian ideology. . . . molded by the Englightment and forged in the revolution. . . . [It is] simultaneously a civic credo, a social vision, and a definition of nationhood." From John Higham, "Multiculturalism and Universalism: a History and Critique," *American Quarterly* 44/2: 197 (my emphasis). For a similar statement of principles, see Gitlin, who calls the United States "the place where the Enlightenment first came down to earth" and defends the utopian possibilities inherent in Myrdal's conception of America as "embryonic humanity itself;" Gitlin, "From Universality to Difference," 24.

8. This analysis is the outgrowth of a few former New Left and liberal–democratic thinkers' attempts to come to terms with the popularity and political success of Reaganism. The conclusion that emerges from this line of reasoning, however— that forms of cultural radicalism and identity politics inherited from the 1960s have helped to undermine the left, by alienating White working men and opening the door to a right-wing populism—has actually been a self-conscious Republican strategy since 1968. This strategy was first formulated by Nixon advisor Kevin Phillips and elaborated in his book *The Emerging Republican Majority* (New York: Doubleday, 1970). For contemporary, left-democratic variations on the Phillips thesis, see Jim Sleeper, *The Closest of Strangers* (New York: Basic Books, 1990); Stephen Fraser and Gary Gerstle, eds., *The Rise and Fall of the New Deal Order: 1930–1980* (Princeton: Princeton University Press, 1989); Thomas Byrne Edsall and Mary Edsall, *Chain Reaction* (New York: Norton, 1991); Harry Ashmore, *Civil Rights and Wrongs* (New York: Pantheon Books, 1994); and Gitlin, "From Universality to Difference." Also, see the provocative debate between Maurice Isserman and Alexander Cockburn about the so-called excesses of 1960s radicalism, "Letters: An Exchange," *The Nation,* 31 October 1994: 507–8.

9. Indeed, the degree to which the architects of the Reagan, Bush, and Clinton presidential victories staked their campaigns on a kind of anti-antiracism, taking-for-granted, and forwarding "common sense" linkages between the politics of racial redress, national fragmentation, the political extremism of the 1960s, and the "pathologies" of Black socialization, has become increasingly clear. The putatively left counterargument that calls for the reinvigoration of an alternative, left-wing populism invariably fails to account for the fact that populism (which Ellen Willis aptly labels "the cultural nationalism of ordinary people"), in large measure names the problem that minority discourses around race (as well as those around gender and sexuality) have always had to confront in the first place. Ellen Willis, "Let's Get Radical," *Village Voice,* 19 December 1994, 33. Thus, for example, the argument that the rightward turn in American politics is the product of a backlash against the excesses of antiracist politics since the 1960s, actually

has it backwards. Rising Black militancy in the 1960s registered in such a profound and disturbing way because it was in itself a direct response to the racist "frontlashing" that has been an implicit or explicit feature of almost every American populism. For a useful analysis and critique of the backlash thesis, see Shiela Collins, *The Rainbow Challenge: The Jackson Campaign and the Future of American Politics* (New York: Monthly Review Press, 1986), 69.

10. Benedict Anderson, *Imagined Communities: Reflections on the Origins and Spread of Nationalism* (London: Verso, 1983).

11. Michael Omi and Howard Winant, *Racial Formation in the United States from the 1960s to the 1980s* (New York: Routledge, Kegan and Paul, 1986), 145.

12. Ibid., 139.

13. Tom Wolfe, *Radical Chic and Mau-Mauing the Flak Catchers* (New York: Farrar, Strauss and Giroux, 1970).

14. The revisionist work on the 1960s that most exemplifies this is Peter Collier and David Horowitz, *Destructive Generation: Second Thoughts About the 1960s* (New York: Simon and Schuster, Inc., 1990). Also see Gitlin, *The Sixties*, 350.

15. Many otherwise admirable accounts of Black liberation politics during the 1960s have this tendency, including Fraser et al. *1968*; Katsiaficas, *The Imagination of the New Left*; Churchill and Wall, *Agents of Repression,* and Eugene Victor Wolfenstein, *Victims of Democracy: Malcolm X and the Black Revolution* (London: Free Association Books, 1989).

16. An analysis of Black liberation politics during the 1960s that scrupulously avoids these pitfalls is significantly not about the Panthers but about the movement that was the most credible Black revolutionary alternative to the Panthers, the Dodge Revolutionary Union Movement (DRUM). See Dan Georgakas and Marvin Surkin, *Detroit: I Do Mind Dying: A Study in Urban Revolution* (New York: St. Martin's Press, 1975). Recent criticism of the so-called White left and the Panthers that nonetheless continues to treat the Panthers as little more than an emblem, includes Adolph Reed, "Tokens of the White Left," *The Progressive* 57.12:18-26. I thank Gordon Lafer for pointing out Reed's essay.

17. For example, see Doug McAdam's brief discussion of the Black Panther Party in his otherwise useful book, *Political Process and the Development of Black Insurgency, 1930–1970* (Chicago: University of Chicago Press, 1982), 182. For a much more egregious example of this phenomenon, see Hugh Pearson, *The Shadow of the Panther: Huey P. Newton and the Price of Black Power in America* (New York: Addison-Wesley, 1994).

18. Elaine Brown, *A Taste of Power: A Black Woman's Story* (New York: Anchor Books, 1992); David Hilliard and Lewis Cole, *This Side of Glory: The Autobiography of David Hilliard and the Story of the Black Panther Party* (Boston: Little Brown and Company, 1993). More recently, the writings of Huey P. Newton and other Panther leaders have been reprinted. Of particular importance and interest are Phillip F. Foner's collection, *The Black Panthers Speak* (New York: Da Capo Press, 1995 [1970]), and Huey P. Newton, *To Die for the People: Selected Writings and Speeches* (New York: Writers and Readers Publishing, Inc., 1995 [1972]).

19. Collier and Horowitz, *Destructive Generation*; Pearson, *Shadow of the Panther*; also Alice Walker, "Black Panthers or Black Punks," *New York Times*, 5 May 1993, A 23.

20. William Gardner Smith, *Return to Black America* (Englewood Cliffs, N.J.: Prentice-Hall Publishers, 1970), 173.

21. Stuart Hall et al., *Policing the Crisis: Mugging, the State and Law and Order* (New York: Holmes and Meier, 1978), 387. The discussion that follows is heavily

indebted to Hall's illuminating comments on the meaning of Panther politics from the vantage point of Blacks in Britain.

22. Manning Marable, *Black American Politics: From the Washington Marches to Jesse Jackson* (New York: Verso, 1985), 57.

23. Bobby Seale, *Seize the Time: The Story of the Black Panther Party and Huey P. Newton* (Baltimore: Black Classic Press, 1991 [1970]), 80.

24. Ibid., 83.

25. Hilliard and Cole, *This Side of Glory*, 232.

26. The writings of the central Black revolutionary figures during the 1960s, in addition to the main Panther leaders, are indispensable sources for reconstructing a sense of the politics of the period. The most important are Eldridge Cleaver, *Soul on Ice* (New York: Dell Publishing, Inc., 1970); Eldridge Cleaver, *Post-Prison Writings and Speeches* (New York: Vintage Books, 1970); James Forman, *The Making of Black Revolutionaries* (Seattle: Open Hand Publishing, Inc., 1985); Angela Davis, *With My Mind on Freedom: An Autobiography* (New York: Bantam Books, 1974); George Jackson, *Soledad Brother* (London: Penguin Books, 1970). For a discussion of the ill-fated Panther–SNCC alliance, see Forman, *The Making of Black Revolutionaries*, 541. For the BPP and DRUM see Georgakas and Surkin, *Detroit: I Do Mind Dying*, 61, 143. For brief discussions of the BPP and the Young Lords, see Foner, *The Black Panther Leaders Speak*, 229–45; and Hilliard, *This Side of Glory*, 229; for the American Indian Movement, see Churchill, *Agents of Repression*; for the Brown Berets, see Carlos Munoz, Jr., *Youth, Identity and Power: The Chicano Movement* (New York: Verso, 1989), 86; for the Prison Movement, see Cummins, *The Rise and Fall of California's Radical Prison Movement*, ch. 5–8; Angela Davis, *If They Come in the Morning: Voices of Resistance* (San Francisco: The National United Committee to Free Angela Davis (NUCFAD), 1971); for Women's and Gay Liberation, see Newton, *To Die For the People*, 152; Echols, *Daring to Be Bad*, 222–23; Karla Jay and Allen Young, *Out of the Closets: Voices of Gay Liberation* (New York: New York University Press, 1992 (1972)); for the BPP and SDS, see Gitlin, *The Sixties*, 348–350; Fraser et al., *1968*, 309–311; Echols, *Daring to be Bad*, 127–28; Andrew Kopkind, "The Real SDS Stands Up (1969)," in *The Thirty Years Wars: Dispatches and Diversions of a Radical Journalist, 1965–1994* (New York: Verso, 1995), 166. Finally, on the centrality of anti-imperialism and internationalism for the Panthers, see Cornel West, "The Paradoxes of the Afro-American Rebellion," in *The Sixties Without Apology,* ed. Sonya Sahres et al. (Minneapolis: University of Minnesota Press, 1984), 53; Hilliard and Cole, *This Side of Glory*, 247, 278; Hall et al., *Policing the Crisis*, 386–88.

27. Arjun Appadurai, "Disjuncture and Difference in the Global Cultural Economy," *Theory, Culture and Society* 7:295–310. Appadurai's important essay outlines protocols for thinking about global cultural flows in terms of the movement of populations, media images, ideologies, technologies, and capital. The various "scapes" corresponding to each instance of movement are unevenly integrated and coordinated across the vast spaces of the global cultural economy.

28. These are the words of scholar–pundit and presidential advisor Daniel Patrick Moynihan, quoted in Collins, *The Rainbow Challenge*, 57.

29. Henry Louis Gates, "Critical Fanonism," *Critical Inquiry*, (Spring 1991).

30. Newton, *To Die for the People*, 92; Hilliard and Cole, *This Side of Glory*, 121.

31. Here I am paraphrasing Stuart Hall who writes that the Panthers forged "a form of Black revolutionary politics alternative to the worlds of low wage work,

hustling, the middle-class politics of Civil Rights and the separatism of cultural nationalism." Hall et al., *Policing the Crisis*, 387.

32. The notion that a Maoist-inflected opposition between "bourgeois" and "revolutionary" becomes the most salient one for radicals during the 1960s (displacing the more orthodox Marxist opposition between the bourgeoisie and the proletariat), is from Frederic Jameson's provocative and important essay "Periodizing the Sixties,"in, *The Sixties Without Apology*, ed. Sonya Sahres et al., 189.

33. C. L. R. James, "The Revolutionary Answer to the Negro Question in the United States (1948)," in *The C. L. R. James Reader* (London: Basil Blackwell, 1992).

34. Omi and Winant, *Racial Formation in the United States*, 32.

35. Huey P. Newton, "We Are Nationalists and Internationalists," in *The Coming of the New International*, ed. John Gerassi (New York: The World Publishing Co., 1971), 575.

36. Essentially, the Panther leaders viewed their local Black nationalist rivals as ineffectual poseurs and political reactionaries. Bobby Seale offered one of the most complete, early statements of the Panther position in 1967: "We're nationalists because we see ourselves as a nation within a nation. But we're revolutionary nationalists. We don't see ourselves as a national unit for racist reasons but as a necessity for us to progress as human beings. We don't fight exploitative capitalism with Black capitalism. We fight capitalism with revolutionary socialism. All of us are laboring people—employed or unemployed, and our unity has got to be based on the practical necessities of life, liberty and the pursuit of happiness. It's got to be based on the practical things like the survival of people and people's right to self-determination, to iron out their problems by themselves without the interference of the police or CIA or armed forces of the USA. We don't care about changing what we wear; we want power—later for what we wear. Dashikis don't free nobody and pork chops don't oppress nobody." Quoted in Hilliard and Cole, *This Side of Glory*, 122.

37. Kobena Mercer, "1968: Periodizing Politics and Identity," in *Cultural Studies*, ed. Lawrence Grossberg et al. (London: Routledge, 1992), 433.

38. Erik Erikson and Huey P. Newton, *In Search of Common Ground* (New York: W.W. Norton & Co., 1973), 133.

39. "Resistance literature" is Barbara Harlow's term, see her *Resistance Literature* (New York: Methuen, 1987).

40. Frantz Fanon, *The Wretched of the Earth* (New York: Grove Press, 1968), 147. Fanon completed this work in 1961, right before he died.

41. Manning Marable, *Blackwater: Historical Studies in Race, Class Consciousness and Revolution* (Dayton: Black Praxis Press, 1981), 193. The idea of the Panther's "counter nationalism", (or in Nancy Fraser's more modest term, their "counter publicity"), is useful because it successfully subverts the false opposition between assimilationism and separatism as the only meaningful political choices for a minority discourse. When understood as "counter discourses," minority discourses can be understood in their "dual character," namely, "as spaces of withdrawal and regroupment," and "as bases and training grounds for agitational activities directed toward wider publics." Fraser, "Re-thinking the Public Sphere," 68.

42. Jameson, "Periodizing the 1960s," 182.

43. Hall et al., *Policing the Crisis*, 387.

44. Seale, *Seize the Time*, 25; Hilliard and Cole, *This Side of Glory*, 120, 183; Newton, *To Die for the People*, 17.

45. Gates, "Critical Fanonism"; also see Cedric Robinson's scathing critique of the uptake of Fanon by contemporary literary critics in "The Appropriation of Frantz Fanon," *Race and Class* 35(1) 1993: 79–91.

46. Eugene Genovese, "The Legacy of Slavery and the Roots of Black Nationalism," in *For a New America: Essays in History and Politics from Studies on the Left, 1959–1967*, ed. James Weinstein and David Eakins (New York: Vintage Books, 1970), 415.

47. Wilson Moses, "Ambivalent Maybe," in *Lure and Loathing: Essays on Race, Identity and the Ambivalence of Assimilation*, ed. Gerald Early (New York: Penguin, 1993), 193.

48. Harold Cruse, *Rebellion or Revolution* (New York: William Morrow & Co., 1968), 23.

49. Ibid., 95. Or, as Cruse puts it still more pointedly, in another context: "The Negro . . . [is] the American problem of underdevelopment (74)."

50. For example, see Harold Cruse, *The Crisis of the Negro Intellectual* (New York: William Morrow & Co., 1967).

51. Cruse, *Rebellion or Revolution*, 95. This goes to the heart of Cruse's entire project, namely, the need to "theorize" Black political struggles: "The crisis of Black and White is also *a crisis in social* theory. (27)"

52. Hilliard and Cole, *This Side of Glory*, 120–22.

53. This is the book Eldridge Cleaver dubbed "the Black bible," in *Post-Prison Writings and Speeches*, 18.

54. Fanon, *Wretched of the Earth*, 80.

55. Ibid., 216, 234.

56. Ibid., 75.

57. Prasnejit Duara, "The Displacement of Tension to the Tension of Displacement," *Radical History Review* 57, (Fall 1993), 63.

58. This phrase was first coined by the great American liberal historian William Appleman Williams; also see Fanon, *The Wretched of the Earth*, 66.

59. Fanon, *Wretched of the Earth*, 98–99.

60. Hilliard and Cole, *This Side of Glory*, 319.

61. Erikson and Newton, *In Search of Common Ground*, 31.

62. I would suggest that Newton's theory was a provocative effort to conceive the lineaments of what Bruce Cummings calls the "post-1945 American realm of action in the world," or the redefinition of a logic of empire without colonies. Bruce Cummings, "Global Realm With No Limit, Global Realm With No Name," *Radical History Review* (1993) 57:46–59. Intercommunalism, then, might be seen as an attempt to name the other face of an imperialism no longer reliant upon territorial possessions, or a "deterritorialized" conception of "national liberation," in which small groups like the Panthers could participate, along with other oppressed communities, like the Cubans, or the Vietnamese. Following Cummings, we might understand the basis of the post-1945 American empire in the following way: (1) in military and territorial terms, it is "an archipelago of military bases" and complexes; (2) in economic terms, it is a disproportionate financial and political influence within the global sphere of multilateral commodity-relations and international state-system—the old U.S. dream of an "open-door empire (51)." To call this an "empire," as Cummings suggests, is clearly something of a misnomer, especially when it comes to defining a world

that was beginning to be decolonized after 1945. During this time "the world-system," as Cummings writes, "did not necessarily need an American empire . . . [though it] did need a hegemon[ist] (53)." This might also help to explain the "ideal" character of American global power (that is, the degree to which it has not always been driven by obvious material interests, but rather by the need to set an example—"empire as a way of life"). Finally, another useful way to describe American global hegemony is through a notion of "ultraimperialism," which implies the end of nationalist autarky, along with the broad cooperation, as opposed to conflict and (imperial) competition of the world's dominant powers. Ultraimperialism was first coined by Karl Kautsky in 1914, at the beginning of WWI. However, it was not until the onset of the so-called American Century and the imposition of the Bretton Woods agreement governing international trade and monetary policy in 1942 that something like ultraimperialism became a reality. Carl Parrini, "The Age of Ultraimperialism," *Radical History Review* (1993) 57:7–20.

63. Clearly Newton's theory possesses its share of wishful thinking, myopia, and, above all, self-importance, since the Vietnamese were in fact struggling for a nation–state of their own. Moreover, the constant refrain that the U.S. was "not a nation, but an empire," and that "the Black people of the empire's heartland" (that is, the Panthers) were "at the center of revolutionary action" in the world, elides the fact that the Panthers' (and the Vietnamese's) primary antagonist was still the American state. Nation–states, in this sense, are hardly "things of the past," but are ordered in specific, functional and hierarchical relations within the world system, relations that have not simply been swept away by forces of capitalist globalization. See Frantz Schurmann's introduction to Newton, *To Die for the People*, xx. Still, I would argue that Newton's thinking is important for three reasons: (1) it acknowledges the "world-ordering" power of the U.S. during this period; (2) it attempts to theorize a relationship between intra- and international conflict and struggle; and (3) it argues that an effective "anti-imperialism" must be based on the understanding that the global power and domestic hegemony of the American state are integrally linked. Also see Michael Geyer, "Concerning the Question: Is Imperialism a Useful Category of Historical Analysis?" *Radical History Review* (1993) 57:68.

64. L. S. Stavrianos, *Global Rift: The Third World Comes of Age* (New York: William Morrow & Co., 1981). My periodization of decolonization is taken from Aijaz Ahmad, *In Theory: Classes, Nations and Literatures* (New York: Verso, 1992), who "designates . . . the years between 1945 and 1975 the high period of decolonization (39)." During this time, Ahmad argues, 1965–75 is especially important for giving rise to revolutionary nationalist struggles with "a distinctly socialist trajectory (30)." On the crisis of U.S. hegemony over the world market by the early 1970s, see Giovanni Arrighi, "Marxist Century, American Century: The Making and Remaking of the World Labor Movement," *New Left Review* 179:45.

65. Richard J. Barnet, and Ronald Muller, *Global Reach: The Power of Multinational Corporations* (New York: Simon and Schuster, 1974), 334.

66. Etienne Balibar and Immanuel Wallerstein, *Race, Nation, Class: Ambiguous Identities* (New York: Verso, 1991), 44.

67. Frantz Fanon, *The Wretched of the Earth*, 98.

68. What Jameson calls "the Fanonian model of struggle," is actually an attempt to replace the proletariat with the "colonized" as the new Subject of History, a move first heralded by Jean-Paul Sartre in his famous essay "Orphee Noir"(1949). Ernesto Laclau emphasizes the populist dimension of successful counter-hegemonic, anticapitalist struggles that effectively articulate

heterogeneous struggles and antagonisms into a single antithetical structure: "the people" vs. "the power bloc," in *Politics and Ideology in Marxist Theory* (London: Verso, 1977), 135. On the Panthers' counter-hegemonic articulations, see Mercer, "1968: Periodizing Politics and Identity," 435. Contemporary criticisms, notwithstanding, the Panther's rhetoric was indeed populist in the sense that Laclau suggests, in particular, in their effort to weld contemporary, anticolonial and anticapitalist ideologies together with the revolutionary, democratic demands of The Declaration of Independence and The United States Constitution. See the last paragraph of the Panthers' famous 10-point program, which begins, "We hold these truths to be self-evident. . . ." Newton, *To Die for the People*, 5.

69. Kwame Nkrumah, *Neo-Colonialism: The Last Stage of Imperialism* (New York: International Publishers, 1966), (the book that purportedly made Lyndon Johnson furious). Stephen Ambrose, *Rise to Globalism: American Foreign Policy, 1938–1980* (New York: Penguin Books,1980), 403.

70. Henri Lefebvre, *The Explosion: Marxism and the French Upheaval* (New York: Monthly Review Press, 1969), 93.

71. Jameson, "Periodizing the 1960s"; Van Gosse arrives at this same fundamental view, by way of a very different route. See Gosse, *Where the Boys Are*.

72. Fanon, *Wretched of the Earth*, 80.

73. "*Malcolm X: Make It Plain*," dir. Orlando Bagwell, Blackside, Inc., 1994.

74. By this account the so-called Congo crisis of 1960 is as important as the Cuban revolution in defining U.S. policy of containing and undermining revolutionary nationalist struggles, as well as crystallizing forms of anti-imperialist opposition within the U.S. itself. Malcolm X, for one, referred frequently to the events in the Congo. It is Bruce Perry who refers to Malcolm X as "America's Lumumba." Bruce Perry, *Malcolm: Life of a Man Who Changed Black America* (Barrytown, N.Y.: Station Hill Press, 1991).

75. Gosse, *Where the Boys Are*, 153–54.

76. Robert F. Williams, *Negroes with Guns* (New York: Mariani and Munsell, 1962), 103.

77. Ibid., 109.

78. This is the basis of Harold Cruse's critique of Williams as a revolutionary without program or substance. See Cruse, *The Crisis of the Negro Intellectual*, 351; also Gosse, *Where the Boys Are*, 154.

79. Forman, *The Making of Black Revolutionaries*, 174.

80. Nikhil P. Singh,"*Pluralism, Decolonization and Postimperial America*," Organization of American Historians, Atlanta, April 1994 (unpublished manuscript).

81. Will Herberg, *Protestant, Catholic, Jew: An Essay in American Religious Sociology* (Chicago: University of Chicago Press, 1983 [1955]). Also see Singh, "Toward an Effective Anti-Racism" (forthcoming).

82. Myrdal, *An American Dilemma*, vol. II, 1021.

83. Van Gosse's fine work offers a wealth of insight into the resurgence of left anti-imperialism by the late 1950s. Gosse argues that support for the Cuban revolution in the face of increasing official hostility was the touchstone for the renewal of activist energies across a spectrum of political commitments. Not only were the most celebrated proto-New Left figures, such as C. Wright Mills, in the forefront of the defense of Cuba, but so were some of the most important African American radicals of the early 1960s, including William Worthy, LeRoi Jones, Malcolm X, James Baldwin, and Robert Williams. The significance of

anti-imperialism and anti-colonialism has been terribly obscured in accounts of Black politics since WW II. Yet the opposition to what Du Bois in *Color and Democracy* (1945) called "imperial-colonialism" may actually be the most reliable and enduring strain of Black radicalism in the twentieth century. By the 1960s, its complex manifestations were visible across a range of activities and events, from Castro's 1960 trip to Harlem and meeting with Malcolm X, to LeRoi Jones's celebrated political "coming-out" in "Cuba Libre" (1960), to Robert Williams' flight and exile, to Martin Luther King, Jr.'s belated opposition to the Vietnam War, and, of course, to the emergence of the Panthers. Van Gosse, *Where the Boys Are*, 147–49. Also, Martin Luther King, Jr., *Trumpet of Conscience* (New York: Harper and Row, 1967). An important recent corrective is Penny Von Eschen, *Race Against Empire: Black Americans and Anti-Colonialism, 1937–1957* (Ithaca: Cornell University Press, 1997).

84. Kobena Mercer, "1968: Periodizing Politics and Identity," 433; Malcolm X, *By Any Means Necessary* (New York: Pathfinder Press, 1970); Williams, *Negroes with Guns*, 124.

85. For the importance of "routes" (as opposed to "roots"), as the governing metaphor for Black radical thinking, see Paul Gilroy, "'It Aint' Where You're From, It's Where You're At'. . . The Dialectics of Diasporic Identification," reprinted in *Small Acts: Thoughts on the Politics of Black Cultures* (London: Serpent's Tale, 1993), 120.

86. Seale, *Seize the Time*, 4; also Paul Gilroy, "A Dialogue with bell hooks," in *Small Acts*, 226.

87. My use of the metaphor of "domestication"is of course deliberately polyvalent, if insufficiently elaborated. The Panthers not only resisted domestication to a narrative of nation, but also to conservative, racialist narratives of family and kinship advanced in the seemingly opposed but ultimately symbiotic discourses of Black cultural nationalism and the Moynihan report. Also see Paul Gilroy, "It's a Family Affair," *Small Acts*, 205.

88. Harold Isaacs, *The New World of American Negroes* (London: Phoenix House, 1963).

89. James Baldwin, "Fifth Avenue Uptown: A Letter from Harlem," in *Nobody Knows My Name* (New York: Dell Publishing Co., Inc., 1961), 79. In 1960, for example, *Ebony* devoted an entire issue to documenting the splendors of Ghanain independence. As Baldwin said at the time, "The image of Nkrumah getting off his plane has an effect on all the other images. . . . tak[ing] a certain sting out of those pictures of the African savage." Quoted in Isaacs, *The New World of American Negroes*, 276.

90. James Baldwin, "An Open Letter to My Sister Angela Davis," in Angela Davis, *If They Come in the Morning*, 19–23; James Baldwin, *No Name in the Street* (New York: Dell Publishing Co., Inc., 1972).

91. James Boggs, *Racism and the Class Struggle: Further Pages from a Black Worker's Notebook* (New York: Monthly Review Press, 1971), 29.

92. Isaacs, *The New World of American Negroes*, 11.

93. Ibid., 13.

94. George Jackson, *Blood in My Eye* (Baltimore: Black Classic Press, 1990), 47.

95. James Baldwin, *The Fire Next Time* (New York: Dell Publishing Co., Inc., 1963); Mercer, "1968: Periodizing Politics and Identity."

96. Here Panther imagery and language were translated immediately into popular idioms and metaphors. Newton suggested that coining the term pig was meant to

dispel the fear image attached to the police in the minds of Black people. Those that think this sort of thing doesn't count in struggles should take note of the fact that the FBI in their attempts to combat the Panther's inventive and effective labeling of the police, circulated an anonymous cartoon lamely deriding the panther as "an animal with a small head." Churchill, *Agents of Repression,* 44. More ambiguously, this moment marks the beginning of the profound, commercial crossover of an explicitly "Black" aesthetic (via "Blaxploitation" genre films and novels) into the mainstream of American and global popular culture. This raises immensely complicated political and theoretical questions that I partially address in the final section of the chapter. I would suggest that in the end there isn't that much that separates the strategic revolutionary vision of George Jackson in *Blood in My Eye* from the literary inventions of Sam Greenlee (*The Spook Who Sat by the Door*) or perhaps even Donald Goines (Al C. Clark, the *Kenyatta* series). For the Panthers' own reflections on popular culture, see Huey Newton's and Bobby Seale's "revolutionary analysis" of Melvin Van Peeble's *Sweet Sweetback's Baadasssss Song*—the pioneering Blaxploitation film—as well as Newton's and Cleaver's admiring references to Gilles Pontecorvo's *Battle of Algiers,* a film that was popular and influential for the entire New Left. Newton, *To Die for the People,* 112–47.

97. Genovese, "The Legacy of Slavery," 415.

98. Balibar and Wallerstein, *Race, Nation, Class,* 18.

99. This is Max Weber's famous axiom for defining the modern state. See *Economy and Society,* vol.II, Ch. IX (Berkeley: University of California Press, 1978); Also see Max Weber, *From Max Weber: Essays in Sociology* (New York: Oxford University Press, 1946), 77–78.

100. Georgakas and Surkin, *Detroit: I Do Mind Dying,* 185.

101. Quoted in Emmanuel Hansen, *The Political Thought of Frantz Fanon* (Ohio: Ohio State University Press, 1977), 6.

102. Cleaver, *Soul on Ice,* 27.

103. Hilliard and Cole, *This Side of Glory,* 115.

104. Boggs, *Racism and the Class Struggle,*39.

105. Harry Haywood, *Black Bolshevik: Autobiography of an Afro-American Communist* (Chicago: Liberator Press, 1978).

106. Quoted in Boggs, *Racism and the Class Struggle,* 41.

107. Newton, *To Die for the People,* 36.

108. In contrast to the Panthers, the Boggs were committed to a project of rewriting a Marxist and historicist theory of class struggle and the state in terms that retained allusions to the struggles of the 1930s and an allegiance to the primacy of the point of production.

109. Homi Babha, "DissemiNation: Time, Narrative and the Margins of the Modern Nation," *Nation and Narration,* ed. Homi Babha (New York: Routledge, 1990), 300. Babha's essay, however, hardly accounts for the kind of active and oppositional spatial determinations represented by groups like the Panthers.

110. If the founding ethos of the post-WW II Civil Rights movement was said to be America's fulfillment of "the main trend in its history," or "the gradual realization of the American Creed," the self-assertion of the ghetto destructured the imaginary space of the nation–state as a place of historicist becoming for Black people and as an integral territorial and ideological unit to which they belonged. Myrdal, *An American Dilemma,* 3. Cleaver cleverly disparaged "the American Creed" as so many failed attempts "to citizenize the Negro." Cleaver, *Post-Prison Writings and Speeches,* 61. For the general reconceptualization of "space" in social

theory and politics, see Edward Soja, *Postmodern Geographies: The Reassertion of Space in Critical Social Theory* (London: Verso, 1989); Neil Smith, *Uneven Development: Nature, Capital and the Production of Space* (London: Basil Blackwell, 1984.)

111. Indeed, it may have been with American Black liberation in mind that Lefebvre offered his own rewriting of Marxist historicism in terms of *la revolution urbaine,* or urban, spatial revolution. Neil Smith, *Uneven Development,* 92.

112. Fanon, *Wretched of the Earth,* 130.

113. Ibid., 129–30.

114. Hilliard and Cole, *This Side of Glory,* 180. The theory of organizing those defined as workless or as Black unemployables should be viewed as the Panther's flexible adaptation of a Marxian emphasis upon the primacy of class struggle. Many radicals (White and Black) during the 1960s had grown entirely skeptical about the militant potential of the organized (predominantly White) working class. Yet despite their reputation as the most anti-White radical group, the Panthers were openly sympathetic to a conception of workers' struggles and viewed themselves in a loose sense as part of a working-class struggle toward socialism. (Recall Bobby Seale, "All of us are laboring people—employed or unemployed," note 38). Yet by giving even greater primacy to the uniquely Black condition of "worklessness" (structural underemployment and ghettoization), the Panthers also tended to embrace a more utopian strand of thinking critical of the idea of labor *tout court.* As Stuart Hall et al. put it, "Those who *cannot* work also discover that they *don't want* to under conditions of alienation and exploitation." Stuart Hall, et al. Policing *the Crisis,* 356; Also Paul Gilroy, "Diaspora, Utopia and the Critique of Capitalism," *There Ain't No Black in the Union Jack* (Chicago: University of Chicago Press, 1991); and Peter Levy, *The New Left and Labor in the 1960s* (Chicago: University of Illinois Press, 1994), 70–72.

115. Fanon, *Wretched of the Earth,* 38.

116. This term was coined by Mike Davis, *City of Quartz: Escavating the Future in Los Angeles* (New York: Vintage Books, 1992), ch. 3. Also see Douglas Massey and Nancy Denton, *American Apartheid: Segregation and the Making of the Underclass* (Cambridge: Harvard University Press, 1993).

117. James N. Blaut, *The National Question: Decolonizing the Theory of Nationalism* (London: Zed Books, 1987), 165.

118. Davis, *City of Quartz,* 298.

119. Babha, "DissemiNation," 300.

120. Barbara Harlow, "Sites of Struggle: Immigration, Deportation, Prison and Exile," in *Criticism in the Borderlands,* ed. Calderon and Saldivar (Durham: Duke University Press, 1991), 150.

121. This is Benedict Anderson's term, quoted in Babha, "DissemiNation," 305.

122. On the historical resonance of Black anticitizenship or the notion of Black people "as enemies rather than members of the social compact," see David Roediger, *The Wages of Whiteness: Race and the Making of the American Working Class* (New York: Verso, 1991), 57. In this vein, Rubin Hurricane Carter, the unjustly imprisoned Black middleweight, described the nation–state for Black people as a little more than a "penitentiary with a flag." Quoted in Bruce Franklin, *Prison Literature in America* (New York: Oxford University Press, 1978), 242.

123. Hilliard and Cole, *This Side of Glory,* 238.

124. *Passing it On: A Story of A Black Panther's Search for Justice,* videotape (Dhoruba Bin Wahad), John Valadez, dir., (New York: First Run Features, 1993).

125. Cummins, T*he Rise and Fall of California's Radical Prison Movement*, 151–86.

126. Davis, *City of Quartz*, 297.

127. Franklin, *Prison Literature in America*, 273.

128. As Hall et al. put it, criminality is a form of "quasi-political" resistance that is ultimately complicit with existing structures of oppression. Despite their immense struggles around this issue, it is important to acknowledge the failure of groups like the Panthers to transform the criminal consciousness into a fully political one. Nonetheless, as Hall et al., put it, "Not to defend that sector of the class which is being systematically driven into crime is to abandon it to the ranks of those who have been permanently criminalised." The Panthers, in other words, were attempting something that remains of the utmost political importance today as more and more Blacks and Latinos (and even Whites) are consigned to a permanently criminalized, anticitizenry, namely, to embrace the possibility of the active politicization of prisoners. Hall et al., *Policing the Crisis*, 398.

129. Stanley Crouch, "The Nationalism of Fools," in *Notes of a Hanging Judge: Essays and Reviews, 1979–1989* (New York: Oxford University Press, 1990), 166; Hilliard and Cole, *This Side of Glory*, 258. David Hilliard is perhaps most eloquent on the Panthers' slide into undisciplined violence and criminal activities by the early 1970s: "Before we've used Cuba, Algeria, and China as examples of revolutionary struggle. Now, Mario Puzo's *Godfather* provides the organization map, a patriarchal family divided into military and political wings (339)."

130. Erikson and Newton, *In Search of Common Ground*, 44.

131. The Panthers were of course famous for carrying guns and law books in their celebrated encounters with the police and in using California law (which at the time allowed for the open carrying of firearms) to justify their activity. This, along with their tendency to quote liberally the *Declaration of Independence* and other founding national texts, makes the Panthers' brand of counternationalism highly ironic, arrayed both within and against-the-grain of American political traditions.

132. Quoted in Churchill and Wall, *Agents of Repression*, 77, 68.

133. A useful way to think of postmodernism is a name for the culturally dominant form of political discursivity in the contemporary, overdeveloped world. Postmodernity might be viewed as a corresponding term defining a social condition, one best characterized by the tremendous flexiblity and global mobility of capital increasingly liberated from the congealed boundaries of nation–states, and the constraints of socially empowered, organized labor. The concepts of postmodernism/postmodernity have obviously constituted a highly charged and politically ambiguous terrain of intellectual debate. In terms of left politics, some have argued that the politics of the new social movements is one salutary aspect of a postmodern condition, which has permitted the liberation of a range of political subjects, identities, desires and possibilities from the shackles of dour, Marxian theoretical predeterminations around the universal primacy of (a highly limited notion of) working-class struggles. By contrast, others have suggested that the characteristic postmodern emphasis upon the fracturing of political subjects, and upon the heterogeneous, local, and contingent nature of contemporary political struggles paradoxically mirrors a world in which the universality of capitalism itself precisely appears as the fragmentation of a global or universal oppositional imaginary (that is, the dream of socialism), and as the generalization of the world-capitalist market, freed from the requirements of any larger legitimating narrative or public principles outside the domain of its own (highly differentiating and privatizing) logic. Frederic Jameson offers a critical Marxian reading of

postmodernism as a new "cultural dominant," in "Postmodernism, or the Cultural Logic of Late Capitalism," *New Left Review* 146:53–92. For a highly problematic, though influential, theory that attempts to replace purportedly outdated master narratives of Marxism with a form of political discursivity suitable to new social movements, see Ernesto Laclau and Chantal Mouffe, *Hegemony and Socialist Strategy* (London: Verso, 1985). The most effective "mapping" of the socioeconomic infrastructure of postmodernity is David Harvey, *The Condition of Postmodernity* (London: Basil Blackwell, 1989). In Harvey's periodization, the dominance of a postmodern form of capitalism coincides with the serious and irreversible weakening of American hegemony in the world market and state–system, beginning around 1973. This period is also marked by a severe crisis of domestic, American hegemony, not only as a consequence of the upheavals of 1968, but also (by the 1970s) as a result of the "fiscal crisis of the state," marked by the unravelling of the "virtuous circle" of intensive accumulation ("Fordism"), which had produced unparalleled, domestic economic growth, prosperity and working class political quiescence, or the dominant features of the official American Century. See also Arrighi, "Marxist Century: American Century." Michel Aglietta, *A Theory of Capitalist Regulation: The U.S. Experience* (New York: Verso, 1979).

134. These numbers have been the subject of intense scrutiny and debate, see Fraser, *1968*, 238.

135. Wini Breines, *Community Organizing and the Left* (New York: Praeger, 1982). Judith Butler, in *Bodies that Matter* (New York: Routledge, 1993), has given one of the most useful and accessible accounts of the complicated notion of "performativity." Performativity pertains to the specific power of discourse itself, the power of naming and ex-nomination, or the ways "terms act rhetorically to produce the phenomenon they enunciate (208)." The power of any performative utterance derives from its "citationality," or its location "within the context of a (pre-existing) chain of binding conventions (225)." The success or realization of any performative act, then, is always provisional, fragile, and revisable. If it gains the power of the "real," it does so because it "echoes prior actions, and accumulates the force of authority through the repetition or citation of a prior, authoritative set of practices (227)." In the work of Butler and politicized postmodernists, the "performative" has become the preferred (liberal) zone of cultural combat—in which "one is implicated in that which one opposes," fighting the power of nominative convention through a process of "resignifying dominant discourses (241)." This, of course, begs the question of historical determination.

136. Jean Genet, *Prisoner of Love* (Middletown: Wesleyan University Press, 1992), 85.

137. Ibid., 84.

138. See *Eyes on the Prize II: A Nation of Law 1968–1971*, (Boston: Blackside, Inc., 1991).

139. Michael Kazin and Maurice Isserman, "The Failure and Success of the New Radicalism," in Gerstle and Fraser, ed. *The Rise and Fall of the New Deal Order*, (Princeton, N.J.: Princeton University Press, 1989), 226.

140. Pierre Bourdieu, "Social Space and Symbolic Power," in *In Other Words* (Stanford: Stanford University Press, 1990), 138. In this sense we must also understand that the state is always performative. As Philip Abrams puts it in slightly different terms, "[The state is] a public reification that acquires an overt symbolic identity progressively divorced from practice as an illusory account of practice." Quoted in Michael Taussig, "Malfecium: State Fetishism," in *Fetishism as a Cultural Discourse*, ed. Apter and Peitz (Ithaca: Cornell University Press, 1993), 220. In other words, if the nation is thought of as an "imagined community"

secured on the terrains of invented traditions and national history, then the state is the just as imaginary site of social reproduction and social security, constituted through the authoritative repetition of that which is deemed to be a proper function of state (that is, policing, diplomacy, social security, waging war, etc.). The collective mobilization of individuals as national subjects then is in crucial ways dependent upon their identification as people subject to a national-state, or the product of a history of phantasmic investments in which the state is the symbolic guarantor of nationality, safety, and social cohesion.

141. Taussig, "Malfecium," 238.

142. Butler, *Bodies that Matter*, 208–9.

143. Newton, *Revolutionary Suicide*, 322.

144. Omi and Winant, for example, critique models of internal colonization because they do not correspond to a stable sense of "territory" that could supply an alternative basis for some form of Black nationhood. They argue further that none of the "national" aspects of oppression presumed by internal colonization models (that is, separate geography, culture, external political rule, extra-economic coercion, etc.,) apply to American Blacks. Omi and Winant, *Racial Formation in the United States*, 145.

145. Davis, *City of Quartz*, ch. 5.

146. Balibar and Wallerstein, *Race, Nation, Class*, 95.

147. Genet, *Prisoner of Love*, 47.

148. Michelle Wallace, *Black Macho and the Myth of the Superwoman* (New York: Dial Press, 1978); Walker, "Black Panthers or Black Punks?" See also Elaine Brown, *A Taste of Power*, and Brown's rejoinder to Walker, "Attack Racism, Not Black Men," *New York Times*, 5 May 1993: A 23.

149. Edmund White, *Genet: A Biography* (New York: Alfred A. Knopf, 1993), 530.

150. Newton, *To Die for the People*, 152–55.

151. See Harvey, *The Condition of Postmodernity* for an explanation of "heterotopia."

152. Mercer, "1968: Periodizing Politics and Identity," 433.

153. Jerry Faber, *The Student as Nigger* (New York: Pocket Books, 1969); John Sinclair, *Guitar Army: Prison Writings* (New York: Douglas Book, Co., 1972).

154. In Jay and Young, *Out of the Closets*, 346.

155. Mercer, "1968: Periodizing Politics and Identity," 434. It is Jesse Jackson who refers to Black struggles in America as "trigger struggles." See R. Radhakrishnan, "Toward an Effective Intellectual: Foucault or Gramsci," in *Intellectuals, Aesthetics, Politics and Culture*, ed. Bruce Robbins (Minneapolis: University of Minnesota Press, 1990), 59.

156. For example, see Cornel West, "The New Cultural Politics of Difference," in *Out There: Marginalization and Contemporary Cultures*, ed. Russell Fergusen et al. (New York: Museum of Contemporary Art, 1990).

157. Robert Young, *White Mythologies: Writing History and the West* (London: Routledge, 1990), 4.

158. See Arjun Appadurai et al."Editorial Comment: On Thinking the Black Public Sphere," *Public Culture* 7.1 (Fall 1994): xii. For the "devaluation" of the citizenship of people of color, see Mike Davis, "Who Killed L.A.: Political Autopsy," *New Left Review* 1993:25.

159. Quoted in Marable, *Black American Politics*, 68.

160. Frantz Fanon, *The Wretched of the Earth*, 83.

Part II

Reflections From The Rank and File

Chapter Three

Once I Was a Panther

Melvin E. Lewis

1.
This poem is for all those who have fallen
those imprisoned
those who can not come home
and the thousand swallow pits
and open graves we live in

 As a child I would get a Black Panther Paper
and we would have political church on the front porch,
in the lunchroom, in the back of study hall
the Panther Paper was our bible, we'd harmonize,
signify, sing some Sam Cooke and the
Six Blind Boys, sing about some new found religion,
political power comes from the barrel of a gun
I'd want to get to Jesus with my hands up and a smile on my
face
if you want to get to heaven it's alright,
if you want to get to heaven it's alright
we wanted to get to heaven free and full

Once I was a Panther
heard shouts in my dreams
saw my heroes murdered in a coldwater flat
on a cold December morning

shotgun pellets and machine gun bullets broke
the frozen Chicago air
tore plaster board and flesh apart
They came in the dark, hidden in a telephone van

left blood running from Peoria to Maywood
left shreiking voices from Memphis to Monroe, La.

Brought my Momma to view Fred Hampton's body
took Slim to George Jackson's funeral
Said, Momma, that's how I want to be buried
a red rose, *A Red Book*, and a Black Panther flag
let Curtis Mayfield sing the dirge
"We people who are darker than blue..."
Ask Tyhimba to open the way
play the drums, pour the libations
for the ancestors to know I'm coming to sit at their feet
Tell the bloods to aim for the middle of the chest

Quit varsity basketball, quit cross country
wanted to do a reverse layup on capitalism
steal its ball, pin its shit to the backboard
Quit varsity b ball
to feed hungry children, to feed my hungry mind
to hear the footsteps of the moving masses
sell Panther Papers in the ice and winter wind
on the corner of Madison & Pulaski
in the spring on Madison & State
in the summer in front of the Englewood Mall el stop
on Saturday morning at Operation Breadbasket

Get yo Black Panther
Get yo Black Panther news
Get yo vanguard newspaper

2
The police arrested me in the subway
people looked, stood as they threatened me,
took me in a blue subway door

Did they take Ruwa Chiri in a subway door
They found him cut in two on the midnight
tracks of the Harlem line

What color were the doors they entered when they
killed long, tall, straight Sam Napier

3
Once I was a Panther
saw what 6 months of solitary confinement
did to 17 year olds
with $200,000 bail, three felony trials waiting,
weighing your life, your mind and movements,
it stopped them, it froze them
it sent them back to their spring memories

I have slept in strange beds
woke early to clean buildings
I have slept with shotguns near
woke early to feed the elders, the youth
I have slept with revolvers replacing dreams
woke early to sing, lumpen songs,
church songs, blues songs
woke early to fly away, fly away
on a Coltrane riff, fly away

Once I was a Panther
people would whisper and point
when I took Communion in my grandmother's church
My uncles would listen and we'd debate
My father would say—Stop all that nonsense
yo goin to get yo self in trouble
My mother would go to the prayer table every Sunday

4
Proud, principled and political
I was a Panther
police stole my books, burned my poems
capital stole my time
Malcolm, Mao, Marx, Ché and Nkrumah
were my road markers.
It's a long lonely road
It's a long dangerous road to the present
to the space above a bird's wings in flight
to the current below the low and melodious Mississippi

They came to high school
6 detectives looking for a 140 lb Black Panther
ideals are heavy, must be controlled or carried away
They carried me away, they carried me away

Voices would whisper, voices would shout
Don't read that, child, that is that black stuff
Don't read that, boy, that is a foreign ideology
Don't think about everybody. Go get yo self a
good job—be a lawyer. Told yo ass bout that movement shit
Old ladies would pinch my chin, u need to shave
I would say, I want to look like Jesus, he had a beard

On the walls of the prisons, they would write
Be African, be a commie
we eat black commies every night
I'd write back; if yo want to see some juju and Jesus
I'll help yo on yo way

They tried to lock me away
Asked my Grandmama to pray for me
A good strong Alabama prayer
A good strong old time country prayer
Together we will pray them away
We will melt them away

Put fire on their asses like squeezing sugar cane
Ask Grandmama about the legends
teach me how to fly, how to fly away

5
Once I was a Panther
Slim would cry in the washroom before demonstrations,
dream sad, sad songs
saw me shot on Madison and Pulaski selling Panther Papers

The principal would stop her, send me messages
they came to my mother's house to my brother's house
my union steward got lost

6

I wanted to be an oceanographer
to study the sea, study the water and wind embrace
listen to the sea's belly, listen to the sea cry
listen to whales sing sweet and hollow songs

Once I was a Panther
wanted to read Cesaire, Fanon and Senghor in French and Wolof
wanted to understand Kiswahii, Umoja
reading French and dodging the draft
dodging dope dealers and fools who said
Man, don't bring that revolution shit here.
Ya'll cause the police to be round here everyday.

It's a long, narrow, lonely path
looking over yo shoulder
saw my shadow, saw my pass
looked over my shoulder
and it said you better move fast

Asked my Aunt Snoot to sing me one those
porch songs that just come up, that tell you it's time
to come out, it's time for me to come out...
Auntie, sing me a powerful song
I need a song to rock me
I need a song to cause the spirit to sing
I need a song to help me testify
I need a song to speak in tongues
roll around the floor, knock over
the woodburning stove and teach me
to fly away, fly away

7

Once I was a Panther
I stole away
My Grandmama prayed

my aunt sang
my Papa mixed herbs to fight the fire and cold metal nights
I stole away to Mexico
to Cuba, to Canada

to New York City,
stole away to Alabama

Went to see my Grandpapa's footsteps
see him fish on a catfish bank
chew tobacco, think stories up and laugh
patch over my left eye
I went to see Huey
to see Cuba libre
to hear wa wa co
to listen to Don Nicolás Guillén

There were no strange beds
No strange calls
We cried when we parted
I flew away, flew away
Once I was a Panther

This poem, this poem is for those who have fallen,
have fought, fought and fallen, fought and flown,
this poem, this poem is theirs and mine
once I was a caged Panther and my Grandmama
taught me how to fly away, fly away
how to melt away bars and stone.
I flew away

This poem first appeared in *Black American Literature Forum,* Volume 24 (Fall 1990).

Chapter Four

Selections from a Panther Diary

Steve D. McCutchen

Editor's Note:

The following contribution comprises excerpts from the diary of Steve D. McCutchen, a ten-year Party veteran who joined the Black Panther Party in Baltimore, Maryland in 1969. In 1972 McCutchen relocated to Oakland when the Central Committee closed most of its organizational units across the nation to marshall support for the political candidacies of Bobby Seale (Mayor) and Elaine Brown (City Council).

The diary selections are drawn from Steve's first year as a member of the Black Panther Party (May 1969–August 1970). This was a critical period in the history of the organization. The Party experienced both rapid growth and intense government harassment. The national leadership of the organization was nearly decimated. Huey Newton remained in prison on a 1968 manslaughter conviction, and Bobby Seale spent jail time in Illinois and Connecticut on conspiracy charges. The other member of the Party's early tripartite leadership, Eldridge Cleaver, resided in exile in Cuba to avoid charges stemming from the April 6, 1968 Panther–police gun battle that took the life of Bobby Hutton. As Chief of Staff, David Hilliard was left with the task of providing national leadership. He too would be arrested during this period. Several Party members, alleged police agents and police officers, were killed during this formative period. McCutchen offers rare insight into the daily existence of a member of the Black Panther Party during this time.

May 1969–

Lt. Charles Butler spoke to Captain Hart on my behalf.[1] Too many conflicts coming and going from office to home and back again. Problems with Dad primarily. He disapproves of the Party . . . doesn't and can't understand.

Captain Hart was impressed with my work with the branch. Lt. Butler vouched for me as did Lt. Boyd (Zeke) and other comrades. I went home for the last time to pick up my clothes and move out, to stay at the Eden Street office. I saw Mom look out the window as we left the apartments. I'll miss being around her, but I want to be closer to my new comrades and the Party. I feel that I belong here.

I'm learning from people who came here before me, mostly older brothers who have welcomed me: Charlie Nelson, Arnold Loney, Ochiki, Eddie [Conway], and Sister Reeva.[2]

The *Red Book* is interesting. I had no idea about the people of the Peoples Republic of China, this thing called socialism, of Ho Chi Minh, or Soviet Russia. I'm learning and enjoying.

Political education classes once a week. I'm about to feed back the ideas from the newspaper and the *Red Book*. These last two months have been comfortable at times, and difficult at other [times]. Panthers are serious about revolution. I still hope I can continue to write, express my ideas about Black people and the struggle we speak of. Comrades tell me to be prepared to die. I hadn't thought about that. Didn't tell anyone that I believe in self-defense, but had no idea that guns would be something primary. "Off the pigs!" is about armed struggle, I'm finding out.

Rally for Malcolm X at Druid Hill Park. Lt. Boyd spoke as did Lt. Butler. Comrades dressed down in Panther blue and black. I think the colors of our uniform impress people. No trouble from the pigs.

Last month twenty-one members were arrested in New York, now fourteen comrades were taken in New Haven. Sister Ericka was on the cover of the newspaper. The FBI and other police agencies are involved against us. We're bigger than I would ever have imagined. Baltimore could be next to get vamped on comrades tell me. We're a threat.

June 1969–

Met some White Panthers from Michigan.[3] They were in Baltimore to visit. Captain Hart talked to them at the office. I thought they were hippies. They partied with us at Arnold Loney's pad.

Our breakfast program for children is at St. Vincent's Church. Charlie Nelson is responsible for the food and preparations. Usually three or four other comrades work with him, then leave to sell papers.

Most comrades are serious; they're pretty mellow brothers, and so is Reeva. Chaka Zulu has a high political education level from what the comrades tell me. I can pick his brain, learn from him when he's around the office. Booty Green is supposed to be a Panther, but he only listens to Captain Hart. One wild nigger.

Some new brothers joined. Raymond [Jones] came from New York. Sherry [Brown] came from Ohio and decided to check us out after reading about the Party. Actually they're supposed to be Panthers in training, except for Raymond. Even some new sisters are working with us. Linda won't join.[4] She's afraid of guns.

Some Panthers still live at home. They're part-time Panthers, at least that's what I understand. Hart explained that was understood at National Hq. that we did that here. Part-time Panthers.[5]

Headline on the cover of the BPP news said that Capitalism Plus Racism Equals Fascism. Some more things to learn. It's not all about being Black and guns. Other things must be learned before the people are ready to pick up the gun.

July 4, 1969–

Field Marshall D.C. from National arrived with Mitch and a lawyer named Turco.[6] A White lawyer with Panthers. Strange. I tried to search them at the front door. Fucked up. Turco was packing, and I missed his piece.

All Panthers had to depart for a general meeting. Hart was criticized for fucking up.[7] D.C. said that the branch might be closed down. Some Panthers were told to get out if they didn't understand what had to be done. Lt. Butler left, Lt. Boyd was expelled.[8] Hart was busted down to Panther.

Spent the day painting the outside of the office. Larry [Wallace] has artist skill and painted a huge sign for the front of the office. The place is starting to look like a Panther office. Mitch made some changes in the chain of command. Kebe is the new defense captain.[9] Reeva is communications secretary. Larry is the O.D. I'm now Lieutenant of Information. The branch may stay open. We'll have to wait. Comrades are walking lightly. Asses are tight here.

Now we [groups of the members] take a hundred papers out into the field. Anyone who can't function full time is a community worker, not a Panther. Revolution is a full-time commitment. I'm impressed with these other comrades, especially D.C. Mitch is a scary brother. Comes up on you out of nowhere. He's leading the political education classes and showing Kebe, Reeva, and Larry how the branch should operate. I learn the details later. I'm not leaving. I came here to be a Panther.

I'll write under the name of Chaka Masai. That's my new name now. After [the great African leader] Chaka Zulu and Masai Hewitt. I like it.[10]

D.C., Mitch, and Turco left. The branch is on its own, but someone will be sent to replace Kebe. National must not think that we can operate by ourselves. We're to contact New York if there are any problems that we're unsure of.

Mom called me. A letter from the government arrived. I had expected something would interfere with my new choice of lifestyle. I've been ordered to report for induction on August 15th. Told Mom that I wasn't going and returned to the office. I can't go into the U.S. military. That's a contradiction to Party beliefs. I didn't want to take the chance of going to Vietnam. If I have to take a stand and fight and maybe die, I'll do it here. I won't go.

Comrades supported my decision to refuse the draft. I'm packing a piece wherever I go now. Don't know whether to be nervous or proud of my decision. I've made a choice, a serious one for me. Mom hasn't told Dad yet. Linda wants to know how I am going to avoid the draft. I have faith in the Party.

New York knows of my situation with the draft.[11] Mitch will pass the information along. I have to stay busy meanwhile.

I seem to have grown by leaps and bounds in a short time. I see things so differently from when I was in school. These experiences are real, they have meaning and, something I never knew about myself until now, I believe like some of the other comrades that I'm living on borrowed time.

Hart sent Donald Vaughn and Arnold by the office with a petition for comrades to sign, to have him reinstated as defense captain.[12] They were allowed to leave the petition. Larry called New York. Anyone who signed that petition was to be expelled from the branch, barred from the office. Booty Green showed up and tried to force his way in. He was met at the door with guns. Now I know that he's either dangerous or stupid.

Larry and Jomo [Melvin] left for New York to get some intensive training at the Harlem office. Kebe is handling things with Reeva. I've been given more responsibility. As one of the comrades with the most time in at the branch and offering full-time duty for the Party, I'm now a part of the chain of command. Feel as though I'm able to make some contributions here. Have some input into constructive things.

Kebe was busted for carrying a machete on the streets. New York thinks we're crazy. Stop fuckin' up down there!

Chaka and Eddie have gone to California for the Party's United Front Against Fascism Conference.[13] Thought that I would get a chance to attend. Seems I'm needed here as I'm one of the few who functions on a daily full-time basis. Besides, there's more than enough that needs to be done here. We've been told that Baltimore needs a lot of attention, a lot of organizing.

New community workers are in and out.[14] After political orientation that I handle, they're invited to attend political education classes, to work with our summer lunch program for children. Neighbors aren't as distant as before. We seem to be more visible, more alive now.

Chaka Zulu and Eddie returned from the Coast. The conference was a success. The chairman [Bobby Seale] has ideas of creating new organizing arms of the Party called Neighborhood Committees against Fascism that would exist side by side with Party branches and chapters. Everyone was told to study more of the literature of revolutionary struggles and to seriously adhere to Party policies and directives. Weekly reports have to be submitted on time and detail our weekly operations. We need to sell more newspapers, establish more programs. Dig deep roots in the community.

Our new defense captain arrived. John Clark from L.A.[15] He spoke with the staff and comrades at the office. A general meeting is scheduled to update members on changes and improvements for the branch. We don't look too bad at first glance. Need more programs and more paper sales though. Basically we're a solid branch.

Shortened my writing name to Lil' Masai. I like it better. John speaks highly of Masai Hewitt, Minister of Education. I feel that I'm in good company with that comrade as a namesake. Power to the People!

August 1969–

John will pass on information concerning my draft situation. Time is growing short. Some decision has to be made soon. I have already declared that I have no interest or desire to report for induction. Mom hopes that I'll change my mind before something happens. If I go into the service, I'm almost sure something is going to happen. I might not come back home alive. That is not a choice I have in mind. Have to stay busy. Have faith in the party.

Kebe was expelled for tampering with Party funds. Some changes in our chain of command here. Sherry Brown has been appointed Lt. of Finance, Charles Jackson designated as Coordinator for the breakfast and lunch programs. Chaka Zulu is designated as Lt. of Education. John, Chaka, and I will lead the cadre political education classes. I will concentrate primarily on the community education classes. Responsibilities are becoming clearer. We're becoming more of a smooth operation cadre. The changes ease the tensions of the last month or so, but we're still not as efficient as other branches or chapters, not yet anyway.

I'll be leaving for New York next week. To avoid the draft. Have to train comrades to take over my duties. A difficult decision, but I'd rather not face the induction and the possibilities of being shipped to Vietnam. Left for dead somewhere. I can struggle here inside of Babylon, take my chances here, and wait until conditions are ripe to participate again here in Baltimore or wherever I'm assigned.

Mom won't see me for awhile. I don't know how long I have to be gone, but I'll be back. Spent some time with Linda. Told my brothers to take care of Mom. Didn't want to talk with Dad. No use in wasting words. He still wouldn't understand me.

August 14, 1969–

Jomo will meet me in New York. I'll be assigned to the Harlem branch office. At least I'll know someone there. Might be homesick.

The Harlem office is busier than ours in Baltimore. They are more organized it seems with a harsher attitude towards the struggle. More sisters involved also. There's Al Carrol, Bashir, Bullwhip, Janet, and a host of comrades who are right on. The pad isn't too far from the 7th Ave. office. The community seems alert and receptive to the Party in Harlem. Have to settle in and see how I fit in. Homesick already.

This place is huge, almost alien compared to Baltimore. Poverty and people everywhere. Haven't seen this kind of mistreatment, poor conditions ever before. A good place for the Party to organize, so many people, Black people that need the Party to do something. I've really been lost all the years before. I'm seeing things about Black people and this system I never imagined could happen. The dreams of school days were either lies or illusions. I'm starting to see truths that had been hidden.

With all the comrades around I still have moments of loneliness here in Harlem. I feel somewhat out of water. I understand what I have committed myself to, but it still leaves many anxious moments, a longing for Baltimore and comrades.

The N.Y. lawyers are busy with the New York 21 case and not much time to consider my draft question.[16] Be patient.

Breakfast program and liberation school are like the ones in Baltimore. More support from some of the businesses and community here. Paper sales aren't all that great. A lot of cultural nationalists here in New York. The arena is more than different here. I know it isn't my place.

D.C. understands my position. Nothing the Party can do to change things for me. Either stay or take my chances in Baltimore. I can function here but not in comfort for some reason. I'm lost.

August 19, 1969–

The pigs snatched Chairman Bobby off the streets in California. The attacks continue on leadership. Comrades must be strong. If there's going to be more efforts against the Party I don't want to be stranded here. We're still short of staff and comrades in Baltimore. Maybe better to take a stand on my home ground than here.

Power to the People!

Mitch spoke with D.C. and Al Carrol. The decision is mine to make. To stay or return to Baltimore. Home. I can leave tomorrow.

Comrades didn't expect me to return or to return so soon. New York couldn't do anything for my situation. I can contribute more in Baltimore where I'm familiar. Good timing. Funds are needed for the lunch program and to sustain our branch. All the help is needed with the Chairman in jail. We have to dig deeper roots against these attacks. Produce or get to steppin'.

We've decided to boycott Roth's Market on Gay St. The manager and owners won't contribute to the programs even after we've explained our position to feed hungry children. They refuse. Jack is heading the picket and the one-on-one discussions with wary customers and inquirers. Good comrade.

More people are stopping by with donations and contributions to the Party. The media is interested in the branch. I'm learning to learn, to accept the different activities and necessities of what we're doing. I never learned anything like this in those years of school on the honor role and from all those after school activities. This is the world I was never prepared to meet.

Roth's Market gave in. They will donate to our program on a weekly basis. Power to the people!

Some of us know that more funds are needed to function. Alternatives are somewhat slim. We went after the places that had some monies. Anything to keep functioning. We took what we could without hurting anyone. The pigs stopped us coming from Catonsville the last time. State police pulled us over. They missed the pocketful of shells I had and couldn't get into the car trunk let alone decide what else to do with us. They were looking for three of us; they didn't have a report about four Black men. That may have saved our asses that night. The media screamed that those responsible were gangsters out of the Capone days. No connection to the Party. Even John was impressed. I did what I thought and believed would help save our branch and add to our struggle. National said to stop the dumb shit! Have to find other ways to raise funds, or else we may still be closed down. Can't do that. I'm past the point of normal longings and interests. The Party is becoming a part of me, and I am becoming a part of it. Now this is my life.

National Distribution increased our papers.[17] John told them that we could handle more. Donations help our fragile condition. We're not starving or desperate and somehow we seem to manage daily. Have faith in the Party, have faith in the people.

September 5, 1969–

Couldn't write until now. Pigs busted us down the street from the office. Took Sherry, Sister Sandy, Raymond, and me down on phony charges. They pulled clubs on the crowd that had gathered peacefully for a park rally on Eden Street. Pigs beat Sherry and me. Threatened to kill us, damn Panthers. My first time in jail. A damn new experience. Somewhat anxious, scared. Didn't know what to expect from the pigs, or what to expect once I was inside. Had my *Red Book* with me. It helped pass the days and fortify my resolve. They tossed me into Q-section at Baltimore City Jail. I remained there for five days until bail for all of us could be raised. I didn't panic during the pig's attack or at the idea of being in jail. Somehow I think it had to happen and I was prepared emotionally for this capture.

September 10, 1969–

Mom told me that Dad almost passed out when the news media flashed the story of my arrest along with other Party members. She said that he nearly collapsed on the couch. Not so much as from concern about me as what his friends and family would say about him, about me. We both laughed. I understand now that many of his interests and understandings have nothing to do with me. Me and my brothers understand something. Be careful. I will. But this is my life. All nineteen years of it.

October 5, 1969–

The pigs came for us again. Trapped us coming from the park on our way back to office. They called out John, Raymond, and me. Said that we had failed to appear for court and had a bench warrant out for us. They blocked off the street like there was a national emergency. They kept us at the Northeastern station until the following day then took us to Baltimore City Jail. This time they put me in N-section. No arraignment or anything, just tossed inside and left. No bail on a damn disorderly conduct and failure to appear.

The pigs want us ba[d]. They don't want the Party to operate here. We must be doing something right.

October 21, 1969–

First time I've spent a birthday in jail. Baltimore lost the World Series. No time for baseball anymore. There's a struggle to think about. No court. No bail.

They called me last night from my cell. No bail release just a transfer to another section. F-section. Maximum security. Going to be here longer than I thought. Have to wait it out. Ride the storm through. Hoover is a determined monster. So am I.

Thanksgiving 1969–

Communications with the office have stopped. No word from comrades in over a week. Must be some problems out there. At least on this section there are brothers who are interested in the Party. I can talk with them about events, they'll listen. The Chairman [Bobby Seale] is in Chicago. Guards bring *The Baltimore Sun* to let us read. Mostly all Black guards here. Most all Black inmates in the jail. All Black on this section. Pitiful that it's Black men who find themselves in the shitholes of society, in places like this. At least when I talk about the Party it gives them something else to focus their attention on besides the usual garbage in the news and their own legal cases.

An article in *The Baltimore Sun* showed that our office was closed. No other comments. And no communication from outside. No response to my letters. Mom hasn't heard anything except that the FBI had been by the house looking for me. They asked questions about the draft. Mom didn't tell them anything. Grip and Pete were standing ready with pool sticks if they tried to get stupid with her.[18] Right on Mom. I'll remember your concern. I'll remember those bastards for harassing you.

December 2, 1969–

They finally released us. John, Raymond, and me. Some Thunderbird to celebrate. The office had moved to 1225 Gay St., and there is a pad down the street in the middle of the block. Things have changed in two months. More community workers. More community support. Chaka Zulu had been busted by the ATF on a weapons charge. More harassment, but they had to let him out as he had bail, and we didn't. Comrades took some initiative, stuck together in one of our first major crises in Baltimore. It's good being among them again. Time to get busy again. I'll see Mom soon.

December 3–9, 1969–

The media announced that the Chief of Staff [David Hilliard] had been busted in California. After a rally. For threatening Nixon. The FBI has been busy tormenting and undermining our leadership and the Party in general. We must persevere.

Now they've murdered Deputy Chairman Fred Hampton. A raid on the Party's pad in Chicago. No shoot-out and two comrades are dead. Murdered in the early morning. We called a press conference at the office. I talked with the media. The Baltimore branch has no response to this government-instigated attack other than to continue organizing and educating the community. The Gas and Electric company has cut off our gas and electricity at the 1225 Gay Street office. Forces are gathering to intimidate our branch and attempt to silence the voices of Panthers in Baltimore. We called on the community to further support us.

News of the L.A. comrades came over the media and was confirmed after calls to National Headquarters. The pigs attacked the office but couldn't get away with any killings this time. The comrades were prepared. They defended the office and held on until the media arrived. Almost five hours they engaged L.A.'s desperados. We will not go quietly in 1969 regardless of what J. Edgar Hoover has said. John tried to get through to comrades at his former point of origin. No luck. Everyone has to wait for the smoke to clear. Entrust the community and the Party with the safety of those comrades and the survival of all other Panthers. This shit is getting out of control. Killers are rampant and anxious to kill us. Baltimore or any other branch or chapter could be next. Security is tightened. All comrades who stay at the office must be prepared for the pigs to attack.

Directives came from National to get out of storefront offices. Get into the community where the pigs can't attack us so easily. Establish Black Community Information Centers (BCIC) in houses that are in the heart of the Black community, surrounded by the masses. Pigs won't be so trigger happy to vamp on our facilities if there is the chance of others being privy to their military-style murderous attacks on our buildings and programs. The pad is now our BCIC, and the old 1225 Gay address is used as our distribution and communications office. We're out of there after dark.

National wants only the BCIC open. Get out of those storefronts altogether. The change seems to be approved of by those in the neighborhood. People are more comfortable in the domestic atmosphere of the BCIC.

Deputy Chairman Fred on the cover of *The Black Panther* brought more interested people to the center. The branch is surviving at this stage of pig repression. I spent a few hours of Christmas with Mom at home. I've changed since leaving home. I almost forget what I used to be.

New Year's Eve 1969—

Comrades weathered the storm. We survived the year. J. Edgar couldn't deliver on his promise to destroy us by the end of the year. All Power to the People!

January 1970—

Staff meetings every Sunday in N.Y. at the Ministry of Information in the Bronx. Larry and I went up to met John. Stayed overnight at the Philadelphia office. Comrades called a drill in the middle of the night, scared the shit out of me. Thought the pigs were vamping on the office. After Chicago and L.A. it's necessary to be more than battle ready twenty-four hours a day.

Juche and the teachings of comrade Kim IL Sung are the new ideas embraced by the Party.[19] More emphasis now on the international struggles. New comrades from the Coast here now to assist at the East Coast chapters and branches. Bay, Jolly, and Rob Webb.[20] John introduced me. Felt comfortable with Bay. He liked my name, Lil' Masai. Wanted to know if I could talk like him on the struggle. Comrades from up and down the East Coast shared ideas. Good feelings about the branches and chapters here. The New York 21 released a tape from the Tombs, "Capitalism Plus Dope Equals Genocide."[21] Cetewayo was the speaker. The brother has a powerful voice and keen insights. Like to meet him someday.

Lots of new materials from National Distribution now. Buttons, posters, Che's *Diary*, Elaine's album, and the Chairman's book due out soon. Keeps the community involved in our support. Spreads the visibility of the Party around. Confounds the enemy. Merges Panthers with community people.

New workers and supporters in to offer help and participate in the struggle. Brother [Paul] Coates out of Cherry Hill doing distribution work in that area. Raymond is recruiting new people, like the sister Connie. Yogi and Bernadette have reached some of the high school youths. Seems they've pulled Ron into work with us. The breakfast program is his interest. Good worker too. Sister J. J. and I having some problems. Can't afford any now. Conditions still too tentative to get apolitical and narrow-minded. Too many personal problems will blind visions of the larger struggle. Must be vigilant on all fronts.

Jack fell by the wayside. Too many personal differences with John and leadership. Some of us must fall due to shortcomings. Some new brothers have stepped in over the weeks to help fill the ranks. Jackie, J.J., and Dippy. Good participation from them all in P.E. classes. Good communications from people in the community.

John was stuck in N.Y. with Rob Bay. Filled in for him on TV program "Brass Tacks." Grandma Nana saw the program and called Mom. Said she was impressed. The audience and panel were impressed also. They had no idea that Panthers could understand the relationship between Huey and Martin Luther King, let alone address other relevant concerns of the community. A good showing for the branch and the Party. Some satisfaction.

February 1970–

Huey's birthday celebration turned out successful. Good turnout from the community considering the weather. Spoke to the audience about the ideas and programs of the Party. Starting to become adjusted to speaking before larger groups and audiences. Good speakers in the cadre. Should lead to a variety of speaking engagements. Good source of funds for the branch.

Rob Bay wanted someone from the branch to accompany Masai to Canada to speak with PLO representatives. John selected me to go. Met Masai at the Bronx Ministry, but couldn't travel with him for lack of any identification. Even Panthers have to have ID to cross into Canada. Had to return without making the trip. Down with pneumonia at the same time. Frustrating combination.

Connie is working at the office after work. Sister has good potential. Feisty and spirited. Good comrade. I enjoy her.

Trial for John, Raymond, and me ended. Buchman did a great job to point out police harassment and evil intentions toward the Party.[22] Each of us took the stand to deliver our views and feelings regarding those arrests and incidents around the Party. Jury could conclude only that we were disorderly. Sentences were suspended and each of us fined $350. Either way we were able to express our views and articulate the goals and some of the intentions of the Party. Still the system sucks. I still hurt from that baton beating. As comrades have written, my patience cries for cessation, my anger cries for vengeance, cold and deadly.

April 1970–

NCCF's coming into existence now. We're not authorized to do any organizing except here. Bay said that we have enough to do here in Baltimore. Take care of the community here first.

Connie is now communications secretary, replacing Reeva and after her J. J.[23] My recommendation that John approved. A personal though still revolutionary interest. If I must criticize myself for that weakness, then I'll do so in good faith. The sister is good for us, for me in that sense.

Jackie, Dippy and I visited the University of West Virginia for a speaking engagement. Drove down there on Thunderbird and Revolutionary fervor. BPP news celebrated Lil' Bobby. I spoke to a packed auditorium. Denounced J. Edgar and the CIA during the speech and condemned the U.S. government and its policies toward oppressed people in the U.S. and around the world. Told the audience the U.S. was nothing but the Lone Ranger, and Tonto wasn't around to help her. The audience understood and did approve. Stayed the next day and spoke to classes on Black History and the history of American oppression. We were well received there. The student body, if ignorant of the Party before, had some understanding of the positions taken by the Party in the interests of Black people. They know that we are the vanguard.

April 28, 1970–

I had been at my Mother's with Connie. Decided to call the office to check in. John told me to get back right away. Sounded important. Something had happened. Jackie and J. J. were involved. I was told that two pigs had been shot. That Jackie and J. J. had been arrested.[24] The news came over WJZ-TV with the account of the event. There was tension in the office while John considered the response. Comrades were worried. I was. I am.

April 29, 1970–

The pigs busted Eddie at his job. Charged him in the attack on the two Baltimore pigs. The media have accused the Party of being involved in the shootings. Told comrades to be watchful out in the streets. Call in every hour for security reasons. No need to prepare a press statement yet. We need more information. Be prepared.

April 30, 1970–

They attacked us this morning. Pigs ran into the breakfast program at the church looking for Panthers. They snatched Larry coming from the pad on Aisquith Street. The vamp was about charges from last year. About something involving a former Panther. Other former members were snatched, Ochiki, Charlie Wyche, Reeva, Jomo, and they're looking for me.

Nixon assaulted Cambodia today also. Things are rampant across the world, but I have to feel it more here than elsewhere. WJZ, WEBB, all the stations are carrying the news. These motherfuckers are serious this time. They're out to get some of our blood. Coates drew down on the pigs. He's busted. The community is responding after the breakfast program was targeted. They have come to our aid. If that is enough.

Mom called the office. Henry Lee talked with her. I did. Frame-up and government repression were the first things to come to mind. We're being attacked like every other branch and chapter of the Party. Told her not to panic. We'll be all right here. If anyone suspicious comes to the house asking about my whereabouts, let me know. Told Mom to be careful. She said she would say a prayer for us. Young comrades reported police cars cruising the area, stopping brothers who fit descriptions of Party members. Can't venture from the office now. More reports from the news media. More warrants are going to be issued. Community people are flocking to the office. Phone lines jammed. We're not isolated. A good sign.

They've targeted damn near the entire branch on charges of murder and conspiracy. Stupid motherfuckers Arnold Loney, Mahoney Kebe, and that infantile Donald Vaughn are pointing fingers. Time to dig in here. This is going to balloon into something ugly. Buchman is going to be busy. [25]

May 1970–

There's a wall of people in the streets protecting the office. People on rooftops—up and down the block. Supporters are bringing medical supplies, food, and volunteering every kind of assistance. Power to the people! Comrades and supporters are selling papers from the sidewalks, car to car. A powerful statement to deter a vamp. The cowards are still subject to come in the night, but the vigil and support keep them at bay for now.

The pigs' attempt to defame us hasn't succeeded. Efforts to intimidate community people and comrades aren't working. Young high school comrades Anita [Stroud] and Patsy [Madden] are mobilizing the students in behalf of the branch and comrades. They're moving in to fill the gaps left by our limited mobility and communication with the outside. The condition is critical this time. Formal charges leveled against me and others in this frame. They needed an excuse to show their colors. Used April 28th events to come after us, but the pigs underestimated our roots. We have dug some deep roots. But deep enough?

Have to stay alert and busy here. Reinforce my confidence in the correctness of our position. This isn't going to blow away soon. These motherfuckers are determined to have their pound of flesh. They won't get any here. Not without putting their own asses up for grabs.

A whole shitload of comrades were dragged into this thing. Besides those busted on the 28th, they have managed to involve at least fifteen comrades. Motherfuckers just tossed in names for the shit. A stew pot of nonsense coming out of the mouths of apolitical hacks. Anyone the pigs can't break or capture is being indicted and hunted.

Mom came to the office. First time she's visited the office. I think she felt comfortable even in the midst of all the traffic in and out and the implications of my situation. She stayed. Talked with comrades. Enjoyed herself. Despite all the horror stories Dad told her, she was relaxed among us. Good for her. Have to hold that memory close. Might be some time before we meet again.

She understands that we're fighting with our backs to the wall. Understands that we've all been there all along, coming off the ropes against the odds and enemies who would deny and destroy. Treacherous motherfuckers would take one of the lighter things from me. Come between one of my few lifelines outside of the Party. I won't forget. Her. Them.

Changes have to be made soon. We can't stay here. The pressure is still there from our hunters to take us. They suspect we're here but won't take the risk of crashing our doors, not with the demonstrated support from the community. The only question for us is when, where, how long will we remain invisible. Subjects of the Hunt?

There'll be some rebuilding after we leave. John has a new cadre around him now. Coates and Connie will be solid for the branch. Fresh blood to replace those who vanished. Hard to reconcile myself with not being near Connie soon. I've grown close to her. A revolutionary love that may breach normal relationships for us. I feel the loss even now. It will be awkward realizing that I miss her. Thought I had slipped past those old feelings. Not yet. Maybe I won't. I feel it now anyway. Some things take time to accept even under these circumstances. Weakness? Selfishness? I accept and understand present duties. Present predicaments. That part of me hasn't fully matured. Political consciousness with a sentimental heart. I'm still a revolutionary regardless.

May 25, 1970–

I'll miss them all, I know that. This is where it all began for me. I'll be back one day. I'm not finished here with these motherfuckers not as long as the Party will have me or long as there is a need. After Fred, I am so revolutionary proletarian intoxicated that I can never be astronomically intimidated.

June 1970–

Thought that I would be homesick again. A different feeling this time around. Maybe it's the city or that the comrades seem to operate with a spirit different from those in N.Y. I'm more confident than last year. The learning has been good for me. This is a new era for me now. Must accept this until something changes. Keep growing. No complacency. Stagnation. Ride this thing out to the end.

Reggie [Schell] assigned me to handle Political Education classes for the cadre. I think Bay or John had something to do with that. Appreciate the confidence and opportunity. Sister Love is dynamic. Good sister. She makes our transition comfortable.

All comrades are safe. Chaka and Sherry. Yogi, Sandy, and I are relieved. We're adjusting easily I sense. The branch is solid, and we seem to fit in. Connie wrote. The beat goes on there.

Wanted to attend the June tenth celebration in D.C. Knew that I would be denied. Stupid of me to even venture the idea. Safety and survival depend on overcoming my personal desires that may compromise our freedom. This is home now.

Rizzo is a monster.[26] His pigs are even more low-lifed than ours. He's deadly and lets anyone and everyone know it. He'll attack his own mother given the urge.

Impressed with the Ministry of Information here. Wes Cook and his cadre supply sufficient and timely material to the community.[27] I can learn from them.

July 1970–

Can't let this day go by. Connie and I had a ceremony. A revolutionary wedding. Reggie served as minister. Jolly disapproved of the activity. Saying that comrades have to be together for at least a year before they can be married. We proceeded anyway. Connie in blue knit with powder blue underneath. Comrades at the event loved it. For now and later this is what I want. It is allowed. It helps me to accept the unknowns. We're out of touch and out of reach physically, but bridge that gap. I think I understand. It's personal.

Vibes. Contradictions. Something that is fomenting within. One comrade trying to blend in, become a part of this branch, in this city. I can't go home, my home. Where are the problems and contradictions? I didn't bring them here with me. Sandra is my comrade and intimate. Perhaps that displeases some people. I'm out of touch and off limits. Day-to-day here. I produce, we produce. Comrades in the same damn struggle. Who would interfere if tomorrow is not guaranteed to any of us? I'm a Panther not some newcomer. I broke the silence of communications. Called Baltimore. John wasn't at the office. Had to speak with comrades—Connie in particular. I am and was moved by emotion. Reason deserted me. Yogi and I took the bus to Baltimore. Reggie was in California. I am temporarily in charge. Violations I know. My responsibility. Personal and political drives moved me. Subjective at first, somewhere the objective fact is hidden.

Just being on the streets in Baltimore somehow invigorated the both of us. Like school kids playing hooky from the overseers. Different overseers this time. Comrades talked, shocked us. But relaxed. Should have anticipated the reaction from John when he returned to the office. Coates was silent.

Yogi didn't budge. Back off. Not this time. I was responsible, but I wanted to talk regardless of the consequences. I jeopardized our office and my comrades. That didn't register then. Through all of the criticisms it was evident that my actions were personal though with good intentions as I viewed them. John is going to talk to Bay about having me expelled. He runs the branch, and I'm not a part of it any longer. Period. Every Panther has roots. Mine are there—in Baltimore. No one denies me that right. No one.

The anger and frustration provoked John. Now I think I understand some other things. I accepted the criticism when we returned to Philly. Reggie and John spoke away from me. Now I'm being treated with a long-handled spoon. Bay can't make a decision from what I can gather. Keep him in the field with papers and out of Baltimore. I acted according to my interests. Didn't want to involve Yogi or any other comrades. First time I've been through this shit. I'm learning something as is everyone else I think. If I have to go back home then what? No Party?

Fieldwork with the other comrades. Perhaps I'm exiled here with no way home. I did what I thought I understood. Panthers don't cry. Maybe I will.

Can't function out of the office any longer. None of us. We threaten the office. Rizzo could vamp any time that we're around. Sister Love is only one comrade, and she has no impact on this branch. I've fucked over our welcome here. Now I have reason to be subjective. I'm still a Panther.

Sandra and her sister Rose live in West Philly.[28] Sandy and I will be here in the community until. Now I am underground, or am I just here? Rose is a bitch in that mainstream American sense, but Sandra is a comrade. That I will respect.

Neither one of us is easy with this situation, but it's understood. I only have one question. Are we still Panthers?

Pilfered credit card numbers to call home. Why not? On our own for the most part. Party communications is minimal and vague. Can't tell you where I am Mom, just take care, hold on. I'm okay. Fuckin' up. Both of us. But the Party isn't involved in this. Get us out of this shit Bay. I think of Connie, again and again. I think of Baltimore. I'm alone I realize. But still I'm Lil' Masai. I'm a Panther.

And the Minister of Defense [Huey P. Newton] is coming home soon.[29]

NOTES

1. Warren Hart was one of the founding cadre members of the Baltimore branch of the BPP and its first defense captain.

2. Arnold Loney was later revealed to be a police agent, while Reeva D. White was the first Communications Secretary of the Baltimore branch.

3. White Panthers were members of the White Panther Party, a White radical organization modeled on the Black Panther Party and based in Ann Arbor, Michigan.

4. Linda was Steve McCutchen's girlfriend and a member of the Forest Park High School's Black Student Union.

5. A part-time Panther was a pejorative term referring to an individual who did not make a full-time commitment to Party activities.

6. Donald Cox, also known as D.C., was one of the field marshals of the Black Panther Party. His responsibilities included recruiting, organizing, and supervising the Party's chapters and branches. Cox was a prolific organizer who enjoyed the respect and admiration of his fellow Party comrades. Arthur Turco, Jr., was a New York lawyer who provided legal assistance to Party members in New York. Mitch, (Henry Mitchell), was the officer of the day for the Harlem branch of the Black Panther Party. Cox was sent to Baltimore, along with Mitchell and Turco, by National Headquarters to improve organizational effectiveness. While D.C., Mitch, and Turco were in Baltimore, or shortly thereafter, suspected police agent Eugene Anderson was allegedly tortured and killed. Cox went into exile in early 1970 after he was charged with complicity in Anderson's murder. Turco was also indicted in the Anderson case, and later acquitted, on conspiracy to commit murder charges. In addition to Cox and Turco, a host of local Party members were arrested on various charges during this period. The Baltimore branch was under constant attack, as were other Panther affiliates, from law enforcement officials nationwide.

7. Hart was accused of operating the Baltimore branch as a social club. He was later demoted from Captain to a rank-and-file member.

8. Charles Butler and Zeke Boyd were expelled from the Party for failure to adhere to the Party's chain of command.

9. Mahoney Kebe, another founding member of the Baltimore branch, was a police agent during his membership in the BPP. He was later expelled from the Party for tampering with organizational funds.

10. Masai [Ray] Hewitt was BPP Minister of Education.

11. The reference to New York refers to the New York chapter of the Black Panther Party. Under the organizational structure of the BPP, the New York chapter was responsible for all East Coast affiliates of the Party, while the Illinois chapter supervised Michigan and Indiana, and Kansas City maintained regional supervision for Iowa and Nebraska. See G. Louis Heath, ed., *Off the Pigs: The History and Literature of the Black Panther Party* (Metuchen, N.J.: Scarecrow Press, 1976).

12. Donald Vaughn was another police agent who infiltrated the Baltimore branch during its formative years.

13. The United Front Against Fascism conference, organized by the Panthers, was a meeting held July 18–21, 1969 in Oakland, California. The attendees included multiple sectors of the American left: White student radicals, members

of the Students for a Democratic Society, Brown Berets, Young Lords, White Panthers, several religious groups, and various other Black organizations, and of course members of the Black Panther Party. Chaka Zulu [Edward Martin] was a founding member of the Baltimore branch of the BPP. Eddie's full name is Marshall Eddie Conway.

14. Community workers were entry level Party members who served at least a year probationary period before achieving full membership status.

15. John Clark of the Los Angeles chapter of the Party was sent to Baltimore by the Central Committee to stabilize the local branch. He was appointed Defense Captain of the Maryland State Chapter of the Black Panther Party and given the responsibility of stabilizing the local branches.

16. The Panther New York 21 were arrested on a host of conspiracy charges, including plotting to bomb five department stores, police stations, subway stations, and the Botanical Gardens in the Bronx. All twenty-one defendants were eventually acquitted of all charges.

17. National Distribution was the headquarters for the production of the Party newspaper which was originally based in San Francisco and later moved to Oakland in 1972.

18. Grip and Pete are the two younger brothers of Steve McCutchen, John "Grip" McCutchen and Maurice "Pete" McCutchen.

19. *Juche* is a concept advocated by Kim IL Sung, then Premier of North Korea. The notion of Juche emphasized the importance of self-reliance.

20. Robert Bay, originally a member of the San Francisco branch, worked closely with the Central Committee. He was assigned to supervise the operations of East Coast affiliates of the BPP. Robert Webb was originally a member of the Washington, D.C. branch of the Black Panther Party. He supported the Cleaver-led faction and was shot to death in New York on March 8, 1971.

21. This tape was later published as a pamphlet and emphasized the Panther interest in combating use of drugs, primarily of heroin, in the Black community.

22. Harold Buchman was a local attorney who represented members of the Baltimore branch of the BPP.

23. There were two members named J. J.: a male named Jack Johnson and a female who served as the Communications Secretary from late 1969 to mid-1970.

24. Jackie Powell was also arrested with J. J. [Jack Johnson] on murder charges on April 30, 1970. Later Marshall Eddie Conway was arrested on the same charge. Jackie later died while incarcerated, and Jack Johnson and Eddie Conway remain in prison.

25. About a year after this entry was written Kebe, Loney, and Vaughn were exposed in court as police agents. While reporting to the Baltimore Police Department, they participated in the torture murder of Eugene Anderson, a police informer who had infiltrated the Baltimore branch. The case against the Panthers collapsed in court once the police involvement in this set up become known.

26. After being moved from Baltimore undercover, Steve and two other Panthers, Sandy and Yogi, were re-established in Philadelphia. Frank Rizzo was the Chief of Police in Philadelphia at this time. During one raid of a Philadelphia BPP office, Rizzo's officers ordered all the arrested Panthers to strip nude. Rizzo was later elected the mayor of Philadelphia.

27. Wes Cook is Mumia Abu-Jamal, a former member of the Philadelphia BPP who is currently on death row for the alleged murder of a police officer. See Jim Fletcher, Tanaquil Jones, and Sylvere Lotringer, eds., *Still Black Still Strong: Survivors of the War Against Black Revolutionaries* (New York: Semiotext(e),

1993), and S.E. Anderson and Tony Medina, eds., *In Defense of Mumia* (New York: Writers and Readers, 1996).

28. Sandra was a member of the Philadelphia BPP, and Rose, a non-Party member, was the older sister of Sandra.

29. Huey P. Newton's 1968 manslaughter conviction was overturned by the state appellate court in July 1970. Newton, who had been incarcerated since October 1967, was released from prison on August 5, 1970.

Chapter Five

"I Got a Right to the Tree of Life": Afrocentric Reflections of a Former Community Worker

Miriam Ma'at-Ka-Re Monges

It is a question of the Third World starting a new history of Man...which will...not forget Europe's crimes, of which the most horrible was committed in the heart of man, and consisted of the pathological tearing apart of his functions and the crumbling away of his unity.[1]
—Frantz Fanon

Panther survival programs, which revitalized life in the African American community, constituted the soul of the Black Panther Party (BPP).[2] According to Bobby Seale, Chairman of the BPP, "The objective of programs set forth by revolutionaries like the Black Panther Party [was] to educate the masses of the people to the politics of changing the system. The politics are related to people's needs, to a hungry stomach, or to getting rid of the vicious pigs with their revolvers and clubs."[3] Perhaps its most enduring legacy, the community service projects of the BPP included free breakfast programs for children, police-alert patrols, liberation schools, sickle cell screenings, free health clinics, free clothing programs, and a wide array of other survival programs.

The Black Panther Party has been the recipient of considerable popular and mass media attention. Between 1992 and 1996, several books, including personal memoirs by Party comrades and a journalistic investigative exposé, were published.[4] Further evidence of the renewed interest in the BPP is the recent production of *Panther,* a movie that provides a fictionalized account of the organization.[5] To be sure, elements of the mercurial rise and tragic demise of the Black Panther Party ensure a captivating narrative. However, melodramatic events depicted in Panther accounts may not accurately capture the substantive dynamics of the organization. Moreover, an over concentration on headline incidents fails to provide adequate "consideration of the tedious day-to-day projects which helped them [Panthers] gain and build their credibility in the community in which they were working."[6] The following essay summarizes my experience as a community worker in the Black Panther Party during the early 1970s. It highlights the manner in which the Party served the interest of African people and offers an assessment of the Panther experiment through an Afrocentric prism.

Critical inquiry is needed in order to discern appropriate lessons from prior African American social movements. Fundamental to this process is to assess systematically both the positive and negative aspects of these movements. Prevailing sensationalistic treatments of the Party that tend to focus solely on the negative aspects undermine this crucial endeavor. These narratives reduce the legacy of dedicated individuals who sought to change America for the benefit of all humanity to gangster escapades and sexual exploits. For example, David Horowitz, a one-time Panther ally and former editor of *Ramparts,* a sixties radical publication, vehemently asserts that Newton and the Party were thugs and criminals masquerading as revolutionaries.[7] Similarly, a recent book by the journalist Hugh Pearson focuses disproportionately on the criminal actions of Huey P. Newton, which precludes a balanced critique of the BPP. In a review of Pearson's *The Shadow of the Panther: Huey Newton and the Price of Black Power in America,* Lori S. Robinson writes,

> Pearson always overshadows the positive with the negative. . . .The book might be capable of discrediting the uplifting legacy of Panthers who struggled, sacrificed and died for Black Power.[8]

Robinson further contends that Pearson's obsessive concentration on the criminal activities of Newton and the squad made it "difficult for the reader *not* to retain a sour impression of the Panthers in general."[9] A different kind of problem is encountered in Elaine Brown's *A Taste of Power: A Black Woman's Story*, which represents a personal odyssey of her sexual liaisons, political transformation and leadership ascendancy, rather than a historical account of the BPP.

The problematic nature of biased evaluations of the Party is further exacerbated by the marginalization of the African American experience in the country's educational process. Seldom is American history taught from the perspective of African American interests. Consequently, the absence of an Afrocentric analytic framework, combined with the virtual invisibility of Black people from the educational curriculum, impair the public's assessment of the Panthers. As a result, a perverse transformation occurs in which the Black Panther Party, a primary target of the government's FBI-directed counterintelligence program (COINTELPRO) becomes the villain.

The goal of COINTELPRO, first launched in August 1967, was to target "Black hate groups" and "expose, disrupt, discredit or otherwise neutralize such groups and their leadership, spokesmen, members and supporters."[10] FBI officers developed and implemented a multitude of tactics and schemes to undermine the effectiveness of the BPP. One frequently employed tactic was an invective letter-writing campaign in which the FBI disseminated fabricated letters to Party leaders and other Panther allies. The FBI also trained and planted agent provocateurs in the BPP. These agent provocateurs would often influence the more impressionable Party members to undertake questionable activities that invariably led to their incarceration. In addition, members of the FBI sowed false stories in the media, which generated mistrust and divisiveness among the Panthers. Of course, Party members were always subjected to constant telephone surveillance and frequent arrests. As a result of these opprobrious machinations, the FBI accomplished its objective to neutralize the Black Panther Party

Suffice it to say, any analysis of the Party should be filtered through the lens of COINTELPRO. The massive assault levied against the Black Panther Party by all three levels of government cannot be overstated. This is not to suggest that Huey Newton and other Panther officials did not abuse their leadership authority. Nor do I contend that the organization was free of sexism. Instances in which female comrades were mentally and physically abused certainly occurred. However, the Party was larger than its national leadership of Huey P. Newton, Bobby Seale, David Hilliard, and others. Concomitantly, it also superseded the chauvinistic behavior of a few male members.

Critics of the Party are often guilty of minimizing the historical significance of the BPP on the basis of the unprincipled actions taken by Panther officials. Excessive attention to the human frailties of Panther leaders discounts the dedication, sacrifice, and collective legacy of the men and women who were committed members of the BPP. To ensure a more balanced interpretation of the BPP, I propose the adoption of the analytical framework of Afrocentricity. The utility of the Afrocentric prism rests upon its fundamental axiom: does the action in question advance the interest of people of African descent? [12] An affirmative response to this critical question provides the basis for gleaning lessons from past African American social movements.

In the Streets

Huey finally had a whole little Black History class going on at the service center when he was community organizer. . .[and] he saw the young people as the basis and foundation of [the liberation struggle]. [13]
—Bobby Seale

Unlike the Niagara movement, the National Association for the Advancement of Colored People, or the Urban League, the Party's origins lie enmeshed among the Black downtrodden. Members of the BPP lived among impoverished African Americans. BPP offices were always located in the center of low-income areas of African American communities throughout the nation. Consequently, Party members formed a "highly developed consciousness of oppression." [14] This heightened consciousness fostered the Party's "conviction that the present existence of the oppressed is a kind of living death." [15]

Panther survival programs assisted African Americans in their struggle against a "living death." In *The Genius of Huey P. Newton*, a 1970 pamphlet distributed by the BPP, Huey explains that "the Panther community programs are attempting to spur the community into action—creative action—to make decisions and regain the dignity of the people."[16] Survival programs of the BPP activated the dormant power lying within Black people, which assisted the process of transforming their negative conditions. Wade Nobles, an Afrocentric psychologist, illustrates the transformative objective undergirding the Party's survival programs:

> The relationship between the social and psychological development of our people and the social structures and institutions (i.e., government, education, health, etc.) designed in theory to affirm our people's being, is ultimately a question of transformation.[17]

Although theoretical constructs of the BPP were imperfect, its commitment to alleviating the oppressive conditions of Black People never wavered. While the Panthers demonstrated a deep desire to empower Black people, unfortunately some Panthers often discounted the significance of Black history. Assata Shakur, a New York Panther, complained that her comrades lacked an understanding of the experience of Black people. She lamented,

> The basic problem stemmed from the fact that the BPP had no systematic approach to political education. They were reading the *Red Book* but didn't know who Harriet Tubman, Marcus Garvey, and Nat Turner were. They talked about intercommunalism but still really believed that the Civil war was fought to free the slaves. A whole lot of them barely understood any kind of history, Black, African or otherwise.[18]

The BPP remains haunted by an anti-White depiction of the organization. This interpretation of the Party belies the Panthers' commitment to revolutionary solidarity with all people. Assata Shakur recalls her political awakening process as a Panther:

> [O]ne of the most important things the Party did was to make it really clear who the enemy was: not the white people, but the capitalistic, imperialistic oppressors. [The Party] took the Black liberation struggle out of a national context and put it in an international context.[19]

The central objective of the Party was to fight the system which oppressed African people. Huey explains, "[W]e [Panthers] don't suffer in the hangup of a skin color, we don't hate white people; we hate the oppressor."[20]

On the other hand, Panther alliances with White supporters have spawned the criticism that the Party was a captive of white interests. Therefore, it was assumed that the Panthers mirrored other civil rights organizations who desired to assimilate into society. While the traditional civil rights organizations fought against the racial restrictive laws that denied Black people full access, these groups rarely protested the skewed distribution of wealth in the United States. Conversely, the BPP denounced the entire structure of American society that denied human rights to Black and other oppressed people. While the Party formed working coalitions with White radical groups, it maintained organizational autonomy by prohibiting White membership in the BPP.

My experience with the BPP began as a college student who participated in a breakfast program at the Ralph Avenue Community Center in Brownsville, a Brooklyn low-income area. A coalition of the Black Panther Party and the Black League of African American Students (BLAC) of Brooklyn College established the free breakfast program, the likes of which are now commonplace in public schools. Party members understood that malnourishment impeded the learning process. Yet in the 1960s and early 1970s, poor children attended school hungry and saddled with the unrealistic expectation that they would master the curriculum. Party members and students cooked and served large pots of grits and eggs. We would then argue over who would wash those gigantic pots. We cajoled supermarkets for donations and we fed hundreds of children. Most importantly, we also nourished their minds with Black history lessons as they ate their meals. Sometimes we fed parents of the children, even though it was not the intent of the program.

A symbiotic relationship existed between the Party and Black students. For example, the Black Panther Party supported the students efforts at Brooklyn College to establish a Black Studies department. On many college campuses across the nation, students protested against racist educational practices and policies. This opposition did not escape the Brooklyn College campus. Tensions surrounding the university's open admissions policy permeated between the majority of students who were middle class and of European ancestry with a family tradition of college attendance, and African Americans and Hispanics, who were generally working-class and first-generation college students. Consequently, cultural and class differences pervaded the Brooklyn campus. Indeed, the entire university was a hotbed of fiery debate and a racially charged environment. Some professors, administrators, and students openly expressed hostility toward the students of color attending the school.

Fortunately, African American and Hispanic students functioned with exceptional camaraderie. I joined BLAC and served on the Central Committee of the organization. The first major activity of the BLAC was an organized protest against the arrest of nineteen student activists. BLAC members besieged the president's office and successfully stopped the daily routine of campus life. BLAC eventually won the release of the incarcerated student activists due in part to an effective coalition between African American and Puerto Rican students and members of the Black Panther Party that extended from the campus to the community.

Through the Ralph Avenue Community Center, we developed a youth program, liberation school and conducted food and clothing drives. We offered karate, cooking, and sewing classes for children in the community. Although not by design, we incorporated rudimentary aspects of the Afrocentric paradigm. We taught African history lessons and sponsored African dance classes. In the 1960s, most people had limited exposure to the history of Black people. Fortunately, we now have voluminous scholarship on the impact of African culture and history. Esteemed elders and scholars have documented the contributions of African people to the various arenas of human civilization, such as ethics, religion, philosophy, engineering, mathematics, and literature.[21]

Members of the Black Panther Party addressed quality-of-life issues in Brownsville through concrete action. Deplorable housing conditions existed in this New York community. Abandoned buildings and substandard housing dominated the landscape. In order to assist community residents to improve their living conditions, Party members organized rent strikes. We learned hard lessons that have remained with me to this day. Our experience made it clear to us that Black people needed to undergo the "transcendence" described by Wade Nobles as "the quality, state or ability to exceed, go beyond or rise above the limits of an experience, condition or situation."[22] Panthers possessed an overriding faith that ordinary people could transform their oppressive conditions. An overriding faith in the imperative of fundamental societal change and its possibility pervaded the membership of the BPP.

I continued working with the BPP well past its coalition with the BLAC. It is difficult to say precisely when my Party experience actually ended since my husband was an imprisoned Panther. My participation with the Party as a college student was not unique. In her autobiography, Assata Shakur also describes working with the Party as a college student. After her departure from the BPP, Assata was later shot during a New Jersey Turnpike gun battle with a state highway patrol officer. Impregnated during her incarceration, Assata gave birth to a baby girl in the midst of hellish prison conditions. Assata eventually escaped from prison and now resides in Cuba where she enjoys political asylum.[23]

Although the lumpen proletariat—the totally disenfranchised class—constituted the core of the Brooklyn branch of the BPP, African American college students also comprised a major contingent of the membership. Notwithstanding the diverse class origins of my Panther comrades, the members remained united in their conviction to serve and defend the Black community. Immediately, everyone received an allotment of the Party's newspaper *The Black Panther* to sell and attended mandatory political education classes. Principally, the political education classes centered on Mao Tse-Tung's *Red Book*, the writings of Malcolm X and Huey Newton, *The Black Panther*, and the works of Frantz Fanon, particularly *The*

Wretched of the Earth.[24] Selections from the *Red Book* were required reading. These classes emphasized the saliency of theory and practice which undergirded Panther activism.

NOMMO—The Generative Power of the Word

Black people throughout the diaspora have retained the oral expression feature of traditional African culture. Molefi Asante asserts that "central to the understanding of the role of vocal expressiveness within the African American community [is] *nommo*, the generative and dynamic quality of vocal expression."[25] I contend that *nommo* contributed to the tremendously rapid growth of the Black Panther Party. Members of the BPP worked street corners selling *The Black Panther* and spreading the word of "revolution" among the people. Panthers on the street spoke a distinct language of protest "framed by characteristic rhetorical and linguistic practices that are products of a special experience, environment, and heritage."[26] Party slogans such as "off the pigs," "political power comes from the barrel of a gun," "seize the time," and "power to the people" galvanized scores of BPP supporters. On occasion, Panther inflammatory rhetoric alienated conservative members of the Black community and left the organization vulnerable to political repression. Members of the BPP countered that extreme oppressive conditions warrant extreme rhetorical responses in order to mobilize opposition to political tyranny. Community work, *The Black Panther* and *nommo* meshed into a powerful liberating force created by Panther activism. Asante illuminates the contours of the rhetoric of resistance:

> The protest speaker's sensitivity to powerlessness in the society frees him or her to utilize the improvisational mechanisms of African American culture. . . In some respects, H. Rap Brown, Eldridge Cleaver, Stokely Carmichael, and Bobby Seale were "jazz artists" in the 1960s. They often chose not to employ *the prevailing behavior* [emphasis in text] of white culture in their verbal responses. The police were "pigs" to Bobby Seale. . . In reply to the charge that the Black Panther used too much profanity, the votarists would argue that the society was profane, poverty was profane, the government was profane, and the American system was the biggest profanity.[27]

Within Stone Walls

For many Party members and their families the politics of the radical sixties and seventies have not dissipated. A host of Party comrades continue to languish in prison as a result of COINTELPRO. Mundo We Langa (David Rice), Marshall Eddie Conway, Albert Nuh Washington, and Ed Poindexter are among the many political prisoners incarcerated in the United States. Their cases like that of other imprisoned African American freedom fighters such as Abdul Majid, Sundiata Acoli, and Sekou Odinga have not received significant public attention and support.[28]

The wives of these incarcerated Party members also endured, albeit unacknowledged, enormous personal sacrifice as well. These sisters have spent much of their adult lives visiting their husbands who were frequently transferred to different prisons. I and my children experienced this lifestyle. My former husband, Pedro Chango Monges, a member of the Party, was incarcerated for ten years. During this period he was transferred to six prisons throughout the East Coast. Visitors were often treated with as much abhorrence as the prisoners themselves. Frequently, families were forced to see loved ones through layers of thick glass and telephone wires. Children grew up playing in prison visiting rooms and conjugal visit trailers. Mothers, such as myself, were forced to nurture and raise children without the support of their imprisoned fathers. We constantly struggled to make sense of these difficult circumstances to our children. Many marriages did not survive this assault; mine was one of those that succumbed to these pressures. Likewise, various Panther children are still living through the deleterious aftermath of COINTELPRO.

Many of us in the middle of the storm survived because of strong support systems. I received tremendous support and encouragement from both my own and former husband's family. Additionally, a group of women who were former Panthers, wives of Panthers, and Panther supporters—Frankye Malika Adams, Odunfonda Adaramola, Dena Greene Brown, and Helen Jones, sustained one another throughout the trying years. We call ourselves the Sisters of Nzingha.[29] We all once lived in New York, but we now reside in various parts of the country. The Nzinghas communicate regularly with each other and come together several times a year to celebrate important occasions.

Conclusion

In retrospect, the Party did not correctly analyze the political, social, and cultural predicament of African people in America. This shortcoming can be attributed to the Panthers' failure to develop a holistic approach to their opposition against racial oppression. Party members emphasized objective reality and historical materialism at the expense of subjectivity. My fellow comrades discounted spirituality, an important feature of the Afrocentric paradigm. The African-centered worldview includes spirituality because in the culture of African people "no line is drawn between the spirit and the physical."[30] The debate between Panther leaders and other Black Powerites over the value of African culture often occurred.

Huey Newton critiqued the misuse of African culture by Papa Doc, the former Haitian dictator when he wrote that "Papa Doc oppresses the people but he does promote the African culture."[31] Huey Newton was not, however, opposed to African culture:

> [T]he Black Panther Party. . . realizes that we have to have an identity. We have to realize our Black heritage in order to give us strength to move on and progress. But as far as returning to the old African culture, it's unnecessary and it's not advantageous in many respects. We

believe that culture itself will not liberate us. We're going to need some stronger stuff.[32]

Nonetheless, Newton failed to fully grasp the richness and depth of African culture. Through the use of African culture, Black people can glean models for liberation. Marimba Ani (formerly Dona Marimba Richards), professor of Black and Puerto Rican Studies at Hunter College in New York, describes the enormous power of African culture in *Let the Circle Be Unbroken:*

> We must turn our spirituality, our ethos, our Africanness into a political tool. We must harness the energies that lie dormant and diffused throughout Pan-Africa, and forge them into a powerful political force for liberation and self-determination. WE ARE A SPIRITUAL PEOPLE BECAUSE WE ARE AN AFRICAN PEOPLE!. . .to deny it is a tactical error. . .we can achieve the balance necessary for creating a healthy new society or revolutionary implications.[33]

She rightfully underscores the essential place of spirituality in the liberation struggle of African people. Conversely, the policy of the Black Panther Party falsely dichotomized spirituality and liberation. We failed to see that these critical concepts were inextricably linked to one another.

Party members were correct, however, in their commitment to community activism. A central tenet of the discipline of Black Studies is the nexus between the academy and the community. Terry Kershaw, an African American studies scholar, stresses the importance of dialogue with the community, an imperative for the Afrocentric scholar:

> Since most Black people, in general, are victims of oppression, a Black Studies which does not emphasize ways of alleviating that oppression will be oppressive. Therefore, the Black Studies scholar must be active in "the community" and cannot afford the "luxury" of objectivity.[34]

Like the Black Panther Party, we all must resist oppression. The African American spiritual "I Got a Right to the Tree of Life" communicates the spirit of the community survival programs that defined the Black Panther Party. An Afrocentric analysis indicates that the members of the Black Panther Party failed to come to terms fully with their African heritage and culture; nonetheless, they valiantly fought to give life to an oppressed people. May the ancestors be satisfied!

NOTES

1. Frantz Fanon, *The Wretched of the Earth* (New York: Weidenfeld, 1961), 315.

2. The terms African, African American, and Black are used interchangeably throughout this chapter.

3. Bobby Seale, *Seize the Time: The Story of the Black Panther Party and Huey P. Newton* (Baltimore: Black Classic Press, [1968], 1970, 1991), 413.

4. Elaine Brown, *A Taste of Power: A Black Woman's Story* (New York: Pantheon Books, 1992); David Hilliard and Lewis Cole, *This Side of Glory: The Autobiography of David Hilliard and the Story of the Black Panther Party* (Boston, Mass.: Little Brown and Company, 1993); Hugh Pearson, *The Shadow of the Panther: Huey Newton and the Price of Black Power in America* (New York: Addison-Wesley, 1994); William Lee Brent, *Long Time Gone: A Black Panther's True-Life Story of His Hijacking and Twenty-Five Years in Cuba* (New York: Times Books, 1996).

5. See *Panther* (Polygram Filmed Entertainment, 1995), and Mario Van Peebles, Ula Y. Taylor and J. Tarika Lewis, *Panther: A Pictorial History of the Black Panthers and the Story Behind the Film* (New York: New Market Press, 1995).

6. Daniel J. Willis, "A Critical Analysis of Mass Political Education and Community Organization As Utilized By The Black Panther Party As A Means For Effecting Social Changing" (Ph.D. diss., University of Massachusetts, 1976), 48.

7. David Horowitz, "Black Murder, Inc.," *Heterodoxy,* March 1993, 15; Peter Collier and David Horowitz, *Destructive Generation: Second Thoughts About the 60s* (New York: Summit Books, 1990).

8. Lori Robinson, "A Panther Caged By His Own Demons," *Emerge,* June 1994, 66.

9. Ibid.

10. United States Senate, "The FBI's Covert Action Program to Destroy the Black Panther Party," *Final Report of the Select Committee to Study Government Operations with Respect to Intelligence Activities* (Washington, D.C.: S.R. No. 94-755, 94th Congress, 2d Sess, 1976), 187.

11. Ward Churchill and Jim Vander Wall, *Agents of Repression: The FBI's Secret War Against the Black Panther Party and the American Indian Movement* (Boston, Massachusetts: South End Press, 1988).

12. See the trilogy of books authored by Molefi Asante on the theory of Afrocentricity. He expands upon the importance of the placement of history in the interest of people of African descent. *Afrocentricity: The Theory of Social Change* (Buffalo: Amulefi Publishing Co., 1980) provides an examination of Afrocentricity as a philosophy. He demonstrates the application of Afrocentricity in a rhetorical analysis found in *The Afrocentric Idea* (Philadelphia: Temple University Press, 1987). In *Kemet, Afrocentricity and Knowledge* (Trenton: Africa World Press, 1990), he delineates the parameters of the discipline of Afrocentricity.

13. Bobby Seale, *Seize the Time,* 105–6.

14. Charles and Betty Lou Valentine, "The Man and the Panthers," *Politics and Society* (Spring, 1972), 2–3.

15. Ibid.

16. Huey P. Newton, *The Genius of Huey P. Newton: Minister of Defense Black Panther Party* (San Francisco: Black Panther Party, 1970), 1.

17. Wade Nobles, *African Psychology: Toward Its Reclamation, Reascension and Revitalization* (Oakland: Black Family Institute Publications, 1980), 97.

18. Assata Shakur, *Assata: An Autobiography* (Chicago: Lawrence Hills Books, 1987), 221.

19. Ibid., 203.

20. Philip Foner, ed., *The Black Panthers Speak* (New York: Da Capo Press, [1970] 1995), 57.

21. See Cheikh Anta Diop, *The African Origin of Civilization: Myth or Reality* (Westport: Lawrence Hill & Co., 1974); *The Cultural Unity of Black Africa* (Chicago: Third World Press, 1987); and *Civilization or Barbarism: An Authentic Anthropology* (New York: Lawrence Hill Books, 1991). Also see Yosef Ben-Jochannon, *African Origins of the Major "Western Religions"* (Baltimore: Black Classic Press, 1971); and Theophile Obenga, *Ancient Egypt and Black Africa* (London: Karnak House, 1992).

22. Nobles, *African Psychology,* 97.

23. Shakur, *Assata*; see also John Castelluci, *The Big Dance: The Untold Story of Weatherman Kathy Boudin and the Terrorist Family that Committed the Brinks Robbery Murders* (New York: Dodd, Mead, 1986); and Evelyn Williams, *Inadmissible Evidence: The Story of the African American Trial Lawyer Who Defended the Black Liberation Army* (New York: Lawrence Hills Books, 1993).

24. *Quotations of Chairman Mao Tse-Tung* (Peking: Foreign Language Press, 1961); Fanon, *The Wretched of the Earth.*

25. Asante, *Afrocentric Idea,* 93.

26. Ibid., 118.

27. Ibid., 116–17.

28. For additional information on African American political prisoners see Spring 1991 and Fall 1991 issues of the *Black Panther Black Community News Service* and contact the Campaign to Free Black Political Prisoners and POWs in the U.S., Kingsbridge P.O. Box 339, Bronx, NY 10463-0339.

29. Frankye Malika Adams was a former Panther and officer of the day of the Brooklyn office. The officer of the day was in charge of supervising branch activities. Odunfon da Adaramola (Gwen Ferguson), also a former Panther, is now a queen in the Yoruba Village of Sheldon, South Carolina. Dena Greene Brown was the wife of Henry "Sha Sha" Brown a former New York Panther, and Helen Jones is an activist who supported African American political prisoners. Our support group is named in honor of Queen Nzingha who waged war against the Portuguese to free her homeland of Angola. My bond with these sisters is very special and enduring.

30. John Mbiti, *African Religions and Practice* (Oxford: Heinemann International, [1969] 1990), 5.

31. Newton, *The Genius of Huey P. Newton*, 14.

32. Ibid.

33. Richards, *Let the Circle Be Unbroken*, 51–52.

34. Terry Kershaw, "The Emerging Paradigm in Black Studies," *The Western Journal of Black Studies* 13. 1 (1989):50.

Chapter Six

"Talkin' the Talk and Walkin' the Walk" : An Interview with Panther Jimmy Slater

Interview conducted by

Charles E. Jones

Editor's Note:

The following chapter is an interview with Jimmy Slater, a nine-year veteran of the Black Panther Party. Slater was raised in Northwest Georgia near the city of Atlanta. After graduating from high school, he migrated with other family members to Cleveland, Ohio, where he eventually joined the Cleveland branch of the Black Panther Party in 1968. He served as a community worker for a year before assuming full membership status in the Party in 1969. Slater was later assigned to Oakland, California, in 1972 to provide assistance to the political campaigns of Chairman Bobby Seale and Elaine Brown. He resigned from the Black Panther Party in 1977 and currently resides in Oakland.

CEJ: Why did you join the Black Panther Party?

JS: I learned about the Black Panther Party from friends and other people who were familiar with the organization. We began to understand the positive community programs that the Panthers had going on throughout the community. So that was one of the reasons why I joined the Black Panther Party. Basically, it was because of the many different positive programs sponsored by the Party.

CEJ: How old were you when you joined the Black Panther Party?

JS: When I became a volunteer worker, I was eighteen. I was between nineteen-and-a-half and twenty years old when I became a full-fledged member of the Party.

CEJ: How long were you a member of the Black Panther Party?

JS: I became a member of the Black Panther Party in the late sixties, (1968), and I left the Party in the mid-seventies (1977).

CEJ: Did you adhere to a particular procedure or process in order to become a member of the Black Panther Party?

JS: Yes, we did. We had to go through a procedure that involved serving as volunteers first and then later being accepted as full members of the Party. Practice was the criterion of the troops; and on the basis of practice, we were called upon to become full-time members. At the time, we really weren't connected with the national headquarters in Oakland.

CEJ: Were you a part of the so-called lumpen sector when you first joined the Party?

JS: Yes, I definitely was a lumpen when I first joined. I felt I would have been considered as one of those lumpen proletarians even though I had a high school diploma. I was one of those brothers out on the street, but every one of my leaders was educated. The Party placed an emphasis on education and always tried to persuade every individual around us to pursue higher education. Education was supported in every way possible by the Black Panther Party. I ended up attending Laney Junior College (Oakland) and going all the way to San Francisco State because of the push from the Black Panther Party. I really didn't have any intention of doing that before I joined the Party.

CEJ: What community programs were offered by your branch?

JS: We had a free health clinic and a free breakfast program in Cleveland. We used to serve out of the Catholic church and a number of the Black churches around. My mother's church was one of those churches. We served breakfast out of the basement. We also had a free clothing program. We utilized the facilities from the churches to set up this program, and we had volunteers—church members, my mother, and a lot of other seniors there who would volunteer to work with us. And they were the ones who really kept the free clothing program going. The free health clinic was blown up. I believe the year was 1969 or somewhere in that area.

CEJ: Who blew up the free health clinic?

JS: Well, we would imagine that the police, COINTELPRO, did. Any positive program that served and mobilized the community was attacked. It was one of the things we had going that served a lot of people who needed free medical aid, and it was attacked to undermine the Party's efforts.

CEJ: How were the Party programs in Cleveland financed?

JS: Basically, from community donations, from us going door-to-door, standing on the corner selling *The Black Panther*, and asking people for donations to serve themselves and their own needs.

CEJ: What was the impact of your branch's community programs?

JS: The impact I felt and still see was something that was very positive. It was really great because there were a lot of, as there are now, poor and oppressed, unemployed individuals out there who needed a number of the services provided by the Party's survival programs. So we had free medical care, the free breakfast program, and when the Angela Davis free breakfast program was implemented, they (governmental officials) weren't giving away free lunch at schools. We don't see free health clinics anymore even though we know that there are people who need free medical aid. At one point, we were testing for sickle cell anemia. We found this to be a very vital need in the Black community because at the time no one was testing Black people for sickle cell anemia.

CEJ: How would you describe the nature of the relationship between your particular branch and the White left?

JS: We had a more or less working relationship. They would come in and volunteer to work with us. I mean they couldn't become members, and we couldn't see them working directly in the Black community because they were not Black and would not have been accepted in the community even though you do have an oppressed White community. Party members felt that White radicals should organize and educate the oppressed White people about similar oppressive conditions in their communities so that there wouldn't be any divisions. We worked with a lot of the so-called White left, the NCCF [National Committee to Combat Fascism] out of Berkeley and a group of coal miners out of Tennessee. So we didn't have a problem working with them; but in terms of them controlling the leadership, that wasn't going to be accepted in the Black community in the first place.

CEJ: What were the positive benefits and/or negative costs of these relationships?

JS: The major benefit was simply gaining solidarity and support. I mean it's always better to have someone working with you than against you if your program is just and right. Basically, many of them [White people] had the same foot on their neck as we had on ours, and a lot of them knew who the ruling class was. They knew that the same individuals who had a foot on their neck had it on ours in terms of keeping us both down and creating a division between the oppressed.

CEJ: Were members of your particular chapter comfortable with that particular relationship, that is, working with the White left?

JS: Well, we didn't work so directly with them. When we sat down and went through a political education class, they were not sitting in there with us. No, they always came when we needed manpower for a particular program. In most cases I've seen, White radicals operated as volunteers, but they did not participate in the decision making of what was done or how the program was led because that wouldn't have been accepted. I mean you're only going to trust White people so far. Now, to volunteer to work with us is one thing. But to participate in the decision making of our internal business and affairs, we weren't comfortable with that from any standpoint.

CEJ: What was the relationship between the Cleveland branch and the local Black elected officials?

JS: The Cleveland chapter was very instrumental in the election of Carl B. Stokes, the first Black mayor of Cleveland [in 1969]. My brother Frank Slater was also a Panther, and he and a lot of other comrades were instrumental in Carl B. Stokes' campaign for the mayor of Cleveland. Angela Davis' brother, Ben Davis, also worked with us in assisting the candidacy of Stokes.

CEJ: When you say, "instrumental," how did Party members assist the Stokes' campaign?

JS: We passed flyers out, went door-to-door. We registered people to vote for Stokes. That was the first time that I became a voter registrar. All of us became voter registrars. We went throughout the community, registered people to vote, and passed out literature and leaflets at churches. A lot of my former comrades worked at campaign headquarters.

CEJ: How was this relationship established? Did Stokes' representatives contact the Black Panther office?

JS: I'm not exactly sure on that, but I do know that it was a strong sense in the Black community of Cleveland to get a Black mayor elected. From understanding Carl B. Stokes' political ideas and views during that time, we couldn't see a better individual to jump behind and support.

CEJ: Did you work in Bobby Seale's 1973 campaign for the mayor's office in Oakland. If so, what was your role?

JS: Definitely, I was a voter registrar again. We canvassed from door-to-door simply giving the overall campaign pitch. Communicating with the masses to go vote for Bobby Seale and support us. Getting flyers out, things like that.

CEJ: Do you recall if there was a great deal of disagreement among Party members about implementing this particular electoral strategy?

JS: From my perspective, there were areas of contradiction, but not anything strong enough to stop the masses of the Panthers from moving in that direction.

CEJ: What was the area of contradiction?

JS: Well, some members didn't want to deal with politics. They didn't feel that it was appropriate to get caught up into politics.

CEJ: In the Cleveland branch, were either work assignments or rank determined on the basis of gender?

JS: No, by no stretch of the imagination because basically it was all looked at from your function and practice. You would prove yourself really through your practice. In terms of gender, I never saw a contradiction there. Now, I'm not speaking for all members, but I didn't see it.

CEJ: Did women hold leadership positions in the Cleveland branch?

JS: Yes, because we had a woman who was a coordinator in the Cleveland chapter. In Toledo, the second-in-command was a sister also. When I got to Oakland, California, Kim was coordinating the West Oakland branch.

CEJ: Did the brothers have difficulty following the orders of sisters who held higher rank?

JS: You know that was something else I only saw with one individual. He ended up getting purged, but we found out he wouldn't have followed the orders of anyone.

CEJ: What type of COINTELPRO tactics were levied against your particular branch?

JS: Every kind that you could name. From the point of planting people among us to creating friction and divisions among comrades within the organization. There were several examples. Now, we would have a peaceful demonstration, and everything is going okay. And then you have a fool out there hollering and talking about murdering and kill the pig. On other occasions, different people would be put in as plants to simply create contradictions and division among the membership.

CEJ: How did your comrades attempt to counteract this repression?

JS: First of all, we defended ourselves. It was imperative not to stand there and roll over and die. First, through political education, trying to educate the community in terms of what was really happening and why it was happening. Education was added to the importance of defending your life. We had political education classes every Wednesday night, which were open to the community.

CEJ: What was the nature of the factional conflict that hampered the Party in 1971?

JS: One aspect of the division was that a lot of the East Coast members didn't want to follow the same by-laws and philosophy of the West Coast. Another thing was that COINTELPRO played a great part by sending leaders of the East Coast fabricated messages that were supposedly from leaders of the West Coast. In other words, COINTELPRO manipulated contradictions and played upon friction within organization. We knew that at one point Huey would get a letter from Eldridge Cleaver. Cleaver would swear up and down he didn't write it. Cleaver would receive a letter from Huey and vice versa. Neither one was writing those letters, but still each of them was tricked into believing that the other was responsible for writing the letters. When the whole time, the FBI agents were fabricating the letters. But to put it bluntly, coming here to Oakland from the East, I did learn what was going on with the policy making. Eldridge Cleaver was one of the biggest contradictions in the Black Panther Party. When we were heading into the political arena, and he was out hollering and screaming these militaristic ideas, it was so counterrevolutionary until all it did was damage the Black Panther Party. The vast majority of the people in the community accepted what Eldridge

Cleaver said, as though it represented the major body of the Black Panther Party, and it really didn't. It wasn't the idea of the vast majority of the Black Panther Party. Also, Eldridge pushed this militaristic line all the way to the hilt. I mean he got Bobby [Hutton] killed.

CEJ: What were your impressions of Dr. Huey P. Newton?

JS: Dr. Huey Newton I felt was a politically sound, great brother. He was a really positive leader. He had a lot of pressure put upon him, and it came from all sides and angles. I found that the brother happened to be one of the strongest individuals that I have known to go through all the negative things that were thrown at him. I felt Huey was one of the great leaders of the Black Panther Party, but this is not to overlook leaders like Bobby Seale and the other Central Committee members that had equal leadership qualities.

CEJ: What factors, other than political repression, contributed to the demise of the Black Panther Party?

JS: One thing that I saw in the beginning of the Panther Party, when we had all the service programs, we always had people bringing in other new people. At some point, that seemed to cease. In other words, the failure to bring in new blood, new members, was one of the most detrimental things that could have happened to the Black Panther Party. Even though we knew that we had COINTELPRO to deal with on one hand and the police on the other. We had spies sitting all around us and working with us in some cases. We found that out after everything had closed down. But the most important thing I saw was the failure to bring in young and new blood. Secondly, while I still don't think capitalism works, you need capital to function in a capitalistic system. Upon reflection, this was one of the areas that I thought we were too liberal about during the Black movement of the sixties. We wanted to give everything away, and we were simply too liberal in our view. We know now that was an error. We had certain things the Black Panther Party had built and established; however, because of our hate for capitalism, we didn't sustain anything. We had buildings and homes. We owned property. We should have learned how to control the economy and to manage those things. Instead, we wanted to fight against capitalism, and now we know that we should have established an economic base. In order to keep the movement going, you've got to have capital.

CEJ: Can the Black Panther Party be revitalized in the 1990s?

JS: The Party can't be repeated because you can't use the same tactics in 1992 as we used in 1967, 1968, and 1970. A lot of the same issues that we addressed during that time we still have to address today, but we can't see really establishing the Black Panther Party using the same platform that we implemented in the late 1960s. Because in the nineties, it's a totally different era and time. So we can see that there will have to be new ideas applied to our current conditions.

CEJ: What is the legacy of the Black Panther Party?

JS: I would think it left a pretty strong legacy. I would have to say the learning center along with the free breakfast program because those were the two things that seemed to always surface. The school and the breakfast program were the two cornerstone projects of the Party.

Part III

Organizational Dynamics

Chapter Seven

"All Power to the People": The Political Thought of Huey P. Newton and The Black Panther Party

Floyd W. Hayes, III, and Francis A. Kiene, III

Recent events have rekindled interest in the Black Panther Party and the significance of its legacy. The absurd murder of Huey P. Newton in 1989 by a young Black man signifies the mounting despair and rage in urban Black America, resulting from the dehumanizing forces of economic impoverishment and social indifference. The concrete situation of dispossession brought the Black Panther Party into existence in the first place. Indeed, the circumstances under which Newton died demonstrate dramatically that urban Black America's economic and social conditions have continued to decline since the 1960s.

The appearance of three recent books has encouraged many to reexamine and reconsider the importance of the Black Panther Party. In *A Taste of Power: A Black Woman's Story*,[1] Elaine Brown writes about her personal development and later rise to power within the Party. The memoir also portrays the role of women in the organization. In another memoir, *This Side of Glory: The Autobiography of David Hilliard and the Story of the Black Panther Party*,[2] the former Black Panther Party Chief of Staff writes a courageous and sensitive account of his life inside and outside of the Party. He recounts personal and political triumph, defeat, and redemption. Both books provide insider views of the Black Panther Party's dynamics, successes, contradictions, and decline.

Hugh Pearson's text, *The Shadow of the Panther: Huey Newton and the Price of Black Power in America*,[3] in effect chronicles the underside of the Black Panther Party. Pearson attempts a cold-blooded, objective analysis of the Party, but his anger and disillusionment with various shadowy aspects of the Panthers seem to cause him to focus unevenly on Newton's and the Panthers' destructive and militaristic tendencies.

All three recent books describe and analyze the social conditions of the 1960s that gave rise to angry groups of urban Black youth who came together to form the Black Panther Party. It is significant that since the end of the 1960s, the social conditions of urban Black America have progressively worsened. America's continued indifference to its urban dispossessed has now produced a generation that is more disillusioned, isolated, angry, and understandably cynical and nihilistic than the generation that joined the Black Panther Party. Many of today's inner-city Black residents have no hope in America nor in themselves; hence, urban areas increasingly are becoming predatory communities where residents prey on each other in a desperate struggle to survive in a dreadful environment.

Similar to the Black Panthers a generation ago, today's urban Black dwellers continue to resist police brutality, racism, and harassment as they engage in angry discourse about the absurdity and despair of living in impoverished urban conditions that make inner city residents outsiders of the American social order. Significantly, the Panthers sought to educate, provoke, and transform American society. Contemporary urban Black youth, inspired by the emerging significance of Malcolm X, appear to have abandoned any expectation of a better future.[4] Hence, they direct mounting rage against each other as well as toward the racialization of power and privilege.

In the late 1960s, the Black Panther Party gained national attention as an organization of defiant young Black men and women committed to resisting by any means necessary what Malcolm X had called America's White power structure. Emerging within the crucible of the Black power movement, these urban revolutionaries symbolized the rejection of Martin Luther King, Jr., and the civil rights establishment's sterile theorizing and ineffectual strategies of nonviolent civil disobedience in the Northern setting.[5] Viewing urban Black communities as colonies occupied by a system of hostile White police, the Panthers fearlessly contested the power of the state to brutalize Black citizens.

Huey P. Newton became the Party's chief theoretician. As such, Newton and the Black Panther Party were central figures in the Black power movement and major contributors in the 1960s and 1970s to the debate over the condition of and proper goals and strategies for the Black population in America. Yet little scholarly work has concentrated on Newton's and the Panthers' political ideas. Therefore, the broad purpose of this paper is to examine, critically but sympathetically, some of the main currents of Newton's political thought and the Black Panther Party's ideology. More specifically, our aim is to probe the evolution of the Party's political ideas.

As a dimension of Black power ideology, Newton's thinking and the Black Panther Party's outlook are significant because they represent the continuation of a tradition of radical African American political thought, dating back at least to W. E. B. Du Bois, that attempts to view the Black struggle through the prism of race and class. Historically, American scholars have struggled with the relationship between the concepts of race and class in trying to understand and explain the changing character of their society.[6] So it was with Huey P. Newton and the Black Panther Party, for they also exhibited the ongoing tension regarding the proper balance between race and class analyses. Through an examination of the development of Newton's and the Panthers' political utterances concerning Black nationalism, revolutionary nationalism, revolutionary internationalism, and revolutionary intercommunalism, as well as the importance of armed struggle and the role of the lumpen proletariat within that struggle, we demonstrate that Newton and the Black Panther Party's efforts to merge aspects of race and class to develop a revolutionary theory and practice were hampered by both internal problems and external pressures facing the Panthers.

Significantly, we recognize the difficulty of dividing the Panthers' political discourse into stages of development. Indeed, we try to show that the Party's rapidly evolving ideas were not fundamental breaks but shifts in emphasis, especially with respect to the concepts of race and class. Although we employ a stages-of-development model for analyzing Newton's and the Panthers' political ideas, it is important not to view this process merely as a linear progression. Rather, the evolving character of their political perspectives is better understood as a dialectical interaction between Black nationalism and revolutionary intercommunalism resulting from the changing social conditions the Panthers confronted. Each transition to a new set of political views represented an attempt to resolve contradictions inherent in the previous system of ideas.

Founding of the Black Panther Party

Although the Civil Rights movement was mainly a Southern phenomenon, its middle-class orientation and nonviolent integrationist ideology became sources of increasing frustration and disillusionment for a broad segment of the Black population in America's Northern and Western cities. A perceived ineffectiveness of the Civil Rights movement in the face of an intransigent, anti-Black power structure served as a catalyst for the development of the more radical Black power movement out of which the Black Panther Party emerged. Huey Newton recalls in his autobiography *Revolutionary Suicide,*

> We had seen Martin Luther King come to Watts in an effort to calm the people and we had seen his philosophy of nonviolence rejected. Black people had been taught nonviolence; it was deep in us. What good, however, was nonviolence when the police were determined to rule by force?[7]

Thus Newton deemed it necessary to create an organization that would focus on the needs of ordinary people and involve members of the lower class. Influenced by Malcolm X's nationalism, Mao Tse-Tung's axiom of "picking up the gun," and Frantz Fanon's and Che Guevara's theories of revolutionary violence, Huey Newton and Bobby Seale founded the Black Panther Party for Self Defense in Oakland, California, in 1966. Newton and Seale planned the Party's platform and program, which Newton actually wrote, delineating "What We Want" and "What We Believe." The program's elements included self-determination for the Black community, decent housing, critical education, full employment for Black people, self defense and the end of police brutality in Black communities, and the freedom of Black prisoners.[8]

Marx and Engels were skeptical that the lumpen proletariat—the rogues, prostitutes, thieves, hustlers, murderers, gamblers, and paupers—could assist in the revolutionary transformation of capitalist society. However, the Panthers took a different position on the lumpen proletariat's role that proved to be one of the most controversial aspects of their political ideology and practice. On this issue, Huey Newton and Bobby Seale drew heavily from a reading of Frantz Fanon's discussion of the colonized lumpen proletariat's revolutionary potential in *The Wretched of the Earth*.[9] Although he employed a Marxian theory of revolutionary change, Fanon pointed out that it had to be sufficiently refashioned to fit the colonial situation. He contended that anticolonial insurrection emerged in the countryside and filtered into the cities by means of the peasantry or the lumpen proletariat who resided at the urban periphery:

> It is within this mass of humanity, this people of the shanty towns, at the core of the *lumpen proletariat* that the rebellion will find its urban spearhead. For the *lumpen proletariat*, that horde of starving men, uprooted from their tribe and from their clan, constitutes one of the most spontaneous and the most radically revolutionary forces of a colonized people.[10]

After introducing Huey Newton to Fanon's text, Bobby Seale saw that Newton grasped the significance of Fanon's view of the lumpen proletariat for organizing the brothers off the street—if the Panthers did not mobilize them, they would become an organized threat to the Panthers. Seale writes,

> Huey understood the meaning of what Fanon was saying about organizing the lumpen proletariat first, because Fanon explicitly pointed out that if you didn't organize the lumpen proletariat and give a base for organizing the brother who's pimping, the brother who's hustling, the unemployed, the downtrodden, the brother who's robbing banks, who's not politically conscious—that's what lumpen proletariat means—that if you didn't relate to these cats, the power structure would organize these cats against you.[11]

Newton, therefore, sought to reach and recruit into the Black Panther Party young men who were disaffected and dispossessed. He often talked about the collective significance of "street brothers," and his responsibility to and affinity with them. In Newton's view, they all shared the same alienation from the American system of oppression:

> The street brothers were important to me, and I could not turn away from the life shared with them. There was in them an intransigent hostility toward all those sources of authority that had such a

dehumanizing effect on the community. In school the "system" was the teacher, but on the block the system was everything that was not a positive part of the community. My comrades on the block continued to resist that authority, and I felt that I could not let college pull me away, no matter how attractive education was. These brothers had the sense of harmony and communion I needed to maintain that part of myself not totally crushed by the schools and other authorities.[12]

Moreover, in advocating the importance of the urban Black lumpen proletariat, Newton arrived at another significant conclusion. He explained that although the development of technology initially expands the middle and working classes, the perpetual specialization and sophistication of the oppressor's technology will ultimately diminish the need of a large labor force.[13] The introduction of computers and the increasing requirement for expertise necessary to operate the new machinery in the age of advanced technology threaten the survival and social development of those who lack the proper knowledge and skills. This understanding led Newton to consider the possibility that the working class could be transformed out of existence; their numbers would continue to decline, increasing the size of the lumpen proletariat.[14]

One of the Party's initial activities was an armed patrol of the Oakland police to ensure that Black residents were not brutalized and were informed of their rights. According to Newton, this effort was key to the Panther's ability to recruit members during the organization's early stages of development. Panthers would talk to the "street brothers" about their right to arm themselves, and the Party's application of this practice through patrolling the police impressed many in the community.[15] One of the most important functions of the Black Panther Party was to provide a number of community programs, which included the free breakfast for children, free health clinics, and liberation youth schools. Although the Panthers sought to portray an image of revolutionary urban guerrillas, it has been argued by some scholars that the Panthers' objectives, as stated in the platform and program, were actually more reformist than revolutionary.[16] Newton pointed out, however, that the Party's community programs were neither revolutionary nor reformist; rather, they were survival programs. He argued that for revolutionary transformation to occur in America, the people had to first possess a fundamental and supportive groundwork that would sustain their potential for existence.[17] Newton admitted that when the Party started in 1966, it maintained basically what were considered self-defense and Black nationalist philosophies.[18] Significantly, Newton's and the Party's ideological perspectives continued to evolve rapidly through several stages, each of which was accompanied by external and internal tensions.

Black Nationalism

Beginning in October 1966, the Black Panther Party initially stressed a race more than a class analysis of the Black situation in America. However, it is important to observe that even at this early stage of development

Newton's and the Party's ideas did not correspond exactly to the Black nationalist outlook as did other Black power organizations of this period, such as Maulana Karenga's Us organization in Los Angeles. Nowhere in the Panther platform and program is there a call for a Black nation; rather, they evaded this issue. In 1968, when Newton was in jail, he had added to Point Ten of the Party's platform, "What We Want," a statement related to the issue of a Black nation. Point Ten originally read: "We want land, bread, housing, education, clothing, justice and peace." To that, Newton added the following:

> And as our major political objective, a United Nations-supervised plebiscite to be held throughout the Black colony in which only Black colonial subjects will be allowed to participate, for the purposes of determining the will of Black people as to their national destiny.[19]

This addition was prompted by the thinking of the Panthers' Minister of Information Eldridge Cleaver, who himself was inspired by Malcolm X's enunciation of this idea. Regarding the issue of whether the Party supported racial integration or separation, Cleaver stated in July 1968 that the Party thought it "too premature" to decide which side it was on.[20] This seeming ambivalence on a basic element of Black nationalism does not, however, contradict the Party's Black nationalist orientation at this time.

The October 1966 Black Panther Party Platform and Program essentially was based on a Black nationalist perspective, for it emphasized the importance of racial solidarity. The document dealt solely with the problems, grievances, and demands of the dispossessed Black population. In this way, it acknowledged Black people's unique identity, which is a primary principle of Black nationalism. The first point of the program proclaims: "We believe that Black people will not be free until we are able to determine our destiny." Self-determination is the essence of the concept of a nation.

During the period when they implemented the police-alert patrols, the Panthers were concerned exclusively with defending Oakland's Black community from police harassment. This again encouraged a view of the Black community's unique and separate identity, which resulted from their oppression and dehumanization by a racialized power system. Other programs of the Party during this period were also largely Black nationalist. For example, the Junior Panther Program for the younger children in the Oakland community taught Black history and revolutionary principles so that these youngsters would "grow up to be men and defend their people in the Black community."[21]

Additionally, Black nationalist themes clearly were predominant in Huey Newton's early thinking. On the issue of Black insurrection, which characterized the nationalist aspirations of Black leaders, such as Denmark Vesey and Nat Turner during slavery, Newton states,

Black people must now move, from the grassroots up through the perfumed circles of the Black bourgeoisie, to seize by any means necessary a proportionate share of the power vested and collected in the structure of America. We must organize and unite to combat by long resistance the brutal force used against us daily.[22]

Here again, it is important to note that at this time Newton spoke exclusively of Black self-determination and of solidarity across class lines—a traditional Black nationalist theme.

In another essay, Newton acknowledges two historic Black nationalist leaders when he states: "Marcus Garvey and Malcolm X were two Black men of the twentieth century who posed an implacable challenge to both the oppressor and the endorsed spokesman that could not be dealt with in any other way than precisely the foul manner recorded by history."[23] Newton then goes on to point out how the Black Panther Party picked up the gun and how other people also should.

In yet another essay, Newton focuses on the Black male psyche. He argues that the Black man's life is "built on mistrust, shame, doubt, guilt, inferiority, role confusion, isolation, and despair." With such a life, the Black man "is dependent upon the White man ('THE MAN') to feed his family, to give him a job, educate his children, serve as the model that he tries to emulate . . . .He Hates 'The Man' and he hates himself. . . .What did he do to be so Black and blue?"[24] Again, the White man's emasculation of the Black man is a common and historic Black nationalist representation, and Black nationalist groups historically have stressed rehabilitation and revitalization of Black manhood. The image of Black aggressiveness and masculinity was the hallmark of the Panthers during the early stage of their development.

What are we to make of the Black Panther Party's early nationalist orientation as adumbrated in its October 1966 Ten-Point Program? One writer views this early statement as naive and reformist.[25] Another argues that the program was "more a statement of grievances and concessions demanded from the White power structure than it is a program to mobilize Black people in escalating struggle for control and power."[26]

Perhaps it would be better not to view the Ten-Point Program as the only guide for understanding the ideological basis of Black Panther actions, even though it was consistently printed on the next to the last page of the Party's weekly newspaper *The Black Panther*. The Panthers themselves acknowledged the unfinished character of the document. For instance, slain Chicago Black Panther leader Fred Hampton once stated: "Our ten point program is in the midst of being changed right now, because we used the word 'White' when we should have used the word 'capitalist.'"[27] Therefore, in order to discover and evaluate the ideological basis for the Panthers' actions, it is necessary to look beyond the Ten-Point Program to other writings and speeches, especially after the Panthers recognized in 1968 that their seemingly nationalist outlook was not sufficient to overturn the historic structures and processes of Black oppression, dehumanization, and dispossession. As a result of this realization, the Panthers modified their ideology and embraced a revolutionary nationalist position. They renounced any type of Black nationalism. As Bobby Seale once stated: "Our ideology is to be constantly moving, doing, solving, and attacking the real problems and the oppressive conditions we live under, while educating the masses of the people."[28]

In this early period, the Black Panthers' repudiation of Black nationalism was based on the continuing contradictions between race and class analyses of the Black situation. As their reading of and thinking about revolutionary literature evolved, Newton and the Panthers saw the increasing importance of class analysis and the limits of the narrow nationalist perspective for understanding the condition of Black and other oppressed people. Thus, the Panthers' disillusionment with what they perceived as reactionary nationalism prompted a transition to revolutionary nationalism.

Revolutionary Nationalism

Newton asserted that the Party adopted a nationalist ideology because they believed that some form of nationhood was the solution.[29] After analyzing history, the Party concluded that colonized people had fought off the yoke of oppression and exploitation in the past by establishing a nation comprising their own racial, ethnic, or cultural group. However, because Black people lacked the power to become a dominant faction in America, thereby making nationhood problematic, Newton was forced to reassess the Panther's nationalist position. This led to the development of revolutionary nationalism, which meant nationalism and socialism.

In *Revolutionary Suicide*, Newton explains that the transformation in his thinking from Black nationalism to socialism was a long and arduous process. While a student at Merritt College in Oakland, Newton supported Castro's Cuban revolution and was thus criticized by others and labeled a socialist. Nevertheless, he believed that if this was socialism, then socialism must be a cogent system of ideas. He was introduced to Marxism around the time of the Black Panther Party's founding through reading Lenin's *Materialism and Empirio-Criticism*.[30] Later, after finishing several volumes of Mao Tse-Tung, Newton embraced the socialist perspective. Summarizing his ideological transformation, he states: "It was my life plus independent reading that made me a socialist—nothing else."[31]

In a 1968 interview with *The Movement*, a White radical periodical, while he was in prison, Newton defined the Black Panther Party as a revolutionary nationalist organization. According to Newton, revolutionary nationalism depended upon "a people's revolution with the end goal being the people in power. Therefore, to be a revolutionary nationalist you would by necessity have to be a socialist."[32] This perspective included a definite role for White radicals, which as Newton defined it was "to first choose his friend and his enemy and after doing this, which it seems he's already done, then to not only articulate his desires to regain his moral standard and align himself with humanity, but also to put this into practice by attacking the protectors of the institutions."[33]

Extremely opposed to the Panthers' rapidly developing revolutionary nationalist perspective was the largely dominant cultural nationalist faction, whose position the Party called "pork chop nationalism." In Newton's words, cultural nationalism is

> a reaction instead of responding to political oppression. The cultural nationalists are concerned with returning to the old African culture and thereby regaining their identity and freedom. In other words, they feel that the African culture will automatically bring political freedom. Many times cultural nationalists fall into line as reactionary nationalists.[34]

According to Newton, an excellent example of reactionary nationalism was Haitian President Francois Duvalier. After kicking out the colonizers, he inserted himself into the role of the oppressor. A clear example of revolutionary nationalism, Newton declared, was the Algerian revolution that Frantz Fanon describes and analyzes in *The Wretched of the Earth*.[35] Significantly then, cultural nationalists view White people and racist oppression as the main enemies, while socialists see the capitalist class and economic exploitation as the primary antagonists. Therefore, as revolutionary nationalists, Newton and the Panthers asserted that their struggle centered on destroying the conditions that generated the twin evils of capitalism and racism.

As a developing revolutionary nationalist, Newton proposed that the Black Panther Party unite with the world's oppressed people who struggle for decolonization and liberation. In the 1960s, Newton, as did numerous other theorists, advanced the position that Black people in America were colonized in much the same way as the people of Africa, Asia, and Latin America, whose countries Western Europeans subjugated in the nineteenth century. Newton argued that the urban police force occupied Black communities in the same fashion that the United States military occupied areas of Vietnam. This was the legacy of the formation of the American political and economic system that was established largely by the violent appropriation of Native American lands and the exploitation of African slave labor. The dislocation and relocation of Africans and their American descendants, along with the dehumanization and exploitation of their labor, represent a form of colonialism—domestic or internal colonialism.[36] It was from a sense of solidarity with other colonized peoples that Newton determined that the Panthers should work with White leftists. This was a significant departure from cultural nationalism.

The Panthers and White Leftists

The Black Panther Party's initial alliance with a White leftist group was with the Peace and Freedom Party in December 1967. This association began in the narrow interest of seeking support to free imprisoned Huey Newton, but it then expanded to include the larger issue of Black liberation within the ideological context of class struggle. The alliance between the Black Panther Party and the Peace and Freedom Party marked the first definite move of the Panthers from a quasi-nationalist to a revolutionary socialist position. As Earl Anthony observes, the controversial alliance with the Peace and Freedom Party also "marked the end of our honeymoon in the Black community in general, and the Black liberation movement in particular. Since 1966 the *modus operandi* of the movement had been to exclude whites. The coalition came in for sharp criticism, publicly and privately, from many quarters."[37]

The alliance, nevertheless, seemed to serve the purposes of the Black Panther Party well. It provided the necessary financial and administrative resources to mount and support the Free Huey Movement. It appears doubtful that the Panthers would have been able to make the Free Huey Movement a *cause celebre* around the country without the supportive machinery and resources of the Peace and Freedom Party. Most Black nationalists feared co-optation in dealing with White organizations. Indeed, if anyone was co-opted in this alliance, it was perhaps the Peace and Freedom Party rather than the Panthers. The influence the Black Panther Party had over the Peace and Freedom Party is suggested by the many Panther leaders who became Peace and Freedom Party candidates for elective office.

Other White leftist groups with which the Panthers had alliances include the Students for a Democratic Society (SDS) and the Gay Liberation Front. At their national council meeting in Austin, Texas, on March 30, 1969, SDS declared its support for the Black Panther Party and passed resolutions to implement that support—by formation of Newton–Cleaver Defense Committees, the printing and distribution of information about the history and development of Black Panther Party programs, and the development and/or strengthening of informal and formal relations with the Panthers.[38]

In a special "Letter from Huey to the Revolutionary Brothers and Sisters about the Women's Liberation and Gay Liberation Movements," Newton calls for the formation of a working coalition with these two groups. To those who opposed the full participation of these groups at revolutionary conferences, rallies, and demonstrations, Newton admonishes,

> Remember, we haven't established a revolutionary value system; we're only in the process of establishing it. I don't remember us ever constituting any value that said that a revolutionary must say offensive things towards homosexuals, or that a revolutionary should make sure that women do not speak out about their own particular kind of oppression. Matter of fact, it's just the opposite: [W]e say that we recognize the women's right to be free. We haven't said much about the homosexual at all, and we must relate to the homosexual movement because it's a real thing. And I know through reading and through my life experience, my observations, that homosexuals are not given

freedom and liberty by anyone in the society. Maybe they might be the most oppressed people in the society.[39]

The Panthers organized these and other radical groups into a National Committee to Combat Fascism at a three-day conference in Oakland, California in July 1969. This association became the most important mechanism for Panther alliances with White groups. Led by Panthers, there were some twenty-five hundred participants, including Students for a Democratic Society, the Young Patriots, Brown Berets, Young Lords, and the Communist Party. The principal proposal of the conference was community control of the police—an issue that dated back to the early days of the Panthers' self-defense activities against police harassment. At this conference, the Panthers had definitely moved beyond a Black nationalist orientation to a class position.[40]

Although not without some contradictions, these various alliances were valuable to the Panthers in providing an assortment of financial and material resources that were otherwise unobtainable. However, as has been indicated, these alliances cost the Panthers a significant loss of credibility within many Black communities, particularly among those with a Black nationalist orientation. Moreover, the Panthers' relations with White leftists were often turbulent and even conflictual. Some White radicals disrespected the intellectual and theoretical leadership of the Panthers, while others literally betrayed them.[41] In some quarters, it seemed that the Panthers were overly concerned with gaining White allies, which drove away some Black allies, and they needed both Black and White allies alike. Many Black Panther Party rallies were attended largely by White radicals and their supporters. This application of the Panthers' revolutionary nationalist orientation and their alliances with White leftists engendered negative reactions in some sectors of the Black community.

Clashes with Cultural Nationalism

Perhaps most influential in the Panthers' strong critical reaction to cultural nationalism were the often deadly conflicts and rivalries they had with various other Black nationalist formations. In establishing their power in the Bay Area during the early days, the Panthers neutralized the influence of other Black nationalist organizations. The first group the Panthers clashed with was the Black nationalist association at the Black House in San Francisco. Eldridge Cleaver had been one of the co-founders of the Black House, which was basically culturally oriented. Prominent figures at the Black House were Black playwrights Amiri Baraka and Ed Bullins. According to Earl Anthony, Black House "was not predisposed to the politics of the Black Panther Party for Self-Defense and had been most critical of the actions of the Party."[42] In response, armed Panthers entered the Black House and gave notice that its members were evicted. "They left the premises, and the Black House was then occupied by [the] Black Panther Party for Self-Defense."[43]

Besides the cultural nationalists of the Black House, the Panthers confronted the members of another Black political organization in San Francisco that called themselves the Black Panther Party of Northern California. Contending that the political struggle was the first priority, this San Francisco-based group accused the Oakland Panthers of being prematurely paramilitary. In contrast, the Newton group believed, following the maxim of Chairman Mao Tse-Tung of China, that "political power grows out of the barrel of the gun."[44] By the end of 1967, the San Francisco-based Panthers had faded from the scene.[45]

Perhaps the most serious and deadliest conflict between the Panthers and a Black nationalist formation was with Los Angeles community leader Maulana Karenga and his Us organization.[46] In search of more support for the Party and the Free Huey Movement, in 1968 the Panthers established an office in the area of Los Angeles where Karenga's organization flourished. Us was a Black cultural nationalist organization under the leadership of Maulana Karenga that emerged after the 1965 Watts insurrection. His members were highly disciplined with a strong commitment to his nationalist ideas. The leading cadre of his organization was the Simba Wachuka (Swahili for *Young Lions*), an army of skillfully trained young men.[47] Earl Anthony, then a captain of the BPP, observed what was destined to be a tragic development:

> At that time the Los Angeles "turf" was almost the exclusive domain of Us, since there were no organization or individual within or without the Black Congress which was strong enough to be its equal politically or militarily. But the Panthers soon began to gain strength and challenge its power, and the first signs of bad blood developed. This rivalry was to develop into a power struggle of tragic proportions.[48]

Disagreements between the Black Panther Party and Us did indeed reach serious dimensions in January 1969. A collision occurred in the context of the campus-based Black Student Union's participation in the selection of a director for the new Black Studies Program at the University of California at Los Angeles. Members of both the Panthers and Us were students in UCLA's High Potential Program—a special entry enterprise for African American, Latino, Asian American, and Native American students who were bright but underachievers in past educational pursuits. The "turf" conflict between the Panthers and Us spilled over to UCLA's campus as both organizations sought to influence the Black Student Union and its agenda.

As a member of the Black Student Union's Community Advisory Committee, Maulana Karenga had participated in the early stages of planning and discussion regarding the selection of the Black Studies Program director. There was no Panther representation. Yet, as a result of their own struggle for a power base at UCLA, both Us and the Panthers came to have substantial stakes in who was chosen director. John Huggins and Alprentice (Bunchy) Carter, both students in the High Potential Program, headed the

Panther contingent at UCLA. A change in the leadership of the Black Student Union resulted in Huggins' later involvement in the Black Studies Program selection process. As the relative influence of the Panthers on the UCLA campus increased in proportion to that of Us, the ongoing tension between these two organizations exploded into an unrelenting power struggle. It all culminated in a bloody shoot-out on January 17, 1969, when three Us members shot and killed Huggins and Carter following a Black Student Union meeting.[49] In the ensuing years, at least two other Panthers were killed in confrontations with members of the Us organization.

The conflict with the Us organization strengthened the Panthers' practical and ideological hostility to cultural nationalism and reinforced their commitment to Marxist Leninism. Hence, the Panthers sought to create a strong vanguard party that went well beyond the Black nationalist world view. They placed Marxism and Leninism in an ideological pantheon along with the ideas and contributions of Che Guevera and Mao Tse-Tung, which were interpreted through the prism of Huey P. Newton. As this development proceeded, social conditions and the character of their overall struggle encouraged the Panthers to embrace a more global view of social revolution.

Toward Revolutionary Internationalism

Although the Panthers kept their revolutionary nationalist views fairly intact during Huey Newton's imprisonment, that changed upon his release in August 1970. Reflecting the impact of an increasingly global consciousness on his thinking, Newton once again transformed the Black Panther ideology but retained the basic elements of revolutionary nationalism as far as coalition politics was concerned. The new Panther ideology represented a transition to revolutionary internationalism.

Newton's new thinking was based on the view that the United States was no longer a nation but an empire that dominated the entire world. Accordingly, the bourgeoisie that Marxist-Leninist adherents sought to defeat was international in character, and Newton believed that "the only way we can combat an international enemy is through an international strategy, unity of all people who are exploited, who will overthrow the international bourgeoisie, and replace it with a dictatorship by the proletariat, the workers of the world."[50] From this perspective, national movements for liberation were to be supported as long as they were also internationalist. Newton declared: "If they are nationalist alone then they are chauvinist. If they are both nationalist and international, they realize that their interests are the same as every other people's interests who are fighting against imperialism."[51]

Of the nationalist aspirations of Black people, Newton believed that their history contradicted any demand for nationhood:

> We feel that Black people in America have a moral right to claim nationhood because we are a colonized people. But history won't allow us to claim nationhood, because it has bestowed an obligation upon us; to take socialist development to its final stage, to rid the world of the

imperialist threat, the threat of the capitalist and the warmonger. Once he is destroyed then there will be no need for nationhood, because the nations won't need to defend themselves against imperialism.[52]

Thus, Newton's concept of revolutionary internationalism suggested the ultimate destruction of nationhood itself so that humankind would develop a sense of mutual friendship throughout the world. To the extent that it called for the solidarity of the "Third World" against Western imperialism, the Black Panthers' internationalist ideas were compatible with other internationalist views, such as those advocated by Pan-Africanist Stokely Carmichael [now Kwame Ture]. The basic difference was that even though Pan-Africanism incorporated an appreciation of Marxist theory and had a global outlook, it did not discount nationalism. Moreover, the Panthers interpreted the Pan-Africanist emphasis on nationalism as synonymous with racial chauvinism, a perspective the revolutionary internationalist Panthers sought to discredit.

The Party took some steps to implement the theory of revolutionary internationalism. Newton offered the National Liberation Front and Provisional Revolutionary Government of South Vietnam an undetermined number of troops to assist in their fight against American imperialism. Nguyen Thi Dinh, Deputy commander of the South Vietnamese People's Liberation Armed Forces, accepted the offer in the following manner: "With profound gratitude, we take notice for your enthusiastic proposal; when necessary, we shall call for your volunteers to assist us."[53]

Newton came under heavy criticism in the United States from such people as Roy Wilkins, the veteran civil rights leader, who questioned Newton's commitment to the advancement of poor urban and rural Black Americans. Newton responded by explaining his ideology of internationalism: "We are internationalist because our struggle must proceed on many fronts. While we feed and clothe the poor at home, we must meet and attack the oppressor wherever he may be found."[54]

In a further attempt to put into practice their theory of revolutionary internationalism, the Panthers officially opened an International Section of the Black Panther Party in Algiers, the capital of Algeria, on September 13, 1970. Algiers had become somewhat of a refuge for fugitive Panthers ever since Eldridge Cleaver surfaced there in June 1969 and was subsequently joined by his wife Kathleen. They and other Panthers there sought to communicate with and issue statements supporting liberation movements in North Korea, North Vietnam, and China.

Revolutionary Intercommunalism: A Higher Phase of Marxist Utopianism

In the face of changing world dynamics, the Panthers' effort to refine the concept of internationalism resulted in a transition to revolutionary intercommunalism. This new ideology was put forward at the turbulent September 1970 Revolutionary People's Constitutional Convention in Philadelphia.

The idea of intercommunalism grew out of the Panthers' fundamental ideological position in internationalism—that the United States was not a nation but an empire that dominated and exploited the world, and that United States imperialism had transformed other nations into oppressed communities: "If a nation cannot protect its boundaries and prevent the entry of an aggressor, if a nation cannot control its political structure and its cultural institutions, then it is no longer a nation, it must be something else."[55] According to the Panthers, this something else—oppressed communities of the world—pointed out serious limitations of both the nationalist and internationalist perspectives. Therefore, the Panthers said: "We must place our future hopes upon the philosophy of intercommunalism."[56] The oppressed peoples of the world needed to work together to overthrow United States capitalism and imperialism under the banner of revolutionary intercommunalism.

As with other Panther ideas, the shift to intercommunalism seemed more of a change in emphasis rather than a complete departure from or break with the Party's earlier internationalist position. Thus, revolutionary intercommunalism stressed the existence of exploited and oppressed global communities and their need for collective revolutionary emancipation. With a flourish of Marxist utopianism, the end goal of intercommunalism was idealistic—nothing short of global socialism was sought. Going beyond revolutionary internationalism, the new ideological position stressed egalitarianism and looked forward, in theory at least, to the abolition of invidious social class distinctions. Reminiscent of Marx's 1875 *Critique of the Gotha Program*, each and every person would be able to take up his or her position in the general division of labor. The Panthers wrote: "We pledge ourselves to end imperialism and distribute the wealth of the world to all the people of the world. We foresee a system of true communism where all people produce according to their abilities and all receive according to their needs."[57]

If there was a cultural lag between the destruction of the oppressive state apparatus and the erection of the new world order based on revolutionary intercommunalism, the Panthers called for "all people in the communities throughout the world to be represented in decision making and participation in direct proportion to their presence in the population under consideration."[58] This call seemed to be a somewhat disguised assent to nationalism in the aftermath of a global socialist revolution. In retrospect, revolutionary intercommunalism was the Panthers' attempt to adapt Marxism to the dynamics of the rapidly changing world of the 1970s. Global class struggle by the world's lumpen proletariat against the world's bourgeoisie and its managerial apparatus (United States imperialism and capitalism) was the means to bring about a new world order—a global, egalitarian community based on socialism. Given this set of circumstances, Newton saw the role of the Black Panther Party as exposing imperialist antagonisms and raising the people's consciousness to the point of undertaking revolutionary social action.[59]

Conclusion

As this essay has shown, the Black Panther Party was an organization whose ideas and activities were in constant evolution in the effort to confront the dynamic character of local, national, and international change and development. The progressive development of Huey P. Newton's and the Panthers' political thought—Black nationalism, revolutionary nationalism, revolutionary internationalism, revolutionary intercommunalism, and the revolutionary role of the lumpen proletariat—represented an effort by a generation of young, dispossessed, and defiant Black Americans to formulate a theory and practice of fundamental social transformation. As their assessment and analysis evolved with respect to Black oppression, specifically, and social domination, generally, the political ideas of Newton and the Panthers changed accordingly.

In some ways, however, the rapidly advancing character of Newton's and the Panthers' thinking proved problematic. Often ideological shifts were not accompanied by sufficient political education so that rank-and-file Panthers could understand fully the new set of ideas. This organizational weakness contributed in some respects to the Party's internal instability. Additionally, the content of ideological changes contributed to problems the Panthers had with rival organizations, especially Black nationalist groups. As discussed in this essay, the Panthers' repudiation of nationalism and embracing of socialism added to mounting ideological conflicts with Maulana Karenga's Us organization and other nationalist groups. It needs to be pointed out, however, that the Black power movement witnessed hard-line ideological positions taken by nearly all politically militant and insurgent theorists, activists, and organizations. Almost everyone despised ideological deviation. This undermined the larger struggle for social justice and human liberation.

The decline and destruction of the Black power movement and the Black Panther Party, brought about by internal fissures and government infiltration and repression, interrupted and redirected the thinking and actions of one of the major Black insurgent formations of the last half of the twentieth century.[60] Emerging in the urban areas of a nation that was largely indifferent to the historic structures and processes of cultural domination, anti-Black racism, and economic dispossession, the idealistic and angry young men and women of the Black Panther Party represented a serious threat, if only for a short time, to the American social order and its system of governance. Viewing themselves as a revolutionary vanguard organization of oppressed urban Black communities, the Panthers seized political space to speak audaciously to the people and to the powerful about justice, liberation, self-determination, and revolution. Arguing that in order to destroy the conditions that engendered ignorance and poverty, the dispossessed themselves needed to take hold of the reins of power, the Panthers demanded the transformation of power relationships within American society and throughout the world.

Yet, three decades after the Panthers fearlessly championed a system of radical social change, the inequitable socio-economic conditions against which they struggled continue and indeed, are worsening for many urban communities in the winding down of industrial manufacturing in advanced capitalism and the expansion of knowledge-based and technically advanced information industries in the post-industrial order.[61] Growing disillusionment, increasing hopelessness, intensifying meaninglessness, and mounting rage have converted many urban communities into predatory zones where residents turn on each other in a desperate and self-destructive attempt to survive in a society that is indifferent to their impoverishment. This often anarchical situation—much worse than the one from which the Panthers emerged thirty years ago—cries out for a positive alternative. Can Huey Newton's and the Panthers' legacy of radical and emancipatory political ideas in the struggle for survival be retrieved on the brink of the twenty-first century? For those suffering intense alienation and despair, the effort to resist social pessimism becomes supreme.

NOTES

1. Elaine Brown, *A Taste of Power: A Black Woman's Story* (New York: Pantheon Books, 1992).

2. David Hilliard and Lewis Cole, *This Side of Glory: The Autobiography of David Hilliard and the Story of the Black Panther Party* (Boston: Little, Brown and Company, 1993).

3. Hugh Pearson, *The Shadow of the Panther: Huey Newton and the Price of Black Power in America* (Reading: Addison-Wesley Publishing Company, 1994).

4. See Mark Baldassare, ed., *The Los Angeles Riots: Lessons for the Urban Future* (Boulder: Westview Press, 1994); Dhoruba Bin Wahad, Mumia Abu-Jamal, and Assata Shakur, *Still Black, Still Strong: Survivors of the U.S. War Against Black Revolutionaries* (New York: Semiotext(e), 1993); Leon Bing, *Do or Die*, (New York: Harper Collins, 1991); Kody Scott, *Monster: The Autobiography of a L.A. Gang Member* (New York: Penguin Books, 1993); Robert Gooding-Williams, ed., *Reading Rodney King, Reading Urban Uprising* (New York: Routledge, 1993).

5. For a recent analysis of the Black power movement, see William L. Van Deburg, *New Day in Babylon: The Black Power Movement and American Culture* (Chicago: The University of Chicago Press, 1992).

6. See Oliver C. Cox, *Caste, Class and Race: A Study in Social Dynamics*, (New York: Monthly Review Press, 1948); Harold Cruse, *The Crisis of the Negro Intellectual* (New York: William Morrow & Company, Inc., 1967).

7. Huey P. Newton, *Revolutionary Suicide* (New York: Writers and Readers Publishing, Inc., 1995), 110.

8. See Philip S. Foner, ed., *The Black Panthers Speak* (Philadelphia: J. B. Lippincott Company, 1970); August Meier, Elliott Rudwick, and Francis L. Brokerick, eds., "Interview with Huey Newton," *Black Protest Thought in the Twentieth Century* (New York: Macmillan Publishing Company, 1971), 495–515.

9. Frantz Fanon, *The Wretched of the Earth* (New York: Grove Press, Inc., 1963), 129-130.

10. Ibid., 103.

11. Bobby Seale, *Seize the Time: The Story of the Black Panther Party and Huey P. Newton* (Baltimore: Black Classic Press, 1991), 30.

12. Newton, *Revolutionary Suicide*, 73–74.

13. Newton, *To Die for the People: The Writings of Huey P. Newton* (New York: Random House, 1972); Newton and Erik H. Erikson, *In Search of Common Ground: Conversations with Erik H. Erikson and Huey P. Newton* (New York: W. W. Norton and Company, 1973).

14. Ibid.

15. Newton, *Revolutionary Suicide,* 73–74.

16. See Manning Marable, "The Legacy of Huey P. Newton," *The Crisis of Color and Democracy* (Monroe: Common Courage Press, 1992), 202–6; for a critique of the Black power movement as a whole, see Harold Cruse, *Rebellion or Revolution* (New York: William Morrow and Company, 1968).

17. Newton, *To Die for the People,* 66–68.

18. Newton and Erikson, *In Search of Common Ground,* 27.

19. Black Panther Party, "What We Want, What We Believe," *The Black Panthers Speak*, ed. Foner, 3–4.

20. Seale, *Seize the Time*, 63; Gene Marine, *The Black Panthers* (New York: New American Library, 1969), 185.

21. Seale, *Seize the Time*, 105.

22. *The Black Panther*, 20 June 1967, 2.

23. Ibid., 3 July 1967, 10.

24. Ibid., 15 May 1967, 18.

25. Marable, "The Legacy of Huey P. Newton," 202–203.

26. James Boggs, *Racism and the Class Struggle: Further Notes from a Black Worker's Notebook* (New York: Monthly Review Press, 1970), 183.

27. Foner, ed., *The Black Panthers Speak*, 143.

28. Seale, *Seize the Time*, 426.

29. Newton, *To Die for the People*, 31–32.

30. See Henry Hampton and Steve Fayer, *Voices of Freedom: An Oral History of the Civil Rights Movement From the 1950s Through the 1980s* (New York: Bantam Books, 1990).

31. Newton, *Revolutionary Suicide*, 70.

32. Foner, ed. *The Black Panthers Speak*, 50.

33. Ibid, 55.

34. Newton, *To Die for the People*, 92; Foner, ed., *The Black Panthers Speak*, 50.

35. Newton, *To Die for the People*; Foner, ed. *The Black Panthers Speak*; Meier, Rudwick, and Broderick, "Interview with Huey Newton," 495–515.

36. See Robert L. Allen, *Black Awakening in Capitalist America: An Analytic History* (Garden City: Doubleday & Company, 1969); Robert Blauner, "Internal Colonialism and Ghetto Revolt," *Social Problems* 16, 4 (Spring 1969): 393–408; Stokely Carmichael and Charles Hamilton, *Black Power: The Politics of Liberation in America* (New York: Random House, 1967); John O'Dell, "A Special Variety of Colonialism," *Freedomways* 7, 7 (Winter 1967), 7–15.

37. Earl Anthony, *Picking Up the Gun: A Report on the Black Panthers* (New York: The Dial Press, 1970), 28.

38. See *Guardian*, 19 April 1969; reprinted in Foner, ed., *The Black Panthers Speak*, 228–229.

39. *The Black Panther*, 21 August 1970, 5.

40. *Newsweek*, 4 August 1969, 35.

41. See Hilliard, *This Side of Glory*, 257–258.

42. Anthony, *Picking Up the Gun*, 21.

43. Ibid, 21; Amiri Baraka Interview with Floyd W. Hayes, III, West Lafayette, Indiana, 28 September, 1994.

44. Mao Tse-Tung. *Quotations from Chairman Mao Tse-Tung* (Peking, China: Foreign Languages Press, 1972), 58.

45. Anthony, *Picking Up the Gun*, 23.

46. Maulana Karenga, *The Roots of the Us-Panther Conflict: The Perverse and Deadly Games Police Play* (San Diego: Kawaida Publications, 1976).

47. Van Deburg, *New Day in Babylon*, 174.

48. Anthony, *Picking Up the Gun*, 73. David Hilliard and Elaine Brown also describe the Panthers' tension-filled experiences with Maulana Karenga and the Us organization; see Hilliard, *This Side of Glory*, 237–40 and Brown, *A Taste of Power*, ch. 8.

49. Gail Sheehy, "Black Against Black: The Agony of Panthermania," *New Yorker*, 16 November 1970, 45–50.

50. *The Black Panther,* 16 January 1971, 10.

51. Ibid.

52. Ibid.

53. *The Black Panther*, 19 January 1971, 10–11.

54. Ibid., 26 September 1970, 12–13.

55. Ibid., 5 December 1970, 7–8.

56. Ibid. Hilliard also discusses the meaning and significance of revolutionary intercommunalism in *This Side of Glory*, 52.

57. Ibid, 8.

58. Ibid.

59. Newton and Erikson, *In Search of Common Ground,* 25–32.

60. See Charles E. Jones, "The Political Repression of the Black Panther Party, 1966–1977: The Case of the Oakland Bay Area," *Journal of Black Studies* 18, 4 (June 1988): 415–34; Karenga, *The Roots of Us–Panther Conflict*; Newton, "War Against the Panthers: A Study of Repression in America"(Ph.D. diss., University of California at Santa Cruz, 1980); Kenneth O'Reilly, *Racial Matters: The FBI's Secret File on Black America, 1960–1972* (New York: The Free Press, 1989).

61. William A. Darity, Jr., and Samuel L. Myers, Jr., with Emmett Darson and William Sabol, *The Black Underclass: Critical Essays on Race and Unwantedness* (New York: Garland Publishing, Inc., 1994).

Chapter Eight

"Serving the People": The Survival Programs of the Black Panther Party

JoNina M. Abron

While speaking about the Black Panther Party (BPP) to college students in a Black American literature class, I was reminded once again that the establishment news media, historians, and political scientists have not provided a full treatment of the BPP. The students (of various ethnic backgrounds) with whom I spoke were surprised yet pleased to learn that the Black Panthers fed hungry children, escorted senior citizens to banks to cash their checks, administered a model elementary school, and tested people for the rare blood disease, sickle cell anemia.[1] Unfortunately, these community service activities lacked the sensationalism of the gun battles between police and BPP members. Not surprisingly, the only recollection of the BPP for many of the students was the Party's confrontations with law enforcement officials. Heretofore, the Panther survival programs have received minimal popular and scholarly attention.

First, this essay addresses the theoretical underpinnings of the survival programs. Secondly, the specific projects constituting the survival programs are described, and finally the essay assesses the impact of the survival programs. From 1972 to 1981, as a member of the Black Panther Party and the last editor of *The Black Panther Intercommunal News Service*, I participated in many of the various survival programs and knew the importance of these service projects to their recipients. It is hoped that this essay proves useful to contemporary young African American activists.

Theoretical Underpinnings

A key philosophical pillar of the Black Power Era of 1965–1975 was the concept of Black self-determination. In the classic treatise, *Black Power: The Politics of Liberation In America,* Black power theorists Kwame Ture (formerly Stokely Carmichael) and Charles V. Hamilton wrote, "Black people in America must get themselves together. [Black Power] is about black people taking care of business—the business of and for black people...If we succeed, we will exercise control over our lives, politically, economically and psychically."[2] To gain such control, Ture and Hamilton urged Black communities to develop experimental programs "out of day-to-day work, out of interaction between organizers and the communities in which they work."[3] The Black Panther Party's survival programs rested upon this idea of self-determination. Panthers established a network of community service projects designed to improve the life chances of African American people. Institutional racism relegated a disproportionate number of African Americans to deplorable housing, poor health care services, an unresponsive criminal justice system, inadequate diets, and substandard education. The Party's survival programs aimed to help black people overcome the devastating effects of racism and capitalism. Panther officials explained,

> [T]he programs, which cover such diverse areas as health care and food services as well as a model school, the Intercommunal Youth Institute, are meant to meet the needs of the community until we all can move to change social conditions that make it impossible for the people to afford the things they need and desire.[4]

In 1971, these community service projects were formally defined as survival programs by Huey P. Newton. However, long before this official pronouncement, many of the specific projects of the survival programs were originally developed by various Panther affiliates to meet the immediate needs of their respective communities. For example, the Party's armed police patrols in Oakland dated back to October 1966, while the Seattle branch initiated one of the early free breakfast programs in 1968.

Political activism constitutes the second pillar undergirding the Party's survival programs. Newton placed a premium on political action to organize the community. He recalled, "When we formed the Party, we did so because we wanted to put theory and practice together in a systematic manner."[5] The desire to serve and empower African American people guided the operations of the survival programs. Dr. Kim Kit Holder, former New York Panther, writes in his dissertation that "[T]he BPP believed that by setting an example with their survival programs they could serve the people as well as demonstrate to them the method of developing people's (community controlled) institutions."[6] Critics, however, contend that the Party abandoned its original revolutionary objective with the adoption of the survival programs. Bobby Seale countered this misperception:

> A lot of people misunderstand the politics of these programs; some people have a tendency to call them reform programs. They're not reform programs; they're actually revolutionary community programs. A revolutionary program is one set forth by revolutionaries, by those who want to change the existing system to a better system. A reform program is set up by the existing exploitative system as an appeasing handout to fool the people and keep them quiet.[7]

Huey Newton explained further,

> We called them survival programs pending revolution...They were designed to help the people survive until their consciousness is raised, which is only the first step in the revolution to produce a new America...During a flood the raft is a life-saving device, but it is only a means of getting to higher ground. So, too, with survival programs, which are emergency services. In themselves they do not change social conditions, but they are life-saving vehicles until conditions change.[8]

Nevertheless, Newton's decision to emphasize community service projects did create intra-organizational strife in 1971. Some members, including Eldridge Cleaver, favored an offensive military policy over the self-help activities of the survival programs. This tactical disagreement, which was exacerbated by the FBI counterintelligence program, ultimately led to the death of several Party members.[9] From 1966–1982, the BPP instituted a host of specific community service projects.[10] The survival projects included police-alert patrols, *The Black Panther Intercommunal News Service*, the breakfast for children program, free medical clinics, the Oakland Community School, free busing to prisons, the free food program, the free clothing and shoes programs, the free ambulance program, sickle cell anemia testing, Seniors Against a Fearful Environment (S.A.F.E.), and the free pest control program. These various community activities are easily categorized into four social policy areas: human sustenance, health, education, and criminal justice.

Human Sustenance

In order to fully develop the human capital of a community, the day-to-day needs of the people must be addressed. Party members understood that in order to maximize one's potential, personal safety, nourishment, and adequate health care were paramount. Unfortunately, for many African Americans, this was not the case. Consequently, the BPP implemented programs to enhance the life chances of the impoverished sector of the African American community. In one of his early political statements, "In Defense of Self-Defense," Newton described the relationship between politics and the material needs of the Black community:

> The masses of Black people have always been deeply entrenched and involved in the basic necessities of life. They have not had time to abstract their situation. Abstractions come only with leisure. The people have not had the luxury of leisure. Therefore, the people have been very aware of the true definition of politics: politics are merely the desire of individuals and groups to satisfy first, their basic needs—food, shelter and clothing, and security for themselves and their loved ones.[11]

Classical philosophers such as Thomas Hobbes note the importance of personal and group security in the formation of the polity.[12] The Party underscored this critical need when it formed the police–alert patrols in 1966. The first, and perhaps the most controversial survival program, the police–alert patrol, aimed to counter the pervasive police brutality in the Black community of Oakland, California. Indeed, the eradication of police brutality was the catalyst which led to the formation of the Black Panther Party for Self-Defense in 1966. Point No. 7 of the BPP Platform demanded "an immediate end to POLICE BRUTALITY and MURDER of Black people" and urged African Americans to form armed self-defense groups to fight "racist police oppression and brutality."[13]

In 1966, California statute permitted an individual to carry a loaded gun in public as long as it was not concealed and did not have a bullet in the chamber. Huey, Bobby, and other Panthers—armed with loaded weapons, cameras, law books, and tape recorders—monitored the police in the Black community of Oakland. These Panther community patrols prevented incidents of police harassment and advised detained suspects of their legal rights. An avid student of the law, Huey gained a reputation for facing down police officers with a loaded shotgun, and for his mastery of the law.[14] The police patrols gained the Party notoriety and respect within the Black community. Of course, this activity also earned the enmity of the police. Furthermore, the police–alert patrols served as a recruiting mechanism during the BPP's formative years. The Party's success in Richmond, California, is a case in point. In April 1967, twenty-two-year-old Denzil Dowell was shot to death by a White deputy sheriff in Richmond. The Dowell family asked the Panthers to investigate the death of Denzil, which was officially ruled a justifiable homicide. The Party organized a series of rallies in which a delegation of "twenty Panthers out there armed with guns, disciplined, standing thirty or forty feet apart on every corner of the intersection were in full view of the local police."[15] Seale recalls, "[w]e were educating the people that we would die for them. This was the position we always took with brother Huey. P. Newton."[16] He further reported that "...just about everybody out there joined the Party that day."[17]

An extension of the Party's original vision to defend the Black community was the creation of the Seniors Against A Fearful Environment (S.A.F.E.) program. The safety of senior citizens was at great peril. One study reported that over a six week period "[o]f the combined total of 249 victims of strong-arm robbery and purse snatching, 48% of the victims (118) were over the age of 50."[18] During Bobby Seale's 1972–1973 mayoral campaign and Elaine Brown's city council bid, the BPP initiated the S.A.F.E. program. In response to a request from a group of senior citizens, the BPP provided free transportation and an escort service. These services permitted the elderly to cash their Social Security and pension checks as well as take care of other monthly errands. When the program started, Seale announced "[T]he Black Panther Party is demanding that muggers and would-be muggers stop these acts. We're calling upon the community to support the program and look out for the welfare of our elderly citizens; if it had not been for senior citizens, we would not be here."[19] S.A.F.E. successfully lobbied the Oakland City

Housing Authority to make major repairs and clean up a low-income residence for senior citizens in downtown Oakland.

Party members mobilized and empowered people by ensuring that the community was informed. Emory Douglas, former BPP Minister of Culture, recounted that "Huey compared the Party's need for a publication with the armed struggle of the Vietnamese. He said that the Vietnamese carried mimeograph machines wherever they went to produce flyers and other literature to spread the word about their fight to free their country. The Party needed to have a newspaper so we could tell our own story."[20] Published April 25, 1967, the inaugural issue of the Party's newspaper, *The Black Panther Community News Service*, was a four-page mimeographed sheet devoted to the death of Denzil Dowell and police brutality in Black America. First published as a monthly paper, *The Black Panther* became a weekly publication in January 1968. The combative editorial of the first issue of *The Black Panther* set the tone of the newspaper for the next four years. After listing the "questionable facts" concerning the police shooting of Denzil Dowell, the editorial stated:

> [T]he white cop is the instrument sent into our community by the Power structure to keep Black people quiet and under control...it is time that Black People start moving in a direction that will free our communities from this form of outright brutal oppression. The BLACK PANTHER PARTY FOR SELF-DEFENSE has worked out a program that is carefully designed to cope with this situation.[21]

Eldridge Cleaver, one of the BPP's most controversial leaders, was the first editor of *The Black Panther*. In December 1966, two months after the founding of the Party, he was paroled from prison as the author of the critically acclaimed, national bestseller *Soul on Ice*. Several months later, Huey invited Eldridge to join the BPP, and Cleaver subsequently became the Party's Minister of Information. During Cleaver's editorship, *The Black Panther* reflected his provocative manner. In one article in which Eldridge criticized the police, whom the Panthers called "pigs," Eldridge wrote: "A dead pig is desirable, but a paralyzed pig is preferable to a mobile pig...In order to stop the slaughter of the people we must accelerate the slaughter of the pigs."[22] The depiction of the police as pigs, generally regarded as dirty, odious animals, was a calculated attempt by the BPP to use words to politicize the Black community and sympathetic whites. Influenced by the German philosopher Friedrich Nietzsche, who believed that concepts of good and evil are used by those in power to maintain control over the powerless, Huey Newton and the Black Panther Party employed "a form of psychological warfare [that] raised the consciousness of the people and also inflicted a new consciousness of the ruling circle."[23]

Provocative articles and cartoons drawn by Emory Douglas and other Party artists, which illustrated the police as pigs, brought *The Black Panther* under close government scrutiny. In a May 15, 1970 memorandum, FBI

Director J. Edgar Hoover declared that the BPP's newspaper was "one of the most effective propaganda operations of the BPP....It is the voice of the BPP and if it could be effectively hindered, it would result in helping to cripple the BPP."[24] Hoover had cause for concern. By 1970, the weekly circulation of *The Black Panther* surpassed 125,000 copies. It sold for 25 cents per copy and was a major revenue resource for the organization. Less than a week after Hoover's memorandum, the San Diego FBI office proposed to spray a foul-smelling chemical on copies of *The Black Panther*. In September 1970, the Committee on Internal Security of the United States House of Representatives investigated the newspaper.[25]

By March 1978 when I became the editor of *The Black Panther*, the membership of the BPP had declined significantly from a high of 5,000 members to less than a couple dozen Panthers. Similarly, the newspaper experienced a significant reduction in personnel from thirteen members in 1974 when I first joined the newspaper staff to six members in 1978. The reduction in the size of the staff and dwindling finances eventually reduced the frequency of the production of the newspaper. It was a weekly publication until 1978. After this the paper experienced sporadic production and ceased publication in 1980. Nevertheless, *The Black Panther* consistently maintained a militant stance on issues affecting Black and poor people. It offered readers an alternative to the mainstream media. One such example was *The Black Panther's* coverage of the Jonestown tragedy. In November 1978, more than 900 Americans, most of whom were Black and members of the People's Temple, a San Francisco church led by Reverend Jim Jones, allegedly committed suicide in Guyana. The staff of *The Black Panther* spent six exhaustive weeks investigating the incident and dedicated an entire issue of the paper to what we described as the Jonestown massacre.[26]

Perhaps the most respected and popular of the survival programs was the free breakfast for school children. Several Bay Area branches, as well as the Seattle, Washington branch of the BPP, established free breakfast programs in 1968. The following year this survival project was nearly uniformly adopted by other Party affiliates in compliance with a 1969 organizational directive issued by Chairman Seale. In addition to selling the Party's newspaper, the breakfast for children programs were a mainstay of Party affiliates. Party chapters in Oakland and New York offered breakfast at multiple sites. Teams of Panthers served a no frill breakfast consisting of eggs, grits, toast, and bacon to children before the school day started. Community churches, nationwide, hosted the Party's breakfast programs. Father Earl Neil, a Black priest of St. Augustine Episcopal Church in Oakland, maintained,

> Black preachers have got to stop preaching about a kingdom in the hereafter which is a "land flowing with milk and honey"...We must deal with concrete conditions and survival in this life! The Black Panther Party...has merely put into operation the survival program that

the Church should have been doing anyway. The efforts of the Black Panther Party are consistent with what God wants...[27]

BPP members solicited financial contributions from community residents and food donations from local businesses to sponsor its breakfast program. Many parents and other community residents volunteered to help implement the breakfast survival project. One woman who volunteered at St. Augustine Episcopal Church breakfast program remembered, "I didn't know the people in the room. I got off on just washing dishes...because to me it was so invigorating just to be part of it. It was so uplifting."[28]

In addition to ensuring that young children received a meal before attending school, the BPP sought to raise public consciousness about hunger and poverty in America. Seale told his audiences that there are "millions of people...who are living below subsistence; welfare mothers, poor white people, Mexican-Americans, Chicano peoples, Latinos, and black people. This type of program, if spread out, should readily relate to the needs of the people."[29]

Moreover, the Party linked the importance of adequate nourishment and educational performance when it asked, "How can our children learn anything when most of their stomachs are empty?"[30] Party members fed thousands of hungry children each school day throughout the nation. This community service program, no doubt, enhanced the stature of the Party. A *Wall Street Journal* story reported that "a sizable number of blacks support the Panthers because they admire other, less-publicized activities of the Party such as its free-breakfast programs for ghetto youngsters, its free medical care program and its war on narcotics use among black youth."[31] Success of the breakfast program attracted the attention of the FBI and became a primary target of the FBI Counterintelligence program. The FBI sent letters to church members discouraging the use of their church for the breakfast programs. Store merchants were dissuaded from donating to the breakfast program while FBI media leaks accused the Party of extortion to finance the free breakfast project and brainwashing school-age children with antiwhite propaganda.[32]

An outgrowth of feeding hungry children was the Party's exposure to other pressing needs of community residents. For example, former BPP member Assata Shakur (formerly JoAnne Chesimard) recalled working in the breakfast program in New York City's East Harlem: "[I]n the middle of winter some of the kids were without hats, gloves, scarves, and boots and wore just some skimpy coats or jackets. When it was possible, we tried to hook them up with something free from the clothing drive."[33] Impoverished adults in the community also lacked basic necessities. Consequently, the Party instituted a number of free programs which involved the distribution of food, shoes, and clothing. During a 1972 community-survival conference, the Panthers distributed more than 10,000 free bags of groceries during the three-day affair. Party members eventually established a food bank to store food needed for periodic mass distributions. In addition, members of the BPP launched massive free shoe and free clothing giveaways. Following his release from prison in May 1971, Bobby Seale returned to Oakland and took charge of the survival programs. Elaine Brown remembers,

> He [Seale] created the most magnificent food giveaways. The big ones became major community events, even reported in the media...Bobby organized a campaign to give away bags of groceries to whole families, with a stalking panther printed on each bag. The community and the press went wild. Bobby's giant good giveaways begat tremendous support for all our other Survival Programs. Even middle-class blacks, heretofore, reluctant to support or be identified with the party, began endorsing it and making contributions.[34]

Health Programs

Panther activism extended to health concerns as well. Members of the BPP sponsored three major programs to address the lack of adequate health services in the Black community. Health related survival projects included free health clinics, sickle cell testing, and a free ambulance service. Since the Party's health programs required medical workers and equipment, the health projects were not as plentiful as some of the other survival programs. One of the first efforts to implement Chairman Seale's 1969 directive to institute free health clinics was undertaken by the Kansas City, Missouri branch of the Black Panther Party, which opened the Bobby Hutton Community Clinic on August 20, 1969. Soon afterwards Party branches in Brooklyn, New York, Boston, Cleveland, Philadelphia, Seattle, Chicago and Rockford, Illinois, created free health clinics. Although medical cadres in the Party received first aid training, the survival of the health clinics depended on health professional workers, such as Dr. Tolbert Small of Oakland, to donate their time. The health clinics offered a variety of services which included first aid care, physical examinations, prenatal care, and testing for lead poisoning, high blood pressure, and sickle cell anemia. An exemplary Party health clinic operated by the Panthers was the Spurgeon "Jake" Winters People's Free Medical Care Center established in January 1970 by the Illinois chapter of the BPP, which "served over 2,000 people within the first two months of its existence."[35] Medical teams from the Winters clinic went door-to-door assisting people with their health problems; the clinic's staff included obstetricians, gynecologists, pediatricians, and general practitioners.

Sickle cell anemia testing was another major health community service program offered by the Black Panther Party. Panthers were at the forefront of an educational and medical campaign to eradicate sickle cell anemia, a rare blood disease that primarily affects people of African descent. In a front page article in *The Black Panther,* entitled "Black Genocide, Sickle Cell Anemia," the Party accused the United States government of refusing to conduct research to find a cure for sickle cell anemia. Five weeks after the publication of this article, the BPP announced that its medical clinics would begin free testing for sickle cell anemia and the sickle cell trait. The Jake Winters Medical Center conducted the Party's first sickle cell testing in May 1971, testing about 600 children in a three-day period. In Houston, Texas, the BPP trained Texas Southern University (TSU) students and community residents to perform testing for sickle cell anemia, hypertension, and diabetes. According to David Hilliard, Chief of Staff of the BPP, the Party "established nine free testing clinics, publicizing the problem so successfully that [President] Nixon mention[ed] sickle cell in that year's health message to Congress."[36]

The Joseph Waddell People's Free Ambulance Service, established in early 1974 by the Winston-Salem, North Carolina branch of the BPP, was another health venture of the BPP. Panthers in Winston-Salem were granted a franchise by the Forsyth County Commissioners and financed their ambulance service with a grant awarded by the National Episcopal Church. It included 24-hour service with a voluntary staff of twenty certified members who received extensive emergency medical technician training. The ambulance service operated for two years.[37]

Educational Programs

From the Party's inception, its leadership attacked what it considered to be a biased and distorted educational process. Hence, the demand for a relevant education was explicitly stated in the organization's ten-point party platform. Specifically, point 5 of the BPP Platform stated: "We want education for our people that exposes the true nature of this decadent American society. We want education that teaches us our true history and our role in the present-day society."[38] The BPP sought to overcome the problem of substandard education with the creation of liberation schools, community political education classes, and the Intercommunal Youth Institute. As early as 1969, the various affiliates of the Black Panther Party instituted liberation schools. Members of the Berkeley branch instituted one of the first liberation schools on June 25, 1969.[39]

According to chairman Bobby Seale, liberation schools taught children "about the class struggle in terms of black history."[40] The lesson plans of these schools included presentations on Party activities, Black history, and current events. Students usually received breakfast and lunch during their attendance of the liberation schools, which "were an outgrowth of the interaction with children of the F.B.P. [Free Breakfast Program]. Frustrated with the lack of time to talk with children, many Panthers were eager to establish liberation schools."[41] Unfortunately, government officials were sometimes successful in convincing community leaders and parents not to cooperate with the Party. Consequently, in some cities, including Omaha and Des Moines, the school program was discontinued. The Party's community political education classes were the educational counterpart for adults. In addition to listening to lectures about the Party's ideology goals and activities, community adults were taught basic reading and writing skills.

The key educational component of the Party's Survival Programs was the Intercommunal Youth Institute. In January 1971, the Oakland chapter established the Intercommunal Youth Institute (later named the Oakland Community School in 1974). According to the Party, the school was established because "we understand clearly that those who can control the mind can control the body. What we have is an educational system which is completely controlled by the power structure."[42] At the beginning, there were twenty-eight students in the school, many of whom were the children of BPP members. Students, ages 2 ½ to 11, attended the institute. They were placed in levels instead of grades, and their placement was made according to their abilities rather than age. Therefore, a student might be in a fourth-level math class but in a first-level English or reading class. Meals were provided and buses transported the pupils to and from school as well as to medical and dental appointments. During the fall of 1973, the Youth Institute was housed in a former church in East Oakland's predominantly Black community. The school graduated its first class in June 1974. At one point, there were 400 children on its waiting list. Ericka Huggins served as the director of the school from 1973–1981. In September 1977, California Governor Edmund "Jerry" Brown Jr. and the California Legislature gave Oakland Community School a special award for "having set the standard for the highest level of elementary education in the state."[43] The last class graduated from the Oakland Community School in 1982.

Criminal Justice Programs

The 1966 version of the BPP ten-point Party platform included two demands concerning the United States criminal justice system. Point 8 demanded, "We want freedom for all Black men held in federal, state, county, and city prisons and jails." In a similar vein, Point 9 demanded, "We want all black people when brought to trial to be tried in court by a jury of their peer group or people from their black communities, as defined by the Constitution of the United States."[44] In the early days of the organization, the Party informed community residents of their constitutional rights. Early issues of *The Black Panther* included a column authored by Huey P. Newton entitled "Pocket Lawyer of Legal First Aid," which noted,

> [Black people] are always the first to be arrested and the racist police forces are constantly trying to pretend that rights are extended equally to all people. Cut [the "Pocket Lawyer"] out, brothers and sisters, and carry it with you...at all time [sic] remember the fifth amendment...Do not resist arrest under any circumstances...Do not engage in "friendly" conversation with officers."[45]

For a time, the BPP newspaper also included a section that explained state and federal gun laws.

Established in Seattle, Washington, in July 1970, the Party's free busing to prisons program provided transportation for families and friends to visit their relatives who were incarcerated in prison. Seattle BPP members recalled, "We found out that many families and friends cannot afford transportation to these prisons to visit their loved ones. The result is that the prisoners feel that no one even cares about them...It [the busing program] gives a chance to establish some type of communication between the community and the prisoners."[46] This program was one of the first survival projects in which I personally participated after joining the Detroit branch of the BPP in 1972. I drove one of the vans that transported families to visit their incarcerated relatives at Jackson State Prison. Having grown up as the sheltered daughter of a minister and a music teacher, I was overwhelmed by my experience at Jackson State Prison, which was my first visit to a penitentiary. Another service that the BPP provided for prison inmates was the free commissary program. BPP members secured donations of personal hygiene items and non-perishable foods and sent care packages to prisoners. The Party also offered attorney referral services for prison inmates.

Legacy of the Survival Programs

Sociologist Herbert H. Haines has suggested that the activities and rhetoric of Black power groups like the Black Panther Party provided a "positive radical flank" for Black progress. According to Haines, Black radicals of the '60s improved the bargaining position of mainstream civil rights groups, which hastened the accomplishment of many of their goals.[47] There is evidence that the Black Panther Party's survival programs contributed not only to the improved bargaining position of civil rights groups, but for all poor people in America. First, in the area of police–community relations, the Party's police–alert patrols educated the public about police brutality. In Oakland, California, the Panthers increased public awareness about the role and actions of the police. A Citizens' Complaint Board to hear allegations of police abuse was established by the Oakland City Council in 1981—fourteen years after the BPP launched its community patrols of the police.

Contemporary incidents of police brutality, the Rodney King case among others, demonstrate that police abuse of African Americans continues. Nonetheless, today, unlike the 1960s, "three strikes and you're out" is the prevailing public attitude toward criminals. This attitude is perhaps understandable, given the rapid growth during the last decade in the sale and use of crack cocaine and its attendant violent crime. Given the contemporary situation, the Black Panther Party's call in 1966 for the "immediate" release of all Blacks in prisons and jails would understandably draw little support. Nevertheless, the Party's observations that Black and poor people are not tried by a jury of their peers and that crime and poverty are inextricably linked remain correct.[48]

The BPP's breakfast program and food give aways also raised public consciousness about hunger and poverty in the United States. The precursor to the present free school lunch program, the Party's free breakfast for children survival program was a popular community service activity. Indeed, Panther activism provides a model of community self-help. Finally, in the area of education, the Black Panther Party established the Oakland Community School in 1971 as an alternative to the substandard education foisted upon the city's low-income and working-class children. However, Oakland, California, must not be singled out. Then, as now, public education is in crisis throughout the United States, particularly in large, urban school districts. Notwithstanding the sincere efforts of parents and teachers to improve education, urban schools are often abandoned. Is it not possible to create Oakland Community Schools throughout America?

More than thirty years have elapsed since Huey P. Newton and Bobby Seale founded the Black Panther Party. Despite the passage of time, however, the Party's quest for "land, bread, housing, education, clothing, justice and peace" remains elusive for far too many Black and poor people in America. Consequently, in recent years there has been a renewed interest in the Black Panther Party, particularly by African American youth. Several former Panthers have written books about their experiences, young artists have "rapped" about the Party, and a major motion picture on the BPP has been produced.[49] What are our young people, who are searching for role models, to make of the sometimes contradictory accounts of the Black Panther Party?

Above all, it must be remembered that the BPP was an organization comprised of young African Americans from diverse social and economic backgrounds. Moreover, Party affiliates throughout the country possessed distinct organizing styles and programs based on the qualities of the local membership and the particular needs of their respective communities. What happened in one chapter of the Party did not necessarily occur in the same manner in another chapter. Furthermore, members of the Black Panther Party were young men and women, many in our teens and twenties. There were, undoubtedly, times when members of the BPP romanticized the Black liberation struggle. As a result, we seriously underestimated the apparatus of the state in the most powerful country in the world. Moreover, we did not always operate democratically and sometimes failed to grasp fully the imperatives of leadership.[50] Lastly, but certainly not least, the BPP was the main target of the FBI's counterintelligence program to destroy the entire Black power movement.[51] The pervasive government repression directed against the Party affected all aspects of organizational life. It developed an atmosphere of mistrust and personal danger among the membership. In the end, the Panthers sought to transform powerless Black and poor people into *powerful*, political individuals in their attempt to actualize the motto of the Black Panther Party "All Power to the People." As Huey P. Newton recalled,

> We knew that this strategy would raise the consciousness of the people and also give us their support...revolution is a process...we offered [the programs] as a vehicle to move [the people] to a higher level...In their quest for freedom...they have to see first some basic accomplishments, in order to realize that major successes are possible.[52]

NOTES

1. JoNina Abron, "The Black Panther Party," lecture by author, English 223, Black American Literature, Western Michigan University, 5 December 1994.

2. Kwame Ture (formerly Stokely Carmichael) and Charles V. Hamilton, *Black Power: The Politics of Liberation* (1967; reprint, New York: Vintage Edition, 1992), xv–xvi.

3. Ibid.

4. Black Panther Party (Guest Editors), "Supplement to the Whole Earth Catalog," *The Co-Evolution Quarterly*, no. 3 (23 September 1974): 7.

5. Huey P. Newton, *To Die for the People* (New York: Writers and Readers Publishers Edition, 1995), 46.

6. Kit Kim Holder, "The History of the Black Panther Party 1966–1972: A Curriculum Tool for Afrikan-American Studies" (Ph.D. diss., University of Massachusetts, 1990), 78.

7. Bobby Seale, *Seize the Time: The Story of the Black Panther Party and Huey P. Newton* (1970; reprint, Baltimore: Black Classic Press, 1991), 412–413.

8. Huey P. Newton, *To Die for the People*, 89.

9. United States Senate, Final Report of the Select Committee to Study Government Operations with Respect to Intelligence Activities, S.R. No. 94–755, 94th Congress, 2d Session (Washington, D.C., U.S. Government Printing Office, 1976), 200–207, which hereafter will be referred to as The Church Committee; Huey P. Newton, "On the Defection of Eldridge Cleaver from the Black Panther Party and the Defection of the Black Panther Party from the Black Community," The Black Panther Intercommunal News Service, 17 April 1971, C–F.

10. Black Panther Party, "Whole Earth Catalog," 5.

11. Huey P. Newton, *To Die for the People*, 89.

12. Thomas Hobbes, *Leviathan Parts I and II* (Indianapolis: Bobbs-Merrill Company, 1958).

13. Philip S. Foner, ed., *The Black Panthers Speak* (New York: J.B. Lippincott Co., 1970), 2–4.

14. Huey P. Newton, *Revolutionary Suicide* (New York: Harcourt Brace Jovanovich, 1973). Reprint, New York: Writers and Readers Publishing, Inc., 1995), 114–115, 120–126, 146–147; Bobby Seale, *Seize the Time*, 153–166. In April, 1967, a California legislator, Donald Mulford, introduced legislation to change a gun statute in California. This bill was designed to disarm the BPP and end its police-alert patrols. On May 2, 1967, Bobby Seale led a group of Panthers to the California State Capitol in Sacramento where he read the Party's "Executive Mandate No. 1," a statement written by Huey, upholding the right of blacks to arm themselves against "terror, brutality, murder and repression" by "racist police agencies."

15. Bobby Seale, *Seize the Time*, 139.

16. Ibid., 136.

17. Ibid., 139.

18. Black Panther Party, "Whole Earth Catalog," 19. The dates of the six week period were August 21 to October 1, 1972.

19. "Seniors Against A Fearful Environment," *The Black Panther*, 16 December 1972, 3 and 11; "S.A.F.E. Wins Victory for Senior Citizen Home," *The Black Panther*, 26 January 1975, 4. Elaine Brown, *A Taste of Power: A Black Woman's Story* (New York: Pantheon Books, 1992), 321–327; Rod Bush, ed., *The New Black Vote, Politics and Power in Four American Cities* (San Francisco: Synthesis Publications, 1984), 323–325; and the following articles in *The Black Panther*: "Unite to Defeat Reading" and "Bobby in Run-Off," 21 April 1973, 3, A, B, and C; "A People's Victory May 15 in Oakland" and "The People's Political Machine Victors," 3 and A, 19 May 1973. On April 17, 1973,in a field of four candidates, Bobby Seale forced the incumbent mayor of Oakland, John Reading, into a run-off election. Defeated by Reading on May 15, Bobby nevertheless won a respectable 40 percent of the vote. Elaine Brown lost her race for Oakland City Council, but garnered over 34,000 votes. The Seale–Brown campaign registered over 30,000 new voters in Oakland, paving the way for the election of the city's first Black mayor, Lionel Wilson, in 1977.

20. JoNina M. Abron,"'Raising the Consciousness of the People': The Black Panther Intercommunal New Service, 1967–1980," in *Voices From the Underground: Insider Histories of the Vietnam Era Underground Press*, ed. Ken Wachsberger (Tempe, AZ: Mica Press, 1993), 348.

21. "Why Was Denzil Dowell Killed?," *The Black Panther*, 25 April 1967, 4.

22. United States, House of Representatives, Committee On Internal Security, *The Black Panther Party: Its Origin and Development as Relfected in Its Official Weekly Newspaper, The Black Panther Black Community News* Service, 91st Congress, 2nd (Washington, D.C.: U.S. Government Printing Office, 1970), 15.

23. Huey P. Newton, *Revolutionary Suicide*, 163–167.

24. The Church Committee, 214.

25. Ibid., 214–215. Also see Seale, *Seize the Time*, 179. Describing the purpose of its study of the Black Panther Party in the preface of the report, the Committee on Internal Security stated, "to determine its origin, history, organization, character, objectives, and activities with particular reference to certain aspects set forth in the committee mandate." The mandate included investigations of groups "which seek to establish a totalitarian dictatorship within the United States, or to overthrow or assist in the overthrow of the form of government of the United States or any State thereof." United States, vi. House of Representatives, Committee on Internal Security, *The Black Panther Party: Its Origin and Development as Reflected in Its Official Weekly Newspaper, The Black Panther Black Community News Service.* 91st Congress, 2d Session. Washington, 1970, vi. For information about incidents of sabotage against the BPP newspaper, see "Repression of the Black Panther Newspaper," *The Black Panther*, 8 August 1970, 11.

26. Abron, "Raising the Consciousness of the People," 357; "The Government Murdered My Sister at Jonestown" and "People's Temple 'Hit List' Exposed As Fake," *The Black Panther*, 29 December 1978, 3. People's Temple was founded by the Rev. Jim Jones, who died at Jonestown. The BPP had developed a close relationship with the People's Temple, whose community programs for the poor in San Francisco and northern California were much like those of the Party. Charles Garry, a long-time attorney for the BPP, was also the attorney for the People's Temple. The BPP believed that People's Temple members, voluntarily moved to Guyana to flee racism and poverty in the United States which the Party considered a serious indictment of life in America. Also see Michael Meirs, *Was Jonestown a CIA Experiment*? (Lewiston, NY: Emellen Press, 1988).

27. Father Earl A. Neil, "The Role of the Church and the Survival Program," *The Black Panther*, 15 May 1971, 11.

28. JoNina M. Abron, "Women in the Black Power Era: Lessons for the 1990's from the 1960's," paper presented at the "Black Women in the Academy, Defending Our Name: 1894–1994" Conference, Boston, Massachusetts, January 1994.

29. Bobby Seale, *Seize the Time*, 414.

30. Ibid., 413–414.

31. Foner, ed. *The Black Panthers Speak*, xiii.

32. The Church Committee, 210–211; see also Charles E. Jones "The Political Repression of the Black Panther Party 1966–1971: The Case of the Oakland Bay Area," *Journal of Black Studies* 18 (1988): 415–434.

33. Assata Shakur, *Assata, An Autobiography* (Westport, Conn.: Lawrence Hill & Company, 1987), 220.

34. Elaine Brown, *A Taste of Power*, 276; Huey P. Newton, *Revolutionary Suicide*, 303.

35. Kit Kim Holder, "History of the Black Panther Party," 112; Jake Winters, a member of the Chicago BPP, and two Chicago policemen died during a shoot-out on November 13, 1969. See Kenneth O'Reilly, *"Racial Matters": The FBI's Secret File on Black America, 1960–1972* (New York: The Free Press, 1989), 311.

36. David Hilliard and Lewis Cole, *This Side of Glory: The Autobiography of David Hilliard and the Story of the Black Panther Party* (Boston, Mass.: Little, Brown and Company), 339;"Black Genocide: Sickle Cell Anemia," *The Black Panther*, 10 April 1971, 1; "The People's Fight Against Sickle Cell Anemia Begins," *The Black Panther*, 22 May 1971, 10; "BPP Trains Houstonians for Free Medical Testing Program," *The Black Panther*, 22 June 1974, 5.

37. "Winston-Salem Free Ambulance Service Opens," *The Black Panther*, 16 February 1974, 3. Joseph "Joe-Dell" Waddell was a member of the Winston-Salem, North Carolina, branch of the BPP. On June 12, 1972, he was pronounced dead of a heart attack at Central Prison in Raleigh, North Carolina. His fellow inmates believed that prison authorities gave Waddell drugs to induce heart failure; Also see Mario Van Peebles, Ula Y. Taylor, and J. Tarika Lewis, *Panther: A Pictorial History of the Black Panthers and the Story Behind the Film* (New York: New Market Press, 1995); *The Black Panther*, 16 February 1974, 3.

38. Huey P. Newton, *Revolutionary Suicide*, 117.

39. G. Louis Heath, ed. *Off The Pigs!*, 107.

40. Ibid.

41. Kit Kim Holder, "History of the Black Panther Party," 99.

42. "Huey P. Newton Intercommunal Youth Institute," *The Black Panther*, 27 March 1971, 1.

43. The Oakland Community Learning Center offered a variety of educational and recreational programs, including G.E.D. classes and martial arts classes. Various community groups in Oakland, such as the Black Veterans Association, also met regularly at the OCLC. See "O.C.L.C.'s 2nd Annual Martial Arts Friendship Tournament Huge Success," *The Black Panther* 29 January 1977, 23. Elaine Brown, *A Taste of Power*, 391–394. Former BPP member Carol Granison and I wrote the curriculum for language arts and the Oakland Community School. I also taught at the school from 1976 through 1981; "Address of Deborah Williams At First Intercommunal Youth Institute Graduation Exercise," *The Black Panther*, 22 June 1974, 2. Also see "S.O.S.: Win $1000 in 'Support Our School' Donation Drive," *The Black Panther*, 2 April 1977, 3; Elaine Brown, *A Taste of Power*, 439.

44. Huey P. Newton, *Revolutionary Suicide*, 117–118.

45. Ibid., 157–159.

46. See the following articles in *The Black Panther:* "People's Free Busing Program," 8 August 1970, 9 and "Behind the Walls," October 1–14, 1979, 8–9. According to Elaine Brown, "The Black Panther Party provided a voice and a hope for thousands of black inmates." See Brown, *A Taste of Power*, 315–316.

47. Herbert H. Haines, *Black Radicals and the Civil Rights Mainstream, 1954–1970* (Knoxville, Tenn.: University of Tennessee Press, 1988), 180–182.

48. Robert Staples, *The Urban Plantation, Racism and Colonialism in the Post Civil Rights Era* (Oakland, CA: Black Scholar Press, 1987), 103–120.

49. In addition to Elaine Brown, among the other former BPP members who have written autobiographies in recent years are David Hilliard (with coauthor Lewis Cole), *This Side of Glory*; Akua Njeri (formerly Deborah Johnson), *My Life With The Black Panther Party* (Oakland, CA: Burning Spear Publications, 1991), and Assata Shakur (formerly JoAnne Chesimard], *Assata, An Autobiography* (Westport, Conn.: Lawrence Hill & Company, 1987). Some of the rap artists who have performed material about the Black Panther Party are Public Enemy and Tupac Shakur. The 1995 film *Panther*—a fictional account of the BPP's early days—was based on a screenplay written by Melvin Van Peebles and directed by his son Mario. See Mario Van Peebles, Ula Y. Taylor, and J. Tarika Lewis, *Panther*.

50. For discussions of the structure and decision-making process of the Black Panther Party, see Brown, *A Taste of Power*, 319–321 and 443–447; and Hilliard and Cole, *This Side of Glory*, 224–225, 246–247, and 250–251.

51. See Jones, "Political Repression," 415–434; Ward Churchill and Jim Vander Wall, *Agents of Repression* (Boston: South End Press, 1988), 63–99.

52. Huey P. Newton, "On the Defection of Eldridge Cleaver from the Black Panther Party and the Defection of the Black Panther Party from the Black Community," *The Black Panther Intercommunal News Service*, 17 April 1971, C–F.

Chapter Nine

Reading the "Voice of the Vanguard": A Content Analysis of The Black Panther Intercommunal News Service, 1969–1973

Christian A. Davenport

The Black Panther Party's image, ideas, and activities created excitement and great controversy during a turbulent time in American cultural and political history. Images of armed Panthers clad in black berets and leather jackets, soundbites of their "Off the pigs" chants and angry anti-American government rhetoric, and headlines describing their often bloody gun battles with police are among the most recognizable and evocative icons of the late 1960s and early 1970s.

One of the most visible manifestations of the BPP during this era was the Party's newspaper *The Black Panther Intercommunal News Service* (hereafter referred to as *The Black Panther*). First published on April 25, 1967 under the auspices of The Black Panther Community News Service, *The Black Panther* was purchased by individuals throughout the nation and in many foreign countries.[1] As the official voice of the BPP, *The Black Panther* provided information on the organization's ideology, activities, and internal affairs. It also included coverage of "mainstream" news events, community political struggles, and revolutionary liberation movements around the world. Poetry and the social-realist artwork of Emory Douglas, the Party's Minister of Culture, were regular features of the newspaper. In fact, *The Black Panther* was an exemplary representative of a "dissident press," which can be defined as those newspapers, newsletters, leaflets, and other printed forms produced by groups that challenge the power relationships, institutions, and policies of the existing social order.[2]

In an effort to gain insight into Party organizational dynamics, previous research has examined *The Black Panther*. JoNina Abron, the last editor of the newspaper, provides a general historical overview of the inner workings of the production of the paper.[3] Jim Mori utilizes multiple issues of *The Black Panther* to trace the Party's ideological development and fluctuation, and Charles Hopkins analyzes selected issues of the paper to confirm the deradicalization of the organization.[4] Carolyn Calloway focused on group cohesion, and John Courtright used the paper as a tool for investigating the political rhetoric of the BPP.[5] Similarly, Charles E. Jones examines the paper in the context of political repression on the BPP, identifying the Party's newspaper as a central target of the tactics used against the Panthers.[6] *The Black Panther* was the subject of investigations by the former Committee of Internal Affairs of the House of Representatives Committee on Internal Security in 1970 and 1971.[7]

The primary objective of this essay is to examine the nature and manner in which the BPP disseminated its political message from 1969 to 1973. Such an examination permits one to capture the essence of the Party's political message while assessing the variance of its political ideas over time. For the period under study (1969–73), every issue of *The Black Panther*, which was published weekly, was examined. The research design of this investigation repairs a glaring weakness of previous research on the Party's newspaper. Previous studies of *The Black Panther* have analyzed only a sample of papers over a specified time period. Although strategies for selecting random issues of a newspaper are widely accepted in conducting a content analysis, the selection and analysis of every issue of a publication during a specific time frame precludes selection bias.

This chapter begins with an overview of the history and functions of the dissident press. It then describes the development and production of *The Black Panther*. The chapter then reports the results of the content analysis and concludes with a discussion of the various lessons discerned from this investigation of the Party's newspaper.

Political Messages and the Dissident Press

Political communication generally involves "the construction, sending, receiving, and processing of messages that are likely to have a significant impact on politics (and the understanding of political dynamics)."[8] The political messages of the state provide a lens for understanding and interpreting political expressions and symbols. Consequently, control over the dissemination of political messages is critical to the maintenance of the existing political–economic regime. In the American context, a small number of companies tend to dominate the production and distribution of political views in the United States.[9] Not only do a few companies monopolize the mass communication industry, but the political message disseminated often reflects the interests and biases of the status quo. On this point, Michael Parenti quite clearly states,

> The basic distortions in the media are not innocent errors, for they are not random; rather they move in the same overall direction again and again, favoring management over labor, corporatism over anticorporatism, the affluent over the poor, private enterprise over socialism, Whites over Blacks, males over females, officialdom over protesters, conventional politics over dissidence, anticommunism and

arms-race militarism over disarmament, national chauvinism over internationalism, U.S. dominance of the Third World over revolutionary or populist nationalist change. The [main-stream] press does many things and serves many functions, but its major role, its irreducible responsibility, is to continually recreate a view of reality supportive of existing social and economic class power.[10]

Despite the lack of adequate capital with which to compete equally in the "marketplace" of political communication, various individuals, and social and political organizations, have produced alternative news organizations that rebut the mainstream press. A host of descriptions—"dissident press," "grassroots press," "alternative press," "radical press," "underground press"—have been used to describe these media outlets. Despite differences in labels, format, message content, and ideological orientation, these alternative modes of communication share several characteristics:

(1) they attempt to create an alternative evaluation of political, social, and economic reality that might provide new insights or different solutions from those that are already current in the mainstream;

(2) they advocate political positions not expressed within the more established media;

(3) they attempt to decrease the legitimacy of existing political and economic relations;

(4) they increase the visibility of the dissident individuals/groups they represent by promoting the group's ideas in order to garner support and/or increase membership;

(5) they help provide an identity for the dissident individuals/groups they represent as well as their constituency; and,

(6) they generate revenue for other activities.[11]

The critical functions identified above underscore the vital role of the dissident press in the organizing efforts of activist groups. Furthermore, the dissident press provides a valuable service to individual citizens. By raising questions, offering divergent viewpoints, and covering topics outside the mainstream, the dissident press ensures that competing sources of political news are available. The importance of this function cannot be overstated. Access to multiple news sources increases opportunities for the citizenry to make informed political judgments. Parenti explains,

When exposed to a view that challenges the prevailing message, the reader is not then simply burdened with additional distortions (of reality). A dissident view provides us with an occasion to test the prevailing beliefs, open ourselves to information that the mainstream media and the dominant belief system have ignored or suppressed. Through this clash of viewpoints we have a better chance of moving toward a closer approximation of the truth.[12]

This process of critical thinking allows for the formulation of sound political judgments and is perhaps the most essential contribution of the dissident press.

Voice of the Vanguard Party: *The Black Panther*

Initially a monthly publication in 1967, *The Black Panther* became a weekly paper in January 1968. The newspaper remained a weekly publication until 1978 when the Party faced financial difficulties. After a period of sporadic publication, it ceased publication in 1980. One of the first major projects undertaken by the BPP was the publication of *The Black Panther*. The newspaper was created in response to the brutal death of Denzil Dowell who was shot in the back by the police in Richmond, California. Huey P. Newton, cofounder of the BPP recalled,

> We had never even thought of putting out a newspaper before. Words on paper had always seemed futile. But the Dowell case prompted us to find a way to inform the community about the facts and mobilize them to action. Lacking access to radio, television, or any of the other mass media, we needed an alternative means of communication.[13]

The initial paper, published in April 1967, was "two sheets of legal-sized mimeographed paper, printed on both sides," with a headline that read, "Why was Denzil Dowell Killed?"[14] By January 1968, the Party produced a more professional product that was published weekly. During the following years, circulation figures indicated a readership of more than a hundred thousand per week.[15]

The Black Panther proved critical to the fortunes of the BPP. Paper sales provided a much needed source of revenue for both local chapters and the national headquarters, which would split a percentage of the profits from the paper. Each rank-and-file member was responsible for selling an allotment of newspapers and received ten cents for each paper sold. Paper distribution provided a central activity for BPP chapters. As the Party's Chief of Staff David Hilliard states, "The paper . . . helps us organize new chapters. '[W]hat do we do?' new members in San Diego or Sacramento want to know. '[S]ell the newspaper,' we answered."[16] Paper distribution also provided a useful mechanism for organizational recruitment. While Party members were out in the streets selling the paper, they were able to talk to different individuals and explain the ideology and activities of the BPP. David Hilliard remembers that

> Huey has always stressed the significance of *The Black Panther*. From my experience on the docks and at Stop the Draft Week I'm well aware of the paper's functions not only to inform but to organize: "Hey, brother," I say, flashing a copy in a stranger's face, "read *The Black Panther*. Find out what's really going on in this country. Open up your mind! Stop being one of the living dead. See what's really happening." If the brother takes the copy, I've made a potential convert; if he refuses, we get into a conversation that lures other people and ends in

a general verbal free-for-all that's probably the most exciting event on the block in the last ten years.[17]

In fact, *The Black Panther* was so vital to the Party that it established a newspaper cadre whose sole responsibility was the production and distribution of the newspaper. Members of the newspaper cadre investigated stories, wrote text, took photographs, drew pictures, and designed the layout of the paper before it went to press on Thursday nights.

Production of the paper was an arduous and physical task that took a toll on the members of the newspaper cadre. No one better represents this tireless effort than Samuel Napier who held the position of National Distribution Manager from 1968 until his death in 1971. Another dedicated comrade of the newspaper cadre was Cindy Smallwood, who was killed in an automobile accident while driving the BPP's passenger van after a long night of Party work.[18] Moreover, even though the BPP was subjected to intense government repression during this period, Party members met the weekly publication deadline for ten years.

The *Black Panther* was an important vehicle for circulating the message of the BPP. An editorial published on March 22, 1970 states,

> We [the BPP] found [that] we as citizens of this country were being kept duped by the government and kept misinformed by the mass media. In an effort to give the facts to the people, the so-called "underground press" developed with various groups setting up newspaper and magazines with differing emphasis. The Black Panther Community News Service was created to present factual, reliable information to the people. The Black Panther Party has been organized to serve the needs of the people of the Black community and to educate and politicize the masses of Black people, but the Black Panther Party realizes that racism can only be eliminated by solidarity among oppressed people and the educating of all people is [*sic*] the news and problems of Black and oppressed people in amerikkka that are dealt with in the Black Panther Party along with international news. The Black Panther Party Community News Service is the alternative to the "government approved" stories presented in the mass media and the product of an effort to present the facts not stories as dictated by the oppressor, but as seen from the other end of a gun.[19]

The preceding discussion clearly demonstrates that *The Black Panther* functioned as a dissident press. It performed multiple functions for the BPP that included establishing and maintaining organizational identity, recruiting members, providing information about political events, generating revenue, and most importantly, conveying the message of the organization. Positions articulated within the paper were clearly divergent from the "mainstream" press. The Panthers offered an anti-war, pro-Viet Cong/North Vietnamese, Marxist analysis of domestic and foreign affairs, while addressing numerous issues that affected poor and oppressed people such as housing, health care, education, police brutality, family structure, crime, and drugs. Lastly, *The Black Panther* employed particular language as well as visual imagery that reflected the alternative orientation of the BPP. Prominent among its pages were words and pictures representing the police as pigs and drawings of armed freedom fighters.

Analyzing the Voice of the Panthers

To investigate the rhetorical and functional role of *The Black Panther*, I conducted a content analysis of the Party's newspaper from 1969–73. A total of 234 individual papers and 5,178 articles were analyzed, which makes this one of the most comprehensive examinations of *The Black Panther* to date.[20] Several factors dictated the selection of the time period (1969–73) for this study. First, by late 1968, the Party had transformed itself into a national organization with chapters in most major cities. By this time, the Panthers were widely featured in the mainstream media and targeted by federal, state, and local authorities as a major domestic threat.[21] The study concludes in 1973 because according to numerous accounts, by 1971 "the Panthers were finished as an effective or influential force."[22] By extending the analysis two more years, we allow for an examination of the newspaper in the aftermath of both the organizational split and the Party's major electoral campaign to win political power in Oakland. Therefore, the time period under investigation (1969–73) encompasses the most important moments in the history of the BPP from its zenith to its decline.

Three elements are the focus of the following content analysis: (1) the kinds of subjects addressed, (2) the frequency with which these subjects are addressed, and (3) the placement of these subjects within the newspaper. Examples of the subjects addressed include the following categories:

(1) *Issues Concerning the Party:* Statements by members, statements of support by other groups, discussion of the various programs or actions they conducted, philosophical and ideological discussions, general reflections about things;

(2) *The Criminal Justice System:* Experiences in court, trials, laws concerning the criminal justice system, prisons;

(3) *Culture:* Poems, discussions about films, art, literature, history;

(4) *Education:* Access to as well as problems with;

(5) *Employment:* Access to, wages, problems with unions;

(6) *Eulogies:* Statements made or stories about people who died;

(7) *Health:* Access to health care, health problems of African Americans;

(8) *Housing:* Access to, rent, problems with;

(9) *Other Struggles:* Foreign and domestic groups that challenged existing authorities;

(10) *Police and Intelligence Agencies:* Brutality and harassment exercised by, laws concerning this subject, or overall activity of;

(11) *Mainstream Politics:* Issues concerning the U.S. government, electoral politics, war, laws not concerning the criminal justice system, the police, or the intelligence community;

(12) *Services:* Welfare, garbage removal, transportation;

(13) *Social Relations:* Issues concerning the family, male/female roles, oppression in general, discrimination, racism.

These subject categories were drawn from the "Black Panther Party Platform and Program: What We Want, What We Believe." Because the ten-point Party platform articulates the objectives of the BPP, it provides an ideal means of identifying salient issues and concerns of the organization.

The frequency with which articles on these subjects appear is derived by counting the number of articles on the topic that are printed within each newspaper. For the purposes of this analysis, this information is presented in percentage form—identifying what percentage of a paper was dedicated to a particular subject. It is expected that those subjects of high priority to the BPP will be discussed more frequently and will fill the most space in the paper. To further identify relative importance of the different subjects, the location of the article is identified by noting the number of the page it appears on. Similar to most content analyses, it is assumed that the more important topics would be placed toward the front of the newspaper.[23]

Identifying the Message of the Panthers

The accompanying tables reveal that the content of *The Black Panther* changed significantly over time. In 1969, each issue of the newspaper contained a large number of articles (averaging approximately thirty-one per issue) and dealt with a significant variety of subjects (averaging approximately six different subjects per issue). Subject variety and the number of articles continued to rise steadily until the latter part of 1970. By this time, the number of stories reported in each issue increased to thirty-eight, and the variety of subjects addressed increased from six to nine. Because the Party underwent significant increases in its membership and received substantial media attention, and underwent ideological changes during this time period (1969 to late 1970) as well, these findings are not unexpected. At the time the group emerged, significant amounts of information became important for establishing group identity within the group itself and in the larger society. Extensive discussion of the Party's revolutionary ideology was warranted because of the membership's lack of familiarity with ideas on the political left (such as, community empowerment and collective economics).[24]

Intense political repression of the Party during this period would also affect the number of topics addressed by *The Black Panther*. During 1969 to the late 1970s, there were a significant number of arrests and deaths of Black Panther Party personnel and members. In addition, the Party experienced a major internal purge in 1969. Moreover, Huey P. Newton's August 1970 release from prison and his new focus on survival programs precipitated increased organization division and confusion.

TABLE 1. TOTAL NUMBER OF ARTICLES

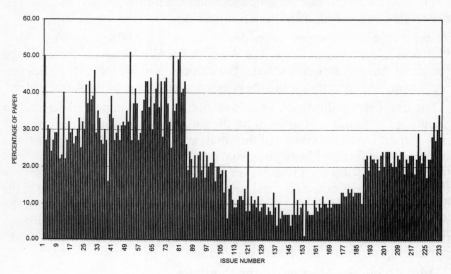

This period of rapid growth and change placed an enormous strain on the membership in general and the newspaper cadre in particular.[25] The toll of all these events is evident in the frequent turnover of editors during the 1969 to late 1970 period, which constituted the greatest turnover in the existence of *The Black Panther*. Within this relatively short time span, four members successively served as editor of the newspaper—Raymond Lewis, Frank Jones, Elbert "Big Man" Howard, and Bobby Heron.

A significant change in content, as measured by the overall number and variety of stories, began in early 1971 when the number of articles decreased to less than ten. In terms of subject variety, a similar downward trend is observed by mid-1972 when the variety of subjects reached only five. With regard to this time period, one could say that the Party changed how it conveyed its message. The message was reduced in size; it was concentrated into a smaller number of stories that dealt with fewer subjects.

An explanation for this pattern involves both external and internal factors. Externally, BPP members and supporters were increasingly subject to greater repression. Internally, the Party experienced great organizational turmoil. During this time, the Panther 21, Geronimo ji Jaga, and Eldridge Cleaver were expelled, and the Party split into factions that differed over tactics. Under these circumstances, a large amount of coverage in *The Black Panther* was allocated to organizational affairs at the expense of covering a broader range of topics. The downward trend indicates that during Elaine Brown's editorship from mid-1970 to late 1972, the paper essentially fulfilled the function of maintaining organizational identity and generating much needed revenue for the Panthers.

Beginning in mid-1972 until the end of the period under investigation, the number and variety of stories increased. In fact, both categories returned to earlier levels. By this time, the Party had reconsolidated itself. Significant attention was given to the electoral campaigns of various Party members, most notably Bobby Seale, and increased attention was given to the various survival programs. The important linkage between BPP activity and the paper was clearly revealed in the series of articles that ran on sickle cell anemia, which occurred simultaneously with the Party's free nationwide testing program for sickle cell anemia.

All of the changes undertaken at this juncture (organizational, ideological, as well as tactical) were quite important to the BPP. Many would argue that the BPP had transformed itself into a new organization, especially when compared with the Party's 1966–69 profile. Consequently, the paper proved crucial in facilitating the "refashioning" of the BPP. The paper expanded discussion of numerous subjects, which enabled Party members as well as concerned individuals to understand new developments. David DuBois' editorship from December 1972 to March 1976 enhanced this process. As Table 2 shows, the content of the message was also altered. There were a greater number of different kinds of stories during the period under review, but issues concerning the Party tended to dominate.

TABLE 2. VARIETY OF ARTICLES

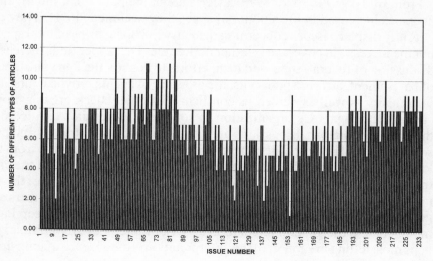

A reader was most likely to see stories about the Party's views and their activities. Considering that *The Black Panther* was "voice of the Vanguard," this attention is not surprising.

The variation in discussion of subjects during this period is notable. From the beginning to the middle of 1969, it was quite common (averaging 48% of the paper's content) to read about the BPP's perspective of the political system or what the relationship was between the police (the "pigs") and the inner city community (the "lumpen"), or a discussion on the difference between the rebellion of anarchists and a Black revolution. During this time, one also finds discussions of police and intelligence agencies (16%), the criminal justice system (16%), and other struggles (13%) as well as some discussion of politics (8%), culture (2%), and education (1%). Predominantly, however, one is struck by the extent to which the Party's ideology suffused the various issues discussed; a discussion of a particular subject was usually linked to the Party's position on that issue. This practice was quite understandable because during this time, Eldridge Cleaver's editorial influence (April 1967–April 1968) was still present —his penchant for long discussions of BPP ideology and equally long interpretations of the political economy.

There were also many discussions about Party activity around the country including the opening of a liberation school in Richmond, California; the development of a National Committee to Combat Fascism, the Brooklyn branch assisting high school students with boycotts, or the founding of the Kansas City branch as well as discussions about organizational purges and the implications for the BPP. When we consider these characteristics, a case can be made that the newspaper was principally serving all of the earlier identified functions of a dissident press.

From mid-1969 to early 1970, articles about the police and intelligence agencies increased in the amount of space they occupied (19%). They did not fully displace issues concerning the Party (38%) in terms of total space, but the increase in coverage is rather noticeable. The reader finds increased discussion of federal, state, and local efforts to destroy the Party: instances of harassment, arrests, shoot-outs, the presence of agents provocateurs, and informants as well as numerous conflicts with other Black organizations, such as Karenga's Us organization in southern California. Additionally, there were numerous discussions of changes in both Party strategy and personnel. Several issues of the paper carried stories about expulsions from the Party. The expulsions of Eldridge Cleaver and various members of the Panther 21 were by far the most memorable. At that time, the function of the paper moved exclusively toward providing an identity for Party members and generating funds for the organization. It appeared important to keep Party members and the general population abreast of internal Party affairs. Perhaps most telling in support of this interpretation is the absence of long theoretical discussions.

The trend toward increased reporting on political and intelligence agencies gave way to increased discussions of the criminal justice system by mid-1971 to late 1972 (as reports on the former decreased to 11% and reports on the latter increased to 20%). Indeed, a close examination of the tables reveals that the "valley" left by decreased discussion of issues concerning the Party (between early 1971 and mid-1972) is "filled" quite substantially by discussions of the criminal justice system.

During that time, we find increased attention given to legal issues—motions made by Panther attorneys, jury selection in the increased number of trials being conducted, and various court rulings. This pattern illustrates the problems confronting the BPP during that period. Several events were occurring directly relevant to the subject matter—the trial involving Bobby Seale and the Chicago 8, the trial of the Panther 21, the trial involving Geronimo ji Jaga (Pratt), and discussions of conditions within American prisons. Discussions of politics (13%), social relations (7%), and other struggles (7%) also increased during this interval.

In late 1972 to mid-1973, there were no long theoretical discussions such as those that occurred in the 1969–70 period. What emerged were more factually based discussions of events rather than ideological postulations. In a sense, articles appearing in *The Black Panther* during this period were less ideological than in the past. Panther news was reported in a journalistic style more in accordance with the dissemination of news by the mainstream media. In addition, discussions of politics increased to 17% and discussion of the criminal justice system increased to 13%. The amount of space allocated to police and intelligence agencies decreased during this time (to 4%) and discussions of social relations decreased as well (to 5%).

What accounts for these changes? It must be remembered that these changes occurred after the BPP had reconstituted itself in Oakland and concentrated its efforts on "reformist" objectives, such as electoral politics and the survival programs. We find that *The Black Panther* fell in line with the new political message put forward by the Party, which was less ideological and more news-oriented. Consequently, the Party faced less repression than it had experienced during the formative years of the organization. By the end of the period under investigation (mid-1973 to the end of the year), the coverage of different topics again changed. Here, as a percentage of all topics covered, politics increased to 26%, police and intelligence agencies to 11%, social relations to 11%, and the criminal justice system to 15%. Additionally, the subjects of housing, education, and employment were given relatively consistent coverage. The number in terms of sheer percentage was still rather small here, but it is clear that consistent attention was given to these subjects.

The location of the article and the importance of different subjects were relatively consistent with the pattern identified above. Several subjects received consistent emphasis during the full time period, while others only appeared at certain times.

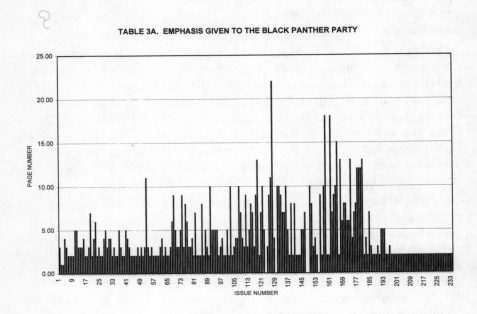

TABLE 3A. EMPHASIS GIVEN TO THE BLACK PANTHER PARTY

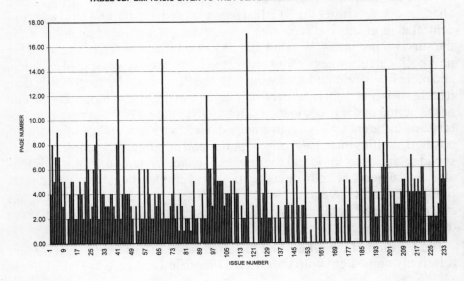

TABLE 3B. EMPHASIS GIVEN TO THE POLICE/INTELLIGENCE COMMUNITY

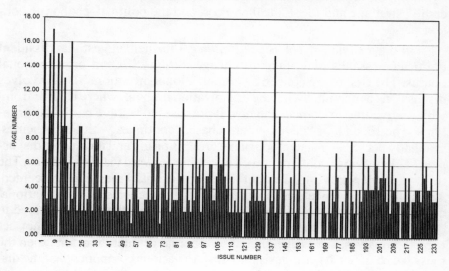

TABLE 3C. EMPHASIS GIVEN TO THE CRIMINAL JUSTICE SYSTEM

Of all the subjects considered, police and intelligence agencies, the criminal justice system, and issues concerning the Party received the most consistent attention. Specifically, stories about the police and intelligence usually appeared on page 3, while the criminal justice system stories usually appeared on page 4. Issues concerning the Party usually appeared on page 4 as well. The importance given to these issues was not consistent throughout the full period. From early 1971 to early 1973, police and intelligence stories received less attention. The placement of housing, health, other struggles, and social relations was somewhat erratic. The data show that the location of these subjects varied from as early as page 2 to as late as page 21 during 1969 to the mid-1970s.

Dissident Political Messages and the Legacy of *The Black Panther Intercommunal News Service*

We have chronicled the path of the BPP by examining all issues of its newspaper *The Black Panther* during the five years from 1969 to 1973. Careful examination of *The Black Panther* discloses the perceptions of the Party and its philosophical and political orientation. More specifically, this examination of *The Black Panther* contributes to the general understanding of how dissident organizations change over time. Political messages disseminated by social movements are usually static configurations, impervious to change. From this perspective, the political message of the Civil Rights movement was about nonviolence, societal integration, and political enfranchisement consistently and without alteration, while the Black nationalist movement was about violence/armed self-defense, separation, and political empowerment. The current study challenges the static view and suggests that the content and functions of dissident political messages are dynamic configurations that change in accordance with organizational leadership, strategic and ideological choices, and the political–economic context.

From the analysis of *The Black Panther*, I further suggest that dissident political messages may undergo change during different organizational phases. The first phase concerns "organizational inception." This involves discussions concerning what the organization is about, where it came from, why it came into existence, and how it proposes to resolve particular problems. The second, or "development phase," continues with these themes, gradually decreasing discussion of the group's origin and increasing discussion of identifying problems as well as putting forward viable solutions. The third phase depends on the extent to which the initial message is accepted. This is the "acceptance phase." If the message is accepted by organizational members, the general audience, and political elites, then it is expected to continue without alteration. If the dissident political message is not accepted, however, and is challenged by external or internal actors, then the message changes. Its emphasis may shift to various components of the dissident message, but most importantly the message is altered in some manner from what it was in phase one. This leads to the fourth phase, or the "regeneration phase." At this point, the dissident group attempts to recreate itself and develop a new message, somewhat similar to the previous one but altered in some manner—one that attempts to eliminate what was contentious from the earlier message. This phase sends the dissident group on a cyclical path of message generation, acceptance or rejection, and alteration. This phase ends either with the demise of the dissident group or its ascendance to power.

By providing an index to the BPP's experience, *The Black Panther* newspaper allows us to place the organization itself into its own "subjective context." As bell hooks suggests, too often African Americans and their activities are "objectified;" we are spoken about and spoken to. [26] Very seldom do oppressed groups have an opportunity to invoke their own understanding of the world. A review of past issues of *The Black Panther* enables us to hear the many voices that existed within the BPP.

However, as can be readily ascertained from the examination conducted here, much work still remains to be done. Obviously, a large part of the Black Panther Party's history remains to be told. *The Black Panther* provides interesting groundwork for investigating dissident political messages, but the relationship between the different strategies used by challengers and "power holders," for example, still needs to be explored further. Additionally, the information provided from 1969–73 must be extended to encompass the entire period of the newspaper's existence (1967–80). Perhaps, after these issues have been addressed, we will have a better understanding of and appreciation for the BPP. If, as the film *Sankofa* reminds us, we must look back in order to go forward, then perhaps *The Black Panther Intercommunal News Service* is a good place to begin. [27]

NOTES

1. Philip S. Foner, ed. *The Black Panthers Speak* (New York: J. B. Lippincott Co., 1970), 9–12.

2. This definition follows from numerous discussions of the dissident press: Richard Askin, "Comparative Characteristics of the Alternative Press"(master's thesis, University of Texas at Austin, 1970); John Downing, *Radical Media: The Political Experience of Alternative Communication* (Boston: South End Press, 1984); Robert Glessing, *The Underground Press in America* (Westport: Greenwood Press, 1970); Lauren Kessler, *The Dissident Press: Alternative Journalism in American History* (Beverly Hills: Sage, 1984); John Sim, *The Grass Roots Press: America's Community Newspapers* (Iowa: The Iowa State Press, 1970); Laurence Leamer, *The Paper Revolutionaries: The Rise of the Underground Press* (New York: Simon and Schuster, 1972).

3. Jo Nina Abron, "'Raising the Consciousness of the People': *The Black Panther Intercommunal News Service, 1967–1980*," in *Voices from the Underground: Volume 1 Insider Histories of the Vietnam Era Underground Press*, ed. Ken Wachsberger (Ann Arbor: Mica Press, 1993).

4. Jim Mori, "The Ideological Development of the Black Panther Party," *Cornell Journal of Social Relations* 12, no. 2 (1977): 137–55 and Charles Hopkins, "The Deradicalization of the Black Panther Party, 1967–1973" (Ph.D. diss., University of North Carolina at Chapel Hill, 1978).

5. Carolyn Calloway, "Group Cohesiveness in the Black Panther Party," *Journal of Black Studies* 8, no. 1 (1977): 55–76; John A. Courtright, "Rhetoric of the Gun: An Analysis of the Rhetorical Modifications of the Black Panther Party," *Journal of Black Studies* (March 1974): 249–267.

6. Charles E. Jones, "The Political Repression of the Black Panther Party 1966–1971: The Case of the Oakland Bay Area," *Journal of Black Studies* 18, no. 4 (1988): 415–34.

7. Committee on Internal Security, House of Representatives, *The Black Panther Party, Its Origin and Development as Reflected in Its Official Weekly Newspaper, The Black Panther Party Black Community News Service* (Washington: U.S. Government Printing Office, 1970). Committee on Internal Security, House of Representatives, *Gun-Barrel Politics: The Black Panther Party, 1966–1971* (Washington: U.S. Government Printing Office, 1971).

8. Doris A. Graber, *Mass Media and American Politics* (Washington: Congressional Quarterly Press, 1993), 305.

9. Michael Parenti, *Inventing Reality: The Politics of News Media* (New York: St. Martin's Press, 1993).

10. Ibid., 8.

11. See Robert Glessing, *Underground Press in America;* John Downing, *Radical Media*; Lauren Kessler, *Dissident Press*, and Robert Smith and Richard Windes, "The Innovational Movement: A Rhetorical Theory," *Quarterly Journal of Speech* 62 (April 1975): 140–153.

12. Parenti, *Inventing Reality*, 3.

13. Huey P. Newton, *Revolutionary Suicide*(New York: Harcourt, Brace & Jovanovich, 1973), 142.

14. Bobby Seale, *Seize the Time* (Baltimore: Black Classic Press, 1991), 147.

15. Several sources are employed here: U.S. Senate Select Committee to Study Governmental Operations, "Supplementary Detailed Staff Reports on Intelligence Activities and the Rights of Americans, Book III," (Washington: U.S. Government Printing Office, 1976); Seale, *Seize the Time*, 179.

16. David Hilliard and Lewis Cole, *This Side of Glory: The Autobiography of David Hilliard and the Story of the Black Panther Party* (Boston: Little, Brown and Company, 1993), 154.

17. Ibid., 149.

18. See "Twenty-eight Black Panther Party Members Murdered by U.S. Government," *The Black Panther*, 30 December 1978–12 January 1979, p. 16.

19. *The Black Panther*, 22 March 1970, p. 2.

20. For the purposes of this study, an article was defined as all written material at least 3 to 4 paragraphs in length. As there were many short articles (1–2 paragraphs), this was done in order to identify what BPP members spent most of their attention on. For those articles that addressed numerous subjects simultaneously I simply coded the subject most frequently addressed within the article itself.

21. Committee on Internal Security, 69.

22. Robert J. Goldstein, *Political Repression in Modern America: From 1870 to the Present.* (Boston: Schenkman/G.K. Hall, 1978), 530.

23. Holsti Ole, *Content Analysis for Social Sciences and Humanities* (Reading, Mass.: Addison-Wesley, 1969).

24. See "The Cold War in Black America, 1945–1954" in Manning Marable, *Race, Reform and Rebellion: The Second Reconstruction in Black America, 1945–1990* (Jackson: University Press of Mississippi, 1991), 13–49 for an explanation.

25. This was done by harassing individuals distributing the paper on the street, intimidating potential printers/distributors and/or unions that were to work on the paper, or pouring damaging substances on newspapers before they were to be mailed to other locations for distribution. See Jones, "Political Repression," and Abron, "Raising the Consciousness."

26. bell hooks, *Killing Rage: Ending Racism* (New York: Henry Holt and Company, 1996).

27. *Sankofa*, VHS 125 min. Mypheduh Films, Washington, D.C. 1994.

Chapter Ten

Back to Africa:
The Evolution of the International
Section of the Black Panther Party
(1969–1972)

Kathleen Neal Cleaver

Author's Note:

Originally, this paper was intended as an introduction to a complex subject that deserved further research, but one so elusive that few scholars would know where to start. The clandestine, or otherwise nonpublic, events that led to the creation of the Black Panther Party's International Section made the existence of extensive documentary records improbable. Fortuitously, the initial obstacles to traditional research did not deter me since my personal involvement in the International Section's formation gave me a basic understanding of its chronology, its main personalities, and the extraordinary political dynamic that sustained its existence. The article published here was adapted from a paper I wrote in 1983 to fulfill Yale University's graduation requirements for history majors. But as this paper remained unpublished for years, available only at Yale's Sterling Memorial Library or from the author, little additional research was conducted.

Initially, the essay started with a focus on three key elements: the unfolding drama of the Black Panther Party during 1969–1971, the relationship between Algeria and the United States during those same years, and finally, the policies of the United States intelligence services towards the International Section of the Black Panther Party. But getting documentary support for the last topic proved exceptionally difficult, and so I concentrated primarily on the first two. I knew where to find the initial sources, certain available documents, and being at Yale University when I wrote this gave me access to knowledgeable individuals. The lack of availability of many documents, combined with certain officials' refusal to divulge information, as well as the paucity of writing about Algeria in English channeled my work into narrative history. Whatever errors of omission or fact remain uncorrected are my responsibility, and I am pleased to make this little known facet of Black Panther Party history available to a larger audience for the first time.

On July 21, 1969, two American astronauts became the first men in history to walk on the moon after the successful landing of the Apollo II spacecraft. In Algiers, Algeria, on July 21, 1969, the First Pan African Cultural Festival opened. Eldridge Cleaver, the Minister of Information of the Black Panther Party, told an American reporter covering the Pan African Festival, "I don't see what benefit mankind will have from two astronauts landing on the moon while people are being murdered in Vietnam and suffering from hunger even in the United States."[1] Former President Lyndon B. Johnson gave a different interpretation to the victorious Apollo mission; to him it meant that America could do anything that needed to be done.[2]

While America celebrated the triumph of science and technology that the moon landing symbolized, African culture was the focus of celebration in Algeria. The colorful crowds that thronged under the festive banners and lights spread above the streets of Algiers represented hundreds of nationalities and ethnic groups from the huge continent, but only a fragment of the staggering diversity of Africa's peoples and cultures. Delegations of artists, musicians, dancers, writers, and political figures from twenty-four African countries flocked into Algiers, along with representatives of six African liberation movements from still colonized areas, as well as an Afro-American contingent that included the Black Panther Party.

The African independence movements of the 1950s and 1960s profoundly influenced Black Americans immersed in the struggle for civil rights and human dignity. The Mau Mau rebellion in Kenya, the rise of Patrice Lumumba in the Congo, and the emergence of independent Ghana under Kwame Nkrumah inspired a new political consciousness among American Blacks. The dramatic transformation of former European colonies into independent African states stimulated a resurgent identification with Africa, and Blacks in America were enthusiastically appropriating their African cultural heritage. After Malcolm X's assassination, the escalating momentum of a dynamic Black nationalism challenged the nonviolent integrationist approach to civil rights, and nearly eclipsed it by 1969.

Surging at the crest of the wave of nationalist protest, the Black Panther Party insisted that Black self-determination was not feasible under American imperialist domination. Although its membership was exclusively Black, the Black Panther Party emphasized "power to the people" far more than Black power and sought to unify the anti-imperialist movements and organizations. On July 21, 1969, back in Oakland, California, a multiracial crowd of over 3,500 radicals and revolutionaries from all over America attended the Black Panther Party conference called to start a "United Front Against Fascism."[3] The Black Panther Party believed the liberation of Blacks from racist oppression and capitalist exploitation required a social revolution to transform the economic and political institutions of the United States, and its presence in Algiers signified its identification with African struggles to end colonialism.

The Organization of African Unity had designated Algeria as the host country for Africa's liberation movements, making Algerian President Houari Boumedienne's continued support for the fight against colonialism significant in the quest for African unity. In his welcoming speech at the opening of the First Pan African Cultural Festival, Algeria's president described the unifying factor in Africa as "anti-colonialist zeal."[4]

Boumedienne stated that "culture is a weapon in our struggle for liberation."[5] His remarks revealed the political dimension of the colorful panorama of African dancers, mounted Berber horsemen, musicians, and uniformed freedom fighters marching in the spectacular parade that opened the Festival.

Algeria officially acknowledged the link between the struggles of Africans and Afro-Americans by extending an invitation to a host of Black artists and political figures to participate in the First Pan African Cultural Festival. The Afro-American contingent included jazz musicians, playwrights, actors and actresses, poets, scholars, writers and political activists, among them Nina Simone, Archie Shepp, Ed Bullins, Dr. Nathan Hare, and Haki Madhubuti, who was then known as Don L. Lee.[6] Stokely Carmichael, who had recently adopted the name Kwame Ture, also arrived at the Festival, but not with the delegation. He no longer lived in the United States but in Guinea, and he came accompanying his wife, exiled South African singer Miriam Makeba, who was a featured performer.

Algeria's Minister of Information, Mohammed Ben Yaya, authorized the Black Panther Party to set up an official exhibit in connection with the Festival. The Panthers transformed a chic office with large plate glass display windows in downtown Algiers into the Afro-American Information Center. Most of the Festival's exhibits and conference sessions were held at the exclusive Club des Pins facility in a suburb of Algiers, but the Afro-American Center was located right in the heart of the city not far from the local office of Al Fatah, the largest and most powerful of the Palestinian liberation movements led by Yasir Arafat. A close bond grew between Fatah and the Panthers as soon as their arrival became public, and Cleaver embraced the Palestinian cause in his speech at the opening of the Festival.

Emory Douglas, the artist whose bold drawings in *The Black Panther* illustrated the Party's revolutionary ideology, had prepared a special exhibition of his art for the Festival. From the moment he taped the first drawing on the Center's bare walls, crowds of Algerians clustered on the sidewalk outside and stared through the windows. Soon large framed posters of Black Panther martyrs and brightly colored drawings showing Afro-Americans holding guns or fighting the police decorated all the walls and windows. The militant spirit the artwork conveyed transcended the language barrier and evoked enthusiastic reactions among the Algerian onlookers.

The Black Panther Party represented an unprecedented development, both ideologically and stylistically, in the centuries-old quest for Black freedom. Its uniqueness derived, in part, from its practical adaptation of the colonial analogy to America's reality. The first point of the Ten-Point Program of the Black Panther Party declared, "We want power to determine the destiny of our black community." The Panthers admired the Algerian revolution and considered its victory a powerful example of the ability of oppressed people to attain power over their destiny. The anti-imperialist stance the Black Panther Party took provided a direct connection to the Algerian hosts. And for Algerians, anti-imperialism was far more than rhetoric: more than a million of them had died fighting the French colonial rulers during their war for liberation.

Algeria's Influence on the Black Panther Party

The crucible of civil war forged the writings of Frantz Fanon, the Black psychiatrist from Martinique who fought alongside Algerian revolutionaries for independence from France. His books became available in English just as waves of civil violence engulfed the ghettos of America, reaching the level of insurrection in the wake of the assassination of Dr. Martin Luther King, Jr. in 1968. Fanon died in 1961, a year before Algeria obtained the independence he had given his life to win, but his brilliant, posthumously published work *The Wretched of the Earth* became essential reading for Black revolutionaries in America and profoundly influenced their thinking. Fanon's analysis seemed to explain and to justify the spontaneous violence ravaging Black ghettos across the country, and linked the incipient insurrections to the rise of a revolutionary movement. The opening sentence of *The Wretched of the Earth* said, "National liberation, national renaissance, the restoration of nationhood to a people... whatever may be the headings used or the new formulas introduced, decolonization is always a violent phenomenon."[7] Fanon's penetrating dissection of the intertwining of racism and violence in the colonial scheme of domination was compelling to Blacks fighting in America; it provided a clearly reasoned antidote to the constant admonition to seek changes peacefully. Fanon explained how violence was intrinsic to the imposition of White colonial domination, and portrayed the oppressed who violently retaliate as engaged in restoring the human dignity they were stripped of by the process of colonization. His analysis of the tortured mentality of the colonized person and the therapeutic nature of fighting to destroy colonial domination provided radical Blacks in America with deep insights—into both their own relationship to a worldwide revolution underway and to the profound kinship between their status in America and that of colonized peoples outside America.

Fanon's discussion of a key element in the process of decolonization—the overt rejection of White cultural domination—illuminated the transition from shame to pride in Blackness that masses of Black Americans experienced during the era of Black power. He wrote,

> The violence with which the supremacy of white values is affirmed and the aggressiveness which has permeated the victory of those values over the ways of life and thought of the native mean that, in revenge, the native laughs in mockery when Western values are mentioned in front of him. In the colonial context the settler only ends his work of breaking in the native when the latter admits loudly and intelligibly the supremacy of the white man's values. In the period of decolonization, the colonial masses mock at these very values, insult them, vomit them up.[8]

Fanon's analysis of decolonization made the connection between the cultural challenge to White domination and the violent rejection of political control by Whites explicit.

Because the African colonial world that Fanon wrote about bore a striking resemblance to the world in which American Blacks lived, his analysis profoundly altered the strategic understanding of Black revolutionaries. According to Fanon,

> The colonial world is a world cut in two. . .The zone where natives live is not complementary to the zone inhabited by settlers. The two zones both follow the principle of reciprocal exclusivity . . .The settlers' zone is strongly built. . .brightly lit . . . an easy going town . . . always full of good things . . . The settlers' town is a town of white people. . . .
>
> The town belonging to the colonial people, or at least the native town, the Negro village, . . . the reservation, is a place of ill fame, peopled by men of ill repute . . . The native town is a hungry town . . . starved of meat, of shoes, of coal, of light . . . a town wallowing in the mire.[9]

But the uniqueness of the colonial context lay in the fact that "economic reality, inequality, and the immense difference in ways of life never come to mask the human realities."[10] Close examination revealed "that what parcels out the world to begin with is the fact of belonging to or not belonging to a given race, a given species."[11] But, Fanon explained, "in the colonies . . . the cause is the consequence, you are rich because you are white, you are white because you are rich."[12] This type of divided world was ended, Fanon explained, when the oppressed appropriated the violence that brought the colonial world into being in the first place:

> The violence which has ruled over the ordering of the colonial world . . . that same violence will be claimed and taken over by the native at the same moment when, deciding to embody history in his own person, he surges into forbidden quarters. To wreck the colonial world is henceforth a mental picture of action, which is very clear, very easy to understand . . . .[13]

The condition of Blacks in the United States, in the perspective of the Black Panther Party, was analogous to that of a colonized people—a captive nation dispersed throughout the White population. We were subjected to what Cleaver called "community imperialism."[14] Cleaver redefined what was usually called the White community as the "mother country," and constantly referred to the Black community as "the colony."[15] Adapting Fanon's analysis helped to clarify the historical relationship between subjugated Blacks and dominant Whites that conventional terms obscured. Viewing Blacks as colonized subjects, instead of so-called second-class citizens, defined the political course the Black Panther Party proposed as a legitimate alternative to the assimilationist thrust of the Civil Rights movement, and justified organizational strategies designed to liberate, instead of integrate, Blacks.

Considering the impact of the international context in which decolonization took place, Fanon saw the breakdown of colonial structures as "the result of one of two causes: either of a violent struggle of the people in their
own right, or of action on the part of the surrounding colonized peoples
which acts as a brake on the colonial regime in question."[16] Fanon pointed
out that,

> A colonized people is not alone. In spite of all colonialism can do, its
> frontiers remain open to new ideas and echoes from the world outside.
> It discovers that violence is in the atmosphere, that here and there burst
> out, and here and there sweeps away the colonial regime.[17]

An eagerness to challenge the colonial administration came from this
knowledge that other colonized peoples had succeeded in putting an end to
their domination. Fanon wrote that the native "openly brandishes the threat
of violence" because "he is conscious of the unusual character of the contemporary situation and . . . he means to profit by it."[18]

From its inception, the Black Panther Party saw the condition of Blacks
within an international context, recognizing that the same racist imperialism
that people in Africa, Asia, and Latin America were fighting against was
victimizing Blacks in the United States. The initial ideological inspiration
of the Black Panther Party came from diverse sources. Stokely Carmichael's call for Black power in 1966 and his creation of the Lowndes
Country Freedom Organization, whose symbol was the black panther,
caught the imagination of Huey Newton and Bobby Seale, two college students in Oakland who were anxious to start a new organization in the wake
of the explosive 1965 Watts uprising. To the revolutionary Black nationalism adapted from Malcolm X, the Panthers added Frantz Fanon's analysis
of colonialism and the necessity for violence, ideas of political organization
taken from Kwame Nkrumah, and theories of guerrilla warfare and political
struggle taken from Che Guevara and Mao Tse-Tung. That was all combined with the revolutionary message of the Declaration of Independence,
which advocated the right to abolish a government that did not meet the
needs of the governed.[19] The strategic importance of Black Americans, in
Panther terms, was that they lived "in the belly of the beast," within striking
distance of the heart of American imperialism.

Eldridge Cleaver's Refuge in Algeria

The press conference Eldridge Cleaver held in Algiers on July 17, 1969
before the formal opening of the Festival was his first public appearance
since disappearing from San Francisco eight months earlier. He became a
celebrated fugitive from the United States, facing several charges of attempted murder stemming from a shoot-out between Oakland police and the
Panthers in April 1968, two days after King's assassination. The gun battle
had left one Panther dead, three policemen wounded, and eight Panthers under arrest. That June, Cleaver was released on bail after being granted a writ
of *habeas corpus.* His book of essays, *Soul on Ice,* became a best seller,

Cleaver ran for President as the candidate of the Peace and Freedom Party, and the national press gave increasingly sensationalized coverage to the Black Panther Party's confrontations with police forces. Months of legal wrangling in California courts ended with his being ordered back to prison that November as a parole violator. Instead of surrendering to prison authorities, Cleaver clandestinely traveled to Cuba.

His arrival in North Africa made it possible to resume face-to-face connection with scores of friends, supporters, colleagues, and comrades that his stay in Havana had interrupted. A series of misunderstandings, disagreements, and outright confrontations with Cuban authorities in Havana had culminated with Cleaver's departure for Algiers.[20] Afterwards, he claimed that "the Cubans reneged on certain promises they had made before I even arrived, such as a permanent, well organized facility, and the right to make broadcasts . . . They had no intention of ever allowing the things that they promised."[21] Bay Area radicals had negotiated Cleaver's asylum with the diplomats at Cuba's United Nations mission in New York. But once he reached Havana, the government extended permission for Cleaver to remain in Cuba as long as he wished as a private citizen only, and insisted that his presence remain unpublicized. After a Reuters wire report revealed that Cleaver was living in Havana in late May of 1969, his stay abruptly ended.

Traveling on a Cuban passport with nothing but a transit visa for Algeria, Cleaver was escorted to Algiers by a Cuban diplomat in early June. Within a week of his arrival, full of distrust for his Cuban sponsor, Cleaver privately initiated an effort to remain in Algeria, where no blockade inhibited communication with the United States. Ultimately, he would seek Algerian backing to establish a base for Black Panther political and military action against the United States, the plan he had hoped to realize in Cuba.

Cleaver's fugitive status posed no handicap in Algeria. Most government officials had been branded as criminals by the French authorities during the guerrilla warfare that raged from 1954 to 1962. These men were concretely aware of the relationship between a revolutionary movement and the established government it challenges, which deems all activity in support of a revolution as criminal. Fugitives from all over Africa and other parts of the world lived peacefully in Algiers as the new nation became host to representatives from nearly every African liberation movement, the Palestinian liberation movement, and several revolutionary groups outside of Africa, including political exiles from Brazil and Canada. Algeria's foreign policy supported all struggles against colonial domination, if not materially, rhetorically.

The absence of official diplomatic ties between Algeria and the United States, however, made Cleaver's presence in Algiers secure. Algeria had broken off diplomatic relations with the United States during the 1967 Egypt–Israel War, in which Algerian troops had fought on the side of Egypt. Egyptian President Nasser was the most widely respected and admired Arab leader in Algeria. His leadership had inspired and supported the rise of their revolutionary nationalist movement. Boumedienne had spent years in Egypt during the Algerian liberation war. As a leading advocate of radical Arab nationalism, Algeria was thrust in perpetual conflict with those conservative Arab states closely allied to the United States, especially Morocco, with whom she had been at war. But American support for Israel had precipitated the formal break. Cleaver faced no threat of being arrested and extradited back to the United States, since the American Embassy had lost its official standing.

But arriving in Algiers under Cuba's aegis was not propitious because Cuba and Algeria were no longer on friendly terms. Cuba had supported the FLN (Front de Liberation Nationale) since 1960 and closely allied itself with Ben Bella's radical government.[22] But when then-Vice President and Defense Minister Boumedienne led a bloodless military coup against Ben Bella in June 1965, Cuban leaders vigorously denounced his action. Boumedienne had staged his coup on the eve of the Second Afro-Asian Conference, a major gathering of the nonaligned and socialist nations planned in Algiers, hoping to block Ben Bella's considerable international prestige from rising. That was far greater than the internal political strength he commanded, which had been eroding since independence.[23] Cuba's socialist leaders refused to support Boumedienne, dismayed that he had overthrown one of Africa's most progressive regimes.[24] The stern, colorless colonel who replaced Ben Bella was virtually unknown outside of Algeria. Even his true name was unknown, Houari Boumedienne being the alias he used during the war. Part of Boumedienne's strategy for asserting Algerian leadership on an international level, one plank in his comprehensive program to place Algeria in the political leadership of Africa, the Arab world, and nonaligned nations, was hosting the First Pan African Cultural Festival.

At the end of May 1969, Emory Douglas, the Black Panther Party's Minister of Culture, accompanied Kathleen Cleaver from San Francisco to Algiers. They left the United States planning to take an Aeroflot flight from Algiers to Havana, but first had to make arrangements for their travel documents in Paris. In Paris for ten days waiting for the visas, Emory and Kathleen became acquainted with Julia Wright Hervé and her husband Henri Hervé, radical Pan Africanist supporters of American and African liberation movements. Julia Hervé generously threw herself into helping the Black Panthers. Ms. Hervé, the daughter of Richard Wright, had spent her childhood in France. She was thoroughly bilingual and bicultural, and astutely immersed in African politics. On several occasions, she traveled to Algiers to help the Cleavers, and her gracious assistance was crucial both to their personal and political goals.

Eldridge Cleaver was smuggled into Algiers disguised as a Cuban and brought directly to the small waterfront hotel where Cuban Embassy officials had insisted on housing Kathleen Cleaver and Emory Douglas. A few days after the Cleavers were reunited, the diplomat in charge of them visited their hotel room. He informed Cleaver that arrangements were underway to hide him at an Al Fatah training camp in Jordan, and he would have to leave Algiers very soon. The reason he gave for this bizarre development was that the Algerian authorities had discovered that Cleaver was in their country and were angry about it.

Kathleen Cleaver, who had not seen her husband since November 1968, was eight months pregnant. The thought of either of them secretly dashing off to Jordan made no sense, and Eldridge suspected he was being double-crossed. The first English-speaking Black person Cleaver met in Algiers was Charles Chikarema, the local representative of ZAPU (Zimbabwe African Peoples' Union). Chikarema himself had been expelled from Cuba years earlier in response to his agitation for better treatment of African students in Havana.[25] Chickarema fully sympathized with the revolutionary aims of the Black Panther Party, with which he was thoroughly familiar, and the Cleavers wholeheartedly endorsed the liberation of Rhodesia. Further, the two men shared hostility towards the Cuban government, so Cleaver turned to Chikarema for help in unraveling the awkward position in which the Cuban design placed him. Chikaerma introduced Eldridge to his friend Elaine Klein, an American woman who was well acquainted with Algeria's governing officials and who at that time worked at the Ministry of Information.

Klein befriended most of the African liberation movements in Algiers and was always ready to help stranded Americans. Once she learned he was in Algiers, Klein was delighted to meet the author of *Soul on Ice* and generously and energetically helped Cleaver's effort to remain in Algeria. A vivacious woman originally from New York, Elaine Klein had attended art school during the 1950s in Paris, where she became an ardent supporter of Algeria's FLN.[26] Klein had moved to Algiers as soon as the FLN won independence and worked as press secretary for Algeria's first president, Ahmed Ben Bella. She had also been a close friend of Frantz Fanon, having accompanied him to the United States when he flew there for medical treatment for his fatal illness.

Klein managed to find out through contacts at the Vietnamese Embassy after their Ambassador had a meeting with President Boumedienne that the Cuban explanation of Cleaver's need to leave in a hurry was baseless: no Algerian official was aware that he was in Algiers. Furthermore, since she was responsible for drawing up the list of Afro-Americans being invited to the Pan African Cultural Festival, she promised to make sure he was formally invited to Algiers.

Klein secured official invitations to the Pan African Cultural Festival for an entire delegation of the Black Panther Party. Along with Eldridge and Kathleen Cleaver and Emory Douglas, who were already in Algiers, the delegation included Chief of Staff David Hilliard and Raymond "Masai"

Hewitt, Minister of Education. As they were the highest ranking officers still out of jail, they agreed to travel to Algiers primarily to consult with Cleaver. Hilliard, who had grown up with Newton in Oakland, was thrust into the position of chief spokesman for the Black Panther Party by accident and was ill-prepared to handle the tremendous responsibility of Party leadership. He depended heavily upon Hewitt, from the Los Angeles chapter, for assistance and advice, but neither of them possessed the magnetism or power that inspired people to follow Newton, Seale, or Cleaver. George Gaines, another Black Panther who had been in prison with Cleaver, insisted on coming to Algiers with them to make sure Cleaver got the full story of what was really going on within the Black Panther Party in America. And Julia Hervé, along with several other French speaking Afro-Americans, came to Algiers to help the delegation prepare for the Festival.

Cleaver had sought sanctuary first in Cuba and then Algeria, but he considered this action a temporary maneuver, not a permanent arrangement. On numerous occasions, he publicly announced his intention of returning to the United States. In a message to the Black Panthers Cleaver said,

> I do not want people to think that I was setting an example of how to deal with the situation by leaving Babylon . . . It was my desire to remain . . . and to continue my participation in the struggle underground. I do not want people to believe that the best thing to do is to leave, but to stay and to continue to struggle and to make it possible for others who have already left to return because that is where my heart is.[27]

When Cleaver's colleague Bob Scheer, the editor of *Ramparts* magazine, arrived in Algiers he cautioned Cleaver against making such statements. According to Sheer, the CIA would probably kill him if he attempted to return to the United States:

> "But what do you think will happen to me if I stay out here for any length of time?" Cleaver asked.
>
> "You'll probably be killed by the CIA," Scheer answered.[28]

The First Pan African Cultural Festival in Algiers

The Pan African Cultural Festival drew immense numbers of people from all over Africa, the Middle East, Europe, and even the United States. All the major hotels overflowed with Festival guests. The Black Panther Party delegation stayed at the elegant, government-run Hotel Aletti in the center of town, which became the meeting place for political groups. Mealtimes in the enormous dining hall turned into a lively round of reunions, meetings, connections, and spontaneous gatherings, followed by further meetings in various parts of the sprawling hotel at all times of day and night.

Despite the scorching heat, Algerians, Africans, Europeans, and Americans jammed the formal opening ceremony at the Afro-American Information Center on July 22, 1969. Julia Hervé, speaking in French, introduced the

Black Panthers to the audience. She remarked that when Malcolm X came to Africa, he was only one man, but the Black Panthers came to Africa as a fully developed organization representing the Afro-American liberation struggle. The crowd enthusiastically welcomed the Black Panthers, and the Algerian visitors to the Center were intensely curious. They crowded in close to the speakers and asked questions that revealed almost total ignorance about the existence of the Black Panther Party, the goals of the Black struggle, and conditions within the United States. The Algerians were convinced, however, that American imperialism was an enemy of their country, and they warmly expressed their solidarity with its Black opponents visiting their home.

Once the Center was opened and competently staffed by French-speaking Afro-Americans Julia had brought from Paris, Cleaver felt free to devote his attention to an intense schedule of meetings. He talked to journalists and political figures from all over the world. He saw his visiting colleagues from the United States and kept a close and frequent round of consultation going with visiting Panther comrades whom he had not seen or talked to since he'd left California.

During the Festival, Cleaver met the Ambassador of the Democratic Peoples' Republic of Korea. Elaine Klein arranged the meeting at the request of the Korean Embassy and served as interpreter, for Cleaver only spoke English and some Spanish, and Algeria's day-to-day language was French. The Korean ambassador extended an invitation to Cleaver to attend the International Conference of Revolutionary Journalists being held that September in Pyongyang. Journalists from countries all over the world would be attending, and the Korean hosts wanted to have a Black Panther there as the representative of the United States.

Cleaver's sojourn in Cuba had not dampened his enthusiasm for socialism, but he viewed Cuba as too closely tied to the Soviet Union to retain any freedom of action. He had learned to expect little from the Communist superpowers. The Korean government was especially sensitive to the problems of small countries and resolutely retained its independence despite its proximity to China and the Soviet Union. Korea's intense hostility to American imperialism appealed to Cleaver, and he anticipated that his trip to Korea would be politically fruitful for the Black Panther Party. He was anxious to resume work on establishing international contacts and winning support for the Black Panther movement among the socialist countries pledged to international proletarian solidarity. Cleaver accepted the invitation to the conference, beginning a long and close association between the representatives of North Korea and the Black Panther Party in Algiers.

After the Pan African Cultural Festival got underway, several Black American fugitives with whom Cleaver had been associated in Havana joined him in Algiers. Two of them, Byron Booth and Clinton Smith, had spent time with Cleaver years earlier in prison, where they all were inspired by Malcolm X to make a commitment to Black revolution. Booth and Smith were adventurous daredevils in their late twenties who had no intention of spending their lives in prison. In January of 1969, they managed to break out of a minimum security prison in Southern California and immediately hijacked a plane to Cuba.[29] When Booth and Smith arrived in Havana, the authorities promptly threw them back in prison. Booth managed to smuggle a message out to Cleaver. The two escaped from the rural labor camp and made their way to his doorstep in Havana. The apartment came to be known as "la casa de las Panteras" because of all the Black fugitives who gathered there.[30] Part of Cleaver's difficulties with his Cuban hosts arose from his attempt to ameliorate the status of Booth and Smith, whom he pressured the Cuban authorities to treat as revolutionaries rather than criminals.

The other fugitives that left Havana to join Cleaver in Algeria were James "Akili" Patterson, his wife Gwen, and their daughter Tanya. In Cuba, they had not experienced any direct conflict with the government. The two first became involved in the Black movement while attending college in California. After being arrested for carrying a concealed weapon, Patterson hijacked a plane to Cuba to avoid going to trial and took his young, pregnant wife along with him. Because Patterson's association with the Black Panther Party could be verified, the Cubans housed the couple in the Havana Libre, the former Hilton Hotel, and provided for their basic needs. They traveled to Algiers believing the public participation of the Black Panther Party in the Pan African Cultural Festival meant that they, as Black revolutionaries, would receive a warmer reception in Algeria than Cuba.

In Havana, the couple was surprised to discover that the government considered emphasis upon Black pride and solidarity subversive to its propagation of communism. The official line was that everyone was equal, and racism no longer existed in their socialist country. But the brief span of the revolution had not entirely destroyed Cuba's legacy of slavery and segregation, and American Blacks felt especially sensitive to the racial stratifications obvious in Havana. The communist government officials were overwhelmingly White, but Cuba's population was racially very mixed. As the Cuban authorities discouraged the formation of racially based organizations, it became clear to the fugitives in Havana that Cuban support for the Black liberation movement in the United States was only for export.

After becoming a fugitive from the United States, Cleaver was declared a "designated national" of Cuba under the Trading with the Enemy Act. This law authorized the Treasury Department to freeze all his assets in the United States and made any American conducting business with him liable to criminal prosecution. Cleaver's departure from Cuba made it legally possible to remove that designation and have the sanctions lifted. Alan Brodsky, one of Cleaver's lawyers from San Francisco, brought the papers that Cleaver needed to sign before an official representative of the United States government to Algiers during the Festival. That meant Brodsky and Cleaver had to visit the American Consul at the American Interests Section of the Swiss Embassy. The former American Embassy in Algiers had merely hoisted the Swiss flag, posted a new sign in its driveway, and withdrawn its Marine Guards, which meant Cleaver could freely enter the Embassy without being arrested. Like the country in which he sought sanctuary, Cleaver was politically antagonistic but economically bound to the United States.

Ironically, his own situation reflected the dual status that he had described as characteristic of Blacks in America:

> Black people in North America have always been plagued by a dual status. We were both slave and Christian, we were both free and segregated, we are both integrated and colonized. In the past this duality has worked to our disadvantage. It kept us running around in circles. Today we propose to turn it to our advantage, in the manner that we have turned blackness from a disadvantage to a rallying point of advantage.[31]

This dual status continued to plague the Black Panthers in their associations with individuals and organizations in the Third World, for their connection to the United States provoked both attraction and distrust.

After the Festival ended in early August, the Afro-American Information Center was closed, and the Black Panthers visiting from America returned home. But the Cleavers, their infant son, who had been born during the Festival, and all the fugitives from Havana remained in Algiers. The Algerian Ministry of Information denied Cleaver's request to turn the Center into a permanent office. His subsequent request to establish some type of Black Panther facility in Algiers was referred to the Council of the Revolution, Algeria's governing body of military officers. Elaine Klein, the intermediary with the Algerian authorities, told Cleaver he would have to meet with Commandante Hoffman to discuss that request. No date was set for that meeting, and she said he would just have to wait.

The lack of any formal relationship to Algeria's government did not prevent the Black Panthers from creating ties with the officially recognized liberation movements or being included in functions where other movements were participants. The FLN invited the Black Panthers to attend a press conference held at their headquarters by Amilcar Cabral, leader of PAIGC (African Party for the Independence of Guinea-Bissau and Cape Verde Islands) on his visit to Algiers. For African liberation movements, Algiers was an ideal center of communication, for both the Western and the socialist press were well-represented in the city. Vietnam's National Liberation Front (NLF) was represented in Algiers as well as the government of the Democratic Republic of Vietnam. The Black Panthers were invited to the NLF's commemorative ceremony to mark Ho Chi Minh's death in September, and Cleaver was warmly welcomed. The lack of any language barrier between the Black Panthers and the representatives of the liberation movements from South Africa and Zimbabwe made associations with them, in personal terms, the closest, but in political terms the Panthers found their strongest support among those directly harmed by United States' policies: the Palestinians, the Vietnamese, and the North Koreans.

No longer guests of the government as during the Festival, the Black Panthers in Algiers needed to find places to live. Housing was scarce, for the capital was filled with rural migrants seeking employment; but jobs were even scarcer. Outside of the international political circles, the Panthers found themselves culturally isolated in the French and Arab speaking Islamic society. Few Blacks lived along Algeria's coastline, and the majority of the inhabitants in Algiers were Berber. Julia Hervé's mother, Ellen Wright, a literary agent in Paris, had visited Cleaver during the Festival. As well as agreeing to negotiate future publishing contracts for him, she advanced him a considerable sum of money in U.S. currency. This highly desirable commodity enabled Cleaver to organize his life privately in Algiers and to support the entire Panther contingent as well. The week before leaving for Pyongyang, Cleaver rented a spacious but bleak apartment on the outskirts of Algiers right on the shore of the Mediterranean. The two families with children moved into the apartment, while the two single men remained in the inexpensive Algiers hotel that had become their residence.

Repression and Ideology Promote International Work

Between 1966 and 1969, the Black Panther Party exploded into a nationwide political movement of men and women who formed chapters in more than thirty cities. Panther offices spread from Oakland to Sacramento, San Francisco, Los Angeles, Seattle, Denver, Kansas City, Des Moines, Chicago, New Orleans, Baltimore, Philadelphia, and New York within a few short years. During his presidential campaign, Richard Nixon stressed the need for "law and order,"and as soon as his administration took office in 1969, the scope and pace of the repression against the Black Panther Party intensified. Arrests, imprisonment, and death decimated the leadership and seemed to be dismantling the Black Panther Party.

In January 1969, two leaders of the Los Angeles branch of the Black Panther Party were shot to death. After a Black student meeting on the UCLA campus, Alprentice "Bunchy" Carter and John Huggins were murdered, apparently by members of Us, a Black nationalist organization led by Maulana Karenga. That April, New York police rounded up more than twenty members of New York's Black Panther Party and jailed them on charges of conspiring to bomb public places. The New Haven branch was shut down in May after nearly all its members were arrested for conspiracy to commit murder. Eventually, fourteen Panthers, including Chairman Bobby Seale, were jailed in New Haven and faced trial on those charges. On December 4, Chicago police raided the home of the Black Panther Party's Deputy Chairman Fred Hampton and murdered him as he slept, along with visiting Illinois Panther leader Mark Clark. The following week, the newly formed SWAT (Special Weapons and Tactics) squad of the Los Angeles police stormed the Central Avenue Black Panther Party headquarters. Although no one was killed during the ensuing shoot-out, eighteen Panthers were jailed on numerous charges and faced a series of expensive trials. In other cities, Panther offices were bombed or set on fire. Police attacks across the country happened with such regularity that it seemed they were being centrally co-ordinated by the government. That year, some twenty Panthers were killed and more than two hundred were imprisoned.[32] The escalating repression threw the movement into such disarray that the creation of any secure underground network was unlikely, and although Eldridge Cleaver never abandoned his desire to return to the United States, he devoted his energy to establishing a base of operation in Africa. By the time Cleaver left Algiers to visit North Korea, the expenses of bail, legal fees, and court proceedings had depleted the Party's funds, and the organization faced severe problems of internal security and discipline. Chairman Bobby Seale faced criminal charges in California, Illinois, and Connecticut. Chief of Staff David Hilliard was under federal indictment for threatening the life of President Nixon.

As the nationwide assault against the Black Panther Party magnified its internal conflict, the beleaguered leadership appropriated an overtly Marxist–Leninist ideology. Marxist theory clarified the role of the Black Panther Party as a vanguard party in the revolutionary struggle for Black liberation and helped to combat the debilitating collapse of intraparty discipline in the wake of the death, imprisonment, or exile of key leaders. Marxism–Leninism provided a useful justification for a policy of internal purges of Party membership across the country and also compelled obedience to Party dictates pursuant to the principle of "democratic centralism."[33] But as the rank and file saw it, the new policy often meant "all centralism and no democracy." Party morale sagged and frustration rose as the Black Panthers found themselves increasingly isolated by their violent confrontations with the police in city after city. However, the adoption of Marxism–Leninism enabled the Party to articulate its basis for international solidarity with the most vigorous antagonists of American imperialism in the ideological currency of the socialist world.

The extraordinary ideological polarization that the Vietnam War provoked led to massive international protests against the United States. The political climate became especially receptive to the Black Panther Party's strident anti-imperialism. More extensively than any previous Black organization, the Black Panther Party cultivated international support in mobilizing mass protests against the legal and political repression of the Party, beginning with its protest effort around Defense Minister Huey Newton's 1968 murder trial in Oakland. This gained international recognition for the Black Panther Party throughout Western Europe. Committees of solidarity with the Black Panthers were formed in Sweden, Denmark, the Netherlands, Belgium, Britain, France, and West Germany. The Scandinavian and the

West German committees were the most dynamic and the best organized as they were tied to strong student movements in countries where socialist parties were well-represented in the national government.

Cleaver's sojourn in North Korea brought the Black Panther Party in touch with the variant of Marxism–Leninism that Premier Kim IL Sung advocated, one that emphasized the concept of *Juche* or self-reliance. This idea became popular with many Black Panthers who were less than fully enthusiastic about the wholesale adaptation of an ideology essentially foreign to their perceived situation. The *Juche* concept justified the flexible translation of the Marxist–Leninist propositions the Panthers made, which traditional Marxists (especially American communists), received with skeptical disdain. For instead of basing their revolutionary strategy upon workers and seeking interracial unity within the working class, the Black Panthers saw the lumpen proletariat—the status to which imperialism had reduced colonized Black would-be workers—as the revolutionary class.

After attending the International Conference of Revolutionary Journalists, which brought representatives of ninety countries to Pyongyang to elicit their support for a propaganda campaign against U.S. imperialism, Byron Booth and Cleaver remained in North Korea.[34] For nearly a month, they traveled across the country, receiving lessons in Marxism–Leninism and Korea's history. *The Black Panther* began featuring the writings of Kim IL Sung regularly after Cleaver and Booth returned from North Korea, and Panther political education classes in the United States began to include pamphlets on Marxism–Leninism printed in North Korea. Back in Algiers, the North Korean representatives became the closest associates of the Black Panther Party, for they were anxious to have a vehicle for disseminating the ideology of Kim IL Sung within the United States.

Algerian Politics Complicates Effort to Create an International Base

The recently arrived Black Panthers, whose knowledge of the internal details of the Algerian revolution was minimal, found the political conflicts swirling around them particularly opaque. The FLN was Algeria's only legal political party, but since its beginning in 1954 it represented an unstable coalition of political perspectives, ranging from liberal to revolutionary.[35] After successfully negotiating Algeria's independence from France in 1962, the FLN suffered several internal crises that its lack of ideological unity left unresolved. Since independence, shifts in the controlling faction had weakened the party, and its ongoing conflicts—both ideological and pragmatic—perpetuated tensions within Algeria's political life that foreigners could not easily grasp. Boumedienne's 1965 coup d'état elevated the army into a dominant position, leaving the revolutionary factions of the FLN fragmented and isolated. Former President Ben Bella remained in Algiers under house arrest, but most of his supporters fled into exile.

Following the 1968 assassination attempt against President Boumedienne, the government imposed strict police control over everyone's movements and kept close watch over political activity. Suppression of opposition was the order of the day. Furthermore, the necessity for clandestine tactics during the war against France left secrecy and intrigue as the hallmarks of Algerian politics. While the hesitation to grant an official status to the Black Panther Party was not explained, it did not take the Panthers long to discover that Algeria's military government was not universally popular. But its imposition of curfews, road blocks, surveillance, infiltration, and other police tactics effectively stifled dissent. Algeria's domestic policies were geared toward maintaining internal stability and achieving economic development under a centrally directed state capitalism. Thus, the country's internal politics seemed to contradict the zealously anti-imperialist stance Algeria adopted in foreign policy. After nationalizing the French oil companies, Algeria undertook extensive negotiations with American corporations to develop its petrochemical industry. By the time the Cleavers arrived in Algiers, American technicians were working in Algerian oil fields, American oil companies had invested in the natural gas industry, and an American company was computerizing the operation of SONATRAC, the government oil corporation. Economic ventures on such a scale presaged the eventual resumption of diplomatic relations with the United States, but under the current political climate, that was prohibited. Nonetheless, high- level Algerian officials were already engaged in planning for this eventuality.[36]

Although the FLN was in charge of the liberation and opposition movements accredited in Algiers, it was no longer the central government. The FLN could merely implement the decisions reached by the Council of the Revolution. Although the relationship between the FLN officials and the Black Panthers seemed cordial and supportive, the power to authorize any concrete change in the Black Panther Party's status lay outside the domain of the FLN.

After Cleaver returned from North Korea, he was notified that the man who could authorize an official status for the Black Panther Party would see him. In his meeting with Commandante Hoffman, Cleaver learned that the Council of the Revolution considered the Black Panther Party an opposition movement, not a liberation movement against colonial domination. The government the Panthers opposed was not just any government, as Hoffman emphasized, but the government of the United States! Although he agreed verbally to grant the Black Panther Party official status, Hoffman did nothing to translate that into reality. The Algerian authorities refused to accede to American pressure to prevent the Black Panther Party from functioning in Algeria, but they also declined to make any concrete indications of their official recognition of the Black Panther Party in Algiers.

After renting another apartment for the Panthers from Cuba, Cleaver turned his own apartment on the outskirts of the city into a Black Panther Party office. Set in the midst of a poor Berber community, the Afro-American outpost was fully equipped with a desk, typewriter, telephone, television, tape recorder, and file cabinets. The apartment filled regularly with European and American visitors who were intensely involved in radical politics. While linked directly to the Panther headquarters in Oakland and to the solidarity committees in Europe, the office and its occupants remained isolated from the neighboring Algerians. The isolation came about in part from the ingrained suspicion Algerians felt towards non-Muslims, in part from their poorly concealed hostility to Blacks, and particularly because of the reluctance of the government to manifest visible support for the Black Panther Party.

An articulate young Jamaican named Connie Matthews, employed by UNESCO in Copenhagen, had helped sponsor Bobby Seale's visit to Scandinavia in 1968. Afterwards, she became active in the Danish Committee for Solidarity with the Black Panther Party. Energetic and dedicated to the Black liberation movement, Connie Matthews became International Coordinator of the Black Panther Party in 1969. She spent several months visiting the Black Panther headquarters in the United States, coordinating activities between the European solidarity committees and the Black Panther Party, writing for the Panther newspaper, and speaking at conferences. She briefly joined the Black Panther delegation to the Pan African Cultural Festival, and that following November Matthews returned to Algiers to collaborate with Cleaver on the international activities of the Black Panther Party in Europe.

The lack of any clear focus for carrying out the revolutionary aims of the Black Panther Party in the Algerian context felt disconcerting to the handful of fugitives in Algiers. Those conditions that stimulated the intense momentum of the Panther movement in the United States did not exist, and the cultural isolation of the Panthers attenuated their sense of belonging to a genuine community. While the Cleavers had been involved with the Party since its inception and had a strong vision of what an international base for the Black Panther Party could accomplish, the contingent of Panthers from Cuba had invested far less of themselves in the movement and found it difficult to sustain any sense of a larger purpose to their presence in Algeria. Frequently, the hijackers' behavior was unscrupulous, and their repeated infractions of discipline forced Cleaver to expel them from the Black Panther Party. With the exception of Gwen Patterson, a gentle, naive woman abandoned by her husband, they all left Algiers by March of 1970. As the momentum of the confrontations between Black Panthers and police forces in the United States continued, the international staff of the Black Panther Party increased as more fugitives seeking to avoid arrest or imprisonment fled to Algiers.

Don Cox, a highly competent Panther organizer from San Francisco, arrived in March 1970. After belatedly discovering that his name was included among twenty-two Panthers indicted for conspiracy to commit murder in Baltimore, he went underground and then left the country. Unlike most of the Panthers, who were young and single, Cox had raised a family and run a printing business in San Francisco before becoming involved in the Black Panther Party. His personal stability and political experience were valuable assets to the new international section of the Party. That June, two fugitives from the New York chapter arrived in Algiers. Sekou Odinga and Larry Mack, who had managed to escape during the mass arrest of New York Panthers and go into hiding in Philadelphia, had hijacked a plane to Guinea and from there came to Algiers. Eventually Odinga's wife and infant twin sons joined him, and Cox's new wife from the San Francisco chapter also came to Algiers.

The Black Panther's international perspective came primarily from studying powerful revolutionary movements, especially those in Cuba, China, Vietnam, and Algeria. The leaders and doctrines that had guided these successful revolutions had inspired Black Panthers and given them enormous confidence in the ultimate success of their own struggle. However, the vast discrepancies between social conditions in the Third World and the United States were, for the most part, overlooked by Panthers studying these movements.

The world into which Panthers came to escape imprisonment in America was an ancient North African society struggling to modernize itself in the aftermath of a vicious war with France, which had ruled the country for 130 years. Bombed out buildings still stood as grim reminders of the war that had left no family in Algeria unscathed. The French colonial past was evident in the striking architecture of the city and the complex bureaucracy of the state, while the daily calls to prayer and veiled women attested to the resurgence of Algeria's Islamic heritage. Arabic was the dominant language, but everyone in Algiers still spoke French, the language of government and commerce. The complicated tribal and ethnic divisions among Arabs, Berbers, and Africans bewildered Panthers accustomed to simple stratifications of color and class, as did the general absence of antagonism towards France. The daily juxtaposition of ancient and modern, North African and French, yielded unending confusion to the Black refugees accustomed to a fast-paced, sophisticated urban life.

Thus, adapting to life in Algiers, where nothing was remotely similar to America, presented a shock for which none of the Panthers was prepared. Few Algerians would discuss their society, their government, or their recent history with any Panthers, who were left to grope for such understanding on their own, whatever assistance they got usually being offered by other foreigners. The tension in Algiers was inescapable and unrelieved by intimate friendship. Government surveillance of the Panthers so inhibited Algerians who were interested in becoming acquainted with the Panthers that interactions remained superficial and frequently uncomfortable. Yet, eventually, as their numbers increased and they managed to make Algerian friends, both within and outside of government circles, the isolation that initially frustrated the Panthers began to diminish.

The breakthrough happened in the spring of 1970. Mohammed Yazid, an influential Algerian politician whose wife was American, took an interest in the Black Panthers. He invited the entire group and Elaine Klein to have dinner at his villa in Blida, a small town west of Algiers. A cordial, cosmopolitan host, Yazid was the first Algerian to display personal hospitality to the Black Panthers. During Algeria's war for independence, Yazid, a brilliant political strategist, had represented the FLN at the United Nations, and although he was no longer active in Algerian politics, he retained many friends and associates within the governing bureaucracy. Elaine Klein, who had worked with Yazid at the UN, encouraged him to help the Black Panthers. His intervention finally won the Black Panther Party the official recognition as an accredited organization in Algiers that Party members had been hoping for since the Pan African Cultural Festival.

The Institute of International Studies, headed by Commandante Hoffman, who was appointed as Mayor of Algiers, authorized the FLN to accord the Black Panther Party all the privileges of an accredited movement. These included the use of a facility provided by the FLN, the right to obtain entrance and exit visas for guests and members of the organization, a monthly stipend, and official identity cards issued by the FLN, which facilitated all organizational activities in the city, such as obtaining a post office box and automobile registration. The Black Panther Party was added to the list of accredited movements and like the rest, was accorded a quasi-diplomatic status in Algeria.

The Black Panther Party's "People's Diplomacy"

Domestically, the Black Panther Party analysis insisted that racism could not be fought with racism, but with solidarity. Unlike most Black nationalist organizations during the 1960s, the Black Panther Party encouraged close cooperation across racial and cultural barriers and engaged in numerous coalitions. Its nationwide coalition with the predominantly White Peace and Freedom Party, begun in 1968, sparked tremendous controversy during the Black Power Era. Stokely Carmichael, among numerous other nationalistic Blacks, denounced the Black Panther Party for its cooperation with Whites and resigned as the Party's Prime Minister in 1969.

The Black Panther Party advocated a full-fledged American Revolution to replace domination by "pig power" with the freedom gained through "people's power." Recognizing that the revolution could not be accomplished by Blacks alone, the Panthers sought to unify all disaffected and oppressed peoples in America to combat the imperialist monopoly of power and transfer control over the country's resources into the hands of the people. In California, the Panthers worked closely with the Brown Berets, a Chicano group similar to the Black Panthers; the Red Guards in Chinatown, and various radical White groups and individuals. In Chicago, Fred Hampton organized the "Rainbow Coalition" combining the Puerto Rican Young Lords, the Chinese-American Red Guards, the Appalachian Whites' group, the Young Patriots, the Black Stone Rangers, and the Black Panther Party, modeling the antiracist direction in which the organization sought to move within the United States. Understanding how intricately Black liberation within America was bound to the destruction of America's imperialist power, Cleaver sought to make international alliances for the Black Panther party with the most aggressive foes of American imperialism in the world.

In Algeria, the kind of tensions and frustrations the Black Panthers experienced bore little resemblance to what the Party faced in the United States, where confrontation with the system was direct and violent. The FLN was only willing to enable the Black Panthers to display their presence publicly, which had symbolic importance in a nation where the United States government was denied formal representation, but the military training facility Cleaver had envisioned never materialized. Having access to the Algerian international base, however, permitted Panthers to communicate directly with the embassies of socialist states from which they sought support. But every effort to secure major financial backing or a site for military training failed.

Although the Panthers had difficulty meeting all of their goals in Algeria, the physical establishment of a political presence outside the United States represented a kind of victory for the Black movement, magnified by the international scope of anti-American sentiment created by the Vietnam War. Later, the Panthers came to realize that their political presence outside the United States also allowed socialist governments to manipulate the Black Panther Party to serve ends that were extraneous to their own goals within America.

In Algiers, the Korean Embassy maintained close relations with the Black Panthers, frequently inviting Panthers for dinners, receptions, or meetings. The occasions tended to be formal, and all conversation required an interpreter. Frequently, Kathleen Cleaver served as translator for these meetings, some of which took place at the Cleavers' residence. During his 1969 visit to Pyongyang, Cleaver had been asked to return to North Korea with a delegation representing progressive Americans. The North Korean diplomats in Algiers were instructed by the newly formed Committee for the Peaceful Reunification of the Fatherland to join the campaign to gain international support for Korea's unification. The major obstacle the committee faced was American political, military, and economic support for the South Korean state. The diplomats were persistent in their effort to secure the American delegation's visit to Pyongyang and energetically provided Cleaver with all the support he needed to get the project moving.

Cleaver delegated the process of selecting the people to visit North Korea to David Hilliard at the Panther headquarters and to his former editor at *Ramparts,* Bob Scheer. Scheer had run for Congress on an antiwar platform in 1966 as one of the first "peace" candidates to challenge the war at the polls, and he became increasingly involved in radical politics and journalism in the

Bay Area. By July 1970, a delegation representing a cross-section of radical organizations was ready to travel to Pyongyang via Moscow, where Cleaver joined them. The individuals represented the antiwar movement, the radical media, the women's liberation movement, the Asian revolutionary group, the Red Guard, and the Black Panther Party. The group of seven women and four men called themselves the American Peoples' Anti-Imperialist Delegation, emphasizing what united them as a group, and what separated them from the American government.[37]

Shortly before Cleaver left to lead the delegation to North Korea, the FLN provided the Black Panther Party with a spacious building for its office in Algiers. After South Vietnam's NLF became recognized as the Provisional Revolutionary Government, its representatives in Algiers were given more prestigious accommodations, and the FLN decided to make a symbolic statement by assigning the National Liberation Front's former quarters to the Black Panther Party. However, disputes within the FLN over who would receive the elegant villa delayed its presentation until June 1970. The new office of the International Section of the Black Panther Party was a beautiful, two-story, white stucco building with a courtyard, all enclosed behind stone walls. It was located in El Biar, a pleasant quarter of Algiers. The Panthers in Algiers spent the summer refurbishing and equipping the villa to be ready for its formal opening ceremony, which would coincide with Cleaver's return from Asia with the entire American People's Anti-Imperialist Delegation.

In Pyongyang, the American Peoples Anti-Imperialist Delegation was greeted with austere, but warm Korean communist hospitality. American guests were a rarity in North Korea, and the Delegation received a showcase tour of the country. They saw meticulous museums commemorating American atrocities during the Korean War and striking evidence of Korea's rapid and successful recovery. They discovered a clean, efficient, industrialized state whose population was highly disciplined. The Delegation's itinerary included attending spectacular cultural and athletic events, visits to factories, schools, the Children's Palace, and meetings with numerous organizations. But their ability to obtain any information outside official channels was tightly circumscribed, for Korea was an enclosed world sealed off from unwanted influences, suffused with the "cult" of Kim IL Sung. His statue, portrait, or photograph appeared at every site, and his name was mentioned in connection with every place the delegation toured or each event they were told about. The "courageous leader of the 40 million Korean people" was given credit for every achievement in the country, making every discussion with the Korean hosts seem to American delegates like listening to preprogrammed statements.

While the Delegation was touring North Korea, Huey Newton was released from prison in California. The California Court of Appeals had overturned his manslaughter conviction in June on procedural grounds and ordered a new trial. On August 5, 1970, Newton was released on $50,000 bail in Oakland pending his new trial.[38] Cleaver, removed from immediate involvement in the fierce intraparty struggle underway, was perplexed to discover that some Panthers greeted Newton's release with suspicions of foul play. He felt jubilant at Newton's freedom and saw it as an unqualified victory for the Black Panther Party. He was excited by the possibility that Newton would be in Algiers for the formal opening of the International Section and was thrilled by the opportunity of seeing Newton in person once again.

But the Delegation's return to Algiers was postponed. An unexpected opportunity presented itself when the Vietnamese ambassador in Pyongyang invited the Delegation to Hanoi. The Black Panther Party had not only consistently opposed the war, but emphasized the parallels between the Black struggle and the war Vietnam's people were fighting against American imperialism. For the revolutionary Panthers, the success of national liberation movements in Asia, Africa, and Latin America were blows against the system that oppressed Blacks in America. *The Black Panther* devoted several pages of each issue to international revolutionary news, much of which focused on Asian resistance to American imperialism. The ability of the Vietnamese to maintain such concerted resistance to the technologically superior American armed forces won the admiration of everyone in the Movement, and opposition to American involvement in the Vietnam War was one point on which agreement among radicals was unanimous. The members of the Delegation leaped at the opportunity to see North Vietnam firsthand (except for Black Panther Party delegate Elaine Brown, who wanted to return to California immediately after she learned that Newton was free).

A significant number of Panther leaders, including Chairman Bobby Seale, had been in the armed forces, and the Black Panther Party paid special attention to the Black soldier. The Party newspaper frequently ran appeals to Black soldiers in Vietnam to oppose the war and to recognize the folly of fighting on behalf of their oppressor. In numerous forums, the Panthers advocated sentiments like those expressed in Cleaver's "Letter to My Black Brothers in Vietnam." He asked the Black soldier to "either quit the army now or start destroying from the inside. Anything else is . . . a form of treason against your own people." The letter insisted that instead of fighting the Vietnamese, Black soldiers should "start killing the racist pigs who are over there giving you orders."[39] One of Newton's first acts following his release from prison was to announce at a press conference that the Black Panther Party would send troops to help the NLF fight in Vietnam.[40]

The NLF also acknowledged a connection between its fight in Vietnam and that of Blacks in America. In 1969 an effort to exchange American P.O.W.s for imprisoned Panther leaders Newton and Seale had been proposed by the NLF through Cleaver in Algiers. The plan was promoted within the United States by antiwar movement activists, but the American government completely ignored it.[41] The Delegation was also invited to China, but it could only visit Peking briefly in transit to Hanoi. The Chinese hosts, the Committee for Friendship with the American People, asked Cleaver to return to China at a later date with an all-Black Panther delegation, however.

In Hanoi, the government honored the visiting Delegation with a celebration marking the International Day of Solidarity with the Afro-American People on August 18, 1970, the day that OSPAAL (Organization for Solidarity with the People of Africa, Asia, and Latin America) had selected to commemorate the anniversary of the 1965 Watts uprising.[42] While in Hanoi, Cleaver broadcast a radio message directed to Black soldiers encouraging them to either refuse to fight, desert, or sabotage the war from within.[43] Their hosts in Hanoi gave the members of the Delegation a packet of 379 letters from P.O.W.s to deliver upon their return to America, but the letters were confiscated by customs agents when they arrived in New York.

The visit to North Korea, North Vietnam, and China was an exercise in what Cleaver termed "people's diplomacy," in direct opposition to the official posture of the American government that withheld recognition from the governments sponsoring the Delegation's trip. In the Asian capitals the Delegation visited, their effort to make a clear distinction between the sentiments of America's people and the policies of the American government was welcome, for such an effort formed part of North Vietnam's diplomatic strategy. The expansion of the antiwar movement in the United States gave encouragement to that strategy, although the extent of domestic opposition to America's role in the war did not indicate any corresponding level of popular support for communist regimes.

This important distinction was lost on the Nixon Administration, however, which viewed the international activities of the Black Panther Party and all other American radicals with alarm. While the CIA insisted that "radical movements in the United States were home-grown, indigenous responses to domestic problems and grievances that had been growing for years," The White House was "preoccupied with the extent of foreign influence on domestic radicals."[44] The CIA investigated the issue of Algerian support for the Black Panther Party sixteen times, but the White House remained dissatisfied with the CIA's conclusion that it was not significant.[45] To satisfy his insistence that the foreign support for American radicals be discovered, Nixon had forty agents and thirty clerks from the FBI assigned to collect intelligence abroad, a policy that the CIA felt was an unwarranted encroachment upon their territory.[46] This international apparatus of the FBI undertook a highly secret campaign of intervention in the internal activities of the Black Panther Party that directly affected the International Section.

When the delegation returned to Algiers in September, the International Section of the Black Panther Party was formally opened. The Panthers invited representatives of all the liberation movements and socialist states to their villa, inaugurating their official establishment within the revolutionary diplomatic community in Algiers. The villa became a kind of embassy of the American revolution, receiving visitors from all over the world. But the Panthers found themselves essentially limited to serving as an information center, conveying news about revolutionary developments within the United States to their associates in Algiers and receiving information from all the movements represented in Algiers. The International Section of the Black Panther Party, however, turned into a magnet for an increasingly diverse crop of fugitives from the United States.

In California, Jonathan Jackson's revolutionary attempt to free several Black prisoners from the Marin County courthouse in August 1970 ended in carnage. Jackson, the judge he kidnapped, and all but one of the escaping prisoners died in the shooting outside the courthouse, and it was later discovered that one of Jackson's guns had been registered to Angela Davis, who then belonged to a small organization advocating freedom for the imprisoned Soledad Brothers. Angela Davis was indicted for murder and soon disappeared.

In Algiers, the Panthers expected to greet the fugitive Angela Davis, but that October the FBI arrested her in New York. However, a few weeks later, LSD guru Dr. Timothy Leary, who was serving time in San Luis Obispo prison on drug charges, was freed by the underground revolutionary Weathermen and quickly brought to Algiers. Leary and his wife were hardly committed to the same goals as the Black Panthers, and they caused so many problems that the Panthers in Algiers eventually put them under house arrest in February 1971. Such autonomous action threw the Panthers into conflict with the local Algerian authorities as well as all of Leary's supporters in the U. S. But far more complex difficulties were facing the International Section of the Black Panther Party.

The community of fugitives kept expanding. Cleaver's wife Kathleen and Cox's wife Barbara Easley gave birth to new babies in Pyongyang, where they were invited as guests of the Democratic Women's Union during the visit of the Delegation. Pete O'Neal, the leader of the Kansas City branch of the BPP, had fled to Algiers with his wife Charlotte, who also had a son in Algiers. Thus, the International Section was faced with the complexities of supporting an expanding community of families. In response, the Panthers organized a communal nursery, published a newsletter, built a library, and made audio and video tapes for distribution in the United States. But the Panther activities possible in Algiers were limited. The International Section could only serve as a base for international activities, as little more than peoples' diplomacy could be carried out.

Impact of Intra-Party Strife

Cleaver was anxious to have Newton visit the International Section and tried to persuade him to travel from Algiers to China with a Black Panther Party delegation. But Newton claimed he was unable to get a passport and seemed unaware of the extent of international activity generated during his imprisonment. Newton's apparent reluctance to come to Algiers disappointed Cleaver, but the new directions Newton adopted after his release were even more disturbing.

Newton assumed the arrogant title of "Supreme Commander" and then modified it to "Supreme Servant of the People." Other than the public statement he issued endorsing gay liberation, most of the reports in *The Black Panther* of Newton's speeches showed him giving an increasingly theoretical analysis divorced from practical merit, which left Cleaver and the entire community of fugitives in Algiers perplexed. His attention became absorbed by the idea of holding a Revolutionary Peoples' Constitutional Convention in Philadelphia to draft a new Constitution. By the time Newton proclaimed the new ideological principle of "intercommunalism,"[47] which was to transcend internationalism, Cleaver reluctantly surrendered all hope that Newton's return would lift the sagging morale that was paralyzing Black Panthers. Unresolved conflicts were tearing the Party apart, and Newton's release did nothing to calm the tensions that had been boiling within the Panther Party since 1969.

David Hilliard had implemented a harshly authoritarian policy that engendered intense resentment. Purges of rebellious Panthers were disrupting entire chapters, and the rank and file across the country were furious at the heavy-handed treatment meted out from Oakland. Transfers of Panthers from chapter to chapter and cultivation of loyalty to the central staff in Oakland kept decision making tightly centralized. Faced with mushrooming trials and arrests, Hilliard had attempted to keep order in the party at the expense of continuing revolutionary activity. The use of expulsions to compel compliance intensified. By the time Newton was released in August 1970, rebellion against Hilliard's tactics was out in the open, and opposition factions were coalescing. Newton failed to investigate the situation himself. Instead, he supported Hilliard's conservative approach and even increased the centralization of leadership and funds in Oakland. Newton's inaction only exacerbated tensions within the BPP. As a result, Party morale sank, membership declined, and hostility toward Hilliard and Newton mounted.

Another source of tension was disagreement among Panthers over the nature of the Black Panther Party. Since 1969, the efforts to build both a mass movement and a vanguard party had always been in conflict and had attracted people with different aims into the Party. But while verbally advocating revolution, the Oakland leadership was actually inhibiting individual members from carrying out revolutionary acts. Also, exacerbating the problems with organizational unity was the level of attention given to arrested members. The Party was devoting its resources to finance the trials of key leaders at the expense of many ordinary Panthers facing trials on serious charges. These members felt slighted and accused the Oakland-based leadership of favoritism.

In Los Angeles, the experience of Panther leader Elmer Geronimo Pratt, (who later changed his name to ji Jaga) who gained a reputation as a genuine revolutionary, is instructive. Before coming to Los Angeles to attend UCLA, he had fought in Vietnam. After leaving the Army, he came to UCLA where he met Alprentice Carter. Pratt was drawn to the revolutionary program of the Black Panther Party, which gave him an entirely different perspective on his situation as a Black man and the role of the U.S. Army in Vietnam. Dedicating himself to the liberation of Blacks within America, Pratt rose quickly in the Party leadership. He used his experience in guerrilla warfare to train the Los Angeles Panthers in revolutionary struggle. His skill as a leader enabled him to maintain discipline more effectively in Los Angeles than was the case in many other chapters, and luck helped him to survive several attempts on his life. When the Panthers found out that no one had been killed during the 1969 SWAT attack on the Los Angeles Panther office, Pratt was credited with the one "victory" in the sustained nationwide assault police were waging against the Black Panthers. He was revered as a hero, and *The Black Panther* praised him as representing "the essence of a revolutionary."

Initially held without bail after being arrested in connection with the attack on the Panther office, Pratt finally won his release in 1970 and promptly went underground. He set up a secret camp in Texas where he began training an underground military force for the Black Panther Party. Shortly after an emissary from Hilliard came to see him in Texas, FBI agents surrounded the apartment where Pratt and his comrades were hiding, arrested them all, and extradited them back to Los Angeles. It was in late December while in jail that Pratt discovered the article in *The Black Panther* denouncing him. In the article, Newton accused him of working for the CIA, of displaying rude and reckless behavior, and announced the expulsion of Pratt , his wife Sandra (Nsondi ji Jaga), and all his associates from the Black Panther Party.[48]

This act rocked the Panther Party. The year before Pratt had been hailed as a revolutionary hero. Cleaver, who personally knew Pratt and couldn't believe the expulsion was warranted, was stunned. It became clear to everyone in Algiers that something was severely askew inside the Black Panther Party. Several long-distance telephone conversations among Cleaver, Hilliard, and Newton did not reveal any satisfactory explanation for the actions of the Central Committee.

The trial of the New York Panthers arrested on bomb conspiracy charges gained intense publicity. The highly controversial case became known as the "New York 21." The Panthers won broad support from numerous political and community groups to win the release of some members of the Panther 21 whose bail was set at ridiculously high levels. Visiting New York in February, Newton denounced Michael Tabor and Richard Moore, two members of the New York 21 who had jumped bail, as "enemies of the people."[49] He also expelled half of the defendants as the trial was in progress in retaliation for the "Open Letter to the Weathermen" that they published in *The East Village Other,* a small underground paper in New York. The publication of the letter, which stridently criticized the leadership of the Black Panther Party for its lack of militancy, was a last resort for dissatisfied Panthers after previous attempts to express their concerns to the leadership in Oakland were ignored.

Michael "Cetewayo" Tabor was a serious, articulate, and thoughtful member of the New York chapter. His pamphlet, "Capitalism + Dope = Genocide," had attracted wide attention in the Party, which had recently initiated a campaign against dope peddlers in the Black community. Tabor, after being pulled into Newton's inner circle, fell in love with Connie Matthews, who was working as Newton's personal secretary while in the United States. The couple got married and planned their escape from Newton's entourage after Tabor's life was threatened by people he termed Newton's "robots." They fled to Algiers in February. The bizarre picture they painted of Newton surrounded by sycophants was unrecognizable to Cleaver and Cox, who hadn't seen Newton since his 1968 trial in Oakland.

The size of the community of fugitives and the leaders collected in Algiers increased the significance of the International Section in the disputes roiling the Party. Panthers everywhere refused to believe that O'Neil, Odinga, Cox, and Cleaver all supported Newton's latest actions. Newton, for his part, anxiously wanted to prove to the disgruntled and antagonized members that there was no division between him and Cleaver. He arranged for a telephone hook-up between San Francisco and Algiers with the host of a television show on which he was to be a guest. The popular A.M. show was broadcast live in San Francisco on February 26, 1971, and also carried on a local radio station. The host Agar Jaiks routinely asked Cleaver if he had anything else he would like to say to the audience at the end of his interview.

Cleaver's answer led to what was later called the "split" in the Black Panther Party. In response, he stated briefly that David Hilliard's actions were destroying the Black Panther Party, that Geronimo and the New York Panthers should be reinstated and given a public apology, and that David Hilliard should be expelled instead.[50] Afterward, an enraged Newton telephoned Cleaver in Algiers and expelled the entire International Section from the Black Panther Party.

Immediately, the New York Panther chapter allied itself with Cleaver, calling for Hilliard's resignation and a public trial of Newton for abusing Party funds. But a few weeks later, the verbal attacks escalated into violence. On March 8, 1971, Robert Webb, a San Francisco Black Panther leader who had moved to New York, was shot to death in the middle of the day on 125th Street in Harlem.[51] The New York Panthers blamed his killing on Huey Newton's henchmen and realized there was no possibility of reconciliation. The Oakland Panthers became known derisively as the "Peralta Street gang," in reference to the location of their headquarters on Peralta Street. The New York Panthers believed that the refusal of the police to do anything about Webb's killing showed complicity between Newton's faction and the police.

Then on April 17, 1971, the circulation manager of *The Black Panther*, Sam Napier, who had been sent to New York to supervise the national distribution of the paper, was murdered in retaliation for Webb's killing. But this time, Panthers were arrested in several states, including Michigan and New York, in connection with Napier's killing. Others were detained as material witnesses. This confirmed the rampant suspicion among New York Panthers that Newton's clique was collaborating with the police in some way.

The Panthers in Algiers aligned with the New York Panthers in a desperate effort to salvage the crumbling Party. Lengthy long-distance phone conversations between New York, Algiers, and San Francisco took place in hopes of pulling together a new Central Committee. The New York chapter began publishing its own newspaper, *Right On*, to counteract *The Black Panther*— now totally under Newton's control. Although the New York Panthers were able to rally a few dedicated people to their side, the attempt to reorganize the entire Party failed. Panthers who aligned themselves with the more radical New York faction were being arrested across the country and faced threats on their lives from Newton's supporters, while those connected with the Newton faction seemed immune from police attention regardless of what they did. The Black Panther Party became irrevocably split, with the line between the two factions drawn in blood. The separation eventually led to the formation of a clandestine Black Liberation Army in New York, composed of former Panthers determined to carry out revolutionary action in isolation from any larger political movement.

Newton took the opportunity to blame all the past mistakes of the Black Panther Party on Cleaver, whom he now claimed had "defected."[52] He set the organization on a new track, "survival pending revolution," emphasizing service projects called "survival programs," such as food giveaways, free medical clinics, free breakfast for children, and other social programs. After Newton's third murder trial ended with a hung jury, the charges against him were dismissed in January 1972. By then the Black Panther Party had completed its transition into a reformist community action group. Newton announced that the Panthers had been wrong to attack the police, that they would return to the church, participate in electoral politics, support Black capitalist ventures, and work within the system.

In the midst of the despair about the split in the Party and the Panthers' growing isolation in Algiers, an invitation to attend an International Conference of Solidarity with the People Under Portuguese Domination arrived in Algiers, addressed explicitly to Cleaver. The Congolese Socialist Youth Union was sponsoring the conference in Brazzaville that April, and had invited delegations from thirty socialist countries and liberation movements. The Panthers learned about their invitation at the last minute from the FLN youth organization.

Next, the Congolese Ambassador in Algiers invited the Panthers to his Embassy to make arrangements for the trip. The Ambassador informed the Panthers that Ernest Ndalla, the first secretary of the Congolese Worker's Party, had personally initiated the invitation. Further, he had asked that the Panther delegation to the conference remain in Brazzaville to attend their May Day celebrations. Panthers enthusiastically welcomed the opportunity to visit the Peoples' Republic of the Congo, especially because Algeria's shallow support left them vulnerable in the climate of uncertainty that followed the split. The recognition that the International Section received from African revolutionaries was crucially important.

Back to Africa

The city of Brazzaville, the capital of the former French Congo, was located directly across the river from Kinshasa, the capital of Zaire (formerly the Belgian Congo). The revolutionary movement in Congo-Kinshasa, where Ché Guevara fought with the African guerrillas, was defeated during the 1960s. When Fidel Castro ordered Guevara to withdraw, it disrupted a strategy that would have linked two military forces, and left the Congolese isolated.[54] The government troops defeated them, but across the river in Congo-Brazzaville, the revolutionary movement succeeded in seizing power. The Peoples' Republic of the Congo was established there in 1969.

The Congo reverberated with historical and cultural associations for Afro-Americans: Congo was virtually synonymous with Africa. The story of a revolution in the Congo would make a powerful statement to Blacks in America. Cleaver planned to document fully the first Black Panther visit to Black Africa. By portraying the Black Panthers' visit to Congo-Brazzaville, Cleaver hoped to project a synthesis of Marxism–Leninism with African culture. In America, the two had become separated and their division produced a weakness in the liberation movement.

The delegation to the Congo was selected in order to best document the trip. Cleaver chose Michael Tabor, who was a good writer; Kathleen Cleaver, who had frequently served as interpreter in Algiers; and Denise Oliver, a lively, articulate member of the New York Panther chapter who was sent to Algiers to coordinate work on the Party newspaper. William Stephens, a young Black American photographer living in Paris, would join the group in Brazzaville to film the trip. A radical French video group in Paris that had been collaborating with the International Section on several projects had agreed to provide Stephens with all the supplies and equipment necessary for the documentary.

As soon as they arrived in Brazzaville, the Panthers attended the receptions, conference sessions, and public rallies held in support of the war against Portuguese colonialism in Africa. Representatives of Guinea-Bissau's PAIGC (African Party for the Independence of Guinea-Bissau and Cape Verde Islands), Angola's MPLA (Popular Movement for the Liberation of Angola), and Mozambique's FRELIMO (Front for the Liberation of Mozambique) were the featured speakers for these events. A host of delegates from socialist youth movements in Eastern Europe, the Soviet Union, Asia, and North Africa expressed their support for the struggle against Portuguese colonialism.

After the conference ended, the Panther delegation devoted several weeks to learning all they could about the Congolese revolution. The delegation had a full-time guide from the Congolese Socialist Youth Union, Comrade Okabande, and he arranged a rich itinerary of travel and meetings with leading government officials. The Panthers toured the main cities, Brazzaville and Pointe Noire. From Pointe Noire on the coast, they traveled by helicopter to an MPLA camp in the hills of the neighboring Portuguese enclave of Cabinda. An English-speaking Army officer who had attended college in San Francisco gave them lessons in the Congo's ethnic composition and its recent history. They went to meetings of the Women's Union, met with the Minister of Education, and attended a special cultural program put on for their benefit by an elite paratrooper unit of the People's Army. Their Congolese hosts were warm, open, and hospitable people who welcomed the delegation of Black Panthers as distinguished visitors.

Meeting Ange Diawara, the Political Commissar of the People's Army, was the most impressive experience of the visit. Diawara invited the Panthers to his office in the Ministry of Civil Air Transport, hosted their visit to the paratrooper camp, and held a dinner for them at his home. He was a fiery, brilliant man totally committed to the revolutionary transformation of the neocolonial Congo into a peoples' state, the task for which he was training the Army.

Diawara, a member of the Political Bureau of the Congolese Worker's Party, had been a leader in the revolutionary youth movement that had overthrown the former government in 1968. After fighting against soldiers sent from Congo-Kinshasa in 1970 to defeat the new government, Diawara had joined the Army.[55] He was engaged in the process of transforming the old colonial Army inherited from the French into a Peoples' Army in which "politics is in command."[55] In the lengthy interview conducted with Diawara, and during their many conversations, the Panthers gained valuable insights into the political contradictions African revolutionaries were fighting, especially concerning the neocolonial stranglehold their countries faced after independence.

The Panthers also met at length with Ernest Ndalla, the member of the Political Bureau in charge of Organization and First Secretary of the Worker's Party. Ndalla gave the Panthers a careful, perceptive Marxist analysis of the realities facing the Congo. He insisted that socialism alone could guarantee independence. He smoothly articulated the revolutionary ideas in the Congolese context that the Black Panthers had raggedly attempted to implement in America.

Cleaver had finally encountered Marxist–Leninists whose analysis made complete sense to him and with whom the Black Panthers could feel at ease. The Panthers were so enthralled with their Congolese hosts that Cleaver asked Ndalla if the International Section of the Black Panther Party could move its headquarters to Brazzaville. But he gave the same answer that everyone gave to that request: "You'll have to ask the President."

President Marien Ngouabi was a soldier whose imprisonment for revolutionary activities had been the catalyst that sparked the overthrow of the previous government.[57] Ngouabi gave the keynote speech at the May Day ceremonies in Brazzaville, and he was clearly the most powerful figure in the Worker's Party. The Panthers were taken to meet Ngouabi at his home, but that brief, reserved encounter gave them no indication of his opinion on their request to relocate to Brazzaville.

The Panther delegation returned to Algiers with photographs, taped interviews, video tape footage, and stacks of other documents from their visit to the Congo. In New York, Denise Oliver supervised the publication of an issue of *Right On* devoted to the Congo, featuring photographs of the May Day demonstrations and excerpts from the interviews with Diawara and Ndalla. Stephens went back to Paris to edit the film, entitled *We Have Come Back*.

The title was taken from an interchange with an old farmer the Panthers met in the countryside. The discussion had to be translated first from English into French, then into Lingala, the dominant Congolese ethnic language, and then into the indigenous language he spoke. Standing in a clearing overlooking the sea, the old man said that the empty countryside used to be filled with people, but so many had been taken away in boats to America. The country could not be great when the people are gone, the man commented. Then Cleaver told him that the Panthers were descendants of those slaves taken away to America. The old man's face lit up, and he exclaimed, "Oh! You have come back!"[58]

The desire to return to Africa was always a powerful undercurrent in the Afro-American experience. The hunger to see the land where their ancestors were captured and brought as slaves to America remained ever present among Blacks struggling to express their identity in a White-dominated world. But few Blacks knew about any reciprocal concern Africans felt about the descendants of those captured slaves. The old man's cheerful welcome struck a deep emotional response among the Panthers, who each felt the joy that comes from being reunited with long lost relatives.

Back in Algiers, the interviews with Ndalla and Diawara were transcribed and translated into English. Along with several other articles about the Peoples' Republic of the Congo, they were published in a small booklet called *Revolution in the Congo.* Far more than Cuban, Chinese, Algerian, or Vietnamese revolutions, the revolution in the Congo could be projected as a model that Afro-Americans could appropriate. Cleaver decided to use the resources and contacts the International Section had built up in Algiers to form an independent communications center for revolutionary movements, which he named the Revolutionary Peoples Communications Network (RPCN). It was to be a new form for linking the groups and individuals that had been brought together through the Black Panther Party before the split, but now lacked any central cohesion. In October 1971, Elaine Klein, Kathleen Cleaver, and Jessica Scott, an Afro-American woman from Frankfurt, West Germany, who worked on the underground newspaper *Voice of the Lumpen,* all traveled to the United States to organize the RPCN.

To raise money for the International Section, Kathleen Cleaver made numerous speeches at colleges and conferences across the country about the international context of the revolutionary struggle in America. While attracting considerable interest, the RPCN was never able to provide substantial organizational cohesion to the scattered newspapers, groups, and individuals it sought to link together. Apathy and defeat seemed generalized in the movement in America, and the fear and confusion generated by the split in the Panther Party posed a major obstacle to anything connected with Eldridge Cleaver. That December, Elaine Klein and Kathleen Cleaver returned to Algiers.

The situation facing the International Section in Algiers was demoralizing. Nothing so far had developed in the effort to move to Brazzaville, and there was no indication of when, or if, the Panthers could expect any reply from the Congolese government. Little relevant work could be accomplished in Algiers. The financial burden of sustaining the fugitive community was growing greater as the resources were dwindling. Cleaver had been made a designated national of North Korea, North Vietnam, and China under the Trading with the Enemy Act after returning from those countries in 1970, and as a result, all his royalties in the United States were blocked. Getting further advances on a contract with an American publisher was very difficult. The other members of the International Section had meager resources. There was no way of earning money in Algiers, as no one could speak the language adequately, nor were their skills marketable in Algiers. Furthermore, the fugitives there without passports or money were unable to go elsewhere. The isolation of the Panthers and their inability to do anything constructive in Algiers wore everyone down and aggravated the inevitable conflicts that close group living provokes.

America's involvement in the war in Vietnam united the entire socialist world and the nonaligned Third World against the United States. Even the European allies did not fully endorse the American role in Vietnam, especially France. But that entire structure of political alignments was upset by President Nixon's visit to the Peoples' Republic of China in February 1972.

The split in the Black Panther Party had prevented Cleaver from taking a Black Panther Party delegation to China in 1971. But a series of Chinese overtures toward the United States were made, beginning with the invitation to the U.S. Table Tennis Team to compete in Peking, moves Cleaver termed "ping pong diplomacy." The revelation that Secretary of State Henry Kissinger had secretly visited Peking in July 1971 struck the revolutionary movements like a thunderbolt. Then the Panthers in Algiers were startled to discover that Huey Newton, his bodyguard Robert Bay, and Elaine Brown visited Peking. The international posture of China was radically changing, and no one in Algiers, not even Mr. Sun, the local representative of New China News Agency, knew what to think.

The press photographs showing Mao Tse-Tung and Richard Nixon shaking hands testified to a meeting that no revolutionary would have ever imagined. Cleaver's statement that any reconciliation between the United States and Communist China would do no good for Black people was attacked by the North Koreans as "revisionist." It became obvious that world-scale preparations for the post-Vietnam War world were being made, and that the future for the fugitive Black Panthers trapped in Algiers was dim.

In late February 1972, a violent clash between the right and the left erupted in Congo-Brazzaville. The Panthers were shocked to learn that one of Ange Diawara's closest collaborators, an Army officer who had been their host in Pointe Noire, was killed on the same day that President Ngouabi visited the city. In Brazzaville fighting had broken out within the Army, and Ange Diawara was reported to be in hiding. Ernest Ndalla had been arrested and imprisoned in the far north, a region of the country inhabited by an ethnic group hostile to Ndalla's tribe. There were reports of hundreds of their supporters being arrested, tortured, and killed.[59] The news was confusing and meager, but it was clear that a violent power struggle had surfaced in the Congo, and the revolutionary element suffered defeat. Ngouabi demoted a host of Army officers and accused Diawara of attempting a coup d'état, for which he would be punished when captured. In Algiers it was impossible to get any accurate account of the events taking place in the Congo. But one thing was clear: the political composition of the Congolese government had drastically changed, and any possibility of ever moving the International Section to the Congo was destroyed.

Black Panthers Expelled from Algeria

The Panthers carefully followed the international news, and recording revolutionary activities was one of their primary occupations. The spring and summer of 1972 brought an upsurge of news of airplane hijacking in the United States and all over the world. That April, Japanese terrorists demanding the release of imprisoned Palestinians hijacked a plane from Rome to Tel Aviv. Numerous travelers were killed in the bloody gunfight that erupted at the airport before the Israelis managed to capture the hijackers. Then on June 2, a young Black man wearing a U.S. Army uniform threatened to detonate a bomb aboard a Western Airline jet flight to Seattle unless his demands were met. In San Francisco, he exchanged half of the passengers for a larger jet capable of crossing the ocean and collected $500,000 in ransom. Then in New York, he exchanged the remaining passengers for a navigator. When the Algerian authorities learned that this jet was headed toward Algiers, they broke their silence toward the Black Panthers. An official who had been unavailable for months suddenly sent word for Cleaver to meet him at the airport. The Panthers were as startled as the Algerians by the hijacking, for only one plane had ever been hijacked to Algiers. In 1968, Palestinian revolutionaries had brought an Israeli jet to Algiers, but the government had returned the plane and reprimanded the hijackers. No subsequent Palestinian hijackings had ever brought planes to Algiers.

Roger Holder, a deserter from the Vietnam War, accompanied by his White girlfriend, Catherine Kerkow, walked off the plane in Algiers carrying a duffle bag stuffed with money. They claimed the money was for the Black liberation struggle. Algerian police took the pair into custody and confiscated their ransom money. But a few days later they released the couple, who had requested political asylum, to the Black Panther Party.

The hijacking stoked a political controversy among Algerian governing officials. The decision to return the ransom money and the airplane to Western Airlines caused intense conflict, which increased the antagonism provoked by the presence of the Black Panther Party in Algiers. The entire incident received no local publicity, but popular sentiment ran high about keeping the ransom and the plane in Algeria. The FLN official who met with the Panthers to explain the government's decision to return the ransom but allow the hijackers to stay explained that Algeria, formerly known as the Barbary Coast, was anxious not to revive its old image as a haven for pirates.

Then on August 1, a collective of Black Americans from Detroit hijacked a Delta Airline flight to Miami and reached Algiers with $1,000,000 in ransom. The arrival of another hijacked plane so quickly after the Algerians had confiscated the ransom money from the first one astonished the Panthers. The Algerian police arrested the hijacking party of three men, two women, and two small girls, and again confiscated their ransom money. The Panthers in Algiers had no idea who these people were or what motivated their actions. But if the Panthers did not defend them, then the group would face severe punishment and possible extradition back to the United States. So the International Section requested that the Algerians release the hijackers to the Black Panthers, who would take responsibility for them.

The group of hijackers were an odd assortment of friends who had shared a house together in Detroit. The group— a married couple, Melvin and Jean McNair, known as Idrissi and Nazinga; their four-year-old daughter; their friend Jean Tillerson, a Oberlin college drop-out, and her three-year-old daughter; and Tillerson's boyfriend, along with his former cellmate from a New Jersey prison, both of whom seemed to have little political consciousness. Their conversation revealed what seemed to the Panthers to be strange spiritist beliefs and vaguely pan-African convictions. Back in America, the collective had been debating whether they should rob a Brinks truck or hijack an airplane, and they chose hijacking because it seemed safer. They came to Algiers because it was in Africa, and to express their sympathy with the revolutionary views of the International Section of the Black Panther Party. When the Panthers questioned them on why they had chosen Algiers after the first hijacker's money had been confiscated, the cohort of hijackers replied that they figured that the newspaper account of the confiscation of money was a lie.

The hostility toward the Panthers among Algerians, from the lowest policeman to the highest official, became blatant after the second airplane arrived. The expulsion of the Panthers from Algeria was being seriously considered as a means of putting a stop to the hijackings. But some quarters would interpret the expulsion of the Panthers as a concession to U.S. imperialism, and this inhibited many Algerian officials from endorsing the proposal. As the Algerian authorities debated the question of what to do about the Black Panthers, the Panthers were looking for some way of coping with the problems caused by being stuck in Algiers.

Years before the Black Panthers arrived in Algiers the indigenous revolutionary elements had been driven out of the country or forced into inactivity. The support authorized to foreign revolutionary elements was purposely confined, for the intent of the support was not to promote revolutionary change but to provide evidence of Algeria's revolutionary foreign policy. Unresolved conflicts within Algeria's political elite had been projected onto the screen of their foreign policy, but when Black hijackers burst through it loaded with American dollars to finance revolutionary action, the government of Algeria was forced to act in terms of its self-interest. By the summer of 1972, the usefulness of the Black Panther Party in Algeria was questionable.

On August 2, Cleaver wrote an open letter to President Boumedienne, which he released to the press after personally delivering a copy to the People's Palace, the official residence of the President. Cleaver explained that he had addressed an "open" letter to President Boumedienne to assure that it gained his attention because his previous efforts to communicate with

Algeria's governing officials had failed. The letter stated that the "heroic struggles and sacrifices of the Algerian people constitute a magnet for the oppressed people of the world" and that it was not Algeria's fault that "the torch of freedom held in the hand of the Statue of Liberty is deprived of its flame by the oppression which the United States' ruling circles heap upon the people of the world, the American people included." Cleaver claimed that "when many countries with glorious revolutionary traditions and traditions of support for struggling people are abandoning the field and making a separate peace with the enemy, we feel that revolutionaries and those fighting for the liberation of the people must . . . renew their dedication and escalate their struggle at all costs."

"As every revolutionary and freedom fighter fully understands," the letter continued, "without the money to organize and finance the struggle, there will be no freedom, and those who deprive us of this are depriving us of our freedom." This was the genuine reason, Cleaver argued, that "the fascist, imperialist ruling circle of the United States is going crazy over the prospects of the one million and a half dollars recently expropriated by these American revolutionaries and freedom fighters coming into the hands of the International Section of the Black Panther Party." Cleaver appealed to President Boumedienne to recognize that he was not asking Algeria to fight the battles of the Afro-American people: "What we are asking is that the Algerian government not fight the battles of the American government for the fascist imperialist ruling circles that are oppressing the whole American people."

The letter referred to an incident during Algeria's war against France in which Boumedienne had been held prisoner in Tunisia and faced the threat of death, while France and Tunisia negotiated the fate of French airplanes shot down over Tunisia. Cleaver said that it was Boumedienne's "personal experience . . . of privation and opposition" that gave him the confidence to believe the President could sympathize with the position of the Black Panthers "as befits a revolutionary warrior for the liberation of his people . . . toward those who are still locked in the struggle for the liberation of their people."[60]

Cleaver's act outraged Algeria's governing officials who were deliberately concealing from the Algerian public their consternation over the hijackings. But Le Monde and other newspapers easily available in Algiers quoted the letter extensively. Cleaver had brought up explosive conflicts raging within the Arab Nationalist world, where United States' support for Israel made conciliatory gestures towards the United States particularly costly. As the Arab masses were bitterly hostile to Zionism, and the united opposition to Israel was crucial to sustaining Arab cohesion, favorable treatment of the United States had to remain unpublicized.

However, Algeria was in the process of negotiating a $1 billion contract for the sale of liquefied natural gas to American oil companies, and the application for that contract's approval was before the Federal Power Commission in Washington, D.C.[61] Because of the absence of formal diplomatic relations between the United States and Algeria, special guarantees had to be provided to protect American investments. The approval of the contract was crucial to the state plans for Algerian economic development. But in its relationship with rival Arab governments for leadership of the Arab nationalist cause, Algeria could not jeopardize its anti-imperialist foreign policy by overt concessions to the United States.

The Algerian reaction to the open letter was far more drastic than anything the members of the International Section had anticipated. In the Muslim culture, a President was seen more as an autocrat than an elected statesman, and public criticism of the President was considered subversive. The Black Panther problem was turned over to the Algiers' Chief of Police. On August 10, as all the hijackers and Panthers remaining in Algiers were assembling for a meeting to decide what to do about the additional responsibility the new arrivals created, Cleaver received a call from the Chief of Police. Within half an hour, two bus loads of policemen pulled up outside the gates and raided the International Section.

The police chief told everyone to remain in the central meeting room while officers searched the entire villa and confiscated all the weapons they found. They kept the building surrounded, and when they had completed their search, the police chief informed the assembled group that no one would be allowed to leave the building until further notice. They disconnected the telephone and the telex machine. Several police remained in the courtyard and inside the villa to prevent anyone from entering or leaving the premises, but the rest departed. For two days the only person the police permitted to come in and out was the Algerian housekeeper who worked at the villa.

The possibility of being put under house arrest had not been anticipated since the official standing of the Black Panther Party was quasi-diplomatic, but the political hostility expressed by the act came as no surprise. The house arrest simply expressed in an extreme manner the Algerian authorities' long standing ambivalence towards the Panthers. A group of high officials from the Council of the Revolution came to the villa several days later to inform the Panthers of the government's decision on their status. The Black Panthers had to leave Algiers. The Panthers were more than willing to leave, but needed to be supplied with passports and money to travel. The Algerian officials refused to provide either. The situation was a stalemate.

Nonetheless, the FLN official who had worked with the Black Panther Party from the beginning authorized the International Section to hold a public gathering at their villa on August 18 to mark the International Day of Solidarity with the Afro-American people. The villa was decorated for the special gathering, and printed invitations were mailed out to the liberation movements, socialist embassies, and press agencies. But when the guests began arriving for the event, Algerian police blocked their entry into the villa. The police directed all the traffic towards the villa to turn away and refused to permit anyone to attend the event. Press photographers had their film confiscated. Other decision makers in the Algerian hierarchy had overruled the approval granted by the FLN.

The abrupt cancellation of the gathering planned for the International Day of Solidarity with the Afro-American People was a fitting commentary on the situation the Black Panthers faced in Algeria. Unresolved internal conflicts concealed from the Black Panthers nonetheless dictated what they could and could not do in Algiers. The brass plaque on the gatepost outside the villa still gleamed in the sunshine, with English and Arabic lettering reading "International Section of the Black Panther Party." But the live presence of the organization in Algiers had come to an end.

Seeking Another Sanctuary

No African country other than Algeria had been willing to risk antagonizing the United States by openly supporting the Black Panther Party as an organization. During the 1960s, American fugitives of all complexions and varieties scattered over the world, but only in Algeria were they able to make any concerted political statement in their sanctuary. The antiwar movement and the Black liberation struggle yielded a bountiful harvest of political exiles who left America or dropped into the underground instead of going to prison. But the essential anonymity of the life of a fugitive, either abroad or underground, eventually leads to the death of his political identity. Whatever the reason for their exile—fleeing bombing charges or drug charges, deserting the Army, leaving to avoid the draft, or preventing incarceration on the criminal charges used for political repression during the 1960s, America's fugitives gradually faded from view except for the International Section of the Black Panther Party.

By choosing to leave the country instead of returning to prison, Cleaver had refused to cease participating in the revolutionary movement developing within the United States. He sought to expand the political vehicle provided by the Black Panther Party onto an international level and to link the movement to transform America to the revolutionary changes underway during the world wide resistance to imperialism. But that vehicle was smashed.

In Algiers many Panthers wanted to move to a Black African country, to experience living in a Black world with their African brothers and sisters. Cleaver came to see the emotional and political identification with Africa as a "skin game" and realized that the kind of problems that America's Blacks faced bore little relationship to the Africans' problems. Cleaver was ready to leave the Third World, and the socialist world, behind him. For he found out that the kind of freedom he dreamed of for Blacks in America was not available within the socialist countries and liberated Third World nations he had visited.

The colony of fugitives in Algiers dwindled from nearly thirty people in 1971 to seven by the summer of 1972, and then was augmented by eight hijackers. Connie and Michael Tabor had left for Zambia before the hijackers arrived. Don Cox's wife and son had already returned to her family in Philadelphia, and Odinga had sent his wife and children back to New York. Pete O'Neal and his wife and son eventually arranged to join a community of Afro-Americans living in Tanzania, where they had friends. Odinga and Mack also headed for Tanzania. Cox planned to return clandestinely to the United States. By January 1973, only the Cleavers and the hijackers were left in Algiers. During the summer, Kathleen Cleaver had sent their children back to the United States, and then spent the rest of the year traveling between Algeria and Europe, investigating the possibility of Cleaver's obtaining political asylum in Switzerland, Italy, and Sweden. Secretly, Cleaver arranged to go to France.

Friends of Elaine Klein in France, who had sheltered Algerian fugitives and supported their independence struggle, provided Cleaver with safe places to stay. Kathleen Cleaver openly moved to Switzerland, taking their personal belongings out of the country little by little. A couple in Paris who owned two adjacent apartments agreed to let Cleaver stay in their empty apartment across the hall. The Left Bank location was ideal, directly across the street from the Institute for Deaf Mutes. A French law passed in 1971 prohibited the extradition of fugitives from France charged with criminal offenses if such charges could be shown to be politically motivated. Clandestinely, Cleaver's wife joined him, and the two lived an underground existence in Paris, concealing their identity and spending most of their time inside.

The French writer Jean Genet had become a supporter of the Black Panther Party during an international campaign to protest Bobby Seale's imprisonment in 1969. After learning about Cleaver's plight, he arranged for his personal attorney, who was active in the Socialist Party, to assist Cleaver in his effort to remain in France. One afternoon, Genet visited the Cleavers in their Paris apartment:

> "Why did you come to France?" he asked Eldridge.
>
> "Because Benjamin Franklin came to France," Cleaver answered. "The French supported the American Revolution then. They believe in '*Liberté, Egalité, Fraternité.*'"

Genet roared with laughter, but Cleaver was serious. The revolution in which he believed— and sought to claim during the Black liberation movement—was fundamentally the unfinished revolution for democracy in America.

Although Cleaver's attempt to gain political asylum in France failed, he and his family eventually obtained residence papers that allowed them to live openly in Paris. Once the Vietnam War ended and the Watergate scandal left Richard Nixon disgraced, Cleaver finally decided to return openly to America in late 1975. It meant he had to surrender to the FBI and return to jail, but Cleaver was convinced that the country had changed, and he returned to face trial in California without fearing it would cost him his life.

Although the historical moment when the International Section of the Black Panther Party evolved flashed briefly, it gave Eldridge Cleaver and a handful of fugitives the opportunity to transform their "disadvantage into a rallying point of advantage," the way he once described the condition of blackness. Over the centuries that America enslaved Blacks, those men and women most determined to win freedom became fugitives, fleeing from the brutal captivity of slavery. Many of their descendants who fought the Black liberation struggle also became fugitives. These men and women refused to endure the captivity awaiting them in retaliation for their systematic effort to win freedom. But unlike runaway slaves, these men and women fought for a more expansive freedom, not merely as individuals, but for an entire nation, and sought in the face of internationally overwhelming odds to build a more humane and democratic political order.

NOTES

1. Eric Pace, "Cleaver Assails Apollo Program," *The New York Times*, 21 July 1969, 40.

2. "Johnson Says Feat Shows 'We Can Do Anything,,'" *The New York Times*, 21 July 1969, 15.

3. Earl Caldwell, "Panthers' Meeting Shifts Aims from Racial Confrontation to Class Struggle," *The New York Times*, 22 July 1969, 21.

4. Eric Pace, "African Nations Open 12-Day Cultural Festival With Parade Through Algiers," *The New York Times*, 22 July 1969, 9.

5. Ibid.

6. See Hoyt W. Fuller, "Algiers Journal," *Negro Digest* (October 1969): 72–87.

7. Frantz Fanon, *The Wretched of the Earth*, trans. Constance Farrington, (New York: Grove Press, 1968), 35.

8. Ibid., 43.

9. Ibid., 38–39.

10. Ibid., 40.

11. Ibid.

12. Ibid.

13. Ibid.

14. Eldridge Cleaver, "Community Imperialism," *The Black Panther*, 18 May 1968, 10; also, reprinted 20 April 1969, 14.

15. Ibid.

16. Fanon, 70.

17. Ibid.

18. Ibid., 74.

19. In the Ten-Point Platform and Program of the Black Panther Party, each point was divided into two sections, the first representing "what we want," the second, "what we believe." In the tenth point, the section explaining what we believe was a quotation of the opening paragraphs of the Declaration of Independence, ending with this sentence in bold type: "But, when a long train of abuses and usurpations, pursuing invariably that same object, evinces a design to reduce them under absolute despotism, it is their right, it is their duty, to throw off such government and to provide new guards for their future security."

20. Henry L. Gates, Jr., "After 'the Revolution': the Odyssey of Eldridge Cleaver," (unpublished manuscript, 1975), 5–8. Gates, then a Ph.D. candidate at Cambridge University, wrote this article after interviewing Eldridge Cleaver for *The New York Times Sunday Magazine*, but it was never published.

21. Ibid., 5.

22. William M. Leo Grande, "Cuban–Soviet Relations and Cuban Policy in Africa," *Cuba in Africa*, eds. Carmelo Meas-Lago and June S. Belkin (University of Pittsburgh: Center for Latin American Studies, 1982), 18.

23. William B. Quandt, *Revolution and Political Leadership: Algeria 1954–1968*, (Cambridge: MIT Press, 1969), 238–239.

24. Jorge I. Dominguez, "Political and Military Consequences of Cuban Policies in Africa," *Cuba in Africa*, 125.

25. Conversation with Charles Chikarema, Hotel Victoria, Algiers, Algeria, June 1969.

26. Don A. Schanche, *The Panther Paradox*, (New York: David McKay Co., 1970), 176.

27. Eldridge Cleaver, "From Somewhere in the Third World," *The Black Panther*, 12 July 1969, 13.

28. Conversation between Robert Scheer and the Cleavers. Hotel Aletti, Algiers, Algeria. August 1969.

29. Byron Booth, "Beyond Demarcation," *The Black Panther*, 25 October 1969, 16. Booth was Deputy Minister of Defense for the International Staff of the Black Panther Party.

30. Gates, 6.

31. Cleaver quoted in John Brown Society, *The Black Panther Movement*, (Ann Arbor: Radical Education Project, 1969), 4.

32. See, "Evidence and Intimidation of Fascist Crimes by U.S.A." *The Black Panther*, 21 February 1970, 1–17.

33. Virtual Murell, "Panther Purge," *The Black Panther*, 25 January 1967, 17.

34. See Eldridge Cleaver, "Solidarity of the Peoples Until Victory or Death!" Address of the Black Panther Party USA to the International Conference on Tasks of Journalists of the Whole World in the Fight Against Racism in Pyongyang, Korea (delivered September 22, 1969); *The Black Panther*, 25 October 1969, 12-16.

35. William B. Quandt, *Revolution and Political Leadership: Algeria 1954–1968*, (Cambridge: MIT Press, 1968), 87.

36. At a formal reception held by the Council of the Revolution in November 1969 to celebrate the anniversary of the beginning of Algeria's war for liberation, a young Algerian official quietly mentioned to Cleaver that Algeria would be resuming diplomatic relations with the United States.

37. The leaders of the delegation were Robert Scheer, editor of *Ramparts* magazine in San Francisco and Eldridge Cleaver. The other participants were Jan Austin, of *Ramparts* and the Peace and Freedom Party; Elaine Brown, Deputy Information Minister, Los Angeles Chapter of the Black Panther Party; Alex Hing, Red Guards, San Francisco; Ann Froines, New Haven Defense Committee for the Black Panther Party and peace activist; Randy Rappaport, Boston Women's Collective; Pat Sumi, of the Movement for a Democratic Military; Regina Blumfield, from the women's liberation movement and the film company Newsreel, and Andy Truskier of the International Liberation School and the Peace and Freedom Party.

38. "Bail Hearing for Huey Newton," *San Francisco Chronicle*, 4 August 1970, 3.

39. Eldridge Cleaver, "Letter to My Black Brothers in Vietnam," *The Black Panther*, 2 May 1970, 10B.

40. "Freed Newton Discusses His Plans for the Future," *San Francisco Chronicle*, 6 August 1970, 6.

41. "Interview with Bobby Seale," *Berkeley Barb*, 14–20 November 1969, 3.

42. "Cleaver and Black Panther Group Attend Hanoi Observance," *The New York Times*, 19 August 1970, 13.

43. "Statement by Eldridge Cleaver to GIs in South Vietnam," *The Black Panther*, 26 September 1970, 14.

44. Seymour M. Hersh, "Alien-Radical Tie Disputed by CIA," *The New York Times,* 25 May 1973, 1.

45. Ibid., 17.

46. Ibid.

47. Huey Newton, "Let Us Hold High the Banner of Intercommunalism," *The Black Panther*, 23 January 1971, F.

48. "On the Purge of Geronimo from the Black Panther Party," *The Black Panther*, 23 January 1971, 7.

49. "Death Here Tied to Panther Feud," *The New York Times*, 10 March 1971, 29.

50. For background information, see Earl Caldwell, "The Panthers: Dead or Regrouping," *The New York Times*, 1 March 1971, 1.

51. "Death Here Tied to Panther Feud," *The New York Times*, 10 March 1971, 29.

52. Huey P. Newton, "On the Defection of Eldridge Cleaver from the Black Panther Party, and the Defection of the Black Panther Party from the Black Community," *The Black Panther*, 17 April 1971, C.

53. One aspect of the COINTELPRO (Counter Intelligence Program) actions the FBI directed against the Black Panther Party included mailing key individuals letters composed by agents over forged signatures of Black Panthers. The letters contained false information to cause distrust and foment disruption, a prime goal of the COINTELPRO operation. Newton was sent letters threatening his life signed by individuals associated with Cleaver's faction, and Cleaver received letters from various Panthers implying that Newton banned all contact with Algiers upon threat of expulsion, that Newton and Hilliard had no interest in what he was doing, and denouncing their actions in the U.S. as absurd. After the split, there were letters discouraging efforts at reconciliation. The letter to President Boumedienne with Newton's signature was included in materials used to document the COINTELPRO actions by investigators for the Church Committee, investigators for the Senate Select committee on Intelligence Activities headed by Senator Church. During a deposition in April 1976 before staff attorneys of the corresponding House Committee headed by Representative Pike, a copy was shown to the author . The Pike Committee was the Intelligence Committee of the U.S. House of Representatives and was responsible for investigating the intelligence operations of the United States Government.

54. Guevara launched his guerrilla struggle in Bolivia after being recalled from the Congo, and was killed there in 1967.

55. *Africasia*, 61(1972): 31.

56. Eldridge Cleaver, "Interview with Ange Diawara," *Revolution in the Congo* (London: Revolutionary Peoples' Communication Network, 1971), 34.

57. *Africasia*, 61(1972): 31.

58. *We Have Come Back*, Paris: Voo Doo production, 1971. Film.

59. *Africasia*, 61(1972): 31.

60. Quotations from "Open Letter to President Boumedienne" taken from full text reproduced in confidential cable from U.S. political affairs officer in Algiers to Secretary of State, Washington, D.C., August 3, 1972. This document was released by the CIA to the Cleavers through their Freedom of Information suit filed in 1976.

61. Benjamin Welles, "U.S. Hears Algerian Police Raided Panthers' Quarters," *The New York Times*, 11 August 1972, 33.

Part IV

Gender Dynamics

Chapter Eleven

Why I Joined the Party: An Africana Womanist Reflection

Regina Jennings

In *Africana Womanism*, Professor Clenora Hudson-Weems provides a useful theoretical framework for explaining why I joined the Black Panther Party in 1968.[1] As creator of the concept "Africana womanism," she cites racism as the dominant challenge to Black people. She contends that Black women have historically subordinated their own needs in the interest of the family and community. When I became interested in the Black Panther Party at the age of sixteen, I knew racism and police brutality intimately, but I had no knowledge or understanding of sexism. I was raised, as most Black women of the 1950s and 1960s were, to accept male dominance and to consider myself a helpmate to men. I joined the Black Panther Party because I wanted to help smash racism in America. I joined the Black Panthers because it was the only organization that faced White America forthrightly without begging or carrying signs for equality and justice. I respected and admired their bold image. However, after being in the Party, I experienced and recognized the existence of a double standard for women. Some brothers in leadership positions were sexist. This was a problem that was left unchecked and weakened the foundation of the Black Panther Party.

In 1968, still in my teens, I took a late plane from Philadelphia to Oakland, California, to join the Black Panther Party. As a runaway since the age of fifteen, a witness to vulgar police brutality, and a victim of racism on my first job, I was ready to become a Panther. Their mystique—the black pants, leather jackets, berets, guns, and their talk—aggressive and direct—attracted me and thousands more across America.

I grew up in Philadelphia in the 1960s where I regularly saw the police do a "Rodney King" on Black people. Attending a school where I learned only about White accomplishments and living in an environment where the elders rarely discussed Black advancement, I grew into an unstable young woman without race pride or self-respect. When I worked in a secretarial pool of about twenty White women who deliberately refused to even speak to me, I experienced the trauma of White racism. I had never been around so many Whites before, and their inhumanity literally drove me toward insanity.

I would walk into this company and speak to each person the way Black people had always spoken to one another in my neighborhood. However, when I spoke to them, they pretended not to see or hear me. I became emotionally distraught and started to sink in a terrible way.

One particularly cruel woman collected money for refreshments. Each day that I foolishly placed my money on my desk for collection marked a day that she held her head contemptuously high and walked by my desk. This insult hurt me in ways I find difficult to express. I decided to personally place my money in her hand. As she made her rounds laughing and talking with all the other secretaries, I arose from my chair and stood in front of my desk. With my money hot in my hand, I waited for her to come my way. As she approached my space, I reached for her hand and she skipped around me. As I watched her walk away, I stood humiliatingly frozen with my hand still extended.

I already knew how to handle weapons; I had lived among people who disregarded the law. I decided to equalize this situation. I decided that murder was a fair and equitable recourse. During this period when I pistol-packed for work, I watched the news about Martin Luther King, Jr. on television. I saw his people police-whipped like dogs. As I planned how I would take this offensive woman off the planet, I fumed at how White Americans generally treated my people. Then one day I saw an eloquent Huey P. Newton being interviewed on film. He was charged with killing one policeman and wounding another. He was discussing race, society, self-defense, and other subjects I failed to comprehend. I saw a marvelous Bobby Seale marching with male and female Panthers with guns at the state capitol in California. I thought I had finally found my calling.

Summer 1968

I spat on Philadelphia
boarded a late plane to Oakland
Oakland land of Huey Newton and Bobby Seale

I looked on the earth
sky down
the geography a map
like the one in Miss Somebody's class

Hating school, counselors, teachers,
and basement books
Hating Black to mean
ugly, evil, dirty sub, shiftless, and slavery

I flew high wolfing at streams
of fat clouds
knowing I would land in San Francisco
and light up on the Golden Gate Bridge

And just like this airplane bursting through clouds
like snow
I would burst
the bloodless murderers
of Blacks

Panther Power

I joined the Black Panther Party with a serious drug habit and with a personal directive to kill White people. When I first showed up at Panther headquarters in Oakland, California, and was asked why I wanted to be a Panther, I said, "I wanna kill all the White people; that's why." I was dressed in my best suede and leather outfit and was sporting a most pronounced cabaret hair-piece. The officer-of-the-day must have been accustomed to all types of people with outrageous reasons for wanting to join the Panthers. After my outburst, he calmly took my name and number and said someone would get in touch with me soon. I immediately became self-conscious—aware of myself, my clothing, and my hair—as I watched the stony Black faces in the office continue their work while ignoring my comment.

On leaving the Panther office, I moved around the Bay area, discovering the ambience of California and the new lingo slightly peppered with southern accents. Black people would say, "Right on sister," when someone agreed with female rhetoric. During the 1960s, Oakland reflected the Black power movement that was electrifying the country. Large bushy Afros, Muslims selling Black ice cream, and hairdressers and barbers stocking new products for natural hair were commonplace.[2] It never occurred to me while I was glorifying in the language, music, and the aesthetics of my people that I was being followed. As the Panthers checked out my Philadelphia and Oakland addresses, they also followed me for well over a week. Some believed I may have been sent by the FBI, but the captain assured them with Panther good humor, "She's too stupid to be from the FBI." He believed my cover and my comments too honest, too loud, and too ridiculous to be serious.

My struggle from drug addict to soldier was a hard-fought personal war. The Panthers, like many people in the Black community, understood my dependency on drugs; and under the leadership of the captain, they helped me gradually to abandon the addiction. The captain assigned me so many activities, as he did other Panthers, and our teachers taught us so vigorously about our importance to our community that I started to care about learning and understanding our situation with an undrugged mind. Never having particularly enjoyed history as taught in school, my attitude completely changed in the Party. The way Panther teachers taught us new recruits, I wanted to devour history books. They taught us from an Afrocentric perspective, whereby the needs and interests of African people determined our perception of the world. I had never considered Black people as a subject of knowledge. I had been taught only to revere White people as the source of world progress. We studied about revolutions in China, Cuba, and Africa. The void I used to fill with drugs was now filled instead with a pure and noble love for my people.

In Oakland, California, the Panthers and the Black community had a mutual love affair. We brought them Black men and women willing to transform the Black community with social programs, to defend where we lived and breathed with our lives. The people brought us food, joy, assurances, hope, and companionship. I remember one week when our office was rather low on food, a gentleman came into the headquarters with a huge deer slung across his shoulders. Fascinated, I crept up close to see the deer, and as I stared into his dead eyes, I felt a connection. I thought of *Bambi,* the Walt Disney film of my childhood. I thought, "how could anyone kill and eat a deer." Many of the Panther brothers were hunters so they cut up the deer meat in the back of the office. I almost fainted. The Panther men in particular laughed at my reaction, but after it was cooked, I refused to eat the meat. Knowing that I was very hungry, some of them chased me around the office and playfully urged me to sample the spicy scented deer. Ironically, as we fed hungry children breakfast, and later gave out bags of groceries to the poor, often times Panthers themselves had little food and certainly very little money. We lived mostly off paper sales. We sold each Panther paper for twenty-five cents. We turned fifteen cents into the office and kept ten cents for ourselves.

Most people know about the breakfast for school children program founded by Huey and Bobby and implemented by the rank-and-file. Panther leadership demanded that businessmen in the Black community donate food to the program. We were taught that businesses that profited from the Black community ought to assist in community development. Panthers arose at dawn to cook and serve hungry children before they attended school. Panthers also stayed afterwards and cleaned the area where the programs were housed. Our first breakfast program was in the basement of Saint Augustine Church pastored by Father Earl Neil.

The free breakfast for school children seems to be common knowledge, but people may not know about the dances we staged for the Oakland youth. We decorated the community centers, halls, or church basements with our colors—blue and black. We hung blue and black streamers and lights and Panther paraphernalia on walls. On vending tables, there were the usual posters and buttons of our national leaders, Kathleen Cleaver, Eldridge Cleaver (The Rage), Bobby Seale, and Huey P. Newton. We sisters attempted to bake cakes and cookies, but we were not very good cooks, and the community people knew it. They usually supplied the food for our dances.

Some of the youth imitated our dress—black pants, blue sweat shirts fronted with prowling panthers. Although this imitation made us feel rather proud, one had difficulty discerning Oakland youth from Panthers. When not on guard duty, we jammed on the dance floor with one another or with community brothers and sisters. Sometimes young males would rap to us sisters while we were dancing under blue/black lights, and we would laugh and urge them to join the Party if they wanted to talk to us. Local Panther male leaders made speeches after playing records— the Isley Brothers, Sly Stone, James Brown— and the youth pretty much listened attentively. Whether or not they joined our organization, we usually won community sympathizers after our events.

I have never known any people like members of the Black Panther Party. Their bravery and courage both humbled and awed me. Some have said that Panthers were crazy, that they wanted to die. Not so. We considered ourselves the vanguard army of Black people, an army not unlike the military vision of Marcus Garvey. We understood that one had to pay a price for freedom in the tradition of Harriet Tubman, Frantz Fanon, and Malcolm X.

In addition to studying revolutions in Africa and Cuba, we studied the *Red Book* of Chairman Mao. The film *The Battle of Algiers* was our orientation theme; yet at core we were Black Americans struggling with issues that pertained directly to our people. Our local leaders organized political education classes regularly for Panthers and community folk where we all learned about the nature of America. In the early morning before dawn, we attended exercise classes before we were vanned to various churches to cook and serve breakfast to our school children. At night we blew the poetry of Alprentice "Bunchy" Carter, who along with John Huggins, was brutally murdered by members of Us, the organization led by Maulana Karenga. We also blew other Panther poetry, plus the precious words of Sonia Sanchez and Haki Madhubuti. Our main purpose from 1968–70, however, was to free Huey P. Newton. Our leaders planned and organized broad-based rallies with diverse Black activist groups: the Brown Berets, a Chicano organization; the Red Guard, an Asian organization; and the Peace and Freedom Party, an organization of White leftist radicals.

Initially, I refused to work with Whites in the Peace and Freedom Party, but my captain threatened me with Panther Party punishment for my initial refusal. Party discipline entailed a marathon of push-ups or pumping X number of laps around the corner. I had not forgotten either the racism of White cops or the racism of my former coworkers. Firmly believing that they hated all Blacks, I saw no value or sense in working with Whites. This belief remained solid until I witnessed how hard some Whites worked on the Free Huey campaigns. However, I always wondered and openly asked why they were not working as aggressively to solve the racism that existed within their own communities.

The captain of the East Oakland branch of the Black Panther Party was well respected by the national Party leadership. All of us in East Oakland thought of him as a friend and sometimes as a father. The rank and file readily understood that for our Party to be effective we had to follow orders. Additionally, between the years of 1968–70, we all felt the pig infiltration of our organization. The pigs were playing dirty tricks on us through letters that pitted one leader against another and through wire taps.[3] Still a young organization, we were unable to discern what was real or fake. We were constantly fortifying our office on the strength of leaks from agents who had turned into supposed sympathizers.

Such infiltration changed whatever sense of normalcy the Panther environment ever had. Our situation was always on the periphery of alarm. The very nature of existing in Oakland, or any place in America for that matter, as a Black group organized to defy the racist oppression of the state entailed constant tension. Add to this the infiltration of pigs who were Blacks like us, and one can only imagine how the Panther environment was continually charged with suspicion and tension. We rank and file lived every day as if it were our last. At times, in a frenzied, scary way, all of us sometimes questioned whether to trust one another; and we all lived together, worked together, studied together, played together, ate together, and drank together. Since we expected either to be killed or to be jailed, we loved one another fully, purely, and platonically unless we decided otherwise.

All I wanted was to be a soldier. I did not wish to be romantically linked with any of my comrades, and even though I gave my entire life to the Party—my time, my energy, my will, my clothes, my money, and my skills; yet my captain wanted more. My captain wanted me.

This man, who had helped me overcome my addiction, who had taught me and others so much about the world, who had stood toe to toe with racist businessmen who initially refused to donate food to our breakfast for school children program, who had organized our office so efficiently that we were considered a model for other branches— the man whom I thought was my friend over time turned into my nemesis. When I repeatedly refused his advances, he made my life miserable. He gave me ridiculous orders. He shunned me. He found fault in my performance. During the early years of the Black Panther Party, there was no democratic procedure for challenging an officer. This was one of the greatest flaws in my beloved organization. There was no external governing board to regulate how the individual offices operated.

Moreover, by this time Kathleen Cleaver was abroad with Eldridge, after he pulled a brilliant masquerade that eluded the authorities and allowed him to escape arrest. The Rage was wanted for parole violation and for his part in the April 6, 1968 shoot-out when Little Bobby Hutton was the first to fall. Indeed, we did have national headquarters in Berkeley where the Central Committee presided, but usually one strong personality held sway of that committee, either Bobby Seale or during his incarceration, David Hilliard. I sought redress from the Central Committee. However, the Central Committee sided with my captain. The all-male panel agreed that I should not behave as a bourgeois woman and bring such values to the Party. They believed that my attitude of sexual abstinence was both foolish and counter-revolutionary.

I lacked maturity and the skill necessary to challenge authoritarian men, so I searched for ways to circumvent the sexism of my captain. I was determined not to leave the Party because I felt there was no other place in America where I could fully be my Black revolutionary self. Besides, I had become a part of the Oakland community. I had store owners and other Oakland people who only purchased papers from me. I assisted senior citizens with their grocery shopping, participated in political organizing, and personally instructed a group of young children in reading. There were homes in the community where I could always get a good meal, and neighborhood residents consistently watched my back.

After a year of transforming myself into a young woman who cared deeply for my people and becoming a fixture within Oakland and enjoying all of its rights and privileges, I found that my captain searched for greater ways to push me out of the Party. He felt that I was not a good influence on the other soldiers; so with the help of local Panther officials, he transferred me out of Oakland and away from a year of diligent and joyous work. He transferred me to National Headquarters where I experienced the same kind of vicious sexism all over again. There were women who came through the Party and would immediately leave because of the vulgar male behavior. There were women in the Party like me who tried to hold on because we understood the power, the significance, and the need for our organization. Black men, who had been too long without some form of power, lacked the background to understand and rework their double standard toward the female cadre. Perhaps, if the Party had external observers—community elders who respected our platform—such unfair practices against women may not have occurred.

All men in the Party were not sexist. In fact, many fought with me against the foolishness of our captain. These men were also ostracized by the leadership. Besides, we were facing so many threatening issues that were larger than the plight of selected female cadre. I am talking about the years when Huey P. Newton faced the gas chamber. I am talking about the years when our offices were being attacked by the police. I am talking about the years of massive Panther arrests. I am talking about the years when our national leadership rotated in and out of prison or transported themselves to countries outside of America. Sexism was a significant factor in weakening the structure of the Black Panther Party. It is important to understand and recognize the proclivities among men, especially as we move toward the 21st century, and especially as Black men make public pronouncements to regain the reigns of leadership for Black America. If women are disrespected, so goes the nation.

Members of the rank and file of the Black Panther Party were a unique group of dedicated warriors who worked years without any recognition, rewards, awards, or monetary inducements to eliminate injustice in America. Nothing impressed me more than the discipline exhibited by my dear,dear brothers and sisters in the Black Panther Party. There is no other experience like being with people who wake up before dawn and retire at night thinking about and working aggressively for our people. Some sisters and brothers with whom I lived, ate, talked long into the night, exchanged clothes, fed children, sold Panther papers, shot targets, drank bitter dogs, and ran midnight missions are dead now. I want you to know how much they perfectly loved you. I want you to know that they were willing to die for you.

Routine

In a Blackberry morning
a bullet rests in each chamber
In a morning of chilled expectation
I shower and jump into Levi's and combat boots
In a mirror providing memory
I fork my big, Black bush
Panthers in the bedroom,
living room, bathroom, growl, laugh, scowl
count weapons and cleanse bodies

In the seedling of a Blackberry morning
we prepare for the knock
of Panthers
standing
around the swimming pool
standing like pieces in a game of chess

I move to secure my place
We walk
unsmiling, sisters and brothers
bursting through doors of damaged glass

In a Panther van we ride
smoking, talking, teasing, listening
Our Captain
mapping the day in a pattern of plans

And outside
the stars pinch inward
and outside
a midnight morning
muses on the daylight

NOTES

1. Clenora Hudson-Weems, *African Womanist: Reclaiming Ourselves* (Troy, Michigan: Bedford Publishers, 1994).

2. "Black" was the actual name of this new ice cream, sold in Muslim restaurants, which was created to honor the power and thrust of the Black power movement. Because we "Negroes" had just made the enormous leap to "Black" as a preferable racial identifier, we consumed and created many things with the title Black.

3. Ward Churchill and Jim Vander Wall, *Agents of Repression: The FBI's Secret War Against the Black Panther Party and the American Indian Movement* (Boston, Massachusetts: South End Press, 1988). Assata Shakur, *Assata: An Autobiography* (Westport, Connecticut: Lawrence Hill and Company, 1987).

Chapter Twelve

"No One Ever Asks, What a Man's Place in the Revolution Is": Gender and the Politics of The Black Panther Party 1966–1971[1]

Tracye Matthews

By the middle of the 1960s, young Black people in the United States were growing weary of civil rights leaders telling them to turn the other cheek so that they could "overcome someday." The inspiring eloquence of Martin Luther King, Jr. had been challenged, even ridiculed, by the fiery message of Malcolm X. For Black youth, who increasingly found themselves trapped in overcrowded Northern urban ghettos, many of the old movement slogans and ideas, particularly nonviolence as a philosophy, were becoming obsolete.[2] In spite of the gains of the Southern Black freedom movement, civil rights organizations and leaders, especially King, were slowly but surely becoming aware of growing dissatisfaction among Blacks with the limitations of hard-won legislation, especially its failure to ensure economic gains and tackle seemingly intractable forms of Southern and Northern racism. The call for "Black Power" became the order of the day.

Beginning in 1964 and continuing each summer through 1968, disillusionment, frustration, and economic disenfranchisement fueled urban rebellions in Black communities across the country.[3] It was within this context that the Black Panther Party for Self Defense (BPP) formed and staked its claim for leadership of the Black masses. In October 1966, Huey P. Newton and Bobby Seale officially founded the Party in Oakland, California, one of many U.S. cities noted for its racist and repressive police force. The main targets of their initial organizing efforts were disaffected urban Black male youth, and their activities centered on addressing police brutality through armed self-defense. Although the actual size of their constituency and membership is a subject of debate, the Party had a significant impact on the consciousness and political developments of the late 1960s and early 1970s both nationally and internationally.

The issues raised by the Black Panther Party remain salient for Black communities at the turn of the twenty-first century. Economic conditions for the

majority of Black people have declined since the late sixties in large measure as a consequence of structural adjustments in advanced capitalism in response to global competition and the shift from industrial to service-based
economies, all of which undermine the security and safety of workers globally. The social consequences of these changes, including more sophisticated and insidious forms of racism and sexism, demand not only new
responses, but also a closer investigation of and learning from past practices
of collective, organized resistance.

Current feelings of dissatisfaction with "traditional" Black middle-class
leadership, especially among young African Americans, are reminiscent of
the sentiments that led to the revolutionary youth movement of the late
1960s in which the Panthers played a critical role. Yet, in spite of renewed
popular interest, the political ideology and inner workings of the BPP still
remain hidden from those most likely to take up the mantle of resistance in
this era. The first two years of the Black Panther Party's development have
been fictionalized, romanticized, and popularized in the recent larger-than-
life Hollywood film *Panther*, complete with a supporting cast that looks like
a BET (Black Entertainment Television) top-forty countdown, a full line of
Panther gear for the nineties, two "Panther inspired" CDs, and a "PAN-
THER 'Power to the People' Sweepstakes" in which the winner receives
$1,000.00 personal empowerment cash.[4] However, the content (or lack
thereof) of this and many of the other contemporary popular sources influencing our collective memory of the Panthers, including movies, hip-hop
magazines and music, and mainstream newspapers, may, in fact, serve to re-
produce rather than rectify mistakes and miscalculations of the past.

The goal of this essay is to provide a perspective on an often-ignored aspect of the history and legacy of the BPP, namely, its gender politics. The
gender ideology of the BPP, both as formally stated and as exemplified by
organizational practice, was as critical to its daily functioning as was the
Party's analysis of race and class dynamics in Black communities. Rather
than the Party's gender politics being secondary to the "larger" struggle
against racism and capitalism, I instead posit that the politics of gender were
played out in most aspects of Party activity and affected its ability to function as an effective political organization.

A comprehensive scholarly analysis of the ideology, activity, successes,
and failures of the Black Panther Party has yet to be undertaken by historians. While there are numerous first-hand accounts written during the late
sixties, as well as several recently published autobiographies and memoirs,
most of these sources are primarily descriptive and do not attempt a sustained investigation of the race, class, or gender politics of the Party.[5] My
purpose here is to begin this process with an examination of the construction
of gender ideology within the context of Panther Party politics from
1966–1971.[6] Gender struggle affected the Party's political ideology and positions taken on a variety of issues, relationships with the larger Black and

progressive political communities, daily working and living arrangements, and the organization's ability to defend itself from state-sponsored disruption. The Party's theory and praxis with regard to issues of gender and sexuality should be viewed as an ongoing, nonlinear process that was affected by factors both internal and external to the organization. This analysis of gender ideology offers insights into the internal politics of Black communities, especially relations of power between and among men and women, and the myriad ways in which these dynamics influence political movements and popular perceptions of them.

Although much of the public rhetoric of the BPP and other Black power organizations tended to center on issues usually defined (by themselves and by scholars) as race and/or class concerns, contestation around the politics of gender formed a significant component of the "hidden (and not so hidden) transcript" in the intracommunity discourse.[7] Evelyn Brooks Higginbotham suggests that race functions as a metalanguage in Western culture and tends to subsume and obscure gender, class, and other social relations. In addition, she argues that scholarly work in women's studies and African American history that are premised on the assumption of racial, gender, and class homogeneity "preclude recognition and acknowledgment of intragroup social relations as relations of power," and overlook crucial micropolitical struggles in Black communities.[8] Drawing on Higginbotham's work, I hope to show how the imagery, rhetoric, and praxis of the BPP contain components of ongoing power struggles, overt and hidden, over gender identity and sexuality. These struggles, in turn, complicate and disrupt romanticized notions of "nation-building" and/or Black unity, both historical and contemporary, that presume the existence of a monolithic Black community and privilege male authority/dominance in the family, politics, and culture.

In my analysis, gender is not to be understood as a discrete category unto itself, but one of several interacting factors, such as race, class, color, age, and sexual orientation, that together make up individual identities, as well as the social terrain upon which we experience our realities. To say that I am examining gender and the politics of the BPP does not mean that this work is solely about sexism in the Party, or women's experiences. Instead, a gender analysis also encompasses the experiences of men; definitions of manhood and womanhood; the interconnections between gender-, race-, and class-based oppression; and the impact of all of these factors on the successes and shortcomings of the BPP.

The category of gender was not as fully politicized and theorized during the late 1960s as it is today, thus one must resist the temptation to impose current standards to measure the feminist, nationalist, or revolutionary credentials of the BPP. Each of these social theories/categories must be understood as being situationally/historically specific. What constitutes feminism or radicalism in one time period is not necessarily recognized as such in another. Nevertheless, it is useful to compare and contrast feminism and race-consciousness across historical periods, examining continuities and ruptures. In addition, it is possible to assess which theories and actions constitute a challenge to status quo relations of power in different eras, and thus to assess the merits of political organizations on their own terms and in their particular historical context.

Ideas about gender and gender roles were far from static within the BPP. As the Party spread numerically and geographically, class and gender diversity within its ranks increased. New members brought new (and old) ideas with them. Despite the initial self-conscious creation by the leadership of a masculine public identity for the Panthers, some women and men in the Party challenged the characterization of the struggle as one solely for the redemption of Black manhood and worked within its constraints to serve the interests of the entire community. The stories of the BPP cannot be reduced to a monolithic party line on "the woman question," or a linear progression from an overtly and overwhelmingly sexist organization to a pro-Black feminist/womanist one. Instead, one must pay attention to internal conflict as well as agreement; overt as well as covert manifestations of this dialogue; change over time; diversity of individual experiences; and internal as well as external influences. While it can justifiably be argued that the BPP at various points in its history was a male-centered, male-dominated organization, this point should not negate the important ideological and practical contributions of its female members or of the men who resisted chauvinistic and sexist tendencies. Indeed, the diversity, both in terms of geography and personnel, of an organization whose existence spanned from Oakland to Algiers and from 1966 to 1982, cannot be understood and appreciated through simplistic explanations or superficial head counts of official leadership roles. As will be shown, Black women were critical players in the BPP, and the Party overall had a significant impact on the political life of an entire generation.

Historian Elsa Barkley Brown, in her essay "African-American Women's Quilting: A Framework for Conceptualizing and Teaching African-American Women's History," explores the polyrhythmic and nonlinear structures of African American material cultures, such as quilting, and their relationship to political and economic aesthetics. The structure of African American women's quilting is, according to Barkley Brown, "in fact illustrative of a particular way of seeing, of ordering the world," and thus, of studying and interpreting history. She shares a piece of wisdom passed on from her mother that is instructive in my effort to incorporate the complexities of everyday life into this narrative. Brown reminds us of what she calls the "essential lessons of the quilt: that people and actions do move in multiple directions at once."[9]

With the intention of recognizing the polyrhythms embedded in this stanza of African American history, I begin this chapter with an overview of the larger socio political context with regard to gender ideology in which the BPP functioned. I continue with an examination of some "official" representations of gender ideology by various BPP spokespersons; and then compare these with the "unofficial" renderings of rank-and-file members. Finally, I present some examples of BPP theory in action in an attempt to assess the day-to-day gender struggle and its implications for the lives of Party members and the life of the Party.

Competing Gender Ideologies

The designation, conscious or otherwise, of specific gender-based roles for women and men within the Black Panther Party began with the Party's inception. Of course, this process did not happen in a vacuum. Thus, it will be helpful first to briefly examine the gendered context in which the Panthers operated. In addition to having their own ideas about the roles men and women should play in society and within the Party, the founders and members were also influenced by competing ideologies and vice versa. These competing ideologies could be either supportive of or opposed to the status quo of American society. Three such ideologies that bear mentioning because of their enormous impact on the period are cultural nationalism, feminism, and the Black matriarchy/tangle of pathology thesis.[10] These three ideological discourses illustrate historian E. Frances White's contention that "counter discourse struggles against both dominant and competing oppositional discourses."[11] In other words, the oppositional rhetoric of the BPP challenged and was challenged by other "alternative" as well as mainstream perspectives. There were, of course, many other important hegemonic and counterhegemonic theoretical constructs vying for prominence. These three are highlighted because of their impact on the consciousness of the period in general and on the BPP specifically.

One of the most popular proponents of Black cultural nationalism, at least on the West Coast in the late 1960s, was the Los Angeles-based Us organization headed by Maulana Karenga. The Us organization stressed the necessity for cultural awareness among Blacks to be gained primarily through the revival of African traditions—real or invented— of dress, language, religion, and familial arrangements as well as the rejection of White supremacy. The relationship between Karenga, the Us organization, and the BPP changed over time just as the Panthers' own ideological positions changed. In the early years of the Party, Karenga participated in meetings and rallies in support of the BPP.[12] However, over time as their respective ideologies were clarified and contradictions exposed, the BPP became scathingly critical of the Us organization. Chiefly, the Party's critique was based on the fact that Karenga's group promoted cultural nationalism and Black capitalism. Drawing on the theories of Frantz Fanon, the Panthers repeatedly asserted that cultural pride was a necessary phase in Black people's political development, but it did not guarantee liberation, nor did Black skin necessarily identify one as an automatic ally.[13] The open conflict between the two organizations came to a head in January 1969 when two prominent Panthers,

John (Jon) Huggins and Alprentice "Bunchy" Carter, were killed by Us members in a shoot-out at a Black Student Union meeting at UCLA.[14] This incident sparked numerous articles and political cartoons in *The Black Panther* that criticized cultural nationalism in general and Karenga in particular. There were even charges leveled that Karenga himself was on the payroll of the FBI and/or various other police and government agencies.[15]

One major component of Us rhetoric called for women's submission to "traditional" male authority, and promoted the notion of complementary gender roles. According to Karenga's teachings,

> What makes a women appealing is femininity and she can't be feminine without being submissive. A man has to be a leader and he has to be a man who bases his leadership on knowledge, wisdom and understanding. There is no virtue in independence. The only virtue is in interdependence . . . The role of the woman is to inspire her man, educate their children and participate in social development. . . . We say male supremacy is based on three things: tradition, acceptance, and reason. Equality is false; it's the devil's concept. Our concept is complimentary [*sic*]. Complimentary [*sic*] means you complete or make perfect that which is imperfect.[16]

Karenga and other proponents of complementary gender roles for men and women rarely addressed the power imbalances between the respective roles prescribed. These theories also tended to rely heavily on biological determinism and notions of "natural order" in assessing and assigning separate roles for Black women and men. In practice, complementary theory often led to ridiculous incidents between Black women activists and members of Us, such as when Panther Elaine Brown was told she had to wait to eat until after the male "warriors" had been fed, and, on another occasion, when Angela Davis was discouraged or prevented from taking on a leadership role because it was deemed a "man's job."[17]

E. Frances White's important article "Africa on My Mind: Gender, Counter Discourse and African-American Nationalism" provides a thorough critique of various strains of Black nationalism, including Karenga's, that "can be radical and progressive in relation to white racism and conservative and repressive in relation to the internal organization of the Black community." As White points out, Karenga and other nationalists construct "collective political memories of African culture . . . that both counter racism . . . and construct utopian and repressive gender relations." In particular, she argues that in "building off conservative concepts of 'traditional' African gender relations before colonial rule, [Karenga] argues that the collective needs of Black families depend on women's complementary and unequal roles."[18]

Although BPP members themselves invoked complementary theory early in the organization's development, the unapologetic male supremacist policies and practices of the Us organization exacerbated the already tenuous relationship between the two organizations.[19] Bobby Seale included the issue of male chauvinism in his public opposition to cultural nationalism in a 1970 interview. He stated that "[c]ultural nationalists like Karenga, are male chauvinists as well. What they do is oppress the Black woman. Their Black racism leads them to theories of male domination."[20] For Seale, the link between racism and sexism was that both were practices of domination that fed upon each other (through some unspecified process). He presented the BPP as a viable alternative to Us and cultural nationalism on the basis of the Panthers' ostensibly more progressive party line on "the gender question." The timing of Seale's statement reflected ongoing, internal Party struggles to reconcile the existence of male chauvinism within its ranks and refine its gender ideology. It may also have been an attempt to deflect negative attention away from the Party's own contradictions on these issues.

A second ideological trend that influenced the social and political terrain of the 1960s is contained under the rubric of feminism and the predominantly White Women's liberation movement (WLM). Many young White women who eventually played leadership roles in this wave of the feminist movement in the U.S. had been previously politically involved and developed their budding gender consciousness in the southern Black freedom movement and the New Left.[21] For example, in 1965, responding to a build-up of gender tensions within Students for a Democratic Society (SDS) and a heightened recognition of their own capabilities, women in the organization pressed that group to issue a statement on women's roles in the movement and women's liberation.[22] The growth of various factions in the Women's movement, such as radical feminism, separatism, lesbian separatism, and women of color caucuses, continued throughout the decade and into the 1970s.[23] Although early proponents of the WLM professed to encompass the issues, needs, and demands of all women, its initial definition of the term *feminism*, and its strategies, ideology, tactics, and membership were dominated by White middle-class women.

The rise in visibility of a feminist Women's movement in the mid-to-late sixties is portrayed as the exclusive domain of White women in most historical texts. While the proliferation of explicitly feminist organizations among White women cannot be denied, some of the earliest stirrings of an incipient gender consciousness can be found in the activities of Black women, especially those in the Student Nonviolent Coordinating Committee (SNCC).[24] Black women in Black (mixed-gender) organizations did not necessarily relate to the label *feminist* as defined by the theories and activities of the predominantly White WLM organizations. However, this lack of identification with the terms "feminist" or "women's lib" should not preclude the recognition that Black women who organized on issues, such as police brutality, racism, poverty, imperialism, and Black women's liberation, had a significant impact on the development of gender consciousness during this time.[25] In fact, their involvement and leadership in these arenas represented a challenge to view all of these issues as indeed Black women's issues, as well as concerns for the community as a whole. Their presence in Black organizations eventually forced a recognition of the sexism in some of those organizations and of the racism and middle-class biases of many White women's organizations. Historian Deborah King reminds us that the history of "Black feminist concerns . . . have existed well over a century. In other words, Black women did not just become feminists in the 1970s."[26] Nor did they need to rely on White women's organizations and theories to define the terms of their womanhood or political interests.

The Black Panther Party came into direct contact with various predominantly White women's liberation groups. The level of these interactions differed between chapters and even varied from person to person. In some areas, local WLM groups organized fundraisers and rallies for Panther political prisoners. For example, an article in *The Black Panther* reported the attendance of more than five thousand people at a rally in support of the Panther New Haven 14 and in protest of the particularly cruel treatment of imprisoned Panther women. According to the author of that piece,

> Black Panther Party Chapters and Branches, and Women's Liberation groups from Massachusetts, Connecticut, New York, New Jersey, Pennsylvania, Maryland, and Washington D.C. participated in the march and rally. Organized by the New Haven Chapter of the Black Panther Party, and Women's Liberation groups mostly from New York, the action exposed the blatantly fascist acts of the Connecticut pigs . . . against the people's servants—the Black Panther Party.[27]

The Party did not have an official position on the ideologies and tactics of WLM organizations until Huey P. Newton's statement, "The Women's Liberation and Gay Liberation Movements" in August 1970, calling for the formation of working coalitions with the revolutionary factions of both movements.[28] Previous to this pronouncement, individual Party members had a variety of critical perspectives. Some of the most thorough and thoughtful critiques of the WLM were forthcoming from Panther women. Panther women (and men) eventually came to the conclusion that the struggle for women's liberation was a part of the struggle against capitalism and as such should be waged by men and women together. According to one former member, there was never a position taken that women's liberation was *not* a part of Black liberation struggle, but the Party felt the need to make more formal pronouncements on the issue in part because of the growth and visibility of the WLM.[29]

Panther sisters stated in a 1969 interview that to the extent that women's organizations don't address themselves to the class struggle or to national liberation struggles they are not really furthering the women's liberation movement, because in order for women to be truly emancipated in this country there's going to have to be a socialist revolution. Their critique of various women's lib organizations grew from this basic premise. In their opinion and experiences, the WLM viewed "the contradictions among men and women as one of the major contradictions in capitalist society...and develop[ed] it into an antagonistic contradiction, when actually it is a contradiction among people. It's not a contradiction between enemies."[30] Panther women also acknowledged that Black women's relationship to Black men was qualitatively different from gender relations between Whites. In a 1971 interview, Kathleen Cleaver stated that

> the problems of Black women and the problems of White women are so completely diverse they cannot possibly be solved in the same type of organization nor met by the same type of activity. . . . I can understand how a White woman cannot relate to a White man. And I feel sorry for White women who have to deal with that type of people [sic].[31]

In addition to such theoretical differences, the BPP women interviewed also questioned the structure and practice of some women's liberation organizations. One sister rejected the anti-male and female separatist structures and strategies employed by some organizations as "illogical . . . because you can't solve the problem apart from the problem. You can't be liberated from male chauvinism if you don't even deal with it—if you run away from it."[32] Although some of the women dismissed the usefulness of women's caucuses and separatist groups outright, others agreed that they should be judged by their practice and reserved commentary until they could assess whether those types of formations furthered the struggle for socialism. Although women in the BPP generally chose not to work in female-only organizations, and most did not think of themselves as feminists, this did not necessarily mean that they accepted male chauvinism or sexism. Most expected to be treated as equals, as revolutionary comrades, by their male counterparts. And some did engage the WLM as well as the men (and other women) in the BPP on issues of gender and Black women's roles in the movement.

A final important piece of the ideological landscape of this period that influenced thinking about gender concerned the alleged structural and cultural deficiencies of the Black family. Daniel Patrick Moynihan's *The Negro Family: A Case for National Action,* written in March 1965 under the auspices of the U.S. Department of Labor, became a cornerstone of intense debate in a variety of settings. Moynihan's report used sociological, historical, anecdotal, and statistical information regarding the status of Black families to draw the conclusions that Black families were matriarchal, that Black men were unable to fulfill the roles required of men in a patriarchal society, and that the resulting pattern of female-headed households was largely responsible for the "tangle of pathology" in which Black people found themselves. According to Moynihan, "the Negro community has been forced into a matriarchal structure which, because it is so out of line with the rest of the American society, seriously retards the progress of the group as a whole and imposes a crushing burden on the Negro male, and in consequence, on a great many Negro women as well."[33] The ideas presented in this report, which suggested a change in focus for the government's civil rights policies, were eventually made public. Responses to Moynihan came from all sectors of Black communities, including academics, grassroots activists, politicians, service providers, artists, and independent intellectuals.[34] While the implications of the Moynihan report on the internal debate in the Black community were important, this was not by any stretch of the imagination the beginning of such discussions about a Black matriarchy, Black male castration, and the like. Moynihan inserted himself, and by extension, the Federal government and the media, into previously existing discussions within Black communities. Moynihan built upon earlier works on Black family structure to buttress his claims, especially E. Franklin Frazier's *The Negro Family in the United States.*[35]

Direct references to the Moynihan report in BPP literature are few. However, engagements of its major theses can be found in writings by Panthers on Black family structure, slavery, and the sexual politics of Black and White race relations. In the 1967 essay "Fear and Doubt," Huey P. Newton wrote that

> he [the Black man] feels that he is something less than a man. . . . Often his wife (who is able to secure a job as a maid, cleaning for White people) is the breadwinner. He is, therefore, viewed as quite worthless by his wife and children. He is ineffectual both in and out of the home. He cannot provide for, or protect his family. . . Society will not acknowledge him as a man.[36]

Newton was not far from Moynihan in his assessment of the dilemmas of Black manhood in general, and Black men's seeming inability to live up to the patriarchal norms of the larger society in particular. In this instance, Newton failed to challenge the notion of men as sole providers for and protectors of Black families while corroborating the opinion that Black women devalued, disrespected, and dominated Black men, and were privileged with economic advantages at the expense of Black manhood.

Discussions within the Party regarding gender roles and relations responded to the thesis of Black matriarchy and cultural pathology in varied and sometimes contradictory ways. Panthers could condemn the racism of the larger society in its assessment of Black families and reject the notion that Black culture is inherently pathological, while at the same time affirming an ideal of male-dominated gender relations. To complicate matters further, Newton's own questioning of the validity and usefulness of "the bourgeois family," which he described as "an imprisoning, enslaving, and suffocating experience," eventually led the Party to experiment with communal living and communal sexual relationships. Although this challenge to traditional nuclear family structures might be perceived as radical, an acceptance of male dominance within these alternative arrangements could diminish their revolutionary potential. This point serves to further illustrate

E. Frances White's analysis of the "interrelationship between dominant and counter discourse." She points out that "as part of the same dialectic counter discourses operate on the same ground as dominant ideology."[37] While the BPP offered fundamental critiques of U.S. society, Party members were socialized by and accepted many of its hegemonic norms.

Although cultural nationalism, feminism, and the Black matriarchy thesis were not the only prominent ideological and popular discourses in the late 1960s and early 1970s, their impact was felt nationally (and internationally). Individual Panther chapters may or may not have had direct contact with organizations or individuals espousing any of these perspectives. Yet their ideas and activities were critical threads in the cultural fabric of this period. As such, they formed a part of the larger framework of competing gender ideologies in which the Party functioned, and their impact was represented in a variety of cultural forms, including fiction, movies, scholarly literature, media, and poetry.[38]

"We'll Just Have to Get Guns and Be Men": The Official Gendering of the Black Panther Party[39]

The creation of gendered space and gender ideology in the Black Panther Party was also the product of various internal dialogues in addition to the external ones cited above.[40] The remaining parts of this essay identify some of these other factors and show interactions among them, as well as a process of change over time in ideology and practice. The ideological development of the BPP was necessarily linked to actual experiences and events; thus, the incorporation of the themes of sexual and gender politics into the Party's overall revolutionary nationalist ideology was an ongoing process affected by concrete material realities.

The increased presence of women, the shift from a paramilitary to a community service focus, the incarceration, assassination, and exile of key male leaders, and the increasing pressures of state-sponsored repression, all affected the internal dialogue about gender roles. With such in mind, it is helpful to recount a few significant events in the history of the BPP that contributed to changes in both the daily reality and public perception of Party life. For example, in early 1968, the BPP dropped "for Self-Defense" from their name in an effort to encourage their recognition as a political Party with a full platform that included, but was not limited to, self-defense and paramilitary activities.

Beginning in late 1968 and early 1969, community service programs, such as the free breakfast for children and free health clinic projects as well as liberation schools and community political education classes, were implemented nationally (with varying degrees of success).[41] Prior to initiating the official "survival" programs, Panther chapters had already been involved in local community struggles for decent housing, welfare rights, citizens' police review panels, Black history classes, and traffic lights on dangerous intersections in Black neighborhoods.[42] The development of an overt and public dialogue within the Party about male chauvinism also intensified in late 1968 and continued throughout 1969. As will become clearer, each of these events influenced the ideological and practical development of the BPP.[43]

Initially, for the Panthers, as for many other Black groups in this period, the quest for liberation was directly linked to the "regaining" of Black manhood.[44] This was evident in much of the Party's early language and ideology about gender roles generally, and men's roles in particular. In fact, the Black Panther Party for Self-Defense was an all-male organization at the outset.[45] From the first issue of the official Party newspaper, *The Black Panther,* leaders Huey Newton, Bobby Seale, and Eldridge Cleaver presented a gendered vision of the Party's potential composition. A recruitment call read:

> The BLACK PANTHER PARTY FOR SELF-DEFENSE really has something going. These Brothers are the cream of Black manhood. They are there for the protection and defense of our Black community . . . BLACK MEN!!! It is your duty to your women and children, to your mothers and sisters, to investigate the program of the PARTY.[46]

Men were the primary recruitment targets of early Panther campaigns. The language in this statement clearly asserted the role of Black men as protectors of women and children—self-defense was a man's job. In a 1968 speech, Bobby Seale went even further to provide an analysis of how the Party's race-, gender-, and class-specific imagery actually aided their recruitment efforts:

> A lot of people ain't gon know what's happening. But the brothers on the block who the man's been calling thugs and hoodlums for four hundred years, gon say, "Them some out of sight thugs and hoodlums up there!". . . Well, they've been calling us niggers, thugs, and hoodlums for four hundred years, that ain't gon hurt me, I'm going to check out what these brothers is doing![47]

Here, Seale continued to create a self-consciously masculine, "lumpen" public identity for the Party that served to mask the numerically greater participation of women by 1968, when the paramilitary functions of the organization were less prominent.[48] Statements such as these, along with the Party's militaristic style and male dominated formal (national) leadership structures, suggested a particular definition of Black masculinity that assumed men had the skill, inclination, and obligation to be warriors, while conversely, women (and children) did not. In many ways this posture was an attempt to counter the racist and anti-working-class brutes, and irresponsible, incapable, and emasculated patriarchs. At the same time that the Party's alternative self-representations of Black manhood elicited responses of pride from sectors of Black communities, they also mirrored the restrictive gender codes of the larger society that limit the options of both women and men. In addition, their public image was interpreted and exploited by mainstream media in ways that capitalized on White people's fear of alleged Black criminality in the form of an armed and dangerous Black male.

While the ten-point platform and program of the BPP ostensibly outlined the needs of the entire Black community, the other rhetoric of Party leaders presented a less gender-inclusive analysis of community concerns.[49] Many early statements by Newton and Seale linked Black oppression to Black male castration and focused squarely on the sexual politics of White supremacy. Consequently, many of the Party's public positions on questions of gender took on increasingly sexual overtones.

Perhaps the most extensive and most often referenced presentation of this strain of sexual politics was given by Eldridge Cleaver in his best-seller *Soul on Ice*.[50] Cleaver joined the BPP in February of 1967. Prior to this, he had been released on parole December 12, 1966 after serving nine years of a one-to-fourteen year sentence for rape. Newton and Seale were impressed by Cleaver's speaking and writing abilities, his commitment to the self-defense philosophy of Malcolm X, and the fact that he had spent time in prison (like Malcolm).[51]

It is an interesting but rarely commented on point that one of the key leaders of the BPP was a convicted and self-described rapist. His reflections on rape in *Soul on Ice* are both illuminating and deeply disturbing. He claims he refined his technique for raping White women by "practicing" on Black women. Although Cleaver repudiates his previous assessment of raping White women as an "insurrectionary act" in the book, he maintains that "the Black man's sick attitude toward the White woman is a revolutionary sickness" which has to be dealt with openly and resolved for the sake of the nation as a whole.[52] These were themes, experiences, and preoccupations that he brought with him to the BPP and to his analysis of sexual/gender politics. *Soul on Ice* was a national best seller and thus was read by a large number of Whites. It was also key reading for BPP members (especially on the West Coast) and often cited as influential by male Party leaders.[53]

Using exaggerated stereotypes and caricatures in *Soul On Ice*, Cleaver describes in some detail his assessment of the historical relationship between Blacks and Whites, and women and men.[54] Black men are described as "supermasculine menials" who, during slavery, were stripped of their mental abilities and castrated by White men, the "omnipotent administrators." White women, allegedly idealized by all men, are dubbed "superfeminine freaks." And Black women, denied any semblance of femininity because of their "domestic role," are characterized as "subfeminine" or "self-reliant Amazons." In addition, Cleaver hypothesizes that Black women hold Black men in contempt because of their inability to be "real men."

In this analysis, Cleaver corroborates other racist and sexist descriptions of slavery and Black male/female relations that cast Black women in the role of collaborators in the oppression/castration syndrome of Black men. According to Cleaver, the interactions among these various groups explain class and racial antagonisms in sexual terms, with the ultimate battle being between "the Omnipotent Administrator and the Supermasculine Menial for control of sexual sovereignty."[55] In fact, what Cleaver describes here is a racialized struggle for male supremacy between Black and White men for sexual access to White women and control over the reproductive (labor as well as childbearing) capacities of Black women. References to capitalism and the material basis of Black oppression are absent. Class struggle is reduced to a psychological power struggle over sexual territory in which sex and women's bodies are commodities to be possessed and controlled by men.

Huey P. Newton often reiterated and expanded the thesis put forward by Cleaver. A vivid example of this is to be found in Newton's exposition on the legacy of slavery in the U.S.:

> The historical relationship between black and white here in America has been the relationship between the slave and the master, the master being the mind and the slave the body... The master took the manhood from the slave because he stripped him of a mind ... In the process the slave-master stripped himself of a body ... This caused the slave-master to become very envious of the slave because he pictured the slave as being more of a man, being superior sexually, because the penis is part of the body... He attempted to bind the penis of the slave ... he psychologically wants to castrate the Black man.[56]

Newton goes on to describe the Black liberation movement in terms of the Black man's search for unity of his body with his mind, in order "to gain respect from his woman. Because women want one who can control...[I]f he [the slave] can only recapture his mind, recapture his balls, then he will lose all fear and will be free to determine his destiny...The Black Panther Party along with all revolutionary Black groups have regained our mind and our manhood."[57] Here Newton reasserts the desirability of Black male domination and Black female acquiescence, while assuming that this pattern has been unduly interrupted. He uses the term "balls" in a metaphorical sense to refer to the courage and bravery required to stand up to the oppressor (which could possibly be attributable to a man or woman). Yet his comment about Black women's alleged desire to be controlled interferes with the notion that phrases like "recapturing our balls" and "regaining our manhood" are merely figures of speech. Instead, this language is linked to specific practices. Its usage in this context seems to preclude the possibility that Black women can be an active part of this process of resistance to oppression and clearly asserts that a rehabilitated Black manhood will be the key to Black liberation. In essence, Black men must learn to be better patriarchs. Black women, too, will be reconstructed in this process by learning not only to respect, but to defer to Black male authority.

These theoretical formulations give us important clues about gender-role construction within the Party as it was put forth by key men in leadership positions. Here, women are all but defined out of an active or productive role in the Black liberation struggle. In male Party leaders' historical analyses, Black women are either viewed as co-conspirators in the castration process or idle sideline observers waiting for Black men to get their balls back. Meanwhile, men are the primary actors and agents of change and the protectors of Black women and children. These formulations reflect assertions in the majority culture that Black men were indeed castrated and are thus less than real men, especially if they do not enforce patriarchy/male dominance in their sexual and familial arrangements. At the same time, such assertions degrade and ignore the historical legacy of Black women and men who reject such gender hierarchies, and they present no viable alternative models of male/female (hetero)sexual interaction.

In hindsight, Newton would write that it "was a common misconception at the time—that the Party was searching for badges of masculinity. In fact, the reverse is true: the Party acted as it did because we *were* men. Many failed to perceive the difference."[58] Needless to say, his own previous public statements did not help clarify this point. In fact, even this reflection fails to address the limitations of such a male-centered definition of politics and continues to discount the importance of Black women to the life of the Party by promoting the misperception that all Panthers were male.

In this context of sexualized representations of race and gender politics, Black men's and women's sexuality—how they defined themselves or were defined by others in terms of their sexual preferences, orientations, and practices—was an open topic of discussion. Expressions of sexuality were often described as directly related to the potential successes or failures of the movement and were integrated into the culture of the movement in both explicit and covert ways. During Eldridge Cleaver's 1968 presidential campaign, he promoted the idea of "pussy power," women's ability to withhold sex in order to compel men to political activism. He told women, "Until he [sic] ready to pick up a gun and be a man, don't give him no sugar. Politics comes from the lips of a pussy. I don't know how you can stand to have them faggots layin' and sucking' on you. You can always have a real man."[59] Here again, sex and women's bodies, in particular, are viewed as commodities to be exchanged in service to the revolution. It can be argued that women and men both use sex/sexuality to exert an influence on the behavior of others in certain situations, and that there are sexual politics and power dynamics at work in most relationships. However, it is one thing to engage in sexual power struggles in personal relationships (which in the context of a political organization/movement also has political implications), it is quite another thing for an influential leader to promote this as a preferred mode of political praxis.

Also implied in this statement is an antigay and heterosexist component to Cleaver's and the BPP's construction of a Black masculine ideal.[60] "Real men" are identified not only by their political commitment to joining the BPP, but also by their participation in "appropriate" sexual practices with partner(s) of the "appropriate" gender. It is important to note that the above commentaries by Cleaver preceded Huey P. Newton's statement on "The Women's Liberation and Gay Liberation Movements," in which he declared that "[t]he terms 'faggot' and 'punk' should be deleted from our vocabulary, and especially we should not attach names normally designated for homosexuals to men who are enemies of the people, such as Nixon . . . Homosexuals are not enemies of the people."[61] The impact of both Cleaver's pronouncement on pussy power and Newton's statement in support of lesbian/gay and women's liberation varied both in terms of acceptance and implementation at the local level.[62]

It is somewhat ironic that Eldridge Cleaver's 1969 statement from exile on the incarceration of Panther Ericka Huggins was one of the earliest and strongest formulations by a male Panther of a nonsexual, revolutionary role for Black women. In 1969, Huggins and thirteen other Panthers were arrested by the FBI on charges of murder, kidnapping, and conspiracy in New Haven, Connecticut. Of the five women imprisoned, three were pregnant and one, Frances Carter, gave birth while under armed guard.[63]

Eldridge Cleaver's statement may seem somewhat uncharacteristic at this point, yet it was likely the product of ongoing dialogue and struggle within the Party. While Cleaver did not clarify the steps that led to his revised perspective, his words reflect an intellectual or rational understanding of Huggins' predicament based on her condition and, possibly, a more intuitive empathy based on his own experiences of incarceration.[64] Cleaver was a very articulate and shrewd political thinker, and thus his statement was as much a tactic to build support for Huggins' defense campaign as it was an edict to Party members. In any case, his comments on this matter merit extensive quotation, for they reveal a significant shift in the public rhetoric about roles prescribed for women in the Party:

> I know Erica [*sic*], and I know that she's a very strong sister. But I know that she is now being subjected to a form of torture that is horrible. . . Let it be a lesson and an example to all of the sisters, particularly to all of the brothers, that we must understand that our women are suffering strongly and enthusiastically as we are participating in the struggle. The incarceration and the suffering of Sister Erica [*sic*] should be a stinging rebuke to all manifestations of male chauvinism within our ranks. . . That we must too recognize that a woman can be just as revolutionary as a man and that she has equal stature. . . . That we have to recognize . . . revolutionary standards of principles demand that we go to great lengths to see to it that disciplinary action is taken on all levels against those who manifest male chauvinism behavior.
>
> Because the liberation of women is one of the most important issues facing the world today. . . I know from my own experience that the . . . demand for liberation of women in Babylon is the issue that is going to explode, and if we're not careful it's going to destroy our ranks, destroy our organization, because women want to be liberated just as all oppressed people want to be liberated.[65]

In this statement, previous disparities between women's and men's roles are discredited, rhetorically at least. Cleaver goes on to say that "if we want to go around and call ourselves a vanguard organization, then we've got to be . . . the vanguard also in the area of women's liberation, and set an example in that area. . . . [S]isters have a duty and the right to do whatever they want to do in order to see to it that they are not relegated to an inferior position."[66] Cleaver challenged the notion of gender-specific role models and called on both women and men to learn from the example set by Huggins. He also argued for a standard of gender equality, not complementary, thus implicitly rejecting the notion that there are or should be specific roles assigned to women and men. Cleaver raises the issue of Black women's liberation and the struggle against male chauvinism to the level of a serious political concern for the Party and the movement as a whole. According to this analysis, female/male relations and the status of women are not solely personal matters, but instead critical political issues that necessitate regulation by disciplinary rules and sanctions. The sense here is that concrete steps are being taken to spread this consciousness to all levels of the Party and to base future actions on this premise of gender equality. However, interviews with former Panthers regarding daily interactions, and leadership and work assignments, suggest that the process of changing gender ideology and praxis was full of contradictions and necessitated ongoing struggle. For example, it is not clear that within the Party there were shared definitions of women's liberation, equality, and male chauvinism. What is clear is that there was variation in the level and pace of change on these issues across chapters and over time.

Elsewhere in Cleaver's statement, he mentions (twice) that Huey Newton had made pronouncements against male chauvinism and called for its eradication from the ranks of the BPP. In fact, point seven on the BPP's "8 Points of Attention" read "do not take liberties with women."[67] While this rule was limited in terms of clarity, detail, and scope, Party members were required to memorize these "points of attention." At the very least, they probably sparked debate and discussion among the rank and file.[68]

Panther women also began to make more prominent public pronouncements on gender relations in 1969. The analysis of gender as part and parcel of class struggle began to permeate "official" Party rhetoric. In July 1969, Panther Roberta Alexander spoke on a panel on women in the struggle at the BPP-sponsored United Front Against Fascism (UFAF) Conference. In her speech, she confirms there indeed is "a struggle going on right now" within the Panther Party and that people are "confused about the Black Panther Party on the woman question." She observes that "Black women are oppressed as a class. . . .They are oppressed because they are workers and oppressed because they are Black. In addition, Black women are oppressed by Black men . . . The problem of male supremacy can't be overcome unless it's a two-way street. Men must struggle too."[69] Alexander confirms the existence of dialogue and debate within the Party on the relationship between race, class, and gender in the Black liberation movement. She presents an analysis of the multiple positions of Black women, who simultaneously negotiate realities shaped by their identities as women, African Americans, and exploited workers.[70] In addition, like Eldridge Cleaver, she calls for a recognition that gender issues and the oppression of women are not solely (or even primarily) Black women's personal problems, but are instead concerns to be addressed by the entire community/movement.

The following September, the Panthers published the article "Sisters," which was widely circulated as a four-page leaflet entitled "Panther Sisters on Women's Liberation." The text of the leaflet is an extensive interview with six anonymous women conducted at Party headquarters.[71] In the interview, Panther women discuss changes that occurred in the Party during the year regarding its position on the role of women in the movement. They attribute these changes to several factors, including the example set for all Party members by Ericka Huggins and revolutionary Vietnamese women; greater political analysis and understanding of the proletarian revolution within the Party; and forces of repression outside the Party. According to these women, "[T]here used to be a difference in the roles in the party because sisters were relegated to certain duties. This was due to the backwardness and lack of political perspective on the part of both sisters and brothers."[72] Regarding the oppression of women, the interviewees reassert the class-based analysis presented earlier at the UFAF. One sister adds that

> I can see since the time I joined the Party that the Party has undergone radical change in the direction of women [*sic*] leadership and emancipation of women . . . because we have come to realize that male chauvinism and all its manifestations are bourgeois and that's one of the things we're fighting against. We realize that in a proletarian revolution, the emancipation of women is primary.[73]

The women in the interview also challenge Black men to rethink their own definitions of manhood. One sister remarks that "it's important that within the context of the struggle that Black men understand that their manhood is not dependent on keeping their Black women subordinate to them because this is what bourgeois ideology has been trying to put into the Black man and that's part of the special oppression of Black women." Although they also mention, "Our men have been sort of castrated," the solution they pose is "to be very sure that the roles are evenly divided," so that men will not have the "fear of women dominating the whole political scene."[74] These Panther sisters corroborate the view that internal struggle around the BPP's ideology and practice regarding gender issues was a dynamic, nonlinear process. They acknowledge intracommunal power relations as well as the influence of external factors. Their reference to the castration of Black men and their concern that they, as women, do not "dominate" or take over political leadership are somewhat ambiguous. Perhaps this statement is both a way of

distancing themselves from what they interpret to be the goals of the pre-
dominately White women's movement as well as a slight nod to the Black
matriarchy thesis. The national hierarchy of the BPP was always predominantly male until Elaine Brown was named chairman in 1974, yet there were
always women in leadership positions, formally and informally, at the local
level. Thus, this statement also can be interpreted as recognition of the
prevalence of women numerically as well as the significance of their contributions to the life of the Party as leaders. It suggests the need for a redefinition of leadership to include those activities and people often thought of
as providing support to officially and publicly credited leaders and a greater
appreciation of the historical prominence of women in Black freedom
movements and organizations.

Old and New Ideas About Gender

*"You might have been a revolutionary for six months, but you been a colo-
nialized slave for eighteen, nineteen, twenty-five years"* [75]

It is important to stress that the above examples of changes in the BPP's
gender ideology are officially sanctioned public pronouncements. They are
the Party's revised self-representations, which stand in contrast to both their
own earlier posturing and to racist and sexist mainstream media portrayals.
In order to render a more complete view of the dialogic process of gender
role/ideological construction, one must consider the perspectives of rank-
and-file members and examine the relationship between Party rhetoric and
actual practice.

The experiences and ideas that individual members brought with them to
the Party varied widely and affected how they functioned within the organization. Some had been involved previously in other political organizations,
while many had not. Some had college training, especially those in leadership positions, while among the ranks there was a predominance of "lumpen" sisters and brothers. These are just a few examples of the diversity
within the BPP.

Because of the heterogeneity of the Party, the articulation and understanding of Party ideology by the leadership and members varied widely and
are not easily reduced to a single interpretation. Such complexity, in combination with periods of rapid growth when the Party structure (especially
screening and political education mechanisms) could not keep pace with rising membership numbers, contributes to the difficulty in tracing gender ideology over time.[76] Nevertheless, an examination of the written and spoken
communication of Party members reveals the complexities of their analyses, and their attempts, as a "vanguard party," to articulate their ideology to
each other and the masses of Black people.

The examples thus far have been drawn from men and women speaking
in an official capacity for the Party. There is, however, evidence in the BPP
newspaper of rank-and-file members' perspectives on questions of gender

politics.[77] These articles are very useful for the insights they present on how members interpreted the Party's and other competing ideologies about gender roles and related them to their own experiences. For example, one unnamed male writer of a 1969 article examines Black women's role in their families and in the revolution. He argues that Black women as a group are primarily cultural nationalists who berate Black men for engaging in armed self-defense. He sees Black men as inherently revolutionary—"consciously or unconsciously." According to him,

> Black women are for the most part selfish and subjective. In past times Black men existed in a matriarchal society, where the women were the only members of the family to work. This condition created a feeling of superiority in Black women . . . To a great extent her attitude explains the high rate of divorce among Panthers and other revolutionaries.[78]

This author's assertions place Black women squarely at the root of many of the problems in Black communities. His statement affirms the basic premise of the Moynihan report that Black families are matriarchal and thus pathological. In this Panther's analysis, "Black women have failed to see that this unbalanced economic condition helped to rob the men of their manhood."[79] According to him, it is female chauvinism and Black women's complicity in the castration of Black men primarily through the receipt of an alleged economic advantage that destroyed relationships and families in the Party and elsewhere. This anonymous Panther was obviously influenced by the pseudohistorical analysis of Black women as domineering matriarchs and was seemingly unaware (or unconvinced) of the revised Party rhetoric highlighting the significance of revolutionary comrade sisters to the movement. His article appeared without commentary or reply; thus it is unclear whether his views were representative of "official" Party ideology, represented significant numbers of male members, or were strictly his own. Thus, while there appeared to be a transition or at least a recognition of some contradictions in the Party's gender ideology, these changes did not always inform the actions or ideas of all members. At the very least, ideological formulations on gender roles were being constantly revised and were open to various interpretations.

Articles by rank-and-file Panther women were also included in early issues of *The Black Panther*. Beginning in late 1968, articles authored by women appeared more frequently and specifically addressed their roles in the movement. These types of articles represented a move by women in the Party, as well as by formal Party leadership, to explicitly recognize women's past contributions and to influence their future participation in Party life and activity.

Two very telling examples of what may be called "prescriptive literature" by Black women in the Panther Party appeared in the same issue, on the same page of *The Black Panther* in September 1968. Each offers characterizations of "Black Revolutionary Women" that partially challenge Moynihan's portrayal of Black women as overbearing and domineering, and at the same time, reinforce traditional middle-class or bourgeois gender norms. Linda Greene writes that the "new phenomenon" of the revolutionary woman

> is, and must be the Black Man's everything. She is a worker. She is a mother. She is a companion, intellectual, spiritual, mental and physical. She is what her man, and what her people need her to be ... She is the strength of the struggle ... She is militant, revolutionary, committed, strong, and warm, feminine, loving, and kind. These qualities are not the antithesis of each other; they must all be her simultaneously.[80]

She goes on to discuss how women must support revolutionary Black men, not distract them, and provide a haven at home for their rejuvenation.

The second article by Gloria Bartholomew, "A Black Woman's Thoughts," supplements Green's piece by giving examples of how Black women could change themselves to better aid the struggle. She begins with the rhetorical question, "What is a Black woman's chief function, if it is not to live for her man?" Then, in what seems to be a direct reference to the predominantly White women's liberation movement, she asserts that "Black women must drop the White ways of trying to be equal to the Black man. The woman's place is to stand behind the Black man, so in the event he should start to fall she is there to hold him up with her strength." According to her five-point inventory, Black women must "find out who you are, ... rid yourself of the inferiority complex about being Black ..., stop playing the role of a man, and take your place beside your man ..., and smile when you pass a brother."[81]

Taken together, these two articles both contradict and complement each other. They should be seen as evidence that their own and the Party's official position on the role of women was still evolving through a process of internal struggle. They may also be signs of openness, in that members engaged each other publicly and expressed diverse perspectives. Neither woman challenges traditionally defined roles for women in heterosexual nuclear family settings, such as nurturer, mother, spiritual family sustainer, and adjunct of men. Roles for men, such as breadwinner, protector, and head of the household, also remained fundamentally unchallenged and were in fact encouraged. At the same time, they present women as standing beside men and use character defining terms that were previously reserved for men, such as militant, intellectual, and committed revolutionary. The overarching themes of both articles define women only as they relate to and support the men in their lives. In sum, "[I]t is what the Black woman can contribute to the Black man that is important."[82] This position was consistent with many of the previously mentioned commentaries of male Party leaders during this period. Their arguments for complementary roles closely mirrored the positions taken by Karenga and other cultural nationalists. Yet it should also be noted that within such traditionally gendered settings, these women were seeking to define a space for themselves in the movement that would value and enhance their potential power as women committed to revolutionary change.

There were also competing views on the appropriate models of a revolutionary Black manhood among rank-and-file members. In her autobiography, Assata Shakur recounts her relationship with Zayd, the Minister of Information in the Bronx. Of him she writes,

> I also respected him because he refused to become part of the macho cult that was an official body in the BPP. He never voted on issues or took a position just to be one of the boys. When brothers made an unprincipled attack on sisters, Zayd refused to participate . . . Zayd always treated me and all the other sisters with respect. I enjoyed his friendship because he was one of those rare men completely capable of being friends with a woman without having designs on her.[83]

Shakur's description of Zayd challenges the popular image of male Black Panther leaders. Zayd's behavior and attitude also presented an alternative construction of male gender roles for other brothers in the Party. He gained the respect of women in the Party through his actions. Yet he also incurred the wrath of some men, according to Shakur, "because he was small and his masculinity was always being challenged in some way by the more backward, muscle-headed men in the party."[84] Shakur's comments raise the question of whether it was not only Zayd's size but also his stance on the "woman question" that was equated with weakness and a lack of appropriate "manhood credentials" (whatever those may have been). In the context of other extremely homophobic and heterosexist comments by some Party members, one could also reasonably raise the question of whether this challenging of Zayd's manhood also may have represented a pejorative commentary about his sexual orientation, whether metaphorical or literal. Recall that Eldridge Cleaver publicly articulated the category of "real men" as being the opposite of "faggots." [85]

Yet even at the expense of being ridiculed, some men in the Party did challenge the predominant thinking and posturing of the times that equated Black heterosexual manhood with male dominance. These Panther men often learned and taught others about alternative models of Black manhood and female–male relations through the example of their interactions with women in the BPP. Harlem branch member Jamal Joseph remembers, with an air of sincere respect and fondness, his interactions with women in the Party and the BPP's contributions to his overall political development. He joined the Panthers at the age of sixteen. According to Joseph, "[G]rowing up in the Black Panther Party . . . it's where I learned not to be a chauvinist. OK. I learned there was no such thing as man's work or woman's work." For Joseph, women like Afeni Shakur, Janet Cyril, and Assata Shakur were some of his "most important teachers and best friends" and had a profound and lasting impact on his ideas about gender and politics in general.[86] Thus, while the popular image of the BPP, both then and now, is that of a male-dominated, macho cult, the reality of Party life deserves a more nuanced description. One must take into account the diverse individual experiences of Party members as well as examine the subtleties to be found in dissecting broad patterns.

Observation and Participation: Quotidian Gender Struggle in Ideology and Practice

Huey P. Newton was often quoted as saying that Black people learned primarily through observation and participation, a point which supports the argument that the events of everyday life were important in shaping the consciousness and practice of Party members.[87] It is critical, then, that we begin to explore the daily struggles over gender and definitions of Black manhood and womanhood and not just moments of extraordinary rupture and conflict (although these, too, are important). I do not mean to suggest that the BPP was a hotbed of critical inquiry on gender issues in the academic sense. Instead, many of these dialogic interactions played themselves out in the daily acts of living and working together. In other words, the actions of Party members often represented their theory.[88] A few examples drawn from the experiences of women in the Party will serve to illustrate the impact of gender politics and power dynamics on everyday life.

The late Connie Matthews, who worked in both the international chapter and Oakland headquarters, recounts that

> [i]n theory, the Panther party was for equality of the sexes . . . On a day-to-day struggle with rank-and-file brothers, you got a lot of disrespect, you know . . . Because, I mean, it's one thing to get up and talk about ideologically you believe this. But you're asking people to change attitudes and lifestyles overnight, which is not just possible. So I would say that there was a lot of struggle and there was a lot of male chauvinism. . . .But I would say all in all, in terms of equality . . . that women had very, very strong leadership roles and were respected as such. It didn't mean it came automatically.[89]

Matthews acknowledges the existence of sexism in the Party, but at the same time highlights the existence of struggle on the part of women (and men) to grapple with the disparities between Party rhetoric and the concrete reality of daily working and living arrangements. She confirms an awareness of the influence of socialization on Party members' ideas and behavior. Yet her quote leaves some ambiguity as to whether she saw chauvinistic "attitudes and lifestyles" as being generated from within, or from outside of Black communities, or both. She also hints at her opinion of the way in which class differences may have affected gender relations in her reference to the "rank-and-file" brothers as being particularly disrespectful.

Statements by Assata Shakur corroborate Matthews' acknowledgments of the daily struggles of women for respect in the Party. According to Shakur,

> [A] lot of us [women] adopted that kind of macho type style in order to survive in the Black Panther Party. It was very difficult to say "well listen brother, I think that . . . we should do this and this."[I]n order to be listened to, you had to just say, "look mothafucka," you know. You had to develop this whole arrogant kind of macho style in order to be heard . . . We were just involved in those day to day battles for respect in the Black Panther Party.[90]

Here, Shakur presents one strategy employed by some women in the BPP to exert authority—participation in presumably masculine styles of behavior and posturing. This approach to political organizing is more authoritarian than democratic and was criticized elsewhere by Shakur.[91] However, Black women's presumption of a style, actions, and words associated with male prerogative potentially undermined the notion of men's inherent aggressiveness or innate leadership abilities that were the basis of masculinist gender ideologies, including some of the BPP's earlier formulations. While this macho posturing by women may have reinforced the notion of Black women as domineering, it also challenged the idea that only Black men should lead and protect Black women. That some women had to modify their public persona in order to be respected is indicative of the extent to which gendered power dynamics pervaded the lives of Party members.

Such intracommunal struggles, which Matthews and Shakur describe, directly affected the organization's culture and ability to function, yet are hidden in analyses that fail to look at gender relations as relations of power. The ways in which women and men understood their respective roles, and the relative exercise of power they brought to bear on their relationships, were not merely personal dynamics, but also political interactions and choices made in the context of the movement. While on a very practical level the dialogue on gender in the Party was affected by the presence of increasing numbers of women, it was, more importantly, the impact of these women's actions that demanded a certain level of respect and recognition from male members.

Female Panthers often tested and stretched the boundaries of the largely masculinized Party structure. Many of these women held low or no formal positions of rank. Yet, their heroic actions thrust them into positions of prominence inside and outside of the Party. Women, such as Joan Bird, Afeni Shakur, and numerous other unnamed rank-and-file members, fought figuratively and literally for the revolutionary principles and platform of the Party. Many were involved in armed confrontation with police authorities alongside Panther men.[92] By so doing, they challenged old Party notions of community defense being a man's job. The brutal treatment of these women by police authorities made it clear to them as well as the entire Black community that they could expect no comfort or benefits from stereotypes of women as fragile and weak and needing to be protected. After all, this construction of womanhood historically had never been applied to Black women by the larger society (even though some nationalists adapted their own variation). Nor could the idea (propagated by Moynihan and even some Panthers) that Black women somehow received special treatment from government agencies or U.S. society in general remain intact. Once these Black women, involved in militant organizing efforts, stepped outside of roles traditionally assigned to women or African Americans, their treatment more closely resembled the experiences of their Black male comrades than those of White women. Racist and sexist government agencies and a racist and sexist mainstream polity responded to Black Panther women as Black people who did not "know their place" with respect to their gender, race, or class.

The above examples attest to the ability of some Black women to carve out a space for their own empowerment within the context of a formally male-dominated organization, often in the face of extreme male chauvinism and harassment from within and without. In her recognition of women as strong leaders in the Party, Connie Matthews legitimizes women's contributions as crucial to the survival of the organization. In so doing, she not only pays respect to the leadership abilities of the well-known (and higher ranking) women in the BPP like Ericka Huggins, Kathleen Cleaver, and Elaine Brown, but also to local female rank-and-file members.

Matthews' claim that women held key leadership roles is echoed in other accounts. Many former Panthers recall that women were responsible in terms of both leadership and personnel for key Party programs, such as the free breakfast programs, liberation schools, and medical clinics; yet the media image of the Party was and is male-centered. The Party also recruited non-Panther "welfare mothers, grandmothers and guardians in the Black community" to help staff breakfast programs in particular.[93] As former Panther Malika Adams pointed out,

> [W]omen ran the BPP pretty much. I don't know how it got to be a male's party or thought of as being a male's party. Because those things, when you really look at it in terms of society, those things are looked on as being woman things, you know, feeding children, taking care of the sick and uh, so. Yeah, we did that. We actually ran the BPP's programs.[94]

Her assessment of the prominence of women not only provides us with the standard participatory history or "women were there too" analysis, but on an even more significant level, argues for new definitions of leadership and politics. As Adams indicates, the types of activities prescribed in these community survival programs often represented an extension of "traditional" roles for women in the family: nurturers, caretakers of children, transmitters of morals, etc. Yet Panther men as well as women staffed the programs, thus potentially challenging narrowly defined male gender roles. These types of movement jobs are often categorized by historians and activists alike as "support work" or "community service" as opposed to "real" political activism.[95] These tasks were the lifeblood of the organization and as such should be understood more accurately as forms of political leadership. Given the context of state repression, these activities took on an explicitly political and public function and were often the sites of intense struggle with state authorities. Thus, public speaking abilities and formal titles were not the sole markers of leadership abilities, a point not missed by the FBI. Panther survival programs were an ideological and practical counter to the misinformation and destruction campaign being waged against the BPP. In fact, many of the FBI's activities against the Party were designed to undermine the free breakfast for children operations and other community based "survival programs." An FBI memo from Director J. Edgar Hoover in 1969 described the free breakfast program as "the best and most influential activity going for the BPP and as such, is potentially the greatest threat to efforts by authorities . . . to neutralize the BPP and destroy what it stands for."[96]

The experiences of Brooklyn-branch member Janet Cyril further illuminate this point. As one of the founding members of that branch, she eventually rose to city-wide coordinator of the free breakfast programs. In the meantime, she was expelled from the Party no less than four times. She argues that this was in part due to her generally anti-authoritarian attitude, which, in her assessment, was even less tolerable because she is a woman. One of her expulsions was for refusing to have sex with a very high-ranking member of the Central Committee of the Party:

> [He] thought he was gon' sleep in my bed with me. And uh, that was
> not happening. And I was given several direct orders which I
> disobeyed quite directly (laugh). And then to top it off, the street I lived
> on had alternate side of the street parking and their car got towed in the
> morning because they overslept.[97]

After this episode, Cyril was expelled for sabotage. She later found out through research in the FBI's Counter Intelligence Program (COINTELPRO) files that the FBI deliberately planted misinformation by using an actual informant, which made it appear that Cyril was the informant. This particular tactic was called "bad-jacketing" or "snitch-jacketing."[98] An FBI internal agency memorandum, she recalls, stated that she should be targeted for "neutralization" because of her effectiveness as an organizer.

This example points to the significance of the community service programs in lending credibility and longevity to the BPP, which was precisely why the FBI made such diligent efforts to undermine them. It also gives a concrete example of the power relations embedded in sexual interactions in that Cyril was expelled at least once for refusing to participate in what some Party members referred to as "socialistic fucking," or engaging in sexual relations ostensibly as a revolutionary duty.[99] In this case, the political impact of the attempted power play by the male leader actually served the interests of the oppressive state apparatus and helped to undermine the effectiveness of one of the Party's key local leaders and programs. Here, the contradictions between the theory and practice of the national leadership with regard to sexual relationships and sexual self-determination directly and adversely affected the Panthers' capacity to function as a viable political organization.

Conclusions

The ideological development of Party members was an ongoing process, ripe with contradiction, and shaped by the material and cultural conditions of the late 1960s and early 1970s. The increasing numbers of women in the Party as rank-and-file members and as leaders and the severity of state repression directed at all Panthers provided the pressure-cooker setting for testing out their new ideas about gender and revolution.

The members of the BPP were themselves products of the larger society. Thus the terrain on which intracommunal debates over gender, class, and race took place was one influenced by the terms of the so-called dominant culture and its agents. The Party was both critic and purveyor of American culture and politics. Panthers decried the class and gender biases of their contemporaries and the larger White society, but at the same time they reaffirmed many of those same shortcomings. A former female member of the Party's Brooklyn branch recalled,

> [W]e could talk about this stuff [gender and sexism]. We could talk about it just as we talked about capitalism and imperialism. But I don't know that we internalized it. I think we saw that our Party line was that there was no difference [between men and women]. We tried to be progressive in our thinking. But I think what we didn't realize was that we were just as much victims of a social condition that perpetuated it and that we carried these traits with us.[100]

She acknowledges that men and women engaged each other in discussions about gender issues, yet basic contradictions remained between theory and practice. Most still did not have full command of the contemporary language and theory of gender politics that was being developed, revised, and disseminated during this period. Many of their shortcomings arose from the lack of experience addressing such concerns in an explicitly political context. This was probably especially true for those who had no previous activist involvement. Their contradictions were part and parcel of the dialectic between hegemonic norms, which reinforced unequal gender roles and power relations between men and women, and intracommunal struggles, which attempted to redefine the terms of this discourse both internally and externally.

Despite their limitations (or perhaps because of them) and the generally dire circumstances in which they found themselves, the BPP was still often ahead of most other Black nationalist organizations and many White leftist and mainstream organizations in their progress on addressing (at least rhetorically) "the woman question." According to Assata Shakur,

> The BPP was the most progressive organization at that time [and] had the most positive images in terms of . . . the position of women in the propaganda . . . I felt it was the most positive thing that I could do because many of the other organizations at the time were so sexist, I mean to the extreme . . . There was a whole saturation of the whole climate with this quest for manhood . . . even though that might be oppressive to you as a human being . . . For me joining the BPP was one of the best options at the time.[101]

Thus, for Shakur and many other Black women seeking involvement in the Black Power Movement and grassroots organizing, the Party presented a viable option. The programmatic focus of the Party after 1968 directly addressed the needs of poor Black women, especially those who were primarily responsible for childrearing. BPP membership could also offer women and men a sense of control over their lives outside the Party. Many, probably for the first time in their lives, were able to contest directly the larger society's representations and perceptions of them and to fight for better treatment from the state apparatus that imposed its policies on their lives and their communities. Through its ideology, rhetoric, imagery, and praxis, the BPP engaged the dominant culture in a debate about the parameters of Black racial and sexual identity and its impact on politics and policy. This was particularly significant given the history of struggles by Black people to be recognized as respectable, fully human beings.[102] They also engaged each other and the larger Black community about what it meant to be a Black woman, man, comrade, revolutionary—not in the abstract—but in the heat of political struggle.

The insidious attempts by the U.S. government to destroy the organization and individual members restricted the development of a more self-reflective theory and practice by BPP members. Party members did not always have the luxury or the space to reflect and revise past errors. Nonetheless, it is somewhat paradoxical and instructive that a movement that was initially so thoroughly male centered in many ways broke ground for subsequent explicitly feminist/womanist activism by Black women and, in some ways, engaged in more nuanced discussions of gender roles than those found in social movements, academic texts, and popular culture in the 1990s. For example, the movie *Panther* fails to treat in any substantial manner the role of women in the Party, not to mention the internal struggles over gender roles and sexist/misogynistic behavior, a point made by many reviewers of the film. However, some of these same cultural critics replicate this error of omission by making summary comments such as, in the sixties "it was believed that the greatest threat to the nation was a black *man* with a gun"[103] and that the film is a "stirring affirmation of black masculinity, an image of what the Panthers could have, and maybe should have, been."[104] Statements like these justify and excuse the movie's inattention to gender politics as critical to the story of the Party and, in effect, further the notion that the central actors and focus of Black struggle should be Black men/manhood. Through an emphasis on "gun barrel politics" in both the film and the reviews, the critical presence and actions of female Panthers are virtually ignored, while the complexities of Black masculinity are constrained by romanticized, flat images of angry, hard bodies with guns.[105]

Many of the intracommunal debates raised by the Black Panther Party have resurfaced once again in the context of a resurgent cultural nationalism in Black communities in the U.S. Unfortunately, both the language and the content of many contemporary discussions reflect little if any recognition of the historical depth of these issues, nor of the progress made, however limited, in addressing them in the past. Black men are once again talked about and talk about themselves as castrated or "endangered species." Black women are often cited as complicit in this process or as succeeding at the expense of Black men. The most popular formulations blame poor and working-class Black women for their alleged inability to raise Black boys/men, and accuse Black women in general of being the willing recipients of alleged special treatment and unearned entitlements from White society. To paraphrase the official recruitment literature from the Million Man March, Black men need to resume their rightful place as patriarchs of Black families and communities.[106]

The interrelationship between the ways Black people are targeted for gender-, class-, and sexual-orientation-specific attacks are unrecognized in our acceptance of linear, "either/or" analyses of problems facing Black communities as a whole. For the sake of so-called Black unity, we often sacrifice or ignore the needs of some of the most oppressed and marginalized sectors of our communities to the detriment of us all. Those who dare to assert our heterogeneity and identify oppressive practices within and between Black communities are silenced and assailed as divisive or assimilationist, as race traitors, or worst of all, as just not authentically, purely Black enough. Witness the virtual gag order and public attacks against those within the community, particularly Black women such as Angela Davis, who disagreed with the Million Man March's gender politics, focus, and agenda (or lack thereof).

We would all benefit from a closer, more complex interrogation and public discussion of historical struggles over these same issues, from slavery to the present, one that does not gloss over mistakes or internal differences, to aid us in redefining our roles and relationships in ways that can nurture and sustain the community and build a progressive movement for the twenty-first century.

NOTES

1. The quote in the chapter title is from an interview with Kathleen Cleaver cited in Philip S. Foner, ed., *The Black Panthers Speak* (Philadelphia: Lippincott, 1970), 145. I wish to thank my dissertation committee members, Elsa Barkley Brown, Robin D.G. Kelley, and Earl Lewis, for critiques of various versions of this chapter. I thank also the Center for Afro-American and African Studies at the University of Michigan, the Ford Foundation, and the Chicago Historical Society for support during research and writing. I am grateful to Charles E. Jones for editorial suggestions and support and to Paul Coates for thoughtful comments. Props to my homies Michelle S. Johnson, David Maurrasse, Melina Pappademos, Barbara Ransby, and Orlando Bagwell for critical comments on this version; Reginald Ball for research assistance; and the rest of y'all for various hook ups—it's all good. Very special thanks to the Panthers who shared pieces of their life stories with me and inspired me. Hopefully, this generation will continue the struggle. And finally, much respect to my mother and my late father who convinced me that I would be and should be a life-long student.

2. There is a lengthy history of armed resistance among Black communities in the U.S. Several studies have noted that many Civil Rights movement participants practiced nonviolence as a strategy, not a philosophy, while at the same time engaging in armed self-defense tactics. For evidence of this, see Gene Marine, *The Black Panthers* (New York: Signet, 1969), 36; Clayborne Carson, *In Struggle: SNCC and the Black Awakening of the 1960s* (Cambridge, MA: Harvard University Press, 1981); Aldon Morris, *Origins of the Civil Rights Movement: Black Communities Organizing for Change* (New York: The Free Press, 1984), 19; and Akinyele Umoja, "Eye for an Eye: The Role of Armed Resistance in the Mississippi Freedom Movement, 1955–1980" (Ph.D. diss., Emory University,1996).

3. *Report of the National Advisory Commission on Civil Disorders [The Kerner Report]* (New York: Bantam Books, 1968; Pantheon Books, 1988), 35–41.

4. The film *Panther* (Gramercy), written by Melvin Van Peebles and directed by his son Mario Van Peebles, opened to mixed reviews from critics and former Panthers alike. For sweepstakes information, see *Young Sisters & Brothers Magazine* 4, 8 (May 1995): 40.

5. For examples of primary sources written in the 1960s and 1970s, see Gene Marine, *The Black Panthers,* and Huey P. Newton, *Revolutionary Suicide* (New York: Harcourt Brace Jovanovich, 1973); G. Louis Heath, ed., *Off the Pigs: The History and Literature of the Black Panther Party* (Metuchen, New Jersey: Scarecrow Press, 1976); and Philip S. Foner, ed., *The Black Panthers Speak, The Manifesto of the Party: The First Documentary Record of the Panthers' Program* (Philadelphia: Lippincott, 1970). For brief scholarly treatments, see Robert Allen, *Black Awakening in Capitalist America* (Garden City, NY: Doubleday & Co., 1969), and Manning Marable, *How Capitalism Underdeveloped Black America* (Boston: South End Press, 1983). There are government hearings and reports on BPP activity such as U.S. Senate, *Final Report of the Select Committee to Study Government Operations with Respect to Intelligence Activities,* 94th Cong., 2d sess., 1976, S. Rept. 94–755. There are also more recently published specialized texts, such as those on FBI repression, which are cited later in this essay.

6. The time period examined in this essay does not include the period during and following the major division within the Party over matters of ideology, practice,

and leadership, and its decline as a national organization. Many important shifts occurred after the split, especially in terms of the numbers of formally recognized female leaders. Some former Panthers believe that the "original" BPP ended in 1970 or 1971; others saw themselves as being part of the BPP until 1981, when the Oakland Community School closed. My dissertation will include this later period.

7. Most scholarly texts on the Civil Rights movement, (White) Women's liberation movement, and Black power movement neglect or minimize any analysis of the issues of gender politics in the Black power movement or BPP.

8. Evelyn Brooks Higginbotham, "African-American Women's History and the Metalanguage of Race," *Signs 17, 2* (Winter 1992): 225, 274. Here she draws on James C. Scott's notions of the infrapolitics and hidden transcripts of everyday resistance in his book *Domination and the Arts of Resistance: Hidden Transcripts* (New Haven: Yale University Press, 1990). Higginbotham adds to this a discussion of hierarchies and power struggles within oppressed communities. See also Robin D. G. Kelley, *Race Rebels: Culture, Politics, and the Black Working Class* (New York: The Free Press, 1994), for a nuanced discussion of infrapolitics and intraracial power dynamics in Black communities.

9. Elsa Barkley Brown, "African-American Women's Quilting: A Framework for Conceptualizing and Teaching African-American Women's History," in *Black Women in America: Social Science Perspectives,* ed. Micheline R. Malson et al. (Chicago: University of Chicago Press, 1988), 9–18. Quote from 17.

10. Daniel Patrick Moynihan, *The Negro Family: The Case for National Action* (Office of Policy Planning and Research, United States Department of Labor, March 1965).

11. E. Frances White, "Africa On My Mind: Gender, Counter Discourse and African-American Nationalism," *Journal of Women's History* 2, 1 (Spring 1990): 80.

12. Us was a member of the Black Congress, an umbrella organization in Los Angeles organized around the principle of "operational unity." The Congress supported "Free Huey" movement activities. See *Harambee* 11, 1 (17 November 1967): 1–2, 8.

13. Two examples of Panther critiques of cultural nationalism are: Linda Harrison, "On Cultural Nationalism," *The Black Panther,* 2 February 1969 and George Mason Murray, "Cultural Nationalism," *The Black Panther,* 3 March 1969.

14. Ward Churchill and Jim Vander Wall, *Agents of Repression: The FBI's Secret Wars Against the Black Panther Party and the American Indian Movement* (Boston: South End Press, 1988). Evidence shows that this shooting was probably instigated by FBI agents within Us and through counterintelligence propaganda circulated between the two organizations. The authors quote a 1968 FBI memo from J. Edgar Hoover encouraging agents to "'fully capitalize upon BPP and Us differences as well as to exploit all avenues of creating further dissension within the ranks of the BPP,'" 42.

15. For example, see *The Black Panther,* 2 February 1969, 3; and 3 March 1969, 4; Newton, *Revolutionary Suicide,* 255; and Louis Tackwood and The Citizens Research and Investigation Committee, *The Glass House Tapes* (New York: Avon Books, 1973), 105.

16. Clyde Halisi, ed., *The Quotable Karenga* (Los Angeles: Us Organization, 1967), 27–28.

17. Elaine Brown, *A Taste of Power: A Black Woman's Story* (New York: Pantheon Books, 1992), 109; Angela Davis *Angela Davis: An Autobiography*

(New York: International Publishers, 1974, 1988), 161. At the time of this incident in 1967, Davis was a founding member of the Black Student Union at the University of California at San Diego.

18. White, "Africa On My Mind," 73–77. The BPP and Us subscribed to revolutionary nationalism and cultural nationalism respectively and thus had widely divergent political perspectives and programs for action. The BPP identified themselves variously as revolutionary nationalists, Marxist–Leninists, and Intercommunalists at different points in time. Despite the diversity of nationalist ideologies, aspects of White's critique are applicable to both organizations.

19. Panthers' critiques of cultural nationalism may have varied regionally. Both my own and sociologist David Maurrasse's interviews with former Party members suggest that New York-based Panthers considered themselves more nationalistic or more rooted in African culture than West Coast Panthers.

20. Bobby Seale. "Bobby Seale Explains Panther Politics," *The Guardian,* February 1970, 4. Us's anti-White polemics were interpreted as Black racism by the BPP.

21. Sara Evans, *Personal Politics: The Roots of Women's Liberation in the Civil Rights Movement and the New Left* (New York: Vintage Books, 1979), 57, 193–95.

22. Alice Echols, *Daring to Be Bad: Radical Feminism in America, 1967–1975* (Minneapolis: University of Minnesota Press, 1989), 34–35.

23. See Echols, *Daring to Be Bad,* for an excellent account of the politics and activities of White radical and cultural feminists.

24. See Robin Morgan, ed., *Sisterhood Is Powerful* (New York: Vintage Books, 1970), xxi. Several key women in the BPP were former members of SNCC, including Kathleen Cleaver and Connie Matthews.

25. Several earlier studies analyze the political activities of Black women in the 1960s through an "either/or" framework—either they were feminists or Black power sympathizers. This does not account for the activities of Black women that incorporated race, gender, and class simultaneously. See for example Evans, *Personal Politics,* 101; Paula Giddings, *When and Where I Enter: The Impact of Black Women on Race and Sex in America* (New York: Bantam Books, 1984), 311, 323; and Echols, *Daring to Be Bad,* 106.

26. Deborah King, "Multiple Jeopardy, Multiple Consciousness: The Context of a Black Feminist Ideology," *Signs* 14, 1 (Autumn 1988). For examples of Black women's writings on the issues of gender and race in this period, see Toni Cade, ed., *The Black Woman: An Anthology* (New York: Mentor, The New American Library, Inc. 1970).

27. Cappy Pinderhughes, "Free Our Sisters," *The Black Panther,* 6 December 1969, 2. Bobby Seale and Ericka Huggins, along with twelve other New Haven BPP members were charged with the kidnapping, murder, and torture of fellow Party member Alex Rackley, who had been falsely identified as an informant by an actual police infiltrator, George Sams. Two Panthers and Sams were convicted. For more on this case, see Ward Churchill and Jim Vander Wall, *The COINTELPRO Papers: Documents from the FBI's Secret War Against Dissent in the United States* (Boston: South End Press, 1990), 146–47, 360.

28. Huey Newton, "The Women's Liberation and Gay Liberation Movements: 15 August, 1970," in *To Die for the People: The Writings of Huey Newton* (New York: Vintage Books, 1972), 152–55.

29. Kathleen Cleaver in a telephone conversation with the author, 27 November 1994.

30. Anonymous, "Black Panther Sisters Talk about Women's Liberation," pamphlet reprinted from *The Movement* (September 1969). The same interview appears as "Panther Sisters on Women's Liberation," in *Off the Pigs!*, ed., Heath, 339–50. Quote from 344. Originally appeared as "Sisters," *The Black Panther*, 13 September 1969, 12.

31. "Black Scholar Interviews Kathleen Cleaver," *Black Scholar* (December 1971): 56.

32. Anon., "Panther Sisters on Women's Liberation" in *Off the Pigs!*, ed., Heath, 348; "Sisters," *The Black Panther*, 13 September 1969, 12.

33. Lee Rainwater and William L. Yancey, *The Moynihan Report and the Politics of Controversy* (Cambridge, MA: The M.I.T. Press, 1967), 75.

34. In this period, cultural productions by Black people directly addressed gender, race, and class issues as they were manifest in all areas of Black life. See Abby Arthur Johnson and Ronald Mayberry Johnson, *Propaganda and Aesthetics: The Literary Politics of African-American Magazines in the Twentieth Century* (Amherst: University of Massachusetts Press, 1979, 1991), especially chapter 6; and William L. Van Deburg, *New Day in Babylon: The Black Power Movement and American Culture, 1965–1975* (Chicago: University of Chicago Press, 1992); and Madhu Dubey, *Black Women Novelists and the Nationalist Aesthetic* (Bloomington: Indiana University Press, 1994).

35. E. Franklin Frazier, *The Negro Family in the United States* (Chicago: University of Chicago Press, 1939, 1948, 1966).

36. Newton, *To Die for the People*, 81.

37. White, "Africa on My Mind," 79.

38. For an analysis of the cultural components and impact of the Black power movement, see Van Deburg, *New Day in Babylon*.

39. Quote from Elaine Brown, "A Black Panther Song," reprinted in Foner, ed. *The Black Panthers Speak*, 31.

40. One should add to the list of external factors the increased attention paid to the role of women in "Third World" revolutions by movements in the U.S. See for example "The Heroic Palestinian Women," *The Black Panther*, 26 July 1969. The impact of the "sexual revolution," "free love," the birth control pill, etc., are also other factors to be examined in my larger work.

41. Heath, ed. *Off the Pigs!*, 96–108.

42. Foner, ed. *The Black Panthers Speak*, xviii–xix; Bobby Seale, *Seize the Time: The Story of the Black Panther Party and Huey Newton* (Baltimore: Black Classic Press, 1991).

43. The Party's various community programs took shape in the context of an overall reorganization effort initiated by the national leadership in January 1969 to address problems associated with rapid growth and increased repression. This reorganization process included provisions for a "three month ban on recruitment and . . . a systematic purge of the party's ranks of 'fools and jackanapes' refusing party discipline, indulging in drugs or petty crime, or operating in a 'purely military' manner—as well as conscious police agents." Heath, ed. *Off the Pigs!*, 8; see also Jim Fletcher, Tanaquil Jones, and Sylvere Lotringer, eds., *Still Black, Still Strong: Survivors of the U.S. War Against Black Revolutionaries, Dhoruba Bin Wahad, Mumia Abu-Jamal, Assata* Shakur (Brooklyn: Semiotext(e), 1993), 229–31.

44. This analogy did not begin with the BPP. It can be traced back to discussions and symbolism in the Civil Rights movement. Recall, for example, the placards of the Memphis sanitation strikers in 1968 that read "I Am A Man." See photo in Henry Hampton and Steve Fayer, eds. *Voices of Freedom: An Oral History of the*

Civil Rights Movement from the 1950s through the 1980s (New York: Bantam Books, 1990), 449. The use of this analogy and, in some cases, its literal interpretation, can also be found in other African-American freedom struggles as far back as the Black abolitionist movement. These various efforts to self-define Black manhood may or may not have included a concomitant focus on the need to "restore" or redefine Black womanhood. For examples, see Frederick Douglass, *Narrative of the Life of Frederick Douglass, An American Slave* (New York: Signet, 1968; orig. published in 1845); Hazel V. Carby, *Reconstructing Womanhood: The Emergence of the Afro-American Woman Novelist* (New York: Oxford University Press, 1987); Paula Giddings, *When and Where I Enter: The Impact of Black Women on Race and Sex in America* (New York: Bantam Books, 1984); and Kelley, *Race Rebels,* especially ch. 5.

45. Although it is not clear exactly when the first woman joined the BPP, we do know that there were women Panthers present at the 2 May 1967 Panther demonstration at the California State Capitol. See Marine, *The Black Panthers,* 63; and Seale, *Seize the Time,* 153. Also see Angela Darlene Brown, "Servants of the People: A History of Women in the Black Panther Party" (B.A. honors thesis, Harvard University, 23 March 1992), 14. Brown names Tarika Lewis, also known as Joan Lewis or Matilaba, as the first woman to join the BPP.

46. "Armed Black Brothers in Richmond Community," *The Black Panther*, 25 April 1967, 5.

47. Bobby Seale, "Free Huey," in *Rhetoric of Black Revolution,* ed. Arthur L. Smith (Boston: Allyn and Bacon, 1969), 177–78, quoted in Van Deburg, *New Day in Babylon,* 12–13; also quoted in Marine, *The Black Panthers,* 66.

48. Elsewhere, Seale wrote that women comprised about sixty percent of the BPP membership by 1968. See Bobby Seale, *A Lonely Rage: The Autobiography of Bobby Seale* (New York: Times Books, 1978), 177. The term lumpen is a shortened version of "lumpen proletarian," a Marxist term used to refer to people who are "below" the stable working class, that is, disaffected, unemployed, uneducated, etc. It is close in meaning to the current term *underclass,* but *lumpen* was used with less of a pejorative connotation by the BPP. Huey Newton called the lumpen class "the unemployables." See Newton, *To Die for the People,* 28.

49. See Appendix A, "What We Want, What We Believe," BPP Platform and Program, reprinted in Foner, ed. *The Black Panthers Speak,* 2–4.

50. Eldridge Cleaver, *Soul on Ice* (New York: Dell, 1968*). Soul on Ice* is a collection of essays and letters written between 1955 and 1967.

51. Seale, *Seize the Time,* 132–34; Newton, *Revolutionary Suicide,* 128–33. At the time of their first face-to-face meeting with Cleaver, neither had read *Soul on Ice,* but they had heard his speeches, and read it soon thereafter. Seale may have read some of Cleaver's articles in *Ramparts* magazine.

52. Cleaver, *Soul on Ice,* 14–16.

53. Seale, *Seize the Time,* 247–48, 266–68. While *Soul on Ice* reflects Cleaver's views before he joined the BPP, the book was more widely read than the subsequently published *Eldridge Cleaver: Post-Prison Writings and Speeches, ed.* Robert Scheer. (New York: Ramparts Magazine/Random House, 1969). In the later collection, commentary on gender politics is almost totally absent except for the repetition of his infamous "pussy power" statement in a speech at Stanford University, and a remark that "all the young chicks in the Black community nowadays relate to young men who are Black Panthers" because the Party supplied "very badly needed standards of masculinity," 143, 203. However, this is not necessarily an indication of a lack of interest or lack of discussion of these issues

by Cleaver. Apparently, Scheer, not Cleaver, decided on the selections to be included since Cleaver was underground and in exile at the time of its publication.

54. Cleaver and other Panthers participated in a larger process of revisionist theorizing about the nature of slavery and its contemporary impact on Black male–female and familial relations. Their discussions were similar to those in academia, as well as in public policy led by Moynihan and the like. The sheer volume of disparaging assessments of Black women's history prompted Angela Davis to write her ground-breaking essay "Reflections on the Black Woman's Role in the Community of Slaves" from jail in 1971. See *Black Scholar* 3 (December 1971): 3–15.

55. Cleaver, "The Primeval Mitosis," in *Soul on Ice,* 176–90.

56. Huey P. Newton, "Huey P. Newton Talks to the Movement" (Chicago: SDS, 1968), reprinted in *Black Protest Thought in the Twentieth Century*, eds. August Meier, Elliot Rudwick, and Francis I. Broderick (New York: Bobbs-Merrill Co., 1965, 1971), 506.

57. Ibid., 506–8.

58. Newton, *Revolutionary Suicide,* 133 (emphasis in original).

59. Robert Igriega, "Eldridge for 'Pussy Power,'" *Open City* (Los Angeles), 9 August 1968, 1; Eldridge Cleaver, "Speech to the Nebraska Peace and Freedom Party Convention," 24 August 1968, 22; Scheer, ed. Eldridge Cleaver. *Post-Prison Writings and Speeches*, 143; Seale, *Seize the Time,* 247. Seale writes that Cleaver also said "power comes out of the barrel of a dick," but I have not seen this corroborated elsewhere. The pussy power statements are by far more prominent. It should also be noted that this theme and practice of women withholding sex in order to influence men's political beliefs and behaviors are not new. See for example Elsa Barkley Brown, "To Catch the Vision of Freedom: Reconstructing Southern Black Women's Political History, 1865–1880," in *To Be a Citizen*, eds. Arlene Avakian, Joyce Berkman, John Bracey, Bettye Collier-Thomas, and Ann Gordon (Amherst: University of Massachusetts Press, forthcoming).

60. This theme is also present in *Soul on Ice,* where Cleaver traces the origins of homosexuality to White men's alienation from their bodies and their consequent envy of Black men's physical strength and heterosexual virility. Presumably, according to this analysis, there are no Black gay men, not to mention Black lesbians. Homosexuality is seen as a "White thing." For more on conservative constructions of sexuality among Black nationalists, see White, "Africa on My Mind," 75, 81–82.

61. Newton, "The Women's Liberation and Gay Liberation Movements: 15 August 1970," in *To Die For the People,* 154. In this statement, Newton still tends to associate homosexuality (and feminism) with Whiteness, a point not to be missed by the inclusion of the statement under the section heading "White America."

62. For one example of a disapproving reaction to Newton's statement from Chicago Panthers, see J. F. Rice, *Up on Madison Down on 75th Street: A History of the Illinois Black Panther Party* (Evanston, IL: J.F. Rice/The Committee, 1983), 53.

63. Cappy Pinderhughes, "Free Our Sisters," *The Black Panther,* 6 December 1969, 2; Anonymous, "New Haven 14 Under Pressure," *Guardian,* February 1970, 6; *The Black Panther*, 25 October 1969, 3. For more on this case, see Churchill and Vander Wall, *The COINTELPRO Papers,* 146–47, 360.

64. Kathleen Cleaver, phone interview with the author, 27 November 1994.

65. Eldridge Cleaver, "Message to Sister Erica Huggins of the Black Panther Party, Excerpt from Tape of Eldridge Breaking His Silence from Somewhere in

the Third World," *The Black Panther*, 5 July 1969, reprinted in Foner, *The Black Panthers Speak*, 98–99.

66. Ibid., 99.

67. See Appendix B, "8 Points of Attention," reprinted in Foner, *The Black Panthers Speak*, 6.

68. Seale, *Seize the Time*, 374–76. The Party never incorporated their position on gender equality into the official BPP Ten Point Platform and Program as did one of their allies, the Young Lords Organization. See Young Lords Organization, "13 Point Program and Platform" (January, 1970), reprinted in Foner, *The Black Panthers Speak*, 237. Point ten on their platform was: "WE WANT EQUALITY FOR WOMEN. MACHISMO MUST BE REVOLUTIONARY . . . NOT OPPRES SIVE." Also see reference to "Machismo is Fascism" by YLO women in Robin Morgan's *Sisterhood is Powerful*, xxvi. The Young Lords were a Puerto Rican street organization turned into a political group based in Chicago and New York.

69. Margie Stamberg, "Women at the UFAF and After," *Guardian*, 2 August 1969, 5.

70. For investigations of the multiple subject positions of Black women, see Deborah King, "Multiple Jeopardy, Multiple Consciousness: The Context of a Black Feminist Ideology," *Signs* 14, 1 (Autumn 1988); and Elsa Barkley Brown, "Womanist Consciousness: Maggie Lena Walker and the Independent Order of Saint Luke," *Signs* 14, 3 (Spring 1989). Both are reprinted in *Black Women in America*, ed., Malson, et al.,

71. Anon., "Panther Sisters on Women's Liberation," in Heath, ed. *Off the Pigs!*, 339. One name mentioned during the interview is "Roberta," presumably the same woman from the UFAF panel.

72. Ibid., 339.

73. Ibid., 341.

74. Ibid., 343 (emphasis added).

75. Jamal Joseph, interview with the author, 30 September 1994; Harlem, New York.

76. On the difficulty of assessing membership numbers, and the inability to standardize screening mechanisms, political education (PE), etc., see Marine, *The Black Panthers*, 179–82, 192; Newton, *Revolutionary Suicide*, 150–51; and Seale, *Seize the Time*, 366–91. All of these problems were exacerbated by increased government harassment and repression.

77. The editing process and policy of the newspaper is unclear. There are many unsigned articles and sometimes contradictory information on political perspectives. Yet these contradictions are worthy of note because they give a sense of the diversity of opinion within the Party in spite of an "official" Party line (or mass line) on a particular issue. For the names of *Black Panther* editorial and writing staff as listed in the paper from 1967–70, see G. Louis Heath, ed., *Black Panther Leaders Speak: Huey Newton, Bobby Seale, Eldridge Cleaver and Company Speak Out Through the Black Panther Party's Official Newspaper* (Metuchen, N.J.: The Scarecrow Press, 1976), 1–3.

78. Anonymous, "'Subjectivism' . . . from a Male's point of view." *The Black Panther*, March 1969, 9.

79. Ibid.

80. Linda Greene, "The Black Revolutionary Woman," *The Black Panther*, 28 September 1968, 11.

81. Gloria Bartholomew, "A Black Woman's Thoughts," *The Black Panther, 28* September 1968, 11.

82. Anonymous, "Black Woman, By a Black Revolutionary" *The Black Panther, 14* September 1968, 6.

83. Assata Shakur, *Assata: An Autobiography* (London: Zed Books, Ltd; and Chicago: Lawrence Hill Books, 1987), 223–24. "Zayd" is presumably Zayd Malik Shakur, who was with Assata Shakur at the 2 May 1973 incident during which he was killed by the New Jersey State Police. For more on this incident, see Fletcher et al., *Still Black, Still Strong,* 205; and Shakur, *Assata,* IX, 3.

84. Ibid, 223.

85. In *Soul on Ice,* 110, Cleaver writes, "Homosexuality is a sickness, just as are baby-rape or wanting to become the head of General Motors." For one official attempt to curtail such language and sentiments, see Newton, "The Women's Liberation and Gay Liberation Movements," in *To Die For the People,* 152–55. For further discussion of Black nationalism and homophobia, see White, "Africa on My Mind;" Cheryl Clarke, "The Failure to Transform: Homophobia in the Black Community," in *Home Girls: A Black Feminist Anthology,* ed. Barbara Smith (New York: Kitchen Table Press, 1983), 197–208; Phillip Brian Harper, "Eloquence and Epitaph: Black Nationalism and the Homophobic Impulse in Response to the Death of Max Robinson," in *Fear of a Queer Planet: Queer Politics and Social Theory,* ed. Michael Warner (Minnesota: University of Minnesota Press, 1993); Isaac Julien, "Black Is, Black Ain't: Notes on De-Essentializing Black Identities," in *Black Popular Culture,* ed. Gina Dent (Seattle: Bay Press, 1992), 255–63; and Isaac Julien and Kobena Mercer, "True Confessions: A Discourse on Images of Black Male Sexuality," in *Brother to Brother: New Writings By Black Gay Men,* ed. Essex Hemphill (Boston: Alyson Publications, 1991), 167–73.

86. Jamal Joseph, interview with the author, 30 September 1994; Harlem, New York.

87. Newton, *To Die for the People,* 15.

88. Barkley- Brown, "Womanist Consciousness," in *Black Women in America,* ed. Mason et al., 194.

89. Connie Matthews, interview with the author, 26 June 1991; Kingston, Jamaica.

90. Assata Shakur, interview with the author, 30 July 1993; Havana, Cuba.

91. Shakur, *Assata,* 204.

92. For specific mainstream media articles, about Joan Bird, see *New York Post,* 14 May, 7 July, 19 December 1970; and *New York Times,* 7 July, 15 July 1970. About Afeni Shakur, see *New York Times,* 15 July 1970. About Ericka Huggins, see *New York Times,* 2 December 1969, and 22 March 1970.

93. Heath, ed. *Off the Pigs!,* 100. See also *The Black Panther,* 7 September 1986, 7. In later years, some of the breakfast programs were in fact wholly taken over by community members, which was a stated goal of the Party.

94. Frankye Malika Adams, interview with the author, 29 September 1994; Harlem, New York.

95. Ibid. Adams goes on to stress that while men also participated in these programs, women clearly organized and led them.

96. "FBI Airtel from Director to SAC's in 27 field offices, 15 May 1969," cited by Huey P. Newton in "War Against the Panthers: A Study of Repression in America (Ph.D. diss., University of California, June 1980), 109.

97. Janet Cyril, interview with the author, 29 September 1994; Brooklyn, New York.

98. For further definition of these terms, see Churchill and Vander Wall, *Agents of Repression*, 49–51.

99. Frankye Malika Adams, interview with author, 29 September 1994; Harlem, New York.

100. Ibid.

101. Assata Shakur, interview with the author, 30 July 1993; Havana, Cuba.

102. In my dissertation, I will explore the construction of Black Civil Rights movement participants as noble, respectable, asexual, and peaceful in juxtaposition to notions of Black urban youth as a riot-prone, extremist, hypersexual menace. This is one of many oppositional dichotomies imposed by mainstream discourses and reinforced by some activists and by many academic studies of this period, such as the now almost played out Malcolm-versus-Martin dyad, nonviolence versus self-defense, accommodation versus resistance, etc. On intracommunal struggle and challenges to these types of false dichotomies, see Kelley, *Race Rebels*. On the topic of respectability and racialized constructions of sexuality, see Higginbotham, "African-American Women's History and the Metalanguage of Race," and Darlene Clark Hine, "Rape and the Inner Lives of Black Women in the Middle West: Preliminary Thoughts on the Culture of Dissemblance," *Signs* 14, 4 (Summer 1989).

103. Michael Eric Dyson, "The Panthers, Still Untamed, Roar Back," review of *Panther* (Gramercy movie), *New York Times,* 30 April 1995, 17, 25 (emphasis added).

104. Michael Robinson, "The Van Peebleses Prowl Through The Panthers' History," *American Visions: The Magazine of Afro-American Culture* 10, 2 (April/May 1995): 16–18.

105. The chronology of events and emphasis on guns in *Panther* closely resembles the structure and content of an anti-Panther government report that summarizes House Committee on Internal Security public hearings on the BPP conducted in 1970 and gives an analysis of the origins, politics, tactics, successes, and failures of the Party. The report also details the anti-capitalist ideology of the BPP, a point easily missed in the film. See House Committee on Internal Security, *Gun Barrel Politics: The Black Panther Party, 1966–1971,* 92d Cong., 1st sess., 1971, H. Rept. 92–470.

106. Frightening parallels can be drawn between this strain of Black thought and current reactionary discourses on the evils of affirmation action and Black single motherhood.

Chapter Thirteen

"The Most Qualified Person to Handle the Job": Black Panther Party Women, 1966–1982

Angela D. LeBlanc-Ernest

In June 1990, I opened *The Vanguard*, a "photographic essay" of the Black Panther Party for Self-Defense (BPP), and was surprised to see a picture of an African American woman wearing all-black attire and holding a shotgun.[1] Previously, I had encountered media images and journalistic accounts of the armed resistance efforts of male Party members. Therefore, I and many others labored under the assumption that BPP women merely prepared breakfast for children and participated in rallies. The full extent to which women served and defended the African American community as members of the Black Panther Party remained obscured. Moreover, analyses of both the prominent role of Panther women in the Party's survival programs and the prevalence of female leadership were nearly nonexistent. The invisibility of women in the narratives of the Black Panther Party is symptomatic of the paucity of scholarly attention devoted to African American women's activism during the Black Power Era (1966–1975). In short, female participation in the BPP has been largely neglected.

This essay examines the roles and activities undertaken by women in the Black Panther Party from 1966 to 1982.[2] To date, extant literature on the Black Panther Party primarily focuses on the first five years of the organization. During this period (October 1966 through April 1971), the BPP stressed armed self-defense, a strategy that contributed to law enforcement's strong stance against the organization. During 1971, after the culmination of intra-organizational tensions, exacerbated by coordinated federal and local police actions, the Party focused on its community programs. This reemphasis led some former Panthers and scholars to argue that 1971 marked the end of the original revolutionary intent of the organization.[3] Nevertheless, focusing only on the Party's revolutionary period limits our understanding of the full participation of Panther women during the post-revolutionary years.

The time frame of this analysis extends from the origins of the BPP in October 1966 to June 1982, which marks the date that the final BPP program, the highly acclaimed Oakland Community School, closed. This approach captures more fully the nature of female participation in the Black Panther Party. The essay begins with a brief overview of the revolutionary years 1966 to 1971 to provide a context for the assessment of female participation in the organization. It then examines the role of women during the period of deradicalization (1971–1974). A discussion of the Party under the leadership of Elaine Brown (1974–1977) follows. Finally, the essay examines the activities undertaken by Panther women during its final phase (1977–1982) and concludes with a discussion of the legacy of women in the BPP.

Women in the Early Years 1966–1971

Women who joined the Black Panther Party were a part of a long tradition of African American women steeped in social service and political activism. During the 19th century, African American women in northern states, such as Pennsylvania and New York, participated in the Free African Societies. Historian Shirley Yee notes the central role of African American female abolitionists in the anti-slavery campaign. Similarly, Paula Giddings documents the activism of Black women during the late-nineteenth and early-twentieth centuries. African American women believed in collective work and therefore formed organizations such as the National Federation of Colored Women. Individual women like Ida B. Wells and Mary Church Terrell, inspired by their race devotion, combated the lynching of African American males and advocated women's suffrage through public speaking, journalism, and agitation. Other Black women such as Anna J. Cooper and Mary McLeod Bethune advanced the interest of the race through education.[4] Bethune founded Bethune-Cookman college, a historically Black college. African American female activism continued well into the 20th century. Amy Jacques Garvey, prolific writer, leader, and historian of the United Negro Improvement Association (UNIA); Claudia Jones, a Communist party activist and political prisoner; Fannie Lou Hamer, a tireless grassroots organizer; and Ella Baker, indefatigable union and community activist, Southern Christian Leadership Conference (SCLC) member, and mother of the Student Nonviolent Coordinating Committee (SNCC), are but a few examples of women of African descent who were the forerunners and torch-bearers to the women in the Black Panther Party.[5]

African American women's activism also appears in Black armed-resistance movements. Evidence of this tradition, albeit limited, is seen in the Louisiana-based Deacons for Self-Defense and Justice. Originally formed in Jonesboro, Louisiana in July 1964, the Deacons defended local Black residents against random, yet frequent, Ku Klux Klan attacks against their neighborhoods. In the tradition of Maria Stewart, Harriet Tubman, and

Queen Mother Moore—women who claimed the right to self-defense, Southern African American women Unita Blackwell, Ora Bryant, Annie Reeves, and Laura McGhee joined the Deacons for Self-Defense. Novelist Louise Meriwether was also an early participant in the armed patrols of the Deacons in Bogalusa, Louisiana.[6] Women who later became members of the Black Panther Party followed the legacy of radical African American female activists of the early 1960s, such as Gloria Richardson who was "the first woman to be the unquestioned leader of a major movement and one of the first major leaders to openly question nonviolence as a tactic."[7]

During the BPP's formative years from 1966 to 1967, the male dominance, paramilitary emphasis, and acceptance of societal gender norms created a distinctly male-oriented organization. Initially, Newton and Seale consciously recruited the "brothers off the block." The two cofounders took pride in their defiant male-based organization. Newton considered the Panthers "proud men, armed with knowledge of the law."[8] Not surprisingly, only men attended the opening of the organization's first office on January 1, 1967. However, Seale recalls a woman who did attend one of the Party's biweekly meetings as early as February. Her presence, according to Seale, stimulated discussion concerning female participation in the BPP. In response to inquiries from rank-and-file members, Seale explained that "[W]e had to make it clear, when asked, that sisters could join the Black Panther Party. We would welcome them."[9]

Thus, the decision of one woman to attend a BPP meeting initiated female participation in the Party. Tarika Lewis (also known as Joan Lewis or Matilaba) is generally recognized as the first woman to officially join the Black Panther Party. A native of Oakland, California, Lewis attended Oakland Tech High School where she cofounded the Black Student Union, which staged sit-ins for Black Studies courses. After high school, Lewis abandoned her earlier plans to become a jazz violinist and joined the BPP. As a Panther, Lewis recalled that her "duty was to open the eyes of the people, to give them hope, courage, understanding; to teach, guide, and pull the cover off what was going on and what should be done about it."[10]

Lewis did not receive special treatment because she was a female. She explained that all organizational rules applying to the male members also were applicable to her. Lewis regularly attended political education classes and learned to disassemble, reassemble, clean, and use firearms. During her first year in the Party, she quickly advanced beyond the rank and file and assumed various leadership positions. Lewis taught drill classes and led political education sessions. However, as a female section leader in an organization still largely controlled by and composed of men, Lewis' abilities and talents were not always respected. She recounted, "When the guys came up to me and said 'I ain't gonna do what you tell me to do 'cause you a sister,' I invited 'em to come on out to the weapons range and I could outshoot 'em."[11] Lewis noted that she earned the respect of many of the men because she "worked just as hard or harder than they did."[12]

Other early female Panther recruits who joined the Black Panther Party in 1967 also participated in BPP physical training, political education classes, and efforts to mobilize the Black community. For example, both Belva Butcher and Majeeda Roman recalled receiving firearms instruction and providing weapons training for their male comrades.[13] Therefore, it was not surprising that on May 2, 1967 women were among the armed Party members who traveled to Sacramento to protest at the California state legislature. Assemblyman Don Mulford proposed legislation to prohibit carrying "loaded weapons within incorporated areas," which would undermine the legal basis of the Party's armed police patrols.[14]

In October 1967 an early morning shoot-out, which left one police officer dead and Huey Newton and another officer seriously wounded, transformed the BPP into a national political movement. BPP chapters were formed in various cities across the United States. The ensuing "Free Huey" campaign attracted a myriad of men and women to the Black Panther Party. Among these early recruits was Kathleen Cleaver, the most prominent and influential woman during the formative stage of the BPP. She joined the Party in November 1967 shortly after moving to California to live with her new fiancé, BPP Minister of Information Eldridge Cleaver. Prior to her participation in the Party, Kathleen had been a student at Barnard College, but she dropped out to work full time in the Student Nonviolent Coordinating Committee.

Kathleen Cleaver provided critical assistance during the early growth of the BPP. She was instrumental in the Free Huey campaign and served as assistant editor of the Party's newspaper. Cleaver would become the first woman to sit on the organization's Central Committee. When she arrived in Oakland in late 1967, most of the Panthers, including the two cofounders, were incarcerated.[15] Cleaver recalled, "I went there [Oakland] in the midst of a total crisis. They didn't really have any organization to speak of at that time."[16] She organized rallies to draw attention to the Newton trial and represented the Party at numerous press conferences and political meetings. Kathleen Cleaver has stated that she was not a victim of overt gender discrimination during her tenure in the Party. She attributed this treatment to her unique status in the organization. First she "came in working with the leaders of the Party so there was not any way for me to be treated differently."[17] Moreover, her status as the wife of Eldridge Cleaver, the Party's respected Minister of Information, may have shielded her from some forms of gender discrimination. Nevertheless, Cleaver does recall that male members sometimes tended to overlook ideas suggested by women during the early years of the Party. According to Kathleen Cleaver,

> If a woman would express an idea, because that idea is coming from a source that they're not looking for an idea from, it [would be]

discounted... They looked to women to help them, to take care of them, to nurture them, to be their mothers, to be their lovers. But they did not look to women for their ideas.[18]

In contrast to Kathleen Cleaver, other Panther women encountered more routine forms of chauvinism during the formative phase. The Party had not yet achieved the desired objective of a gender-neutral organization. Initially, the Party adopted a gender-based hierarchy in which men and women reported to officers of the same sex. One female comrade recalled, "I can remember that when I came into the Party over a year ago, at that time David Hilliard was National Headquarters Captain, and there was another sister who was National Captain for women."[19] The Panther/Pantherette designation aptly illuminates the influence of societal norms during the formative years of the self-professed revolutionary organization.

As the Black Panther Party expanded in 1968, so did women's participation in Party activities. By the latter part of the year, the sheer increase in the number of women partially accounts for the expansion of their participation. In his autobiography *A Lonely Rage*, Bobby Seale estimated that women represented approximately sixty percent of the BPP's membership in 1968.[20] During the fall of 1968, Panther women discussed their role as revolutionary Black women in the pages of *The Black Panther*. A series of articles appeared in the September issues of *The Black Panther* that documented the process of self-definition by Panther women.[21] Ironically, however, these articles reflected and reinforced prevailing patriarchal societal norms. A common theme underlying the three articles emphasized the supportive role to be assumed by the genuine "Black" woman. For example, one female Party member suggested that once the Black woman fulfills her family responsibilities, "she then becomes an artist, existing solely for the purpose of helping the Black man achieve the heights of his ambition."[22] Similarly, in another article, Panther member Linda Greene defined the revolutionary Black woman as "a Black man's everything ... [who] fulfills the needs of her Black man when they are made known to her and when they are not evident she will and does seek them out."[23] Although these articles lacked the ideological sophistication of later gender statements, the essays signaled the impending challenge to the vestiges of chauvinism in the Party. Indeed, by late 1968, gender contestation led to the elimination of the Panther/Pantherette hierarchy.

The year 1969 was a watershed period for the participation of women in the BPP. During this year, local and national law enforcement officials waged their strongest attack against the BPP leadership. Newton remained in prison while appealing his voluntary manslaughter conviction in the shooting death of police officer John Frey. Bobby Seale, the other cofounder, spent much of the year incarcerated in New Haven, Connecticut, on charges stemming from the May 1969 murder of Alex Rackley, a BPP member and suspected FBI informant. Eldridge Cleaver, the third member of the

Panthers' early leadership, was in exile in order to avoid revocation of his parole due to his participation in the April 6, 1968, police shoot-out that left 16-year-old Bobby Hutton, the first BPP recruit, dead. The Party's Chief of Staff, David Hilliard, who was responsible for administering the organizational affairs during this period, was arrested at the close of the year on charges of threatening to kill the President of the United States. Many of the Party's local leaders were also targets of police harassment during this period.[24] This leadership vacuum underscored Panther June Culberson's prognosis that "[I]t is a necessity that we [women] be given equal rank according to acquired abilities."[25] Expansion of female participation became critical for the organization to function effectively.

The Party's decision to close ranks further contributed to the increased opportunities for women to fill nontraditional female roles. Party leaders in January 1969 prohibited individuals from joining the BPP for a three-month period in an attempt to curtail infiltration by police informants. Consequently, a greater reliance was placed upon the current membership rather than new recruits to implement Party programs. Concurrently, the national leadership initiated the expulsion of suspected police informers and insubordinate Party members.[26]

During this state of organizational flux, women in the Party emerged as national and local Party leaders. Some assumed the rank and duties left unoccupied by the departure of their male comrades, while other women filled prominent local leadership positions from the onset. Under both patterns of leadership succession, the individual's talents, skills, and performance formed the selection criteria for advancement in the BPP. Both Kathleen Cleaver and Patricia Hilliard held influential positions at the national level, Communications Secretary and Finance Secretary respectively. In Panther affiliates throughout the nation, Elaine Brown, Ericka Huggins, Barbara Sankey, Ann Campbell, Afeni Shakur, Yvonne King, and Audrea Jones were among many women who became influential leaders in their respective chapters during the revolutionary phase of the BPP.

For example, in Los Angeles, Elaine Brown advanced in the leadership hierarchy after the deaths of two leading members of the Southern California Branch of the Black Panther Party, Alprentice "Bunchy" Carter and John Huggins. David Hilliard appointed Elmer "Geronimo" ji Jaga (Pratt) to the leadership position of the Branch and Elaine Brown to the post of Deputy Minister of Information.[27] Brown's Los Angeles comrade, Ericka Huggins, holds the distinction of the first woman to open a BPP chapter where she served as Deputy Chairman. Born and raised in Washington, D.C., Ericka left Lincoln University in Pennsylvania in November 1967 to become active in the Black liberation struggle. She and her husband John Huggins of New Haven, Connecticut, moved to Los Angeles and eventually became members of the Southern California Branch of the BPP. After her husband was killed along with "Bunchy" Carter during a melee with members of the

Maulana Karenga-led "Us" organization on the campus of UCLA on January 17, 1969, Huggins relocated to New Haven where she buried her late husband. At the behest of local community residents, Huggins contacted the Central Committee and requested permission to establish a New Haven chapter of the Black Panther Party. The chapter became functional in April with the establishment of a free breakfast program. Huggins also worked in concert with local residents and Yale University students to establish a liberation school for local youth. Additionally, she conducted political education classes. Huggins and other members of the New Haven branch as well as National Chairman Bobby Seale were indicted for the murder of Alex Rackley. However, she and Seale were eventually acquitted on May 24, 1971.[28]

Female leadership was particularly significant in the Illinois chapter of the BPP. By mid-1969 women in Chicago occupied "responsible positions on the central staff" of the local Panther affiliate. Examples included "a woman section leader, a woman field secretary, and a woman on the security staff."[29] Barbara Sankey, Ann Campbell, and Yvonne King also held important policy positions in the Illinois chapter of the Black Panther Party. Sankey, raised on the west side of Chicago, joined the Panthers after hearing about Huey Newton's murder trial in 1968. Shortly thereafter, she became the director of three free breakfast program sites in the city. Ann Campbell held the Communications Secretary post while Yvonne King's positions included Deputy Minister of Labor and Field Secretary.[30] On the East Coast, the Boston branch exemplified the prevalence of women's leadership in the BPP. Audrea Jones became the Captain of the Boston branch after Doug Miranda was transferred to Connecticut to work on the New Haven 14 case. Miranda, a founding member of the Boston Panther unit, attributed Audrea's appointment to her impressive skills, which made her the most qualified person to assume the captain's position.[31]

Paradoxically, the proliferation of female leadership in the Party occurred in the midst of gender inequality within the organization. The perpetuation of the traditional domestic gender roles still posed problems in some Party chapters. During a visit to one Panther chapter, Seale noted,

> Twenty or so dudes were there one night and we were sitting down to eat; ten or twelve sisters were laboring in the kitchen. Now a sister fills up a plate with the product of her labor and she brings it in, says "Here you are brother." Then the brother starts eating and he looks up and says "Bring the hot sauce."[32]

Sexual harassment, which on occasion took the form of sexual coercion, was an additional problem. Women in the Party complained of various male officers who attempted to sleep with them by exploiting their rank. For example, in 1970 Regina Jennings attributed sexual harassment for her decision to leave the Oakland branch.[33] However, she later returned to the Party in Philadelphia in 1972.

Indeed, the process of establishing a gender-neutral organization was an on-going dynamic process. Roberta Alexander notes,

> For the last several months in our Party there have been struggles over this question [of gender inequality]. These struggles have gone through the whole gamut of possible real problems; have gone through women leadership; women being able to be armed, to defend themselves as well as the brothers; on whether or not the women do all the typing or whether or not they take part in the armed self-defense and the running of the offices, not just behind the typewriters; and it goes down to the sexual levels, whether or not the women are supposed to do so and so for the cause of the Revolution, etc.[34]

Geographical distinctions, different personnel, and varied levels of ideological maturity precluded a monolithic female experience. This diversity was evident in Chicago, where Party members declared in a May 1969 interview that "women's liberation is not perceived as a problem in the Illinois Party."[35] Likewise, Panther women in the Boston chapter noted the absence of gender discrimination.[36] Among these diverse experiences was the voice of June Culberson of the Southern California chapter. On May 4, 1969, *The Black Panther* published Culberson's powerful articulation of a feminist-based model of the Black revolutionary woman drawn from the experience of female freedom fighters of the liberation movements in China, Vietnam, and Cuba. Similar to Anna J. Cooper's *A Voice from the South by a Black Woman from the South*, which underscored a woman's right to self-definition, Culberson argued that "the time has come for this subject of the revolutionary woman to be discussed and dealt with from inside out—by a woman."[37] She noted that women "have fought in revolutions for the liberation of their people. We have examples of the Chinese women, the Vietnamese women, and the Cuban [women]."[38]

Culberson challenged her male comrades to act in accordance to the organization's principle of gender equality:

> You tell us that we are the backbone of the Party and yet you won't allow us to put this into practice for fear that if you really help us get politically educated, we might learn a little more than you do, or may shoot little straighter. This is a hangup the brothers will have to overcome because while they are taking the time to do this, some thing is left undone—the political education of the sisters.[39]

Culberson maintained that this manifestation of chauvinism not only hampered organizational effectiveness but also precluded the equal treatment of women in the Party. Culberson declared that female comrades in the organization "would like to be regarded as Panthers not females (Pantherettes), just Panthers."[40]

Dedication and courage exhibited by Panther women in the throes of government repression reinforced Culberson's advocacy for the eradication of gender distinctions among members of the Black Panther Party. During

1969, the BPP experienced intense surveillance and harassment from local law enforcement personnel and FBI officials. Local police officers frequently raided Panther facilities throughout the year. Numerous Party members were arrested on a host of assorted charges, while at least six other Panthers lost their lives in violent confrontations with the police. At the close of the year on December 29th, the American Civil Liberties Union issued a press release of its national survey of police–Panther relations and concluded that "the record of police actions across the country against the Black Panther Party forms a *prima facie* case for the conclusion that law enforcement officials are waging a drive against the black militant organization resulting in serious civil liberties violations."[41] Women in the Black Panther Party did not escape the government's assault against the organization. Ironically, an unanticipated, yet significant, consequence of the repression of the BPP resulted in a heightened awareness of the gender contradictions within the Party.

Two women, Joan Bird and Afeni Shakur, were among the Panthers of the New York 21 arrested in April 1969 on conspiracy charges to bomb police stations, a city commuter train, the Bronx Botanical Gardens, and five department stores. Although both women, along with their male comrades, were eventually acquitted of all charges in April 1971, they nonetheless experienced brutal treatment during incarceration.[42] Judicial officials required $100,000 bail for each member of the Panther 21. All defendants "were put under 24-hour solitary lock-up, denied access to library, medical and recreational facilities and were not allowed to meet jointly with counsel."[43]

Born in New York City in 1949, Joan Bird lived in Harlem as a child. She joined the New York chapter of the BPP in the fall of 1968 while attending Bronx Community College. Prior to her arrest on conspiracy charges in April, Bird was detained on charges of felonious assault upon local police officers, during which time she suffered police abuse. She recalled,

> I was found in the car by the pigs and they dragged me out and began
> to beat and stomp on me and use heavy blackjacks and beat and kicked
> me in the stomach, lungs, back, and handcuffed me . . .telling me that
> I had better tell them the truth or else they were going to kill me.[44]

Afeni Shakur, the other female member of the New York 21, was born in 1947 in Lumberton, North Carolina, and spent her early childhood years living in North Carolina and Norfolk, Virginia. At the age of eleven she moved to New York with her mother and sister. After listening to a speech delivered by Eldridge Cleaver in 1968, Afeni Shakur accepted Cleaver's challenge to join the Panthers. She remembered, "Eldridge dared people, he just said I dare you to go to the political education class tomorrow, PE, and join the Black Panther Party. And I went."[45] Soon after she joined the New York chapter, Shakur ascended to the position of section leader. This further illustrated the distinctive pattern of leadership in the BPP stimulated by government repression. The arrest of two leading male members created the vacant section leader position. At the urging of her male comrades, Shakur assumed the leadership post. She explained,

> I didn't have any leadership ability because I'm just not a brilliant person, but, they did, you know, and every time I'd tell them that I shouldn't be in any position like that, they would just look at me and tell me there's nobody else to do it. That's how they justified it.[46]

The imprisonment of Ericka Huggins and other women of the New Haven 14 offers illustration of the indirect effect of political repression. Huggins and five other women, who included Peggy Hudgins, Rose Smith, Francis Carter, Jeannie Wilson, and Maude Francis, were members of the New Haven 14 arrested in the murder of Alex Rackley. Three of the women, Carter, Smith, and Francis, were pregnant when arrested and two gave birth while in prison. According to one news report of their incarceration, "life has been anything but easy for the three pregnant women." Furthermore,

> Shortly after their arrival at Niantic, outside searchlights were installed which keep their rooms lit all night (they are locked in their individual rooms at 9 p.m.). Police maintain a patrol by car and foot outside the windows, often shining a spotlight into the rooms. The noise from walkie-talkies combined with the lights to make sleep extremely difficult.[47]

From exile, Eldridge Cleaver sent a recording of a letter to Ericka Huggins that was published in *The Black Panther* on July 5, 1969. This letter entitled "Message to Sister Erica Huggins of the Black Panther Party," addressed Huggins' status and exemplary revolutionary behavior. He wrote, "the incarceration and the suffering of Sister Erica should be stinging rebuke to all manifestations of male chauvinism within our ranks." Cleaver extolled the courage and commitment of Huggins and other Panther women: "Let it be a lesson and an example to all of the sisters, particularly to all the brothers, that we must understand that our women are suffering strongly and enthusiastically as we are participating in the struggle."[48] Cleaver's seminal letter of support for gender equality within the ranks of the Party concluded,

> But, I'm saying that it's mandatory, the Minister of Defense Huey P. Newton has said it is mandatory that all manifestations of male chauvinism be excluded from our ranks and that sisters have a duty and the right to do whatever they want to do in order to see to it that they are not relegated to an inferior position, and that they're not treated as though they are not equal members of the Party and equal in all regards.[49]

A constellation of intra-organizational factors, such as gender contestation, the dedicated and courageous actions of Panther women, and the ideological maturation of both female and male Party members, fueled the process of establishing a more gender-neutral Black Panther Party. By the end of 1969, it was increasingly difficult to discount the exemplary actions of female Panthers.[50] The December 8, 1969, gun battle between the

Panthers and the Los Angeles Police Department is a case in point. During the police raid of the local Panther headquarters, Party members held the police at bay during a five-hour shoot-out. Among the eighteen Party members arrested on a host of charges, six were women. Each of the six female Panthers—Evon Carter, Tommye Williams, Renee Moore, Kathy Kimbrough, Sandra Pratt, and Sharon Williams—suffered injuries. Overcome by tear gas upon emerging from the building, Sharon Williams was thrown over a banister and kicked and beaten so severely that she suffered rib and kidney damage. Furthermore, after her arrest she did not receive medical attention for three days.[51] According to Bobby Seale, the bravery displayed by the Los Angeles Panther women compelled men in the Party to begin "to see that the sisters can get arrested, too, just the same as the brothers. I know that the community can see this in the recent shoot-out in L.A. where the sisters were in there too, battling, defending just as hard as the brothers."[52]

On May 29, 1970, the voluntary manslaughter conviction of Huey Newton was reversed. His release from prison in August furthered the process of eradicating gender inequality in the BPP. Elaine Brown remembered,

> As to the relationship between men and women, he [Newton] stated, openly, and often, that it was that of comrades (a term without gender). He further commanded that personal relations be stripped of possessive pronoun referents, i.e., "my" woman/man. He forbade the use of the Cleaver-inspired term "pussy power." Finally, Huey was fond of saying of himself: "I'm not a man, I'm not a woman, I'm a plain-born child."[53]

In Newton's post-prison statement concerning women's liberation August 15, 1970, he declared that "we [members of the Black Panther Party] recognize the women's right to be free."[54] Newton's commitment to gender equality would positively impact gender dynamics in the Party. While at times leadership efforts were uneven, opposition to sexism during the revolutionary phase of the Party laid the groundwork for the expansion of female participation during its subsequent years.

Politics, Women, and Reproduction

Shortly after his release from prison in August 1970, Huey Newton began to redirect the ideological orientation of the Party. He believed that during his absence, the BPP had drifted away from the Black community under Eldridge Cleaver's leadership. Newton maintained,

> They [White radicals] had been drawn to the Party by Eldridge's rhetoric, and their views had come to influence too many of our activities. I made up my mind that we could not let white radicals define the struggle for us; they knew too little about the Black experience and life in Black communities.[55]

Consequently, the Party re-emphasized community programs to bolster support from the Black community. However, this redirection of the Party came amidst lingering tensions within the organization. Disagreements over strategy, allocation of organizational resources, and the unilateral decision making of the Central Committee persisted within the BPP. The expulsion of the highly respected Geronimo ji Jaga by Newton on January 23, 1971, brought latent organizational tensions to the surface. Over the course of the next three years, the Party was transformed from a nationwide organization to a progressive locally based group influential in Oakland Bay Area politics. During this transition, intraparty strife and programmatic shifts significantly impacted female participation.

In February 1971, a factional split within the Party materialized. One faction supported Huey Newton's emphasis on community programs, while other members aligned with Eldridge Cleaver, who advocated guerrilla warfare. Cleaver's support of the New York 21, who were expelled earlier by the Central Committee, exacerbated past differences. Newton expelled members of the New York 21 because of their letter of support that declared the Weathermen Underground as the true vanguard of revolutionary struggle in the United States. An armed splintered branch of the Students for a Democratic Society, the Weathermen Underground took credit for the bombing of the home of John Murtaugh, the presiding judge in the New York 21 case. Members of the New York 21 accused National Headquarters of favoritism regarding bail payment of incarcerated Party members in the nationally distributed letter.[56]

Subsequent intraparty strife exacted a severe toll on the organization's membership. Almost immediately, Party comrades were forced to choose sides between the two Panther leaders. As a result of this conflict, many members of the BPP were expelled. Others left to escape the turmoil. And some members were killed. Kathleen Cleaver was among the members expelled by the Central Committee.[57]

Assata Shakur voluntarily left the BPP because of disaffection with the national leadership. A member of the New York chapter from 1969 until 1971, Assata attended City College of New York during her stint in the Party. She participated in the medical cadre, the breakfast program, and the liberation school of the New York chapter. Despite her dissatisfaction with previous Central Committee decisions, Shakur remained in the BPP. However, after the expulsion of her fellow New York Panthers whom she admired, Shakur explained that she eventually became "[s]ick and disgusted" and "decided it was time for me to leave the Party."[58] Assata would join the Black Liberation Army soon after leaving the BPP.

By the end of the summer in 1971, Newton consolidated the BPP's re-emphasis on community service programs, which he renamed the Party's "survival programs." Between 1971 and 1974, the Party expanded the scope of its community projects. Several additional survival programs were established, including a free ambulance service, free plumbing and maintenance, free pest control, and free food give-aways. The Party also created a sickle cell anemia research foundation to test for the disease.[59]   Many of these programs were implemented by Panther affiliates across the nation. Panther women provided critical assistance and invaluable leadership service. The Party's survival programs depended on abilities rather than personal attributes. Consequently, as one Party member explained, "If you showed talent and ability, you got the job."[60]

Application of the merit principle was most evident in the leadership of the Party's school. An outgrowth of the organization's Intercommunal Youth Institute (established in January 1971), the Oakland Community School became a model of alternative education in Oakland. The Party sought "to establish a progressive educational program that poor and oppressed people could use as a model. . . [and]. . .to save Black and poor children from the miseducation of the city's public schools."[61] Women directed the school from its inception until 1981. From 1971 to 1973, Brenda Bay directed the Intercommunal Youth Institute. In 1973, Ericka Huggins was appointed to the director's position while Donna Howell served as the codirector. Huggins would head the Party's educational apparatus until 1981. As director, her duties included curriculum development, fund raising, and public relations. In 1977, the school received a commendation for its innovative curriculum from the California State Legislature.[62]

Despite the lessening of overt political repression levied against the BPP as a result of the Party's focus on community projects, members of the organization remained subject to police harassment. As previously noted, Panther women were certainly not secure from the actions of the police. The abduction and brutal beating of Carol Rucker, a San Francisco Panther, is proof that police abuse did not distinguish between male and female Party members. According to Rucker's account of the ordeal,

> They [police officers] threatened me to answer, until one reactionary pig came in and started beating me and knocking me into the wall. My hands were still handcuffed behind my back, so I was unable to control myself from falling. I fell into the wall and hit my head, and after that I was unconscious. . . They pulled me out of the car, searched me again and then kicked me down and then drove off.[63]

She reported that the police "made a joke about killing a Panther sister by having sexual intercourse with her until she would die."[64] In describing her mistreatment, Rucker's experience was testimony to Eldridge Cleaver's 1969 letter that urged male comrades to consider BPP women as revolutionaries because they received similar mistreatment from police as the men. Indeed, Rucker's physical and mental abuse offered evidence of the nondiscriminating nature of state repression.

The lives of other Panther women were directly threatened. On January 4, 1972 in High Point, North Carolina, the police raided the Angela Davis Day-Care Center where Haven Henderson, a Party member, was "vehemently pushed from the doorway" and threatened by a policeman who put his gun to the back of her head. According to another woman present, Eva

Thompson, the occupants were all held at gun-point while the police conducted "a phony man-hunt." In spite of their harassment, both women continued to serve as teachers in the center.[65]

An entrée into electoral politics constituted the second manifestation of the programmatic shift in the Party. Party leaders sought to empower the local African American community in Oakland. On May 13, 1972, Bobby Seale and Elaine Brown announced their candidacies for local political office in the city. Seale ran as a mayoral candidate while Brown sought a seat on the city council. To mobilize resources for the Seale/Brown campaigns, National Headquarters issued a directive that ordered its members to cease operations in their local chapters and report to Oakland. While all of the Party's affiliates did not close immediately, the transfer of members to Oakland enhanced female participation in the BPP. This redeployment of Party members resulted in the concentration of a highly educated female cohort in Oakland. Between October 1972 and May 1973, women represented approximately 45% of the total membership and more than 85% of the female members had some level of college education.[66] This highly skilled group of women would assume a prominent role in the electoral efforts of the organization. Indeed, Audrea Jones and Joan Kelley served as codirectors of the Seale–Brown campaign. Herman Smith headed the historic Seale–Brown campaign.[67]

Bobby Seale and Elaine Brown campaigned as representatives of the people. "The thing that we can do," Brown announced, "is to represent the people's true interests and needs on the city council and transform the power that the existing council has, to serve the needs of the people."[68] Seale and Brown mounted a campaign against Oakland's entrenched economic and political interests, which were unresponsive to the needs of minority and poor communities. Neither of the mayoral candidates garnered a majority of the vote, forcing a run-off election which Seale lost. Brown received 34,845 votes, approximately 33% of the vote. Although the BPP failed to win either office, the Party's extensive grassroots campaigning in the election would lay important groundwork for the 1977 victory of the city's first African American mayor, Lionel Wilson.[69]

Members of the Black Panther Party also campaigned for positions on the boards of federally funded community programs, including model cities and community action programs, in the East Bay Area. Among the Panther political candidates were a number of women. For example, in June 1973, Ericka Huggins and Audrea Jones were elected to the Berkley Community Development Council (BCDC) in Berkley, California, a committee responsible for directing federal funds to "meaningful programs for the poor." Huggins stated that she "witnessed the oppression of poor and oppressed people and . . . found it hard to ignore the unending harassment, poverty and racism Black and poor people of this country have had to face."[70] Panther women were also among the ten-member slate who attempted to win positions on the West Oakland Planning Committee (WOPC), the policy-making Board of Directors for the Model Cities Program of Oakland. Among the candidates for a seat on the WOPC were Ruth Jones, Earlene Coleman, Marion Hilliard, and Millicent Nelson. BPP participation also extended to other national Party affiliates. In Chicago, for example, Yvonne King, Lynn French, Ernestine Crossley, Pamela Jones, and Beverlina Powell campaigned for seats on the city's Model Cities Board.[71]

After the BPP's transformation into a national organization, reproductive policy constituted an important point of discussion among the Party's membership. Motherhood and family issues constituted a recurring issue. In 1971, Akua Njeri (formerly Deborah Johnson) left the Illinois Branch of the BPP in Chicago because she found it too difficult to care for her infant while a full-time Party member. According to Njeri,

> Before. . .you were by yourself, you could really sleep anywhere and you could work all night. But when you have the responsibility of children, you can't do that. . . There was no structure set up to work within the Party, to continue to work in the Breakfast program, to continue to sell the newspaper. It was the demand to do it all or nothing. You would have to explain why you had to go take your child to the doctor, go through some struggle with that.[72]

Therefore, Njeri left the Party because she "didn't think it was her [Njeri's mother] full responsibility to take care of him [Njeri's son] while I continued to do Party work."[73]

An increasing number of Panther women were having children. Between April and July 1972, five Panther women gave birth, and by December of the same year, there were three more newborns. These eight new babies were in addition to the 21 pre-schoolers and 48 children at the Intercommunal Youth Institute. The growing number of children created additional hardships for a financially strapped BPP.[74] Fortunately, the majority of the Party members tended to be younger and therefore were childless. A reflective Elaine Brown notes,

> Those who did come into the Party with children found it very difficult to manage a home life with life in the Party. Hindsight suggests that most members of a settled family might have considered it untenable to join. . . in the late Sixties, given the kind of commitment required: every day of one's life and one's life itself.[75]

A 1972 position paper by Audrea Jones dealt with birth control policy in the organization. Jones, the leader at the Boston branch, remained in Oakland after her return from China as a member of a Panther-led delegation of twenty people. She served as codirector of Bobby Seale's mayoral campaign and also directed the George Jackson Free Health Clinic. In her position paper, Jones noted the need for a shift in the Party's policy regarding birth control and family planning. She cited the financial and manpower strain on the organization caused by the increasing number of children born to Party members. She wrote, "Our experience has been one of groups of sisters becoming pregnant at approximately the same time. As a result, we have had bulk increases in financial expenses and bulk decreases in manpower during the pregnancies, and the child care staffs are experiencing similar problems after the babies are born."[76] She noted that Panther children needed financial assistance for food, clothing, shelter, and health care. In addition, lost manpower due to child rearing hampered the implementation of the Party's survival programs. Basically, pregnant mothers confronted numerous difficulties in carrying out the full-time duties of a Party member.

Jones challenged the BPP not to expect women to bear the sole responsibility for birth control. In her opinion, such a policy was "backward and unprogressive." Instead, Jones suggested that both women and men attend BPP clinic-sponsored birth control classes. She wrote, "these classes would not only consist of the pros and cons of various birth control devices and methods, but also, and most importantly, the responsibility and necessity for us to do so." The concerns raised by Jones were addressed in a Central Committee meeting on August 16, 1972. These issues included, "setting a policy of Planned Parenthood in the Party. . . the establishment of a policy for expectant mothers. . . [and] a designated period of recuperation after child birth."[77]

The Jones position paper also addressed the Party's directive on dating non-Party members. She requested that the Party clarify its "outside dating" policy and restrict members from parenting children with non-Party individuals. For Jones, ideological training was necessary for members to understand the full responsibilities of parenthood. Therefore, she suggested that Planned Parenthood be a part of the political education discussions. Furthermore, because much of the membership was young in age, Jones believed the BPP would benefit from collective decision-making in regards to having children. In essence, she proposed a four-step program:

> (1) A comrade sister and brother should first decide between themselves that they wish to have a child. (This is usually not the case. Many of the pregnancies are *not* planned.)

> (2) Discussions between them and a Review Committee, which would consist of Responsible members (and should include Finance Secretary, Personnel, and the Ministry of Health) should occur.

> (3) Based upon the discussions and the objective conditions, the Review Committee would then make recommendations to the entire Central Committee.

> (4) The Central Committee would then make a decision as to the feasibility at that time.[78]

The issues addressed in Jones' position paper never became mandatory organizational policy. However, the BPP leadership did initiate a policy in 1974 directing members to use birth control. When JoNina Abron, a member of the Detroit branch, arrived at Party headquarters in Oakland during the winter of 1974, she encountered a Central Committee directive instructing all Party members to use birth control. Abron remembers some members adhering to the policy, and others disregarding it all together.[79] Indeed, there is evidence that Panther women made their own decisions regarding reproductive issues. For example, Elaine Brown revealed that she had always made the final decision for her personal life. She explained that "I never went along with that program. I always bought my own contraceptives." Brown recalls that "having or not having a child, or having or not having an abortion, was left as an individual decision."[80]

In 1973, Newton established new dormitories to house the Panther children who were matriculating at the Party's school. Residence facilities at the Oakland Community School permitted greater flexibility for BPP parents. Panther women such as Lu Hudson benefited from the new organizational initiative to add dormitories to the school. Hudson enrolled her son Derrick in the Oakland Community School while she remained in Baltimore to continue her Party work. Hudson credited her son's attendance at the Party's school with making it easier to perform her duties as a BPP member. [81]

Women in the Forefront 1974–1977

During the fall of 1974, the Black Panther Party faced a leadership vacuum with the departure of its two cofounders. Bobby Seale resigned, while Huey Newton went into self-exile in Cuba rather than face prosecution on a host of felony charges.[82] Before leaving the country for Cuba, Newton appointed Elaine Brown as Chairperson of the Black Panther Party in his absence. Prior to her assumption of the leadership mantle of the Party, Brown held a number of important posts during her six-year tenure in the organization. She previously served as the Deputy Minister of Information for the Southern California chapter, and while in Oakland, Brown held the position of editor of the organization's newspaper. Brown was also among the early Panther women to have a seat on the Party's Central Committee.

In contrast to Brown's assumption of previous leadership positions in the organization, her appointment as chairwoman of the BPP met with some disapproval. She remembered "there was never any criticism raised as to my gender when I took on the various leadership positions. When, however, Huey was forced into exile and I became the leading member of the Party, there was some resistance."[83] She attributed the initial resistance to the fact that Huey Newton "had become the absolute leader and centerpiece of the Party."[84] Consistent with organizational practice in the BPP, Newton appointed Brown without input from the membership. Notwithstanding this mild opposition, Brown does insist that the "toughest and truest" men in the BPP supported her leadership.[85]

During Brown's tenure as Party spokesperson, women increased their participation in Party affairs and the BPP expanded its role in Oakland's local politics. As leader of the organization, Brown filled vacant Party positions with women. Female participation on the Central Committee reached an all-time high. In addition to Brown, four other women served on the Central Committee during Brown's 1974–1977 tenure. Among the organization's ten-member decision-making body were Ericka Huggins, Phyllis Jackson, Joan Kelley, and Norma Armour. Jackson coordinated campaign workers, Huggins directed the Oakland Community School, and Armour coordinated organizational finances. Joan Kelley was administrator of activities such as the survival programs and legal matters.[86]

During these years, the Party continued its earlier efforts to enhance the political empowerment of the city's African American and poor communities. Embarking upon a citywide plan for community revitalization, Brown explained that the Party sought "to engage all segments of the Oakland power structure, 'politicians' as well as capitalists. We operated in any arena that affected our goal of building a base there," she continued, "including striking at a new organization of drug dealers and . . .the Mafia-run garbage business."[87] Effective grassroots political organizing helped to counter the negative publicity from Newton's rash of arrests. As part of this revitalization effort, Brown campaigned a second time for an Oakland council seat in 1975. Her platform mirrored that of her and Seale's 1973 election bid. During her campaign against incumbent Raymond Eng, she advocated affordable housing, increased employment, better education, improved safety for senior citizens, and the elimination of job discrimination against women.[88] Although Brown won a larger percentage of the vote during her second city council bid (41% in 1975 compared to 33% in the 1973 campaign), she failed to win the election.[89] In addition to Brown, other Panther women were at the forefront of the BPP's enlarged electoral focus. In May 1976, Ericka Huggins became the first African American woman elected to the Alameda County School Board. The Party ventured into presidential politics when both Ericka Huggins and Elaine Brown led a slate of delegates to the 1976 National Democratic Party Convention in support of Governor Jerry Brown's candidacy for president.[90]

Under Brown's leadership, the BPP continued to build its influence in Bay Area politics. Panther leaders were often keynote speakers at local rallies and symposiums of labor and progressive organizations. For instance, in June 1976, Huggins delivered the keynote speech at a rally held by striking members of the Alameda County public employees. Brown addressed Black law students during the students' annual conference and spoke at a rally protesting the extradition of Native American activist Dennis Banks. She headed a delegation that lobbied Governor Brown for jobs in the construction of the Grove-Shafter Freeway. The Brown-led delegation successfully secured 4,000 jobs in return for support of the freeway's reconstruction. Under Brown, the BPP provided critical assistance in the successful 1977 electoral campaign of Mayor Lionel Wilson, the first African American mayor of Oakland. Wilson made several joint campaign appearances with Elaine Brown, and members of the BPP registered Alameda County voters. Food giveaways during the campaign of John George, the first African American to serve on the Alameda Board of Supervisors, also demonstrated the Party's expansive role in local Black political insurgency.[91]

Several political appointments of Panther women further indicate the growing influence of the BPP in Oakland city politics. For example, in 1977 the newly elected Mayor Lionel Wilson appointed Brown to his transition team. Supervisor John George also appointed Brown to his executive committee. Elaine Brown served on the Board of Directors for the Oakland Community Housing Corporation, an agency responsible for allocating funds for low-income replacement housing. In September 1977, Mayor Wilson appointed Phyllis Jackson to Oakland's Civil Service Commission. In the same year, Jackson, like Brown, secured an appointment to John George's executive committee. Other Panther women appointees included Joan Kelly, who held a seat on the Alameda County Juvenile Delinquency Prevention Committee.[92]

All of these women were central figures in the Party hierarchy during Newton's absence. As a result of their leadership, the Party increasingly focused on issues of concern to women. In several speeches Elaine Brown indicted the Oakland city government for employing such a low number of women. Joan Kelly addressed a reproductive rights rally in Oakland where she stressed "women's rights to self-determination in all arenas of life."[93] Moreover, the Party's newspaper featured several articles discussing incidents of forced sterilization at home and abroad.

On July 3, 1997, Newton returned to the United States and was met at the San Francisco airport by a jubilant crowd of Party members and Bay Area community supporters. This "welcome home" rally culminated two years of BPP organizing. Newton's return led to a shift in the composition of the BPP leadership. Several key members, primarily women, lost their municipal and county positions after city audits revealed mismanagement of funds. In addition, Newton's heavy reliance on the Squad (an all-male group of Party members loyal to Newton) generated negative publicity. Former Southern California member Shareef Abdullah recalls that Squad members would visit the Compton, California branch to promote the military wing of the organization.[94] Subsequently, some women resigned while others simply left the Party. Phyllis Jackson relinquished her Oakland Civil Service Commission position. Similarly, Elaine Brown resigned from several city government appointments, quit the Party, and eventually left the city of Oakland.[95] Newton stated that he would not shift any of the women's leadership roles because "the Party had operated on course and been strengthened" during his self-imposed exile in Cuba.[96] Soon after returning, Newton announced that "he was not climbing back into his poster image, and that the party leadership shared equally between men and women would remain as it had during his exile," a statement Brown says "enraged" chauvinistic men in the

Party who had not been pleased with the prominence of the largely female leadership during Newton's absence.[97]

While Newton initially agreed not to remove women from the BPP leadership, he did not provide resistance to chauvinist actions that resulted in female members' departure. In her autobiography, *A Taste of Power*, Elaine Brown cites the re-emergence of chauvinistic attitudes as the reason for her resignation from the BPP in November 1977. She also notes that Newton was suspicious of Phyllis Jackson and Norma Armour, who oversaw Party finances. By late November, both Jackson and Armour resigned from the Party and left Oakland. According to Brown, the brutal beating of the school's codirector, whose jaw was broken after verbally criticizing a male member's work performance, finally pushed her completely away from the Party.[98] When Brown left the BPP at the close of 1977, the Party was quickly approaching its demise. Under her leadership the BPP gained responsibility as a genuine force in Bay Area politics. Moreover, female participation significantly increased while Brown was chairperson. Most importantly, her departure was another signal of the demise of the BPP.

Final Years and Legacy 1977–1982

Newton's return from Cuba marked the beginning of the dissolution of the Black Panther Party. Between 1977 and 1982, the negative publicity generated by Newton and the Squad offset the positive impact of the few remaining Party programs. Party energies were largely concentrated on maintaining Newton's freedom during the final years of the organization. During the course of a two-year period, 1978–79, Newton faced three major courtroom trials. In each instance, the Party launched massive legal mobilization efforts. By 1980, the BPP had but 27 members according to an organizational report.[99]

Women directed the few remaining community programs. Ericka Huggins, the most prominent female member remaining in the Party after Elaine Brown's resignation, served as the Oakland Community School director until 1981. She was a thirteen-year member (1968–1981) of the organization. Huggins attributed her decision to remain a Panther, in spite of Newton's erratic and criminal behavior, to her commitment to the students of the OCS. Huggins attributes her eventual resignation from the Party to Newton's increasing drug problems.[100] Another Panther still active during the final phase of the BPP was JoNina Abron. A nine-year BPP veteran, she originally joined the Detroit branch in 1972 after earning a master of arts degree in journalism from Purdue University. During the early part of 1974, Abron reported to the national headquarters in Oakland and became highly visible in Party activities until her resignation in 1981. She served as editor of the Party's newspaper from March 1978 until 1980, when the paper ceased production. During this period, Abron worked full-time on a number of Party projects, including Huey P. Newton's and Johnny Spain's legal defense, the BPP's legal suit against the FBI, the Panther newsletter (formerly the newspaper), and coalition work with other local and international organizations. Like numerous other Panthers, she eventually experienced work burnout. In the end, Abron noted that she "had done all that [she] could do."[101]

During the last years of the BPP, its few remaining members were severely overwhelmed by the sheer volume of organizational duties and activities. According to Abron, some members wanted Newton to declare publicly that the Party was officially disbanded, but he never did.[102] While the definitive date of the official demise of the Black Panther Party remains unclear, we do know that the formal closing of the school in 1982 concluded the last program sponsored by the BPP. Female Party members continued to serve in the BPP until the final days of the OCS.

An enduring commitment to service undergirds the legacy of female participation in the BPP. Many former members of the Party have continued to work on behalf of the community. They are now employed in service-oriented professions and credit their chosen occupations to their prior activism in the Black Panther Party. For example, several former Panther women assigned to the Oakland Community School retained an interest in education. Katherine Campbell, a former teacher and child-care center worker in Oakland Community School until 1979, worked as a substitute teacher at a San Francisco elementary school and is currently completing her degree requirements for drug-rehabilitation work at the University of California at Berkeley. JoNina Abron also opted for a career in education. After leaving the BPP in 1981, Abron accepted a position with *Black Scholar*. She eventually became managing editor of the publication and is currently a tenured associate professor in the English department at Western Michigan University.[103]

Regina Jennings, a member of the Oakland chapter from 1970–1972 and the Philadelphia branch from 1972–1974, says that education has also occupied her post-Party career. She is now a poet and a writer. She also holds a Ph.D. degree in African American Studies and teaches at Franklin and Marshall College. Jennings stressed that "people lost their jobs, went to jail and protested to create [African American studies] programs." She recalls that the BPP was often at the forefront of the demand for African American Studies in both secondary and higher education. Ericka Huggins also works in both the educational and community service spheres. Huggins has been an adjunct professor in the Women's Studies Department at San Francisco State University. She also directed a program with the Shanti Project for HIV-positive individuals and their families in underprivileged areas of San Francisco and currently is a trainer–consultant for the Harvard Medical School-sponsored Mind/Body Education Initiative in which she teaches stress management.[104]

Kathleen Cleaver, who divorced Eldridge Cleaver in the mid-1980s, completed a Bachelor's degree in history and a law degree from Yale University. While at Yale, she participated in the pro-divestment from South Africa campaigns and union organizing in New Haven. After graduating from law school, Cleaver clerked in the Third District Court of Appeals of the United States for Judge Leon Higginbotham. She briefly practiced corporate law before accepting an appointment on the faculty at Emory University's School of Law. According to Cleaver, she wanted to study what she experienced as a member of the BPP.[105]

Lu Hudson also pursued a legal career after her stint in the Party. She served as the director of the Party's free legal services programs throughout the 1970s. Hudson first joined the BPP in Baltimore in 1970 and transferred to the Oakland branch in 1972 to work on the Seale/Brown campaign. She recalls being prompted to join the Party after realizing that the images of the Panthers in *The Black Panther* differed from those in the news media. She could not understand why members of an organization that fed children were being murdered. As a child Hudson wanted to become a lawyer. During a brief assignment to New Haven, she worked with famed Panther lawyer Charles Garry on the New Haven 14 case. Once she relocated to Oakland, Hudson requested a legal affairs work assignment within the Party. Her duties included making legal referrals, soliciting businesses to donate funds, securing bail funds for Party members, and supervising student interns in the legal affairs program. Hudson decided to attend law school, but found it difficult to balance school responsibilities with her full-time Party duties. She explained, "I had to make a choice between doing it [making bail for Panther members] and learning it." She opted to stay in the Party. When she eventually left the organization, Hudson obtained a law degree.[106]

Upon leaving the BPP, Elaine Brown undertook a host of diverse activities. For example, she briefly attempted to establish a musical career. While a member of the BPP, Brown recorded two albums, *Seize the Time* in 1969 and *Until We're Free* in 1973. She worked as a paralegal and later as a freelance writer for *Essence* magazine. Currently, Brown lives in Atlanta, Georgia, where she is developing a community school modeled on the Party's famed Oakland Community School.[107]

Akua Njeri is but one example of a female Panther still engaged in political activism. She is a member of the African People's Socialist Party (APSP), now based in St. Petersburg, Florida, and is also the president of the National People's Democratic Uhuru Movement, a grassroots organization led by the African People's Socialist Party. Njeri describes her current political activism as a "continuation of the Panther legacy." Akua Njeri was a member of the Chicago branch of the Black Panther Party and the fiancée of Fred Hampton, the popular leader of the Chicago Panthers. Hampton was killed with Mark Clark in the infamous December 4, 1969 police raid. In 1992, Njeri campaigned for the First Congressional seat of Illinois. Interestingly, one of her opponents included then-alderman Bobby Rush, a former Chicago Panther. [108]

Clearly, the Panther women highlighted in the above discussion are only a small sample of the many members of the Party who happened to be women. Countless other former Panther women, like their male comrades, entered various careers ranging from business to public service occupations. However, not all Panthers experienced professional success. Many, both women and men, have found it difficult to overcome the psychological trauma of the political repression resulting from their activism in the BPP.

Women who participated in the Black Panther Party represented another important link in the chain of African American women activists that dates back to the abolitionist efforts of Maria Stewart and Harriet Tubman. Panther women, like their foremothers, dedicated themselves to serving and defending the African American community. They also sought to transform America by struggling against racist, classist, and sexist oppression and exploitation. In the words of Belva Butcher, "I felt that we were giving the community life, blood, and oxygen to their [Black people's] problems."[109] It is hoped that this essay helps to ensure that the commitment, dedication, and sacrifice of members of the Black Panther Party, particularly the women, are not forgotten.

NOTES

Acknowledgments: I thank everyone who has entered, remained in, or exited my life. I would not be where I am without your massive gifts of love and encouragement. I give special thanks to my parents and relatives for their willingness to grow with me to discover and understand my passion for reclaiming our legacies. My interest in the Panthers grew out of an August 27th, 1989 newspaper article about Huey Newton's death five days earlier. Since then I have been blessed to receive intellectual, emotional, and financial support from numerous individuals and institutions. Thanks everyone, especially Gerald Gill, Catherine Clinton, Trei Martin, the Harvard Afro-American Studies Department, Clayborne Carson, Estelle Freedman, Troy Christmas, Gibson Ernest, the Martin Luther King, Jr. Papers Project Staff, the Black Panther Party Research Project Staff, and numerous Panthers who I have met, will meet, or may never meet. Without each of you, this project would not be. Thank you, Professor Charles E. Jones, for your patience, insightful comments, and ever-present support.

1. The title of this essay is a quote from Doug Miranda, a former Massachusetts Branch leader, interviewed by the author in Boston, MA. In context, Miranda explains why Audrea Jones was chosen as leader to replace the male leadership that had been transferred to New Haven, Connecticut, to work on Bobby Seale's and Ericka Huggins' trial. Prior to this, Bobby Seale had stated the same sentiment in 1980: "It wasn't just based on just because she was a female. It was based on *she* or *he* who was qualified to do the work." (Bobby Seale, telephone interview with unknown interviewer, Clayborne Carson Collection, March 13, 1980.) For the photographic essay on the BPP during its early years, see Ruth-Marion Baruch and Pirkle Jones, *The Vanguard: A Photographic Essay on the Black Panthers* (Boston: Beacon Press, 1970).

2. This essay is largely based on my undergraduate senior honor's thesis, which has been significantly revised and expanded. See Angela Darlean Brown, "Servants of the People: A History of Women in the Black Panther Party 1966–1981," Senior thesis, Afro-American Studies, Harvard University, 1992. Pre-1990 exceptions to the oversight of BPP women include the section entitled "Black Panther Women Speak" in Philip S. Foner, ed. *The Black Panthers Speak* (New York: Da Capo Press [1970], 1995), 145–66; Assata Shakur, *Assata: An Autobiography* (Westport, CT: Lawrence Hill and Company, 1987).

3. Robert Goldstein, *Political Repression in Modern America 1978*, (New York: Schenkman Publishing, 1978); Charles Hopkins, "The Deradicalization of the Black Panther Party," Ph.D. dissertation, University of North Carolina, 1978.

4. Shirley Yee, *Black Women Abolitionists: Study in Activism, 1828–1860* (Knoxville, TN: University of Tennessee Press, 1992); Paula Giddings, *When and Where I Enter: The Impact of Black Women on Race and Sex in America* (New York, NY: W. Morrow, 1984); Louise D. Hutchinson, *Anna J. Cooper: A Voice From the South* (Washington, DC: Smithsonian Press, 1981); Doris C. Lefall and Janet L. Sims, "Mary McLeod Bethune–The Educator," *Journal of Negro Education* 45 (Summer, 1976): 342–359.

5. Robin D.G. Kelley, "Jones, Claudia (1915–1965)," Darlene Clark Hine, ed., *Black Women in America: An Historical Encyclopedia* (New York: Carlson Publishing, 1993): 647–648; Mark Naison, *Communists in Harlem During the Depression*, (Urbana, IL: University of Illinois Press, 1983); Barbara Ransby, "Baker, Ella Josephine," Hine, ed., *Black Women in America: An Historical*

Encyclopedia, 70–74; Joanne Grant, Fundi: *The Story of Ella Baker* (New Day Films, 1981); Charles Payne, "Ella Baker and Models of Social Change," *Signs* 14 (Summer 1989): 885–889; Kay Mills, *This Little Light of Mine: The Life of Fannie Lou Hamer* (New York: Plume, 1994); Ula Taylor, "Garvey, Amy Euphemia Jacques (1896–1973)," Hine, ed. *Black Women in America: An Historical Encyclopedia*, 482–483; Karen S. Adler, "Always Leading our Men in Service and Sacrifice: Amy Jacques Garvey, Feminist, Black Nationalist," *Gender and Society* 6 (1992): 346–375.

6. Akinyele K. Umoja, "Eye for an Eye: Armed Resistance in the Mississippi Freedom Movement," unpublished dissertation, Emory University, 1996, 188–189 and 242–243; From: Frederick Brooks To: Oretha Castle-North Louisiana Director of CORE, Jackson Parish, Jonesboro, Louisiana," Gwendolyn Hall Papers, Box 3, Folder 14, Amistad Research Center, Tulane University; Vicki Crawford, "Blackwell, Unita (1933–)," Hine, ed. *Black Women in America: An Historical Encyclopedia*, 138–140; Rita Dandridge, "Meriwether, Louise," Hine, ed. *Black Women in America: An Historical Encyclopedia*, 783–784.

7. Paula Giddings, *When and Where I Enter: The Impact of Black Women on Race and Sex in America,* 290–291. Also see, Annette K. Brock, "Gloria Richardson and the Cambridge Movement," in Vickie L. Crawford, Jacqueline Rouse and Barbara Woods, eds. *Women in the Civil Rights Movement: Trailblazers and Torchbearers 1941–1965* (Bloomington Ind.: Indiana University Press, 1993), 121–144. See James Turner's introduction for a discussion of the influence of David Walker's advocacy of armed resistance on Maria Stewart's political thinking. Also, see Kai Jackson "Telling Off: Black Feminist Narrative and the Civil Rights Movement in the Oral Narratives of Queen Mother Audley Moore," unpublished paper presented at "In Their Own Right: Women's Solutions to Black-White Issues of Race, Class, and Gender, 1895–1985," conference sponsored by Spelman College and Georgia State University, November 12–14, 1995, Atlanta, GA.

8. Huey P. Newton, *Revolutionary Suicide* (New York : Ballentine, 1973), 135.

9. Bobby Seale, *A Lonely Rage* (New York: Bantam, 1979), 203.

10. J. Tarika Lewis, "Voices of Panther Women," video of conference proceedings at the University of California at Berkeley, 26 October 1990. J. Tarika Lewis, Presentation to the Black Panther Party Research Project, Stanford University, Stanford, California, July 28, 1997.

11. Ibid.

12. Ibid.

13. Belva Butcher and Majeeda Roman, "Voices of Panther Women" video of conference proceedings at the University of California at Berkeley, 26 October 1990.

14. Gene Marine, *The Black Panthers* (New York: Signet, 1969), 62–63; and Seale, *Seize the Time*, 153.

15. Kathleen Cleaver, interview by author, Brighton, MA, 10 November 1991.

16. Ibid.

17. Ibid.

18. Julia Hervé, "*Black Scholar* Interviews Kathleen Cleaver," *Black Scholar* 2 (December 1971): 55–56.

19. "Panther Sisters on Women's Liberation" in G. Louis Heath, ed. *Off The Pigs!: The History and Literature of The Black Panther Party*, (Metuchen, NJ: Scarecrow Press,1976), 340.

20. Bobby Seale, *A Lonely Rage: The Autobiography of Bobby Seale* (New York: Times Books, 1978), 177.

21. See, A Black Revolutionary, "Black Woman," *The Black Panther*, 14 September 1968, 6. Linda Greene, "The Black Revolutionary Woman," *The Black Panther*, 28 September 28 1968, 11. Gloria Bartholomew, "A Black Woman's Thoughts," *The Black Panther*, 28 September 1968, 11.

22. "Black Woman," *The Black Panther*, 14 September 1968, 6.

23. Linda Greene, "The Black Revolutionary Woman," *The Black Panther* 28 September 1968, 11.

24. For various accounts of this incident see Seale's *Seize the Time*, 269–273; Ward Churchill and Jim Vander Wall, *Agents of Repression: The FBI's Secret Wars Against the Black Panther Party and the American Movement* (Boston, MA: South End Press, 1990), 42–43; and Elaine Brown, *A Taste of Power: A Black Woman's Story* (New York: Pantheon Books, 1992), 156–170.

25. June Culberson, "The Role of the Black Revolutionary Woman" *The Black Panther*, 4 May 1969, 9.

26. Heath, ed., *Off The Pigs!*, 92; "Kathleen Cleaver" (from New York Radio Address) *The Black Panther*, 4 January 1969, 2; and Seale, *Seize the Time*, 373–392.

27. Brown questionnaire responses, 3; Brown, *A Taste of Power*, 186.

28. See Angela D. Brown "Ericka Huggins" in Hine, ed., *Black Women in America: An Historical Encyclopedia*, 589–90; Ericka Huggins interview by the author, San Francisco, California, January 4, 1992; "Pigs Conspiracy Against Conn. Panthers" *The Black Panther*, 31 May 1969, 5.

29. C. Clark Kissinger, "Serve the People," *Guardian*, 17 May 1969, 7.

30. Ibid.

31. Doug Miranda interview by the author, Cambridge, MA, 9 December 1991.

32. Seale, *A Lonely Rage,* 178.

33. Regina Jennings telephone interview by the author, 2 February 1992.

34. Roberta Alexander, "UFAF Women's Panel: Roberta Alexander at Conference," *The Black Panther*, 2 August 1969, 7.

35. Kissinger, "Serve the People," 7.

36. Anonymous interview by the author, San Francisco, CA, 25 January 1992. Audrea Jones interview by Charles E. Jones, Rahway, New Jersey, 14 June, 1997.

37. June Culberson, "The Role of the Black Revolutionary Woman," *The Black Panther*, 4 May 1969, 9.

38. Ibid.

39. Ibid.

40. Ibid.

41. "News Release Issued by the American Civil Liberties Union" in Phillip S. Foner, ed., *The Black Panthers Speak* (New York, Da Capo Press), 263–264; Rudy Johnson, "Joan Bird and Afeni Shakur, Self-Styled Soldiers in the Panther Class Struggle" *New York Times*, 19 July 1970, 53.

42. Murray Kempton, *The Briar Patch: The People of the State of New York versus Lumumba Shakur et al.* (New York: Dell Publishing Company, 1973), 14.

43. Chris Wilson, "Panther Women Held in Jail," *Guardian*, 18 October 1969, 6; and Raquel Campos, "Panther Trial Begins in New York City," *Guardian*, 31 October 1970, 6.

44. Kuwasi Balagoon et al., eds., *Look For Me in the Whirlwind : The Collective Autobiography of the New York 21*, (New York: Vintage Books, 1971), 103, 304–305.

45. Ibid., 125, 288–90.

46. Ibid, 293.

47. Wilson, "Panther Women Held in Jail," 6.

48. Eldridge Cleaver, "Message to Sister Ericka Huggins of the Black Panther Party,"in Phillip S. Foner, ed. *The Black Panthers Speak*, 98–99.

49. Ibid.

50. Seale, *Seize the Time*, 398.

51. "The Victors," *The Black Panther*, 10 December 1969, 1; "The People Speak," *The Black Panther*, 20 December 1969, 13; Churchhill and Vander Wall, *Agents of Repression*, 82–85.

52. Seale, *Seize the Time*, 398.

53. Brown questionnaire responses, 4; Seale, *Seize the Time*, 394; and Ericka Huggins interview.

54. Huey P. Newton, "The Women's Liberation and Gay Liberation Movements: August 15, 1969," in *To Die For The People*, 152–155.

55. Newton, *Revolutionary Suicide*, 333.

56. Huggins interview, 24 January 1992; Lu Hudson, Interview by Angela Darlean Brown, 27 October 1991; Johnny Spain, Interview by Angela Darlean Brown, Palo Alto, California, 9 August 1996; Ronald Freeman, Interview with Angela Darlean Brown, Los Angeles, California, 4 October 1996.

57. "Enemies of the People," *The Black Panther*, 13 February 1971, 13; Murtaugh had revoked bail for two NY 21 members on bail after Tabor and Moore jumped bail; Newton, *Revolutionary Suicide*, 339; Assata Shakur, *Assata: An Autobiography* (Chicago, IL: Lawrence Hill Books, 1987), 232; "An Open Letter to the Weathermen Underground from the Panther 21," *East Village Other Newspaper* is the original cite for the publication of the NY 21 article. Referenced in "Enemies of the People," *The Black Panther*, 13 February 1971, 13. There is no one version of the split which occurred in March of 1971. Newton, *Revolutionary Suicide*, 339; *The Black Panther*, 17 February 1971: 17; Hugh Pearson, *Shadow of the Panther: Huey Newton and the Price of Black Power in America* (Menlo Park, CA: Addison-Wesley Publishing, 1994), 230–31; Also see Roland Freeman, Interview with Angela Darlean Brown, Los Angeles, California, 4 October 1996; Brown, *A Taste of Power*, 261–267; Deacon Alexander, Interview with Angela Darlean Brown, Los Angeles, California, 10 October 1996; Arthur League, Telephone interview with Angela Darlean Brown, 22 September 1996; Churchill and Vander Wall, *Agents of Repression*, 65–66.

58. Shakur, *Assata,* 230, 232.

59. Black Panther Party (guest editors), *Supplement to the Whole Earth Catalog: The CoEvolution Quarterly* (23 September 1974); *The Black Panther*, 23 September 1974, 1, 19, 23.

60. Anonymous Interviewee, Interview by the author, San Francisco, California, 25 January 1992.

61. "Oakland Community School: A History of Serving the Youth Body and Soul," *The Black Panther*, 16 October 1976, 4

62. "Creative Curriculum, 150 Students, Oakland Community School Expands Services to Youth," *The Black Panther*, 18 September 1976, 4 and 16 October 1976, 4; Ericka Huggins, Interview with Angela Darlean Brown, San Francisco,

CA, 24 January 1992; David Hilliard and Lewis Cole, *This Side of Glory: The Autobiography of David Hilliard and the Story of the Black Panther Party* (Boston: Little, Brown and Company, 1993), 321, 326; Donna Howell, Telephone interview with Angela Darlean Brown, 23 April 1993.

63. "Panther Kidnapped and Beaten by Special Gestapo Pigs," *The Black Panther*, 6 February 1971, 7.

64. Ibid.

65. "Angela Davis Day-Care Center Raided," *The Black Panther*, 29 January 1972, 9.

66. This data is compiled from Skills Survey Sheets, Series 2, Box 4, Folders 4–5, Central Committee Info., Newton Foundation Records (NFR), Stanford University.

67. Audrea Jones interview by Charles E. Jones, Rahway, New Jersey, 14 June 1997.

68. "We Were Victorious: Interview with Elaine Brown," *The Black Panther*, 28 April 1973, 3.

69. "Chairman Bobby Seale for Mayor!" *The Black Panther*, 20 May 1972, special supplement pp. A, C; Charles Houwer, "Strong Seale Showing—Reading Faces Runoff," *San Francisco Examiner*, 18 April 1973, 18; Rod Bush, "Black Enfranchisement, Jesse Jackson and Beyond" in *The New Black Vote* (San Francisco: Synthesis Publications, 1984), 13–52.

70. "Panthers Sweep Berkeley Elections!" *The Black Panther* 10 June 1972, 2; "Vote August 19, 1972," *The Black Panther* 12 August 1978, special supplement D; "B.P.P. Withdraws from Poverty Program," *The Black Panther*, 3 November 1973, 5.

71. "Chicago Model Cities Election—Dec. 19th People's Candidates Campaign for Public Offices," *The Black Panther*, 7 December 1972, 6.

72. Akua Njeri, *My Life with the Black Panther Party* (Oakland, CA: Burning Spear Publications, 1991), 45, 46.

73. Ibid., 45.

74. "From: Audrea Jones, To: Responsible Members. . .Re: Establishment of Birth Control Policy for Party Members," July 22, 1972, 1.

75. Brown, questionnaire responses, 5. There were numerous Party members throughout the country who joined the BPP with children in addition to those who had children after they joined. My discussion of women during the "revolutionary phase" explores inherent tensions for some parents.

76. "From: Audrea Jones, To: Responsible Members. . .Re: Establishment of Birth Control Policy for Party Members, July 22, 1972," Series 2, Box 18, Folder 1, Health Cadre Reports, NFR, Stanford University; "To: All Comrades of the Central Body, From: Comrade Bobby, Re: Agenda Items to be Discussed, Date: August 16, 1972," Series 2, Box 4, Folders 4–5, Central Committee Info., NFR, Stanford University.

77. "From: Audrea Jones, To: Responsible Members. . . Re: Establishment of Birth Control Policy for Party Members, July 22, 1972," Series 2, Box 18, Folder 1, Health Cadre Reports, 2, NFR, Stanford University.

78. Ibid.

79. JoNina Abron, Telephone interview with the author, 31 January, 1992. Audrea Jones' July 1972 document supports Abron's recollection of the directive.

80. Elaine Brown, questionnaire responses, 7.

81. Lu Hudson, Telephone interview, October 1991.

82. Wallace Turner, "Huey Newton Denies Murder and Assault," *New York Times*, 22 November 1977, 11.

83. Brown questionnaire responses, 7.

84. Ibid.

85. Ibid.

86. Elaine Brown, *A Taste of Power*, 3, 4, 357, and 362; "The Black Panther Party et al., Plaintiffs v. Edward Levi, et al., Defendants. Plaintiff Black Panther Party's Responses to Interrogatories of the Federally Represented Defendant" (1978), 14. Series 2, Box 38, Folder 11–13, BPP vs. Levi Folder, NFR, Stanford University.

87. Brown questionnaire responses, 10.

88. "Elaine Brown's Candidacy Prompted by Her Concern over Oakland Conditions," *The Black Panther*, 4 January 1975, 5.

89. Elaine Brown Candidacy for Oakland City Council Threatened," *The Black Panther*, 9 November 1974, 3; Alan Cline, "Widener's Close Win; Moderates Voted in the East Bay," *San Francisco Examiner*, 16 April 1975, 18.

90. Mel Assagi, "Black Panthers Today: Pussycats? Or Stalking Cats?" *Sepia*, September 1977, 28; "Elaine Brown Announces Candidacy," *The Black Panther*, 28 December 1974, 3; "Tony Kline, John George, Elaine Brown 1–2–3 in 8th District Caucus for Brown," *The Black Panther*, 17 April 1976, 14.

91. Brown questionnaire responses, 6 December 1991, 10; Rod Bush, "Introduction: Black Politics and Oakland Development," in Rod Bush, ed., *The New Black Vote* (San Francisco, CA: Synthesis Publications), 1984, 323–325.

92. "Black Panther Wins Seat on County Board," *The Black Panther* 22 May 1976, 1+; "B.P.P. Member Appointed to Civil Service Commission," *The Black Panther* 24 September 1977, 3; Assagi, "Black Panthers Today: Pussycats? Or Stalking Cats?" *Sepia* September 1977, 28.

93. "750 Rally For Reproduction Rights," *The Black Panther*, 1 October 1977, 11. Abron Interview, 31 January 1992; "Elaine Hits City Government on Women," *The Black Panther*, 23 June 1973, 3; "Israeli Doctors Sterilize Arab Women," *The Black Panther*, 9 February 1974, 17; "New Sterilization Guidelines," *The Black Panther*, 2 March 1974, 9.

94. "Welcome Home Huey," *The Black Panther*, 5 July 1977, 1+; Brown questionnaire responses, 7; Peter Collier and David Horowitz, *Destructive Generation: Second Thoughts About the '60s* (New York, NY: Summit Books, 1990), 160; and also see Shareef Abdullah, Personal interview with Angela Darlean Brown, Los Angeles, California, 4 October 1996, B. Kuaku Duren, Interview with the author, Los Angeles, California, 21 September 1996.

95. Hugh Pearson, *The Shadow of the Panther*, p. 280–282.

96. "Huey Speaks to BPP Members on Return from Cuba 8/3/77; Return from Cuba/E.B. Leadership; Huey P. Newton at P.E. Class, 3 August 1977," NFR, Series 6, Box 6, Folder 15.

97. Elaine Brown, *A Taste of Power*, 441; "Huey Speaks to BPP Members on Return from Cuba 8/3/77; Return from Cuba/E.B. Leadership; Huey P. Newton at P.E. Class, 3 August 1977" NFR, Series 6, Box 6, Folder 15.

98. The exact date of Brown's departure is unclear. There are several resignation letters from Elaine Brown in the NFR Collection. For documentation supporting the October 18, 1997 date see "Elaine Brown resigns from the BPP," Series 2, Box 41, Folder 4, Elaine Brown-Corresp., NFR, Stanford University. For documentation supporting the November 16, 1977 date, see "Statement of Elaine

Brown Re: the Black Panther Party," November 16, 1977, Series 2, Box 41, Folder 4, Elaine Brown-Corresp., NFR, Stanford University. *The Black Panther* carried a letter of Brown's resignation in the 26 November 1977 issue. BPP member Regina Davis' jaw was broken (Donna Howell is Regina Davis in Brown's autobiography.), and Newton acknowledges his compliance; Brown explains this event as the final straw in her decision-making process. Brown, *A Taste of Power*, 444–449; Donna Howell, Personal interview by the Author, 23 April 1993; See also Hugh Pearson's *Shadow of a Panther*, 280.

99. "JoNina Abron to Huey Newton, 10/1/80 Report," Series 2, Box 4, Folder 12, [Direction of the Party by JoNina Abron], NFR, Stanford University. This statement is supported by the various resignation explanation letters in "Reports on Comrades," Series 2, Box 4, Folder 19, NFR, Stanford University. The author has conducted over a dozen interviews with members who were in the BPP until the final years and many of them state this reason, among others, to explain their departure.

100. See Angela D. Brown, "Ericka Huggins (1948–present)" Hine, ed., 589–90. Also see Newton, *Revolutionary Suicide*, 340; "Case Against Chairman Bobby and Ericka Dismissed," *The Black Panther*, 29 May 1971, 6; Gail Sheehy, *Panthermania: The Clash of Black Against Black in One American City* (New York, NY: Harper & Row Publishers, 1971), 113, 117–118, 121.

101. Abron interview.

102. Ibid.

103. Katherine Campbell interview by the author, San Francisco, California, 25 January 1992; Campbell interview, 8 August 1996; Abron interview.

104. Regina Jennings, Huggins interview, Stanford, California, 2 December 1992; Huggins, Black Panther Party Research Project Seminar, Stanford University, July 15, 1997, in Author's collection, Regina Jennings, "A Panther Remembers," *Essence*, February 1991, 122.

105. Kathleen Cleaver, Interview by the author.

106. Lu Hudson, Interview by the author.

107. Elaine Brown, "Tough Love!" *Essence*, December 1988, 70; Elaine Brown, History 204f Presentation, Stanford University, in Author's Collection, 20 November 1995.

108. Njeri, *My Life with the Black Panther Party*, ii; Salim Muwakkil, "In the Nation," *In These Times*, 22–28, January 1992, 7.

109. Belva Butcher, "Voices of Panther Women," Conference at the University of California at Berkeley, 26 October 1990.

Part V

Decline of
The Black Panther Party

Chapter Fourteen

Lumpenization: A Critical Error of The Black Panther Party

Chris Booker

The Black Panther Party (BPP) in its ascendant phase embodied the highest aspirations of a generation of radical African American youth. At the peak of the organization's national influence, spanning the years 1969 to 1970, the BPP attracted a broad swath of African Americans to its ranks, leading many to conclude that the Party was indeed the "vanguard" of the Black liberation movement. While there were many countervailing forces within the BPP, college students, working- and upper-middle class members, and the lumpen element dominated Party dynamics, particularly during the zenith of the organization. This essay analyzes the Black Panther Party from its birth in Oakland, California in 1966 to its demise as a national political force in 1971. An examination of the development of the Black Panther ideology reveals an early decision to focus recruitment, role modeling, and orientation in the African American lumpen proletariat. The following analysis maintains that the decision to mold the Black Panther Party from the Black lumpen placed the organization on a course of instability. It is further contended that the emphasis on the lumpen was a decisive factor in the BPP's eventual decline as a national political force.

The Black Panther Party's political programs, stressing long-standing social, economic, and cultural needs of African Americans, inspired thousands to combat racial oppression. Many of these young adults were committed not only to the liberation of Black people in the United States, but also to that of downtrodden people throughout the world. According to the ideological doctrine of the BPP, the African American lumpen proletariat was to spearhead the revolution against capitalist and racist exploitation. Contrary to conventional Marxist thought, Panther theoreticians saw the lumpen as the potential leading revolutionary force within the African American community. Immediately prior to the actual formation of the Black Panther Party, Bobby Seale indicated that he and Huey Newton gave considerable thought to the political qualities of the Black *lumpen* class:

> We would argue with and somewhat change our friends' Marxist views that the lumpen never did anything but pillage and/or ignore the

> revolutionary cause altogether. We downed that view when it came to
> applying it to the black American ghetto-dweller because we were off
> the block too, Stagolees.[1]

To be sure, the Party's conception of the lumpen was much broader than that identified by traditional Marxists. Seale explains that "we are saying that our lumpen proletariat, even though they get into illegitimate activity, okay, it was also the Black mother who had to scrub Miss Anne's kitchen floors, right?"[2] Panther strategists envisioned a Fanon-like transformation of the "forgotten" African American into a world actor.

The primary thesis of this essay is that the criminal element within the lumpen developed a modus operandi that created a sociocultural milieu inimicable to a stable political organization. The modus operandi of the lumpen (or lumpenism) entailed the adoption of values and behavior of the hustler/criminal element of society which included misogyny, undisciplined and illegal behavior, weak political loyalties, and a proclivity toward intimidation and violence. To a large extent, this phenomenon was evident in the organizational dynamics of the Black Panther Party. Clearly other factors—political repression, tactical disagreements, and authoritarianism—all contributed to the ultimate demise of the Party. However, in order to draw important lessons from the Panther experience, it is crucial to ascertain the role that lumpenism played in the Party's fall from national prominence.

Origin of the Black Panther Party

Huey Percy Newton was born February 17, 1942, in Oak Grove, Louisiana, and named after the very popular Louisiana politician Huey P. Long. Newton's family moved to Oakland after his second birthday. His father worked at the Naval Supply Depot as a laborer and also served as a part-time Baptist minister, while his mother was a full-time housewife. Early in life Newton grew to know the hostility of the local police: "[T]he police were very brutal to us even at that age. There would be a policeman in the movie house, and if there was any disturbance, we would get kicked out and the police would call us niggers."[3]

While he was at Merritt College, Huey Newton searched for an organizational vehicle that would lead the struggle for Black liberation. He became involved in the Afro-American Association, an organization he initially believed could lead a mass movement. Just as for many others of his generation, this period was one of debate and discussion of a variety of ideologies, strategies, and tactics. Newton quickly acquired a reputation on campus as a skillful debater who documented his rhetoric with facts. This allowed him to "shoot down" his opponent, further enhancing his reputation. Newton had a healthy respect for research, study, and logical thinking that was followed by action. This intellectual characteristic was infused into the initial thrust of the Black Panther movement.[4]

At Merritt College, Newton met Bobby Seale, who was five years older than Newton. At this point, Seale had considerably more experience on the street and in the workforce than Newton. During his youth, Seale moved to Los Angeles and worked while attending high school. During a Harlem Globetrotters basketball game, according to Seale, he and a friend "found" a purse and went into the men's restroom to search it and discovered twenty-seven dollars. They returned to watch the remainder of the basketball game, but while leaving a guard stopped them at a woman's request. After a brief discussion, Seale and his friend were arrested for stealing the woman's purse. In court, Seale was let off with a warning, since he did not have a criminal record, and instructed by the judge to join the Air Force. He did join the Air Force, but was subsequently discharged after spending a stint in the military jail. Later, Seale found employment as a sheet-metal mechanic on the Gemini missile project, gambled, played drums, and attended college part-time during his off hours. Seale recalled that during this period, he fell "into the trap of projecting an air of having some cool, well-kept hustle. It wasn't really me, but it allowed me to feel more relaxed around other working-class hustlers."[5]

The initial friendship of Huey P. Newton and Bobby Seale proved quite productive. Seale initiated a drive to organize the African American students on campus. Skeptical, Newton believed that it was necessary to balance the "do-nothing activity of the blacks on campus" with that of the "brothers off the block."[6] The new organization, the Soul Students Advisory Council, soon became split between those who favored campus cultural enrichment programs and other members who advocated community mobilization. According to Seale, "Huey said to all these cats on the central committee of the SSAC that we are going to have to show the brothers on the block that we have an organization that represents the community and we're going to have to show it in a real strong fashion."[7] Newton argued that African Americans must arm themselves.

This disagreement eventually led to Seale's and Newton's resignation from the campus organization. The impetus for their departure was a crisis which ensued following the unapproved spending of monies from the organization's treasury on the bail for Newton and Seale. After several heated verbal exchanges which nearly erupted into a physical altercation, Newton and Seale declared, "We resign. We're going to the black community and we intend to organize in the black community and organize an organization to lead the black liberation struggle."[8]

Both Seale and Newton expressed contempt for the "cowards" who were "scared" and opposed the idea of armed self-defense. Seale accused these "cultural nationalists" of "trying to act bad on campus like they were bad dudes off the block." According to Seale, Newton remarked,

"If they think they're bad, we're going to get our shit." So he called up his boys—the pimps, thugs off the block (people always call them thugs)—and he called up his nephew, who, like the brothers on the block, just liked to fight.[9]

Seale declared that they "were going to kick ass that day." Fortunately, no serious violence took place. Eventually, Newton and Seale left the Soul Students Advisory Council; they declared it hopelessly riddled with futile ideas of "reforming" the system.[10] Newton and Seale decided to form an organization that would patrol the police and safeguard the rights of African American citizens. "A law book, a tape recorder, and a gun," Huey said, "that's all we would need. It would let those brutalizing racist bastards know that we mean business."[11] They agreed to accept arrests nonviolently and keep their guns in plain view when they patrolled the police in order to comply with the law. Seale and Newton vowed to "do battle only at the point when a fool policeman drew his gun unjustly."[12]

According to Seale, the 10-point Panther program was drawn up very quickly. Late one evening in October 1966, Huey Newton dictated the future organization's program to Seale who wrote Newton's words down verbatim. The name of the organization was derived from the Lowndes County Freedom Organization of Alabama that featured a black panther as its campaign symbol. At this early stage, it was evident that the Panthers adopted a unique position toward the role of violence and weapons in their political practice. In one incident, Panthers, Seale and Newton included among them, took their guns to a birthday party because they wanted to patrol the police on the way there. After they entered the house, a wave of panic ensued. Newton told the hostess that the guns symbolized the goals of a new Black organization. Seale remembered that the hostess then told Newton that she did not want weapons in her house. Newton failed in his attempt to calm the people, so the hostess then asked him and the other Panthers to put the guns into a closet. Twenty minutes later, the police appeared and asked the Panthers if they were carrying guns. The Panthers finally agreed to leave and angrily denounced the hostess as "a nigger bourgeois bitch" for calling the "white swine racists on us."[13]

By New Year's Day 1967, the Black Panthers moved into their first storefront office. Shortly thereafter, twenty-five people turned up for a meeting at the new office, and the organization began to attract new members. Weeks later Panthers began to sell *The Red Book*, Mao Tse-Tung's *Quotations from Chairman Mao,* in order to raise money for the organization. Amid the radical political climate of Berkeley and the University of California campus, this proved to be an effective fund-raising method.

With the largest Black rebellions in recent history bolstering their recruitment efforts, the Black Panther Party rode a wave of militancy and attracted young Black men and women en masse to its ranks. The compelling anger of the increasingly politically aware masses made it possible for an African

American militant organization to utilize less than optimal strategies and still experience rapid growth. The Party's membership grew to an estimated five thousand members with thirty-two branches spread over fifteen states.[14] The organization attracted many members directly after their release from jail.[15] However, unlike the Nation of Islam, which reoriented and reformed its recruits, the Panthers did not attempt to thoroughly reshape these individuals. Newton explained his approach:

> Instead of trying to eliminate these activities—numbers, hot goods, drugs—I attempted to channel them into significant community actions. . . . Many brothers who were burglarizing and participating in similar pursuits began to contribute weapons and material to community defense.[16]

The Panthers did try, however inconsistently and unevenly, to rehabilitate the purely antisocial tendencies of its criminalized members.[17] In addition, the Party also recruited on campuses as well as in all other sectors of the community, which helped to mitigate the impact of lumpen behavior.[18]

Rise of the Black Panther Party

The growth and development of the Black Panther Party was hardly smooth, gradual, or well calibrated. Quite to the contrary, the Panthers' rise to national prominence was marked by at least six key events that enhanced the organization's prestige, publicized its existence and objectives, and sharpened the hostility of the American establishment against it. The first of these key events involved providing security for the widow of Malcolm X, the late Betty Shabazz. The Black Panther Party and competing Bay Area militant organizations challenged each other for the responsibility of protecting Shabazz during her visit. The Black Panther Party for Self-Defense, the group's earlier name, went all out to impress both the public and their rivals with its degree of organization, determination, and discipline. When the date of Betty Shabazz's arrival came, the Panthers, twenty strong, marched with her into the *Ramparts* magazine office and caused an immediate panic among the staff. An armed confrontation soon developed after the police confronted the Panthers outside the building. As earlier planned, Shabazz was whisked away. Angered by the reception of the police, Newton reportedly taunted one "big fat racist pig" to draw his gun. Newton faced him down with the challenge: "Draw it, you cowardly dog!" The officer backed down with Newton laughing in his face. Aided by the media, this incident quickly became part of the rapidly growing legend of the Panthers.[19]

A second spurt in the membership of the Black Panther Party came following the April 1, 1967, slaying of Denzil Dowell, a twenty-two-year-old African American youth of Richmond, California. Neighborhood residents were thoroughly convinced that Dowell was a victim of police murder, and his brother contacted the Panthers to assist in an investigation of the incident. Finding discrepancies in the police account of the incident, the Panthers decided to sponsor a community rally. The aim of this rally was to educate the residents on the necessity of self-defense. The Panthers' investigation led them to the conclusion that Dowell's murder was not an isolated event. Rather, they concluded that there was a pattern of police shootings of Black youth by Richmond police officers.[20] Approximately one hundred and fifty people attended the Panthers' community rally in North Richmond. Seale and Newton made speeches, while twenty other members handled security tasks. Soon afterwards, the Panthers held a second rally and began recruiting prospective members from the community. The brother of Denzil Dowell, George Dowell, was one of these new recruits. Dowell noted that the Panthers made him "feel like they were really interested in the people, and they knew what they were doing."[21] Later, in the same community, the Panthers accompanied a group of Richmond parents on a visit to a junior high school where a teacher had reportedly "beat up and slapped down a couple of black kids in school. "[22]

Chance was also a significant factor in the expansion of the Party. An early key event, which constitutes the third factor in the growth of the BPP, was the recruitment of former prisoner and acclaimed author Eldridge Cleaver. His lengthy involvement with the criminal justice system, level of politicization, and unique personality proved to be a significant influence on the still-developing politics of the Black Panther Party. As an adolescent and young adult, Cleaver was involved in petty theft, drugs, and felonies, including rape and assault. In prison, Cleaver became a Black Muslim, a follower of Malcolm X. He left prison as the famous author of *Soul on Ice,* which instantly gave Cleaver celebrity status. The addition of Cleaver to the Panther organization during its formative stage bolstered the Party's prestige.[23] Cleaver's membership also lent the impression of a Panther monopoly on the Black revolutionary leadership of the period. This perception grew in June 1967, when the Panthers boldly and successfully "drafted" Stokely Carmichael (now Kwame Ture) as their prime minister. H. Rap Brown and James Forman would later join the Party's ranks. The announcement of a "merger" with the Student Nonviolent Coordinating Committee (SNCC) and of joint activities with the Detroit-based League of Revolutionary Black Workers (LRBW) further cemented the impression that the African American revolutionary left was uniting under the banner of the Black Panther Party.[24]

However, John Watson, a former leader of the League of Revolutionary Black Workers and editor of its organ *The Inner City Voice,* indicated that his organization was always conscious of its differences with the Panthers. The League's focus on the potential and key role of the African American working class clashed with the Panthers' emphasis on the lumpen. Watson indicated that the League took steps to prevent the emergence of a strong Panther branch in Detroit by organizing the initial local Panther branch themselves. Geschwender writes in his study on the League that "the degree to which the League was successful in this attempt may be seen in the April

24, 1969 statement by Panther Chief of Staff David Hilliard that the majority of DRUM (Dodge Revolutionary Union Movement) and FRUM (Ford Revolutionary Union Movement) members were Panthers."[25] The early Black Panther chapter in Detroit was involved in supporting the activities of these factory-based organizations. The succeeding Black Panther organization in Detroit subsequently clashed with the League of Revolutionary Black Workers over a range of different issues.[26] Eventually, these heated confrontations put an end to the cooperation and joint activities of the two organizations.

A fourth catalyst in the growth of the Black Panther Party was the May 2, 1967, Panther "invasion" of the California State Assembly during the debate on the Mulford bill, pending legislation that banned the carrying of loaded firearms in incorporated areas of the state. An armed delegation of Panther "lobbyists" descended on the state capital to protest the pending legislation. The publicity from this event gave the Black Panther Party international exposure.[27] The shoot-out involving Huey Newton and two Oakland police officers on October 28, 1967 constitutes the fifth formative event in the rapid growth and development of the BPP. Newton was stopped by officer John Frey, who carried a list of license plate numbers of Panther-owned vehicles. Newton and officer Herbert Heanes were seriously wounded, while Frey was slain. Although Newton was found innocent of assault charges related to the Heanes shooting, he was convicted on charges of voluntary manslaughter for the death of officer Frey.[28] A news photo showing a seriously wounded Huey Newton stretched over a hospital cot once again gave the Black Panthers national publicity.[29] The significance of this incident stems largely from the importance the Panthers placed on securing Newton's release from jail. This objective immediately forced the organization to make pivotal decisions: to ally with the White liberal Peace and Freedom Party, to hire Charles Garry, and to build broad coalitions with less radical Black political formations. Through the Free Huey campaign, the Panthers became a national organization. Free Huey rallies were held in all parts of the country. Even internationally, the existence of the Black Panther Party became known. Free Huey rallies were held in France, Germany, Sweden, as well as in Dar Es Salaam, Tanzania.[30] The Panthers pushed this process at every opportunity. On July 24, 1968, they delivered a portfolio of information on the case to the Cuban mission and vowed to inform all United Nations members about the status of Huey Newton's trial. The Panthers also inquired about the possibility of obtaining non-governmental status in the world body.[31]

National publicity about the Black Panther Party stimulated new interest in the organization. Almost independent of the leadership's capacity for effective outreach, the organization grew nationally by leaps and bounds. Driven by a hunger on the part of hundreds of thousands of young African Americans to contribute to an uncompromising organization committed to social justice, hundreds of individuals flocked to the Party. Organizational growth was in tandem with the enhanced administrative skills of the Party's leadership. For example, during this period Hilliard's responsibilities grew to include reviewing the weekly reports of some thirty branches, offering advice to national Party units when necessary, overseeing relations with the media, and supervising the production of the Party's newspaper, *The Black Panther*. In addition, Hilliard regularly directed political education classes and other Panther events. In short, his busy schedule bore a great resemblance to that of a CEO of an emerging national firm.[32]

Another critical incident in the Panthers' rise was the April 6, 1968, shoot-out between Party members and the Oakland police. Two days after the assassination of Martin Luther King, Jr., a struggle over tactics emerged between Eldridge Cleaver and David Hilliard. Cleaver was determined to register an armed Panther response to the murder of Dr. King. This would set an example for the whole of Black America as well as demonstrate the Panthers' vanguard role in the revolution. According to Hilliard, Cleaver's plan was to carry a cache of arms from one side of town to the other and, on the way, ambush some police officers. While searching for a police car to assault, Cleaver reportedly felt an irresistible urge to urinate. After he had stepped away from the convoy of Panther cars and into the bushes, a police car spotted Cleaver. A gun battle ensued between the Panthers and the police, which forced Eldridge Cleaver and Bobby Hutton to take shelter in a basement of a home. After Cleaver and Hutton were finally forced to surrender, the police ordered them to run to a squad car. Cleaver could not comply with this order because of a wounded leg, but Hutton was gunned down after following the police request. According to Cleaver, his life was spared only because of the intervention of a crowd of community residents.[33] The publicity generated by this event, notably major articles in *Ramparts* and lesser-known leftist publications, heightened the Panthers' prestige and support nationally. Of course, in between these six key events were countless, daily organizing efforts by members of the Party.

Panther Conception of the Black Community

> When people got a problem they come to the Black Panther Party for help and that's good. Because like Mao says, we are supposed to be ridden down the path of the social revolution and that's for the people.[34]
> — Fred Hampton

The Black Panther Party officially targeted three "levels of oppressors": the "greedy, exploiting, rich, avaricious businessman" who exploited the Black community; "the misleading, lying, tricky, demagogic politician" who played upon the community's woes; and "the atrocious, murdering, brutalizing, intimidating, fascist, pig cops."[35] The Black community that confronted these enemies was perceived as deeply divided into a prosperous Black middle class and an impoverished working class and lumpen proletariat. The latter population was, in Eldridge Cleaver's view, a blend of working class and lumpen individuals. In "On Lumpen Ideology," Cleaver wrote that when "workers become permanently unemployed, displaced by the streamlining of production, they revert back to their basic lumpen condition."[36] From its inception, the Panthers championed the interests of the least prosperous section of the community, and, at times, evinced an hostility toward the Black middle class.

Panther officials saw the role of the African American lumpen proletariat as the vanguard of the more docile working class. Eldridge Cleaver, the most eloquent spokesperson for this view, maintained that Newton provided the "ideology and the methodology for organizing the Black urban lumpen proletariat."[37] No longer would they be "the forgotten people," lying on the bottom but would instead be the "vanguard of the proletariat."[38] The Black Panther Party's definition of the lumpen proletariat, while different from that of the then established Communist and left-wing parties, shares many common elements. While Marx distinguished the lumpen from the poor who received relief from the state, there is, nonetheless, conformity with the other elements of Cleaver's definition:

> The Lumpen proletariat are all those who have no secure relationship or vested interest in the means of production and the institutions of a capitalist society. That part of the "Industrial Reserve army" held perpetually in reserve, who have never worked and never will, who can't find a job; who are unskilled and unfit; who have been displaced by machines, automation, and cybernation, and were never retrained or invested with new skills; all those on Welfare or receiving State Aid.
>
> Also the so-called "Criminal Element," those who live by their wits, existing off that which they rip off, who stick guns in the faces of businessmen and say "stick em up" or "give it up!" Those who don't even want to work and can't relate to punching some pig's time clock, who would rather punch a pig in the mouth and rob him than punch that same pig's time clock and work for him, those whom Huey P. Newton calls "the illegitimate capitalists." In short, all those who simply have been locked out of the economy and robbed of their rightful social heritage.[39]

Kathleen Cleaver concurs that the lumpen have an unstable relationship to the labor market with jobs that are "irregular and usually lowly paid—with the exception of criminal activities."[40] Contrary to much of orthodox Marxist theory, the Black Panther Party theoreticians viewed the line separating the Black proletariat from the class of the Black lumpen proletariat as a tenuous and fragile one that often resulted in a blending of the two classes.

Notwithstanding disagreements over the precise location of the Black lumpen in the context of the United States class system, Panther strategists followed the lead of Huey P. Newton who saw the Black lumpen as the potential leading revolutionary force within the African American community. The fearlessness exhibited by the "brothers off the block" made them attractive recruits for the Panther style of revolutionary politics. Newton reasoned that if the courageous brothers off the block were politically organized around revolutionary principles then the Black lumpen could play an invaluable role in the liberation struggle. According to Seale,

> Huey wanted brothers off the block—brothers who had been out there robbing banks, brothers who had been pimping, brothers who had been peddling dope, brothers who ain't gonna take nothing, brothers who had been fighting pigs—because he knew that once they get themselves together in the area of political education (and it doesn't take much because the political education is the ten-point platform and program), Huey P. Newton knew that once you organize the brothers he ran with, he fought with, he fought against, who he fought harder than they fought him, once you organize those brothers, you get niggers, you get black men, you get revolutionaries who are too much.[41]

On the other hand, scholars and activists alike have been pessimistic about the revolutionary potential of the lumpen class. Specifically, they argue that individuals of the lumpen class are unsuitable for the rigors of revolutionary action because this sector not only tends to lack loyalty and discipline, but is also prone to the use of intimidation and violence when resolving disputes.[42] Epstein, for example, finds "grounds for caution, if not, pessimism, about the potential of the urban 'non-working class.'"[43] Nevertheless, the Party's theoreticians did not heed this warning. Instead, Panther leaders emphasized the revolutionary potential of the Black lumpen as a whole without giving adequate attention to the dangerous tendencies of various sectors within this class. This crucial oversight would prove detrimental for Party fortunes.

Panther Power: From the Barrel of the Gun

Central to the goal of achieving political power was the Black Panther insistence that millions of African Americans take up arms. Huey P. Newton's call for African Americans to "pick up the gun" had its immediate roots in the ideology of Malcolm X, pervasive nationwide police brutality, the experience of the Southern Civil Rights movement, and worldwide decolonization movements. The key role of the doctrine of self-defense was stressed by Newton in the Party's first position paper "In Defense of Self-Defense Executive Mandate Number One":

> Black people have begged, prayed, petitioned, demonstrated and everything else to get the racist power structure of America to right the wrongs which have historically been perpetrated against Black people. All of these efforts have been answered by more repression, deceit, and hypocrisy. As the aggression of the racist American government escalates in Vietnam, the police agencies of America escalate the repression of Black people throughout the ghettoes of America. Vicious police dogs, cattle prods and increased patrols have become familiar sights in Black communities. City Hall turns a deaf ear to the pleas of Black people for relief from this increasing terror. The Black

Panther Party for Self-Defense believes that the time has come for
Black people to arm themselves against the terror before it is too late.[44]

In response to a rash of police raids on Panther dwellings, an imprisoned
Huey Newton issued "Executive Mandate No. 3" on March 1, 1968. This
mandate was an internal Panther directive that reinforced the Party's commitment to armed self-defense:

> We draw the line at the threshold of our doors. It is therefore mandated
> as a general order to all members of the Black Panther Party for
> Self-Defense that all members must acquire the technical equipment to
> defend their homes and their dependents and shall do so.[45]

The penalty for violating this mandate was expulsion from the
organization.

Early in 1969 in his essay the "Functional Definition of Politics," Newton
described the Panthers' view of politics as "war without bloodshed" and war
as "politics with bloodshed." For the masses of impoverished and struggling
African Americans Newton maintained that armed self-defense was critical
to the empowerment of Black people. Newton wrote, "Black people can develop self-defense power by arming themselves from house to house, block
to block, community to community, throughout the nation."[46] As in many
aspects of Black Panther ideology, the examples of protracted conflicts with
underdeveloped nations figured heavily in the molding of its position. This
particular concept would appear to have drawn inspiration from the Cuban
Committees for the Defense of the Revolution, the Chinese militia, and the
Vietnamese National Liberation Front (NLF). On more than one occasion
Newton argued that there "is a great similarity between the occupying army
in Southeast Asia and the occupation of our communities by the racist police."[47] The Party's firm demand that the "racist dog policeman must withdraw from our communities or face the wrath of an armed people" is
analogous with "the NLF's and North Vietnamese demands for the immediate withdrawal of U.S. troops from their nation."[48]

In his *Sechaba* interview, Newton indicated the Panthers' ideological debt
to Third World revolutionary movements:

> I think that not only Fidel and Ché, Ho Chi Minh and Mao and Kim IL
> Sung but also all the guerrilla bands that have been operating in
> Mozambique and Angola, and the Palestinian guerrillas who are
> fighting for a socialist world. I think they all have been a great
> inspiration for the Black Panther Party.[49]

The Cuban revolution, as interpreted by Ché Guevara and Regis Debray's
influential *Revolution in the Revolution?*, was an important influence on the
Panthers. In an interview with a New Left paper, *The Movement,* Newton
described the guerrilla fighter as "a very unique man," thus contrasting his
views with those of "Marxist-Leninist orthodox theories." Echoing Debray,
Newton maintained that the political Party should be in control of the mili-

tary arm of the organization. In other words, the guerrilla combined political and military roles. "Debray says 'poor the pen without the guns, poor the gun without the pen,'" asserted Newton. The ideal Panther was to be a "guerrilla" who "is the military commander and the political theoretician all in one."[50]

The Black Panther Party stressed the sacrifice of one's life for the future of the Black masses. Newton's unusual concept of "revolutionary suicide" is a marriage of a sense of dignity and need to sacrifice for the common good. Shortly after Newton's release from prison in 1970 in a speech at Boston College, he elaborated upon this concept. Reflecting upon the perpetual state of siege inflicted by the federal government's relentless attacks, Newton tied the concept of revolutionary suicide to the question of organizational self-defense. Declaring that the Black Panther Party would not tolerate the destruction of Black people, Newton saw it as tantamount to "reactionary suicide" if the Panthers remained passive in the face of fascist attacks upon the Party. He declared, "[W]e will not die the death of the Jews in Germany. We would rather die the death of the Jews in Warsaw" and "where there is courage, where there is self-respect and dignity, there is a possibility that they could emerge victorious."[51] Revolutionary suicide meant that the Panthers would not be repressed easily. One *Black Panther* article authored by New York State prisoners of the Jonathan P. Jackson Commune lauded those qualities that make the new man, the revolutionary guerrilla fighter: "love, devotion, and dedication to the people and the ideals of revolution."[52]

One important reason for Panther endorsement of armed struggle was the contention that the United States was on the brink of transformation into a fascist society. The Party made the following prediction:

> As the struggle intensifies, and reaches toward higher levels, the power structure responds with increased levels of repression; insanely murderous violence, and terror, in futile attempts to intimidate or destroy all opposition to its inhuman system. As each day passes, we must cope with more killings and frame ups; more maniacs with license to kill us at will; more pigs, more busts, more laws—a slow, but sure and purposeful trend toward the establishment of an open fascist dictatorship led by the Nixons, Agnews, Mitchells and Hoovers, and avidly encouraged by the avaricious, power-mad, super-rich hogs of Babylon—Rockefeller, DuPonts, Hunts, Gettys, Mellons, Kennedys, and Company.[53]

George Jackson maintained in his "Tribute to Three Slain Brothers" that the United States "brought fascism to its highest arrangement." He contends that the sophistication of the United States' brand of fascism is based on its subtlety. It already existed as reflected in an "immediate and violent response to all truly revolutionary threats" involving scores of distinct police agencies.[54] Yet, those advocating picking up the gun, as the BPP did, put themselves at risk when the membership is prone to undisciplined behavior. Bobby Seale complained,

> In the early days of the Party, we had to try a number of times to show brothers that they were breaking rules, and eventually tell them that they were no longer members of the Party and that they didn't represent the Party anymore.[55]

This discipline problem was compounded when ". . .brothers identified only with the gun."[56] Seale identified this element of the Party as "jackanapes." According to Seale, the jackanape "centers things only around himself; he's still selfish. He thinks his pot and wine are above the Party. He thinks his gun is something that he can use at will to rip off stuff for himself."[57] Individuals from the street element of the lumpen stratum demonstrated a greater likelihood to engage is such behavior. For example, William Brent, a prison associate of Eldridge Cleaver, robbed a gas station in broad daylight while traveling in the Party's newspaper van and was expelled from the Party.[58]

Alliances of the Black Panther Party

The Marxist–Leninist-tinted lenses of the Black Panther Party led it to support revolutionary alliances with progressive and working-class Whites, non-White ethnic groups, radical women, and others who would follow their leadership as the vanguard party. The Black Panther Party's official position on Whites, as a race, differed profoundly, in theory, from their cultural nationalist rivals. Without minimizing the extent of racism in American society, the Party did not view the White community, unlike their Black power counterparts, as a monolith of hard-core racism. This analysis of the fabric of racism allowed the Panthers more strategic and tactical flexibility regarding building alliances and coalitions with Whites. While recognizing that impoverished Whites often displayed the most extreme racial prejudices, the Party felt secure enough to plan alliances with poor Whites in American cities and in regions such as Appalachia. In Chicago, they encouraged the growth of the Young Patriots Party, a Panther-inspired organization of second-generation, displaced Appalachian youth. Overall, they were optimistic that White racism could be eradicated under socialist conditions. Consistent with their Marxist outlook, the Panthers argued that the White bourgeoisie had a material interest in the perpetuation of racism, but that the White working class had a self-interest in combating it. Newton once said, "We don't hate white people; we hate the oppressor. And if the oppressor happens to be white then we hate him."[59]

This sense of solidarity, consistent with Marxist–Leninist internationalism, was extended to the young "white revolutionaries who are sincere in attempting to realign themselves with mankind, and to make a reality out of the high moral standards that their fathers and forefathers only expressed."[60] In an essay from prison, Black Panther Ericka Huggins illustrated the universalism of Panther rhetoric: "Change, destroy and rebuild. It is time for us to build a world free of selfishness, racism, narrow nationalism and the desire of any group of people to claim this world as their own. The universe belongs to the people—to live to create—for each other."[61] Consequently, as a Black revolutionary organization, the Black Panther Party was the most notable militant and revolutionary Black organization that actively sought alliances with White allies. The Panthers were officially optimistic with regard to the eventual elimination of White racism and believed in racial equality. However, the lumpen modus operandi often adversely impacted the Panthers' relationships with its White allies. Clearly, the personal and organizational behavior of the White organizations contributed to such conflict, yet, even by the Panthers' own admission, the Party was not always truly willing to cooperate on an equal basis with their White allies. Moreover, these functional coalitions were often undergirded by a heavy-handed intimidating style characteristic of the lumpen sector.

The most important early biracial alliance of the Black Panther Party was with the Peace and Freedom Party. The Panther motive for seeking the alliance was a burning thirst for resources, both to build the organization and to defend Huey P. Newton. On one occasion, Bobby Seale frankly recalled the heavy-handed tactic the Panthers used to obtain money from the Peace and Freedom Party. He remembered that members of the Peace and Freedom Party initially refused and claimed that they did not have any money. Cleaver and Seale called them "liars" at that point, and later asked them, "Are you cats going to be racists and jiving around and go back on your word, or are you cats going to be able to go out and hustle that money?"[62] Seale admits that he used anger and rejection of White liberals as a tactic, one that Cleaver also utilized to receive the money.[63]

Other examples of intimidation, characteristic of lumpen behavior, include the aftermath of a conference in Montreal, at which the Panthers boldly asserted that they had "dominated" the event.[64] Also, during a late-1968 Young Socialist Alliance national conference, a Panther representative abruptly denounced the group and called an African American leader of the organization a "clown" for requesting that the Panther wind down his speech.[65] Finally, at the Black Panther-sponsored United Front Against Fascism Conference in Oakland on July 18–20, 1969, the Weathermen faction of the Students for a Democratic Society disagreed with the Panther demand for community control of the police in White areas on grounds that it would "undermine the fight against White supremacy."[66] This mild disagreement infuriated the Panthers who denounced the group:

> SDS had better get their politics straight because the Black Panther Party is drawing some very clear lines between friends and enemies. And that we're gonna make it very clear that we're not going to be attacked from any of those motherfu—kers . . . We'll beat those little sissies, those little schoolboys' ass if they don't straighten up their politics. So we want to make it known to SDS and the first person

motherf—ker that gets out of order better stand in line for some kind of disciplinary actions from the Black Panther Party.[67]

As Kirkpatrick Sale observed, this "was not exactly the kind of fraternalism SDS thought it had been establishing with the Panthers."[68] Julius Lester, a well-known African American intellectual activist of the period who was also a past recipient of Panther verbal abuse remarked, "The contempt shown SDS in this instance cannot be said to exemplify the conduct and attitudes one has a right to expect (and demand) from anyone claiming to be revolutionary."[69]

The Party's most notable effort to forge a racial alliance was with the Student Nonviolent Coordinating Committee. Despite the fact that the Panthers were able to work with individual SNCC leaders for a period, including H. Rap Brown, Stokely Carmichael, and James Forman, the two organizational structures never formally merged. Other SNCC members also achieved prominence as Panther leaders, including the charismatic Don Cox or "DC" and Carver "Chico" Neblett, who were both field marshals in rank.[70] Many factors accounted for Panther–SNCC difficulties—radically different organizational histories, demographically contrasting constituencies, divergent ideological perspectives, and different leadership styles—all undoubtedly contributed to the conflict between the two groups. For example, Lester reports that following a June 1968 SNCC meeting, the organization "reaffirmed its independence from the Black Panther Party by voting not to adopt the Panther ten-point program as its own;" they saw it as "reformist" not revolutionary."[71] Moreover, the intimidation tendency akin to the lumpen modus operandi played a significant role. Although James Forman denied that he was tortured by the Panthers, as several accounts allege, he did state that he refused to work "in an organization where I felt my personal security and safety were threatened by internal elements."[72] Stokely Carmichael, who was drafted into the Black Panther Party in June 1967, resigned from the Panther organization by letter in August 1968. His letter read, "I cannot support the present tactics and methods which the Party is using to coerce and force everyone to submit to its authority."[73] Intimidation replaced a principled basis of a relationship founded on mutual respect within these alliances. Inevitably, the effect was negative and corrosive for both parties. For some Whites, it led to "flunkeyist" attitudes and, no doubt, their ultimate disillusionment as activists sympathetic to the African American cause of social justice. For African Americans, the Panther "gorilla" tactics at times precluded the united front necessary to wage effective opposition to racial oppression.

"The Other Half": Women and the Black Panther Party

Consistent with socialist tradition, the Black Panther Party theoretically upheld the equality of women in all spheres of life. Yet the evidence indicates that this philosophical principle was also adversely impacted by lumpen behavior. Formally, the Black Panther Party position contrasted sharply with that of their ideological opponents—the cultural nationalists—who held that women were unfit for overall leadership and should be restricted to supportive and subordinate roles. The Black Panthers were vehement in their rejection of the cultural nationalists' conservative position on women. Fred Hampton once described their differences with the Los Angeles-based Us on this question:

> You think we scared of a few karangatangs, a few chumps, a few male chauvinists? They tell their women, "Walk behind me." The only reason a woman should walk behind a faggot like that is so she can put a foot knee-deep in his ass.[74]

Although the experiences of female comrades and the practice of gender equality in the Party were uneven and varied, the Black Panther Party surpassed the tepid commitment to gender-neutral organization exhibited by the other radical and mainstream (Black and White) organizations of the period. Women such as Elaine Brown, Ericka Huggins, Kathleen Cleaver, and Joan Bird were all prominent members of the Black Panther Party. Indeed, Elaine Brown was the leader of the Party from 1974–77 following its demise as a national political formation. Members of the Black Panther Party sought to eradicate gender-based roles and leadership rank. Seale explains,

> So we have to progress to a level of socialism to solve these problems. We have to *live* socialism. So where there's a Panther house, we try to live it. When there's cooking to be done, both brothers and sisters cook. Both wash the dishes. The sisters don't just serve and wait on the brothers. A lot of black nationalist organizations have the idea of regulating women to the role of serving their men, and they relate this to black manhood. But a real manhood is based on humanism, and it's not based on *any* form of oppression.[75]

Nevertheless, the Party, for the most part, fell short of this goal. A contributing factor to its failure to establish a gender-neutral organization was the prominence of values and behavior more closely aligned with the hustler element of the lumpen class. The issue of gender equality within the organization was an ongoing struggle throughout the existence of the Party. For example, Roberta Alexander's speech at the Panther-sponsored United Front Against Fascism Conference noted the controversy over women's role in the organization. She said that the battles within the Party over women's equality had run "the whole gamut" of possible problems, the issues involving whether women could use arms as well as men, whether they were confined to office work, and whether men deserve sex because of their revolutionary activity. Unequivocally, Alexander declared that African American women are "oppressed by black men and that's got to go."[76] Kathleen Cleaver also felt that suggestions from women received less consideration despite the key logistical role undertaken by women since the early days of the Party.[77]

June Culberson's May 1969 essay, "The Role of the Revolutionary Woman" stresses that Panther women rejected the "Pantherettes" designation and demanded to be called Panthers like their male comrades.[78] Yet, ironically, the essay, uncompromising in its demand for equal rights for women within the organization, cites Eldridge Cleaver's *Soul on Ice*, which includes the author's account of raping Black women to prepare for the eventual rape of White women, as support for her position. Culberson wrote that many of the male Panthers "still haven't had an understanding" of Cleaver's book because "they are still trying to hang the women up by their own feelings of inferiority."[79]

Also instructive is an article which appeared in *The Black Panther* celebrating a lumpen lifestyle based on the exploitation of women. Al Carroll's article, "On Illegitimate Capitalist [sic] 'The Game'" praises the attributes and contributions of "pimps and whores" to the African American freedom movement. This endorsement of a purely lumpen lifestyle demonstrated the unstable, mutually contradictory political practice of the Panthers. Carroll wrote,

> Historically speaking pimps played a major role in the colony during a depression. . . .Here is a person (some might disagree, mainly the sisters) . . . that had what a lot of people didn't have. Pimps and whores have always been of some constructive help or use in the colony. I've known them to buy groceries for mothers and their children.[80]

Carroll regarded pimping as a necessary means of survival for African Americans. He explains that when a "sister dug on a brother," if "that particular sister wanted to continue her relationship with this brother," certain acts followed:

> In other words she had to get this blood's particular type of theory so she could start implementing it or putting it into practice. This process is called "Turning-out"...a change from the old to the new way of survival...If that was the way Black men had to do it to survive and be recognized [as] men then I would say that was a good thing and not a bad thing.[81]

While this article is quite unusual in its blatant sexism and explicit justification for exploitative practices, the reality of its inclusion in *The Black Panther* indicates the range of tolerance for the practices and lifestyles of the Black lumpen class.

This tolerance was also exemplified by the infamous pussy power slogan popularized by Party members. In a speech at Stanford, Cleaver, in remarks specifically directed to "the ladies," reminded the women of the seriousness of the situation and then called for "pussy power." Apologizing to "the Victorians who have had their morals ruffled," he posits both a "revolutionary" and a "counterrevolutionary" form of sex. Advising women to tell their male mates "that they're going to have to become part of the solution or don't call you up on the telephone anymore...Tell them to go away...You can put them under more pressure than I can with speeches. You can cut off their sugar"[82]

Male–female relationships in the lumpen culture are undergirded by a lack of respect. The significance of the reality and legend of the Black pimp, for instance, is a good example of the material factor anchoring sexism within the male-dominated lumpen sociocultural milieu. Unfortunately, lumpen values impacted gender dynamics in the Party, particularly during its formative years.

Lumpenism and Political Repression

Lumpen behavior also made the organization susceptible to government repression. The Black Panther attitude and practice with respect to violence stand out in their uniqueness from all preceding organizations in African American history. On the one hand, the Panthers announced that they opposed spontaneous violence, including rioting, and called for disciplined tactical use of violence within the framework of a long-term strategy. However, in reality, as evidenced by their own documents, the Black Panther Party, generally indirectly, encouraged spontaneous violence against representatives of the government, especially the police.

Imprisoned Panther George Jackson held that "any serious organizing of people must carry with it from the start a potential threat of revolutionary violence."[83] The assumption that a massive and sustained armed uprising on the part of African Americans would be necessary to realize their deeply rooted desires was taken seriously. For example, in *The Black Panther*, Field Marshall Don Cox occasionally contributed a column on guerrilla strategy and tactics. In one issue, he discussed the problems associated with the spontaneous formation of guerrilla units. Pointing out common errors, Cox wrote that all too often "much attention is given to a plan up to the point of execution without giving the same attention to evasion and escape."[84]

The Party's newspaper also occasionally printed instructions on how to make homemade weapons and bombs. In January 1971, the paper reprinted Scanlan's "Guerrilla Acts of Sabotage and Terrorism in the United States, 1965–1970," which blurred the lines between political violence and sheer acts of vandalism.[85] Eldridge Cleaver once gave an example of the type of information revolutionaries need to know: "Simple little things like the fact that all the lights should be broken out in Babylon [Cleaver's term for the United States]."[86] On many other occasions, throughout their existence as an organization, the Panthers seemed to reduce politics entirely to a question of military action. Shortly before his assassination, Fred Hampton of the Chicago branch, said in reference to the police, "If you kill a few, you get a little satisfaction. But when you kill them ALL you get complete satisfaction."[87]

The early decision to target the lumpen for both recruitment and as a model for behavior set the stage for the later problems the Black Panther

Party experienced with maintaining organizational discipline. Black Panther leaders openly acknowledged that there was a problem with Party discipline—more so in some chapters than others. David Hilliard, for instance, noted "one of Los Angeles's problems is discipline."[88] John Seale recalled "A lot of people came into the Party brought a lot of violence with them."[89]

On repeated occasions, the Panthers found themselves embroiled in armed conflict with the police because of the spontaneous actions of their members. Long-time Panther leader David Hilliard notes several incidents when Panthers initiated violence on a whim. Once Hilliard himself recalls an incident on New Year's Eve when, after guzzling a large amount of alcohol at his sister B.B.'s house, Hilliard decided to "carry out a guerrilla action" by firing on a police car with his pistol. The incident startled Bobby Seale, who stood next to Hilliard. Since it occurred so quickly, Seale did not have a chance to discourage Hilliard from committing the act. While Hilliard's shot missed, incidents such as this presented the government ample opportunities to exploit the Panthers in the effort to dismantle their Panther organization.[90]

While the Party adopted a formal structure of rules and internal regulations consisting of twenty-six rules, eight "points of attention," and three main rules of discipline to combat such problems. However, with its rapid rush to national fame characterized by the spontaneous formation of chapters across the nation, the BPP rules were often ignored.[91] Consequently, the Panthers relied on physical coercion to ensure discipline among the membership. The daily practice of chapters reflected great attention to "discipline," which tended to entail some form of violence. Rice's description of the Chicago Black Panther Party illustrated this observation:

> Discipline was applied democratically. Every member shared work and responsibilities...Being late for a meeting meant a slap in your face or a kick in the ass, depending on your sex. The Minister of Labor...got slapped once for being late, and according to her it worked. A slap in the face, or a kick in the ass made the Illinois Party the most effective, most dependable organization she has ever worked for before or since.[92]

During the formative years, the BPP also instituted a tactic called mudholing—"putting the victim in the center and stomping him down" to ensure discipline.[93] The lumpen model of behavior contributed to a persistent problem of the inflammatory and exaggerated rhetoric of the Panthers. Such rhetoric needlessly alienated people from the Party and left it dangerously vulnerable to attack from the government. While it is true this malady afflicted many left-wing and Black power organizations during this period, it reached new levels with the Black Panther Party. David Hilliard, for example, unraveled during perhaps the most important speech of his political life. During the height of the FBI–police collusion to destroy the Black Panther Party, Hilliard had an opportunity to favorably influence the huge crowd assembled at the San Francisco Moratorium demonstration against the war in Vietnam. After assailing the presence of so many American flags in the crowd and praising Ho Chi Minh, Hilliard concluded his brief presentation by saying,

> We say down with the American fascist society. Later for Richard Milhous Nixon, the motherf—er. Later for all the pigs of the power structure. Later for all the people out here that don't want to hear me curse because that's all I know how to do. That's all that I'm going to do. I'm not ever going to stop cursing, not only are we going to curse, we're going to put it into practice some of the shit that we talk about. Because Richard Nixon is an evil man.[94]

Denouncing President Nixon for sending federal agents to destroy the Black Panther Party Breakfast for Children Program, Hilliard's anger at the president builds to the point where he finally says, "F—k that motherf—king man. We will kill Richard Nixon. We will kill any motherf—er that stands in the way of our freedom."[95] Not only was an opportunity to gain valuable political support to ward off repression from the government squandered, the Panthers' adversaries used this statement to launch new attacks upon the Party. Shortly after the speech, Hilliard was indicted by a federal grand jury for threatening to kill the President of the United States.

Eldridge Cleaver was largely responsible for lending credibility to the notion of a lumpen political party in Black America. His ability to engage in counterproductive and wild political rhetoric was on a world-class level. During one interview, Cleaver was asked why he used the term *Babylon*. After explaining that it signified a decadent society and that the term originated in the Bible, he suddenly blurted out, "F—k the Bible."[96] On another occasion, Cleaver said that had he been elected president in 1968, he would not have "entered the White House but I would have burned it down and turned it into a museum of a monument to the decadence of the past."[97] Despite the popularity of such rhetoric among sections of the left, it alienated many African Americans.

In 1969, FBI Director J. Edgar Hoover deemed the Black Panther Party the chief security threat to the security of the nation. After the Party was declared a threat to "national security," it marked a turning point in the government's effort to destroy the Panthers. Thereafter, the government allowed the more extensive use of wiretaps and bugging without court approval. Special units and squads were established in cities where the Panthers operated. FBI offices across the country were instructed to disrupt and neutralize the Black Panther Party.[98] Undoubtedly, the undisciplined behavior of various lumpen members enhanced the FBI's ability to disrupt Party activities. FBI actions inflicted considerable damage to the already unstable infrastructure of the BPP.

Conclusions: The Lumpen and the Decline of the Party

The population of African American lumpen has dramatically expanded since the Reagan-era cutbacks of social programs, the economic recession of the early 1980s, the progressive deterioration of Rust Belt industries, and the increase in crack cocaine abuse. Given the continued social, economic, and political frustrations of African Americans, the temptation of movement organizers and activists to look to the lumpen as a source of power and resources will continue to be attractive. However, the experience of the Black Panther Party strongly suggests that its survival, development, and institutionalization were undermined by the ascendancy of the criminal element of the lumpen in the Party. The reckless, erratic, and often violent behavior associated with this sector served to alienate many people from the organization, chronically destabilize it, and render it more vulnerable to the FBI–police onslaught.

To be sure, the Black Panther Party was nothing like the type of criminal or quasi-criminal organization that some have depicted. Rather, the Panthers' legacy is that of a Black political group that relied on recruiting a social element that existed on the fringes of legality for its daily existence. The lumpen element was, however, part of a broad segment of African Americans attracted to the BPP. Indeed, college students, persons from middleclass backgrounds, working people, and individuals from marginal working and lumpen backgrounds all flocked to the Party's banner of serving and defending the Black community.

Nevertheless, the influence of that segment closely aligned with the criminal element created a crisis, one that would contribute to the demise of the organization. One important lesson gleaned from the experience of the Black Panther Party is that organizations that seek to focus their recruitment on the lumpen should have effective mechanisms to reform new members. The Nation of Islam, for example, recruits heavily from prisons, but stresses personal transformation with much apparent success. By promoting the personalities and lifestyles of the lumpen, the Black Panther Party contributed to its own demise. Clearly, one of the basic functions of the military and police apparatus of the state is to thwart challenges to the existing economic and political order. In the case of the Black Panther Party, the task of the state was eased by the organization's endemic instability. At times not only did the underlying lack of discipline undermine the morale of the organization, but it also made the calculated disruptive efforts of informers and undercover agents more effective.

Abandoning its lumpen emphasis would have been necessary for the organization to resume its initial development and growth. Instead, the Black Panther Party, declined as a national political formation by mid-1971. While the Black Panther Party emerged as an important political force in Oakland for a period (1974–1977) before degenerating into a semi-political criminal organization, it would never again attain its past glory. For a brief period, the Black Panther Party offered hope to a generation of youth who realized that, unless fundamentally altered, the American political, economic, and social arrangement would not allow for the full participation of African Americans in the foreseeable future.

The shortcomings and failures of the Black Panthers should not be allowed to overshadow its significant achievements. The heady idealism of the Party's dedication and genuine empowerment of thousands of African Americans should all be remembered. The love of Panthers for their people materialized in survival programs, such as the Breakfast for Children Program and Free Health Clinics, whose success created embarrassment and consternation in establishment circles. Furthermore, any assessment of the achievements of the Black Panther Party is compounded by the difficult task of calculating the indirect impact of the BPP. An incalculable number of agreements to expand Black enrollment, employment, or representation were indirectly facilitated by the actions of the Black Panther Party. Indeed, there is little doubt that the Party raised the level of struggle for African American equality. Ignoring the impact of the Black Panther Party and other Black militant organizations distorts our understanding of radical African American social movements. At its peak, the Panthers' slogan, "All Power to the People," resounded across the globe as a defiant echo of the African American determination to win a meaningful freedom and achieve genuine democracy. Future generations will inevitably build on this sentiment, and hopefully avoid the mistakes of the Black Panther Party.

NOTES

1. Bobby Seale, *A Lonely Rage* (New York: New York Times Book Co., Inc., 1978), 153.

2. Bobby Seale, interview by Ronald Stephens, Philadelphia, 1989, 14.

3. Gene Marine, *The Black Panthers* (New York: Signet Books, 1969), 13.

4. Ibid., 27.

5. Seale, *A Lonely Rage*, 110–111.

6. Ibid., 145.

7. Bobby Seale, *Seize the Time* (Baltimore: Black Classic Press, 1991), 30.

8. Ibid., 33.

9. Ibid., 32.

10. Ibid, 33.

11. Seale, *A Lonely Rage*, 153.

12. Ibid, 154.

13. Ibid., 155; Seale, *Seize the Time*, 74.

14. *The Black Panther*, 1 November 1969, 20.

15. Seale, *Seize the Time*, 65.

16. Huey P. Newton, *Revolutionary Suicide* (New York: Harcourt, Brace and Jovanovich, 1973), 127.

17. See "Rules of the Black Panther Party" in early issues of *The Black Panther* and Appendix C of this volume.

18. Ibid., 126–127.

19. Eldridge Cleaver, *Post-Prison Writings and Speeches* (New York: Ramparts Books, 1969), 35.

20. Marine, *The Black Panthers*, 57–60.

21. Ibid., 60.

22. Ibid.

23. Eldridge Cleaver, *Soul On Ice* (New York: Delta Books, 1968).

24. "SNCC, Panthers Announce Merger,"*Guardian*, 24 February 1968, 1.

25. James A. Geschwender, *Class, Race and Worker Insurgency: The League of Revolutionary Black Workers* (Cambridge: Cambridge University Press, 1977), 142.

26. John Williams, interview by Charles E. Jones, Detroit, MI, 24 July 1993.

27. Marine, *The Black Panthers*, 66.

28. David Hilliard and Lewis Cole, *This Side of Glory: The Autobiography of David Hilliard and the Story of the Black Panther Party* (Boston: Little, Brown, and Company, 1993), 208.

29. Hugh Pearson, *The Shadow of the Panther: Huey Newton and the Price of Black Power in America* (Reading, MA: Addison-Wesley Publishing Company, 1994), 146–7.

30. Edward M. Keating, *Free Huey* (New York: Dell Publishing Co., 1970); Marine, *The Black Panthers*, 185.

31. Marine, *The Black Panthers*, 185.

32. Hilliard and Cole, *This Side of Glory*, 220.

33. Eldridge Cleaver, *Post-Prison Writings*, 89–93.

34. Fred Hampton, "You Can Murder a Liberator, But You Can't Murder Liberation," in *The Black Panthers Speak*, ed. Philip S. Foner (Philadelphia: J.B. Lippincott Company, 1970), 138–144.

35. Ibid.

36. Eldridge Cleaver, "On Lumpen Ideology," Black Scholar 3 (November–December 1972): 9.

37. Eldridge Cleaver, "On the Ideology of the Black Panther Party," (Black Panther Party, San Francisco, pamphlet, 6 June 1970), 7.

38. Ibid.

39. Ibid.

40. Kathleen Cleaver, "On the Vanguard Role of the Black Urban Lumpen proletariat," pamphlet (London: Grass/Roots Publications, 1975).

41. Seale, *Seize the Time*, 64.

42. Clarence J. Munford, "The Fallacy of Lumpen Ideology." *Black Scholar* 4 (July–August 1973): 47–51. Henry Winston, "Crisis of the Black Panther Party," in *Strategy for a Black Agenda*, ed. Henry Winston (New York: International Publishers, 1973), 214.

43. David G. Epstein, "A Revolutionary Lumpen Proletariat? " *Monthly Review* (December 1969): 55.

44. Huey P. Newton, "In Defense of Self-Defense Executive Mandate Number One," in *The Black Panthers Speak*, ed. Philip S. Foner (New York: J.B. Lippincott, 1970; reprint, New York: Da Capo Press, 1995), 40.

45. Huey P. Newton, "Executive Mandate No. 3," *The Black Panther*, 16 March 1968.

46. Huey P. Newton, "Functional Definition of Politics," in *The Black Panthers Speak* ed. Foner, 46.

47. Ibid, 47.

48. Ibid.

49. Huey P. Newton, "Interview with *Sechaba*," *The Black Panther*, 2 January 1971, 2.

50. Huey P. Newton, "Huey Newton Talks to the Movement about the Black Panther Party, Cultural Nationalism, SNCC, Liberals and White Revolutionaries," in *The Black Panthers Speak*, ed. Foner, 60.

51. Huey P. Newton, "Let Us Hold High the Banner of Intercommunalism and the Invincible Thoughts of Huey P. Newton, Minister of Defense and Supreme Commander of the Black Panther Party," *The Black Panther*, 2 January 1971, A–H.

52. "Brothers in the New York State Concentration Camp from the Jonathan P. Jackson Commune," *The Black Panther*, 9 January 1971, 8.

53. "To All Brothers of Misfortune," *The Black Panther*, 16 January 1970, 6.

54. George Jackson, "A Tribute to Three Slain Brothers," *The Black Panther*, 16 January 1970, 9.

55. Seale, *Seize the Time*, 365.

56. Ibid., 368.

57. Ibid, 380–381.

58. See William Lee Brent, *Long Time Gone: A Black Panther's True-Life Story of His Hijacking and Twenty-Five Years in Cuba* (New York: Times Books, 1996).

59. Huey P. Newton, "Huey Newton Talks to the Movement," in *Black Panthers Speak*, ed. Foner, 54.

60. Ibid, 54.

61. Ericka Huggins, "Revolution in Our Lifetime," *The Black Panther*, 9 January 1971, 5.

62. Seale, *Seize the Time*, 213.

63. Ibid.

64. Raymond Lewis, "Montreal: Bobby-Seale-Panthers Take Control" *The Black Panther*, 21 December 1968, 5–6. "Uneasy lies any person who collided with a BLACK PANTHER during the weekend...THE BLACK PANTHER PARTY did not attend the Hemispheric Conference to "End the War in Vietnam" at Montreal. The BLACK PANTHER PARTY dominated it. 'They simply took up and carted around big pieces of the conference with them, admitted a member of the organizing committee.'"

65. An incident personally observed by the author.

66. Kirkpatrick Sale, *SDS* (New York: Vintage Books, 1974), 590.

67. Ibid., 590.

68. Ibid.

69. Ibid., 591.

70. Clayborne Carson, *In Struggle: SNCC and the Black Awakening of the 1960's* (Cambridge: Harvard University Press, 1981), 283.

71. Julius Lester, *Revolutionary Notes* (New York: Grove Press, 1969), 144.

72. Pearson, *The Shadow of the Panther*, 163.

73. Ibid., 164.

74. Fred Hampton, "You Can Kill a Revolutionary But You Can't Kill a Revolution," *The Black Panther*, 16 January 1970, 12.

75. Seale, *Seize the Time*, 403.

76. Roberta Alexander, "UFAF Women's Panel: Roberta Alexander at Conference," The Black Panther, 2 August 1969, 7.

77. Julia Heave, "Black Scholar Interviews Kathleen Cleaver," *Black Scholar* 2 (December 1971): 54–59.

78. June Culberson, "The Role of the Revolutionary Woman," *The Black Panther*, 4 May 1969, 9.

79. Ibid.

80. Al Carroll, "On Illegitimate Capitalist 'The Game,'" *The Black Panther*, 20 June 1970, 7.

81. Ibid.

82. Cleaver, *Post-Prison Writings*, 143.

83. Eric Mann, *Comrade George: An Investigation into the Life, Political Thought and Assassination of George Jackson* (New York: Perennial Library, 1974), 6.

84. Don Cox, "Organizing Self-Defense Groups," *The Black Panther*, 23 January 1971, 6.

85. Dan Scalan, "Guerrilla Acts of Sabotage and Terrorism in the United States, 1965–1970," *The Black Panther*, 2 January 1971, 9.

86. Lee Lockwood, *Conversations with Eldridge Cleaver—Algiers* (New York: Delta Books, 1970), 95.

87. Hampton, "You Can Murder a Liberator," in *The Black Panthers Speak*, ed. Foner, 138–150.

88. Hilliard and Cole, *This Side of Glory*, 234.

89. Ibid.

90. Ibid., 151–152.

91. Alphonso Pinkney, *Red, Black and Green: Black Nationalism in the United States* (New York: Cambridge University Press, 1970), 98.

92. J. T. Rice, *Up on Madison, Down on 75th, Part One*, pamphlet (Evanston, Ill.: The Committee, 1983), 23.

93. Ibid.

94. David Hilliard, "If You Want Peace, You Got to Fight For It," *The Black Panthers Speak*, ed. Foner, 128–130.

95. Ibid.

96. Lockwood, *Conversations with Eldridge Cleaver*, 53.

97. Ibid., 117.

98. See Ward Churchill and Jim Vander Wall, *Agents of Repression: The FBI's Secret Wars Against the Black Panther Party and the American Indian Movement* (Boston: South End Press, 1988); Charles E. Jones, "The Political Repression of the Black Panther Party, 1966–1971: The Case of the Oakland Bay Area," *Journal of Black Studies* 18 (June 1988), 415–434; and Kenneth O'Reilly, *Racial Matters: The FBI's Secret File on Black America, 1960–1972* (New York: The Free Press, 1989).

Chapter Fifteen

The Black Panther Party: State Repression and Political Prisoners

Winston A. Grady-Willis

Political repression has been defined as "government action which grossly discriminates" against individuals and organizations that seek to change the existing political order.[1] The Black Panther Party was the primary target of such repression in the United States for the better part of its existence as a political organization. This essay analyzes the systematic and comprehensive government assault by local, state, and federal police agencies against the Party.[2] Such state activity did not occur within a historical vacuum. It represented the most developed manifestation of decades of repression—intensified in this context by state racism—waged against those activists deemed a threat to the political economy of the United States.

Authorities at the federal, state, and local levels employed a variety of tactics in their assault on the Black Panther Party and other Black political organizations. The tactics included mandating arrests and detention, deployment of informants and agent provocateurs, the use of disinformation, electronic surveillance, and assassinations. The Federal Bureau of Investigation (FBI) was the driving force behind employment of these tactics through both its counterintelligence program and its support of local police agencies.

The FBI and other agencies had specific targets for police action. Black Panther Party activities, such as its free breakfast program, became government targets as were Panther alliances with Black and White political groups alike. Some of the most successful federal counterintelligence measures targeted the Panther leadership itself, including the effort to divide the Central Committee between 1970–71.

State political repression directed against the Black Panther Party severely circumscribed the organization's effectiveness. Revolving arrests and detention distracted Panther activists from community organizing, and repeatedly raising bail depleted Party funds. The most devastating, lasting impact of state political repression, short of death itself, has been the ongoing incarceration of members of the BPP and other radical African American activists of the Black Power Era. Indeed, many of these activists, including Sekou Odinga and Sundiata Acoli, remain incarcerated despite overwhelming evidence of their innocence.

Overview

Political repression in the United States has been complex and often subtle in nature. Historically, repression "American style" has tended to be legalistic, constrained to a degree by certain procedures, and conducted at the federal, state, and local levels.[3] The sophistication of such a repressive apparatus does not make it any more benign, however, especially in relation to African American activists. This point has been confirmed throughout the twentieth century since the conviction and imprisonment of Marcus Garvey, leader of the Universal Negro Improvement Association (UNIA), on mail fraud charges.

Garvey was unaware that John Edgar Hoover, an ambitious young attorney in the Justice Department, had initiated a two-year battle beginning in 1919 to imprison or deport the UNIA leader. Hoover had been particularly distressed by a speech Garvey made that summer at New York City's Carnegie Hall in which the Black leader advocated retaliatory violence in the wake of lynchings in the southern United States. By early 1920, the UNIA had been heavily infiltrated. Agent–informants code named WW, C-C, and *800* submitted regular reports to Hoover. James Wormley Jones was agent '800.' Jones was a former Army captain who became the chief administrative officer of the African Legion, the UNIA's paramilitary unit. Hoover also relied on intelligence gathered from Harlem businessman Herbert Simeon Boulin, another FBI informant. Boulin was a native Jamaican and a friend of Garvey.[4]

After an unsuccessful attempt to stop Garvey from returning to the United States following a fund-raising trip to the Caribbean in 1921, Hoover settled on a scheme to charge the UNIA leader with mail fraud. Aware that the Black Star Line shipping venture was near bankruptcy, federal authorities tried to prove that Garvey had urged his followers to buy stock in the failing operation with the intent to defraud. Although it was obvious that Marcus Garvey did not profit a penny from the entire venture, an all-White jury convicted him of mail fraud on June 21, 1923, in New York City. The United States deported Garvey four years later as an "undesirable alien."[5]

The Bureau of Investigation (BOI), formed in 1906, had established a name for itself by helping to repress the Industrial Workers of the World, anarchists, and various antiwar activists during the World War I period.[6] Aided by the American Protective League, the BOI operated as a "secret political police force" investigating German immigrants and suspected draft resisters. From late 1919 until early 1920, Attorney General A. Mitchell Palmer oversaw the arrest and detention of thousands of White activists in an attempt to deport "subversives." Police departments in larger cities began establishing intelligence units in the years following the Palmer Raids. It was during this time that J. Edgar Hoover rose in the ranks of the BOI and became its director in 1924. Hoover immediately changed the agency's name to the Federal Bureau of Investigation, giving the FBI an added sense of autonomy from the larger Justice Department.[7]

The FBI continued its efforts to stifle radical dissent during the World War II era. Congress aided Bureau activities with the passage of two pivotal laws in 1941. The Alien Registration (Smith) Act made it illegal to advocate the overthrow of the United States government, and the Voorhis Act required "all subversive organizations having foreign links" to be registered with the federal government. As the FBI pressed forward in its efforts to imprison or silence those thought to be Communists, the agency did nothing, however, to disrupt the cozy relationship several U.S. corporations enjoyed with Nazi Germany. Indeed, J. Edgar Hoover and his agents looked the other way when Standard Oil, International Telephone and Telegraph, Chase Bank, and General Motors helped arm and finance Hitler's genocidal war machine.[8]

The Cold War ushered in yet another wave of repression aimed at those suspected of being members of the Communist Party or its sympathizers. For Black radical activists such as scholar W. E. B. DuBois, entertainer Paul Robeson, and politician Ben Davis, Jr., Cold War politics linked racism and anti-Communism. In February 1951, scholar–activist W. E. B. DuBois —ironically, Garvey's principal rival during the 1920s—found himself handcuffed and in court for his activities on behalf of world peace. Authorities indicted him for an unusually overt political offense: "failure to register as an agent of a foreign principle." Gerald Horne, a student of radical movements, has noted that elder DuBois (who was acquitted because of mass public support) could be arrested at all was proof positive that one cannot truly "comprehend the Cold War itself without comprehending its sharp racist edge."[9]

The 1960s witnessed key changes within the state repressive apparatus at both the national and local levels. At the national level, FBI officials realized that "the old-style anti-Communism" of the past decade would draw criticism from the general public. Instead of conducting open witchhunts, the federal government began to rely more on covert operations. The FBI used counterintelligence measures in the electoral campaigns of socialists, such as Judy White who ran for governor of New York in 1966 and Paul Boutelle who was a candidate in the 1969 mayoral race in New York City.[10]

At the local level, the Law Enforcement Intelligence Unit, initiated in the late 1950s and early 1960s, established a network in which over one hundred fifty local and state police agencies shared information obtained on a number of activists. In a separate, yet related development, the Law Enforcement Assistance Act spurred the further militarization of local police agencies. Departments acquired assault rifles, personnel carriers, and other military technology, partly in response to the growing number of protests and rebellions in Harlem (1964), Watts (1965), Detroit (1967), and a number of other African American urban communities.[11]

In 1960, FBI Director J. Edgar Hoover decided to expand the scope of the Bureau's counterintelligence operations against "subversives" to include *independistas*, activists in the Puerto Rican independence movement. Three years after the initiative against the *independistas,* Hoover ordered that Martin Luther King, Jr. become the object of government surveillance. Hoover launched the campaign to discredit the civil rights leader shortly after King's historic "I Have a Dream" speech in 1963. The Bureau sought to expose King's "association" with alleged "known Communists," such as advisers Jack O'Dell and Stanley Levinson. The Bureau also monitored intimate details of the SCLC leader's personal life. Although Levinson's working relationship with King survived the Bureau's campaign, O'Dell resigned.[12] At one point, the Bureau launched a concerted but unsuccessful effort to drive Martin Luther King, Jr., to commit suicide. King remarked, "They are out to get me, harass me, break my spirit."[13]

In August 1967, after four years of eavesdropping on the life of Martin Luther King, Jr., J. Edgar Hoover expanded FBI operations to include Black protest groups. This counterintelligence initiative, commonly referred to as COINTELPRO, sought to disrupt and "neutralize" a number of "Black Nationalist Hate Groups." He intended to prevent:

> 1. the formation of a Black political front, 2. "rise of a messiah," 3. violence directed at the state, 4. the gaining of movement credibility, 5. and long-range growth of organizations, especially among young people.[14]

Organizations targeted included the Southern Christian Leadership Conference, Student Nonviolent Coordinating Committee, Revolutionary Action Movement, and the Nation of Islam. Ironically, the Black Panther Party was not one of the groups targeted in the 1967 directive.

Despite the rapid ascendancy of the Black Panther Party, J. Edgar Hoover did not add the organization to the COINTELPRO hit list until the fall of 1968. The FBI director made up for lost time, however, when he declared that the Party was "the greatest threat to the internal security of the country."[15] Former Panther activist Dhoruba Bin Wahad asserted that the FBI's counterintelligence program "was in effect a domestic war program, a program aimed at countering the rise of Black militancy, Black independent political thought."[16] By the summer of 1969 the Black Panthers had become the central focus of COINTELPRO and eventually became the target of 233 out of 295 total counterintelligence operations directed at African American political groups.[17]

One of the tactics used most by police agencies at all levels in their domestic war against Black Panthers and other African American activists was arrest (often through raids) and detention. In a March 4, 1968 memorandum,

J. Edgar Hoover informed the special agent in charge of the FBI's Albany, New York office about the success the Philadelphia office had in encouraging the local police to move on the Revolutionary Action Movement (RAM). RAM was a clandestine Black radical group that had been formed in the years prior to the assassination of one of its earliest members, Malcolm X. "[RAM members] were arrested on every possible charge until they could no longer make bail. As a result, RAM leaders spent most of the summer in jail."[18]

Police treatment of Party Chairman Bobby Seale was but one example of how police agencies utilized arrest and imprisonment. One month before Hoover sent the memorandum to the Albany FBI office, Oakland police raided the home of Bobby and Artie Seale, ostensibly arresting them for possession of a sawed-off shotgun. As it turned out, police found neither person's fingerprints on the weapon. A likely objective of this arrest was to drain Party resources. In August 1969, police arrested Seale on conspiracy to riot charges following the turbulent Democratic National Convention in Chicago. Immediately after Seale posted bail for the Chicago charge, authorities rearrested him and charged him with conspiracy to commit the murder of New Haven Panther Alex Rackley.[19]

In addition to arrest and detention, police agencies used both physical and electronic surveillance in their effort to neutralize the Black Panther Party. An excellent example of the use of this tactic was the surveillance of Huey Newton's apartment upon his release from jail in August 1970 after three years of political imprisonment following the death of an Oakland police officer. San Francisco FBI agents paid building engineer Roger DuClot to help them enter Newton's apartment, where they placed a microphone inside a wall. The Bureau also paid for the rental of the apartment adjacent to Newton's. There, undercover agent Don Roberto Stinnette engaged in physical surveillance of his activist neighbor. At one point the FBI even staged a "shoot-out" in the hallway between Stinnette and police in which no one was injured. This COINTELPRO action failed, because Newton had the good sense not to enter the hallway.[20]

Another tactic employed by the FBI was the use of various disinformation techniques. "Snitch-jacketing" or "bad-jacketing" was one of the techniques utilized most often to discredit radical African American activists. Ironically, a snitch-jacket was a document, usually anonymous, that accused an activist of being an informant or agent provocateur.[21] Since there were informants within the movement, this tactic was often utilized successfully.

Although the Black Panther Party exposed some informants and undercover agents, many worked for the FBI or local police undetected. Arguably, one of the first Panther FBI informants on the West Coast was none other than Earl Anthony, author of *Picking Up the Gun*. Anthony became an informant–agent provocateur after FBI agents Robert O'Connor and Ron

Kizenski threatened to move forward with an investigation supposedly linking him to the bombing of a local draft board office. "There were soon so
many of us," Anthony recalled, "that we were informing on each other."[22]

The Illinois chapter of the Party, led by a brilliant young activist and
"ghetto diplomat" named Fred Hampton, came under increasing scrutiny
from federal and local authorities. The FBI "hired" William O'Neal, who
had been arrested for car theft and (curiously) impersonating an FBI agent,
to work as an agent provocateur and informant for the Bureau. In return for
his services O'Neal had charges dropped against him, and he received a
monthly stipend from 1969–72 that amounted to thirty thousand dollars.
Thanks in part to the work of O'Neal and other informants, the FBI would
amass in the span of two years a twelve-volume, four thousand-page surveillance file on Hampton.[23]

If Chicago represented an advanced level of police–FBI cooperation, the
repression of the Black Panther Party in New York City was an example of
local police playing a leading role. Undercover police officers from the New
York City police department's Bureau of Special Services (BOSS) had a
history of infiltrating Black political organizations. Ray Wood had successfully infiltrated both the Revolutionary Action Movement and the more
moderate Congress for Racial Equality. Eugene Roberts was a police agent
while serving as the bodyguard for Malcolm X before joining the Panthers.
Wood and Roberts, along with undercover cop Ralph White, provided the
bulk of state testimony during the eight-month, Panther 21 conspiracy
trial.[24]

These undercover agents testified along with other state witnesses that the
Panthers on trial (which included the New York leadership) conspired to
blow up three police precinct buildings, a school, six sites along the New Haven railroad, five department stores, and the Bronx Botanical Garden. In
May 1971, the jury for the case delivered a not guilty verdict on all charges
after only four hours of deliberation.[25] The jury's verdict could not, however, give back to Panther defendants two years of lost time organizing and
helping to empower the urban Black community of New York City. The incarceration of radical Black activists before and during the trial was a hallmark of political repression during the COINTELPRO era.[26]

That agencies other than the FBI took part in the political repression of the
Black Panther Party underscores the systematic nature of the entire operation. The Internal Revenue Service (IRS) established an Activist Organizations Committee at the behest of President Richard M. Nixon. Former
Panther leader Huey Newton elaborated on the significance of this clandestine group in his 1980 dissertation. "In essence then, the IRS formed a covert
group within the agency for the purpose of selecting out organizations for
special enforcement of the tax laws solely on the basis of their political beliefs." The Party was one of the original twenty-two groups named by the
IRS committee in 1969. A specific tactic utilized by this covert group

involved serving third parties, such as publishers or banks, with summonses seeking information on the Panthers.[27]

No counterintelligence strategy would have been complete without the involvement of the Central Intelligence Agency (CIA). The domestic intelligence activities of the CIA became a matter of public knowledge in the wake of the Watergate hearings. By providing "technical assistance," CIA agents helped the White House "plumbers" burglarize the office of psychiatrist Daniel Ellsberg, the man who disclosed the Pentagon Papers.[28] Radical Black activists were already aware of the CIA's pivotal role in the assassination of Patrice Lumumba in the Congo in January 1961 and in the destabilization of Kwame Nkrumah's regime in Ghana in February 1966.[29] Yet few realized the extent of the agency's activities in the United States. The CIA recruited Blacks to spy on the Black Panther Party in this country and in Africa with the intent of "neutralizing" the organization abroad.[30] Investigations conducted by the U.S. Senate into three CIA domestic–security operations of the late 1960s and early 1970s revealed that each focused on Panther activists in some way. Project CHAOS involved opening the mail of groups on the agency's "watch list." Project RESISTANCE entailed intelligence gathering on a number of radical organizations. The third CIA program, Project MERRIMAC, which lasted from 1967–73, called for the specific infiltration of Black political groups.[31]

Panther Repression

The state repressive apparatus targeted specific activities and political relationships of the Black Panther Party. The FBI's counterintelligence program targeted Panther relationships with other Black political groups. Informant Earl Anthony was part of the FBI effort to exacerbate problems in the precarious alliance between the Black Panther Party and Student Nonviolent Coordinating Committee (SNCC). According to Anthony, the FBI tapped the phones of both the Panther and SNCC leadership circles. The Bureau obtained information indicating that SNCC leaders, especially James Forman, wanted to end the alliance and would seek "protection" from the Nation of Islam, if necessary.[32]

A group of Panthers led by Eldridge Cleaver went to Forman's SNCC office in July 1968. The Panthers sought to intimidate the SNCC leader. According to Anthony, Eldridge Cleaver ordered two Panthers to place what turned out to be unloaded guns at Forman's head: "He screamed for his life, as Cleaver taunted him with insults." With Forman's office bugged, FBI agents were privy to the entire scene. Shortly after this brutal and unprincipled Panther power play, Bureau agents "gloatingly" told Anthony "that their seeds of dissension were spreading everywhere."[33]

FBI agents were not exaggerating when they boasted to Anthony. In September 1968, only two months after the incident in James Forman's office, the FBI placed an anonymous phone call to Stokely Carmichael's (Kwame Ture's) mother, and falsely advised her that several Panthers were out to kill him and that he should "hide out." The former SNCC leader apparently took the call seriously and left for Africa the next day.[34]

One of the Bureau's most successful counterintelligence measures involved a series of violent confrontations between the Black Panther Party and the Us organization in southern California in 1969. The FBI capitalized on the already existing ideological battle between the two groups and orchestrated the January 17, 1969, deaths of Panthers Alprentice "Bunchy" Carter and John Huggins by Us members during a heated student meeting on the UCLA campus. Evidence that came to light years after the shootings pointed to possible direct FBI involvement. Not long after the UCLA shootings, the Bureau sent a number of derogatory cartoons, supposedly done by Us members, to five Panthers and two underground newspapers in the San Diego area.[35] Representatives of the two groups met in both March and April 1969 to attempt to settle their differences. In response, the FBI's San Diego office distributed more inflammatory cartoons. On April 4, 1969, several Panthers initiated a bloodless confrontation at San Diego's Southcrest Park. In retaliation, Us members "roughed up a female BPP member" at a Party political education meeting later that day. During the spring and summer of 1969, Us members killed Black Panthers John Savage and Sylvester Bell, and authorities implicated the Party in the bombing of the San Diego office of the Us organization. Not surprisingly, FBI agents in San Diego boasted of their apparent success in instigating further violence between the Black Panther Party and Us.[36]

The FBI's successful effort in exacerbating the Panther–Us conflict in southern California shows how far the Bureau went to repress the Black liberation movement as a whole and the Black Panther Party specifically. Us leader Maulana Karenga has noted, however, that the Panthers and Us were not blameless. Both groups often looked to the gun as a final arbiter of conflicts; both had succumbed to a "gang rivalry" mentality. Nevertheless, Karenga is correct in his assertion that the ultimate responsibility for the conflict rested with the U.S. government and its counterintelligence program.[37]

One of the most coordinated moves to destroy the Black Panthers via FBI–local police cooperation took place outside the Party's California home base. A primary concern of police and FBI officials following the activities of the Illinois chapter of the Party was the leadership's ability to negotiate and form alliances with lumpen street groups and larger underworld organizations. Panther leaders in Chicago maintained that they were targets of the Gang Intelligence Unit and Task Force of the Chicago Police Department because of their efforts to establish a tenuous alliance with the Black Disciples, a youth street gang. In May 1969, the Chicago police ransacked the headquarters of the Disciples not long after the formation of the alliance. The Party leadership in Chicago responded to the police raid in militant solidarity with the Disciples. " The Black Disciples, the Black Panthers and all other segments of the people are saying to the pigs: it's either/or—either—they stop their repressive acts of barbarism, or we're going to start shooting."[38]

State Political Repression of the Black Panther Party		
Tactic	**Target**	**Impact**
Harassment	All Party Members	Disrupted daily organizing
Arrest and Detention	All Party Members	Drained bail funds; removed activists from needed organizing; provided police agencies with surveillance opportunities; harassment and political imprisonment
Surveillance	All Party Members and Activities	Intelligence gathering by both physical and electronic means
Snitch-Jacketing	Party Leaders, Allies, and Supporters	Discredited the targeted individual by suggesting he/she was an informant or agent provocateur; provided general disinformation
Forged Letters	Party Leaders	Provided recipient with ; disinformation regarding a potential threat to his/her position or life; discredited others
Paid Informants and Undercover FBI/Police Agents	All Party Members	Provided the FBI and local police with physical surveillance and gathered intelligence; provided testimony, often perjured, in Panther trials
Agents/ Provocateurs	All Party Members	Exacerbated both existing internal and external problems with other groups; created new problems.
Assassination	Party Leaders	Eliminated key activists through state murder.

Table 1

The FBI also knew that Fred Hampton was close to negotiating a pact with Jeff Fort and the Blackstone Rangers (later called the Black P. Stone Nation), a well-organized and armed group that dominated Chicago's Black underworld. Hampton's efforts to politicize the Rangers highlighted for both local and federal authorities the significance of a potential merger between the two groups. With the Blackstone Rangers numbering three thousand, the Black Panther Party's national membership would double instantly.[39]

When Chicago Bureau agents got wind that Jeff Fort had misgivings about a possible alliance with the Party, they quickly suggested COINTELPRO action. On January 30, 1969, J. Edgar Hoover authorized an anonymous letter be sent to "Brother Jeff" of the Rangers: "I'm not a Panther, or a Ranger, just black. From what I see these Panthers are out for themselves, not black people. I think you ought to know what they're up to, I know what I'd do if I was you. You might here [sic] from me again."[40] As Fort pondered what he had just received in the mail, the FBI's Chicago office sent a number of false letters to various Panthers implying that Jeff Fort wanted to "off" Fred Hampton. As was the case in southern California, the FBI had managed to exacerbate existing tensions between groups while creating a host of additional concerns among organization leaders.

A high level of coordination between the FBI and local police in Chicago was a primary reason for the repression of the Black Panther Party in that city. The Bureau consolidated its forces with both the Gang Intelligence Unit of the Chicago police and the Cook County state attorney's office. State's Attorney Edward V. Hanrahan insured that the Special Prosecutions Unit of his office focused on Party activities. Hanrahan's attorneys were able to convict Hampton on a charge of stealing seventy dollars worth of ice cream in 1967. In turn, the FBI furnished Hanrahan with intelligence on the Black Panther Party. As a result, police raided Party headquarters in Chicago on four occasions in 1969.[41]

Party Chairman Bobby Seale was particularly disturbed by the ferocity of the police raids in Chicago, noting that police stormed the office "like Eliot Ness with sledgehammers. I mean, our press, all of our IBM typewriters that had been donated by the white radicals, our newspapers. . . and then set the whole building on fire. This is what the FBI and Chicago police did." The issue for Seale was one of naked state terror. "The idea on the part of the police was to pysch the community up. To terrorize us out of existence."[42]

The fourth police raid, which occurred in the early morning hours of December 4, 1969, was the culmination of police and FBI efforts in the Windy City. Only a month earlier, Hampton, since released from prison, had traveled to California to meet with the Party's national leadership. Hampton learned that in the "near future" he would become Chief of Staff, becoming the major spokesperson for the Black Panther Party.[43] FBI informant William O'Neal, who had become the head of security for the Panther office, prepared dinner and soft drinks for Hampton and other comrades on the night of December 3, 1969. Fred Hampton ate his last supper unaware that O'Neal had provided the FBI and local police with a detailed floor plan of the apartment Panther activists called home.[44]

At approximately 4:00 a.m., a contingent of Chicago police stormed the Panther apartment, ostensibly to raid illegal weapons. They came armed with an M–1 carbine, a Thompson submachine gun, twenty-five "lesser" weapons, and an illegally obtained search warrant. The police fired a total of ninety shots, killing Fred Hampton and Mark Clark in cold blood and leaving several Party members wounded. The lone Panther round fired was a reflex shot by Mark Clark. In another act of repression police charged the (mostly wounded) survivors of the massacre, including Hampton's pregnant fiancée Deborah Johnson, with attempted murder and aggravated assault and imposed bail at a hundred thousand dollars. Chicago authorities eventually dropped the charges. In the spirit of plantation generosity, William O'Neal received a $300.00 bonus from the FBI.[45]

The predawn raid that assassinated Mark Clark and Fred Hampton ignited a firestorm of protest. A blue-ribbon commission of inquiry chaired by moderate Black political leader Roy Wilkins and former U.S. Attorney General Ramsey Clark condemned the police action in a 1973 report, noting that "of all violence, official violence is the most destructive."[46] The report asserted that the hour of the raid, absence of notice, and excessive use of police firepower, "all were more suited to a wartime military commando raid than the service of a search warrant." The commission also contended that it was "highly probable" that Fred Hampton had been drugged with secobarbital, most likely placed in his soft drink by O'Neal. Despite the commission's findings and a victorious lawsuit in which the survivors and families of the deceased Panthers received $1.85 million to share, it came as no surprise that neither Edward Hanrahan nor any of the police officers and FBI agents involved saw the inside of a prison cell.[47]

Another form of repression aimed at the Party was the effort by the FBI to cause a rift between the Panthers and White radical political organizations. The Bureau was equally vigilant in targeting White radical activists. The FBI engaged in 290 disruptive actions against New Left groups alone between the 1968 student protests at Columbia University and the spring of 1971. Federal officials designed most of these counterintelligence measures to keep "targets from speaking, teaching, writing or publishing."[48]

The counterintelligence campaign also made life difficult for White supporters of the Party, irrespective of organizational affiliation. In July 1969, the Bureau's Los Angeles office attempted to stifle relations between the Party and Donald Freed, a White writer who led a California "Friends of the Panthers" support group. The FBI sent a condescending letter to several Party members, supposedly from the White support group. The letter listed six precautions Whites "should keep in mind" when associating with the Black Panther Party. The FBI also utilized snitch-jacketing, distributing leaflets at a park near a Panther-sponsored conference in Oakland that claimed that Freed was a police informant.[49] The FBI kept close tabs on entertainers, such as actress Jane Fonda, who was a supporter of the Panthers as well as a vocal antiwar activist. The Bureau even sent bogus letters to employers whose employees supported the Party. One such letter went to top executives at Union Carbide concerning one of its employees. The fictitious author of the letter threatened not to buy stock in a company "whose ranking employees support, assist, and encourage any organization which openly advocates the violent overthrow of our free enterprise system."[50]

Panther activities were also targets of repression, especially the organization's free breakfast program. J. Edgar Hoover was extremely perturbed by the overwhelming success of the program, calling it a "real long range threat to American society."[51] Apparently, Hoover's primary concern was that children would be "propagandized." As Huey Newton has written, however, being propagandized "simply meant they were taught ideas, or an ideology, the FBI and Hoover disliked."[52] The Bureau directed most of its efforts at destabilizing the program by targeting its supporters. The FBI's New York City office persuaded a Father Steltz to renege on his offer of church space for the community program. The Bureau descended to new depths, however, when it placed a number of calls from "parishioners" to a Catholic bishop protesting the activities of Father Frank Curran. The San Diego priest was an FBI target because he offered his church and services to the Party for its breakfast program. Father Curran soon received a "permanent assignment" transfer from San Diego to New Mexico.[53]

Part of the effectiveness of COINTELPRO was its ability to make the most of larger societal contradictions that also existed within the liberation movement. An example of this was the FBI's ability to use the homophobia of many persons in and outside of the Party to its own advantage. In September 1968, the Chicago FBI office included in its strategy a fraudulent letter written by "a black friend" that was sent to a leader of a lumpen group called the *Mau Maus*. This letter insinuated that two members of the Panther leadership in Chicago were homosexual lovers. "The Panthers need real black men for leaders," the letter stated, "not freaks."[54]

When Party leader Huey Newton called for marginalized groups, including homosexuals, to "unite with the Black Panther Party in revolutionary fashion" in the summer of 1970, the FBI took action. The FBI approved a plan to mail forged letters from so-called Panther sympathizers to Party Chief of Staff David Hilliard protesting Newton's statement.[55] The FBI's effort to capitalize on rampant homophobia spoke to the need to confront honestly sexism and homophobia within the Black Panther Party, not to mention the larger society.

During a critical period when the Party was soul-searching on issues such as sexism and homophobia, the FBI struck a COINTELPRO coup de grace directly at the Party's national leadership. The bureau sought to drive a permanent wedge between Huey Newton and the exiled Eldridge Cleaver who was now residing in Algeria. While Newton had begun to emphasize the establishment of community programs and the building of the Party's mass base, Cleaver asserted from Algiers the need for urban guerrilla warfare.[56]

In March 1970, the FBI launched a "concerted program" to divide the Black Panther Party. FBI agents drafted an anonymous letter to David Hilliard so that it appeared to have been written by Connie Matthews, the Party's representative in Scandinavia. The fictitious letter claimed that Eldridge Cleaver "ha[d] tripped out. Perhaps he ha[d] been working too hard," and urged Panther leaders in California to "take some immediate action before this becomes more serious." On August 19, 1970, the day of Newton's release from prison, the Philadelphia FBI office released a bogus letter suggesting that David Hilliard and Eldridge Cleaver were the true leaders of the Party. The letter argued that "Huey Newton is useful only as a drawing card."[57]

After the Panthers sponsored the relatively unorganized November 1970 Revolutionary People's Constitutional Plenary Session in Washington, D.C., the FBI mailed a number of bogus letters criticizing Huey Newton's handling of the event to the exiled Eldridge Cleaver. Such letters were part of the Bureau's effort to divide the Party leadership. The Boston FBI office sent a letter from a fictitious White radical, "Lawrence Thomas of Students for a Democratic Society." The "SDS" letter stated that any "unity or solidarity which existed between the Black Panther Party and the white revolutionary movement before the convention has now gone down the tube . . . . No longer can the Party be looked upon as the 'Vanguard of the Revolution.'"[58]

The Impact of Repression

The immediate impact of the domestic war waged against the Black Panther Party was nothing short of internal chaos. By the winter of 1971, the barrage of COINTELPRO letters sent to various persons in the Party came to shattering fruition. Eldridge Cleaver criticized Newton for expelling a number of Party members on a February television program. Newton then expelled the entire "Intercommunal Section" located in Algeria, including Eldridge Cleaver. Kathleen Cleaver recalled the level of confusion that ensued in executive testimony before the U.S. Senate's Select Committee on Intelligence Activities in April 1976. According to Cleaver, "We did not know who to believe about what. . . . It was a very bizarre feeling."[59]

The state of chaos brought about by the flurry of letters touched every member of the Panther Central Committee. David Hilliard remembered that Huey Newton had even received letters before his release from prison that supposedly indicated that other Panther leaders wanted to kill him: "It was the FBI's work to keep us all confused. We were getting letters from everybody. Phones were tapped. They created mass distrust."[60]

At one point, New York Panther leader Dhoruba Bin Wahad (Dhoruba Moore) jumped bail during the Panther 21 trial when he suspected that Huey

Newton, in the midst of the leadership rift with Eldridge Cleaver, wanted him dead. "We were right in the middle of madness that we couldn't understand," Bin Wahad explained. "We felt we were going to get killed by someone and we didn't know who."[61] In February 1971, the FBI sealed the issue by sending to Oakland via special delivery a bogus letter that claimed the New York Panthers "were conspiring" to murder Newton.[62]

Violence between members of the two rival Panther "factions" followed the confusion. In one of the starkest examples of such internecine violence, members of the Cleaver group killed fellow Panther Sam Napier in New York City. Napier was Distribution Manager of the Party newspaper and considered part of the Newton camp. Napier's murder was allegedly in retaliation for the death of Robert Webb, thought by many in the Cleaver camp to have been killed by supporters of Newton. Hilliard spoke to the significance of COINTELPRO in his 1993 autobiography: "They employ every kind of deviousness to put us at one another's throat, make us appear like gangsters and thugs, niggers killing niggers."[63] Noting that Panther activities were already "in a state of chaos," the FBI's New York office notified J. Edgar Hoover that it "will in the immediate future submit counterintelligence proposals against the Cleaver faction of the BPP designed to widen the existing rift within the BPP."[64]

Mumia Abu-Jamal—a former Philadelphia Black Panther currently incarcerated as a political prisoner on death row—recalled leaving the Party during the period of the Newton–Cleaver split: "I felt that it was proper to fight the system, but when the system can manipulate you into fighting your own, then the system wins and the people lose."[65]

The most lasting impact, perhaps, of state repression of the Black Panther Party was the effort of the federal government not only to disrupt the group, but to imprison many of its key activists. The FBI, in conjunction with state and local law enforcement agencies, conducted a fierce campaign to incarcerate some of the most tenacious and dedicated activists of the Black Panther Party and Black liberation movement. This legal repression continued after the Party's actual demise as an effective radical activist African American national organization.

Amnesty International officially recognizes over five thousand "prisoners of conscience" worldwide. The human rights group defines prisoners of conscience as those individuals "who have been imprisoned for their beliefs, race, ethnic origin, sex, language or religion, and who have neither used nor advocated violence." Although the London-based human rights group has monitored the cases of a handful of activists in the United States, such as Leonard Peltier of the American Indian Movement, no U.S. political prisoner currently falls under the group's narrow definition of a prisoner of conscience.

Black radical activist and scholar Angela Davis knows something about being incarcerated for one's political beliefs. She remained behind bars as a political prisoner in an outrageous attempt on the part of the federal government to implicate her in the August 7, 1970 prison break led by 16-year-old Jonathan Jackson at the Marin County Hall of Justice.[66] She offered this more expansive definition of political imprisonment in 1971:

> There is a distinct and qualitative difference between one breaking a law for one's own individual self-interest and violating it in the interests of a class or a people whose oppression is expressed directly or indirectly through that particular law. The former might be called a criminal (though in many cases he is a victim), but the latter, as a reformist or revolutionary, is interested in universal social change. Captured, he or she is a political prisoner.[67]

There are over a hundred political prisoners and prisoners of war (POWs) currently being held in U.S. prisons.[68] That group includes Puerto Rican activists (who consider themselves prisoners of war engaged in a colonial liberation struggle), African Americans from the Black liberation movement, Native American freedom fighters, and radical White activists. The largest number of those incarcerated for political activity are Blacks. The bulk of them were associated at one time or another with the Black Panther Party.[69]

Since political prisoners have not been acknowledged officially in this country, activists have almost always stood trial for specific "criminal" offenses. Dhoruba Bin Wahad, a former Panther 21 member and political prisoner for some nineteen years, asserted that most people in the U.S. operate under the erroneous assumption that all prisoners are criminals who have been afforded due process. U.S. law enforcement agencies "have *consistently* criminalized the legitimate movements of oppressed people, and in so doing have. . . rendered the activists that come from these movements 'criminals'. . . ."[70]

Imprisoned African American activists have not lost sight, however, of the institutional racism that links the judicial and penal systems and affects much of the general prison population. The often inhumane double standard applied to Blacks and other people of color in the criminal justice system may help to explain why these prisoners as a group tend to be more politicized than other inmates. A Black prisoner convicted of a criminal offense may also benefit from the work of political prisoners and other activist inmates in addition to his or her own consciousness-raising efforts. [71]

One of the clearest examples of a Black inmate who went on to become politicized—indeed, radicalized—while in prison, was George Jackson. At age eighteen, Jackson was sentenced to an indefinite term for a seventy-dollar robbery of a gas station. The imprisoned Jackson not only went on to be named Field Marshal of the Black Panther Party, but founded a guerrilla group called the *People's Army*. George Jackson along with his comrade inmates John Cluchette and Fleeta Drumgo comprised the Soledad Brothers. Prison officials had the three inmates indicted for the retaliatory murder of a White prison guard at Soledad. Given the organizing activities of the

Soledad Brothers, the rationale behind the indictment was a political one. George Jackson died on August 21, 1971, a year after his brother Jonathan, at the hands of guards at San Quentin prison. Jackson died having spent the entirety of his adult life in the California prison system.[72]

The legal cases of most political prisoners associated with the Black Panther Party resemble that of Geronimo ji Jaga (Elmer Geronimo Pratt). Geronimo ji Jaga was a highly decorated combat paratrooper while in the Vietnam War. He became disillusioned with U.S. intervention in Vietnam, however, and returned to his native Louisiana a changed man in 1968. He left the South to attend UCLA as a student in the High Potential Program. He also joined the Black Panther Party.[73]

The Panther leadership named Geronimo ji Jaga leader of the Southern California Chapter of the Party after the January 1969 Us shootings at UCLA. He "became instrumental" in forming the Afro-American Liberation Army (later changed to Black Liberation Army), an underground military cadre. He went to trial for the robbery and first degree murder of Caroline Olsen, a White woman who had been playing tennis with her husband Kenneth on December 18, 1968. The murder occurred in Santa Monica at the same time the FBI was aware that Geronimo ji Jaga was in Oakland on Party business. In the confusion and distrust surrounding the Newton–Cleaver rift (he was in the Cleaver camp), no one in the Newton faction would testify at ji Jaga's trial on his behalf.[74]

Geronimo ji Jaga's 1972 conviction was not due solely, however, to a refusal of Party comrades to testify on his behalf. Police informant Julius Carl "Julio" Butler, who is currently a Los Angeles attorney, was the prosecution's key witness in the trial. Ji Jaga had demoted and later expelled Butler in August 1969 when he suspected him of being an informant. During the trial Butler denied being an FBI or LAPD informant, or that he had even been expelled.[75]

Butler's questionable testimony was not Geronimo ji Jaga's only problem. Ji Jaga's attorneys and a number of grassroots activists uncovered other repressive machinations conducted by police agencies at the time of his trial. A number of FBI surveillance documents that supported ji Jaga's alibi mysteriously disappeared. Kenneth Olsen, who survived the assault, identified another man as one of the two attackers a year before he placed ji Jaga at the scene of the crime. In light of these revelations, California Superior Court Judge Everett W. Dickey reversed the 1972 conviction on June 10, 1997, ending a staggering 27 years of incarceration for the Panther leader, the first eight of which Geronimo ji Jaga spent in solitary confinement. A month after his release from prison, ji Jaga pressed for support of those activists who remained behind bars: "Those brothers need our support 1,000 percent. They need that letter every now and then." Ji Jaga drew a connection between doing such support work and participating in the larger Black liberation struggle. He said, "We have to conquer the fear of freedom. We have to be audacious, like the Panthers."[76]

One of the U.S. government's most extensive efforts to legally repress a radical Black activist came against former Panther and Black Liberation Army member Assata Shakur (JoAnne Deborah Chesimard). Shakur went to trial on eight separate occasions on seven different charges between April 1971 and March 1977 before being convicted of killing a state trooper during a May 1973 shoot-out on the New Jersey Turnpike. The conviction occurred despite evidence that she was seriously wounded during the confrontation and unable to fire a single shot. [77]

Attorney Lenox Hinds has written that Assata Shakur "understates the awfulness of the condition in which she was incarcerated."[78] The revolutionary Black activist was not allowed books or exercise. During both the time she spent recovering from an injury to her median nerve from the turnpike shooting and her later pregnancy, prison authorities undertook a concerted effort to deny her adequate medical attention. As a female prisoner, Assata Shakur was also subject to vaginal as well as anal strip searches. Shakur spent a great deal of time in solitary confinement and was always under twenty-four-hour surveillance. At one point, she spent four consecutive months in solitary confinement in the Middlesex County Jail for Men in New Jersey. Lengthy periods "in the hole" had a profound effect on her. Shakur recalled, "When someone asked my name I stammered and stuttered. My voice was so low everyone constantly asked me to repeat myself. That was one of the things that always happened to me after long periods of solitary confinement: I would forget how to talk."[79] Assata Shakur's nightmare as a political prisoner ended in 1979 when members of the Black Liberation Army aided her escape from prison. Shakur fled to socialist Cuba where she received political asylum and continues to live on the island.[80]

Longtime freedom fighter Sundiata Acoli (Clark Squire)—who had also been convicted in connection with the 1973 New Jersey Turnpike incident—remains a political prisoner today, serving a sentence of life plus thirty years. Acoli survived for five years in "a cell smaller than the Society for the Prevention of Cruelty to Animals required space for a German shepherd" at Trenton State Prison.[81] Authorities then moved him to the notorious maximum security federal prison at Marion, Illinois, the U.S. facility condemned by Amnesty International. Currently housed at Leavenworth, prison officials denied parole to Sundiata Acoli for the next twenty years in December 1993. Acoli's lawyers have presented an appeal of the parole denial.[82]

Assata Shakur has noted that during her years in the Party, one of the comrades she respected most was Dhoruba Moore, known today as Dhoruba Al-Mujahid Bin Wahad. It took Bin Wahad nineteen years before he set foot outside a prison a "free" man. Bin Wahad was a self-employed painter and "artist for the free press" before joining the Black Panther Party in New York

City. An articulate Panther leader, he had assumed the post of field secretary for the state of New York by the time he and other defendants went to trial in the Panther 21 case in October 1970. Following the acquittal of the Panther 21 in May 1971, the FBI intensified its efforts to imprison radical Black activists in New York.

President Richard Nixon, Attorney General John Mitchell, FBI Director J. Edgar Hoover and assorted local law enforcement officials at a White House meeting on May 28, 1971, launched a counterintelligence campaign called NEWKILL [New York Police Killings] ostensibly aimed at securing indictments for a number of recent police killings. As part of this newly established NEWKILL investigation, Bin Wahad and other New York Panthers were primary targets because of their support for the underground Black Liberation Army.[83] When police arrested Dhoruba Bin Wahad and other Panthers for the armed robbery of a Bronx social club on June 4, 1971, they provided themselves with a NEWKILL opportunity. Bin Wahad and comrade Jamal Joseph targeted the Triple O club as a known after-hours "dope den" and meeting place for local drug dealers.[84] Police charged Bin Wahad with attempted murder in the machine gunning of patrolmen Nicholas Binetti and Thomas Curry on May 19, 1971, claiming that Bin Wahad used the same weapon in the June attempted robbery. Law enforcement authorities savored the arrest because the policemen were wounded near the home of Manhattan District Attorney Frank Hogan, the man who unsuccessfully prosecuted the Panther 21. The Black Liberation Army had claimed responsibility for the shooting, which occurred on the birthdate of Malcolm X.[85]

Dhoruba Bin Wahad's 1973 conviction (after two mistrials) on the attempted murder charges was a clear-cut case of state legal repression. The Panther leader received a twenty-five-years-to-life sentence for a crime he maintained he did not commit. Twelve years of litigation by Bin Wahad and his attorneys revealed prosecutorial misconduct and an FBI cover-up. Through the Freedom of Information Act, Bin Wahad was able to obtain more than three hundred thousand pages of FBI documents that indicated he was the victim of a sophisticated act of political repression. The key witness for the prosecution, a paranoid schizophrenic who had been kept in "protective custody" for twenty months, perjured herself on the stand. Another prosecution witness recanted his testimony, and the district attorney's office withheld evidence during Bin Wahad's trial.[86]

The overwhelming evidence in Dhoruba Bin Wahad's favor finally led to a reversal of his conviction in March 1990. Bin Wahad's release and hard-fought right to a new trial did not erase, however, the memories of being held as a prisoner of conscience for nearly twenty years. Bin Wahad recalled that solitary confinement and the sensory deprivation it entailed placed him and other incarcerated activists in a "prison within a prison." Having spent eight of his nineteen years as a political prisoner in solitary confinement, Bin

Selected Political Prisoners Who Were Former Members of the Black Panther Party

Activist	BPP Branch	Imprisoned
Mumia Abu-Jamal	New York	1982 (Death Row)
Sundiata Acoli (Clark Squire)	New York	1973
Herman Bell	Oakland	1973
Marshall Eddie Conway	Baltimore	1970
Mark Cook	Walla Walla	1976
Bashir Hameed (James York)	New York	1981
Robert Seth Hayes	New York	1973
Teddy Jah Heath	New York	1973
Mundo We Langa (David Rice)	Omaha	1970
Abdul Majid (Anthony LaBorde)	New York	1981
Maroon (Russell Shoats)	Philadelphia	1972
Jalil Abdul Muntaqin (Anthony Bottom)	San Francisco	1973
Baba Odinga (Elmore Johnson)	New York	1973
Sekou M. A. Odinga (Nathaniel Burns)	New York	1981
Ed Poindexter	Omaha	1970
Albert Nuh Washington	San Francisco	1971

Note: This table contains the names of fifteen current political prisoners and prisoners of war who were associated with the Black Panther Party. Some were arrested after they entered the underground Black Liberation Army. Mumia Abu-Jamal's imprisonment on death row stems from his support of the MOVE organization in the wake of the August 8, 1978, predawn bombing raid approved by the then mayor of Philadelphia, Wilson Goode. Mark Cook's imprisonment occurred as a result of his work with CONVENTION, a prisoner's rights and labor group. See issues of *The Black Panther Community News Service* (especially Spring 1991 and Fall 1991). This table is by no means an exhaustive one. For more detailed information, including addresses, on these freedom fighters, as well as others such as Mutulu Shakur (himself an active supporter of political prisoners before he was incarcerated in 1982), Ruchell Cinque Magee (since 1966) and Hugo Pinell (since 1964) who were not involved directly with the BPP, contact the Campaign to Free Black Political Prisoners and POWs in the U.S., Kingsbridge Station, P.O. Box 339, Bronx, NY 10463–0339. Also consult issues of the resurrected *Black Panther Black Community News Service* (see Spring 1991 and Fall 1991).

Table 2

Wahad was well equipped to elaborate on its significance as a mechanism of control:

> Tyranny is very strange. The tyrant, despite the access that he or she may have to the instruments of power and control, always fears the individual who will speak out against their prerogatives or their tyranny—whether this individual is armed or just has the clothes on his or her back. . . . But when an individual does not care about the coercive instruments of the state, and calls into question the moral and ethical credibility of the tyrant, then the tyrant has a very serious problem. And the way that they deal with this problem is by isolating this individual as if he or she has a virus, as if he or she has something that's contagious.[87]

Dhoruba Bin Wahad got the chance to deliver the message that there are political prisoners in the United States to Nelson and Winnie Mandela during a June 1990 Harlem rally welcoming the South African couple. He was speaking for imprisoned comrades Sundiata Acoli, Bashir Hameed, Abdul Majid, Sekou Odinga, then-imprisoned Geronimo ji Jaga, and countless others when he told the Mandelas that "African-American people and their movement for liberation have been criminalized just as the ANC [African National Congress] was criminalized by the racist, fascist regime in South Africa."[88]

Bin Wahad's outspoken discussion of the issue of political prisoners sparked a failed bid by the Manhattan district attorney's office to have him reincarcerated. The legal odyssey of Dhoruba Bin Wahad—who finally had his criminal charges dropped in February 1995—has implications for current political prisoners and prisoners of war. His case may have a direct bearing on the legal struggles of other incarcerated activists, most notably those activists from the Black liberation movement incarcerated in the state of New York.

One such case involves the New York 3—Herman Bell, Jalil Abdul Muntaqin (Anthony Bottom), and Albert Nuh Washington. These former Panthers have been fighting for a new trial since their 1975 conviction for the Harlem murders of two police officers in the spring of 1971. COINTELPRO and NEWKILL documents obtained through the Freedom of Information Act indicate that prosecutors also suppressed evidence at the trial of the New York 3. A ballistics expert concealed test results that proved that the alleged weapon could not have been used in the killings. Furthermore, the prosecution's "star witness" had been tortured with cattle prods to obtain perjured testimony. Lawyers for the New York 3 have petitioned the United States Supreme Court for review of their case.[89]

In struggling to win the release of and make conditions better for political prisoners in the United States, grass-roots organizations such as the Campaign to Free Black Political Prisoners/P.O.W.s in the United States (New York City) have begun to expose the issue. Freedom Now, a short-lived but highly active group based in Chicago, sponsored an international tribunal in

New York City to address the issue of human rights violations in this country in the winter of 1990. Panther activists like Safiya Bukhari-Alston, who endured nearly nine years of "almost total isolation" as a political prisoner, have begun the difficult process of confronting post-traumatic stress disorder similar to that generally attributed to veterans of the Vietnam War. [90] What other concerned activists will do to confront this legacy of struggle against repressive forces remains to be seen.

Conclusion

An analyst of the Vietnam War noted in 1971 that "the predominant American objective was not victory over the enemy but merely the avoidance of defeat and humiliation."[91] The primary objective of the U.S. government was nothing short of victory, however, in its covert domestic war against the Black Panther Party and other radical Black political groups. Party activists most certainly knew that the FBI and local police agencies were out to destroy the organization. Why, then, were they unable to do anything substantive about it? As political prisoner Herman Bell has indicated, the inexperience of many Panther leaders and the Party's overall youth hindered the organization in this instance. Bell went further, however: "Given the level of sophistication, unlimited man-power and resources available" to the federal government's repressive machinery, it was not only understandable that the Party met its eventual demise, but "remarkable . . . that the Party lasted as long as it did."[92]

There are lessons to be learned from the repressive war waged against the Black Panther Party. Current and future activists will have a better understanding of how to better guard against infiltration and disinformation techniques. They will realize the need to generate effective and consolidated support in the African American community through principled day-to-day activism. It is also vitally important that current activists be sophisticated enough to understand that certain internal contradictions of groups such as the Black Panther Party provided easier opportunities for state repression. As COINTELPRO's manipulation of homophobia within the movement indicated, the powers that be will not hesitate to exploit any weakness that otherwise progressive movements present.

Finally, those who consider themselves activists in this day and time cannot overlook the dual need to press for the release of and make survival conditions better for those all-but-forgotten freedom fighters who remain incarcerated as political prisoners and prisoners of war. These activists of the frontline have a great deal to impart to those currently doing grassroots work in Black communities; for they are a living testament to the resiliency of the centuries-old Black liberation movement. As important, however, they are husbands and wives, fathers and mothers—and in many instances, grandfathers and grandmothers who continue to have the most productive years of their lives snatched away by a repressive system that is as cowardly as it is sophisticated.

NOTES

1. Robert Justin Goldstein, *Political Repression in Modern America: From 1870 to the Present* (Cambridge: Schenkman Publishing Company, 1978), xvi.

2. This essay grew out of a chapter of my 1993 master's thesis at the African Studies and Research Center, Cornell University. I would like again to thank Professors James Turner and Margaret Washington, who supervised completion of the thesis. Professor Akinyele Umoja and Tracye Matthews offered constructive comments on the paper at the 1994 annual meeting of the Association for the Study of Afro-American Life and History. Scot Brown and Tanaquil Jones were kind enough to make valuable corrections and comments. I owe a special debt of gratitude to Professor Charles E. Jones for his suggestions in making recent revisions.

3. Charles E. Jones, "The Political Repression of the Black Panther Party, 1966–1971: The Case of The Oakland Bay Area," *Journal of Black Studies* (June 1988): 415–21.

4. Emory J. Tolbert, "Federal Surveillance of Marcus Garvey and the UNIA, "*Journal of Ethnic Studies*, 14, 4 (Winter 1987): 27–31, 36.

5. Ibid., 37–43. See also, Tony Martin, *Race First: The Ideological and Organizational Struggles of Marcus Garvey and the Universal Negro Improvement Association* (Dover: The Majority Press, 1976), Ch. 9.

6. For an extended treatment of political repression during this period, see Robert K. Murray, *Red Scare: A Study in National Hysteria, 1919–1920* (New York: McGraw Hill, 1964) and Murray Burton Levin, *Political Hysteria in America: The Democratic Capacity for Repression* (New York: Basic Books, 1971).

7. Ward Churchill and Jim Vander Wall, *Agents of Repression: the FBI's Secret Wars Against the Black Panther Party and the American Indian Movement* (Boston: South End Press, 1988), 19–26. See also, Huey P. Newton, "War Against the Panthers: A Study of Repression in America"(Ph.D. diss., Univ. of California at Santa Cruz, June 1980), 19–21. Newton's dissertation was republished by Writers and Readers Publishing, Inc. in 1996.

8. Ibid., 24; See also Churchill and Vander Wall, *Agents of Repression*, 32 and Charles Higham, *Trading with the Enemy: An Expose of the Nazi-American Money Plot, 1933–1949* (New York: Delacorte Press, 1983), preface.

9. Gerald Horne, *Black and Red: W. E. B. Du Bois and the Afro-American Response to the Cold War, 1944–1963* (Albany: State University of New York Press, 1986), Ch. 14, 62.

10. Nelson Blackstock, *COINTELPRO: The FBI's Secret War on Political Freedom* (New York: Anchor Foundations, 1975), 150, 42.

11. Maxwell Stanford (Akbar Muhammad Ahmad), "Revolutionary Action Movement (RAM): A Case Study of an Urban Revolutionary Movement in Western Capitalist Society" M.A. thesis, Atlanta Univ., 178). See also Jim Fletcher et al., eds., *Still Black, Still Strong: Survivors of the U.S. War Against Black Revolutionaries* (New York: Semiotext(e), 1993), 19.

12. David Garrow, *The FBI and Martin Luther King, Jr.: From "Solo" to Memphis* (New York: W. W. Norton and Company, 1981), 115; Churchill and Vander Wall, *Agents of Repression*, 58.

13. Garrow, *The FBI and Martin Luther King*, 134.

14. U.S. Congress. Senate. *Book III: Final Report of the Select Committee to Study Government Operations with Respect to Intelligence Activities* (Washington, D.C.: S.R. No. 94–755, 94th Congress, 2d Sess., 1976), 187. This influential report, researched and drafted by the Senate subcommittee headed by Frank Church (D–Idaho), was critical of the FBI's counterintelligence program. The report argued in part that "the chief investigative branch of the federal government, which was charged by law with investigating crimes and preventing criminal conduct, itself engaged in lawless tactics and responded to deep-seated social problems by fomenting violence and unrest."

15. Ibid., 188.

16. Bin Wahad quoted in Fletcher et al., *Still Black*, 18.

17. U.S. Senate, *Book III*, 188. Churchill and Vander Wall, *Agents of Repression*, 44–51.

18. Fletcher et al., *Still Black*, 244. Former RAM activist Max Stanford (Akbar Muhammad Ahmad) made a convincing case for Malcolm's involvement in the group in his Master's thesis. See Stanford, "Revolutionary Action Movement," 96–107. An FBI report done after Malcolm's assassination mentioned his "affiliation with the Revolutionary Action Movement." The FBI report focused on a four-page memorandum written by a RAM official in New York City titled "Malcolm Lives: Analysis of the Assassination." See Clayborne Carson, Malcolm X: The FBI File (New York: Carroll and Graf Publishers, Inc., 1991), 431–32.

19. Fletcher et al., Still Black, 225–32.

20. Newton, "War Against the Panthers", 76–79, 81–82. See also FBI Memorandum from Special Agent Wilbert J. Weishkirch to SAC, San Francisco, 28 February 1973, and FBI Memorandum for J. G. Deegan to W.R. Wannall, 26 August 1974.

21. Ibid., 70.

22. Earl Anthony, *Spitting in the Wind: The True Story Behind the Violent Legacy of the Black Panther Party* (Malibu: Roundtable Publishing, Inc.,1990), 38.

23. U.S. Senate, *Book III*, 222–23. FBI Memorandum from Chicago Field Office to National Headquarters, 8 December 1969. See also, Churchill and Vander Wall, *Agents of Repression*, 64–65.

24. Peter L. Zimroth, *Perversions of Justice: The Prosecution and Acquittal of the Panther 21* (New York: The Viking Press, 1974). See also, Rick Hornung, "The Last Caged Panther," *The Village Voice*, 19 September 1989, 14.

25. Ibid., 16.

26. Dhoruba Bin Wahad, interview with author, 16 June 1990, New York City. This interview aired on WKCR-FM. Charles E. Jones has indicated in his work on the organization in the Oakland area that because of such legal repression, "the Party was unable to devote the time and resources needed to build a mass political organization." See Jones, "Political Repression of Black Panther Party," 423.

27. Newton, "War Against the Panthers," 14–15.

28. Stanford J. Ungar, *FBI: An Uncensored Look Behind the Walls* (Boston: Little, Brown and Company, 1976), 479.

29. The assassination of Patrice Lumumba drew a firestorm of protest worldwide, including a number of demonstrations in New York City led by Black activists. Karl Evanzz, *The Judas Factor: The Plot to Kill Malcolm X* (New York: Thunder's Mouth Press, 1992), 97–116, 313. See also, Kwame Nkrumah, *Revolutionary Path* (New York: International Publishers, 1973), 324–25.

30. "CIA Reportedly Recruited Blacks for Surveillance of Panthers," *New York Times*, 17 March 1978, A1.

31. Newton, "The War Against the Panthers", 120–21, 125n.

32. Anthony, *Spitting in the Wind*, 49.

33. At the time James Forman denied a report in the *New York Times* that guns had been placed at his head. He may have been guided by a desire not to split the movement further. Forman, *The Making of Black Revolutionaries: A Personal Account by James Forman* (New York: The Macmillan Company, 1972), 457. See also, Anthony, *Spitting in the Wind*, 199.

34. U.S. Senate, *Book III*, 199.

35. Newton, "War Against the Panthers," 104–6; Churchill and Vander Wall, *Agents of Repression*, 42–43; U.S. Senate, *Book III*, 194. See also, M. Ron Karenga, "A Response to Muhammad Ahmad," *Black Scholar* (July–Aug. 1978): 55–56.

36. U.S. Senate, *Book III*, 194.

37. Karenga, "Response to Mohammad Ahmed," 55–56. See also, Karenga, "Kawaida and Its Critics: A Sociohistorical Analysis," *Journal of Black Studies*, (Dec. 1977), 133–34.

38. Phil Hamlin, "Groups Vow End to Police Brutality," *The Black Liberator* (Chicago), May 1969, 1, 9.

39. U.S. Senate, *Book III*, 197–198.

40. Ibid.

41. Churchill and Vander Wall, *Agents of Repression*, 66–68.

42. Henry Hampton and Steve Faver, eds., *Voices of Freedom: An Oral History of the Civil Rights Movement from the 1950's through the 1980's* (New York: Bantam, 1990), 530–31.

43. Churchill and Vander Wall, *Agents of Repression*, 69.

44. Ibid., 68. See also, Churchill and Vander Wall, *The COINTELPRO Papers: Documents form the FBI's Secret Wars Against Domestic Dissent* (Boston: South End Press, 1990), 138–41.

45. Churchill and Vander Wall, *Agents of Repression*, 69–75. Kenneth O'Reilly, *"Racial Matters": The FBI's Secret File on Black America, 1960–1972* (New York: The Free Press, 1989), 311–14. O'Neal's last report to the FBI prior to the 4 December predawn raid indicated that there were no illegal weapons in the apartment.

46. Roy Wilkins and Ramsey Clark, *Search and Destroy: A Report by the Commission of Inquiry into the Black Panthers and the Police* (New York: Metropolitan Applied Research Center, Inc. 1973), preface.

47. Ibid., preface, and 176. See also, Churchill and Vander Wall, *Agents of Repression*, 76–77; O'Reilly, *"Racial Matters,"* 312.

48. Goldstein, *Political Repression in America*, 451–52.

49. U.S. Senate, *Book III*, 208–9.

50. Ibid., 209.

51. Ibid., 188.

52. Newton, "War Against the Panthers," 55.

53. Fletcher et al., *Still Black*, 250; U.S. Senate, *Book III*, 210–11.

54. Ibid., 199.

55. Ibid., 202.

56. Jones, "Political Repression of the Black Panther Party," 429. Huey Newton discussed the growing leadership divide within the Party in *To Die for the People* (New York: Random House, 1972), which includes the essay "On the Defection of Eldridge Cleaver from the Black Panther Party and the Defection of the Black Panther Party from the Black Community." See also, David Hilliard and Lewis Cole, *This Side of Glory: The Autobiography of David Hilliard and the Story of the Black Panther Party* (Boston: Little, Brown and Company, 1993), 301–2 and 323–24.

57. Both letters quoted in U.S. Senate, *Book III*, 201–2.

58. Ibid., 204.

59. Ibid., 206–7.

60. Hilliard quoted in "Prisoner of War," by Reginald W. Major and Marcia D. Davis, *Emerge*, June 1994, 34.

61. Hornug, "The Last Caged Panthers," 14.

62. Hornung, "The Last Caged Panthers," 14–16. The FBI circulated a fictitious letter in which Dhoruba Bin Wahad accused another Panther of being an informant in June 1970. The Bureau then suggested approaching Bin Wahad to become a possible informant, but never did so.

63. Hilliard and Cole, *This Side of Glory*, 221.

64. Fletcher et al., *Still Black*, 265; . U.S. Senate, *Book III*, 206–7. See also Anthony, *Spitting in the Wind*, 119–20, and 33–34. FBI informant Earl Anthony has asserted that six Panthers died in 1971 during the violence between the rival factions within the Party.

65. Fletcher et al., *Still Black*, 151.

66. On August 7, 1970, Jonathan Jackson, the younger brother of prison revolutionary George Jackson, attempted to free inmates James McClain, Ruchell Magee, and William Christmas. Jackson and his comrades were able to hold off authorities momentarily by taking five hostages, including Judge Harold Haley. Jackson, McClain, Christmas, and Haley all died in the gun battle which ensued. Authorities indicted Ruchell Magee and Angela Davis for the murder of Judge Haley despite Davis's being nowhere near the scene of the incident. Police implicated Davis because the gun Jonathan Jackson carried was registered in her name.

67. Angela Y. Davis, *If They Come in the Morning: Voices of Resistance* (New York: The Third Press, 1971), 22.

68. The Freedom Now Campaign for Amnesty and Human Rights for Political Prisoners in the U.S. adopted the cases of ninety-eight political prisoners and prisoners of war, thirty-nine of whom were Black activists, before the organization's demise in the early 1990s. Dhoruba Bin Wahad of the Campaign to Free Black Political Prisoners/P.O.W.s in the United States has placed the overall total at closer to one hundred fifty. Obtaining a precise figure for the number of political prisoners currently incarcerated in the United States is a difficult task, in part because the U.S. government does not acknowledge the existence of such prisoners. Andrew Young came under severe fire as U.S. Ambassador to the United Nations in 1979 when he admitted that there were "hundreds if not thousands" of U.S. political prisoners in the midst of President Jimmy Carter's international human rights campaign. See Richard Dhoruba Moore, "U.S. Black Political Prisoners: A Threat to America's International Human Rights Campaign," *Black Scholar* (March–April 1979):17.

69. Bin Wahad interview, 16 June 1990.

70. Ibid.

71. Assata Shakur, *Assata: An Autobiography* (Westport, Connecticut: Lawrence Hill and Company, 1987), 59; Bin Wahad interview, 16 June 1990. For a thorough discussion of Blacks and the criminal justice system, see Bruce Wright's *Black Robes, White Justice* (Secaucus: Lyle Stuart, Inc., 1987), Ch. 7.

72. For a fuller account of George L. Jackson's life as a political prisoner see his *Blood in My Eye* (Baltimore: Black Classic Press, 1990, [1972]) and *Soledad Brother: The Prison Writings of George Jackson* (New York: Random House, 1970). See also, Churchill and Vander Wall, *Agents of Repression*, 94–98; Jo Durden-Smith, *Who Killed George Jackson?* (New York; Alfred A. Knopf, 1976), foreword.

73. Major and Davis, "Prisoner of War," 32–34; Churchill and Vander Wall, *Agents of Repression*, 78–79.

74. Major and Davis "Prisoner of War," 79–88. See also, O'Reilly, *Racial Matters*, 323.

75. Major and Davis "Prisoner of War," 32–34.

76. Edward J. Boyer, "Pratt Strides into Freedom," *Los Angeles Times*, 11 June 1997, A1 and A17. Judge Dickey ruled that Los Angeles County Prosecutors had "suppressed" evidence in the 1972 trial that would have led the jury to reach a different verdict. See also, Geronimo ji Jaga, Speech at Freedom Celebration, 12 July 1997, (Decatur, Georgia: New Afrikan Peoples Organization).

77. Assata Shakur, *Assata: An Autobiography* (Westport, Connecticut: Lawrence Hill and Company, 1987), xii–xiii. Panther comrade Zayd Shakur died during the Turnpike shooting.

78. Lenox Hinds, "Foreword," *Assata: An Autobiography* (Westport, Connecticut: Lawrence Hill and Company, 1987), x.

79. Ibid., 83.

80. Churchill and Vander Wall, *COINTELPRO Papers*, 308.

81. Lori S. Robinson, "Other Political Prisoners," *Emerge*, June 1994, 33.

82. Ibid.

83. Robert J. Boyle, "COINTELPRO: The 19-Year Ordeal of Dhoruba Bin-Wahad," *Covert Action Information Bulletin*, no. 36. See also Dhoruba Moore, "Strategies of Repression Against the Black Movement," *Black Scholar* (May–June 1981), 15.

84. "Passin' It On." Documentary. (Nosotros Moving Pictures, Inc., 1992).

85. Hornung, "The Last Caged Panther," 16. See also, "Panther's Conviction Reversed," *Daily News*, (New York) 16 March 1990, 29.

86. "Ex-Panther in Prison Says Evidence Was Concealed," *New York Times*, 7 April 1989, B6. See also Timothy Clifford, "Convicted Activist Claims Frame-Up," *New York Newsday*, 19 April 1988, 19; and William Kunstler, "The Continuing Ordeal of Dhoruba Al-Mujahid Bin Wahad," *City Sun* (New York City), 28 March 1990, 5.

87. Bin Wahad interview with author, 16 June 1990, New York City.

88. "Political Prisoners Embrace Nelson Mandela at Rally," *Freedom Now! Bulletin* (Chicago), July–Aug. 1990.

89. "Former Black Panther Party Members Argue for New Trial," *The Challenger* (Buffalo), 20 March 1991, 21. See also Robinson, "Other Political Prisoners," 33.

90. Safiya Bukhari-Alston, interview with Tanya Steele and Rosemari Mealy, 21 March 1992, New York City. This interview aired on WBAI-FM.

91. Max Frankel, "The Lessons of Vietnam," *The Pentagon Papers* (New York: Quadrangle Books, Inc. 1971), 639.

92. Herman Bell, "The BPP and Political Prisoners," *The Black Panther Black Community News Service Memorial Issue* (Spring 1991), 11.

Chapter Sixteen

Explaining the Demise of
The Black Panther Party:
The Role of Internal Factors

Ollie A. Johnson, III

Huey P. Newton and Bobby Seale, twenty-four and thirty years old respectively, founded the Black Panther Party for Self-Defense (BPP) on October 15, 1966 in Oakland, California, because they wanted an organizational vehicle to contribute concretely to the social, economic, and political uplift of Black people.[1] Newton and Seale maintained that the recent gains of the Civil Rights movement failed to adequately address the needs of the masses of Black people. Central to the Black power movement of the late 1960s and early 1970s, the BPP represented the most prominent radical African American political organization of this period, with established chapters in many states throughout the United States and an active International Section in Algeria headed by Eldridge and Kathleen Cleaver.[2] At their peak, the Black Panthers were in the forefront of a multiracial and transnational struggle for fundamental social change in the United States and abroad. The Party's demise continues to intrigue scholars, progressive activists, and the general public. The debate has become centered on whether external or internal factors led to the fall of the BPP.

The main purpose of this essay is to contribute to our understanding of the eventual decline of the Black Panther Party.[3] In particular, I explore various reasons for the transformation of the BPP from a national and international organization with approximately five thousand members in forty chapters in 1969 to a local organization with fewer than fifty Panthers in the Oakland, California area by 1980.[4] Most scholarly studies of American social movements during the 1960s put forth the view that multiple factors account for the eclipse of these movements.[5] Among those factors identified are state political repression, ideological errors, an inexperienced and youthful membership, intraparty strife, strategic mistakes, and the cult-of-personality phenomenon. This essay examines the role and impact of internal factors in the demise of the Black Panther Party.

Robert Michels and other scholars have developed a social theory concerning political organizations and political systems.[6] Michels' view, known as "elite theory," is that popular, revolutionary, and democratic socialist organizations are confronted with a paradox, namely, that despite their attempts at equitable membership participation, the necessity for organization leads to oligarchy.[7] Thus, political activists attempting to expand democratic practice inevitably produce unequal organizational relationships. The iron law of oligarchy holds that a numerical minority will gain and misuse power and control within a political organization because of technical and psychological factors.[8] Technically, it is difficult for large numbers of the membership to process the many complex issues facing the organization in a timely and effective manner, which results in the overreliance on a small group of leaders. Psychological factors pertain to the unequal distribution of information, knowledge, and competence within the organization. Consequently, the uninformed members tend to defer to those individuals who are knowledgeable about organizational affairs. Both types of factors give elites a clear advantage over the mass membership in organizational operation. As Cassinelli states, "The exercise of power has a conservative effect, and the leader tends to use all his power to retain his position of power. The leader comes to regard the organization, and his own office, as more important than the professed goal of the organization."[9]

Elite theory is employed to argue that the BPP's decline was in part due to oligarchization. At a critical point in the Party's development, the leadership centralized organizational power. This process changed the Party's organizational structure and facilitated significant abuse of power by the leadership. From 1970–74, the Party changed from a large, decentralized, revolutionary organization to a small, highly centralized, reformist group. By 1974, great responsibility had been placed in the hands of a single individual—Huey P. Newton—who often used this power irresponsibly and destructively. While the tenure of Elaine Brown renewed Panther influence and partially halted the decline of the organization during the self-imposed exile of Newton, his return to leadership in July 1977 signaled the eventual demise of the BPP. The depletion of organizational resources spent on numerous Newton criminal trials, coupled with the resurgence of authoritarianism and criminal behavior, ultimately undermined the organization.

Historical Overview

The history of the BPP can be divided into at least four phases. The first phase extended from the birth of the Party in 1966 until the major Party split in 1971. In retrospect, these were the Party's glory years. During its first year and a half, however, the Party was essentially a California phenomenon that began as a small group of young Black men and women working to protect and serve the Black community. The BPP initiated "policing the police" in Oakland because of widespread police brutality. Panthers demanded their right to observe police officers during an arrest and referred to the local, state, and national laws that ensured them that right. More importantly, the Panthers patrolled the streets with guns. When confronted by the police, they would vigorously explain their constitutional right to carry weapons.

This boldness impressed the local Bay Area Black community. The Party first gained state and national recognition in May 1967 when Party members led by Chairman Seale marched into the California state legislature to protest a bill to prohibit individuals from carrying loaded guns. At this point, the Party probably had less than one hundred members. In October 1967, when Huey P. Newton was shot and charged with killing an Oakland police officer, the incident became a catalyst for the national growth of the Party.[10]

In 1968 Party membership dramatically expanded nationwide following the deaths of Dr. Martin Luther King, Jr. and Bobby Hutton (one of the first members of the Party), and the summer's urban protests and rebellions. In 1969–70, the Black Panther presence was felt in almost every major city in the country, and the BPP gained thousands of recruits. However, even during the peak period (1968–70) of the organization's membership, the Party lost members to government repression and organizational purges that attempted to weed out government infiltrators and agent provocateurs.[11]

During this period, serious political and ideological differences developed within the Party. Panthers outside of California complained about their lack of involvement in decision making at the national level. After many violent confrontations with police officers, national Party leaders began to downplay armed self-defense and place greater emphasis on community service programs, especially the popular free breakfast programs for children, free health clinics, and liberation schools. However, some Panthers in other parts of the country disagreed with these policies. Consequently, internal conflicts that were manipulated by the FBI emerged, which led to a major schism within the organization. The 1968–70 period culminated in a series of Party purges and expulsions that were confirmed by Newton and the Central Committee.[12]

The second phase began in spring 1971 with a struggle for the soul of the BPP and ended after the defeat of Seale and Brown in the 1973 Oakland municipal elections. By summer 1971, Newton's supporters had won the internal war. Many of the Panther comrades who dissented joined the Black Liberation Army or other revolutionary groups. Despite this internal conflict, the BPP maintained its organizational integrity as a progressive Black political formation with a firm base in the San Francisco Bay Area and several strong chapters throughout the country.

In 1972, the national leadership decided to call all Party members to Oakland to gain local political power by running Bobby Seale for the office of mayor and Elaine Brown for a city council position. Many members went to California while others refused and left the Party. The BPP invested in local electoral politics in an unprecedented way. However, the decision to close virtually all of the Party's chapters and mount an electoral campaign precipitated a nearly irreversible process of organizational contraction and decline. In Oakland, Panthers worked round the clock registering voters, organizing, and mobilizing the Black community, attending and promoting rallies, and participating in countless campaign meetings. During this period, the BPP also moderated its language and emphasized its reformist rather than its revolutionary image. Reflective of this deradicalization, the Panthers registered as Democratic Party members for the local election. Despite this concentrated electoral effort, the BPP failed to capture the city hall of Oakland. Elaine Brown lost her bid for a seat on the city council while Seale was defeated in a run-off election after placing second in the general election.[13]

The third phase began after the Party's electoral defeat, was intensified by Seale's resignation from the Party in 1974, and culminated with Elaine Brown's departure from the BPP in November 1977. This phase was largely characterized by small organizational membership, successful Panther involvement in Oakland politics, and questionable security activities. Seale's mayoral defeat and resignation prompted an exodus of Party members. During this period, Newton consolidated organizational power. The absence of organizational accountability combined with Newton's addiction to alcohol and drugs led to increasingly erratic and violent behavior that generated negative publicity for the Panthers. In August 1974, Brown assumed the mantle of leadership of the Party. Before Newton fled to Cuba to avoid criminal charges, he appointed Brown chairperson of the BPP. Brown worked to increase BPP influence with local economic and political elites.[14]

The fourth phase, which signaled the final demise of the Party, began in the summer of 1977 with Newton's return to the United States. Although Newton was acquitted of felony murder charges, his resumption of organizational power proved fatal to the Black Panther Party. It was during this period that Elaine Brown left the Party. While some Party members worked on the few remaining positive institutions of the BPP, such as the community school and newspaper, Newton and his security squad engaged in activities that continued to defame the organization. These activities included drug and alcohol abuse, violent behavior against Party comrades and members of the community, and the misappropriation of Party funds.[15] The BPP formally ended with the closure of the Oakland Community School in 1982.

External Factors: Government Repression

Many writers persuasively argue that the BPP was destroyed by the combined repression of the local, state, and national governments. While there is evidence to support this contention, it nonetheless provides an incomplete picture for several reasons. Consequently, a review of this interpretation is in order. Ward Churchill and Jim Vander Wall suggest that the Federal Bureau of Investigation (FBI) "was founded, maintained and steadily expanded as a mechanism to forestall, curtail and repress the expression of political diversity within the United States."[16] Consistent with the above assertion, the FBI considered the BPP an unacceptable participant in American politics and society. In 1968, FBI Director J. Edgar Hoover described the BPP as the greatest internal threat to the nation's security. As one historian noted,

> The Black Panthers attracted the nation's attention, so J. Edgar Hoover decided that they had to be destroyed. Launched in the lame-duck months of Lyndon Johnson's presidency, the Panther campaigns had entered their most repressive phase before the Nixon administration began to pressure the FBI to do more. Hoover's pursuit of the Black Panther Party was unique only in its total disregard for human rights and life itself.[17]

Given the extensive FBI effort to crush the BPP, Churchill and Vander Wall write that "under the weight of such ruthless, concerted and sustained repression—and despite the incredible bravery with which many of its members attempted to continue their work—the Black Panther Party simply collapsed."[18]

Indeed, the government's attack on progressive and radical Black groups was systematic and vicious. The argument for the government's destruction of the BPP is based partially on the fact that the BPP was the victim of almost 80 percent of the 295 FBI authorized "actions" against Black political groups. The FBI's covert action program against the BPP began in 1968 and continued until 1971 when the Bureau allegedly terminated all of its counterintelligence programs (COINTELPRO) against domestic groups because of security leaks. The COINTELPRO against the Panthers was in reality part of a program initiated in August 1967 against a diverse group of Black organizations identified as "Black Nationalist Hate Groups" by the FBI. Among the targeted African American political organizations were the Southern Christian Leadership Conference (SCLC), the Student Nonviolent Coordinating Committee (SNCC), the Revolutionary Action Movement (RAM), and the Nation of Islam (NOI). Several prominent individuals were also identified as targets of COINTELPRO. They included Martin Luther King, Jr., Stokely Carmichael, H. Rap Brown, Maxwell Stanford, and Elijah Muhammad. Although the Panthers eventually received the bulk of the FBI's attention, the BPP was not an original target of COINTELPRO. As the BPP gained national and international prominence, the FBI attempted to promote violent conflicts between the BPP and other Black power groups, encourage BPP internal dissension, undermine Panther support, and provoke local police attacks on the BPP. With such repressive tactics, in many instances, the FBI succeeded in neutralizing the Party's political programs.[19]

The BPP was confronted with comprehensive government repression that took diverse forms. All Panthers were subject to police surveillance and harassment. Police officers regularly harassed both the leadership and rank-and-file Party members. They issued parking and traffic tickets for minor and/or nonexistent violations and often arrested Party members on trumped-up charges. Court fines for traffic violations and unjustifiable arrests forced the BPP to allocate time and money to legal matters rather than organizing in the Black community. Between December 1967 and December 1969, the Party paid more than two hundred thousand dollars in bail-bond premiums, money the BPP would never recover. During the same period, at least twenty-eight Panthers were killed.[20] These deaths, which occurred early in the Party's history, were usually the result of conflicts with local police and FBI-inspired intra-party strife and external conflicts with other Black power organizations. Consequently, Panthers were often beset with a siege mentality, unsure who to trust and uncertain about when they might meet death. New York Panther Dhoruba Bin Wahad, formerly Richard Moore, recalls,

> I felt I was in a war. I would walk down a street and if kids threw firecrackers, man, I would duck. The only reason we wouldn't shoot back was that we had a policy to see who it was first. It stayed that way until I was arrested. You could see by some of the photos how I looked. I looked like one of the POW's in the early stages of the battle outside Laos—you know, Vietnam. I was completely shell shocked. I had a combat mentality.[21]

In its destructive program against the BPP, government agencies attacked top chapter leaders in particularly brutal and sophisticated ways. Two brief examples of effective government repression illustrate this point. Created in November 1968, the Illinois chapter of the BPP was one of the most active and productive in the country. Led by charismatic leader Fred Hampton, the Illinois chapter initiated a free breakfast for children program, operated a free health clinic, and brokered a truce among some of Chicago's most violent and notorious street gangs. Hampton and fellow Panther Bobby Rush led the Illinois chapter in sponsoring massive "Free Huey" rallies and other well-attended street demonstrations. The chapter's success in organizing effectively gained the attention of law enforcement at the local, state, and national levels. In fact, FBI informers infiltrated the chapter and attempted to undermine its activities. In one of the clearest examples of this conspiracy, the FBI coordinated activities and shared information on the Illinois BPP with state, county, and local police officials. These efforts culminated in the murder of Illinois BPP leaders Fred Hampton and Mark Clark on December 4, 1969 by Chicago police officers. Several other Panthers were also wounded in the 4 a.m. police raid on the Panther apartment.[22]

The situation of Elmer "Geronimo" ji Jaga (Pratt) provides another example of the United States government's attempt to destroy the BPP. On August 24, 1994, ji Jaga was denied parole for the twelfth time by the California State Board of Prison Terms. A former BPP leader, ji Jaga was incarcerated in California prisons for twenty-seven years. In June 1997, ji Jaga was released from prison after a judge overturned his prior conviction. The available evidence suggests that ji Jaga was a victim of the FBI's effort to "neutralize" Panther leaders. After spending two years in prison on an unrelated charge, ji Jaga was convicted in 1972 by a Los Angeles jury for the 1968 murder of a Santa Monica woman. Three of the case's four crucial

points involve the FBI. First, and without FBI interference, immediately after the attack, the victim's husband gave a description of the murderer that
did not resemble ji Jaga. Four years later, the husband identified ji Jaga in
a police lineup. Unlike the other men in the lineup, ji Jaga was wearing clothing similar to the type worn by the murderer as described by the victim's
husband. Second, the prosecution's chief witness Julius C. Butler, a former
Panther, denied under oath that he worked for any law enforcement agency.
The FBI also denied under oath that Butler was an informant. In 1979, newly
declassified FBI documents showed that not only had Butler met with FBI
agents, he had also supplied them with information about ji Jaga. Third, the
FBI infiltrated the group of friends and attorneys who planned ji Jaga's trial
defense. Finally, ji Jaga argued that he was in Oakland on the day of the murder, December 18, 1968. Mysteriously, the FBI claimed that their tapes of
wiretaps on Panther phones in Oakland and Los Angeles for that month had
been destroyed. According to ji Jaga, those tapes would have confirmed his
presence in Oakland. In freeing ji Jaga, the California judge considered the
aforementioned points. At this time, the District Attorney's office has not
taken a position on a ji Jaga retrial.[23]

Ji Jaga's true crime seems to have been that as a rank-and-file member and
then Deputy Minister of Defense, he was a tremendously effective Panther.
Ji Jaga's effectiveness as a member of the Black Panther Party was partly
due to his military experience. He served in Vietnam as a paratrooper and
"participated in a series of highly classified missions, garnering some eighteen combat decorations—including the Silver Star, Bronze Star (for valor),
Vietnamese Cross of Gallantry, and the Purple Heart. Despite his military
heroics, ji Jaga was disenchanted with the nature of the war, the military system, and the social order that spawned them."[24] Ji Jaga taught other Panthers
the basics of self-defense, military strategy and tactics, and political organizing. He worked in the BPP's Southern California chapter and contributed
to its early popularity and community respect.[25] The unjust imprisonment of
ji Jaga and the murders of Fred Hampton and Mark Clark were not isolated
incidents. Panther leaders and rank-and-file members were constantly harassed and incarcerated by law enforcement throughout the United States
during all phases of the Party's history. Several Panthers remain in prison
today because of their Panther affiliation and background.[26]

To counteract the onslaught of government repression, the Party developed several measures, which included purging suspected infiltrators, improving ties with traditional community groups, and intensifying its
community survival programs.[27] In short, the Black Panther Party was the
target of systematic and comprehensive (overt and covert) political repression by all three levels of government. Nevertheless, the singular focus on
government repression fails to explain the complex factors leading to the demise of the BPP. We must examine the role of internal factors to fully understand the decline of the Black Panther Party.

Demise of the BPP: Internal Factors

Elite theory does not posit that large political organizations will inevitably decline. Rather, elite theory holds that the leaders of such organizations will generally attempt to increase their power, often at the expense of the organization. In addition, rank-and-file members are usually unable to control their leaders. Oligarchization, as described earlier, helps to account for how Party leadership contributed to the decline of the BPP. In this respect, the leadership contributed decisively to the eventual collapse of the organization in three ways, which include (1) intra-party conflict, (2) strategic organizational mistakes, and (3) a new authoritarianism by Huey P. Newton. In examining the role of these factors, I review the four main phases of the Party's history to highlight how critical these factors were in the eventual demise of the Party. I argued earlier that the first phase began with the Party's birth in 1966 and lasted until the 1971 split within the Party. Newton's release from prison in August 1970 represented the crucial point in this phase.

During this initial period the BPP grew from a small group based in the San Francisco Bay Area to a national and international organization. The BPP created a three-tiered structure to accommodate its rapid expansion. At the highest level, the Party's governing body, the Central Committee, comprised BPP founders Huey P. Newton as Minister of Defense and Bobby Seale as Chairman, along with Minister of Information Eldridge Cleaver, Deputy Minister of Information Frank Jones, and Chief of Staff David Hilliard. The Central Committee was always based at national headquarters in the Bay Area. The intermediate level was formed by state regional chapters such as Illinois, Maryland, and New York. The leaders of these chapters were chosen, or if self-selected, confirmed by Chairman Seale or a representative of national headquarters. Local branches represented the BPP at the ground level. The rank-and-file members would report to branch or chapter leaders depending on Party organization development in a specific geographic area.[28] An overview of the Party's organizational structure can be seen in Table 1.

The state and local pattern of organization varied significantly from place to place. Finally, community workers were members of the Black community who desired to be Panthers, but who were not official members. They often performed various Party duties, such as selling the Party newspaper, *The Black Panther*, working in the free breakfast programs, and attending political education classes. Their status became somewhat difficult to distinguish from that of rank-and-file members after 1969 because police infiltration made the Party discontinue formally accepting new members.[29]

An important fact of this early period is that the most prominent Panther, Huey P. Newton, did not participate directly in the building of the national BPP. That task was carried out primarily by leaders Bobby Seale, Eldridge Cleaver, Chief of Staff David Hilliard, and state and local leaders throughout the country.[30] Because Newton was arrested for the murder of a police officer in Oakland, California in October 1967 and was eventually convicted of voluntary manslaughter in September 1968, he was not released from prison until August 1970 after his lawyers gained a new trial on appeal. In prison, Newton became a device for recruitment and his life the subject of a national and international "Free Huey" campaign. Newton achieved mythic status among many Black and radical activists as a political prisoner capable of facing down vicious white racist cops.

Despite problems of every description, the BPP's first four years were its most successful in terms of growth in chapters and membership, effectiveness, and prestige.[31] Perceived by many African Americans as a fearless radical political group, the BPP challenged and called national and international attention to police brutality, poverty, socioeconomic inequality, and the Vietnam War. The Party's success stemmed fundamentally from its ability to inspire African American youth and young adults to work for their people. Sharon Harley, a member of the Washington, DC, chapter, reflects on her experience:

> For me it was an opportunity to be with people who I thought were right on or who were really smart or politically savvy. . . .They were willing to risk their lives for their people. The people being mainly described as poor, black, but also, in various points we identified with people of color throughout the world who were struggling against oppression.[32]

The Party was winning the hearts and minds of many African Americans who were impatient with the Civil Rights movement's perceived emphasis on gradual and legislative change.[33] Although each chapter had a distinct political culture depending on its locality, all Party organizational entities were influenced by the founders' organizing principles of democratic centralism and strict discipline. According to these two principles, members' opinions were sought on diverse issues, but after decisions were made, they were to be implemented promptly and without further question.[34] The early Panther armed patrols, the military experience of Seale and many other members, and the Party's militant rhetoric gave the BPP a paramilitary image and a commitment to disciplined action. The Panthers considered themselves at war with an oppressive capitalist and racist political system. To ensure organizational discipline, Party leaders utilized corporal and other punishment when a member violated Party rules or risked a fellow comrade's life unnecessarily. For example, Seale once ordered a Panther beaten by his Party comrades for raping a female member.[35]

Intra-Party Conflict: The Early Signs of Decline

During the second phase (1971–1973/4), intra-party conflict racked the Party. The seeds of this conflict were planted after Newton's release from prison in August 1970. Once a free man, Newton worked to gain the recently imprisoned Seale's freedom and to strengthen the Party's community service programs. At this time, Eldridge Cleaver was in exile in Algeria heading

Black Panther Party Organizational Framework, 1967–1968

Level of Organization	Units and Positions of the Organization
National	**Central Committee**
	Minister of Defense,
	Chairman,
	Minister of Information,
	Deputy Minister of Information,
	Chief of Staff
	Communications Secretary,
	Field Marshals,
	Minister of Education,
	Prime Minister,
	Minister of Justice,
	Minister of Foreign Affairs,
	Minister of Religion,
	Minister of Culture,
	Minister of Finance
Regional	**State Chapters**
	Chapter Leaders
Local	**City Branches**
	Branch Leaders
	Rank-and-File Members

Source: Taylor and Lewis, 31; Holder, 16–26. Note: The BPP's International Office was developed more fully in 1969 and 1970.

Table 1

the International Section of the BPP. Newton and Cleaver, two of the Party's most prominent members and leaders of the Central Committee, increasingly differed on strategy and tactics. Newton downplayed self-defense and police confrontation. Cleaver, however, advocated violent revolution and urban guerrilla warfare. Cleaver failed to recognize that the emphasis on military action isolated the BPP from the community thereby reinforcing its image as a gang of super-revolutionaries. On the other hand, Newton was unprepared and overwhelmed by a national organization built largely in his name. In late 1970, he toured the country speaking at major political events and visiting Panther chapters. As a public speaker, Newton greatly disappointed his followers. As David Hilliard, Newton's lifelong friend, remembers,

> Huey's great in small sessions, enthusiastic, intense, funny. But before
> large groups he freezes; his voice gets high—the soprano that used to

be a cause of fights back in school—and his style stiffens; he sounds academic, goes on incessantly, and becomes increasingly abstract, spinning out one dialectical contradiction after another.[36]

Newton did not inspire his audiences in the manner of Cleaver, Seale, and other Panther leaders such as Chicago's Fred Hampton and New York's Cetewayo (Michael Tabor).[37]

The stylistic and substantive differences between Cleaver and Newton reflected deeper schisms within the Party that manifested in conflicts between national headquarters and state chapters. A case in point was the friction between Oakland and the New York chapter, one of the largest in the country with local branches in Harlem, Brooklyn, Queens, the Bronx, and other parts of the state. The New York State chapter lodged several complaints with the national leadership while Newton was in prison. New York leaders assumed that with the release of Newton their grievances would be addressed. Unfortunately, Newton's release only exacerbated the tensions between the New York chapter and Oakland. New York leaders tended to agree with Cleaver that the Party should emphasize military action. However, other substantive disagreements were readily apparent. New York Panthers noted that the lack of chapter representation on the Central Committee hampered their local organizing efforts. Moreover, African American nationalism was very strong among New York Panthers exemplified by the adoption African names, the display of the Red, Black, and Green flag symbolizing the Black Nation, and frequent participation in Black cultural events. Conversely, national headquarters emphasized class over race and experienced numerous and sometimes fatal conflicts with Black cultural nationalists.[38]

Consequently, the BPP national leaders prohibited New York Panthers from working closely with cultural nationalists. Moreover, New York Panthers resented the national leadership's deemphasis of local organizing around housing issues and drugs in the Black community. Instead, Oakland placed greater emphasis on the free breakfast, clothing, and health care issues. In short, New York leaders felt that their lack of representation on the Central Committee prevented the national leadership from appreciating the importance and distinctiveness of local conditions.[39]

Disagreements over the distribution of material resources also fueled intra-party strife. To operate its programs, the BPP received funds from various sources: lawyers' groups, church organizations, community organizations, and individuals. Party leadership also raised funds via speaking engagements.[40] The Panthers also received thousands of dollars from wealthy White, and sometimes famous, supporters.[41] Bert Schneider, the Hollywood movie producer, personally contributed large sums of money and secured the Oakland penthouse apartment occupied by Newton after his release from prison.[42]

Party chapters were required to contribute a certain percentage of paper sales and other income to the national headquarters for organizational maintenance. Increasingly, members of the other Panther affiliates felt exploited by the national office. Party members in New York, Illinois, and other chapters became concerned when reports surfaced that Newton and other national leaders were living in penthouse apartments and extravagant homes. Diana Lin Tiatt, a Panther from the Brooklyn branch, recalls,

> It seemed like they were taking everything in California. I don't know where the money was going. We were turning in our paper money . . . . People gave us contributions. . . . I went to various people. We went to various well-to-do people and they gave us contributions, mostly checks or whatever. We turned everything in. We turned every dime in. . . . Then we found out that people were living good. . . . some local, but mostly Californians. . . I started hearing these rumors that they were living in penthouses. . . and all kinds of stuff. That makes you look like sort of a chump or a fool, when you're going without. . . .Nobody forced me to do any of that. I willingly gave. And I willingly did everything. And I was happy to be there to do that. But then things started breaking down. And rumors, and rumors, and rumors.[43]

Intra-party disputes combined with government repression finally culminated in the splintering of the Party. Newton, in the Central Committee's name, confirmed the split by expelling several well-respected Party leaders. In early 1971, Newton expelled Geronimo ji Jaga, Connie Matthews, Michael "Cetewayo" Tabor, and Dhoruba Moore, as well as the entire New York 21 after proclaiming them "enemies of the people."[44] Several attempts to reverse these expulsions were ultimately unsuccessful. Eldridge and Kathleen Cleaver and others argued that as Central Committee members they should have been informed prior to the expulsions. The Cleaver-led faction argued for reinstatements of the purged Panthers. Newton and the national leadership rejected this view. On February 26, 1971, Newton and Cleaver agreed to discuss Party differences during a local San Francisco television program in which Eldridge Cleaver phoned in from Algeria. They promptly began to argue and expelled each other from the organization. This intra-party strife continued throughout the year. The New York leadership as well as various Party members scattered across the nation aligned with Cleaver.[45]

Organizational factional conflict reached a deadly level when Robert Webb, a West Coast Panther originally who sided with the Cleavers and the New York Panthers, was murdered on March 8, 1971.[46] Six weeks later on April 17, 1971, Samuel Napier, Distribution Manager of *The Black Panther*, was tortured and killed in New York allegedly in retaliation for Robert Webb's death.[47] Both Napier and Webb were respected and beloved members of the Party. Such internecine warfare created general fear in the Party and prompted many Panthers to abandon the organization.[48] According to Seale's recollection, approximately thirty to forty percent of the BPP left as a result of this internal conflict.[49]

As previously noted by both activists and scholars, intra-party conflict was fostered and abetted by governmental officials. Unbeknownst to Newton and Cleaver, in March 1970 the FBI initiated a program to divide the two Panther leaders. The FBI also conspired to permanently divide the New York chapter from national headquarters. Years later, Newton would reflect on the government's successful attempt to divide the Party. In conducting research for his 1980 doctoral dissertation, Newton discovered: "For three solid weeks a barrage of anonymous letters flowed from FBI Headquarters. The messages became more and more vicious."[50] Newton's behavior was clearly affected by the government's psychological warfare and disinformation campaigns.[51] These counter-intelligence activities continued throughout 1970–71 and certainly weakened the Party's effectiveness, but proved not to be the sole determinant of its demise.

In late 1971 and early 1972, Newton and Seale regained control of the Party and intensified and expanded its involvement in the Black community. New BPP programs included the Samuel Napier Youth Intercommunal Institute, the Free Busing to Prisons Program, the People's Free Clothing Program, and the George Jackson People's Free Medical Research Health Clinics.[52] In August 1971, the Panthers initiated a boycott of Bill Boyette's liquor store in Oakland. The boycott began after Cal-Pak, a local group of Black business owners, refused to give money directly to the BPP for its community service programs. As Cal-Pak's president, Mr. Boyette claimed to support the actual programs, but he rejected the heavy-handed demand for money and the lack of public accountability for ensuring that donations would, in fact, go to the programs. Only the intervention of Congressman Ronald Dellums led to a compromise that ended the boycott in January 1972.[53] The Party's new activities demonstrated Panther engagement in local community affairs but also signaled the Party's ideological and political transformation from revolutionary to reformist views.

Strategic Organizational Mistakes: The 1973 Election

In 1972, the BPP made what proved to be a strategic mistake that led to an unfortunate concentration of power in Newton's hands. In that year, the Party decided to mount a campaign to capture the Oakland mayoral and other local offices. Toward this goal, the Central Committee agreed to close all chapters outside of Oakland, California in order to support Bobby Seale's mayoral candidacy.

In an attempt to preempt more state chapter rebellions and increase the BPP's power in Oakland, Newton presented the Central Committee with two bold ideas: (1) the Party should run Bobby Seale, leading a full slate of Panther candidates for local office, for mayor of Oakland and (2) the Party should close all chapters outside of Oakland and redeploy all Panthers and their resources (money, cars, office materials, etc.) to Oakland to work on the campaign and consolidate the Party at its birthplace.[54]

Newton's proposal reflected his evolving thought on the nature of power. At the Party's founding, Newton defined power as the ability to define a phenomenon and make it act in a desired manner. He and Seale related power to the use of political violence. Consequently, they adopted Mao's credo that "political power comes from the barrel of a gun" for the Party. But as a result of his studies in prison, fatal Panther shoot-outs with police, and the recent internal Party warfare, Newton's original definition of power evolved into the new theory of intercommunalism.[55] In Newton's new thinking, the Party gave more serious attention to the political and economic dimensions of power and de-emphasized its earlier military focus.

Newton believed that if the Party gained political control of Oakland, it could promote an ambitious economic development plan that included turning the city's port into a highly profitable state of the art facility, promoting local Black business, and implementing new human and social service programs. The Central Committee enthusiastically supported the idea of acquiring political power in Oakland, but was initially divided on the necessity of dismantling the national organization. Chairman Seale led the opposition to breaking down the chapters on strategic and tactical grounds. Strategically, he saw no need to take this action because the Party was already strong in Oakland and had excellent local organizers. Tactically, Seale reasoned that the national headquarters lacked the resources necessary (money, houses, apartments, and jobs) to receive over a thousand members from around the country on short notice. More importantly, the Party had organizational commitments and existing service programs in operation around the country. According to Seale, the Party could not and should not fold its chapters.[56] In retrospect, Audrea Jones, former Massachusetts chapter leader, Central Committee member, and the only woman to lead a state chapter, agreed with Seale's early assessment:

> It [the closing of all chapters outside California] was a major mistake. I think that it was a major mistake. It was a national organization with viable structures in communities. I think people felt abandoned by that. There was great support for the Party in local chapters and branches. People had . . . put themselves out to be part of that. To just close down clinics and close down breakfast programs. I mean the whole idea was to organize these things to the extent that things could be taken over. But there was a hole left.[57]

A large contingent of Panthers from outside the Bay Area also shared Seale's opinion. When the membership received the new directive from the Central Committee, many members refused to uproot their lives and move thousands of miles from home. These Panthers simply left the Party. The leaders of the various state chapters expressed misgivings with the Central Committee's directive to close their respective Party units. In addition to running community programs, they had comrades in jail and on trial for various charges who required legal assistance.[58]

On the positive side, members were happy to finally get to know and work with all the Party comrades from around the country. This infusion of new energy reinvigorated many of the Bay Area community service programs. Members also benefited from the ideological and political training provided by the national leadership. On the negative side, some Panthers new to the Bay Area, were disappointed in the intellectual capacity and lack of preparation of various national leaders who were teaching political education classes. Compounding this problem was the limited contact between most Party members and the Party's main leader, Huey P. Newton. Party cadres wanted to interact more with Newton but were constantly told that he was busy writing. Paul Coates, leader of the Maryland chapter, experienced this problem:

> Now Huey, who is the teacher, or who was supposed to be the teacher, is busy writing a book . . . but he can't come down to the masses. So I'm frustrated with this, too. Huey never made his presence felt at that time. This is after he was out of jail. He never really made his presence one with the masses.[59]

After weeks of debate and individual lobbying of Central Committee members by Newton and Seale, the Committee decided to close all chapters temporarily and to dismantle them gradually over the course of the year (1972). Newton had won the day by accepting Seale's recommendation of a staggered closing of chapters and arguing finally that Party members would eventually take their new campaign skills and governing experience (obviously anticipating victory) and return to their home cities and replicate the Oakland experience of gaining local power. In the end, Seale accepted this view and threw himself into organizing Oakland and running for mayor.[60]

During 1972 and early 1973, Panthers converged on Oakland from all parts of the country. The BPP concentrated the majority of its resources on Seale's mayoral bid and Elaine Brown's campaign for a city council seat. Panthers registered voters, distributed campaign literature, and participated in campaign meetings and rallies throughout 1972–73.[61] Even though both races were competitive, Seale and Brown lost their elections. Seale ran second in the initial three-person race. In the run-off election, he captured 43,719 votes, but lost to incumbent Mayor John Reading who received 77,634 votes.[62] The impact of the electoral defeat was devastating on the Party because its members had invested so much time and effort in the campaigns.

Shortly after the election, many Panthers resigned from the Party because of disappointment, exhaustion, and disillusionment. Their departure represented the beginning of the end of the BPP's second phase. According to Seale, the Party had five hundred members at this point. The organization initially gained its popular support and national prominence as an antisystem party that selectively supported progressive politicians (for example, Ron

Dellums) and ran symbolic candidates (Newton for Congress in 1968 while he was in jail), served the Black community, and offered a systemic critique of American society and politics.

In the 1973 election, the BPP formally entered the electoral process. However, the decision to invest almost all of its political and material resources in the 1973 elections proved to be a critical strategic mistake by the Party leadership. From that point on, the Party never recuperated its size, prestige, and effectiveness. The Party's future efforts remained confined to the Oakland Bay area.[63]

Authoritarian Politics: The Final Demise

The last two phases of the BPP's history were characterized by a sharp contrast between the Party's constructive activities and its increasing authoritarianism.[64] This latter development was the third major internal factor contributing to the BPP's decline. Authoritarianism emerged as early as 1971 but expanded dramatically after the 1973 electoral defeat. The decision to close down all chapters outside of Oakland not only reduced the size of the BPP, it also changed the Party's organizational structure. Most importantly, Newton increasingly centralized power. During most of the BPP's first phase, state regional leaders developed their own contacts and relationships with various institutional and local individual supporters. Consequently, despite the lack of representation on the Central Committee, they still maintained relative autonomy based on their personal contacts and geographical distance from national headquarters. After 1972, Newton required that all money coming into the Party go directly to him. Then he would distribute it to the BPP's relevant programs. Newton created several corporate entities to store the Party's money. He also diverted money from Party programs to support his personal activities.[65] Party members tended to accept this centralization of money and power by Newton because of their excessive worship and later fear of him as a leader. This pattern of behavior is consistent with elite theory. The leader took clear steps to increase his power, and the organization's members failed to prevent this concentration of power and resources.

The Party's last two periods, 1973–77 and 1977–82, witnessed numerous incidents of abuse of power resulting from Newton's centralization of authority within the BPP. Whereas Party leaders would discipline members for violations of Party rules in the first phase (1966–71), in the subsequent periods, Newton began to assault Party members and innocent bystanders on personal whim. These outbursts by Newton usually occurred in his penthouse apartment or in one of the Panther-owned or controlled establishments, such as the Lamp Post Restaurant and Bar in Oakland. Two such reported outbursts occurred in August 1974. In the first event, Newton allegedly stepped out of his car on a Monday evening, a little before midnight, and shot Kathleen Smith in the jaw for calling him "baby." Kathleen Smith, a prostitute, had been working on the Oakland streets that evening with her friend Crystal Gray. The gunshot damaged Smith's spine and sent her into a coma. She died three months later. Gray was an eyewitness and identified Newton as the murderer. Less than two weeks later, Newton pistol-whipped Preston Callins in Newton's penthouse apartment. Callins, a tailor, had offered to make Newton some dress suits at a discount price. During their conversation, Callins innocently referred to Newton as "baby" and Newton became enraged. He smashed a gun into the back of Callins' head and continued to brutalize him until Callins finally struck Newton back and attempted to leave the apartment. Bleeding profusely, Callins stumbled out of Newton's apartment only to be caught and forced back into the apartment where he was repeatedly tortured.[66] Newton's behavior was partially the result of serious alcohol and drug abuse. After his release from prison in 1970, Newton's celebrity status brought him a regular flow of alcohol, drugs, and other substances that he consumed recklessly.[67]

Other BPP abuses during this phase were of a more organizational nature. In 1972, the Central Committee created the Party's security cadre.[68] Its original purpose was to provide security for Panther leaders, especially the Party's candidates for public office. In addition, Newton believed that to consolidate political power in the city of Oakland, the Party would have to gain complete control of both legal and illegal affairs. This meant regulation of the city's vices or underworld activities. Newton reasoned that Oakland's criminal class would only understand violence. So, the Party's security cadre protected the Party's leaders while trying to force Oakland's criminal groups to pay the Party money for the right to continue their activities.[69] Apparently, during 1973–74 only Newton was privy to the full extent of the Party's growing activities and multiple organizational units, which included political and extra-political wings of the Party. Even Bobby Seale, co-founder of the BPP, did not know the extent of Newton's substance abuse, extortion of local crime organizations, misappropriation of Party funds, and violence against fellow Party comrades and members of the community. The BPP's decline accelerated in 1974 with the departure of several key Panther leaders. Seale resigned July 31, 1974, after a major argument with Newton.[70] Audrea Jones and other Panthers left the Party shortly after Seale's resignation.[71]

Newton might have caused the demise of the BPP then had he not gone into exile in Cuba in August 1974. Newton fled the U.S. to avoid a series of felony counts related to the Smith murder and the assault of Preston Callins. Newton returned to the United States three years later to face these charges on which he was later acquitted. In Newton's absence, Elaine Brown became the Party's leader and managed to recuperate some of the Party's respectability. Brown appointed more women to leadership positions in the Party. Ericka Huggins guided the community school, and Black women such as Phyllis Jackson, Joan Kelley, and Norma Armour handled financial and administrative tasks.[72] At this time, the Party, with less than two hundred members, returned to its roots as a local Oakland organization. Brown also successfully secured government and private financial support for several Panther programs.

In 1975, she ran another impressive campaign for Oakland City Council and finished second. However, her campaign was seriously hampered by drug charges and accusations that she was involved in the murder of Betty Van Patter, a White woman who had been hired to put the Party's financial records in order.[73] Brown was also former California Governor Jerry Brown's delegate to the 1976 Democratic Party's National Convention.[74] During her leadership, the BPP played a key role in the election of the first Black mayor of Oakland, Judge Lionel Wilson, in 1977. At the same time, Brown continued the BPP's violent underground operations and tended to rely on corporal punishment to maintain her authority over Party comrades.[75]

The final stage of the Party lasted from 1977–82. In August 1977, Newton returned to the U.S. In response, Brown, citing a lack of mental and physical strength, resigned from the Party. She too has claimed to have been beaten by Newton.[76] Following Newton's return, the security cadre increased its involvement in criminal activities. Under Newton's guidance, the Party began to lose all legitimacy. For example, on October 23, 1977, the security cadre contributed greatly to discrediting the Party's remaining image when a botched assassination attempt of Crystal Gray (the eyewitness to the murder of Kathleen Smith) resulted in the death of Panther Louis Johnson and the wounding of another.[77] During this phase, there were revelations of gross financial mismanagement of private and government grants. The Party discontinued several community programs beginning in the late 1970s. The last issue of *The Black Panther* was published in 1980, and the school closed in 1982 because of a lack of money, some of which Newton was eventually convicted of embezzling.[78]

Conclusion

The BPP emerged at a time of great political activity and excitement at the possibility of radical social change in the U.S. In their work, the Panthers contributed significantly to making America a more democratic, egalitarian, and humane society. Party members led the movement to end police brutality and create civilian police- review boards. The BPP's free breakfast programs became a catalyst for today's free meals to poor school children. More than most progressive political groups, the Party highlighted, connected, and protested U.S. oppression abroad and U.S. injustice at home. The revolution was not achieved, but important reforms were.

The rise of the Party was rapid and dramatic; its fall, slow and embarrassing. The BPP's experience provides a guide for a new generation of Black activists. Members of the Black Panther Party were committed activists who read and studied a wide body of revolutionary literature in order to understand and improve the plight of their people. They applied the teachings of

European, Asian, African, and Latin American revolutionaries to the African American condition. Party theoreticians also drew on the revolutionary writings of the founding fathers of the United States, especially the Declaration of Independence and the Constitution. Perhaps their most important influence was Malcolm X. Black Panthers sought Black power and liberation "by any means necessary."[79] Their genius was to transform their radical analyses into practical programs affecting the daily lives of the masses of Black people. However, like many revolutionaries, the Panthers were young and impatient, and they made mistakes. The confluence of three internal factors (intra-party conflict, strategic organizational errors, and a rise in party authoritarianism) contributed directly to the demise of the BPP. As a result of these forces, the Party dismantled its national organizational apparatus, concentrated its remaining resources in one geographic area, and lodged organizational authority in a single person.

Elite theory asserts that leaders usually have more power and influence in organizations than the rank-and-file membership. Nonetheless, the membership has the responsibility of holding top leaders accountable to an organization's principles. The BPP's decline might have been averted if an effective system of intra-party democracy and financial accounting had been instituted. Black America has frequently suffered because "Great Men" have gained too much power within leading organizations and groups. Government repression, intra-organizational conflict, and strategic mistakes are likely to occur in radical social movements. These factors become increasingly detrimental for an organization when combined with an unwarranted concentration of power in one or a few leaders. Such a combination of forces eventually undermined the Black Panther Party.

NOTES

1. Huey P. Newton, *Revolutionary Suicide* (New York: Harcourt Brace Jovanovich,1973), 99–114; Bobby Seale, S*eize the Time* (Baltimore: Black Classic Press, 1991), 44–69. The original and revised versions of the BPP's 10 Point Platform and Program illustrate the founders' diverse concerns.

2. Alphonso Pinkney, *Red, Black, and Green: Black Nationalism in the United States* (Cambridge: Cambridge University Press, 1976), 98–126; Manning Marable, *Race, Reform, and Rebellion: The Second Reconstruction in Black America, 1945–1990.* Revised Second Edition (Jackson: University of Mississippi, 1991), 108–110.

3. I want to thank many friends and colleagues for comments and criticism. From the University of Maryland at College Park, graduate students Pam Burke, Todd Burroughs, Margo Plater, and Delgreco Wilson provided important research assistance and feedback. Faculty members Ken Conca, Mark Graber, Ted Gurr, Paul Herrson, Joe Oppenheimer, Clarence Stone, Eric Uslaner, and Bruce Williams read and discussed early drafts with me. Outside the University of Maryland, Black politics scholars Charles E. Jones and Robert C. Smith offered penetrating and constructive critiques. Unfortunately, I was unable to incorporate all of their suggestions. Monifa Akinwole contributed a helpful and vigorous critique. Special thanks to the Black Panthers who agreed to give interviews.

4. There is ongoing debate regarding the membership figures for the BPP. The above numbers are from Bobby Seale, former chairman of the BPP from 1966 to 1974. Seale argues that Party membership peaked at around 5,000 in late 1968 and into 1969. He says that the BPP had approximately 3,000 members in February 1971 following the major split between Huey Newton and Eldridge Cleaver. Seale states that the Party had 1,250 members in early 1973 during his mayoral election campaign and 500 after his electoral defeat. He believes that there were 200 members in the Party when he resigned on July 31, 1974. Seale's estimates are based on his observations and numbers given him by Party leaders from around the country. Interview by author, September 24, 1994, Philadelphia, PA. Most academic and journalistic estimates of Party membership are lower with membership peaking at around 2000 in 1968 and 1969. The BPP did not keep formal membership rolls or lists. Party membership fluctuated greatly throughout the Party's history. Seale's figures should probably be seen as estimates of a constantly fluctuating membership.

5.See for example, Anthony Oberschall, *Social Movements: Ideologies, Interests, and Identities* (New Brunswick: Transaction Publishers, 1993); Jo Freeman, ed. *Social Movements of the Sixties and Seventies* (New York: Longman, 1983); Doug McAdam, *Political Process and the Development of Black Insurgency, 1930–1970* (Chicago: The University of Chicago Press, 1982).

6. Robert Michels, *Political Parties: A Sociological Study of the Oligarchical Tendencies of Modern Democracy* (New York: The Free Press, 1962). For direct applications of elite theory to American politics and society, see the work of Thomas R. Dye, especially, *Who's Running America? The Bush Era*, 5th ed. (Englewood, NJ: Prentice-Hall, 1990) and Thomas R. Dye and Harmon Zeigler, *The Irony of Democracy: An Uncommon Introduction to American Politics* (Pacific Grove, CA: Brooks/Cole Publishing Company, 1990).

7. Oligarchy refers to an organizational or political situation in which top leaders are unconstrained and uncontrolled in their decisions and activities.

8. Michels, *Political Parties*, 61–106.

9. C.W. Cassinelli, "The Law of Oligarchy," *American Political Science Review* (1953), 773–784. Thanks to Professor Clarence Stone for emphasizing the importance of this article.

10. Ula Y. Taylor and J. Tarika Lewis, "Part 1—The History," in *Panther: A Pictorial History of the Black Panthers and the Story behind the Film* (New York: Newmarket Press, 1995), 26–51.

11. On the role of agent provocateurs, see Gary T. Marx, "Thoughts on a Neglected Category of Social Movement Participant: The Agent Provocateur and the Informant," *American Journal of Sociology*, no. 2 (1974), 80. I would like to thank Professor Robert C. Smith for calling my attention to this article.

12. Clayborne Carson, "Foreward," *The Black Panthers Speak*, edited by Philip S. Foner (New York: Da Capo Press, 1995), xii–xvi.

13. Taylor and Lewis, *Panther*, 99–124.

14. Elaine Brown, *A Taste of Power: A Black Woman's Story* (New York: Pantheon Books, 1992), 311–450.

15. Taylor and Lewis, *Panther*, 120–128. See Hugh Pearson, *The Shadow of the Panther: Huey Newton and the Price of Black Power in America* (Reading, MA: Addison-Wesley Publishing Company, 1994) for the view that excessive violence, sexism, and elitism permeated the Party from the beginning. Pearson exaggerates the early negative activities of Party members by describing real and alleged wrongs committed by specific Party members and then generalizing this behavior throughout the Party.

16. Ward Churchill and Jim Vander Wall, *Agents of Repression: The FBI's Secret Wars Against the Black Panther Party and the American Indian Movement*, Corrected Edition (Boston, MA: South End Press, 1990), 12.

17. Kenneth O'Reilly, *"Racial Matters": The FBI's Secret File on Black America, 1960–1972* (New York: The Free Press, 1989), 294.

18. Ward Churchill and Jim Vander Wall, *The COINTELPRO Papers: Documents from the FBI's Secret Wars Against Dissent in the United States* (Boston, MA: South End Press, 1990), 164.

19. U.S. Congress. Senate. *Book III, Final Report of the Select Committee to Study Governmental Operations with Respect to Intelligence Activities*. 94th Cong., 2d sess., 1976.

20. Charles R. Garry, "A Survey of the Persecution of the Black Panther Party," *The Black Panthers Speak*, edited by Philip S. Foner (New York: Da Capo Press, 1995), 257–258. The recent book by Frank Donner, *Protectors of Privilege: Red Squads and Police Repression in Urban America* (Berkeley: University of California Press, 1990) also highlights how local police departments often harassed Black Panthers in cities around the country.

21. Jim Fletcher, Tanaquil Jones, and Sylvere Lotringer, eds. *Still Black, Still Strong; Survivors of the U.S. War Against Black Revolutionaries—Dhoruba Bin Wahad, Mumia Abu-Jamal, Assata Shakur* (New York: Semiotext(e), 1993), 10.

22. Lynn French, "The Murder of Fred Hampton," Photocopy, 21–30; Churchill and Vander Wall, *Agents of Repression*, 64–77.

23. *Oakland Tribune*, 5 May, 1987, A–9; *Oakland Tribune*, 6 May 1987, A–6; *San Francisco Examiner*, 12 January 1986; Court TV's *Lock & Key*, "Geronimo Pratt," 23 November 1994; Associated Press "Judge Orders New Trial for Former Panther" *The Washington Post*, 30 May 1997, A20; B. Drummond Ayres, Jr. "A Black Panther is Free at Last" *New York Times*, 15 June 1997, Section 4, 2.

24. Churchill and Vander Wall, *Agents of Repression*, 77.

25. Heike Kleffner, "The Black Panthers; Interviews with Geronimo ji Jaga Pratt and Mumia Abu-Jamal," *Race & Class* 35. 1 (1993), 9–18.

26. Herb Boyd, *Black Panthers: For Beginners* (New York: Writers and Readers Publishing, Inc., 1995), 126, 128; Fletcher et al. *Still Black, Still Strong*, 10.

27. Huey P. Newton, *To Die For the People* (New York: Writers and Readers Publishing, 1995), 44–75.

28. Taylor and Lewis, *Panther*, 31; Kit Kim Holder, "The History of the Black Panther Party, 1966–1971, A Curriculum Tool for African American Studies," (Ph.D. diss., University of Massachusetts, 1990), 16–26.

29. Holder, "The History of the Black Panther Party, 1966–1971," 6–26; Paul Coates, interview by author, Baltimore, MD, 10 September 1994; Sharon Harley, interview by author, College Park, MD, 7 September 1994. See the bibliography for a list of the author's interviews with Party members. These personal, semi-structured interviews ranged from approximately one to five hours. In all of the interviews, the author covered the following topics: personal history and background, participation in the Black Panther Party, and government surveillance and repression of the BPP.

30. With Newton incarcerated from 1967 to 1970, Cleaver out of the country after April 1968, and Seale travelling frequently and also in and out of prison between 1968 and 1971, Hilliard assumed major national leadership for the BPP from 1968 to 1971. He often spoke to the media on the Party's behalf and gave guidance to chapter leaders around the country. The Party's top leaders (Newton, Seale, and Cleaver) were never free to meet together and formulate policy after 1967. As a result, many national leadership decisions regarding organization, finances, legal representation, discipline, and membership became Hilliard's responsibilities. Phone interview with David Hilliard by the author, 6 August 1997; Audrea Jones interview by the author, Rahway, NJ, 30 October 1994; Coates, interview.

31. In addition to lethal government repression, these problems included constant fund raising for legal fees and Party programs, Panther isolation/rejection by family members/friends, and competition with other political groups.

32. Harley, interview.

33. Pinkney, *Red, Black and Green*, 115–116.

34. Coates, interview; Jones, interview.

35. Seale, September 24 interview. Although almost all the Panthers interviewed agreed that there was sexism in the BPP, their opinions varied greatly on the extent of the problem. See Pratt interview for a short statement; Kleffner, 14; see Elaine Brown's *A Taste of Power* for another view.

36. David Hilliard and Lewis Cole, *This Side of Glory: The Autobiography of David Hilliard and the Story of the Black Panther Party* (Boston: Little, Brown and Company, 1993), 302.

37. Hilliard and Cole, *This Side of Glory*, 302, 313, 318, 321; Pearson, *The Shadow of the Panther,* 226–227.

38. On these conflicts, see the perceptive short essay by a leading protagonist and Black cultural nationalist, Maulana Karenga, *The Roots of the Us–Panther Conflict: The Perverse and Deadly Games Police Play*, (San Diego: Kawaida Publications, 1976) as well as other essays in this volume.

39. Holder, "The History of the Black Panther Party, 1966–1971," 259–261. Panthers from other chapters complained about the unrepresentative nature of the

Central Committee. For New Jersey Panthers' complaints, see the *Newark Star-Ledger*, 7 August, 1969, 7. In this article, Panther leader Carl Nichols noted that the Central Committee was dominated by California Panthers.

40. Seale, *Seize the Time*, 178–181.

41. Lynn French, interview by author, Washington, DC, 27 September 1994; Jones, interview.

42. Brown, *A Taste of Power*, 209, 262–264.

43. Diana Lin Tiatt, interview by author, New York, NY, 25 September 1994.

44. The New York 21 were top New York Panthers indicted and arrested on bomb conspiracy charges in 1969 and given very high bails. They wrote a letter to the Central Committee explaining their situation and requesting urgent legal and financial assistance. The Central Committee was not acting promptly on their request so they wrote a letter to the underground Weathermen, a predominantly White revolutionary political group, requesting support. This second letter is the alleged reason for their expulsion. See *Right On*, 3 April 1971, 8 and Hilliard and Cole, 320.

45. Holder, "The History of the Black Panther Party, 1966–1971," 275–277; Shakur, *Assata*, 230–233.

46. *Right On*, 3 April 1971, 3.

47. Jim Fletcher, Tanaquil Jones, and Sylvere Lotringer, eds. *Still Black, Still Strong; Survivors of the U.S. War against Black Revolutionaries: Dhoruba Bin Wahad, Mumia Abu-Jamal, Assata Shakur* (New York: Semiotext(e), 1993), 238–241.

48. For one example, see interview with Mumia Abu-Jamal, Kleffner, "The Black Panthers," 18–19.

49. Seale, September interviews. See note 4 for Seale's view on the evolution of Party membership.

50. Huey P. Newton, "The War Against the Panthers: A Study of Repression in America," (Ph.D. diss., The University of California at Santa Cruz, 1980), 87. Our understanding of the BPP will increase greatly as more Panthers write memoirs and scholarly analyses of the Party and the Black power movement.

51. Newton, "The War Against the Panthers: A Study of Repression in America," 70–83.

52. Pinkney, *Red, Black and Green*, 112–115.

53. Coates, interview; Flores Forbes, interview by author, New York, NY, 25 September 1994; Pearson, *The Shadow of the Panther*, 241–246.

54. Seale, September interviews; Brown, *A Taste of Power*, 276–285.

55. Seale, September interviews. For a broad discussion of Newton's views, see John T. McCartney, *Black Power Ideologies: An Essay in African American Political Thought*, (Philadelphia: Temple University Press, 1992), 133–150.

56. Seale, September interviews; Hilliard and Cole, *This Side of Glory*, 326–329; Brown, *A Taste of Power*, 276–281.

57. Jones, interview.

58. Coates, interview; Hilliard and Cole, *This Side of Glory*, 326–327. A few state chapters were allowed to exist after the directive to close chapters was sent. For example, the Illinois office in Chicago and the office in Winston–Salem remained open.

59. Coates, interview.

60. Seale, 24 September interview.

61. JoNina Abron, interview by author, Oakland, CA, 31 October 1986.

62. Taylor and Lewis, 123–124; Rufus P. Browning, Dale Rodgers Marshall, and David H. Tabb, *Protest Is Not Enough: The Struggle of Black and Hispanics for Equality in Urban Politics* (Berkeley: University of California Press, 1984), 65, 114; Rod Bush, ed. *The New Black Vote: Politics and Power in Four American Cities* (San Francisco: Synthesis Publications, 1984), 323–326.

63. Seale, September interviews; Abron, interview; Forbes, September interview.

64. By authoritarianism, I mean a system of governance characterized by limited popular participation, illegitimate use of violence, and a lack of respect for basic civil liberties and human rights.

65. Seale, September 24 interview; Pearson, *The Shadow of the Panther*, 236.

66. Kate Coleman with Paul Avery, "The Party's Over," *New Times: The Feature News Magazine*, 10 July 1978, 33–35. On Callins' blood in Newton's penthouse, see Brown, *A Taste of Power*, 356.

67. Pearson, *The Shadow of the Panther*, 225; Forbes, September interview.

68. Bobby Seale states that Newton had created the Party's first, short-lived underground military wing while in prison between 1967 and 1970. Seale, September interviews.

69. Apparently, the original BPP goal also included the eventual elimination of these activities. Forbes, September interview.

70. Elaine Brown argues that Newton also physically beat Seale during this incident. Brown, *A Taste of Power*, 348–353. Seale has denied to this author that he was beaten by Newton, Seale, September 24 interview.

71. Jones, interview; Forbes, September interview; Hilliard and Cole, *This Side of Glory, 373–378.*

72. Brown, *A Taste of Power*, 408–412.

73. Ibid., 363–367.

74. Coleman, "The Party's Over," 35–36, 41.

75. Brown, *A Taste of Power*, 368–371.

76. Ibid., 356, 437–450.

77. Coleman, "The Party's Over," 22–47.

78. Taylor and Lewis, *Panther*, 126–128.

79. William W. Sales, Jr., *From Civil Rights to Black Liberation: Malcolm X and the Organization of Afro-American Unity* (Boston: South End Press, 1994), 180–181. This excellent book highlights theoretical, ideological, and organizational problems related to radical Black politics in the United States.

Part VI

Legacy of
The Black Panther Party

Chapter Seventeen

Set Our Warriors Free:
The Legacy of the Black Panther
Party and Political Prisoners

Akinyele Omowale Umoja

In 1993, my friend Makungu Akinyela and I had the opportunity to visit five cities in the Basque Country in northern Spain. Basque nationalists have waged a national liberation movement against Spanish occupation that dates back to the Second World War. In each town we visited, there was broad support for Basque political prisoners. Bulletin boards in local bars exhibited letters from political prisoners written to residents of the neighborhood. In the Basque town of San Sebastian, a major square displayed large photographs of over twenty Basque political prisoners. Makungu and I lamented that in the United States, there is not this degree of broad support for political prisoners. Indeed, the overwhelming majority of Black political prisoners are not known outside the small circles of activists in the Black community. Unlike the Basque national liberation movement, the issue of amnesty for incarcerated activists and freedom fighters is not a high priority on the agenda of Black leadership in the United States.

The issue of political prisoners is an important aspect of the legacy of the Black Panther Party (BPP). In the late 1960s and early 1970s, the Black Panther Party played a critical role in championing the call for amnesty and the defense of political prisoners. Human rights advocates in the United States have defined political prisoners as "people who have made conscious political decisions, and acted on them, to oppose the United States government, and who have been incarcerated as a result of those actions."[1] More than one hundred inmates in U.S. prisons have been identified by human rights groups as political prisoners. Nearly fifty percent of these political prisoners are of African descent. Approximately one-third of these were members of or were affiliated with the Black Panther Party. Consequently, there are more political prisoners from the Black Panther Party than any other political formation in United States prisons.[2] The continued incarceration of Black political prisoners reminds us of the Black Panther Party and the low-intensity warfare waged against it by the agencies of the United States government.

This essay examines the role of the Black Panther Party in working for the freedom of Black and other political prisoners in the United States. It also explores the current status of Black political prisoners in the United States and evaluates the legal and political efforts made to secure their freedom. Although this is a scholarly endeavor, this essay is informed by my twenty-four years of activism in support of Black political prisoners.

Black Panther Party and Political Prisoners

The issue of political prisoners was crucial to the rise of the Black Panther Party. Huey Newton, co-founder and Minister of Defense of the Black Panther Party for Self-Defense, became one of the most celebrated political prisoners in American history. After being stopped by police on the evening of October 28, 1967, Newton was involved in a shooting incident. When the smoke cleared, one Oakland policeman was dead, and another officer and Newton were seriously wounded. Newton claimed that he blacked out after being shot and did not know who shot Officer John Frey. The BPP co-founder was charged with murder, kidnapping, assault, and attempted murder. However, on September 28, 1968, an Alameda County jury found Newton guilty only of manslaughter.[3]

In the course of defending Newton, the BPP believed that relying solely on litigation was insufficient in cases in which the defendants were Black revolutionaries. According to the Panthers, the indictment and incarceration of activists was political, and therefore it was necessary to mobilize public pressure to successfully challenge the charges of a racist, capitalist, and repressive government. The legal and the political campaigns to win the freedom of Huey Newton became the major priority of the organization. Panther leaders Bobby Seale, Eldridge Cleaver, and Kathleen Cleaver traveled to cities and college campuses nationwide to rally support for Huey Newton. In the Panther mobilization for the defense of Newton, the BPP leader was projected as a hero who had defended himself from racist police. To many Black youth in the United States, Newton became a virtual symbol of Black resistance. Support for Newton was equated with support for Black people's right to armed self-defense and the right of Black people to bear arms, which were central issues for the Black Panther Party.

Panthers mobilized significant popular support for the freedom of Newton. On February 17, 1968, seven thousand people attended a Free Huey rally at the Oakland Auditorium on Newton's twenty-sixth birthday. On this occasion, $10,000 was raised for Newton's legal defense. In addition to Panther leaders Bobby Seale and Eldridge Cleaver addressing this assembly, leaders of the Student Nonviolent Coordinating Committee— Stokely Carmichael, H. Rap Brown, and James Forman, as well as representatives of the White leftist Peace and Freedom Party, attended the rally and expressed their support for Huey Newton.[4] The next day, on February 18, 1967, a similar event was held at the Los Angeles Sports Arena. On July 15, 1968, five thousand people participated in a Free Huey rally at the Alameda County

Courthouse during the beginning of Newton's trial. The next year, on May 1, 1969, when Newton's case was appealed to the California Supreme Court, over ten thousand people demonstrated for the Panther leader's release.[5] These high-profile events and other efforts of the BPP were responsible for making the defense of Newton a *cause celèbre* within the Black liberation movement and leftist circles. Newton became a national symbol of resistance and a Black folk hero. Panther mobilization to free Huey also served as a marketing and recruiting campaign for the organization. In addition, mobilizing support for Huey Newton provided a vehicle for building solidarity with radical and liberal forces outside the Black community. After he served three years in jail, Newton's prior manslaughter conviction was overturned by an appellate judge on August 5, 1970. Newton's case is a rare occasion when a Black man was exonerated in the murder of a White police officer. The political mobilization of the Black Panther Party in support of Newton must be considered a distinguishing factor in the prosecution's failure to convict the Panther leader on murder charges. The BPP work in defense of Newton serves as one of the high points in the political mobilization strategy to free radical political prisoners.

The BPP also successfully mobilized significant political support in the trials of Bobby Seale, Ericka Huggins, and other Panther defendants in New Haven, Connecticut, and the New York 21. Seale, Huggins, and the New Haven defendants were arrested for the murder of Alex Rackley, a Panther and suspected police informant. BPP national leadership placed priority on the New Haven case. Thousands of Panther supporters demonstrated in New Haven in support of the New Haven 14. President Kingman Brewster of Yale University declared publicly that he believed Black revolutionaries could not receive a fair trial in the United States. Brewster's statements were published in *The New York Times* and were utilized by the New Haven 14 legal defense team to win legitimacy for the claim that Seale, Huggins, and the others were political prisoners persecuted for their Party membership. Although BPP national leaders Seale and Huggins were exonerated, several other New Haven defendants were eventually convicted for the murder of Rackley.[6]

The New York 21 comprised the primary leadership of the BPP in New York City. They were indicted in April 1969 on a variety of charges, including arson; conspiracy to commit armed robbery; conspiracy to commit murder; conspiring to bomb department stores, subways, and police stations; and possession of explosives. Bail was set at $100,000 for most of the New York Panther defendants. The Panther 21 case received national notoriety and broad support from radical activists, students, and White liberals. After a lengthy trial during which most of the New York 21 remained incarcerated for twenty-six months, it took a mere two hours of deliberation for a jury to acquit the New York Panthers.[7] As in the case of Huey Newton, political mobilization was instrumental to achieving the acquittals of the New Haven and New York Panthers. Although Newton was clearly an organizational priority, in its early years the BPP also lent critical assistance to other political prisoners who were not Party comrades. The Party's newspaper, *The Black Panther*, with a circulation of a hundred thousand, regularly updated its readership on the plight of Huey Newton, other incarcerated Panthers, and the political prisoners of the Black liberation movements and radical organizations. In the March 16, 1968 issue of *The Black Panther,* three articles appeared on political prisoners who were not members of the BPP. These individuals included H. Rap Brown, who was under house arrest in Manhattan, New York; Cleveland Sellers, a SNCC activist incarcerated after a student protest in Orangeburg, South Carolina; and LeRoi Jones (now Amiri Baraka) who was incarcerated on charges related to the 1967 uprising in Newark, New Jersey. Highlighted also in that issue were the cases of Benjamin Spock, the internationally renowned pediatrician, who faced charges of advocating resistance to the draft, and Chicano activist Reis Tijeria.[8] The wide circulation of *The Black Panther* transmitted information about the U. S. government's repression of radical activists in the United States and similar activities taking place in the international community. The Black Panther Party would later play a supportive role in the defense efforts of Angela Davis, Joanne Little, the Soledad Brothers, and the San Quentin Six.

One of the controversies that confronted the Panthers in their legal defense efforts was criticism from the Black community that the Panthers often retained White counsel. Dozens of people left Newton's defense committee after a White California Bay Area lawyer, Charles Garry, was selected to lead the Newton legal defense team. A number of Bay Area Black attorneys were considered, but BPP held the opinion that Black legal talent in the area lacked experience in successfully litigating capital murder cases. Panther leadership also questioned whether the local Black attorneys possessed the political will to resist the political pressure from Oakland's White power structure in the murder trial of a Black revolutionary. Garry, on the other hand, had reasonable success in defending clients in capital cases and a history of supporting civil rights and progressive causes. His willingness to defend Newton without consideration of financial compensation also attracted Panther leaders. Despite the arguments in support of Garry, several members left the BPP's legal defense committee.[9]

In 1968, a symposium of radical Black attorneys criticized the BPP for not using Black lawyers in the defense of Huey Newton. They argued that the legal defense of the Black revolution should be directed by Black attorneys. The BPP responded to this criticism with attacks on the commitment of the majority of the Black legal community. In the May 18, 1968 issue of *The Black Panther*, Panther Chairman Bobby Seale and BPP Central Committee member Kathleen Cleaver responded in two articles—"Black Lawyers are Jiving" by Seale and "Black Power, Black Lawyers, and White Courts" by Cleaver. Cleaver acknowledged the efforts of a few Black attorneys who unselfishly offered their services to the Black liberation movement. Those whom Cleaver acknowledged included Howard Moore, the General Counsel for the Student Nonviolent Coordinating Committee (SNCC); Floyd McKissick, then national Director of the Congress of Racial Equality (CORE); C. B. King, activist and attorney for the Black Freedom Movement in southwest Georgia; and William Patterson, supporter of Communist causes and participant in the Scottsboro Boys' defense. While citing these exceptions and acknowledging that there were others, Cleaver severely criticized the Black legal community for failing to offer their services as advocates for the Black liberation movement. She also condemned the majority of Black lawyers who wanted to "cash in" or profit financially from the notoriety of popular Black causes.[10] The dialogue between progressive elements and the BPP served as a catalyst in the establishment of the National Conference of Black Lawyers (NCBL) in 1968. The NCBL became an association and cadre of Black attorneys that championed the causes of the Black liberation movement and marginalized elements of the Black community.[11]

Repression, Organizational Weakness, and Panther Prisoners

As the BPP began to grow into a national revolutionary movement, it became a priority target for national, state, and local law enforcement. In 1968 and 1969, hundreds of BPP members were arrested across the United States on a variety of charges, from hitchhiking and profanity to murder and armed robbery. As the repressive arm of the United States government exerted its counter-insurgency campaign, the number of political prisoners from the radical Black Panther Party significantly increased in the jails and prisons across the nation. Nationally and locally, the BPP depleted valuable resources on legal costs and bail monies for incarcerated comrades.[12]

The BPP was overwhelmed by the number of imprisoned members. Its inability to devote equal attention, financially and politically, to all of the Party's political prisoners created tension within the ranks of the organization. One such example was the tension between the national BPP leadership (based in Oakland) and the New York 21. Concerns emerged within the New York Panthers about what was perceived as a lack of financial support from the BPP national leadership for the legal defense of the New York 21. The FBI further exploited this acrimony, which intensified the schism within the organization. Aware of friction between the New York BPP chapter and the national leadership, the FBI initiated a campaign to split the BPP. FBI operatives drafted and disseminated disinformation letters and leaked stories to media sources to increase tension and undermine internal unity in the BPP. A telegram from the Washington office of FBI Director J. Edgar Hoover to the New York office, dated June 18, 1970, reveals the agency's desire to divide the BPP. In this communication, Hoover's office gives the New York FBI office the authority to "discreetly furnish data to [deleted] ... in an effort to obtain news media publicity highlighting friction between

East and West Coast BPP leadership personnel."[13] In January 1971, a clear sign of discord in the BPP was the open letter to the Weather Underground from the New York Panther 21 criticizing "self-proclaimed 'vanguard' parties (a veiled reference to the national leadership of the BPP)" for abandoning the incarcerated New York Panthers.[14] On February 13, 1971, the headline of *The Black Panther* identified New York 21 defendants Michael Cetewayo Tabor and Richard Dhoruba Moore (Dhoruba Bin-Wahad) and Newton's personal secretary, Connie Matthews, as "Enemies of the People" and announced their expulsion from the BPP.[15] Tabor, Moore, and Matthews disappeared from public life and their whereabouts were unknown to BPP leadership. Tabor and Matthews, who were married, eventually surfaced in Algeria and were received by Eldridge Cleaver and the International Section of the BPP.[16] In February 1971, the New York chapter of the BPP held a press conference in Harlem calling for the expulsion of Huey Newton and David Hilliard and for a new Central Committee to lead the BPP that would include Bobby Seale, Eldridge Cleaver, Kathleen Cleaver, and Donald Cox.[17] The division and eventual split with the national BPP made it more difficult to mobilize support for Panther political prisoners.

One casualty of the division within the BPP was Geronimo ji Jaga (Pratt). Ji Jaga was a Vietnam veteran, a member of the elite Green Beret Special Forces, who joined the Los Angeles BPP in 1968. He became a political prisoner on December 8, 1969, along with eighteen of his comrades, after Los Angeles Panthers were arrested in three simultaneous pre-dawn raids of BPP offices in South Central Los Angeles. Panthers in the Los Angeles Central Headquarters engaged in a five-hour standoff with the Los Angeles Police Department and its SWAT forces before their arrest.[18] After being released on bail, on August 11, 1970, ji Jaga failed to appear in court to face charges of conspiracy to assault with intent to commit murder and assault with a deadly weapon. Ji Jaga went underground to organize clandestine support for the military wing of the BPP, the Black/Afro-American Liberation Army. On December 8, 1970, ji Jaga and other underground BPP/BLA members were captured in Dallas, Texas. While he was underground, the FBI escalated efforts to isolate ji Jaga from the national BPP leadership. At this time, assisted by previous FBI "divide and conquer" tactics, Newton had become estranged from Eldridge Cleaver. During the schism between the two BPP leaders, ji Jaga was identified by Newton as a political ally of Cleaver. Recognizing this opportunity, the FBI operatives spread rumors within the BPP that ji Jaga wished to eliminate key members of the national leadership.[19] On January 23, 1971, BPP Minister of Defense Huey Newton released a statement purging Geronimo, his wife Sandra Holmes Pratt, Will Stafford, Wilfred Holiday, and George Lloyd. This statement, published in *The Black Panther*, accused ji Jaga of "counter-revolutionary" behavior, including threatening the lives of Newton and BPP Chief of Staff David Hilliard. Newton's statement warned, "Any Party member or community worker who attempts to aid them or communicate with them in any form or manner shall be considered part of their conspiracy to undermine and destroy the Black Panther Party."[20] Newton's directive adversely impacted much of the political and financial support for the legal defense campaigns of ji Jaga and the other Los Angeles BPP political prisoners.

The internal weaknesses of the BPP combined with the counter-insurgency efforts of the U. S. government intensified factionalism and led to the split of the BPP. Factionalism and the split in the BPP not only affected the effort to mobilize support for ji Jaga but weakened its ability to wage dynamic campaigns for other Panther political prisoners.

While the Party's legal campaign efforts lost momentum as a result of intra-party strife, significant mobilization efforts on the behalf of political prisoners continued. In 1974, the National Task Force for COINTELPRO Litigation and Research was initiated by former Panther 21 defendant Afeni Shakur and Republic of New Afrika activist and community health worker Mutulu Shakur. Afeni and Mutulu organized a team of lawyers and researchers to review thousands of recently released counter-intelligence files of the FBI. In the COINTELPRO files of the FBI, the National Task Force found evidence of government misconduct in the cases of Black political prisoners. The National Task Force developed a legal strategy to challenge the convictions of Panther and other Black liberation movement prisoners. The COINTELPRO legal strategy served to resuscitate efforts to overturn the convictions of Panther political prisoners such as Dhoruba Bin-Wahad, Geronimo ji Jaga, and the New York Three. The essence of the COINTELPRO legal strategy was to expose government misconduct, particularly the coercion of witnesses to offer false testimony, the manufacturing of evidence, or the withholding of vital evidence in the conviction of radical activists. By exposing the illegal tactics used by police and prosecutors, the lawyers sought to establish a legal basis for the acquittal of revolutionaries faced with politically motivated charges. [21]

The 1990 release of Dhoruba Bin-Wahad is an example of the efficacy of the COINTELPRO strategy. In 1973, Bin-Wahad was convicted of wounding two police officers in an "ambush attack" in New York in 1971 and sentenced to serve twenty-five years to life in prison. Bin-Wahad's legal defense team filed motions in 1975 demanding release of his COINTELPRO files. Years later the courts ordered the FBI to release documents to Bin-Wahad and his lawyers. The COINTELPRO files clearly demonstrated that the FBI, New York police intelligence units, and New York state prosecutors conspired to coerce witnesses to offer false testimony against Bin-Wahad. Due to the exposure of the FBI's COINTELPRO program, Bin-Wahad's conviction was vacated in 1990 after he had served nineteen years, and he was then released on bail.[22]

The COINTELPRO litigation was also successful in the overturning of the prior conviction of Geronimo ji Jaga after he endured 27 years of unjust incarceration. Along with the case of Mumia Abu-Jamal, ji Jaga's case has received the greatest amount of attention among political prisoners. After ji Jaga was acquitted on charges related to the December 8, 1969 police raids on Los Angeles BPP offices, he was charged and convicted in 1972 for the 1968 murder of White school teacher Caroline Olson, in Santa Monica, California. Ji Jaga and his lawyers insisted that at the time of the murders, ji Jaga was 350 miles north of Santa Monica in Oakland, California. The National Task Force for COINTELPRO Litigation and Research initiated a legal defense for ji Jaga on the basis that FBI surveillance of ji Jaga could determine where he was at the time of the 1968 murder. In ji Jaga's case, COINTELPRO files have shown that during the trial FBI representatives perjured themselves concerning whether the Bureau was engaged in electronic surveillance of ji Jaga. FBI files released to ji Jaga's defense team also provided evidence that a key witness against ji Jaga, former Panther Julius Butler, was an FBI informant. Butler claimed he heard ji Jaga confess to murdering Olsen. During ji Jaga's trial, Butler denied being an FBI informant while being cross-examined by ji Jaga's attorney Johnnie Cochran. The release of COINTELPRO documents and corroboration by former FBI agents have exposed Butler's employment as an FBI informant. Several of the jurors in Pratt's case have stated they would not have voted to convict Pratt had they known Butler's relationship to the FBI. Through its paid informants, the FBI also infiltrated ji Jaga's legal defense team and leaked trial strategy to the FBI. On May 29, 1997, California judge Everett W. Dickey ruled that the role of Butler's testimony and the suppression of evidence by the prosecutors biased the earlier conviction.[23]

Similiar to ji Jaga's case, the New York 3—Herman Bell, Albert "Nuh" Washington, and Jalil Muntaqin—have sought release based on revelations of government misconduct in their respective cases. Bell, Washington, and Muntaqin were all members of the Black Liberation Army (BLA), which began as a clandestine armed wing of the Black Panther Party. As the political repression of the BPP and other Black liberation movement forces intensified, several Panthers went underground and joined the ranks of the Black Liberation Army. Units of the BLA carried out military actions, including acts of retaliation against police officers with racist reputations, the expropriation of funds from financial institutions, attacks on drug dealers in Black neighborhoods, and assistance in the escape of fellow incarcerated members. In the early 1970s, federal agents and local police conducted a White House-initiated "search and destroy" campaign, code named "Newkill," to eliminate the BLA. Bell, Washington, and Muntaqin were all captured during this nationwide man-hunt. In 1975, Bell, Washington, and Muntaqin were convicted for the murder of two New York city police officers and sentenced to life imprisonment. COINTELPRO files on Bell, Washington, and Muntaqin reveal ballistic evidence presented by the prosecution to convict the three BLA members was contradicted by FBI laboratory reports. Despite the prior knowledge of the FBI, the New York police, and the prosecutors, this pivotal information was concealed from defense lawyers.

Lawyers for Bell, Washington, and Muntaqin have also cited illegal coercive measures utilized by police, including torture, to obtain testimony against the New York 3.[24] In addition to securing the freedom of Bin-Wahad and ji Jaga, the exposure of COINTELPRO files has demonstrated the lengths to which the U.S. government has gone to disrupt radical movements and organizations. The work begun by the National Task Force for COINTELPRO Litigation and Research clearly illustrated that BPP, BLA, and other Black liberation movement prisoners were not common criminals but political captives of a low-intensity war initiated by the United States government.

Another significant development in the effort to free BPP political prisoners was the liberation of Assata Shakur from Clinton State Prison for Women in New Jersey. A member of the BPP and the BLA, Assata Shakur was incarcerated in May 1973 after a shooting incident between New Jersey State troopers and Shakur and two other BPP/BLA members, Zayd Shakur and Sundiata Acoli. When the smoke cleared, a New Jersey state trooper and Zayd Shakur were dead, and Assata Shakur was severely wounded. Acoli was captured by police days later, eventually tried, convicted for murder, and sentenced to life plus thirty years. Once in government custody, Shakur was tried and acquitted in five separate trials. Finally she was tried for the deaths of the New Jersey police officer and Zayd Shakur. Evidence presented in court supported her claim that she did not fire a weapon during the May 1973 battle between the police and the Panthers. Additional evidence also indicated that Shakur had been shot twice in the back while her arms were up to surrender. In spite of the evidence that demonstrated her innocence, an all-White jury in Middlesex County, New Jersey convicted Shakur. She was sentenced to "life plus sixty-five years."[25]

On November 2, 1979, Shakur escaped as a result of a commando-styled raid by her comrades on a penal facility in Clinton, New Jersey. After a national search for her whereabouts, in 1988 Shakur reappeared in Cuba where she was granted political asylum by the Cuban government. Four individuals, former Panther Sekou Odinga, Mutulu Shakur, and two White radical activists Marliyn Buck and Sylvia Baraldini, were subsequently arrested, tried, and convicted for charges related to the liberation of Assata Shakur.[26] The liberation of Assata Shakur from incarceration was an inspirational spark to the Black Liberation movement in the United States. After her liberation from captivity, Assata became a symbol of resistance for the insurgent Black movement in the United States. In New York, three days after her escape, more than five thousand demonstrators organized by the National Black Human Rights Coalition carried signs saying, "Assata Shakur is Welcome Here."[27] Even today several hip-hop artists, including Public Enemy, X-Clan, Digable Planets, 2Pac, and Paris have written songs that recognize her as a "shero."

Contemporary Panther Political Prisoners

When examining the ranks of contemporary political prisoners, one discovers different categories of incarcerated activists. Individuals such as Marshall "Eddie" Conway, Romaine "Chip" Fitzgerald, Mondo we Langa (David Rice), Ed Poindexter, and Sundiata Acoli were incarcerated when the Black Panther Party was still a viable national political force. Their supporters maintain that the nearly thirty-year prison terms that each of these political prisoners has served is linked to their revolutionary politics.

Romaine Fitzgerald, imprisoned since September 1969, has been incarcerated longer than any Black Panther political prisoner. He was accused of charges stemming from a shoot-out involving three members of the BPP and two California Highway police officers and the murder of a security guard.[28] The length of Fitzgerald's incarceration for a single murder is twice as long as that imposed on others charged with the same offense in the state of California. Fitzgerald's arrest and conviction came during a time period when the Los Angeles branch was in disarray. In 1969, two of the Los Angeles BPP's leaders, Alprentice "Bunchy" Carter and John Huggins, were murdered. The murders of Carter and Huggins were the result of an antagonistic conflict with a rival Black nationalist group, the Us organization. The F BI manipulated both organizations with "divide-and-conquer" tactics that created heightened hostilities and led to gun battles. Besides the internecine warfare with Us, an intensified wave of repression initiated by the LAPD, which included raids on Panther offices, was waged against the Los Angeles BPP in 1969. As a result, Fitzgerald received limited support from his comrades, who were engaged in their own battle for survival in a hostile climate.

In the case of Marshall "Eddie" Conway, questionable evidence led to his conviction in the shooting death of a Baltimore police officer. Conway, a leading member of the Baltimore BPP, has been incarcerated since April 1970. Although he has maintained his innocence throughout the entire ordeal, Conway was charged and convicted of the murder of a Baltimore police officer and the attempted murder of two other members of the police force. In the case against the Baltimore Black Panther leader, prosecutors relied on the testimony of a paid jailhouse informer, who claimed Conway confessed to the murders while awaiting trial. One of the police officers also testified. The officer identified Conway's picture from two stacks of police photo albums. However, Conway's photo was the only one placed in both stacks. Moreover, he was represented by a court-appointed attorney whom he only briefly met twice prior to trial. Conway believed he was targeted because he exposed several police informants and operatives within the Baltimore BPP. It should be noted that at the time of his arrest, at least twenty-one members or supporters of the Baltimore BPP were either prisoners or fugitives.[29]

Mondo we Langa (formerly known as David Rice) and Ed Poindexter were members of the Omaha, Nebraska Committee to Combat Fascism, an arm of the BPP. They were convicted for the August 17, 1970, bombing death of local police officer Larry Minard. Prosecutors used the testimony of fifteen-year-old Duane Peak, who admitted to planting the bomb and identified Langa and Poindexter as conspirators. Since their conviction in 1971, Langa and Poindexter have uncovered an FBI memorandum that reveals the federal agency withheld evidence favorable to the Omaha activists' defense. A United States District Court also ruled that some of the evidence used in the trial was illegally obtained. No remedy resulted from the United States District Court ruling because the United States Supreme Court refused to review the case. Supporters of Langa and Poindexter also question the testimony of Peak and believe that police coerced Peak into implicating Langa and Poindexter in the death of Minard.[30]

The history of the 1960s demonstrates that the United States government waged an insurgency war against the Black Panther Party and other Black liberation movement organizations. Amnesty has not been offered to these incarcerated Black activists or Panthers living in exile, such as Assata Shakur. The continued captivity of Fitzgerald, Conway, Langa, Poindexter, and other Black Panther political prisoners is an indication that the hostility between the United States government and the Black Panther Party has not subsided.

Prisoners of War

Some of the BPP political prisoners classify themselves as prisoners of war. According to international law, prisoner of war [P.O.W.] is a status for captured combatants of an armed conflict between states or of subjugated peoples fighting for national liberation.[31] This interpretation was put forth by Geronimo ji Jaga and his co-defendants as early as 1971.[32] Former BPP members and political prisoners Sundiata Acoli, Sekou Odinga, Bashir Hameed, Abdul Majid, and Kojo Bomani Sababu, and the late Kuwasi Balagoon have identified themselves as members of the Black Liberation Army.[33] Captured BLA members added a new dimension in the struggle to free Black political prisoners. Between the mid-1970s and the early 1980s, several of the captured BLA members claimed prisoner-of-war status during their legal proceedings. By identifying themselves as prisoners of war, Black radicals argued in federal and state courts that international law pertaining to the treatment of captured combatants applied to Black revolutionaries in the United States.

The prisoner-of-war position has been significantly influenced by the political perspectives of the New Afrikan Independence Movement. In the 1970s, many BLA members and prisoners began to identify with the political goals of the Provisional Government of the Republic of New Afrika (RNA). The RNA was a movement initiated by five hundred Black nationalists at the Black Government Conference in Detroit in 1968. The participants of this conference declared their independence from the United States government and called for the formation of a self-governing Black nation–state in the deep South. Mississippi, Louisiana, Alabama, Georgia, and South Carolina were identified as the national territory of the proposed Black nation–state, and "New Afrika" was chosen as the name of the nation.[34] When RNA leadership and members were arrested in government raids on their offices in Mississippi, the New Afrikan legal defense challenged the jurisdiction of the United States courts over Black people who declared their allegiance to the Republic of New Afrika.[35] In November 1971, PGRNA officials waged an information campaign at the United Nations in New York to win support for RNA political prisoners from the international community. In their appeal to the international community, incarcerated RNA members in Mississippi were identified as prisoners of war. PGRNA literature provided the following definition of a prisoner of war, which is based on a United States military field manual:

> A guerrilla may, in time of war, have legal status: When he is captured, he is entitled to the same treatment as a regular prisoner of war if he: (1) is commanded by a person responsible for his subordinates. (2) wears a fixed and distinctive sign recognizable at a distance. (3) carries arms openly. (4) conducts operations in accordance with the laws and customs of war.[36]

The RNA efforts to assist its political prisoners were supported by the "East Coast" faction of the BPP. The New York chapter and other Panther chapters had by this time split from the Oakland-based national leadership. New York Panthers were visible at RNA press conferences in the city. The New York consulate of the PGRNA and the New York Panthers developed a working relationship that included selling each other's newspapers and jointly organizing forums and rallies.[37] On August 18, 1973, PGRNA activists organized the International African Prisoners of War Solidarity Day in Jackson, Mississippi to demand the release of RNA, Black Panther, and other Black Liberation Movement political prisoners, including H. Rap Brown and the Wilmington 10. Over three thousand people attended this event, making it the largest Black freedom rally in the South since the major rallies of the 1960s. Many members of the "East Coast" BPP faction attended this rally, and Safiya Bukhari (Bernice Jones) represented the New York BPP and spoke to the mobilization participants about the cases of incarcerated Panthers and BLA members.[38] The politics of the RNA influenced the members of the East Coast BPP, some of whom would become members of the BLA. Not only did New York Panthers support RNA efforts in New York, but many began to identify themselves as citizens of the Republic of New Afrika.

As the ideological perspectives of the New Afrikan Independence Movement began to gain influence within its ranks, captured Black Liberation Army members began to argue they were New Afrikan prisoners of war. In January 1975, BLA members Safiya Bukhari and Masai Ehehosi were on trial in Norfolk, Virginia for attempted robbery, attempted murder, and the illegal possession of a weapon. Bukhari, the former Communications Secretary of the New York BPP, and Ehehosi, a veteran of the United States military and former Communications Secretary of the Jersey City, New Jersey branch of the BPP Black Panther Community News Service, declared to the court that they were citizens of the RNA and combatants of the BLA and that American courts had no jurisdiction over them.[39]

In his statement to the court in December 1981, the late Kuwasi Balagoon declared that he was a prisoner of war. Balagoon and White radical anti-imperialists Judy Clark and David Gilbert were being tried for armed robbery and murder related to the October 20, 1981, action by the Revolutionary Armed Task Force (RATF), in Nyack, New York. The RATF, a coalition of BLA and White revolutionaries, attempted to take 1.6 million dollars from an armored truck in Nyack, New York. In a communiqué after the incident in Nyack, the BLA claimed responsibility for the action and stated that the taking of money from U. S. institutions, including the October 20th attempts, were revolutionary expropriations to finance the movement and arm Black people to face a growing trend of White supremacist militias.[40] Balagoon, a former New York Panther and defendant in the New York 21 trial, argued that the actions of the BLA and the RATF on the 20th of October were acts of "New Afrikan soldiers" to "encourage New Afrikan people to defend themselves from genocide by the American [N]azis." In his statement, Balagoon declared,

> I am a prisoner of war and I reject the crap about me being a defendant, and I do not recognize the legitimacy of this court. The term defendant applies to someone involved in a criminal matter, an internal search for guilt or innocence. It is clear that I've been a part of the Black Liberation Movement all of my adult life and have been involved in a war against the American imperialist, in order to free New Afrikan people from its yoke. [41]

Balagoon's demand to be considered a P.O.W. was not recognized by the prosecution and the judge in this case. Balagoon was convicted and given a life sentence. Kuwasi Balagoon died on December 13, 1986, of pneumonia induced by the AIDS virus. Up until his last days, he maintained his commitment to the revolutionary ideals he embraced in the BPP and the BLA.

Days after the Nyack incident, former Bronx, New York section leader and member of the International Section of the BPP Sekou Odinga was captured after an ambush by a joint task force of FBI agents and New York police. Odinga's comrade, BLA member Mtayari Sundiata, was killed in the armed battle with New York police officers. Odinga, a fugitive since the arrest of the New York Panther 21 in April 1969, was charged with nine counts of felony violations, including RICO (Racketeering Influenced Corrupt Organization Act) conspiracy, bank robbery, and murder charges. Federal prosecutors argued Odinga was the leader of a unit of the BLA, called "the Family" (activist forces call this group the "New Afrikan Freedom Fighters" wing of the BLA), which was responsible for the liberation of Assata Shakur and several expropriations from financial institutions in New York, New Jersey, and Pennsylvania. According to FBI informants and evidence seized by police, proceeds from the expropriations were utilized by this unit of the BLA to support an alternative health clinic in Harlem, youth camps, political mobilization in the New York area, and freedom fighters in Zimbabwe. Odinga represented himself in court and argued that he was a New Afrikan freedom fighter and therefore should be accorded prisoner-of-war status.[42] Odinga claimed that his actions were military rather than of a criminal nature. In his opening statement to the court on April 19, 1983, Odinga stated,

> The United States of America would have you believe that I am a criminal, that we all are criminals. That just isn't so. I am a New Afrikan soldier, and we have an absolute right to fight for our freedom. That is a human right. That is not a right you have to ask or beg for. Like all people who want to be free, what is necessary to exercise that right is to stand up like men and women and exercise it. If it calls for fighting, then we fight.[43]

To no avail, Odinga was convicted of two counts of the RICO indictment and sentenced to forty years in federal prison, twenty years on each count.

While not confirming his involvement in the escape of Assata Shakur, RNA activist and community health worker, Dr. Mutulu Shakur, during his 1988 trail, filed motions for his charges to be considered by an international tribunal. In pre-trial motions, Shakur and his attorney Chokwe Lumumba argued the charges for which he was indicted, particularly those related to Assata's liberation, were a result of a political act by Black revolutionaries seeking national liberation for the colonized New Afrikan nation from the United States government. Shakur cited American law's recognition of political prisoners in the political offense exception clause. The political offense exception clause is a federal statute that prevents foreign political activists from being extradited to escape political persecution. Shakur and his lawyers argued the political offense exception clause also applied to him, given the political nature of the charges and his revolutionary New Afrikan nationalist politics. Shakur also argued that the 1977 protocols, proposed as amendments to the 1949 Geneva Convention, which defined treatment of prisoners of war for the international community, applied to him. The 1977 protocols, never ratified by the United States, provided a definition of prisoner of war that was inclusive of the clandestine resistance of national liberation movements. New York federal judge Charles Haight required the federal government, including the Departments of State and Defense, to respond to Shakur's motion and his claims that the United States government did not have jurisdiction over him in this case. Ultimately, Haight rejected Shakur's motion and the New Afrikan activist was convicted and sentenced to sixty years in federal confinement.[44] In 1990, in response to an argument by his lawyers, Judge Haight considered an investigation by Shakur's defense team to seek a transfer of Dr. Shakur to Zimbabwe. Shakur had been a friend of the national liberation movement of Zimbabwe in its fight against White-settler colonialism. A doctor of Chinese medicine and acupuncture, Shakur and his legal team anticipated that his health care skills could be used in postcolonial Zimbabwe.[45] Although the efforts by Shakur's legal team were unsuccessful in winning his release, they were significant in expanding the terrain on which political prisoners would seek relief.

At least seven of the currently incarcerated Black political prisoners identify themselves as prisoners of war. The identification with the New Afrikan Independence Movement is also significant to contemporary campaigns for the release of Black political prisoners because at least thirteen of today's captured Black activists, including former BPP members Sekou Odinga, Sundiata Acoli, and Jalil Muntaqin identify themselves as New Afrikans. Before his release, Geronimo ji Jaga also identified himself as a "New Afrikan prisoner of war."[46] The prisoner-of-war position has not been popular or successful in winning freedom for incarcerated Black revolutionaries, but it has provided a political basis for New Afrikan insurgents to explain their actions in the language of international law in America's courts. It is clear that the United States government sanctioned the initiation of a counterinsurgency war, including the FBI's COINTELPRO program, against the Black Panther Party, the Republic of New Afrika, and other Black liberation movement organizations. The Black Liberation Army was a political response to increased state repression of the revolutionary Black movement in the United States. BLA and other revolutionary nationalist military groups saw themselves as soldiers fighting to defend the integrity of the Black liberation movement and Black people from this counterinsurgency war. In that context, Sekou Odinga, Sundiata Acoli, and Russell "Maroon" Shoats are certainly prisoners of war.[47]

Current Status of Black Political Prisoners

Currently in U.S. prisons, there are dozens of incarcerated men and women who have identified themselves and have been recognized by human rights groups as political prisoners and prisoners of war. What distinguishes the incarceration of these men and women from other prisoners? How are political prisoners in the United States treated differently from other incarcerated individuals?

Human rights advocates argue there are several features that distinguish political prisoners from other incarcerated individuals. These distinguishing features include assigning maximum sentences, isolation, and sensory deprivation. Political prisoners generally receive longer sentences than other individuals convicted on the same charges. Human rights advocates see the rendering of maximum sentences to political prisoners as a punitive measure to keep insurgent activists out of their communities as long as possible. Geronimo ji Jaga has stated that if he had really committed the murder he was convicted of, he would have been released sooner. Ji Jaga served over twenty-seven years in California prisons for murder, while the average time served for first-degree murder in that state is 4.5 years. Ji Jaga argues that his incarceration was due to his political beliefs and revolutionary activity.[48] In 1984, the two White radical anti-imperialist prisoners Timothy Blunk and Susan Rosenburg were sentenced to fifty-eight years in federal prison for the illegal possession of dynamite. This sentence is the highest for anyone in U.S. history convicted for a possessory offense. Blunk and Rosenburg had a history of supporting radical Black/New Afrikan and Puerto Rican causes. Supporters of Blunk and Rosenburg compare their sentence to others who have been convicted for more serious crimes to demonstrate the political nature of their imprisonment. For example, Dennis Malvesi, an anti-abortionist, received seven years for actually bombing abortion clinics across the United States. Right-wing survivalist Edward Hefferman was sentenced to serve from six months to two years for the possession of a thousand pounds of dynamite and eighteen pipe bombs.[49]

The political ideology of Black/New Afrikan and other revolutionary groups has also been used as a justification to deny parole. In 1987, BLA prisoner Masai Ehehosi was told by a Virginia parole board that he was not eligible for parole because of his views on armed struggle. The parole board told Ehehosi that he was "contrary to ever be able to adapt" because of his "ideas on revolutionary violence."[50] Prior to being released on bond in 1997, Geronimo ji Jaga was also denied parole. In a 1988 parole hearing for ji Jaga, Los Angeles District Attorney Dianne Vianni argued that the California parole board should deny ji Jaga parole because "he is still a revolutionary man." Even though his conduct had been exemplary during his incarceration, the California state parole board found ji Jaga unsuitable for parole.[51] In 1994, after twenty-one years in prison, Sundiata Acoli was denied parole by the New Jersey Parole Board, which gave him a "twenty-year hit," meaning Acoli would not be eligible for parole for another ten years. The parole board stated Acoli was given the twenty-year hit because of his membership in the BPP and BLA and his identification as a "New Afrikan P.O.W. (Prisoner of War) who had contributed to the theory and practice of the New Afrikan Independence Movement." The political history and contribution of Acoli was utilized by the parole board to demonstrate that "he had not changed appreciably during his incarceration and was in need of extensive counseling/therapy . . . to address his anti-social behavior."[52] The cases of Ehehosi and Acoli are similar to Nelson Mandela, who was asked by the apartheid government of South Africa to renounce the armed struggle as a condition for release. Acoli and other political prisoners remain incarcerated because they maintain their commitment to New Afrikan self-determination and liberation and refuse to repudiate their prior activism in the BPP and other revolutionary movements.

Political prisoners are commonly subjected to isolation and sensory deprivation, which are used by the penal system for behavior modification. Visitation and telephone contact are also limited. In prison facilities utilizing sensory deprivation (often called "control units"), prisoners are placed in an environment without natural light and fresh air, or physical contact with other human beings. These and other behavior-modification measures are intended to break strong-willed individuals. Although these control units are a growing trend in American prisons, political prisoners, particularly, have been assigned to these facilities as a means of coercing them into abandoning their movement, associations, and political beliefs. In 1987, White radical anti-imperialist prisoners Silvia Baraldini and Susan Rosenburg, and Puerto Rican independence fighter Alejandrina Torres were held in an experimental special control unit at Lexington federal prison for women in Kentucky. The "High Security Unit" (HSU) where they were housed had individual cells designed for sensory deprivation. The entire environment was painted white in each cell, which was thirty feet underground, with florescent lights shining twenty-four hours a day. The women were also routinely strip searched by male guards. They received no contact visits and even their attorneys had difficulty seeing them. In developing a case to oppose these conditions, the American Civil Liberties Union obtained psychologist Richard Korn to investigate the effects of the HSU on inmates. Dr. Korn concluded that HSU was designed to "force ideological conversion." Amnesty International also challenged the United States concerning HSU at Lexington as violating the international standards for treatment of prisoners. After three years of protests by the supporters of Baraldini, Rosenburg, and Torres and several human rights organizations, the HSU at Lexington was closed. In response to a federal law suit filed by the attorneys of Baraldini and Rosenburg, a federal judge found the United States government had violated the First Amendment rights of the activists and ordered the Federal Bureau of Prisons to desist from using political beliefs or association as the basis for transfer to an institution.[53] Unfortunately however, isolation and sensory deprivation remain a growing trend in the American penal system, and political prisoners continue to face these conditions as punitive measures because of their political ideology and practice. In an interview, New Afrikan P.O.W. Sundiata Acoli commented on the treatment of political prisoners. Acoli stated,

> Our daily existence is harsher than most other prisoners because the government does everything possible to break us. They send us to the harshest prisons . . . as far away from family, friends, and attorneys as possible. They lock us down for many years in isolation units while cutting off our communications with most of the outside world. They tamper with our food, try to break up our families, and treat them rudely when they visit, fail to provide adequate medical care, aggravate and provoke us. They try to set us up to be brutalized or killed by guards or preferably by other prisoners. All this, and more, to try to break our spirits and/or to make us proclaim to the world that we were wrong to struggle.[54]

The United States government utilizes a policy of criminalization in regards to its incarceration of insurgent activists and revolutionaries. Although Black Panther and other political prisoners were often targeted by the counter-insurgency apparatus of the U.S. state, they were arrested, tried, and convicted of violations of the criminal code. Some criminal violations developed from the political and military confrontations between insurgent activists and federal, state, and local police, but other charges were manufactured to remove radical political activists from their communities. By criminalizing political detainees, the United States government can boldly make the claim that it holds no political prisoners. In making such a claim, the federal government can piously challenge the human rights records of other regimes, such as Cuba, China, or the Sudan. Through an effective policy of criminalization, the United States government is able to maintain its image as a citadel of democracy and a champion of human rights.

One of the challenges in building a viable movement for the freedom of political prisoners in the United States is to effectively confront the U.S. government's strategy of criminalization. Since the decline of the BPP as a national revolutionary movement, no political force has been able to champion the cause of political prisoners in the same dynamic way as the mobilization in defense of Huey Newton. Mumia Abu-Jamal and ji Jaga received some national media attention, but most political prisoners receive little if any material, legal, or political support.

As in the case of Newton, Seale, and Huggins in New Haven, and the New York 21, we know that Black revolutionaries can win legal battles with political mobilization and popular support to supplement their legal strategy. The experience of Mandela and the political prisoners of the African National Congress, the Pan-Africanist Congress, and other Black freedom fighters in South Africa demonstrates the impact of a dynamic mass movement and international pressures. As with the Basque movement, the issue of freedom for Mandela and other South African political prisoners was at the top of the agenda of the freedom movement in South Africa. The current nationally recognized Black leadership has not made political prisoners a priority agenda item. The issue of freedom for political prisoners was not emphasized and received only token remarks at the 1995 Million Man March.

Mainstream Black leadership has, for the most part, ignored or deemphasized the issue of political prisoners, but radical New Afrikan organizations have continued to organize support for the freedom of political prisoners and prisoners of war. In 1978, as a result of a petition by the National Conference of Black Lawyers, a body of international jurists visited New Afrikan political prisoners and other prisoners and determined that there were several individuals who were incarcerated and received extreme sentences because of their radical politics. In 1990 and 1992, international tribunals were organized by representatives of the New Afrikan, Puerto Rican, American Indian, Chicano-Mexican, and White anti-imperialist liberation movements. In both instances, an international panel of human rights advocates, scholars, and lawyers found that the United States has political prisoners. International jurists also found the United States guilty of human rights violations because of its counter-insurgency war on revolutionary Black activists. In 1989, Ahmed Obafemi of the New Afrikan Peoples Organization made a presentation to the United Nations Commission on Human Rights in Geneva, Switzerland that charged the United States with violating the human rights of New Afrikan political prisoners and prisoners of war. Since that year, representatives of the December 12th Movement, a human rights organization based in New York City, have returned to Geneva to offer more evidence of political incarceration in the United States.[55]

As a result of this work, Maurice Glele, a representative of the High Court of the African Republic of Benin, was sent to the United States to investigate American racial discrimination on behalf of the United Nations Committee on Racism and Racial Discrimination. In his report, Glele acknowledged the existence of political prisoners. In 1994, the December 12th Movement also sent a delegation to the African state of Zimbabwe to request that the African government allow New Afrikan political prisoners to receive dual citizenship and the opportunity of repatriation, contingent on the grant of amnesty by the United States.[56]

That same year, former Panther political prisoner Dhoruba Bin-Wahad presented a resolution at the Seventh Pan-African Congress in Kampala, Uganda that called for, among other things, a recognition of the existence of Black political prisoners in the United States, petitions to the United Nations Commission on Human Rights in their behalf, and the acceptance of freed political prisoners in progressive African nations. The assembly of progressive African states and Pan-Africanist organizations endorsed the resolution Wahad presented on behalf of the North American delegation to the Pan-African Congress.[57] In 1995, thousands of people inside and outside the United States, marched in the streets to protest the imminent execution of former BPP activist and progressive journalist Mumia Abu-Jamal. After a massive international outpouring of support to halt the execution of Abu-Jamal, Pennsylvania judge Albert Sabo, who originally sentenced him after the activist was convicted of murdering a Philadelphia police officer, postponed the execution of Abu-Jamal to hear additional evidence for a retrial.[58] In August 1994, the New Afrikan Liberation Front (NALF) was formed. NALF is a coalition of revolutionary nationalist organizations brought together by New Afrikan political prisoners, which include Geronimo ji Jaga, Sekou Odinga, Sundiata Acoli, Jalil Muntaqin, and Mutulu Shakur. In 1996, the NALF initiated a campaign to lobby the Congressional Black Caucus to call hearings on the FBI's COINTELPRO program and investigate the relationship between New Afrikan political prisoners and prisoners of war and the FBI's counter-insurgency programs.[59]

Although these and other efforts have been essential for continuing legal defense for political prisoners, because of inadequate human and material resources, the contemporary New Afrikan insurgent movement has not organized a dynamic campaign for the freedom of political prisoners and prisoners of war. During my 1993 visit to the Basque Country, I realized that the struggle for the freedom of political prisoners in their movement was an intrinsic part of the Basque people's national consciousness and resistance. In the movement against apartheid in South Africa, Mandela's freedom was tied to the overthrow of the White settler regime and Black freedom. The development of a dynamic movement for the freedom of New Afrikan political prisoners and prisoners of war will only occur with the growth of an insurgent movement on behalf of Black communities in the United States.

NOTES

1. National Committee to Free Puerto Rican Prisoners of War and the National Committee to End the Marion Lockdown, eds., *Can't Jail the Spirit: Political Prisoners in the United States* (Chicago: Editorial Coqui Publishers, 1988), 21–22.

2. Ibid. *Can't Jail the Spirit* contains biographies of Black, Puerto Rican, Native American, and White Anti-Imperialist political prisoners; *Crossroad* 7 (May–June 1996): 14. *Crossroad* provides a list of "Black, African-American, and New Afrikan Political Prisoners and Prisoners of War."

3. Bobby Seale, *Seize the Time: The Story of the Black Panther Party and Huey P. Newton* (Baltimore, Md.: Black Classic Press, 1991), 188; David Hilliard and Lewis Cole, *This Side of Glory: The Autobiography of David Hilliard and The Black Panther Party.* (Boston: Little, Brown, and Company, 1993), 130–31; Gilbert Moore, *Rage* (New York: Carroll and Graf, 1993), 34–35.

4. Gilbert Moore, *Rage*, 73; Bobby Seale, *Seize the Time*, 222.

5. Jim Fletcher, Tanaquil Jones, and Sylvere Lotringer, eds., *Still Black, Still Strong: Survivors of the War Against Black Revolutionaries* (New York: Semiotext(e), 1993), 229–30.

6. Hilliard and Cole, *This Side of Glory*, 248–50, 294; Also see Donald Freed, *Agony in New Haven: The Trial of Bobby Seale and Ericka Huggins and the Black Panther Party* (New York: Simon and Schuster, 1973).

7. Ibid, 248, 280–81; Kuwasi Balagoon, Joan Bird, Robert Collier, Richard Harris, Ali Bey Hassan, Jamal Joseph, Abayama Katara, Kwando Kinshasa, Dhoruba Moore, Baba Odinga, Shaba Om, Curtis Powell, Afeni Shakur, Lumumba Shakur, Clark Squire, Cetewayo Tabor, *Look for Me in the Whirlwind: The Collective Biography of the New York 21* (New York: Random House, 1971), 363–64; Fletcher, Jones, and Lotringer, eds., *Still Black, Still Strong*, 10–12, 230; Michael T. Kaufman, "Reactions to the Verdict: Joy, Surprise and Silence," *The New York Times*, 14 May 1971, 20.

8. The following articles all appeared in *The Black Panther*, 16 March 1968: "Eyewitness Report on Orangeburg Massacre," 6, 11; "Let Rap Rap," 7; H. Rap. Brown, "A Letter from Prison to My Black Brothers and Sisters (written 2 February 1968)," 7; "Nashville . . . A Black Concentration Camp," 10. Sellers explains the 1968 ordeal at South Carolina State in "Eyewitness Report." "Let Rap Rap" and "A Letter from Prison" deal with government repression targeting SNCC Chairman H. Rap Brown. In "Nashville," cases of political prisoners, including Rap Brown, LeRoi Jones, Reies Tijerina, Eddie Oquendo, and Benjamin Spock, are discussed.

9. Seale, *Seize the Time*, 203–7. Attorney Charles Garry was very effective in representing the BPP in court. In the *voir dire*, or examination process for the purpose of selecting jurors, Garry was a master at eliminating jurors who had a predisposed bias against the BPP.

10. In the 18 May 1968 issue of *The Black Panther*, see Bobby Seale, "Black Lawyers Are Jiving" and Kathleen Cleaver, "Black Power, Black Lawyers, and White Courts," both on p. 5.

11. Chokwe Lumumba, interviewed by author, 4 January 1997, Atlanta, Georgia; Roger Wareham, interviewed by author, 4 January 1997, Atlanta, Georgia. Lumumba and Wareham are both attorneys who actively work on behalf of political prisoners.

12. For examples of the large number of charges faced by BPP members across the United States in 1969 and 1970, see "Pig Brutality," *The Black Panther*, Saturday, 21 February 1970, 4–10. "Pig Brutality" is a detailed list of arrests, bail designation, and disposition of cases of Panthers across the United States.

13. Fletcher, Jones, and Lotringer, eds., *Still Black, Still Strong* , 253.

14. E. Tani and Kae Sera, *False Nationalism, False Internationalism* (Chicago: A Seeds Beneath the Snow Publication, 1985), 209.

15. Black Panther Party Central Committee, "Enemies of the People," *The Black Panther*, 13 February 1971, 12–14.

16. Herb Boyd, *The Black Panthers for Beginners* (New York: Writers and Readers, 1995), 94–97.

17. Fletcher, Jones, and Lotringer, eds., *Still Black, Still Strong*, 239–40.

18. "What Really Happened In Los Angeles," *The Black Panther*, Saturday, 20 December 1969, 12.

19. Afro-American Liberation Army, *Humanity, Peace and Freedom* (Los Angeles: Revolutionary Peoples Communications Network, 1972), 4–5, 12–13; Ward Churchill and Jim Vander Wall, *Agents of Repression: The FBI's Secret War Against the Black Panther Party and the American Indian Movement* (Boston: South End, 1988), 79–87. *Humanity, Peace, and Freedom* contains articles from Geronimo ji Jaga and Los Angeles BPP prisoners.

20. Huey Newton, "On the Expulsion of Geronimo from the Black Panther Party," *The Black Panther* (Saturday) 23 January 1971, 7.

21. Mutulu Shakur, interviewed by author, 19 December 1996, Atlanta, Georgia.

22. Ward Churchill, "The Third World at Home: Political Prisoners in the U.S.," *Z Magazine* (June 1990), 90; Committee to Free Puerto Rican Prisoners of War, *Can't Jail the Spirit*, 104–6; Fletcher, Jones, and Lotringer, *Still Black, Still Strong*, 11–15.

23. Churchill, "Third World at Home," 90; "Eighteen Years of Fighting for Freedom," *Death to the Klan* (special edition "Free Geronimo Pratt") Spring 1988, 1, 4; National Black Human Rights Coalition, *Free Geronimo Pratt* (Los Angeles: Soulbook, 1979), 1–4.

24. Churchill, "Third World at Home,"90; also see *The Black Panther* (memorial issue), Spring 1991, 14–15 published by the Black Panther Newspaper Committee for profiles on Herman Bell, Albert "Nuh" Washington, and Jalil Muntaqin.

25. May 19th Communist Organization, *To Free Assata Shakur and African Prisoners of War* (New York: Madame Binh Graphics Collective, 1979), 2–3, 20–21; Also read Assata Shakur's autobiography, *Assata: The Autobiography of a Revolutionary* (New York, Lawrence Hill, 1988).

26. "Assata is Free," *Breakthrough: The Political Journal of the Prairie Fire Organizing Committee* 4 (Winter 1980): 1, 12–13; Committee to Free Puerto Rican Prisoners of War, *Can't Jail the Spirit*, 71,144, 153; Assata Shakur, *From Somewhere in the World: Assata Shakur Speaks, Message to the New Afrikan Nation* (New York: New Afrikan Women's Organization, 1980), inside cover; John Castellucci, *The Big Dance: The Untold Story of Weatherman Kathy Boudin and the Terrorist Family that Committed the Brinks Robbery Murders* (New York: Dodd, Meade, and Company, 1986),138–47. "Assata is Free" contains Shakur's statement written days prior to her escape from Clinton Correctional Institution and a statement from the Black Liberation Army Coordinating Committee claiming responsibility for the liberation of Assata. The biographies of Sekou Odinga, Marilyn Buck, and Sylvia Baraldini in *Can't Jail the Spirit* speak of these activists and Mutulu Shakur being tried and convicted for charges related to the

liberation of Assata. *From Somewhere in the World* is a statement by Shakur one year after her liberation and while she was still underground. A brief statement concerning her escape is on the inside cover of the pamphlet. *The Big Dance* basically gives an account based on police, FBI informants, and media versions of Assata's liberation.

27. The author was present at this rally on 5 November 1979. The event was a march from Harlem to the United Nations offices in New York calling for "Human Rights and Self-determination for the Black Nation." The statement from Assata mentioned in note 26, printed in *Breakthrough,* was distributed at this rally.

28. "Political Prisoners' Update (partial list),"distributed at the 20th Anniversary Celebration of the Black Panther Party, Oakland, California, 11–13 October 1996; "Petition to Free Romaine Fitzgerald from California State Prison," flyer, n.d.

29. Speech by W. Paul Coates, 1993; Paul Coates, "Update on Political Prisoners in Baltimore: Marshall Eddie Conway," *The Black Panther: Black Community News Service* 1 (memorial issue) Spring 1991, 1, 15.

30. Erin Schutlte, "Fight Continues for Political Activist's Release," *Daily Nebraskan,* 8 June 1995,1; Committee to Free Puerto Rican Political Prisoners of War, *Can't Jail the Spirit,* 75; "Rice-Poindexter Case History Countdown to Justice Fact Sheet," *The Black Panther* 1 (Fall 1991): 3, 18–19.

31. Kwame Afoh, Chokwe Lumumba, Imari Obadele, and Ahmed Obafemi, *A Brief History of Black Struggle in America* (Baton Rouge: House of Songhay, 1990), 56–58; Committee to Free Puerto Rican Prisoners of War, Can't Jail the Spirit, 22; *Crossroads Support Network, Who Are New Afrikan Political Prisoners and Prisoners of War* (Chicago: Spear and Shield Collective, 1990), 6.

32. "Interview with L.A. P.O.W.s," *Humanity, Freedom and Peace,* 7. In Los Angeles, Panthers Geronimo ji Jaga and Ronald Freeman are interviewed from the Los Angeles County Jail. The activists are referred to as P.O.W.s.

33. Sundiata Acoli, Sekou Odinga, and Kuwasi Balagoon are mentioned elsewhere in this essay. Biographies of Bashir Hameed, Abdul Majid, and Kojo Bomani Sababu appear in *Can't Jail the Spirit.* Hameed and Majid are known as the Queens Two. Hameed joined the BPP in Oakland in 1968. He moved to New Jersey in 1969 and attempted to reorganize the Jersey City branch of the BPP. Majid was a member of the Brooklyn branch of the BPP. In 1981, Majid and Hameed became suspects after two New York police officers were shot, with one dead and the other wounded. After three trials, Hameed and Majid were convicted and sentenced to 33-1/3 years to life. Kojo Bomani Sababu was never a member of the BPP, but was recruited into the BLA in prison by Kuwasi Balagoon and Andaliwa Clark. In December 1975, he was captured and later convicted of charges of engaging in expropriation of banks and killing drug dealers operating in Black neighborhoods in New Jersey. In 1996, he was charged and convicted, along with incarcerated Puerto Rican nationalist Oscar Lopez Rivera (who also identified himself as a prisoner of war) and two Puerto Rican activists, Dora Garcia and Jaime Delgado, of conspiring to escape by using firearms, explosives, and a helicopter. Sababu has received multiple life sentences for all of the incidents mentioned above.

34. Chokwe Lumumba, *The Roots of the New Afrikan Independence Movement* (Jackson, Miss.: New Afrikan Productions, 1991), 3. Afoh, Lumumba, Obadele, and Obafemi, *History of Black Struggle,* 36.

35. Afoh, Lumumba, Obadele, and Obafemi, *History of Black Struggle,* 37, 52–57; "RNA Freedom Fighters: A Continuing Episode of Human Rights Violations in Amerika," *Breakthrough 4* (Winter 1980): 1, 25–30.

36. "Law of Land Warfare," *The New African 4* (August 1972): 9, 16. The criteria for prisoner of war cited here are based on the 1949 Geneva Prisoner of War Convention. In 1977 new amendments were proposed that were inclusive of clandestine national resistance fighters who generally don't wear a "fixed and distinctive sign" or uniform or openly carry weapons. Captured soldiers of clandestine resistance groups from the Puerto Rican and New Afrikan Independence movement would argue the 1977 amendments applied to them.

37. Ahmed Obafemi, interview by author, 20 December 1996, Birmingham, Alabama; Chokwe Lumumba, interview by author, 22 December 1996, Birmingham, Alabama.

38. "Spying on the Republic of New Africa," the Leesha Faulkner Civil Rights Collection. The Faulkner Collection contains Mississippi state government surveillance records on the PGRNA's activities in Mississippi from 1969–73, including the international African Prisoner of War Solidarity Day. The involvement of "East Coast" Panther factions is noted in Mississippi state surveillance.

39. Masai Ehehosi, interview by author, 28 December 1996, Chicago, Illinois; Safiya Bukhari, "Coming of Age: Notes from a New Afrikan Revolutionary," *African Prisoner of War Journal* 7, 1988, 12; Afoh, Lumumba, Obadele, and Obafemi, *History of Black Struggle*, 42.

40. "On the Strategic Alliance of the Armed Forces of the Revolutionary Nationalist and Anti-Imperialist Movements: A Black Liberation Army Communiqué in *America The NationState: The Politics of the United States from a State–Building Perspective*, ed. Imari Obadele (Baton Rouge, La.: Malcolm Generation, 1995), 390–91.

41. Kuwasi Balagoon, *Trial Statement of New Afrikan Revolutionary Kuwasi Balagoon* (Patterson, New Jersey: Patterson Anarchist Collective, 1994), 3.

42. Committee to Free Puerto Rican Prisoners of War, *Can't Jail the Spirit*, 86–87; "RICO Test Case for Counter-Insurgency, 1983," *Let Your Motto Be Resistance: Newsletter of Resistance* 1 (April 1983): 1, 24–25.

43. Sekou Odinga quoted in "New Afrikan Freedom Fighters Day", *By Any Means Necessary: Organ of the New Afrikan People's Organization* 1 (August/September 1984): 1, 12.

44. "Memorandum from Dr. Mutulu Shakur to Judge Charles Haight," 26 November 1987; *United States of America v. Mutulu Shakur* (defendant), United States District Court Southern District of New York, Affidavit 3 sss 82 Cr. 312 (CSH); Shakur outlines his position on prisoner of war status and the application of the political offense exception clause to his case in his memo to Judge Haight. The U.S. government, including the Departments of State and Defense, responded to Shakur's motion in *United States v. Mutulu Shakur*. Watani Tyehimba, interview by author, 24 December 1996, Atlanta, Georgia; Tyehimba was a New Afrikan political prisoner who participated in Shakur's defense team. Roger Wareham interviewed by author, 4 January 1997, Atlanta, Georgia. Wareham, an attorney and member of the December 12th Movement, has been in the forefront of raising American human rights violations in the international community.

45. Jonathan Lubell, interviewed by author, 5 January 1997, New York City; Tyehimba interviewed by author. Lubell is a member of Shakur's legal team. He and Tyehimba were a part of the team who visited Zimbabwe on Shakur's behalf.

46. New Afrikan political prisoners and prisoners of war identify themselves in *Can't Jail the Spirit*. The Crossroads Support Network in its pamphlet *Who Are New Afrikan Political Prisoners and Prisoners of War?* provides a list of

incarcerated New Afrikan revolutionaries. Russell "Maroon" Shoats is not mentioned in either publication.

47. "The Statement of Russell "Maroon" Shoats," *Black Panther* 4 (Winter 1995): 1, 22,25. Russell "Maroon" Shoats was a member of the Philadelphia branch of the BPP. He was arrested and tried for the death and wounding of police officers after a series of retaliatory guerrilla raids on Philadelphia police stations. The raids were in response to repression against the BPP and incidents of police brutality, including the shooting of a Black youth in the summer of 1970. Shoats was convicted and given a "natural life sentence."

48. Churchill, "Third World at Home," 90.

49. Ibid, 91; Committee to Free Puerto Rican Prisoners of War, *Can't Jail the Spirit*, 147–48, 179–80.

50. Ehehosi interview by author. Masai Ehehosi was paroled in 1988. He remains active in the New Afrikan Independence Movement.

51. Churchill, "Third World at Home," 90.

52. Letter from Sundiata Acoli Freedom Campaign to Supporters, dated 15 March 1994.

53. Churchill, "Third World at Home," 95–96; Committee to Free Puerto Rican Prisoners of War, *Can't Jail the Spirit*, 131, 144,179–180.

54. Sundiata Acoli quoted in "So What's It Like to be a Political Prisoner or P.O.W.?" *The Source: The Magazine of Hip-Hop Music, Culture, and Politics*, October 1995, 73, 79.

55. Ahmed Obafemi interview by author, 20 December 1996 Birmingham, Alabama.

56. Roger Wareham, interview.

57. "Seventh Pan-African Congress Called to Support Political Prisoners and P.O.W.s Held by the U.S.," *Crossroads* 5(September 1994): 3, 9.

58. S.E. Anderson and Tony Medina, "If the Threat of Death Can Unite . . . and Ignite," *In Defense of Mumia* (New York: Writers and Readers, 1996), 1–4.

59. William Pleasant, "New Black Nationalist Organization Launched," *Daily Challenge,* 20 September 1995; "Black Nationalist Organizations Unite at Historic Atlanta Summit: The New Afrikan Liberation Front is Launched," *The City Sun*, 27 September to 3 October 1995, 10; Sekou Odinga, Hanif Shabazz Bey, Mutulu Shakur, Kojo Bomani Sababu, Jaili Muntaqin, Jihad Mumit, Sundiata Acoli, Geronimo ji Jaga Pratt, "A Statement in Support of Consolidation from New Afrikan Freedom Fighters in Lewisburg, toward the objective of a National Liberation Front," in *NALF: New Afrikan Liberation Front* (New York: NALF, 1995), 5.

Chapter Eighteen

To Fight for the People:
The Black Panther Party
and Black Politics in the 1990s

Clarence Lusane

As the twentieth century comes to a close, the Black community confronts daunting economic, social, and political challenges. Global economic restructuring, driven by new technologies and a reconfigured capital–labor relationship, is shaping the economic destiny of millions of African Americans in ways that are deeply disturbing and injurious. The debilitating consequences of these changes over the last two decades have contributed to an African American social calamity: devastating homicide rates, excessively high rates of incarceration, unprecedented substance abuse and trafficking, and infant mortality rates that rival those of the developing world. Furthermore, the dismantling of the "welfare state" by conservative policy makers has meant deteriorating housing, decreased access to health care, environmental calamity, and an abandonment of public education for the Black community (and others).

To successfully confront these conditions necessitates a new leadership that is bold, committed, and visionary, a leadership that has yet to appear in a significant and sustained way. An important part of the task of this new leadership is to project a vision for the nation, not only for the Black community. The leadership group that emerged during the last period of heightened activism in the Black community in the 1950s, 1960s, and early 1970s, that is, Civil Rights leaders and Black elected officials, appears to have reached its historic limit. Qualitatively tied to a perspective that assumes a benevolent welfare state and for the most part, politically wedded to the fortunes and foibles of the Democratic Party, the generation of national leadership that now dominates Black politics simply cannot adequately address the challenges confronting the Black community or the challenges that will confront the nation in the years ahead. This inadequacy is not simply a critique of individuals. Indeed, there are many committed and skilled "leaders," elected and otherwise, in the Black community. Yet, the hard truth is that virtually every strategy employed by the current Black leadership has failed to arrest the increasing hardship faced by millions of African Americans.

Similar leadership issues confronted the young men and women who initiated the first Black Panther chapter three decades ago. Their brash fearlessness was part of a new period in Black politics that called for a radical stance and agency to challenge centuries-old questions of class and race power. As the essays in this volume document, the Panthers forged an oppositional discourse and political organization across the nation that transformed the nature and conception of Black politics and American politics. The Panthers were critical in radicalizing a generation of Black, White, and Latino activists, as well as seniors, gays, and other sectors of society who felt left out and discarded. Picking up the baton from earlier efforts of the Student Nonviolent Coordinating Committee and post-Nation of Islam Malcolm X, the Panthers also internationalized the African American freedom movement and inspired followers and imitators from Jamaica to England. They brought into sharp focus the repressive role of the modern capitalist state, at both the federal and local levels, and the degree to which conservative, reactionary forces would go to co-opt, hamper, and eliminate a revolutionary Black movement.

For contemporary Black politics, the legacy of the Panthers provides both an opportunity and a danger. As a transformative moment in politics, the early Panther period is rich in lessons in the vicissitudes and challenges facing African Americans in their struggle for equality and inclusion. A possible uprising of America's inner-city dispossessed led by community-based intellectuals with little tolerance for compromise and pacifism has always been a danger just below an apparent tranquil political and social surface. Ghetto rebellions in the mid-1960s, rhetorically inspired by groups like the Black Panthers, League of Revolutionary Black Workers, and the Republic of New Africa, among others, shattered assumptions of a complacent Black community. The Panthers, along with other organizations, taught the nation and the world that shadows could become flesh and that the desire for justice knows no bounds. That the Panthers failed to realize what can honestly be called their democratic revolution does not diminish the significance of their existence or the spirit of struggle they sought to evoke.

Yet, there is also a danger lurking in the Panther legacy. There are many, including some former Panthers, who see the period through a limited, one-sided, and often romantic prism. In these accounts, the Panthers emerge as ghetto heroes and sheroes devoid of human frailties, strategic misjudgment, and individual evolution. Historical myth-making of this kind, driven by ignorance or ideology, runs the risk of constructing urban legends and fables built on rumor and campfire stories, when critical reflection and inspired interpretation are desperately needed. For those who would make the Panthers less than they were or more than they could be, a rectification and reiteration of the contributions and contradictions they generated are urgently required.

The commodification of the Panther odyssey—resounding in the canyons of Hollywood as scripts about the Panthers make the rounds—must be combated by accurate historical contextualization and reflective analysis unfettered by partisan interests and self-serving political agendas. Spike Lee's *Malcolm X*, a narrative journey of grand speculation, celebrity construction, and ideological confusion, demonstrates the problem of popularization that emerges in the unstable marriage of Black history and White Hollywood. *Panther*, a shameful amalgamation of conspiracy theories, action-movie antics, and political sophistry, was the first strike of what could be a barrage of Panther and Panther-like Hollywood films. For African Americans, this danger resonates even more profoundly in the current period where public platforms are generously offered to some of the most racist theories and views imaginable.

Even without the buying and selling of Pantherism, any effort at popularization and explanation of the Panthers and their significance must battle a broad, conservatively reconstructed history of the 1960s where radicals, rebels, and revolutionaries of every stripe are demonized, discredited, and defeated. However, it is not just on the terrain of history that this battle must be fought. A struggle must also be waged on the grounds of the ongoing political discourse regarding racism, the politics of class and gender relations, and ideological dominance. It is the permanent war for the imagination of the masses of African Americans that links the Panthers with contemporary Black struggles.

This essay evaluates lessons to be learned—in some cases, relearned—from the Black Panther Party experience. In this light, it is critical to examine the similarities and differences between the political economies of the 1960s and the 1990s, questions of strategy and political program, leadership issues, the development and significance of genderized struggles within the Black community, and, finally, the issue of revolution.

African Americans and the New Global Political Economies

Race and racism continue to be profound determinants in the life and destiny of African Americans. Racism is manifest in White supremacist theories, doctrines, public policies, and political initiatives. It is driven, bolstered, and reinforced by a capitalist social system—a system that the Black Panthers unsuccessfully sought to overthrow and that despite its open wounds, still flexes its considerable muscles. Yet, the contemporary struggle of the Black community for freedom and justice takes place on a qualitatively different global and national landscape from the one that confronted the Panthers. In the mid-1960s, U.S. capitalism sustained a global military, economic, and political hegemony that provided the conditions for a functional, though fragile, welfare state. Workers in the United States enjoyed the highest standard of living in the world, held the ideological view that it deserved such and, perhaps more important, was prepared to give political support to the government and corporate militarists who allegedly were committed to fighting to preserve that standard. As nation–states go, the United States on the surface appeared, to many people, to hold a permanent global dominance and growing prosperity that would certainly endure throughout the twentieth century and perhaps, to the end of the twenty-first. The Panthers emerged at the height of U.S. economic dominance. From manufacturing to agriculture to the service sector, U.S. products were the envy of the world. Despite great political reluctance, U.S. political leaders were able to address, at a minimal level, the material demands raised by the Panthers and other Black political leaders of the time. Both guns and bread were doled out as anti-poverty programs spread, Civil Rights legislation was passed, and Blacks were allowed into the political system in unprecedented numbers. President Lyndon Johnson's "Great Society" programs to bring social peace were generated not only from the movement below, but also from the leadership above. The liberal wing of capital recognized the value and utility of ending Jim Crow segregation and helping to develop a Black middle-class that (it was hoped) was unlikely to rebel against a system that it would have a stake in.

In the 1990s, the United States and its working class face a qualitatively different global economic order. The post-Cold War, post-industrial corporate restructuring, and unequal technological breakthroughs have created an economic situation that is fluid and no longer principally controlled by U.S. companies. The shift from monopoly capitalism to global capitalism is the defining economic phenomenon of this historic period. As political economist Robert Ross notes, that process has critically changed the relationship between capital and labor, with labor coming up on the short end.[1] While capital, to some degree, has always had the ability to extend beyond national borders, the contemporary stage of global capitalism provides a mobility that gives capital unprecedented productive agility and seriously undermines labor's ability to protect its gains or advance its interests. These transformations have put global and national capital in a strong position to demand and win changes in state policies that further its interests and hegemony. The dismantling of the welfare state that had disproportionately benefited African Americans is the top agenda item in this period.

Driven by higher profits, desire for close proximity to natural resources, access to local markets, and most critical, cheap labor, large and medium-size corporate investors have fled the United States and Europe with all deliberate speed. The high wages and relative job stability enjoyed by the Western working class for decades are fast-disappearing components of an industrial era that no longer exists. In manufacturing, labor's major weapon, the strike, has become impotent as capital is no longer held hostage to production shutdowns. Consequently, labor militancy has been severely curtailed under the new balance of power. Strikes involving a thousand or more workers numbered about three-hundred yearly in the 1960s; in 1991, there were only forty such strikes.[2] Labor has lost control over job cuts, wages, and work rules, and in some instances, has given back benefits won in the past. These are all tactical moves by labor to hold on to jobs that are rapidly leaving the country. Another consequence of capital's new-found authority is that union membership in the United States has fallen during the 1980s by close to a half-million—one-third of its total.[3] This is especially harmful to African Americans workers who are more likely to be members of unions than Whites—21 percent to 15 percent. The wage differential that comes from being in a union is about 33.8 percent higher than for non-union workers; for blue collar workers, the difference ranges from 157.3 percent to 278.3 percent higher.[4]

In 1950, one-third of all U.S. jobs were in manufacturing. Many of these jobs were held by African Americans. By the mid-1980s, only 20 percent of U.S. jobs were in manufacturing, and by the early 1990s, the number had fallen to 16 percent. Jobs that were lost in the United States washed ashore in other lands where labor revolts were unheard of or brutally suppressed. In the 1980s, the loss of millions of manufacturing jobs was central to the diminished fortunes of the middle class in the United States and to increased national poverty. In 1981, 20.2 million people worked in manufacturing. A decade later, that number had shrunk to 18.4 million—a decline of 1.8 million workers. At the same time, the number of people who became 16 years of age or older grew by 19.4 million individuals.[5]

Companies that symbolized America's global corporate dominance in the past joined the exodus. General Electric, the company that hired super-patriot Ronald Reagan as its spokesperson, cut 25,000 domestic jobs while adding 30,000 foreign positions. RCA cut 14,000 domestic jobs while adding 19,000 globally. No company was more an icon of America's manufacturing might and the rewards won by the industrial working class than the Ford Motor Company. However, in the last two decades, competition from foreign auto makers forced the company to cut its workers worldwide from 506,500 to 390,000. More than 80,000 hourly and 16,000 salaried workers were let go, reducing the number of hourly workers by 47 percent (although productivity increased by 57 percent). Most of those cuts occurred in the United States where Ford spent $28 billion to automate its old and new plants. The number of robots used by Ford, for example, rose from 236 to 1,300. It is estimated that in the United States during the 1970s, between 32 and 38 million jobs disappeared.[6]

In the last thirty years, even prior to the North American Free Trade Agreement (NAFTA), 1,800 plants that employ a half-million workers have been built in Mexico. The overwhelming number of these plants have been set up by U.S. companies, although nailing down the ownership of globalized factories has become a research science all its own.

The lost manufacturing jobs have been replaced by low-wage work, which generally offers fewer benefits and more exploitative working conditions—that is, no labor unions or collective bargaining power. These often

sub-minimal wage jobs include positions in retail sales, food service, jani-
torial services, home keeping, and low-level health care delivery. These
waiters/waitresses, janitors, maids, health aides, fast food workers, and others work full-time jobs, yet constitute a class of the working poor who fall
below the poverty line. They usually do not have unemployment, retire-
ment, or health insurance benefits. This situation is likely to worsen as the
new trend in employment practice shies away from full-time work with
benefits. In the period 1980–87, half of all new jobs went to temporary and
part-time workers.[7] This phenomenon is even taking place in Japan, perhaps
the most stable economy in the world. In 1980, Japan had one agency for
temporary workers. By 1985, there were more than 150, and today the
number is several hundred.[8]

In this era, job competition takes place on a global scale. Workers are no
longer just competing with their next-door neighbors for that potential new
job, but with 700 million people around the world who are unemployed and
subjected to the vicissitudes of global capital. In addition, in the next twenty
years, 700 million more people will reach the legal working age in the Third
World. This means that about 38 million people more than the number of existing jobs will be searching for work where there is none to be found.[9]

There is a domestic price to pay for the new globalization as more in more
industrial corporations downsize or relocate their operations. In a sense, it
did not matter whether former manufacturing workers stayed or went. In
nearly all cases, they saw a sharp drop in their quality of life. The new economic nomads, for example, earned 43 percent less in their new employment than during their auto-making days.[10] The thrust of tens of thousands
of workers into poverty also meant that there were fewer tax dollars available to address the social needs of the (growing) poor.

Studies have shown that unemployment generates a slew of negative social consequences. A study by Dr. Harvey Brenner of Johns Hopkins University concluded that a one percent increase in the unemployment rate leads
to 37,000 deaths, 920 suicides, 650 homicides, 4,000 admissions to mental
hospitals, and 3,300 admissions to state prisons over a six-year period.[11] The
Fordus and McAliden report, prepared for the Joint Economic Committee
of the United States Congress, also highlighted the adverse social impact of
increased unemployment.[12]

One area in which the contradictions of the new period are exposed is in
the growing gap between the highest paid and the lowest paid. Widening income inequality is a defining character of the moment. While the rich were
getting richer, the poor and the middle class were getting poorer. In the
1980s, for those with incomes under $20,000, their incomes increased by
only 1.4 percent. Those with incomes from $20,0000–$50,000 had an increase of 44 percent. In stark contrast, those with incomes of more than $1
million had an increase of 2,184 percent.[13]

All of these developments have been nothing less than catastrophic for the Black community. Historically, low-skill, entry-level employment, particularly in the manufacturing sector, has been the chief means out of poverty for young Black males. Those days are gone. As economist Jeremy Rifkin points out, technological changes have had a devastating economic impact on Black workers. Mechanization and technological innovation, among other factors, ended the sharecropping system and displaced millions of Black farm laborers in the 1940s and 1950s. In 1949, only 6 percent of cotton harvesting was mechanical. By 1964, only fifteen years later, that number had jumped to 78 percent, and by 1972 was 100 percent. [14]

Hardly two decades later, the children and grandchildren of sharecroppers, who migrated North to Chicago, Detroit, Pittsburgh, Cleveland, New York, and other cities, have been jolted by the new technologies of the 1980s and 1990s. One consequence is that in 1995, the Black community confronts an official poverty rate of 33.1 percent or more than 10 million people, a rate which is higher than the rate for Hispanics (30.6 percent), Asians (15.3 percent), or Whites (12.2 percent).[15] Close to half of all Black children live in poverty. In the Black community, poverty is partly driven by the fact that women, who are disproportionately unemployed or earn minimum wage, head 47 percent of all Black families.[16] In 1994, the median income was $32,960 for Whites; $19,532 for Blacks; $22,886 for Latinos; and $38,347 for Asian-Pacific Islanders. Black median income is still only 59 percent that of Whites, essentially what it was thirty years ago. Black median income is only 50 percent of Asian-Pacific Islanders, and 85 percent of Latinos.[17]

Another factor increasing the poverty rate is the high dropout rate of young Blacks and Latinos. Since 1979, real wages of dropouts have fallen by 20 percent while the incomes of those with four years of college or more have risen by 8 percent.[18] The Black civilian labor force comprises about 14.4 million, which constitutes 11.1 percent of the nation's total labor force.[19] In the last two decades, the Black unemployment rate has been roughly three times that of Whites. In 1993, the Black unemployment rate was 13.4 percent while the White unemployment rate was 5.2 percent.[20] Blacks made up 21.7 percent of the nation's unemployed.

Demands for capital to invest in the inner cities—demands emanating from Black conservatives, liberals, and nationalists alike—remain mostly romantic. As political scientist Hilbourne Watson notes, although Black purchasing power is a significant $265 billion, from the vantage of global capital, there is no logical reason to invest its productive capacities in the Black community, or Appalachia for that matter.[21] Nor should the illusion that Black businesses will solve the Black employment crisis be fostered. In 1993, *Black Enterprise's* top 100 industrial and automotive companies collectively employed only 45,628 Blacks.[22] While this is a twenty-two percent increase over the previous year, it accounts for only one percent of the current Black labor force, and like other capitalist businesses, those Black businesses with the potential to grow are capital intensive (e.g., media, technology) rather than labor intensive (e.g., manufacturing). In virtually every Black community, non-Blacks own the majority of businesses. In Washington, D. C., although Blacks are 65 percent of the population, they own less than ten percent of the city's businesses. In Los Angeles, according to the last census, one of every ten Koreans owns his/her own business; for Blacks it's one out of every 67.[23]

The downturns in the economy in recent years have also been felt unevenly across racial lines. According to *The Wall Street Journal,* "[B]lacks were the only racial group to suffer a net job loss during the 1990–91 economic downturn."[24] African Americans lost close to 60,000 jobs at the companies surveyed by the Equal Employment Opportunity Commission. At companies such as W. R. Grace, Bank America, ITT, Sears, Roebuck and Co., Coca Cola, Safeway, Campbell Soup, Walt Disney, and General Electric—all of whom have gone global, Blacks lost jobs at a rate twice that of Whites. The jobs lost by Blacks at these companies covered the entire spectrum from entry-level positions to management. These economic retreats alone go far in explaining—though by no means justifying—the move by so many young and unemployed African Americans into the underground economy, particularly the illegal drug trade.[25]

In the United States, one dynamic that has grown is the unprecedented crisis of violence confronting youth, particularly Black youth. In 1979–1991, 50,000 American children were killed by violence. Each day, thirteen children die from gunfire while another thirty are injured by bullets. In 1991 alone, children under ten years old who died from gun violence were twice the number of U.S. troops killed in the Gulf War and Somalia combined. In the 1980s , there was a major increase in young people killing other young people. Between 1982 and 1991, arrests for juvenile murder/man-slaughter grew by 93 percent.[26] The rise in drug trafficking and violence opened the door for the criminalization of Black youth in massive numbers. Conservative policy makers and academics have lamented the growth in the so-called underclass, an all-too-obvious synonym for Black inner-city residents. This sector of society, the base upon which the Black Panthers built themselves, has become the enemy of choice for many. Progressives have challenged the notion of a predatory underclass. As political scientist Mack Jones and others note, a racialized underclass has always existed in the United States:

> [T]he presence of the Black underclass is not a result of either
> malfunctioning of the American economic process or the pathology of
> the members of the underclass. The underclass results from the sum of
> the routine systemically prescribed actions of the constituent elements
> or institutions of the political economy.[27]

Yet, it is undeniable that in the last fifteen to twenty years the extent of deterioration among the Black poor has grown sharper and its underclass existence appears permanent. In the 1980s, a fairly conscious assault on labor and the Black community by the Reagan administration, in collaboration with Congress, destroyed all hope of economic opportunity for Black youth. Initiating what political scientist Keith Jennings calls "economic genocide,"[28] Reagan dropped policy napalm bombs on the Black poor. Under the theme of anti-communism, Reagan ballooned the military budget by going after "programs targeted to low-income families and individuals—one tenth of the federal budget."[29] Cuts in these programs constituted nearly one-third of the 1981–83 budget cuts.[30]

In the years, 1981–1986, job training funds were "reduced from $7.6 billion to $3.6 billion or 52 percent in real terms, and it is argued that had the President's budget proposals been accepted each time, funding for job training programs would have fallen 62 percent below the funding level for the 1981 fiscal year."[31] As a result of these policies and the normal operations of the labor marketplace, by 1986, Black youth unemployment was officially 39.3 percent.[32] According to the National Urban League, Black teenagers suffered the sharpest increase in unemployment since 1960 of all groups. [33]

Nearly a decade later, little had changed. In the midst of the 1994 economic recovery, Black teen unemployment continued to rise. In January 1994, official Black teen unemployment was 32 percent; by May of the same year, it rose to 40 percent (males, 44 percent; females, 37 percent).[34] In contrast, the May unemployment rate of White teens was 15 percent. While 60 percent of White youth who have either graduated or dropped out from high school hold full or part-time jobs, only 33 percent of Black youth in the same situation are employed as such.

Strategy and Politics

The fight for economic justice is fought more often than not on the battlefield of politics and public policy. The issue of political representation was also one that the Black Panthers sought to address. In 1966, the year the Panthers were formed, one year after the passage of the Voting Rights Act, there were less than three hundred Black elected officials in the entire nation.[35] Although over half of all Blacks lived in the South and were majorities in many jurisdictions, the region had virtually no Black elected officials.[36] This lack of representation legitimized the claims of Black radicals that the political system was unresponsive, hopelessly racist, and opposed to the interests of the average African American. In California, the political appearance of Maxine Waters and Ron Dellums, both of whom would later become members of Congress, and the charismatic and dynamic Willie Brown, the powerful former Speaker of the California State Assembly and now the first Black mayor of San Francisco, was years away. Oakland was ruled by a White political power structure that felt little need to address the needs of African Americans, Latinos, or the poor. In 1964, there were no political

buffers or brokers between the demands of the Black community and a re-
sistant White political elite.[37]

The unsuccessful 1973 political campaigns of Bobby Seale for mayor and
Elaine Brown for city council were a recognition that community power
also entailed power over public policy. Although neither Seale nor Brown
won, they galvanized an electorate that had been slumbering and forced a
run-off election in what was generally assumed to be an unassailable election. Their efforts opened the door for the successful 1977 mayoral campaign of Lionel Wilson, a politically moderate African American.[38]
Wilson's successful bid for office would be followed by a string of political
victories by African Americans and Latinos in Oakland and across the state.

Nationally, much has changed since that period. In 1996, there were more
than 8,500 Black elected officials in the United States, including mayors,
city council members, and more than forty members of Congress.[39] In the
last three decades, an African American—L. Douglas Wilder—has held the
governor's seat in Virginia, a Southern state no less.[40] Blacks are or have
been mayors in almost every major city, including Detroit, Chicago, New
York, Los Angeles, Cleveland, Philadelphia, Atlanta, and Seattle.

The Rev. Jesse Jackson's two insurgent runs for the Democratic Party
nomination in 1984 and 1988 were no less remarkable. He won 3.5 million
votes in 1984 and nearly 7 million in 1988.[41] Other Blacks, including activists and politicians Ron Daniels (1992), Lenora Fulani (1988 and 1992), and
Alan Keyes (1992 and 1996), have also launched presidential campaigns as
Republicans, third party candidates, and independents. In 1995, retired Gen.
Colin Powell, the first and only Black head of the Joint Chiefs of Staff, was
strongly sought after to run for the Republican Party presidential nomination for the 1996 elections, but he declined.

Political representation has also grown in terms of appointed positions. In
1992, President Clinton made history by appointing five African Americans
to his cabinet: Lee Brown, Director of the National Office of Drug Control;
Jesse Brown, Secretary of Veterans Affairs; Hazel O'Leary, Secretary of
Energy; Ron Brown, Secretary of Commerce; and Mike Espy, Secretary of
Agriculture. Clinton also chose Dr. Joycelyn Elders, an African American
physician, to serve as Surgeon General. These appointments along with dozens of others at the local and state level have made African Americans highly
visible in the nation's political system. It should be noted that all five of the
African Americans originally appointed to Cabinet positions by President
Clinton are no longer members of the Cabinet. Jesse Brown resigned, Ron
Brown was killed in a plane accident, Lee Brown resigned, and Mike Espy
and Hazel O'Leary left their posts under the cloud of controversy.

Perhaps most stunning has been the path traveled by Blacks inside the
Democratic Party. It was a long struggle, nearly impossible to see in the mid-
sixties, from the challenge of Fannie Lou Hamer and the Mississippi Freedom
Democratic Party and their effort to merely win a seat at the 1964 Demo-

cratic National Convention to the 1988 crowning of Ron Brown as Chairman of the Democratic National Committee. Without a doubt, institutional Black politics has come of age. Yet, the successful strategy of "putting Black faces in high places" has yielded few clear gains for the masses of African Americans. Neither the Black Panthers nor others who advocated a strategy of moving from what Bayard Rustin called "protest to politics" could have predicted the nearly magical co-opting effect of political office that transformed erstwhile radicals and rebels into functionaries and apologists.[42] Many Black elected officials find themselves merely treading water—struggling to keep their head above the policy waters, but unable to move forward. The rude discovery that being in office is not the same as being in power shocked many newly elected Black officials and the Black community. The structural and institutional constraints of a political system that forces the development of political blocks and compromise on policy have generally meant that African Americans moved from being relatively powerless minorities outside the system to relatively powerless minorities inside the system.

Even more disheartening, the awakening to the realization that the political gains of the past three decades have meant little in advancement for millions of African Americans takes place in the era of the Republican "Contract With America." The 1994 occupation of Congress by Republican conservatives, who are fighting hard to implement an anti-Black, anti-progressive, pro-corporate, and pro-moralist policy agenda, is potentially the greatest setback to Black progress since perhaps the end of the first Reconstruction. And yet, given the rightward thrust of the Democratic Party, it is not clear by any means that a Democratic return to power in Congress will necessarily result in a turnaround for the Black community.

The Panthers flirted with but never resolved the issue of Black involvement in and relationship to third-party politics. Since the 1930s, Black electoral engagement has taken place on the terrain of the Democratic Party. Despite the fact that Southern Democrats were the principal defenders of segregation in the region, even Blacks in the South have remained loyal to the Democrats. There was a logic to this behavior because of the role that the national Democratic Party played in promoting and supporting Civil Rights concerns.[43] However, it took the gut-busting efforts of Fannie Lou Hamer, Jesse Jackson, and countless others to force the party to integrate Blacks more fully into its hierarchies.[44] Meanwhile, the Republican Party pursues what has been called the "Southern strategy" of pursuing White voters by exploiting racial fears coded in issues like busing, affirmative action, welfare, and crime.[45] In recent years, following numerous losses in the presidential races in the 1970s and 1980s, the Democratic Party, led by the Democratic Leadership Council (DLC), adopted a strategy of its own to court White middle-class voters. Under the leadership of Bill Clinton, a former chair of the DLC, the Democratic Party has dramatically shifted to the right with only token nods to the liberal wing of the party.

While the Black need for a third-party option has reached a new urgency in the 1990s, there are three reasons that little significant effort in that direction has occurred. First, despite posturing and public declarations of dissatisfaction with the Clinton administration, traditional Black leaders remain committed to the Democratic Party. In the late 1980s, Jesse Jackson's National Rainbow Coalition (NRC) was perhaps the best hope for a progressive break from the Democratic Party, but Jackson never seriously sought to sever his relationship to the party. Thus, the NRC went from being a potential mass third-party effort to being an impotent arm of Jackson's various operations.[46] The NRC and Operation PUSH have been merged into a single organization, Rainbow/PUSH Coalition, headed by Jackson. The Achilles heel of contemporary Black politics continues to be the clientage relationship that nearly all national Black organizations have to the Democratic Party, which leaves little incentive for a leadership call for a mass break by the Black community from the major parties.

Second, efforts by some Black activists to run outside of the two-party system have been weak at best.[47] These candidates, despite progressive programs, have had little grassroots or elite support, scarce financial resources, and no chance of penetrating the media monopolies. They received faint support by the Black community and almost none from Whites.

Third, most independent and third-party attempts have been distinctly White. In the independent campaign of H. Ross Perot, for example, few people of color were present nor were issues critical to their communities raised.[48] Recent progressive efforts, such as the New Party, the Labor Party, and others, also had few visible African Americans in their leadership. The New Party, to its credit, has run a number of African Americans under its banner. Challenges by some Black activists to the Whiteness of the independent and third-party movements, most notably by long-time progressive Ron Daniels, has led to some remolding and an effort by these groups to become more inclusive.

Despite the problems of Black involvement in third parties, this is an option that must be explored by African Americans.[49] The two major parties have abandoned any pretense of advocating or implementing redistributive policies or social programs to address the discrimination and inequality that African Americans still face. As long as the Black vote– indeed, Black political participation– is principally centered in the Democratic Party, the Black community can expect little relief. The inability of traditional Black leadership to break the bond with the Democratic Party means that new leadership that can articulate a new agenda and political program for the Black community must emerge.

Who Shall Lead Them?

Leadership issues are more critical than ever in the Black community as more and more people feel a political vacuum in the face of conservative attacks. For African Americans, a number of important leadership questions have yet to be answered: What kind of leadership is needed by the Black community at the dawn of the twenty-first century? What should be the relationship between national and local Black leaders and organizations? How are issues of gender equity to be resolved? What ideological direction should the Black community pursue?

In the 1960s, the Black Panthers, SNCC, and a host of new organizations had to snatch leadership from those who held it. While it is true that these groups made history, it is also true that history made them. The times generated new leaders to address the realities of that period, but that new leadership emerged imperfect and incomplete.[50] As these organizations sought to meet the swirl of demands that arose, they also sought to define their long-term mission and purpose. Along these lines, the Black Panthers developed their ten-point program for Black liberation that reflected the political context of the 1960s. Parroted to a great degree from the scroll advocated by the Nation of Islam, the ten-point Panther program achieved rhetorical significance even as it failed to address a number of critical political and strategic concerns.[51]

Black leadership for the twenty-first century will have more demanded of it than at any other time in history. It must carry the best traditions of past leadership — the ability to effectively articulate Black concerns; steadfastness in the face of co-optation, challenge, and adversity; determination to advance a Black political agenda; willingness to put collective interests over individual interests; and so on. At the same time, it must address the new world that has evolved. The new technologies, globalized economies, multipolar politics, conservative hegemony, new racial paradigms, and issues of gender equity and equality will qualitatively shape the thinking and practice of future Black leadership.[52] There is little historical experience to rely on for the period ahead, and how Black leadership prepares itself to survive, thrive, and prosper in the next period cannot be scripted. Yet, preparation is a must as Black America enters a new century under conditions in some ways not dissimilar from that of the last turn of the century: conservatives controlling all or most of government, the propagation of racist genetic theories, the rise of White nationalist movements, and efforts at Black political disenfranchisement.

This situation explains, to some degree, why in the mid-1990s Black leadership is in a state of flux. The most visible challenge to traditional Black leadership has been the movement and leadership to emerge around the October 16, 1995 Million Man March (MMM) event.[53] It would be a gross exaggeration to state that the traditional Black leaders were displaced as a result of the MMM. No Black elected officials were unelected that day. No

Civil Rights leaders resigned their posts. No Black appointees quit their offices. It is undeniable, however, that a transition of sorts is occurring in which both Black nationalism and conservatism appear to be growing among African Americans.[54]

As noted above, the Republicans' anti-Black "Contract With America" set the political context for fairly dramatic changes in Black political activism. Interpreted by many as a sign of the failed politics of liberal Black leadership, Black nationalist rhetoric and behavior have grown substantially. Increasing racial polarization, most egregiously displayed around the O. J. Simpson verdict, moved even pro-integrationist Black leaders to give a nod to the impulse of Black nationalism.[55]

One unexpected development was the mega-hype surrounding the potential entry of retired General Colin Powell into the 1996 presidential race.[56] The Powell-for-President effort provided a convenient alternative for many conservatives and moderates to the rhetorical fires of Minister Louis Farrakhan and Rev. Jesse Jackson. The conservative celebration of Powell's post-Black persona served to justify a politics of retreat from racial equality and government intervention. For his part, Powell teased the political establishment, the post-O. J. Simpson media cartels, and some in the Black community down to the last second before he declared that he was not a candidate (and that he was a Republican). It is uncertain to what extent a Powell candidacy would have realigned Black voters away from the Democratic Party because his commitment to a Republican Party agenda would most likely have seriously diminished his standing in the Black community. His potential candidacy vastly overshadowed the potential candidacy of Jesse Jackson who spent several years telling anyone who would listen that he too would possibly run as a candidate if he felt that Clinton had not and would not address the issues important to his constituents.

The effort to get Powell on the ballot was not a Black community imperative. Both Powell and the Black community were clear on this point. What was unclear was why Black leaders refused to expose Powell's alliances with some of the worst enemies of the Black community. Instead, Powell won awards and kudos from a large number of Black organizations and was appointed to the Board of Trustees of Howard University. The reluctance to criticize the popular Powell appears to be rooted not only in political pragmatism, but also reflects a major concession to narrow nationalism and the inability of contemporary liberal Black leadership to pose a credible and viable alternative.

In the 1990s, Black nationalist politics, for the first time in at least a generation, has been able to assert leadership and reach a significant sector of the Black community on a number of issues. The two most notable efforts are the campaign to save journalist and former Black Panther activist Mumia Abu Jamal from execution and of course, the MMM. In the case of Jamal, a global mobilization was galvanized and helped to highlight the continuing issue of police harassment and judicial racism that are still highly charged issues for the Black community.[57] The resulting publicity forced liberal Black leadership to ultimately speak out on a case that they otherwise would have left dormant.

Without a doubt, however, the zenith of Black nationalist politics in this period was the MMM. The March was in the tradition of mobilization advocated by the Black Panther Party. Politically, it signaled a resurgence of nationalist leadership and the mobilization capabilities of charismatic leaders such as Louis Farrakhan. Whether this situation is transitory remains to be seen, but the event placed Farrakhan, the former Reverend and now Minister Ben Chavis Muhammad, and a number of other previously ostracized activists in a more central role in the debate over the direction and ideology of Black politics. It also highlighted the issue and debate over gender equality in the Black community. The gender politics of nationalism, which relegates Black women and Black women's issues to the sidelines, at best, consistently asserted itself whether in its crude misogynist form or in the manner of what writer bell hooks calls "benevolent patriarchy."[58]

Can the leadership and movement around the MMM serve the Black community's needs in the period ahead? Overall, the MMM movement lacks strategic direction, political purpose, and a progressive agenda. Its brother organization, the National African American Leadership Summit, which is under the controversial and increasingly embattled leadership of Chavis, is also desperately searching for its political footing. In the aftermath of the event, many have become frustrated with the inability of the MMM's leaders to move forward on their claim that they can resolve the problems confronting the Black community in a more dynamic fashion than the current leadership. Despite confusion and problems occurring at the national center, a number of local activists around the country have reportedly used the MMM as a springboard for renewed community organizing. Large mass meetings have been held in cities such as Chicago, Philadelphia, and elsewhere, and a number of organizations, including the NAACP and the National Urban League, have reported upsurges in membership requests since the march. Organizers declare that a new sense of hope and struggle has occurred.

Yet, whatever the MMM may have achieved at the spiritual level, it has had virtually no effect on the legislative and political assaults against the Black community that are taking place in the halls of Congress, in state houses, and in municipal offices. Budget cuts—real and coming—in programs that benefit the Black community are the name of the game. Attacks on welfare recipients, driven by the continued demonization of Black women, go on with the collaboration of both major parties. The politics of *states' rights*, historically a phrase that connoted the scheming machinations of White supremacy, has edged its way back into political discourse as a legitimate, if not preferred option, for public-policy expression. None of these concerns has been addressed by the MMM leaders in any sustained or politically useful manner.

The movement's lack of—even disdain for—a political agenda, its patriarchal and anti-gay tone and tenor, its blame-the-victim chiding, and its social and moral conservatism are a genuine reflection of the crisis state of national Black leadership overall. The projection of a Black male supremacist politics is a throwback and has engendered a number of organized responses including the inspiration for at least one new organization, African American Agenda 2000, which was mainly organized by Black women poised to fight for a progressive, inclusive agenda.

It actually is not surprising that Black nationalist leadership would assert itself in this period. Black nationalist politics, the Rainbow Coalition notwithstanding, have never disappeared as a political resource in the Black community and at various historic points, has dominated Black politics.[59] The politics of Black nationalism are driven by several factors in this era: the sanctioning and validation of institutional racism by conservative policy makers, manifest racism in every arena of popular culture, the devastating impact of globalized economies on White workers and their response, and just low-down, unashamed personal racism. While these factors affect all ideological trends in the Black community, spontaneous identity politics in the absence of genuine coalition politics is more easily asserted and offered as a simple explanation to complex social relations. Thus the Million Man March phenomenon (and other smaller but similarly tense racial manifestations) is not only to be expected, but may be a necessary catharsis for a people under siege.

Much of the left and progressive movement is quick to dismiss the 1994 elections as merely the result of a small ideologically driven and organized conservative electorate that does not "truly" represent the views of most Americans. However, for many in the Black community, it is seen as a recognition that White America, at least voting White America, has not only rejected equality as a goal of public policy, but in fact, has come to embrace punishment of the poor as politically expedient and necessary.[60]

Liberal Black leaders—Black elected officials and civil rights leaders—have not satisfactorily addressed the issues facing large numbers of poor and working-class Blacks. Nor have these leaders been able to put the brakes on the assault on the civil rights gains that many middle-class Blacks depend on for their stability and future. Many of these leaders, with the best resources they can muster and with a genuine commitment to progressive politics, acknowledge that they simply can do nothing more. At every level, the political crisis has grown.

In Congress, under Republican rule, Black politics has been reduced to floor speeches and press releases. The dethroning of the Congressional Black Caucus (CBC) has had a significant impact in terms of the substantive and symbolic resistance that many had come to use as a mobilizing and organizing resource in public policy battles. In 1995, although it was able to keep Clinton's feet to the fire around affirmative action, the CBC was unable to save the nomination of Dr. Henry Foster for Surgeon General or halt the legislative blitzkrieg of the Republicans in Congress.[61] The embarrassing resignations and convictions of Reps. Mel Reynolds (D–IL) and Walter Tucker (D–CA) on charges of child molestation and bribery, respectively, were low points for the CBC.[62] Two Black members ran for governor of Louisiana—Reps. William Jefferson (D–LA) and Cleo Fields (D–LA)—and both were soundly defeated. There were also defeats in the Supreme Court on several redistricting cases, thus forcing Rep. Fields, Rep. Cynthia McKinney (D–GA), and other Black representatives to at least contemplate dusting off their resumes. The CBC also lost a couple of its veteran members. Rep. Cardiss Collins (D–IL), a House member for over two decades, retired; and Rep. Kweisi Mfume (D–MD) shocked many Black political observers when he announced that he was leaving Congress to begin his job as the new president and CEO of the NAACP. All in all, 1995 was a year the CBC would rather forget.

They are not alone. A coup d'état was pulled off by Newt Gingrich (R–GA) in Washington, DC, and the city is now being run by the appropriately-named Financial Control Board. Mayor Marion Barry's rhetoric of resistance did not go far, and in any case, for many it appears insincere. Yet, ironically, his voice remains one of the few arising from Black municipal leaders challenging the direction of public policy oozing out of Washington. In other cities, such as Seattle, Detroit, or Atlanta, to name a few, more accommodating Black mayors have come into office and offer little opposition to Gingrich or for that matter, President Clinton. In fact, Black elected officials have suffered not only their own cutbacks and attacks from Washington, but have also had the thankless job of trying to explain and defend the Clinton administration.

On the Civil Rights front, the stunning decision by Mfume to resign from Congress to take over the leadership of the NAACP raised and furrowed plenty of eyebrows. The highly respected former head of the CBC has a herculean task on his hands to bring the NAACP back to financial stability and political relevance. Few even knew that Mfume was a candidate for the position (previously called Executive Director) that had been open since the ignoble firing of former Executive Director Benjamin Chavis in August 1994.[63] Up until the last minute, many felt that the NAACP search committee would cautiously select someone from inside the organization.

It is easy to see why the NAACP would select Mfume. The well-respected Congressman brought stature, street smarts, and rich political experience to the job. At the time, he was only 47 years old, which makes him relatively young by NAACP standards, and he apparently still has the energy to wrestle with the work ahead that everyone associated with the NAACP acknowledges will be difficult at best. Mfume obtained a promise from board chair

Myrlie Evers-Williams that an effort would be made to restructure the board, making it smaller and more manageable. In addition, the title of the former executive director position was changed to reflect the new duties and vision that Evers-Williams and others have for whoever will lead the NAACP into the next century. Mfume's strengths include his experience and knowledge of the public policy process, particularly as it relates to Capitol Hill. His goal of transforming the NAACP into a progressive version of the Christian Coalition is informed, of course, by his nine years in Congress. How Mfume will handle other political questions is another matter.[64]

The relationship of the NAACP to various Black nationalist leaders, Louis Farrakhan to name the most obvious, may be tricky. Mfume faced criticism a couple of years ago with his CBC colleagues when, as chair of the CBC, he announced a "covenant" between the CBC and the Nation of Islam (NOI). Criticized by other Black members, denounced by some Jewish leaders, and attacked in the press, Mfume "moon walked" and created some space between himself and the Nation of Islam.[65] However, Mfume was perhaps the most visible Black Congressman involved with the NOI-initiated Million Man March. He spoke at the event and committed himself to participate in post-Million Man March activities. While the NAACP did not endorse the MMM, many of its leaders and members enthusiastically participated.[66] If the NAACP is to become even a shadow of its historic self, it must not only negotiate its relationship to Black nationalism, but also address the issue of how independent it will be from the Democratic and Republican Parties. Mfume's swearing-in was held at the Department of Justice and was attended by President Bill Clinton and other Democratic Party officials. This hardly signaled an independent stance.

And then there is Jesse Jackson. In November 1995, Jackson held a press conference and announced that he was returning to Chicago to resume his former position as head of Operation PUSH, the organization he abandoned to launch his National Rainbow Coalition (NRC).[67] Neither Jackson nor the NRC made great strides in Washington, DC. Although he was elected the "shadow" Senator of the city in 1990, the position carries no authority, is not funded, and remains an obscure political post to most people in DC. As the city deteriorated under the iron rule of the Control Board and token leadership of DC Mayor Barry, Jackson played virtually no role in the city's struggle against Congress.

The move to Chicago seems to be calculated along several lines. First, Jackson certainly wants to capitalize on the political base that his son, Rep. Jesse Jackson, Jr. (D–IL), acquired when he won the congressional seat vacated by Reynolds. Second, living in Chicago made Jackson a more visible force at the 1996 Democratic National Convention held in Chicago. It was much more difficult for Clinton and his anti-Jackson advisors, of whom there are plenty, to deny Jackson political space on his own turf. Third, it is also no accident that Chicago also happens to be the home base of Minister Louis Farrakhan of the Nation of Islam.

All of these changes at the national level obscure the grassroots leadership that has developed in recent years in the Black community. From struggles around economic empowerment to fighting police abuse, countless activists have taken on leadership roles to build and rebuild Black civil society. At the core of this emerging leadership is a progressive vision for the future that is willing to confront corporate power, government neglect, and even Black elected and appointed officials.

Black women are the spark and soul of this new leadership for the present and the future. Although Black women historically have been at the core of organizing and mobilizing in the Black community, they have been denied the strategic and visionary role they deserved.[68] The public face of Black politics has too often been male, even when it was clear and well-known that women were carrying the load. Women will have a unique leadership role around issues of concern to women (and children), in particular, but also around broader topics in the Black community and society. In every field, whether political, economic, cultural, or social, Black women's contributions will be indispensable.

New leadership will also be more multigenerational. Black youth and Black seniors have too often been relegated to token status and have not been allowed to participate equally and effectively in the struggles of the Black community. The wisdom of age and the energy of youth must be blended into a leadership structure that is inclusive in ways that have not existed in the past, but are required for the future.

Talking About Revolution—Still

In the 1960s, the Black Panthers and other radicals, Black and White, called for revolution. The view that the United States as constituted was hopelessly committed to a racist and capitalist social order that exploited workers and people of color both within and without was popular and widespread. Depending on who was talking, revolution meant "socialist revolution," "Black revolution," "Pan-African revolution," and many other things. The success of national liberation movements in Asia, Latin America, and Africa inspired the revolutionary movement in the United States.[69] However, those successes were not duplicated at home. Although significant reforms were won from the state, most would agree that the revolution was more or less crushed and that defeat and retreat were the state of affairs by the mid-1970s.

As the end of the century approaches, what does "revolution" mean? The dismantling of the Soviet Union, the fall of the Eastern European socialist states, the accommodationist politics of China, and the sobering of Third World liberation movements have dramatically transformed the notion of revolution and leftist politics on a global scale and in the United States. The debate over reform or revolution remains, but with critical and challenging questions that contemporary radicals must face: Can the United States be reformed in a way that is meaningful and useful to the Black community and other dispossessed groups? If not, in what form would a new political system appear, and how will it be brought about?

A new vision of revolution must begin with the firm belief that millions of lives and destinies are being destroyed and wasted by the current arrangements of economic and state power.[70] The hegemonic power of transnational corporations and their representatives in the state apparatus must be opposed with the utmost sense of urgency. One of the most important contributions of the BPP to Black politics was the Party's position that it was not just Whites who oppressed Blacks, but that the overthrow of a system of corporate and political power had to be the objective of Black resistance. At the most fundamental level, this means constructing a local-to-global movement for radical and participatory democracy. It has to be a core assumption of a new revolutionary movement that corporate authority is not sacrosanct and that public policy must be driven by the imperatives of greater democracy, not greater profit. Winning people to a progressive and meaningful vision of social transformation and the belief that struggling for such a vision is necessary will be the most important goal of activists in the period ahead.

Most critical will be the development of new models and institutions of democracy. In the twentieth century, neither the right nor the left adequately resolved the issue of political participation, either internal to those movements, nor external in the broader society. Both leftist and right-wing party and organizational structures, including the militarized, top-down form of the BPP, have been profoundly undemocratic in their nature and praxis. New notions and conceptions of democracy and citizen participation must be forged and implemented to shatter the cynicism that remains so widespread. The search for identity and meaning that has gripped millions opens possibilities that are gloriously hopeful and profoundly frightening. It is doubtful that with the complex pressures of post-industrial society many people will be inspired to join in the daily grind of running society, but millions can be won to see the value of democratic ventures when citizens believe that their concerns can be heard and addressed. On the other hand, to create a democratic order is not necessarily human destiny, and fascism in this age would take on the most depraved and disillusioned features, which only science fiction has hinted about.

There are theoretical as well as organizational tasks that must be accomplished. Stubborn challenges abound in addressing and explaining radically new racial paradigms, the creation of new democratic institutions, and the nature of class and gender dynamics in the Black community in the era of globalization. The radical theoretical frameworks of the past, from Marxism to feminism to post-modernism, cannot be dogmatically adopted nor wholeheartedly dismissed. Constructing a new paradigm will involve blending, mending, and the synthesizing of numerous approaches that can provide direction and analytical power.

To initiate a new era of progressive activism will require a broad solidarity and unity that embraces and transcends the Black community. As did the Panthers in their heyday, mass mobilization and organization of America's dispossessed must occur. While much of this will be self-generated, veteran activists and analysts must play a critical role in bringing a reflective experience to the struggle. The institutionalization of Black politics led to delegitimization of disruptive mass mobilization as a central tactic in the movement, thereby reducing contemporary civil rights marches to the politics of symbolism manifest in anniversaries of anniversaries, *ad nauseam*. These events have mainly served to keep the Civil Rights movement, bereft of ideas and thrust, on life support. Mobilization in the days and years ahead must be disruptive and have the single objective of stopping the system from functioning as usual. It should be clear that this means a great deal of personal risk—physical and financial. The movement must, therefore, imbue a spirit of resistance and commitment that can weather the storms that are coming. Belief and hope will be necessary resources for future activists.

It is important to distinguish adventurism from mass mobilization. Many have summed up the Panther experience as one die-hard urban guerrilla war against the state, and it must be stated honestly that some Panthers, including many Panther leaders, engaged in and encouraged adventurism. This is a strategy that is doomed to failure. It is a strategy that has little to do with the transformation of society and everything to do with a lack of faith in the capacities of masses of people to redirect their lives and the society they live in.

The South African experience provides some insight into our needs. One of the great lessons to grasp is the role of the civil society, or what some refer to as the third sector. As technology reduces the number of people necessary to work in private industry or government—also reducing the work week—building the civil society will not only be necessary but possible. The responsibility of public policy and the private sector will be to guarantee that a livable wage and appropriate benefits are available for those who dedicate their lives to service to the community and society. The effort to build the civil society still continues in this period. This is not a conservative call for volunteers to take on the tasks that they are ill-equipped to do while allowing the government to relinquish responsibility for resolving conditions that it had a role in creating and helps to perpetuate. In the final analysis, the goal of any revolution should be to make people's lives better, healthier, more livable. If the legacy of the Black Panthers—themselves a product of the resistance of oppressed people throughout time— is to have meaning, then the next generation of activists must take up the challenge and charge into history with all the audacity and courage that they can muster.

NOTES

1. Robert J. S. Ross, "The Relative Decline of Relative Autonomy: Global Capitalism and the Political Economy of State Change," in *Changes in the State: Causes and Consequences*, ed. Edward S. Greenberg and Thomas F. Mayer (Newbury,Calif.: Sage Publications, 1990), 208–9.

2. Ibid., 311.

3. Richard J. Barnet and John Cavanaugh, *Global Dreams: Imperial Corporations and the New World Order* (New York: Simon and Schuster, 1994), 313.

4. Ibid.

5. Donald L. Barlett and James B. Steele, *America: What Went Wrong* (Kansas City: Andrews and McMeel, 1992), xi.

6. Ibid., 268.

7. Ibid., 293.

8. Ibid., 340.

9. United Nations Development Program, *Human Development Report 1992* (New York: United Nations, 1992), 6. Many will not be satisfied to stay home and suffer, but will instead take to the road where some will end up in the United States. On a global scale, about 75 million people emigrate from poor countries to the more developed nations each year. It should be noted that the belief that immigrants to the United States are an economic drain on the nation is erroneous. While immigrants receive $5 billion in welfare, they pay $90 billion in taxes. This fact is critical given the increasingly severe anti-immigrant fever of the 1990s, which appears most notably in the form of the Proposition 187—known popularly as "Save Our State (SOS)" proposal—in California. Passed on the November 1994 ballot, Proposition 187 denies public education, health services, and other opportunities to children of illegal immigrants. See John Roemer and Marta Sanchez-Beswick, "Can SOS Be Stopped?" *San Francisco Weekly*, 24 August 1994, 13–15.

10. Barnet and Cavanaugh, *Global Dreams*, 291.

11. Barry Bluestone, "Deindustrialization and Unemployment in America," *Review of Black Political Economy* 13 (Fall 1983): 34.

12. Cited in Jeanne Prial Fordus and Sean McAliden, *Economic Change, Physical Illness and Social Deviance*, report prepared for the Subcommittee on Economic Goals and Intergovernmental Policy of the Joint Economic Committee, 14 July 1984.

13. Barlett and Steele, *America: What Went Wrong*, 1.

14. Jeremy Rifkin, *The End of Work: The Decline of the Global Labor Force and the Dawn of the Post-Market Era* (New York: G.P. Putnam's Sons, 1995), 71.

15. Bureau of Census, "Census Bureau Announces Number of Americans in Poverty Up for Fourth Year Although Poverty Rate Unchanged; Household Income and Health Care Coverage Drop," press release, 6 October 1994.

16. Associated Press, "Urban League Asks Support for Self-help," *The Washington Post*, 21 January 1994, A3.

17. Bureau of Census, "Census Bureau Announces Number of Americans in Poverty Up for Fourth Year Although Poverty Rate Unchanged; Household Income and Health Care Coverage Drop," press release, 6 October 1994."

18. Aaron Bernstein, "The Global Economy: Who Gets Hurt?" *Business Week*, 16 May 1993, 124.

19. Frank McCoy, "No Real Recovery for Black Jobs or Income," *Black Enterprise*, June 1994, 188.

20. Frank McCoy, "Can Clinton's Urban Policies Really Work?" *Black Enterprise*, June 1994, 182.

21. Hilbourne Watson, "The Pain of NAFTA—or the Pain of Globalization," *Third World Viewpoint*(Spring 1994):19.

22. Alfred Edmond, "Coming on Strong," *Black Enterprise*, June 1994, 78.

23. Barnet and Cavanaugh, *Global Dreams*, 302.

24. Rochelle Sharpe, "In Latest Recession, Only Blacks Suffered Net Employment Loss," *The Wall Street Journal*, 14 September 1993, A1.

25. For a more detailed analysis of the impact of the drug crisis on the Black community, see Clarence Lusane, *Pipe Dream Blues: Racism and the War on Drugs* (Boston: South End Press, 1991).

26. Barbara Vobejda, "Children's Defense Fund Cites Gun Violence," *The Washington Post*, 21 January 1994, A3.

27. Mack H. Jones, "The Black Underclass As Systemic Phenomenon," In *Race, Politics, and Economic Development: Community Perspectives*, ed. James Jennings (New York: Verso, 1992), 53.

28. Keith Jennings, "Understanding the Persisting Crisis of Black Youth Unemployment," In *Race, Politics, and Economic Development: Community Perspectives*, ed. James Jennings (New York: Verso, 1992), 154.

29. Ibid.

30. Ibid.

31. Congressional Black Caucus, *The Quality of Life Alternative Budget* (Washington, D.C.: Congressional Black Caucus, 1990), 57.

32. National Urban League, *The State of Black America 1993* (New York: National Urban League, 1994), 183.

33. National Urban League, *The State of Black America 1986* (New York: National Urban League, 1987), 214.

34. Steven Pearlstein and DeNeed L. Brown, "Black Teens Facing Worse Job Prospects," *The Washington Post*, 4 June 1994, A1 and A6.

35. Linda Williams, "Black Political Progress in the 1980s: The Electoral Arena," In Michael Preston, Lenneal Henderson, and Paul Puryear, *The New Black Politics: The Search for Political Power* (New York: Longman, 1987), 111.

36. Ibid.

37. See Tomas Almaguer, *Racial Fault Lines: The Historical Origins of White Supremacy in California* (Berkeley: University of California Press, 1994).

38. See Rod Bush, *The New Black Vote: Politics and Power in Four American Cities* (San Francisco: Synthesis, 1984), 317–371.

39. See David Bositis, *The Congressional Black Caucus in the 103rd Congress* (Washington, DC: Joint Center for Political and Economic Studies, 1994).

40. See Charles E. Jones and Michael L. Clemons, "A Model of Racial Crossover Voting: An Assessment of the Wilder Victory," In *Dilemmas of Black Politics:*

Issues of Leadership and Strategy, ed. Georgia Pearsons (New York: Harper Collins, 1993).

41. Frank Clemente, ed., *Keep Hope Alive: Jesse Jackson's 1988 Presidential Campaign* (Boston: South End Press, 1989), 233–234.

42. Bayard Rustin, "From Protest to Politics: The Future of the Civil Rights Movement," *Commentary*, 39(1965): 25–31. Also see Robert C. Smith, *We Have No Leaders: African Americans in the Post-Civil Rights Era* (Albany, NY: State University of New York Press, 1996).

43. Taylor Branch, *Parting the Waters: America in the King Years,1954–63* (New York: Simon and Schuster, 1988).

44. See Lorenzo Morris, ed., *The Social and Political Implications of the 1984 Jesse Jackson Presidential Campaign* (New York: Praeger, 1990).

45. Kevin Phillips, *The Emerging Republican Majority* (Garden City, NY: Anchor Books, 1970) and Thomas Byrne Edsall and Mary Edsall, *Chain Reaction: The Impact of Race, Rights and Taxes in American Politics* (New York: Norton, 1992).

46. See Adolph Reed, Jr., *The Jesse Jackson Phenomenon: the Crisis of Purpose in Afro-American Politics* (New Haven: Yale University Press, 1986) and Sheila Collins, *The Rainbow Challenge: The Jackson Campaign and the Future of U.S. Politics* (New York: Monthly Review Press, 1986).

47. See Clarence Lusane, *African Americans at the Crossroads: The Restructuring of Black Leadership in the 1992 Elections* (Boston: South End Press, 1994.)

48. Ibid.

49. See Hanes Walton, *The Negro in Third Party Politics* (Philadelphia: Dorrance, 1969).

50. William L. Van Deberg, *New Day in Babylon: The Black Power Movement and American Culture, 1965–75* (Chicago: University of Chicago Press, 1992).

51. The Black Panthers entitled their program "What We Want, What We Believe." The Nation of Islam under the leadership of Elijah Muhammad titled its program "What the Muslims Want, What the Muslims Believe," which appeared in each issue of their newspaper *Muhammed Speaks.* See Ruth-Marion Baruch and Pirkle Jones, *The Vanguard: A Photographic Essay on the Black Panthers* (Boston: Beacon Press, 1970).

52. See Charles Green, ed., *Globalization and Survival in the Black Diaspora* (Albany, NY: State University of New York Press, 1997) and Clarence Lusane, *Race in the Global Era: African Americans at the Millennium* (Boston: South End Press, 1997).

53. See *The Black Scholar*, Fall 1995, for a range of articles on the Million Man March. Also Haki Madhubuti and Maulana Karenga, *Million Man March/Day of Atonement: A Commemorative Anthology: Speeches, Commentary, Photography, Poetry, Illustrations, Documents* (Chicago: Third World Press, 1995).

54. Michael C. Dawson, *Behind the Mule: Race and Class in African-American Politics* (Princeton, NJ: Princeton University Press, 1994), 182.

55. See Toni Marshall and Claudia Brodsky Lacour, eds., *Birth of a Nation'hood: Gaze, Script, and Spectacle in the O.J. Simpson Case* (New York: Pantheon Books, 1997).

56. See Colin Powell, *My American Journey* (New York: Random House, 1995).

57. See Mumia Abu-Jamal, *Live From Death Row* (Reading, MA: Addison-Wesley Publishers, 1995).

58. bell hooks interview by the author on WPFW-FM, Washington, DC, October 16, 1995; see also Nikol G. Alexander, "A World Without Feminism?: Reading Gender In(to) Nationalist Politics" and "Selling Black: Black Public Intellectuals and the Commercialization of Black and Black Feminist Studies (Or Race, Class, and Gender Go to Market)." Both papers are on file with author.

59. Alphonse Pinkney, *Red, Black, and Green: Black Nationalism in the United States* (New York: Cambridge University Press, 1976).

60. See Ronald Walters, *Black Presidential Politics in America: A Strategic Approach* (Albany: State University of New York Press, 1988), 193.

61. Kevin Merida, "Foster Nomination Fails as Vote Blocked Again, Surgeon General Hopeful's Bid Effectively Dead," *The Washington Post*, 23 June 1995, A1 and A9.

62. Kathryn Wexler and William Clairborne, "Rep. Tucker Convicted of Extortion; Congressman Took Bribes While Mayor of Compton, Calif.," *The Washington Post*, 9 December 1995, A1 and A8; and Edward Walsh, "Reynolds Sentenced to 5 Years for Sex Offenses, Obstruction; Illinois Congressman Misused a 'Job for Life,' Judge Says," *The Washington Post*, 29 September 1995, A2.

63. Edward Walsh, "Chavis Fired by NAACP," *The Washington Post*, 21 August 1994, A4; and Edward Walsh, "Chavis Accused of Hiding Payment," *The Washington Post*, 27 August 1994, A3.

64. Susan Baer, "Building Coalitions, Realizing Ambitions, Kweisi Mfume Comes Into His Own," *The Baltimore Sun*, 11 August 1993, 1.

65. Editorial, "The Black Caucus Gets Mugged," *The New York Times*, 25 September 1993, 22; and William Raspberry, "One that Fell Out of the Sky," *The Washington Post*, 20 September 1993, A19.

66. David J. Dent, "Million Man March: Whose Reality?" *Black Renaissance*, vol. 1(fall 1996): 58–69.

67. See Kevin Merida, "Jackson to Return to Helm of Chicago-Based Operation PUSH," *The Washington Post*, 2 December 1995, A11.

68. See Angela Davis, *Women, Culture, and Politics* (New York: Vintage Books, 1990) and Beverly Guy Sheftall, ed., *Words of Fire: An Anthology of African-American Feminist Thought* (New York: The New Press, 1995).

69. The Black Panthers and others were influenced by the writings of Ho Chi Minh (Vietnam), Frantz Fanon (Martinique), Ché Guevera (Cuba and Latin America), Amilcar Cabral (Guinea Bissau and Cape Verde), and Mao Tse-Tung (China).

70. See William Greider, *One World Ready or Not: The Manic Logic of Global Capitalism* (New York: Simon & Schuster, 1997); David C. Korten, *When Corporations Rule the World* (West Hartford, CT: Berrett-Koehler Publishers and San Francisco: Kumarian Press, 1995); Benjamin R. Barber, *Jihad vs. McWorld: How the Planet is Both Falling Apart and Coming Together and What This Means for Democracy* (New York: Times Books, 1995); and Jerry Mander and Edward Goldsmith, eds., *The Case Against the Global Economy and For a Turn Toward the Local* (San Francisco: Sierra Club Books, 1996).

CONTRIBUTORS

Charles E. Jones is the founding Chair and Associate Professor of the Department of African-American Studies at Georgia State University. He earned a Ph.D. in Political Science in 1985 at Washington State University. He received a M.A. degree from the University of Idaho and a B.A. degree from Fayetteville State University in 1976. He previously taught at Old Dominion University (1983–1994) where he served as the Director of the Institute for the Study of Minority Issues and Associate Professor of Political Science. His past research projects have focused on African Americans in the legislative process and Black electoral success in majority-White districts. He has published articles in *The Journal of Black Studies, Legislative Studies Quarterly, Southeastern Political Review, Phylon, The Western Journal of Black Studies,* and *National Political Science Review.* Currently, Professor Jones is completing a co-edited volume with Robert A. Holmes entitled *Black State Legislative Behavior: A Comparative Analysis* and a co-authored book with Judson L. Jeffries entitled *Vanguard of the People: An Analytic History of the Black Panther Party, 1966–1982.*

JoNina M. Abron is an Associate Professor of English at Western Michigan University where she teaches journalism. A former managing editor of *Black Scholar* magazine, she currently serves on its board of advisors. A member of the Black Panther Party for nine years, Dr. Abron served as the last editor of the Party's newspaper, *The Black Panther Intercommunal News Service.* Her recent publications include "Comrade Sisters: Two Women of the Black Panther Party," co-authored with Madalynn C. Rucker, in *Unrelated Kin, Race and Gender in Women's Personal Narratives* (1996), and "Raising the Consciousness of the People: The Black Panther Intercommunal News Service, 1967–1980," in *Voices from the Underground, Insider Histories of the Vietnam Era Underground Press* (1993). Currently, Dr. Abron is completing a manuscript on political activists of the Black Power Era.

Christopher B. Booker has a Master of Arts in Sociology from the University of Michigan. He earned a B.A. in Sociology from Wayne State University in 1974. Booker is the author of two forthcoming books entitled *Broken Promises, Dashed Hopes: The History of Blacks and the Presidency in America* (Franklin Watts Publishing) and *A Social History of the African American Male, 1619–1997* (Greenwood Press). He has also authored several book chapters and scholarly articles.

Kathleen Neal Cleaver is an Assistant Professor of Law currently visiting at Cardozo School of Law in New York City. In 1966 she dropped out of Barnard College to work full time with the Student Nonviolent Coordinating Committee. In 1967 she moved to the San Francisco Bay Area where she became the Black Panther Party's Communications Secretary. She received a B.A. in History from Yale University in 1984. In 1989 she received a J.D. from Yale Law School. She taught at Emory University School of Law from 1992 to 1994. She was awarded fellowships at the Bunting Institute of Radcliffe College, the W.E.B DuBois Institute of Harvard University, and the Schomburg Center for Research in Black Culture of the New York Public Library to complete the memoir *Memories of Love and War.* Her articles have been published in numerous magazines and newspapers including *Ramparts, The Village Voice, The Boston Globe,* and *Transition.* She has contributed scholarly essays to *Critical Race Feminism, Critical White Studies, and The Promise of Multiculturalism* (in press 1998).

Christian A. Davenport is currently an Associate Professor in Political Science at the University of Colorado at Boulder. He received his B.A. degree in Political

Science in 1987 from Clark University and earned a Ph.D. in Political Science in 1991 from the State University of New York at Binghamton. His research interests include comparative politics, political repression, and conflict. Davenport's scholarly publications have appeared in the *American Journal of Political Science, The Journal of Politics, Political Research Quarterly,* and *The Journal of Political and Military Sociology.* Professor Davenport is the past recipient of the Leaders of Tomorrow award from *Ebony* magazine.

Winston A. Grady-Willis is a Ph.D. candidate in History at Emory University. He received his B.A. degree in History (1987) from Columbia University. He earned a M.A. degree in African-American Studies (1993) from Cornell University. Winston's masters thesis was entitled "The Leadership of the Black Panther Party". His dissertation examines the Black power movement in Atlanta, Georgia. He is the recipient of several awards and fellowships, including a Mellon dissertation fellowship, and the author of a chapter in Black Prison Movements USA. Grady-Willis was recently appointed as an Assistant Professor in the Department of African-American Studies at Syracuse University.

Floyd W. Hayes, III, is an Associate Professor in the Department of Political Science and African-American Studies at Purdue University. He earned a Ph.D. degree in government and politics from the University of Maryland in 1985. He received a M.A. degree in African Area Studies from the University of California at Los Angeles and a B.A. degree in Political Science and French from North Carolina Central University. Mr. Hayes has held faculty appointments at numerous colleges and universities, including the University of California at Los Angeles, Princeton University, Swarthmore College, Morgan State University, Cornell University, and San Diego State University. He has published extensively in several journals, including *Urban Education, The Journal of Ethnic Studies, The Western Journal of Black Studies, Black World,* and *The Journal of Black Studies.* Hayes also is the editor of the anthology *A Turbulent Voyage: Readings in African American Studies* . Currently, he is working on a book entitled African American Cynicism: Cultural Crosscurrents in a Postindustrial-Managerial Polity.

Judson L. Jeffries is an Assistant Professor in the Department of Political Science at Purdue University. He earned a Ph.D. in Political Science at the University of Southern California in 1997. He received a M.A. in Public Policy from the State University of New York at Binghamton. As an undergraduate, he attended Norfolk State and Old Dominion Universities where he completed his B.A. in Political Science. In the past, Dr. Jeffries has been awarded prestigious fellowships at the John F. Kennedy School of Government at Harvard University, Tufts University, and Indiana University. His published research includes "Douglas Wilder and the Continuing Significance of Race: An Analysis of the 1989 Gubernatorial Election" in the 1995 issue of *The Journal of Political Science.*

Regina Jennings is an Assistant Professor of English at Franklin and Marshall College. She is also a former member of the Black Panther Party. Professor Jennings received a B.A. degree in English (1985), a M.A. in English and Creative Writing (1987), and a Ph.D. in African American Studies from Temple University. Professor Jennings essays and poetry appear in *Sage: A Scholarly Journal of Black Women, Essays in Film and Literary Criticism, Essence Magazine, Shooting Star Review,* and *Full Moon.* She is a columnist for *The Black Suburban Journal.* In addition, she has presented numerous scholarly papers and poetry readings. She is currently completing her autobiographical memoir entitled *Vanguard Girl: A Female Panther Remembers.*

Ollie A. Johnson, III, is an Assistant Professor of Government and Politics and Afro-American Studies at the University of Maryland at College Park. He received his B.A. degree in Afro-American Studies and International Relations from Brown

University in 1984 and a M.A. in Brazilian Studies from Brown University in 1986. Professor Johnson received his Ph.D. in Political Science from the University of California at Berkeley in 1993. He is a former American Political Science Association Black Graduate Fellow and California Regents Fellow.

Francis A. Kiene, III, is a Ph.D. student and Graduate Teaching Fellow in the Department of Sociology at the University of Oregon, Eugene. His dissertation examines the life, political thought, and political assassination of Fred Hampton, the late Deputy Chairman of the Chicago branch of the Black Panther Party. Mr. Kiene holds a M.A. degree in American Studies from Purdue University (1996). He also received a B.A. degree in Sociology and African-American Studies from Purdue (1994). He is the 1994 recipient of the Howard G. McCall Award for Distinguished Leadership at Purdue University.

Angela D. LeBlanc-Ernest earned a doctorate in History from Stanford University. In 1992, she received a B.A. degree in Afro-American Studies from Harvard University where she graduated Magna Cum Laude. Her dissertation examines the survival programs of the Black Panther Party. She is the past recipient of several fellowships, including the Mellon Dissertation Fellowship, the Ford Foundation Dissertation Fellowship, the Dorothy Danforth Compton Fellowship, and the Nathan Huggins-Benjamin Quarles Award from the Organization of American Historians. Her publications include several entries in *Facts on File* and in *Black Women in the United States*: *An Historical Encyclopedia*. She is currently the director of the Black Panther Party Research Project at Stanford University.

Melvin E. Lewis was a community worker with the Chicago branch of the Black Panther Party from 1970 to 1972. He was awarded a Bachelor of Arts by the University of Illinois at Chicago and has done graduate work at American University and George Mason University. Mr. Lewis received the Larry Neal Poetry Award and a Significant Illinois Poet Award. His poetry has appeared in the following anthologies: *Dial-A-Poem, Chicago! 1981–1991*; *NOMMO*: *A Literary Legacy of Black Chicago 1967–1987*, *WPFW 89.3 FM Anthology*, and *Fast Talk, Full Volume: An Anthology of Contemporary African-American Poets*. Mr. Lewis has also published his poetry in numerous periodicals. Presently, he coordinates the Remote Video Encoding program of the United States Postal Service in the Mid-Atlantic Area.

Clarence Lusane earned a Ph.D. in Political Science from Howard University. He received his B.A. degree in Communication Studies from Wayne State University in 1976. Before entering graduate school at Howard University in 1992, Dr. Lusane worked for over fifteen years as a journalist. He is the author of five books, the latest of which is *Race in the Global Era: African Americans at the Millennium* (1997). He has taught and done research at Columbia University's Institute for Research in African American Studies, Medgar Evers College's DuBois Bunche Center for Public Policy, and Howard University's Center for Drug Abuse Research. Currently, Dr. Lusane is an Assistant Professor in the School of International Service at American University where he teaches in the area of global race relations.

Tracye Matthews is currently a Public Historian and the former project coordinator of the Neighborhoods: Keepers of Culture program of the Chicago Historical Society. She is also a Ph.D. candidate in History at the University of Michigan. She earned a M.A. in History (1992) and a B.A. in Psychology (1988) from the University of Michigan. Ms. Matthews is the recipient of a Ford Foundation Dissertation Fellowship (1996) and a Drusilla Dunjee Houston Memorial Scholarship (1992) from the Association of Black Women Historians. Her dissertation explores gender dynamics in the Black Panther Party. She has presented more than a dozen papers at professional conferences and is the co-author of "Black Popular Culture and the Transcendence of Patriarchal Illusions" in *Race and Class* (1993). A political activist, Ms. Matthews serves on the board of several community organizations and is the recipient of several community awards.

Steve D. McCutchen is currently a teacher with the Oakland Public Schools. A Baltimore native, Mr. McCutchen is a ten-year veteran of the Baltimore and Oakland branches of the Black Panther Party (1969–1979). As a rank-and-file member, Mr. McCutchen served as the former director of the Oakland Community Learning Center's Martial Arts Program. His martial arts students were featured in an article published by *Black Belt* magazine on June 30, 1975. Steve continues his political activism in the Oakland Bay area.

Miriam Ma'at-Ka-Re Monges is an Assistant Professor of Sociology/Social Work with major responsibility to African American Studies at California State University at Chico. She earned a doctorate in African American Studies at Temple University in 1995. She received a B.A. degree in Early Childhood Education from City University of New York, Brooklyn College (1973) and a M.S.W. from Temple University (1979). In addition, Professor Monges was a former community worker of the Black Panther Party. Professor Monges is the author of *KUSH: The Jewel of Nubia* (Africa World Press) and "Reflections on the Role of Female Deities and Queens in Ancient Kemet," which appeared in the *Journal of Black Studies*.

Nikhil Pal Singh is currently an Assistant Professor of History and American Studies at New York University. He earned a Ph.D. in American Studies from Yale University in 1995. His scholarly publications have appeared in *Radical History Review* and *Race and Reason,* and a chapter will be published in the forthcoming anthology entitled *Beyond Pluralism* (U. of Illinois Press). Professor Singh is a former Whiting Fellow in Humanities at Yale University.

Akinyele Omowale Umoja is an Assistant Professor of African-American Studies at Georgia State University. Professor Umoja received his Bachelor of Arts degree in African-American Studies at California State University at Los Angeles. Dr. Umoja earned a Master of Arts in American Studies (1991) and also holds a Ph.D. in American Studies from Emory University (1996). Dr. Umoja's dissertation thesis is entitled *Eye for an Eye: The Role of Armed Resistance in the Mississippi Freedom Movement.* As a community activist in Los Angeles and Atlanta for over twenty-two years, Professor Umoja's scholarship is informed by his experiences as a political activist. He is also a founder and board member of the Malcolm X Center for Self-Determination in Decatur, Georgia.

Appendix A

October 1966 Black Panther Party
Platform and Program

What We Want
What We Believe

1. *We want freedom. We want power to determine the destiny of our Black Community.*

   We believe that black people will not be free until we are able to determine our destiny.

2. *We want full employment for our people.*

   We believe that the federal government is responsible and obligated to give every man employment or a guaranteed income. We believe that if the white American businessmen will not give full employment, then the means of production should be taken from the businessmen and placed in the community so that the people of the community can organize and employ all of its people and give a high standard of living.

3. *We want an end to the robbery by the CAPITALIST man of our Black Community.*

   We believe that this racist government has robbed us and now we are demanding the overdue debt of forty acres and two mules. Forty acres and two mules was promised 100 years ago as restitution for slave labor and mass murder of black people. We will accept the payment in currency which will be distributed to our many communities. The Germans are now aiding the Jews in Israel for the genocide of the Jewish people. The Germans murdered six million Jews. The American racist has taken part in the slaughter of over fifty million black people; therefore, we feel that this a modest demand that we make.

4. *We want decent housing, fit for shelter of human beings.*

   We believe that if the white landlords will not give decent housing to our black community, then the housing and the land should be made into cooperatives so that our community, with government aid, can build and make decent housing for its people.

5. *We want education for our people that exposes the true nature of this decadent American society. We want education that teaches us our true history and our role in the present-day society.*

We believe in an educational system that will give to our people a knowledge of self. If a man does not have knowledge of himself and his position in society and the world, then he has little chance to relate to anything else.

6. *We want all black men to be exempt from military service.*

We believe that Black people should not be forced to fight in the military service to defend a racist government that does not protect us. We will not fight and kill other people of color in the world who, like black people, are being victimized by the white racist government of America. We will protect ourselves from the force and violence of the racist police and the racist military, by whatever means necessary.

7. *We want an immediate end to POLICE BRUTALITY and MURDER of black people.*

We believe we can end police brutality in our black community by organizing black self-defense groups that are dedicated to defending our black community from racist police oppression and brutality. The Second Amendment to the Constitution of the United States gives a right to bear arms. We therefore believe that all black people should arm themselves for self-defense.

8. *We want freedom for all black men held in federal, state, county and city prisons and jails.*

We believe that all black people should be released from the many jails and prisons because they have not received a fair and impartial trial.

9. *We want all black people when brought to trial to be tried in court by a jury of their peer group or people from their black communities, as defined by the Constitution of the United States.*

We believe that the courts should follow the United States Constitution so that black people will receive fair trials. The 14th Amendment of the U.S. Constitution gives a man a right to be tried by his peer group. A peer is a person from a similar economic, social, religious, geographical, environmental, historical, and racial background. To do this the court will be forced to select a jury from the black community from which the black defendant came. We have been, and are being tried by all-white juries that have no understanding of the "average reasoning man" of the Black community.

10. *We want land, bread, housing, education, clothing, justice and peace. And as our major political objective, a United Nations-supervised plebiscite to be held throughout the black colony in which only black colonial subjects will be allowed to participate, for the purpose of determining the will of black people as to their national destiny.*

When, in the course of human events, it becomes necessary for one people to dissolve the political bands which have connected them with another, and to assume, among the powers of the earth, the separate and equal station to which the laws of nature and nature's God entitle them, a decent respect to the opinions of mankind requires that they should declare the causes which impel them to the separation.

We hold these truths to be self-evident, that all men are created equal; that they are endowed by their Creator with certain unalienable rights; that among these are life, liberty, and the pursuit of happiness. *That, to secure these rights, governments are instituted among men, deriving their just powers from the consent of the governed; that, whenever any form of government becomes destructive to these ends, it is the right of the people to alter or to abolish it, and to institute a new government, laying its foundation on such principles, and organizing its powers in such form, as to them shall seem most likely to effect their safety and happiness.* Prudence, indeed, will dictate that governments long established should not be changed for light and transient causes; and, accordingly, all experience hath shown, that mankind are more disposed to suffer, while evils are sufferable, than to right themselves by abolishing the forms to which they are accustomed. *But, when a long train of abuses and usurpations, pursuing invariably the same object, evinces a design to reduce them under absolute despotism, it is their right, it is their duty, to throw off such government, and to provide new guards for their future security.*

(Reprinted from *The Black Panther*, 9 August 1969, 26.)

Appendix B

8 Points of Attention

1) Speak politely.
2) Pay fairly for what you buy.
3) Return everything you borrow.
4) Pay for anything you damage.
5) Do not hit or swear at people.
6) Do not damage property or crops of the poor, oppressed masses.
7) Do not take liberties with women.
8) If we ever have to take captives do not ill-treat them.

3 Main Rules of Discipline

1.) Obey orders in all your actions.
2.) Do not take a single needle or piece of thread from the poor and oppressed masses.
3.) Turn in everything captured from the attacking enemy.

(Reprinted from *The Black Panther*, 9 August 1969, 27.)

Appendix C

RULES OF THE BLACK PANTHER PARTY
CENTRAL HEADQUARTERS
OAKLAND, CALIFORNIA

Every member of the BLACK PANTHER PARTY throughout this country of racist America must abide by these rules as functional members of this party. CENTRAL COMMITTEE members, CENTRAL STAFFS, and LOCAL STAFFS, including all captains subordinate to either national, state, and local leadership of the BLACK PANTHER PARTY will enforce these rules. Length of suspension or other disciplinary action necessary for violation of these rules will depend on national decisions by national, state or state area, and local committees and staffs where said rule or rules of the BLACK PANTHER PARTY WERE VIOLATED.

Every member of the party must know these verbatim by heart. And apply them daily. Each member must report any violation of these rules to their leadership or they are counter-revolutionary and are also subjected to suspension by the BLACK PANTHER PARTY.

THE RULES ARE:

1. No party member can have narcotics or weed in his possession while doing party work.

2. Any party found shooting narcotics will be expelled from this party.

3. No party member can be DRUNK while doing daily party work.

4. No party member will violate rules relating to office work, general meetings of the BLACK PANTHER PARTY, and meetings of the BLACK PANTHER PARTY ANYWHERE.

5. No party member will USE, POINT, or FIRE a weapon of any kind unnecessarily or accidentally at anyone.

6. No party member can join any other army force other than the BLACK LIBERATION ARMY.

7. No party member can have a weapon in his possession while DRUNK or loaded off narcotics or weed.

8. No party member will commit any crimes against other party members or BLACK people at all, and cannot steal or take from the people, not even a needle or a piece of thread.

9. When arrested BLACK PANTHER MEMBERS will give only name, address, and will sign nothing. Legal first aid must be understood by all Party members.

10. The Ten Point Program and platform of the BLACK PANTHER PARTY must be known and understood by each Party member.

11. Party Communications must be National and Local.

12. The 10-10-10-program should be known by all members and also understood by all members.

13. All Finance officers will operate under the jurisdiction of the Ministry of Finance.

14. Each person will submit a report of daily work.

15. Each Sub-Section Leader, Section Leader, Lieutenant, and Captain must submit Daily reports of work.

16. All Panthers must learn to operate and service weapons correctly.

17. All Leadership personnel who expel a member must submit this information to the Editor of the Newspaper, so that it will be published in the paper and will be known by all chapters and branches.

18. Political Education Classes are mandatory for general membership.

19. Only office personnel assigned to respective offices each day should be there. All others are to sell papers and do Political work out in the community including Captains, Section Leaders, etc.

20. COMMUNICATIONS—all chapters must submit weekly reports in writing to the National Headquarters.

21. All Branches must implement First Aid and/or Medical Cadres.

22. All Chapters, Branches, and components of the BLACK PANTHER PARTY must submit a monthly Financial Report to the Ministry of Finance, and also the Central Committee.

23. Everyone in a leadership position must read no less than two hours per day to keep abreast of the changing political situation.

24. No chapter or branch shall accept grants, poverty funds, money or any other aid from any government agency without contacting the National Headquarters.

25. All chapters must adhere to the policy and the ideology laid down by the CENTRAL COMMITTEE of the BLACK PANTHER PARTY.

26. All Branches must submit weekly reports in writing to their respective Chapters.

(Reprinted from *The Black Panther*, 9 August 1969, 27.)

Selected Bibliography

Books

Abron, JoNina M. "'Raising the Consciousness of the People': The Black Panther Intercommunal News Service, 1967–1980.'" In *Voices From the Underground: Insider Histories of the Vietnam Era Underground Press*, edited by Ken Wachsberger. Tempe, AZ: Mica Press, 1993.

——. "Women in the Black Power Era: Lessons for the 1990's from the 1960's." In *Black Women in the Academy, Defending Our Name: 1894–1994*, edited by Robin Kilson. New York: Carlson Publishers, 1996.

Abu-Jamal, Mumia. *Live From Death Row*. Reading, MA: Addison-Wesley Publishers, 1995.

Afoh, Kwame et al. *A Brief History of Black Struggle in America*. Baton Rouge, LA: House of Songhay, 1991.

Ahmad, Aijaz. *In Theory: Classes, Nations and Literatures*. New York: Verso, 1992.

Alinsky, Saul D. *Rules for Radicals: A Practical Primer for Realistic Radicals*. New York: Vintage Books, 1971.

Allen, Robert. *Black Awakening in Capitalist America*. Garden City, NY: Doubleday, 1969.

Almaguer, Tomas. *Racial Fault Lines: The Historical Origins of White Supremacy in California*. Berkeley, CA: University of California Press, 1994.

Ambrose, Stephen. *Rise to Globalism: American Foreign Policy, 1938–1980*. 2d revised edition. New York: Penguin Books, 1980.

Anderson, Benedict. *Imagined Communities: Reflections on the Origin and Spread of Nationalism*. London: Verso, 1983.

Anderson, S. E., and Tony Medina. "If the Threat of Death Can Unite...And Ignite." In *In Defense of Mumia*, edited by S. E. Anderson and Tony Medina. New York: Writers and Readers, 1996.

Anthony, Earl. *Picking Up the Gun: A Report on the Black Panthers*. New York: The Dial Press, 1970.

——. *Spitting in the Wind: The True Story Behind the Violent Legacy of the Black Panther Party*. Santa Monica, CA: Roundtable Publishing, 1990.

Arlen, Michael J. *An American Verdict*. New York: Anchor Books, 1974.

Arrighi, Giovanni. "Marxist Century: American Century." In *A Theory of Capitalist Regulation: The U.S. Experience*, edited by Michel Aglietta. New York: Verso, 1979.

Asante, Molefi. *The Afrocentric Idea*. Philadelphia: Temple University Press, 1987.

——. *Afrocentricity: The Theory of Social Change*. Buffalo, NY: Amulefi Publishing Co., 1980.

——. *Kemet, Afrocentricity and Knowledge*. Trenton, NJ: Africa World Press, 1990.

Asante, Molefi, and Kariamu Welsh-Asante. *African Culture: The Rhythms of Unity*. Trenton, NJ: Africa World Press, 1990.

Ashmore, Harry. *Civil Rights and Wrongs: A Memoir of Race and Politics*. New York: Pantheon Books, 1994.

Balagoon, Kuwasi et al., eds. *Look For Me in the Whirlwind: The Collective Autobiography of the New York 21*. New York: Vintage Books, 1971.

Baldassare, Mark, ed., *The Los Angeles Riots: Lessons for the Urban Future*. Boulder, CO: Westview Press, 1994.

Baldwin, James. "An Open Letter to My Sister Angela Davis." In *If They Come in the Morning: Voices of Resistance*, by Angela Davis, et al. San Francisco: The National United Committee to Free Angela Davis (NUCFAD), 1971.

——. "Fifth Avenue Uptown: A Letter from Harlem." In *Nobody Knows My Name: More Notes of a Native Son*. New York: Dell Publishing Co., 1961.

——. *No Name in the Street*. New York: Dial Press., 1972.

Balibar, Etienne, and Immanuel Wallerstein. *Race, Nation, Class: Ambiguous Identities*. New York: Verso, 1991.

Baraka, Amiri (LeRoi Jones). "Black Liberation/Socialist Revolution." In *Daggers and Javelins: Essays of Amiri Baraka (LeRoi Jones)*. New York: Quill, 1984.

Barber, Benjamin R. *Jihad vs. McWorld: How the Planet is Both Falling Apart and Coming Together and What This Means for Democracy*. New York: Times Books, 1995.

Barlett, Donald L., and James B. Steels. *America: What Went Wrong?* Kansas City: Andrews and McMeel, 1992.

Barnet, Richard J., and John Cavanaugh. *Global Dreams: Imperial Corporations and the New World Order*. New York: Simon and Schuster, 1994.

Barnet, Richard J., and Ronald E. Muller. *Global Reach: The Power of the Multinational Corporations*. New York: Simon and Schuster, 1974.

Baruch, Ruth Marion, and Pirkle Jones. *The Vanguard: A Photographic Essay on the Black Panthers*. Boston: Beacon Press, 1970.

ben-Jochannon, Yosef. *African Origins of the Major "Western Religions."* Baltimore: Black Classic Press, 1991.

Bhabha, Homi K. "DessemiNation: Time, Narrative and the Margins of the Modern Nation." In *Nation and Narration*, edited by Homi K. Bhabha. New York: Routledge, 1990.

Bing, Leon. *Do or Die*. New York: HarperCollins Publishers, 1991.

Blackstock, Nelson. *COINTELPRO: The FBI's Secret War on Political Freedom*. 3rd edition. New York: Anchor Foundations, 1988.

Blaut, James M. *The National Question: Decolonizing the Theory of Nationalism*. London: Zed Books, 1987.

Bober, Arie, ed. *The Other Israel: The Radical Case Against Zionism*. Garden City, NY: Anchor Books, 1972.

Boggs, James. *Racism and the Class Struggle: Further Pages from a Black Worker's Notebook*. New York: Monthly Review Press, 1971.

Bositis, David. *The Congressional Black Caucus in the 103rd Congress*. Washington, DC: Joint Center for Political and Economic Studies, 1994.

Bourdieu, Pierre. "Social Space and Symbolic Power." In *In Other Words: Essays Towards a Reflexive Sociology*, translated by Matthew Adamson. Stanford, CA: Stanford University Press, 1990.

Boyd, Herb. *Black Panthers for Beginners*. New York: Writers and Readers Publishing, 1995.

Branch, Taylor. *Parting the Waters: America in the King Years, 1954–1963*. New York: Simon and Schuster, 1988.

Breines, Wini. *Community Organization in the New Left, 1962–1968: The Great Refusal*. New York: Praeger, 1982.

Brent, William Lee. *Long Time Gone: A Black Panther's True-Life Story of His Hijacking and Twenty-Five Years in Cuba*. New York: Times Books, 1996.

Brisbane, Robert. *Black Activism: Racial Revolution in the United States 1954–1970*. Valley Forge, PA: Judson Press, 1974.

Brock, Annette K. "Gloria Richardson and the Cambridge Movement." In *Women in the Civil Rights Movement: Trailblazers and Torchbearers 1941–1965*, edited by Vickie Crawford, Jacqueline Rouse and Barbara Woods. Bloomington: Indiana University Press, 1993.

Brown, Elaine. *A Taste of Power: A Black Woman's Story*. New York: Pantheon Books, 1992.

Brown, Elsa Barkley. "African-American Women's Quilting: A Framework for Conceptualizing and Teaching African-American Women's History." In *Black Women in America: Social Science Perspectives*, edited by Micheline R. Malson, et al. Chicago: University of Chicago Press, 1990.

——. "To Catch the Vision of Freedom: Reconstructing Southern Black Women's Political History, 1865–1885." In *To Be a Citizen*, edited by Arlene Avakian, John Bracey, and Ann Gordon. Amherst, MA: University of Massachusetts Press. Forthcoming.

——. "Womanist Consciousness: Maggie Lena Walker and the Independent Order of Saint Luke." In *Unequal Sisters: A Multi-Cultural Reader in U.S. Women's History,* edited by Carol DuBois and Vicki L. Ruiz. New York: Routledge, Chapman & Hall, Inc., 1990.

Browning, Rufus P., Dale Rodgers Marshall and David H. Tabb. *Protest is Not Enough: The Struggle of Blacks and Hispanics for Equality in Urban Politics*. Berkeley, CA: University of California Press, 1984.

Buhle, Mari Jo, Paul Buhle, and Dan Georgakas, eds. *Encyclopedia of the American Left*. Urbana, IL: University of Illinois Press, 1992.

Bush, Rod. "Introduction: Black Politics and Oakland Development." In *The New Black Vote,* edited by Rod Bush. San Francisco: Synthesis Publications, 1984.

Bush, Rod, ed. *The New Black Vote: Politics and Power in Four American Cities*. San Francisco: Synthesis Publications, 1984.

Butler, Judith. *Bodies that Matter: On the Discursive Limits of "Sex."* New York: Routledge, 1993.

Cade, Toni, ed. *The Black Woman: An Anthology*. New York: The New American Library, 1970.

Carby, Hazel V. *Reconstructing Womanhood: The Emergence of the Afro-American Woman Novelist*. New York: Oxford University Press, 1987.

Carmichael, Stokely (Kwame Ture), and Charles V. Hamilton. *Black Power, The Politics of Liberation*. New York: Vintage Edition, 1992.

Carson, Clayborne. Foreword to *The Black Panthers Speak*. Philip S. Foner, ed. Reprint, New York: Da Capo Press, 1995.

Carson, Clayborne. *In Struggle: SNCC and the Black Awakening of the 1960s*. Cambridge: Harvard University Press, 1981.

——. *Malcolm X: The FBI File*. New York: Carroll and Graf Publishers, 1991.

Cashman, Sean D. *African-Americans and the Quest for Civil Rights, 1900–1990*. New York: New York University Press, 1991.

Castellucci, John. *The Big Dance: The Untold Story of Kathy Boudin and the Terrorist Family that Committed the Brink's Robbery Murders*. New York: Dodd, Mead and Co., 1986.

Chevigny, Paul. *Cops and Rebels: A Study of Provocation*. New York: Random House, 1972.

Chicago Gay Liberation. "Working Paper for the Revolutionary People's Constitutional Convention." *In Out of the Closets: Voices of Gay Liberation*. New York: Douglass Book Corporation, 1972).

Chisholm, Shirley. *The Good Fight*. New York: Bantam Books, 1974.

Churchill, Ward, and Jim Vander Wall. *Agents of Repression: The FBI's Secret Wars Against and Black Panther Party and the American Indian Movement*. Boston: South End Press, 1988.

——. *The COINTELPRO Papers: Documents from the FBI's Secret Wars Against Domestic Dissent*. Boston: South End Press, 1990.

The Citizens Research and Investigation Committee. *The Glass House Tapes*. New York: Avon Books, 1973.

Clarke, Cheryl. "The Failure to Transform: Homophobia in the Black Community." In *Home Girls: A Black Feminist Anthology*, edited by Barbara Smith. New York: Kitchen Table Women of Color Press, 1983.

Cleaver, Eldridge. "Message to Sister Ericka Huggins of the Black Panther Party." In *The Black Panthers Speak,* edited by Phillip S. Foner. Philadelphia: Lippincott, 1970; reprint New York: Da Capo Press, 1995.

Cleaver, Eldridge. *Post-Prison Writings and Speeches*. New York: Vintage Books, 1970.

———. *Soul on Ice*. New York: Dell Publishing Inc., 1970.

Clemente, Frank, ed. with Frank Watkins. *Keep Hope Alive: Jesse Jackson's 1988 Presidential Campaign: A Collection of Major Speeches, Issue Papers, Photographs, & Campaign Analysis*. Boston: South End Press, 1989.

Cohen, Robert Carl. *Black Crusader: A Biography of Robert Franklin Williams*. Secaucus, NJ: Lyle Stuart, 1972.

Collier, Peter, and David Horowitz. *Destructive Generation: Second Thoughts About the Sixties*. New York: Summit Books, 1989.

Collins, Patricia Hill. *Black Feminist Thought: Knowledge, Consciousness and the Politics of Empowerment*. Boston: Unwin Hyman, 1990.

Collins, Sheila. *The Rainbow Challenge: The Jackson Campaign and the Future of American Politics*. New York: Monthly Review Press, 1986.

Cox, Oliver C. *Caste, Class and Race: A Study in Social Dynamics*. New York: Monthly Review Press, 1948.

Crouch, Stanley. *The All-American Skin Game, or, The Decoy of Race: The Long and the Short Of It, 1990–1994*. New York: Pantheon Books, 1995.

———. "The Nationalism of Fools." In *Notes of a Hanging Judge: Essays and Reviews, 1979–1989,*edited by Stanley Crouch. New York: Oxford University Press, 1990.

Crouchett, Lawrence, Lonnie G. Bunch, III, and Martha Kendall Winnacker. *Visions Towards Tomorrow: The History of the East Bay Afro-American Community 1852–1977*. Oakland: Northern California Center for Afro-American History and Life, 1996.

Cruse, Harold. *The Crisis of the Negro Intellectual*. New York: William Morrow & Co., 1967.

———. *Rebellion or Revolution?* New York: William Morrow & Co., 1968.

Cummins, Eric. *The Rise and Fall of California's Radical Prison Movement*. Stanford, CA: Stanford University Press, 1994.

Darity, William A., Jr. et al. *The Black Underclass: Critical Essays on Race and Unwantedness*. New York: Garland Publishing, 1994.

Davis, Angela. *Angela Davis: An Autobiography*. New York: International Publishers, 1988.

———. *Angela Davis: With My Mind on Freedom: An Autobiography*. New York: Bantam Books, 1974.

———. *If They Come in the Morning: Voices of Resistance*. San Francisco: The National United Committee to Free Angela Davis (NUCFAD), 1971.

———. *Women, Culture and Politics*. New York: Vintage Books, 1990.

Davis, Mike. *City of Quartz: Excavating the Future in Los Angeles*. New York: Vintage Books, 1992.

Dawson, Michael. *Behind the Mule: Race and Class in African-American Politics*. Princeton, NJ: Princeton University Press, 1994.

Delaney, Martin. *The Condition, Elevation, Emigration and Destiny of the Colored People of the United States*. 1852. Reprint, Baltimore: Black Classic Press, 1993.

Diop, Cheikh Anta. *The African Origin of Civilization: Myth or Reality*. New York: Lawrence Hill & Co., 1974.

———. *Civilization or Barbarism: An Authentic Anthropology*. Brooklyn, NY: Lawrence Hill Books, 1991.

——. *The Cultural Unity of Black Africa: The Domains of Patriarchy and Matriarchy in Classical Antiquity*. Chicago: Third World Press, 1978.

Dominguez, Jorge I. "Political and Military Consequences of Cuban Policies in Africa." *Cuba in Africa*, edited by Carmelo Meas-Logo and June S. Belkin. University of Pittsburgh: Center for Latin American Studies, 1982.

Donner, Frank. *Protectors of Privilege: Red Squads and Police Repression in Urban America*. Berkeley, CA: University of California Press, 1990.

Douglas, Frederick. *Narrative of the Life of Frederick Douglas: An American Slave*. 1845. Reprint, New York: Signet, 1968.

Downing, John. *Radical Media: The Political Experience of Alternative Communication*. Boston: South End Press, 1984.

Dubey, Mau. *Black Women and The Nationalist Aesthetic*. Bloomington,: Indiana University Press, 1994.

DuBois, W.E.B. *Color and Democracy: Colonies and Peace*. New York: Harcourt, Brace and Company, 1945.

Durden-Smith, Jo. *Who Killed George Jackson?* New York: Alfred A. Knopf, 1976.

Dye, Thomas R. *Who's Running America? The Bush Era*. 5th edition. Englewood, NJ:Prentice-Hall, 1990.

Dye, Thomas R., and Harmon Zeigler. *The Irony of Democracy: An Uncommon Introduction to American Politics*. 8th edition. Pacific Grove, CA: Brooks/Cole Publishing Company, 1990.

Dyson, Michael Eric. "Screening the Black Panthers." In *Between God and Gangsta Rap: Bearing Witness to Black Culture*, edited by Michael Eric Dyson. New York: Oxford University Press, 1996.

Echols, Alice. *Daring to be Bad: Radical Feminism in America, 1967–1975*. Minneapolis: University of Minneapolis Press, 1989.

Edsall, Thomas Byrne, and Mary Edsall. *Chain Reaction: The Impact of Race, Rights, & Taxes in American Politics*. New York: Norton, 1991.

Erikson, Erik, and Huey P. Newton. *In Search of Common Ground: Conversations with Erik H. Erikson and Huey P. Newton*. New York: W.W. Norton & Co., 1973.

Eschen, Penny Von. *Race Against Empire: Black Americans and Anti-Colonialism 1937–1957*. Ithaca, New York: Cornell University Press, 1997.

Evans, Sara. *Personal Politics: The Roots of Women's Liberation in the Civil Rights Movement and the New Left*. New York: Vintage Books, 1979.

Evanzz, Karl. *The Judas Factor: The Plot to Kill Malcolm X*. New York: Thunder's Mouth Press, 1992.

Fairbarn, Geoffrey. *Revolutionary Guerrilla Warfare*. Baltimore: Penguin Books, 1974.

Fanon, Frantz. *The Wretched of the Earth*. New York: Weidenfeld, 1961. (New York: Grove Press, 1968.)

Farber, Jerry. *The Student as Nigger: Essays and Stories*. New York: Pocket Books, 1969.

Fletcher, Jim, Tanaquil Jones, and Sylvere Lotringer, eds. *Still Black, Still Strong: Survivors of the U.S. War Against Black Revolutionaries—Dhoruba Bin Wahad, Mumia Abu-Jamal, Assata Shakur*. New York: Semiotext(e), 1993.

Foner, Philip S., ed. *The Black Panthers Speak*. Philadelphia: Lippincott, 970; reprint New York: Da Capo Press, 1995.

Forman, James. *The Making of Black Revolutionaries: A Personal Account*. New York: The Macmillan Company, 1972.

Frankel, Max. "The Lessons of Vietnam." In *The Pentagon Papers: The Defense Department History of United States Decision making in Vietnam*, edited by The Beacon Hill Press. Boston: Quadrangle Books, 1971.

Franklin, Bruce. *Prison Literature in America: The Victim as Criminal and Artist*. New York: Oxford University Press, 1978.

Fraser, Ronald et al., *1968: A Student Generation in Revolt*. New York: Pantheon Books, 1988.

Fraser, Steve, and Gary Gerstle, eds., *The Rise and Fall of the New Deal Order: 1930–1980*. Princeton, NJ: Princeton University Press, 1989.

Frazier, E. Franklin. *The Negro Family in the United States*. Chicago: University of Chicago Press, 1939.

Freed, Donald. *Agony in New Haven: The Trial of Bobby Seale, Ericka Huggins and the Black Panther Party*. New York: Simon and Schuster, 1973.

Freeman, Jo, ed. *Social Movements of the Sixties and Seventies*. New York: Longman, 1983.

Garrow, David. *The FBI and Martin Luther King, Jr.: From "Solo" to Memphis*. New York: W.W. Norton and Company, 1981.

Genet, Jean. *Prisoner of Love*. Hanover, NH: Wesleyan University Press, 1992.

Genovese, Eugene. "The Legacy of Slavery and the Roots of Black Nationalism." In *For a New America: Essays in History and Politics from Studies on the Left, 1959–1967*, edited by James Weinstein and David W. Eakins. New York: Vintage Books, 1970.

Georgakas, Dan and Marvin Surkin. *Detroit: I Do Mind Dying: A Study in Urban Revolution*. New York: St. Martin's Press, 1975.

Geschwender, James A. *Class, Race and Worker Insurgency: The League of Revolutionary Black Workers*. Cambridge: Cambridge University Press, 1977.

Giddings, Paula. *When and Where I Enter: The Impact of Black Women on Race and Sex in America*. New York: Bantam Books, 1984.

Giddins, Anthony. *Capitalism and Modern Social Theory: An Analysis of the Writings of Marx, Durkheim and Max Weber*. New York: Cambridge University Press, 1971.

Gilroy, Paul. "Diaspora, Utopia and the Critique of Capitalism," In *There Ain't No Black in the Union Jack: The Cultural Politics of Race and Nation*. Chicago: University of Chicago Press, 1991.

——. "'It Ain't Where You're From, It's Where You're At': Dialectics of Diasporic Identification." In *Small Acts: Thoughts on the Politics of Black Cultures* . . London: Serpent's Tale, 1993.

——. "It's a Family Affair." In *Small Acts: Thoughts on the Politics of Black Cultures*. London: Serpent's Tale, 1993.

Gitlin, Todd. *The Sixties: Years of Hope, Days of Rage*. New York: Bantam Books, 1987.

Glessing, Robert. *The Underground Press in America*. Westport, CT: Greenwood Press, 1970.

Goldstein, Robert Justin. *Political Repression in Modern America: From 1870 to the Present*. Cambridge, MA: Schenkman Publishing Company, 1978.

Gooding-Williams, Robert, ed., *Reading Rodney King, Reading Urban Uprising*. New York: Routledge, 1993.

Gosse, Van. *Where the Boys Are: Cuba, Cold War American and the Making of a New Left*. New York: Verso, 1993.

Graber, Doris A. *Mass Media and American Politics*. 4th edition. Washington, DC: Congressional Quarterly Press, 1993.

Grande, William M. Leo. "Cuban-Soviet Relations and Cuban Policy in Africa." In *Cuba in Africa*, edited by Carmelo Meas-Lago and June S. Belkin. Pittsburgh: University of Pittsburgh Center for Latin American Studies, 1982.

Greider, William. *One World Ready or Not: The Manic Logic of Global Capitalism*. New York: Simon & Schuster, 1997.

Grimshaw, William J. *Bitter Fruit: Black Politics and the Chicago Machine, 1931–1991*. Chicago: University of Chicago Press, 1992.

Grossberg, Lawrence, Cary Nelson, and Paula Treichler, eds. *Cultural Studies*. New York: Routledge, 1992.

Halisi, Clyde, ed. *The Quotable Karenga*. Los Angeles: Us Organization, 1967.

Hall, Stuart et al. *Policing the Crisis: Mugging, the State and Law and Order*. New York: Holmes and Meier, 1978.

Farber, Jerry. *The Student as Nigger: Essays and Stories*. New York: Pocket Books, 1969.

Hampton, Henry, and Steve Faver, eds. *Voices of Freedom: An Oral History of the Civil Rights Movement from the 1950's through the 1980's*. New York: Bantam, 1990.

Hansen, Emmanuel. *Frantz Fanon: Social and Political Thought*. Columbus, OH: Ohio State University Press, 1977.

Harlow, Barbara. *Resistance Literature*. New York: Methuen, 1987.

———. "Sites of Struggle: Immigration, Deportation, Prison and Exile." In *Criticism in the Borderlands: Studies in Chicano Literature, Culture and Ideology*, edited by Hector Calderon and Jose David Saldivar. Durham, NC: Duke University Press, 1991.

Harper, Phillip Brian. "Eloquence and Epitaph: Black Nationalism and the Homophobic Impulse in Response to the Death of Max Robinson." In *Fear of a Queer Planet: Queer Politics and Social Theory*, edited by Michael Warner. Minneapolis: University of Minnesota Press, 1993.

Harris, Louis, et al. *The Harris Survey Yearbook of Public Opinion 1970: A Compendium of Current American Attitudes*. New York: Louis Harris and Associates, 1971.

Harvey, David. *The Condition of Postmodernity: An Enquiry into the Origins of Cultural Change*. London: Basil Blackwell, 1989.

Hayden, Tom. *Reunion: A Memoir*. New York: Random House, 1988.

Haywood, Harry. *Black Bolshevik: Autobiography of an Afro-American Communist*. Chicago: Liberator Press, 1978.

Heath, Louis, ed. *The Black Panther Leaders Speak: Huey P. Newton, Bobby Seale, Eldridge Cleaver and Company Speak Out Through the Black Panther Party's Official Newspaper*. Metuchen, NJ: Scarecrow Press, 1976.

———, ed. *Off the Pigs!: The History and Literature of the Black Panther Party*. Metuchen, NJ: Scarecrow Press, 1976.

Herberg, Will. *Protestant, Catholic, Jew: An Essay in American Religious Sociology*. Garden City, NY: Doubleday, 1955; reprint, Chicago: University of Chicago Press, 1983.

Higham, Charles. *Trading with the Enemy: An Expose of the Nazi-American Money Plot, 1933–1949*. New York: Delacorte Press, 1983.

Hill, Norman, ed. *The Black Panther Menace: America's Neo Nazis*. New York: Popular Library, 1971.

Hilliard, David, and Lewis Cole. *This Side of Glory: The Autobiography of David Hilliard and the Story of the Black Panther Party*. Boston: Little, Brown and Company, 1993.

Hine, Darlene Clark, ed., *Black Women in America: An Historical Encyclopedia*. New York: Carlson Publishing Inc., 1993.

Hirsch, E.D., Jr. *Cultural Literacy: What Every American Needs to Know*. New York: Vintage Books, 1988.

Hobbes, Thomas. *Leviathan Parts I and II*. Reprint, Indianapolis: Bobbs-Merrill Company, 1958.

Holden, Matthew. *The Politics of the Black "Nation."* New York: Chandler, 1973.

Holsti, Ole. *Content Analysis for the Social Sciences and Humanities*. Reading, MA: Addison-Wesley, 1969.

hooks, bell. *Killing Rage: Ending Racism.* New York: Henry Holt and Company, 1996.

Horne, Gerald. *Black and Red: W.E.B. DuBois and the Afro-American Response to the Cold War, 1944–1963.* Albany: State University of New York Press, 1986.

Hudson-Weems, Clenora. *Africana Womanism: Reclaiming Ourselves.* Troy, MI: Bedford Publishers, 1994.

Hutchinson, Louise. *Anna Julia Cooper: A Voice From the South.* Washington, DC: Smithsonian Press, 1981.

Isaacs, Harold. *The New World of Negro Americans.* London: Phoenix House, 1963.

Jackson, George. *Blood in My Eye.* Baltimore: Black Classic Press, 1990.

———. *Soledad Brother: The Prison Letters of George Jackson.* New York: Random House,1970.

James, C.L.R. "The Revolutionary Answer to the Negro Question in the United States (1948)." In *The C.L.R. James Reader*, edited by Anna Grimshaw. London: Basil Blackwell, 1992.

James, Marlise."Charles Garry, Chief Defense Counsel of the Black Panther Party." In *The People's Lawyer,* edited by Marlise James. New York: Holt, Reinhart and Winston, 1973.

Jameson, Frederic. "Periodizing the Sixties." In *The Sixties Without Apology, edited by Sohnya Sayres, et al.* Minneapolis, Minnesota: University of Minnesota Press, 1984.

Jay, Karla, and Allen Young. *Out of the Closets: Voices of Gay Liberation.* New York: Douglas Book Corporation, 1972. Reprint, New York: New York University Press, 1992.

Jennings, James. *The Politics of Black Empowerment: The Transformation of Black Activism in Urban America.* Detroit: Wayne State University Press, 1992.

Jennings, Keith. "Understanding the Persisting Crisis of Black Youth Unemployment." In *Race, Politics, and Economic Development: Community Perspectives*, edited by James Jennings. New York: Verso, 1992.

John Brown Society. *The Black Panther Movement.* Ann Arbor, MI: Radical Education Project, 1969.

Johnson, Abby Arthur, and Ronald Mayberry Johnson. *Propaganda and Aesthetics: The Literary Politics of African-American Magazines in the Twentieth Century.* Amherst, MA: University of Massachusetts Press, 1979.

Jones, Charles E. and Michael Clemmons. "A Model of Racial Crossover Voting: An Assessment of the Wilder Victory." In *Dilemmas of Black Politics: Issues of Leadership and Strategy*, edited by George A. Persons. New York: Harper Collins Publishers, 1993.

Jones, Mack H. "The Black Underclass as Systemic Phenomenon." *In Race Politics and Economic Development: Community Perspective*, edited by James Jennings. New York: Verso, 1992.

Julien, Issac. "'Black Is, Black Ain't': Notes on De-Essentializing Black Identities." In *Black Popular Culture*, edited by Gina Dent. Seattle: Bay Press, 1992.

Julien, Issac, and Kobena Mercer. "True Confessions: A Discourse on Images of Black Male Sexuality."In *Brother to Brother: New Writings By Black Gay Men*, edited by Essex Hemphill. Boston: Alyson Publications, 1991.

Karenga, Maulana Ron. *Kawaida Theory: An Introductory Outline.* Inglewood, CA: Kawaida Publications, 1982.

———. *The Roots of the Us-Panther Conflict: The Perverse and Deadly Games Police Play.* San Diego: Kawaida Publications, 1976.

———. "Society, Culture and the Problem of Self-Consciousness: A Kawaida Analysis." In *Philosophy Born of Struggle: Anthology of Afro-American Philosophy from 1917*, edited by Leonard Harris. Dubuque, IA: Kendall/Hunt, 1982.

Katsiaficas, George. *The Imagination of the New Left: A Global Analysis of 1968*. Boston: South End Press, 1987.

Kazin, Michael, and Maurice Isserman. "The Failure and Success of the New Radicalism." In *The Rise and Fall of the New Deal Order, 1930–1968*, edited by Steve Fraser and Gary Gerstle. Princeton, NJ: Princeton University Press, 1989.

Keating, Edward M. *Free Huey*. New York: Dell Publishing Company, 1970.

Kelly, Robin D.G. *Into the Fire–African-Americans Since 1970*. New York: Oxford University Press, 1996.

———. "Jones, Claudia (1915–1965)." In *Black Women in America: An Historical Encyclopedia,* edited by Darlene Clark Hine. New York: Carlson Publishing, 1993.

———. *Race Rebels: Culture, Politics and the Black Working Class*. New York: The Free Press, 1994.

Kempton, Murray. *The Briar Patch: The People of the State of New York v. Lumumba Shakur et al.* New York: Dell Publishing Company, 1973.

Kessler, Lauren. *The Dissident Press: Alternative Journalism in American History*. Beverly Hills: Sage, 1984.

King, Martin Luther, Jr., *Trumpet of Conscience*. New York: Harper and Row, 1967.

Kopkind, Andrew. "The Real SDS Stands Up (1969)." In *The Thirty Years Wars: Dispatches and Diversions of a Radical Journalist, 1965–1994*, edited by Andrew Kopkind. New York: Verso, 1995.

Korten, David C. *When Corporations Rule the World*. West Hartford, CT: Berrett-Koehler Publishers; San Francisco: Kumarian Press, 1995.

The Labor Institute. *Corporate Power and the American Dream: Toward an Economic Agenda for Working People*. New York: The Labor Institute, 1996.

Laclau, Ernesto. *Politics and Ideology in Marxist Theory: Capitalism, Fascism, Populism*. London: NLB, 1977.

Laclau, Ernesto, and Chantal Mouffe. *Hegemony and Socialist Strategy: Towards a Radical Democratic Politics*. London: Verso, 1985.

Lader, Lawrence. *Power on the Left: American Radical Movements Since 1946*. New York: W.W. Norton, 1979.

Leamer, Laurence. *The Paper Revolutionaries: The Rise of the Underground Press*. New York: Simon and Schuster, 1972.

Lefebvre, Henri. *The Explosion: Marxism and the French Revolution*. New York: Monthly Review Press, 1969.

Lemke-Santangelo, Gretchen. *Abiding Courage: African American Migrant Women and the East Bay Community*. Chapel Hill: University of North Carolina Press, 1996.

Lester, Julius. *Revolutionary Notes*. New York: Grove Press, 1969.

Levin, Murray Burton. *Political Hysteria in America: The Democratic Capacity for Repression*. New York: Basic Books, 1971.

Levy, Peter. *The New Left and Labor in the 1960s*. Urbana, IL: University of Illinois Press, 1994.

Lockwood, Lee. *Conversations with Eldridge Cleaver— Algiers*. New York: Delta Books, 1970.

Lumumba, Chokwe. *The Roots of the New Afrikan Independence Movement*. Jackson, MS: New Afrikan Productions, 1991.

Lusane, Clarence. *African Americans at the Crossroads: The Restructuring of Black Leadership in the 1992 Elections*. Boston: South End Press, 1994

———. *Pipe Dream Blues: Racism and the War on Drugs*. Boston: South End Press, 1991.

McAdams, Doug. *Political Process and the Development of Black Insurgency, 1930–1970*. Chicago: University of Chicago Press, 1982.

McCartney, John. T. *Black Power Ideologies: An Essay in African-American Political Thought*. Philadelphia: Temple University Press, 1992.

Madhubuti, Haki and Maulana Karenga. *Million Man March/Day of Atonement: A Commemorative Anthology: Speeches, Commentary, Photography, Poetry, Illustrations, Documents*. Chicago: Third World Press, 1995.

Major, Reginald. *A Panther is a Black Cat*. New York: W. Morrow, 1971.

Malcolm X. *By Any Means Necessary: Speeches, Interviews, and a Letter*. New York: Pathfinder Press, 1970.

Mander, Jerry and Edward Goldsmith, eds. *The Case Against the Global Economy and For a Turn Toward the Local*. San Francisco: Sierra Club Books, 1996.

Mann, Eric. *Comrade George: An Investigation into the Life, Political Thought and Assassination of George Jackson*. New York: Perennial Library, 1974.

Mao Tse-Tung. *Quotations from Chairman Mao Tse-Tung*. Peking, China: Foreign Languages Press, 1972.

Marable, Manning. *Black American Politics: From the Washington Marches to Jesse Jackson*. New York: Verso, 1985.

———. *Blackwater: Historical Studies in Race, Class Consciousness and Revolution*. Dayton, Ohio: Black Praxis Press, 1981.

———. *How Capitalism Underdeveloped Black America: Problems in Race, Political Economy and Society*. Boston: South End Press, 1983.

———. "The Legacy of Huey P. Newton." In *The Crisis of Color and Democracy: Essays on Race, Class, and Power,* edited by Manning Marable. Monroe, ME: Common Courage Press, 1992.

———. *Race, Reform and Rebellion: The Second Reconstruction in Black America, 1945–1990*. Jackson, MS: University Press of Mississippi, 1991.

Marine, Gene. *The Black Panthers*. New York: Signet, 1969.

Marshall, Toni and Claudia Brodsky Lacour, eds. *Birth of a Nation'hood: Gaze, Script, and Spectacle in the O.J. Simpson Case*. New York: Pantheon Books, 1997.

Martin, Tony. *Race First: The Ideological and Organizational Struggles of Marcus Garvey and the Universal Negro Improvement Association*. Dover, MA: The Majority Press, 1986.

Massey, Douglas, and Nancy Denton. *American Apartheid: Segregation and the Making of the Underclass*. Cambridge: Harvard University Press, 1993.

Mbiti, John. *African Religions & Practice*. London: Heinemann International, 1969. Reprint, Portsmouth, NH: Heinemann International, 1990.

Meier, August, Elliott Rudwick, and Francis L. Broderick, eds. *Black Protest Thought in the Twentieth Century*. New York: Macmillian Publishing Company, 1971.

Mercer, Kobena. "'1968': Periodizing Politics and Identity." In *Cultural Studies*, edited by Lawrence Grossberg, et al. London: Routledge, 1992.

Michels, Robert. *Political Parties: A Sociological Study of the Oligarchical Tendencies of Modern Democracy*. New York: The Free Press, 1962.

Moore, Chuck. *I Was A Black Panther*. Garden City, NY: Doubleday, 1970.

Moore, Gilbert. *Rage*. New York: Carroll and Graf Publishers, 1993.

Morgan, Robin, comp. *Sisterhood is Powerful: An Anthology of Writings from the Women's Liberation Movement*. New York: Vintage Books, 1970.

Morris, Aldon. *Origins of the Civil Rights Movement: Black Communities Organizing for Change*. New York: The Free Press, 1984.

Moses, Wilson. "Ambivalent Maybe." In *Lure and Loathing: Essays on Race, Identity and the Ambivalence of Assimilation*, edited by Gerald Early. New York: A. Lane/Penguin, 1993.

Moynihan, Daniel Patrick. *The Case for National Action: The Negro Family*. Office of Policy Planning and Research, United States Department of Labor, March, 1965.

Munford, Clarence J. *Production Relations, Class and Black Liberation: A Marxist Perspective in Afro-American Studies*. Amsterdam: B.R. Gruner Publishing Co., 1978.

Munoz, Carlos, Jr. *Youth, Identity and Power: The Chicano Movement*. New York: Verso, 1989.

Murray, Robert K. *Red Scare: A Study in National Hysteria, 1919–1920*. New York: McGraw Hill, 1964.

Myrdal, Gunnar. *The American Dilemma: The Negro Problem and Modern Democracy*. New York: Harper, 1944; New York: Pantheon Books, 1962.

Naison, Mark. *Communists in Harlem during the Depression*. Urbana, IL: University of Illinois Press, 1983.

National Committee to Free Puerto Rican Prisoners of War and the National Committee to End the Marion Lockdown, eds. *Can't Jail the Spirit;Political Prisoners in the United States*. Chicago: Editorial Coqui Publishers, 1988.

National Urban League. *The State of Black America 1986*. New York: National Urban League, 1987.

——. *The State of Black America 1993*. New York: National Urban League, 1994.

Newton, Huey. *The Genius of Huey P. Newton: Minister of Defense Black Panther Party*. San Francisco: Black Panther Party, 1970.

——. *Revolutionary Suicide*. New York: Harcourt Brace Jovanovich, 1973. Reprint, New York: Writers and Readers Publishing, 1995.

——. *To Die for the People: The Writings of Huey P. Newton*. New York: Random House, 1972.

——. *War Against the Panthers: A Study of Repression in America*. New York: Harlem River Press, 1996.

——. "We Are Nationalists and Internationalists." In *The Coming of the New International: A Revolutionary Anthology*, edited by John Gerassi. New York: The World Publishing Co., 1971.

Newton, Huey, and Ericka Huggins. *Insights and Poems*. San Francisco: City Light Books, 1975.

Newton, Huey, and Erik H. Erikson. *In Search of Common Ground: Conversations with Erik H. Erikson and Huey P. Newton*. New York: W.W. Norton and Company, 1973.

Newton, Michael. *Bitter Grain: Huey Newton and the Black Panther Party*. Los Angeles: Holloway House Publishing Company, 1991.

Nkrumah, Kwame. *Neo-Colonialism: The Last Stage of Imperialism*. New York: International Publishers, 1966.

——. *Revolutionary Path*. New York: International Publishers, 1973.

Nobles, Wade. *African Psychology: Toward Its Reclamation, Reascension and Revitalization*. Oakland, CA: Black Family Institute Publications, 1980.

Obadele, Imari Abubakari (Milton Henry). *Free the Land!: The True Story of the Trials of the RNA-11 in Mississippi and the Continuing Struggle to Establish an Independent Black Nation in Five States of the Deep South*. Washington, DC: House of Songhay, 1984.

——."The Republic of New Africa: 'We Are the Government for the Non-Self-Governing Blacks Held Captive in the United States.' " In *Black Nationalism in America,* edited by John Bracey. Washington, D.C.: House of Songhay, 1984.

Obenga, Theophile. *Ancient Egypt and Black Africa*. London: Karnak House, 1992.

Oberschall, Anthony. *Social Movements: Ideologies, Interests and Identities*. New Brunswick, NJ: Transaction Publishers, 1993.

Omi, Michael, and Howard Winant. *Racial Formation in the United States: From the 1960s to the 1980s*. New York: Routledge, Kegan and Paul, 1986.

O'Reilly, Kenneth. *"Racial Matters": The FBI's Secret File on Black America, 1960–1972.* New York: The Free Press, 1989.

Parenti, Michael. *Inventing Reality: The Politics of News Media.* 2nd edition. New York: St. Martin's Press, 1993.

Pearson, Hugh. *The Shadow of the Panther: Huey P. Newton and the Price of Black Power in America.* Reading, MA: Addison-Wesley, 1994.

Perry, Bruce. *Malcolm: Life of a Man Who Changed Black America.* Barrytown, NY: Station Hill Press, 1991.

Phillips, Kevin. *The Emerging Republican Majority.* New York: Doubleday, 1970.

Pinkney, Alphonso. *Red, Black and Green: Black Nationalism in the United States.* Cambridge: Cambridge University Press, 1976.

Powell, Colin. *My American Journey.* New York: Random House, 1995.

Presley, Cora. *Kikuyu Women: The Mau Mau Rebellion and Social Change in Kenya.* Boulder, CO: Westview Press, 1992.

Quandt, William B. *Revolution and Political Leadership: Algeria 1954-1968.* Cambridge: MIT Press, 1969.

Radhakrishnan, R. "Toward an Effective Intellectual: Foucault or Gramsci." In *Intellectuals, Aesthetics, Politics and Culture,* edited by Bruce Robbins. Minneapolis: University of Minnesota Press, 1990.

Rainwater, Lee, and William L. Yancey. *The Moynihan Report and the Politics of Controversy.* Cambridge: The MIT Press, 1967.

Rajshekar, V.T. "The Black Untouchables of India: Reclaiming Our Cultural Heritage." In *African Presence in Early Asia,* edited by Ivan Van Sertima and Runoko Rashidi. New Brunswick, NJ: Transaction Publishers, 1988.

Rashidi, Runoko. "Dalits: The Black Untouchables of India." In *African Presence in Early Asia,* edited by Ivan Van Sertima and Runoko Rashidi. New Brunswick, NJ: Transaction Books, 1988.

Reed, Adolph, Jr. *The Jesse Jackson Phenomenon: the Crisis of Purpose in Afro-American Politics.* New Haven, CT: Yale University Press, 1986.

Richards, Dona Marimba. *Let the Circle Be Unbroken: The Implications of African Spirituality in the Diaspora.* Trenton, NJ: The Red Sea Press, 1980.

Richards, Marilyn, ed. *Maria W. Stewart, America's First Black Woman Political Writer: Essays and Speeches.* Bloomington, IN: Indiana University Press, 1987.

Rifkin, Jeremy. *The End of Work: The Decline of the Global Labor Force and the Dawn of the Post-Market Era.* New York: G.P. Putnam's Sons, 1995.

Roediger, David. *The Wages of Whiteness: Race and the Making of the American Working Class.* New York: Verso, 1991.

Rose, Tricia. *Black Noise: Rap Music and Black Culture in Contemporary America.* Middletown, CT: Wesleyan University Press, 1994.

Ross, Robert J. S. "The Relative Decline of Relative Autonomy: Global Capitalism and the Political Economy of State Change." In *Changes in the State: Causes and Consequences,* edited by. Edward S. Greenberg and Thomas F. Macer. Newbury Park, CA: Sage Publications, 1990.

Sale, Kirkpatrick. *SDS.* New York: Vintage Books, 1974.

Sales, William W., Jr., *From Civil Rights to Black Liberation: Malcolm X and the Organization of Afro-American Unity.* Boston: South End Press, 1994.

Schanche, Don A. *The Panther Paradox.* New York: David McKay Co., 1970.

Scott, James C. *Domination and the Arts of Resistance: Hidden Transcripts.* New Haven, CT: Yale University Press, 1990.

Scott, Kody (Sanyika Shakur). *Monster: The Autobiography of an L.A. Gang Member.* New York: Penguin Books, 1993.

Seale, Bobby. "Free Huey." In *Rhetoric of Black Revolution,* edited by Arthur L. Smith. Boston: Allyn and Bacon, 1969.

————. *A Lonely Rage: The Autobiography of Bobby Seale*. New York: Times Books, 1978.

————. *Seize the Time: The Story of the Black Panther Party and Huey P. Newton*. 1970. Reprint, Baltimore: Black Classic Press, 1991.

Sera, Tani E., and Kae Sera. *False Nationalism, False Internationalism*. Chicago: A Seeds Beneath to Sow Publication, 1985.

Shakur, Assata. *Assata: An Autobiography*. Westport, CT: Lawrence Hill and Company, 1987.

————. *From Somewhere in the World: Assata Shakur Speaks—Message to the New Afrikan Nation*. New York: New Afrikan Women's Organization, 1980.

Sheehy, Gail. *Panthermania: The Clash of Black Against Black in One American City*. New York: Harper & Row Publishers, 1971.

Sim, John. *The Grass Roots Press: America's Community Newspapers*. Ames, IA: Iowa State University Press, 1970.

Sims, Charles R. "Armed Defense." In *Black Protest: History, Documents and Analyses, 1619 to the Present*, edited by Joanne Grant. Greenwich, CT: Fawcett World Library, 1968.

Sinclair, John. *Guitar Army: Prison Writings*. New York: Douglas Books, 1972.

Singh, Nikhil. "Toward an Effective Anti-Racism." In *Politics and Theory in the Black World*, edited by Manning Marable. New York: Verso. Forthcoming.

Skolnick, Jerome H. *The Politics of Protest: A Task Force Report Submitted by the National Commission on the Causes and Prevention of Violence*. New York: Simon and Schuster, 1969.

Sleeper, Jim. *The Closest of Strangers: Liberalism and the Politics of Race in New York*. New York: W.W. Norton, 1990.

Smith, Neil. *Uneven Development: Nature, Capital and the Production of Space*. London: Basil Blackwell, 1991.

Smith, Robert C. *We Have No Leaders: African Americans in the Post-Civil Rights Era*. Albany, New York: State University of New York Press, 1996.

Smith, William Gardner. *Return to Black America*. Englewood Cliffs, NJ: Prentice-Hall Publishers, 1970.

Soja, Edward. *Postmodern Geographies: The Reassertion of Space in Critical Social Theory*. London: Verso, 1989.

Staples, Robert. *The Urban Plantation, Racism and Colonialism in the Post Civil Rights Era*. Oakland, CA: Black Scholar Press, 1987.

Stavrianos, L.S. *Global Rift: The Third World Comes of Age*. New York: William Morrow & Co., 1981.

Tackwood, Louis E., and The Citizens Research and Investigation Committee. *The Glass House Tapes*. New York: Avon Books, 1973.

Taussig, Michael. "Malfecium: State Fetishism." In *Fetishism as Cultural Discourse*, edited by Emily Apter and William Peitz. Ithaca, NY: Cornell University Press, 1993.

Thompson, Robert Farris. *Flash of the Spirit: African & Afro-American Art & Philosophy*. New York: Vintage Books, 1984.

Travis, Dempsey. J. *An Autobiography of Black Politics*. Chicago: Urban Research Press, 1987.

Tucker, Robert C., ed. *The Marx-Engels Reader*. New York: W.W. Norton and Company, 1978.

Turner, W. Burghardt, and Joyce Moore Turner, eds. *Richard B. Moore, Caribbean Militant in Harlem: Collected Writings, 1920–1972*. Bloomington, IN: Indiana University Press, 1988.

Ungar, Sanford J. *FBI: An Uncensored Look Behind the Walls*. Boston: Little, Brown and Company, 1976.

Van Deburg, William L. *New Day in Babylon: The Black Power Movement and American Culture, 1965–1975*. Chicago: University of Chicago Press, 1992.

Van Peebles, Mario, Ula Y. Taylor, and J. Tarika Lewis. *Panther: A Pictorial History of the Black Panthers and the Story Behind the Film*. New York: New Market Press, 1995

Wallace, Michelle. *Black Macho and the Myth of the Superwoman*. New York: Dial Press, 1978.

Walters, Ronald. *Black Presidential Politics in America: A Strategic Approach*. Albany, NY: State University of New York Press, 1988.

Walton, Hanes. *The Negro in Third Party Politics*. Philadelphia: Dorance, 1969.

Weber, Max. *From Max Weber: Essays in Sociology*. New York: Oxford University Press, 1940.

Weisbrot, Robert. *Freedom Bound: A History of America's Civil Rights Movement*. New York: W.W. Norton, 1991.

West, Cornel. "The New Cultural Politics of Difference." In *Out There: Marginalization and Contemporary Culture*, edited by Russell Ferguson, et al. New York: New Museum of Contemporary Art, 1990.

——. "The Paradoxes of Afro-American Rebellion." In *The Sixties Without Apology*, edited by Sohnya Sahres, et al. Minneapolis: University of Minnesota Press, 1984.

White, Edmund. *Genet: A Biography*. New York: Alfred A. Knopf, 1993.

Wilkens, Roy, and Ramsey Clark. "The Black Panthers, 1968–1969 'How Serious and Deadly the Game.'" In *Voices of Freedom: An Oral History of the Civil Rights Movement from the 1950's through the 1980's*, edited by Henry Hampton and Steve Fayer, with Sarah Flynn. New York: Bantam Books, 1980.

——. *Search and Destroy: A Report by the Commission of Inquiry into the Black Panthers and the Police*. New York: Metropolitan Applied Research Center, Inc., 1973.

Williams, Evelyn. *Inadmissible Evidence: The Story of the African-American Trial Lawyer Who Defended the Black Liberation Army*. Chicago: Lawrence Hills Books, 1993.

Williams, Juan. *Eyes on the Prize: America's Civil Rights Years, 1954–1965*. New York: Viking-Penguin, 1987.

Williams, Linda. "Black Political Progress in the 1980s: The Electoral Arena." In *The New Black Politics: The Search for Political Power*, edited by Michael Preston, Lenneal Henderson, and Paul Puryear. New York: Longman, 1987.

Williams, Robert. *Negroes with Guns*. New York: Marzani and Munsell, 1962.

Winston, Henry, ed. "Crisis of the Black Panther Party." In *Strategy for a Black Agenda; A Critique of New Theories of Liberation in the United States and Africa*. New York: International Publishers, 1973.

Wolfe, Tom. *Radical Chic and Mau-Mauing the Flak Catchers*. New York: Farrar, Straus and Giroux, 1977.

Wolfenstein, Victor. *Victims of Democracy: Malcolm X and the Black Revolution*. London: Free Association Books, 1989.

Wright, Bruce. *Black Robes, White Justice*. Secaucus, NJ: Lyle Stuart, 1987.

Yee, Shirley. *Black Women Abolitionists:Study in Activism*. Knoxville: University of Knoxville Press, 1992.

Young, Robert. *White Mythologies: Writing History and the West*. London: Routledge, 1990.

Zimbroth, Peter L. *Perversions of Justice: The Prosecution and Acquittal of the Panther 21*. New York: The Viking Press, 1974.

Journal Articles

Adler, Karen S. "Always Leading Our Men in Service and Sacrifice: Amy Jacques Garvey, Feminist, Black Nationalist." *Gender and Society* 6 (1992): 346–375.

Appadurai, Arjun. "Disjuncture and Difference in the Global Cultural Economy." *Theory, Culture and Society* 7 (1990): 295–310.

Appadurai, Arjun et al. "Editorial Comment: On Thinking the Black Public Sphere." *Public Culture* 71 (Fall 1994): xii.

Arrighi, Giovanni. "Marxist Century, American Century: The Making and Remaking of the World Labor Movement." *New Left Review* 179 (1990):29–65.

Assagi, Mel. "Black Panthers Today: Pussycats? Or Stalking Cats?" *Sepia* 28 (1977): 24–29.

Barron, Sahu. "A New Order in Babylon: The Revolutionary Legacy of the Black Panther Party." *Liberation!: Journal of Revolutionary Marxism* (December 1989): pp. 4–5.

Bernstein, Deborah. "Conflict and Protest in Israeli Society: The Case of the Black Panthers of Israel." *Youth and Society* 14 (1984): 129–151.

Black Panther Party (Guest Editors). *Co-Evolution Quarterly: Supplement to the Whole Earth Catalog*, no. 3 (23 March 1974).

"Black Scholar Interviews Kathleen Cleaver." *Black Scholar* 2 (December 1971): 54–59.

Bluestone, Barry. "Deindustrialization and Unemployment in America." *Review of Black Political Economy* 12 (3) (Fall 1983): 27–42.

Bukhari, Safiya. "Coming of Age: Notes from a New Afrikan Revolutionary." *African Prisoner of War Journal* 7 (1988): 10–15.

Calloway, Carolyn R. "Group Cohesiveness in the Black Panther Party." *Journal of Black Studies* 8 (September 1977): 55–74.

Cassinelli, C.W. "The Law of Oligarchy." *The American Political Science Review* 47 (1953): 773–784.

Cleaver, Eldridge. "On Lumpen Ideology." *Black Scholar* 3 (1972): 2–10.

Collins, John. "Oodgeroo of the Tribe Nonnuccal." *Race and Class* 35 (1994): 77–87.

Courtright, John A. "Rhetoric of the Gun: An Analysis of the Rhetorical Modifications of the Black Panther Party." *Journal of Black Studies* 4 (1974): 249–267.

Cummings, Bruce. "Global Realm With No Limit, Global Realm With No Name." *Radical History Review* 57 (1993): 46–59.

Cunningham, Kitty. "Black Caucus Flexes Muscle On Budget and More?" *Congressional Quarterly Weekly Report*, July 3, 1993, 1711–1715.

Davis, Angela. "Reflections on the Black Woman's Role in the Community of Slaves." *Black Scholar* 2 (December 1971): 3–15.

Davis, Mike. "Who Killed L.A.?: Political Autopsy." *New Left Review* (1993): 3–28.

Dent, David J. "Million Man March: Whose Reality?" *Black Renaissance* 1(Fall 1996): 58–69.

Duara, Prasnejit. "The Displacement of Tension to the Tension of Displacement." *Radical History Review* 57 (Fall 1993): 60–64.

Echols, Alice. "We Gotta Get Out Of This Place: Notes Toward a Remapping of the Sixties." *Socialist Review* 92, no. 2 (1992): 9–33.

Fraser, Nancy. "Rethinking the Public Sphere: A Contribution to the Critique of Actually Existing Democracy." *Social Text* 25/26 (1990): 56–80.

Gates, Henry Louis. "Critical Fanonism." *Critical Inquiry* 17, no. 3 (Spring 1991): 457–470.

Geyer, Michael. "Concerning the Question: Is Imperialism a Useful Category of Historical Analysis?" *Radical History Review* 57 (1993): 65–72.

Gitlin, Todd. "From Universality to Difference: Notes on the Fragmentation of the Idea of the Left." *Contention* 2, no. 2 (Winter 1993): 15–40.

Henderson, Errol A. "Black Nationalism And Rap Music." *Journal of Black Studies* 26 (January 1996): 308–339.

Hervé, Julia. "Black Scholar Interviews Kathleen Cleaver." *Black Scholar* 2 (1971): 55–66.

Higginbotham, Evelyn Brooks. "African-American Women's History and the Metalanguage of Race." *Signs* 17, no. 2 (Winter 1992): 251–274.

Higham, John. "Multiculturalism and Universalism: A History and Critique." *American Quarterly* 44, no. 2 (1993): 195–256

Hine, Darlene Clark. "Rape and the Inner Lives of Black Women in the Middle West: Preliminary Thoughts on the Culture of Dissemblance." *Signs* 14, no. 4 (Summer 1989): 912–920.

Jameson, Frederic. "Postmodernism, or the Cultural Logic of Late Capitalism." *New Left Review* 146 (176): 53–92.

Jones, Charles E. "The Political Repression of the Black Panther Party, 1966–1971: The Case of the Oakland Bay Area." *Journal of Black Studies* 18, no. 4 (June 1988): 415–421.

Karenga, Maulana Ron."Kawaida and Its Critics: A Sociohistorical Analysis." *Journal of Black Studies* 7 (December 1977): 133–134.

——."A Response to Muhammad Ahmad." *Black Scholar* 9 (July–August 1978): 55–56.

Kershaw, Terry. "The Emerging Paradigm in Black Studies." *The Western Journal of Black Studies* 13, no. 1 (1989): 45–51.

King, Deborah. "Multiple Jeopardy, Multiple Consciousness: The Context of a Black Feminist Ideology." *Signs* 14, no. 1 (Autumn 1988): pp. 42–72.

Kleffner, Heike. "The Black Panthers; interviews with Geronimo ji Jaga Pratt and Mumia Abu-Jamal." *Race & Class* 35, no. 1 (1993): 9–18.

Lane, Alycee J. "Newton's Law." *BLK* (March 1991): 11.

Leffall, Doris C., and Janet L. Sims. "Mary McLeod Bethune—The Educator." *The Journal of Negro Education* 45 (1976): 342–359.

McLemore, Leslie B. "Black Political Socialization and Political Change: The Black Panther Platform as a Model of Radical Political Socialization." *Negro Educational Review* 26 (1975): 155–166.

Marx, Gary T. "Thoughts on a Neglected Category of Social Movement Participant: The Agent Provocateur and the Informant." *American Journal of Sociology*, no. 2 (1974): 402–442.

Moore, Richard Dhoruba. "Strategies of Repression Against the Black Movement." *Black Scholar* 12 (May–June 1981): 10–16.

——. "U.S. Black Political Prisoners: A Threat to America's International Human Rights Campaign."*Black Scholar* 10 (March–April 1979):17–22

Mori, Jim. "The Ideological Development of the Black Panther Party." *Cornell Journal of Social Relations* 12, no. 2 (1977): 137–155.

Munford, Clarence J. "The Fallacy of Lumpen Ideology." *Black Scholar* 4 (July–August 1973): 47–51.

Parrini, Carl. "The Age of Ultraimperialism." *Radical History Review* 57 (1993): 7–20.

Payne, Charles. "Ella Baker and Models of Social Change." *Signs* 14 (1989): 885–899.

"RNA Freedom Fighters: A Continuing Episode of Human Rights Violations in Amerika." *Breakthrough* 4, no.1 (Winter 1980): 26–30.

Robinson, Cedric. "The Appropriation of Frantz Fanon." *Race and Class* 35, no. 1 (1993): 79–91.

Robinson, Michael."The Van Peebleses Prowl Through the Panthers' History." *American Visions: The Magazine of Afro-American Culture* 10, no. 2 (April/May 1995): 16–18.

Rustin, Bayard. "From Protest to Politics: The Future of the Civil Rights Movement." *Commentary* 39(1965): 25–31.

Singh, Nikhil Pau. "Toward an Effective Anti-Racism." *Race and Reason* 3 (1997): 67–70.

Smith, Robert C. "Black Power and the Transformation from Protest to Politics." *Political Science Quarterly*, 96 (1981): 431–44.

Spartacist League. "Rise and Fall of the Panthers: End of the Black Power Era." *Marxist Bulletin* 5 (1978): 34–45.

Tolbert, Emory J. "Federal Surveillance of Marcus Garvey and the UNIA." *Journal of Ethnic Studies* 14, no. 4 (Winter 1987): 27–31, 36.

Valentine, Charles, and Betty Lou Valentine. "The Man and the Panthers." *Politics and Society* 2, no. 3 (Spring 1972): 273–286.

White, E. Frances. "Africa On My Mind: Gender, Counter Discourse and African-American Nationalism." *Journal of Women's History* 2, no. 1(Spring 1990): 73–97.

Windes, Richard. "The Innovational Movement: A Rhetorical Theory." *Quarterly Journal of Speech* 62 (April 1975): 140–53.

Dissertations, Theses, and Other Unpublished Works

Alexander, Nikol G. "A World Without Feminism?: Reading Gender In(to) Nationalist Politics" and "Selling Black: Black Public Intellectuals and the Commercialization of Black and Black Feminist Studies (Or Race, Class, and Gender Go to Market)."

Askin, Richard. "Comparative Characteristics of the Alternative Press." Master's thesis, University of Texas at Austin, 1970.

Brown, Angela Darlean. "Servants of the People: A History of Women in the Black Panther Party." Senior thesis, Harvard University, 1992.

Cleaver, Kathleen. "The Evolution of the International Section of the Black Panther Party in Algiers 1969–1972." Senior essay, Yale University, 9 December 1983.

Gates, Henry Louis, Jr. "After the Revolution: the Odyssey of Eldridge Cleaver." (unpublished interview, 1975), 5–8.

Holder, Kit Kim. "The History of the Black Panther Party 1966–1972: A Curriculum Tool for Afrikan-American Studies." Ph.D. diss., University of Massachusetts, 1990.

Hopkins, Charles. "The Deradicalization of the Black Panther Party, 1967–1973." Ph.D. diss., University of North Carolina at Chapel Hill, 1978.

Matthews, Tracye A. "Myth, Meaning and Macho: Black Popular Culture and Remembrances of the Black Panther Party." Paper presented at "The Black Panther Party Revisited: Reflections and Scholarship." A 30th Anniversary Commemorative Conference of the Founding of the Black Panther Party, Department of African-American Studies, Georgia State University, Atlanta, GA, 24–5 October 1996.

Newton, Huey P. "War Against the Panthers: A Study of Repression in America. Ph.D. diss., University of California at Santa Cruz, 1980.

Singh, Nikhil P. "Protestant, Catholic, Jew: An Essay in American Religious Sociology." Paper presented at the annual meeting of the Organization of American Historians, Atlanta, GA., April 1994.

Stanford, Maxwell (Akbar Muhammad Ahmad). "Revolutionary Action Movement (RAM): A Case Study of an Urban Revolutionary Movement in Western Capitalist Society." Masters thesis, Atlanta University, 1986.

Umoja, Akinyele. "Eye for an Eye: The Role of Armed Resistance in the Mississippi Freedom Movement, 1955–1980." Ph.D. diss., Emory University, 1996.

Black Panther Newspaper Articles

"Address of Deborah Williams At First Intercommunal Youth Institute Graduation Exercise." *The Black Panther*, 22 June 1974, p. 2.

Alexander, Roberta. "UFAF Women's Panel: Roberta Alexander at Conference." *The Black* Panther, 2 August 1969, p. 7.

"Angela Davis Day-Care Center Raided." *The Black Panther,* 29 January 1972, p.9.

Anonymous. "Black Woman, By a Black Revolutionary." *The Black Panther*, 14 September 1968, p. 6.

Anonymous. "'Subjectivism'...from a Male's Point of View." *The Black Panther*, March 1969, p. 9.

"B.P.P. Member Appointed to Civil Service Commission." *The Black Panther,* 24 September 1977, p. 3.

"B.P.P. Withdraws from Poverty Program." *The Black Panther*, 3 November 1973, p. 5.

Bartholomew, Gloria. "A Black Woman's Thoughts." *The Black Panther*, 28 September 1968, p. 11.

"Behind the Walls." *The Black Panther*, 1–14 October 1979, pp. 8–9.

Bell, Herman. "The B.P.P. and Political Prisoners." *The Black Panther Black Community News Service Memorial Issue*, Spring 1991, p. 11.

"Black Genocide: Sickle Cell Anemia." *The Black Panther*, 10 April 1971, p. 1.

Black Panther Party Central Committee. "Enemies of the People." *The Black Panther*, 13 February 1971, pp. 12–14.

"Black Panther Party Trains Houstonians for Free Medical Testing Program." *The Black Panther*, 22 June 1974, p. 5.

"Black Panther Wins Seat on County Board." *The Black Panther,* 22 May 1976, p. 1+.

"Black Woman." *The Black Panther*, 14 September, 1968, p. 6.

"Bobby in Run-Off." *The Black Panther*, 21 April 1973, p. 3, A, B, and C.

Booth, Byron. "Beyond Demarcation." *The Black Panther*, 25 October 1969, p. 16.

"Brothers in the New York State Concentration Camp from the Jonathan P. Jackson Commune." *The Black Panther*, 9 January 1971, p. B.

Brown, H. Rap. "A Letter from Prison to my Black Brothers and Sisters (written 2 February 1968)." *The Black Panther*, 16 March 1968, p. 7.

Bukhari-Alston, Safiya. "The Question of Sexism Within the Black Panther Party." *Black Panther Community News Service*, Fall/Winter 1993, p. 3.

Carroll, Al. "On Illegitimate Capitalist 'The Game.'" *The Black Panther*, June 20, 1970, p. 7.

"Case Against Chairman Bobby and Ericka Dismissed." *The Black Panther*, 29 May 1971, p. 6.

"Chairman Bobby Seale for Mayor!" *The Black Panther*, 20 May 1972, special supplement, pp. A, C.

"Chicago Model Cities Election—December 19th People's Candidates Campaign for Public Offices." *The Black Panther*, 7 December 1991, p. 7.

"Cindy Smallwood—A Short and Dedicated Life." *The Black Panther*, 10 February 1973, p. 4.

Cleaver, Eldridge. "Community Imperialism." *The Black Panther*, 18 May 1968, p. 10.

———."From Somewhere in the Third World." *The Black Panther*, 12 July 1969, p. 13.

———. "Letter to My Black Brothers in Vietnam." *The Black Panther*, 2 May 1970, p. 10B.

———."Message to Sister Ericka Huggins of the Black Panther Party, Excerpt from Tape of Eldridge Breaking His Silence from Somewhere in the Third World." *The Black Panther*, 5 July 1969.

———."Solidarity of the Peoples Until Victory or Death!" The Black Panther, 25 October 1969, pp. 12–13.

———. "Statement to GIs in South Vietnam." *The Black Panther*, 26 September 1970, p. 14.

Coates, Paul. "Update on Political Prisoners in Baltimore: Marshall Eddie Conway." *Black Panther: Black Community News Service* 1, Spring 1991, pp. 1, 15.

Cox, Don. "Organizing Self-Defense Groups." *The Black Panther*, 23 January 1971, p. 6.

"Creative Curriculum, 150 Students, Oakland Community School Expands Services to Youth. *The Black Panther*, 18 September 1976, p. 4.

Culberson, June. "The Role of The Black Revolutionary Woman." *The Black Panther*, 4 May, 1969, p. 9.

Duren, B. Kwaku. "We Demand Peace, Justice and Reparations." *The Black Panther International Newspaper: The Official Newspaper of the New African American Vanguard Movement*, Summer 1996, p. 1.

"Elaine Brown Announces Candidacy." *The Black Panther*, 28 December 1974, p.3.

"Elaine Brown's Candidacy for Oakland City Council Threatened." *The Black Panther*, 9 November 1974, p. 3.

"Elaine Brown's Candidacy Prompted by Her Concern Over Oakland Conditions." *The Black Panther*, 4 January 1975, p. 5.

"Elaine Hits City Government on Women." *The Black Panther*, 23 June 1973, p.3.

"Enemies of The People." *The Black Panther*, 13 February 1971, p.13.

"Eyewitness Report on Orangeburg Massacre." *The Black Panther*, 16 March 1968, pp. 6, 11.

"Fred Hampton Film." *The Black Panther*, 24 July 1992, p. 13.

"The Government Murdered My Sister at Jonestown." *The Black Panther*, 29 December 1978, p. 3.

Greene, Linda. "The Black Revolutionary Woman." *The Black Panther*, 28 September 1968, p. 11.

Hampton, Fred. "You Can Kill a Revolutionary But You Can't Kill a Revolution." *The Black Panther*, 16 January 1970, p. 12.

Harrison, Linda. "On Cultural Nationalism." *The Black Panther*, 2 February 1969, p. 3.

"The Heroic Palestinian Women." *The Black Panther*, 26 July 1969, p. 7.

"Huey P. Newton Intercommunal Youth Institute." *The Black Panther*, 27 March 1971, p.1.

"Israeli Doctors Sterilize Arab Women." *The Black Panther*, 9 February 1974, p. 17.

Jackson, George. "A Tribute to Three Slain Brothers." *The Black Panther*, 16 January 1970, p. 6.

"Let Rap Rap." *The Black Panther*, 16 March 1968, p. 7.

Lewis, Raymond. "Montreal: Bobby-Seale-Panthers Take Control." *The Black Panther*, 21 December 1968, pp. 5–6.

"The Murder of Fred Hampton." *The Black Panther*, 10 July 1971, p. 12.

Murray, George Mason. "Cultural Nationalism." *The Black Panther*, 3 March 1969, p. 4.

Neal, Father Earl A. "The Role of the Church and the Survival Program." *The Black Panther*, 15 May 1971, p. 11.

"New Sterilization Guidelines." *The Black Panther*, 2 March 1974, p. 9.

Newton, Huey P. "Executive Mandate No. 3." *The Black Panther*, 16 March 1968, p. 1.

——. "Let Us Hold High the Banner of Intercommunalism." *The Black Panther*, 23 January 1971, p. F.

——. "Let Us Hold High the Banner of Intercommunalism and the Invincible Thoughts of Huey P. Newton, Minister of Defense and Supreme Commander of the Black Panther Party." *The Black Panther*, 2 January 1971, pp. A–H.

——. "On the Defection of Eldridge Cleaver from the Black Panther Party and the Defection of the Black Panther Party from the Black Community." *The Black*

Panther Intercommunal News Service, 17 April 1971, Supplemental Section, p. C.

"O.C.L.C.'s 2nd Annual Martial Arts Friendship Tournament Huge Success." *The Black Panther*, 29 January 1977, p. 23.

"Oakland Community School: A History of Serving the Youth Body and Soul." *The Black Panther*, 16 October 1976, p. 4.

"On the Purge of Geronimo from the Black Panther Party." *The Black Panther*, 23 January 1971, p. 7.

"Panther Kidnapped and Beaten by Special Gestapo Pigs." *The Black Panther,* 6 February 1971, p. 7.

"Panthers Sweep Berkeley Elections!" *The Black Panther*, 10 June 1972, p. 2.

"The People Speak." *The Black Panther*, 20 December 1969, p. 13.

"The People's Fight Against Sickle Cell Anemia Begins." *The Black Panther*, 22 May 1971, p. 10.

"People's Free Busing Program." *The Black Panther*, 2 August 1970, p. 9.

"The People's Political Machine Victors." *The Black Panther*, 19 May 1973, p. 3 and A.

"People's Temple Hit List Exposed As Fake." *The Black Panther*, 29 December 1978, p. 3.

"A People's Victory in Oakland." *The Black Panther*, 19 May 1973, p. 3 and A.

"Pig Brutality." *The Black Panther*, 21 Saturday 1970, pp. 4–10.

Pinderhughes, Cappy. "Free Our Sisters." *The Black Panther*, 6 December 1969, p. 2.

"Pregnant Black Woman Brutally Murdered by L.A. Police." *The Black Panther*, 20 November 1971, pp. 3, 4.

"Repression of the Black Panther Newspaper." *The Black Panther*, 8 August 1970, p. 11.

"Rice-Poindexter Case History Countdown to Justice Fact Sheet." *The Black Panther* 1, Fall 1991, pp. 3, 18–19.

"S.A.F.E. Wins Victory for Senior Citizen Home." *The Black Panther*, 26 January 1975, p. 4.

Scalan, Dan. "Guerrilla Acts of Sabotage and Terrorism in the United States, 1965–1970." *The Black Panther*, 2 January 1971, p. 9.

Seale, Bobby. "Black Lawyers Are Jiving." *The Black Panther*, 18 May 1968, p. 5.

——. "Black Power, Black Lawyers, and White Courts." *The Black Panther*, 18 May 1968, p. 5.

"Seniors Against a Fearful Environment." *The Black Panther*, 16 December 16 1972, p. 3 and 11.

"750 at Rally for Reproduction Rights." *The Black Panther,* 1 October 1977, p. 11.

Shoats, Russell. "Statement of Russell 'Maroon' Shoats." *The Black Panther* 4, Winter 1995, pp. 1, 22, and 25.

"S.O.S.: Win $1000 in 'Support Our School' Donation Drive." *The Black Panther*. 2 April 1977, p. 3.

"To All Brothers of Misfortune." *The Black Panther*, 16 January 1970, p. 6.

"Tony Kline, John George, Elaine Brown 1–2–3 in 8th District Caucus for Brown." *The Black Panther*, 17 April 1976, p. 14.

"Twenty-eight Black Panther Party Members Murdered by U.S. Government." *The Black Panther*, 30 December 1978–12 January 1979, p. 16.

"Unite to Defeat Reading." *The Black Panther*, 21 April 1973, pp. 3, A, B, and C.

"The Victors." *The Black Panther*, 10 December 1969, p. 1.

"Vote August 19, 1972." *The Black Panther*, 12 August 1978, special supplement D.

"We Were Victorious: Interview With Elaine Brown." *The Black Panther*, 28 April 1973, p. 3.

"Weekend of Solidarity with the Cuban Revolution." *The Black Panther*, 24 July 1971, p.13.

"Welcome Home Huey!" *The Black Panther*, 5 July 1977, p.1+.

"What Really Happened in Los Angeles." *The Black Panther*, 20 December 1969, p. 12.

"Why Was Denzil Dowell Killed?" *The Black Panther*, 25 April 1967, p. 4.

"Winston-Salem Free Ambulance Service Opens." *The Black Panther*, 16 February 1974, p. 3.

Other Newspaper Articles

"Alien-Radical Tie Disputed by CIA" *The New York Times*, 25 May 1973, p. 1.

Applebome, Peter. "Bitter Racial Rift in Dallas Board Reflects Ills in Many Other Cities." *New York Times*, 27 June 1976, p. A1–A8.

Arnold, Martin. "N.A.A.C.P. Will Give $50,000 to Aid Panther-Police Inquiry." *New York Times*, 14 May 1970, p. 34.

Associated Press. "Judge Orders New Trial for Former Panther," *Washington Post*, 30 May 1997, A7.

Associated Press. "Urban League Asks Support for Self-help." *Washington Post*, 21 January 1994, p. A3.

Ayres, B. Drummond, Jr., "A Black Panther is Free at Last." *New York Times*, 15 June 1997, sec. 2.

Baer, Susan. "Building Coalitions, Realizing Ambitions, Kweisi Mfume Comes into His Own." *Baltimore Sun*, 1 August 1993, p. 1.

"Bail Hearing for Huey Newton." *San Francisco Chronicle*, 4 August 1970, p. 3.

"Baltimore Police Raid Panther Headquarters." *Guardian*, 9 May 1970, p. 5.

Bennett, Allegra. "Claws of the Panthers: Elaine Brown Surviving the 'Trauma' of Huey Newton and the Party." *Washington Times*, 22 March 1993, p. D2.

Bigart, Homer. "U.S. Troops Flown In For Panther Rally; New Haven Braces for Protest By 20,000." *New York Times*, 1 May 1970, p. 1.

"The Black Caucus Gets Mugged." *New York Times*, 25 September 1993, p. 22.

"Black Nationalist Organizations Unite At Historic Atlanta Summit: The New Afrikan Liberation Front is Launched." *The City Sun*, 27 September–3 October 1995, p. 10.

"Black Panther Men Accused of Plot." *London Times*, 27 November 1968, p. 6.

"Black Panther Party for Shirley Chisholm." *New York Times*, 28 April 1972, p. 4A.

"Black Panther Pleads Guilty in Slaying." *New York Times*, 2 December 1969, p. 59.

"Black Panthers Form Party." *New York Times*, 19 January 1972, p. 6.

"The Black Panthers—Two Paths." *New York Times*, 24 August 1989, 24A.

Bond-Staples, Grace. "Drugs, Racism, Urban Neglect Lead to Black Panther Revival." *Fort Worth Star-Telegram*, 6 September 1991, pp. 1, 13.

Boyer, Edward J. "Pratt Strides Into Freedom." *Los Angeles Times*, 11 June 1997, pp. A1; A17.

Brown, Malaika. "Social Movement: Picking Up the Power." *Los Angeles Sentinel*, 6 July 1995, p. 1.

"C.I.A. Reportedly Recruited Blacks for Surveillance of Panthers." *New York Times*, 17 March 1978, p. A1.

Caldwell, Earl. "The Panthers: Dead or Regrouping. " *The New York Times*, 1 March 1971, p. 1.

Campos, Raquel. "Panther Trial Begins in New York City." *Guardian,* 31 October 1970, p. 6.

Clancy, Paul. "Black Panther Co-Founder Slain." *USA Today*, 23 August 1989, p. A2.

Clark, Robin. "Bobby Seale Has Praise, No Tears for Huey Newton." *Washington Post*, 24 August 1989, p. A3.

Cleaver, Eldridge. "Black Panther Black Racism." *Open City: Weekly Review of the L.A. Renaissance*, 27 December–2 January 1968, p. 1.

Clifford, Timothy. "Convicted Activist Claims Frame-Up." *New York Newsday*, 19 April 1988, p. 19.

Cline, Alan. "Widener's Close Win; Moderates Voted in the East Bay." *San Francisco Examiner,* 16 April 1976, p.14.

Craig, Sarah. "Panther Leader Slain: Early Gay-Rights Supporter Gunned Down." *Windy City Times* (Chicago), 8 August 1989, p. 6.

Darnton, John. "New Haven is Looking with Foreboding to the Murder Trial of Bobby Seale, The Black Panther Leader," *New York Times*, 22 March 1970, p. 57.

"Death Here Tied to Panther Feud." *The New York Times*, 10 March 1971, p. 29.

Delaney, Paul. "Blacks in New Orleans Say They Are Sheltering Panther Leader Wounded in Police Raid." *New York Times*, 20 September 1970, p. 60.

"Democrats Seek to Retain the Young." *New York Times*, 20 May 1972, p. 3A.

Easton, Nina J. "The-60's-Aren't-Dead File: There Are Five Black Panther Movies in the Works." *Los Angeles Times*, 21 July 1991, p. 26.

Endicott, William. "Black Panthers Controlled by Communists Senate Unit Says." *Los Angeles Times*, 4 August 1970, p. 1.

"Ex-Panther in Prison Says Evidence Was Concealed." *New York Times*, 7 April 1989, p. B6.

"Former Black Panther Party Members Argue for New Trial." *The Challenger* (Buffalo), 20 March 1991, p. 21.

Gorney, Cynthia. "Huey Newton, Co-Founder of Black Panthers, Is Slain in Oakland." *Washington Post*, 23 August 1989, A6.

Graham, Renee. "She Still Believes in Panthers." *Boston Globe*, 22 February 1993, p. 32.

Hamlin, Phil. "Groups Vow End to Police Brutality." *The Black Liberator (Chicago)*, May 1969, pp. 1, 9.

Hevesi, Dennis. "Huey Newton Symbolized the Rising Black Anger of a Generation." *New York Times*, 23 August 1989, p. B7.

Houwer, Charles. "Strong Seale Showing—Reading Faces Runoff." *San Francisco Examiner,* 18 April 1973, p. 18.

"Huey Newton Killed; Was a Co-Founder of Black Panthers." *New York Times*, 23 August 1989, p. A1.

Igriega, Robert. "Eldridge for 'Pussy Power.'" *Open City* (Los Angeles), 9 August 1968, p. 1.

"Interview with Bobby Seale." *Berkeley Barb*, 14–20 November, p. 3.

Johnson, Ruby. "Joan Bird and Afeni Shakur, Self-Styled Soldiers in the Panther 'Class Struggle.'" *New York Times*, 19 July 1970, p. 53.

Kaufman, Michael T. "Reactions to the Verdict: Joy, Surprise and Silence." *New York Times*, 14 May 1971, p. 20.

Kershaw, Alex. "The Return of the Black Panthers." *Weekend Guardian* (London, England), 22–23 August 1992, pp. 10–11.

Kissinger, C. Clark. "Serve The People." *Guardian*, 17 May 1969, p. 7.

Kunstler, William. "The Continuing Ordeal of Dhoruba Al-Mujahid Bin Wahad." *The City Sun* (New York), 3 March 28– April 3, 1990, p. 5

"Law of Land Warfare." *The New African*, 4 August 1972, pp. 9, 16.

Lelyveld, Joseph. "New Haven Panther Trial Sees Color Slides of Tortured Victim," *New York Times*, 15 July 1970, p. 45.

Lopez, Nora. "Black Panther Leaders Plan To Be Armed At School Board." *Dallas Morning News*, 12 June 1996, p. 38A.

McNulty, Jennifer. "Huey Newton Slain In Street." *Tampa Tribune*, 23 August 1989, p. 1A.

——. "Newton, Co-Founder of Black Panthers, Shot To Death." *Virginia Pilot* (Norfolk, VA), 23 August 1989, p. 1A.

Merida, Kevin. "Foster Nomination Fails as Vote Blocked Again, Surgeon General Hopeful's Bid Effectively Dead." *Washington Post*, 23 June 1995, pp. A1 and A9.

——. "Jackson to Return to Helm of Chicago-Based Operation PUSH," *Washington Post,* 2 December 1995, p. A11.

Montgomery, Ed. "Dismay Grown in Sausalito on Black Panther as Principal." *San Francisco Sunday Examiner and Chronicle*, 17 August 1969, p. 4A.

Nelson, James B. "McGee Plans Panther Militia." *Milwaukee Sentinel*, 1 March 1990, p. 1.

"New Afrikan Freedom Fighters Day." Quotation by Sekou Odinga. *By Any Means Necessary: Organ of the New Afrikan People's Organization* (New York) 1, August/September 1984, pp. 1, 12.

Oelsner, Lesley. "Joan Bird Freed on $100,000 Bail: Black Panther Let Out 15 Months After Jailing." *New York Times*, 7 July 1970, p. 32.

"Panther Co-Founder Shot to Death." *Richmond Times-Dispatch*, 23 August 1989, p. A2.

"Panther's Conviction Reversed." *Daily News*, 16 March 1990, p. 29.

Parish, Norman. "Black Panthers Co-Founder Critical of McGee's Plan." *Milwaukee Journal*, 6 March 1990, p. 1, 2B.

Pearlstein, Steven, and DeNeed L. Brown. "Black Teens Facing Worse Job Prospects." *Washington Post*, 4 June 1994, pp. A1 and A6.

Pleasant, William. "New Black Nationalist Organization Launched." *Daily Challenge,* 20 September 1995, p. 1.

Raspberry, William. "One that Fell Out of the Sky." *Washington Post,* 20 September 1993, p. A19.

Roemer, John, and Marta Sanchez-Berwick. "Can SOS Be Stopped?" *San Francisco Weekly*, 24 August 1994, pp. 13–15.

"SCLC To Aid 21 Panthers." *Omaha World-Herald* (Omaha, Nebraska), 24 January 1970, p. 4

"SNCC, Panthers Announce Merger." *National Guardian.* 24 February 1968, p. 1.

Schutlte, Erin. "Fight Continues for Political Activist's Release." *Daily Nebraskan*, 8 June 1995, p. 1.

Seale, Bobby. "Bobby Seale Explains Panther Politics." *The Guardian*, February 1970, p. 4.

"17 'Panthers' Arraigned in Sacramento Court: 'Invasion' Cases Continued." *San Francisco Examiner*, 4 February 1967, p. 6.

Sharpe, Rochelle. "In Latest Recession, Only Blacks Suffered Net Employment Loss." *Wall Street Journal*, 14 September 1993, p. A1.

Shenker, Israel. "For Alinsky, Organizers Clutch Key to the Future." *New York Times*, 6 January 1971, p. 39.

Stamberg, Margie. "Women at the UFAF and After." *The Guardian*, 2 August 1969, p. 5.

Sullberger, A.O. "H.U.D. to Foreclose on Soul City, Troubled 'New Town' in Carolina." *New York Times*, 29 June 1979, p. 12A.

——. "Soul City and U.S. Agree on Plan to Liquidate Town." *New York Times*, 5 June 1980, p. 16A.

Turner, Wallace. "Huey Newton Denies Murder and Assault." *New York Times*, 22 November 1977, p. 11.

Vobejda, Barbara. "Children's Defense Fund Cites Gun Violence." *Washington Post*, 21 January 1994, p. A3.

Walker, Alice. "Black Panthers or Black Punks?" *New York Times*, 5 May 1991, p. A23.

Walsh, Edward. "Chavis Accused of Hiding Payment."*Washington Post,* 27 August 1994, p. A3.

———."Chavis Fired by NAACP."*Washington Post,* 21 August 1994, p. A4.

———."Reynolds Sentenced to 5 Years for Sex Offenses, Obstruction; Illinois Congressman Misused a 'Job for Life,' Judge Says." *Washington Post,* 29 September 1995, p. A2.

Walton, A. Scott. "Veteran of Black Panthers Calls New Play 'A Travesty.'"*Atlanta Journal/ Constitution,* 22 January 1995, p. C2.

Watson, Hilbourne. "The Pain of NAFTA—or the Pain of Globalization." *Third World Viewpoint,* Spring 1994, p. 19.

Wexler, Kathryn and William Clairborne. "Rep. Tucker Convicted of Extortion; Congressman Took Bribes While Mayor of Compton, Calif." *Washington Post,* 9 December 1995, pp. A1 and A8.

Wickham, DeWayne. "In Newton's World His Murder Was A Natural Death." *Rochester Democrat and Chronicle* (Rochester, NY), 28 August 1989, p. 6A.

Wilkerson, Isabel. "Call for Black Militia Stuns Milwaukee." *New York Times,* 6 April 1990, p. A2.

Wilson, Chris. "Panther Women Held in Jail." *Guardian,* 18 October 1969, p. 6.

Wooten, James T. "Integrated City Rising on an Old Plantation." *New York Times,* 25 July 1972, p. 24.

Interviews and Speeches

Abdullah, Shareef. Interview by Angela LeBlanc-Ernest. Los Angeles, CA, 4 October 1996.

Abron, JoNina. Interview by Ollie Johnson. Oakland, CA, 31 October 1986.

Abron, JoNina. Telephone Interview by Angela LeBlanc-Ernest. 31 January 1992.

Adams, Frankye Malika. Interview by Tracye Matthews. Harlem, NY, 29 September 1994.

Alexander, Deacon. Interview by Angela LeBlanc-Ernest. Oakland, CA, 10 November 1991.

Alston-Bukhari, Safiya. Interview by Tanya Steele and Rosemari Mealy. WBAI-FM Radio, New York City, 21 March 1992.

Anonymous Interview. Interview by Angela LeBlanc-Ernest. San Francisco, CA, 25 January 1992.

Campbell, Kathleen. Interview by Angela LeBlanc-Ernest. San Francisco, CA, 25 January 1992.

Cleaver, Kathleen. Interview by Angela LeBlanc-Ernest. Brighton, MA, 10 November 1991.

Cleaver, Kathleen. Telephone Interview by Tracye Matthews. 27 November 1994.

Coates, Paul. Interview by Charles E. Jones. Baltimore, MD, 21 April 1993.

Coates, Paul. Interview by Ollie Johnson. Baltimore, MD, 10 September 1994.

Cyril, Janet. Interview by Tracye Matthews. Brooklyn, NY, 29 September 1994.

Duren, B. Kuaku. Interview by Angela LeBlanc-Ernest. Los Angeles, CA, 21 September 1996.

Ehehosi, Masai. Interview by Akinyele Umoja. Chicago, IL, 28 December 1996.

Forbes, Flores. Interview by Ollie Johnson. New York, NY, 25 September 1994.

Freeman, Ronald. Interview by Angela LeBlanc-Ernest. Los Angeles, CA, 4 October 1996.

French, Lynn. Interview by Ollie Johnson. Washington, DC, 27 September 1994.

Harley, Sharon. Interview by Ollie Johnson. College Park, MD, 7 September 1994.

Hilliard, David. Telephone Interview by Ollie Johnson. 6 August 1997.

hooks, bell. Interview on WPFW-FM. Washington, DC, 16 October 1995.

Howell, Donna. Telephone Interview by Angela LeBlanc-Ernest. 23 April 1993.

Hudson, Lulla. Interview by Angela LeBlanc-Ernest. Portland, Maine, 27 October 1991.

Huggins, Ericka. Interview by Angela LeBlanc-Ernest. San Francisco, CA, 24 January 1992.

Huggins, Ericka. Interview by Angela LeBlanc-Ernest. Stanford, CA, 2 December 1992.

Jennings, Regina. Telephone Interview by Angela LeBlanc-Ernest. 2 February 1992.

ji Jaga, Geronimo. "Speech at Welcome Home Freedom Celebration." Decatur, GA (New Afrikan Peoples Organization), 12 July 1997.

Jones, Audrea. Interview by Ollie Johnson. Rahway, NJ, 30 October 1994.

Jones, Audrea. Interview by Charles E. Jones. Rahway, NJ, 14 June 1997.

Joseph, Jamal. Interview by Tracye Matthews. Harlem, NY, 30 September 1994.

League, Arthur. Telephone interview by Angela LeBlanc-Ernest. 22 September 1996.

Lubell, Jonathan. Interview by Akinyele Umoja. New York, NY, 5 January 1997.

Lumumba, Chokwe. Interview by Akinyele Umoja. Atlanta, GA, 4 January 1997.

Lumumba, Chokwe. Interview by Akinyele Umoja. Birmingham, AL, 22 December 1996.

Miranda, Doug. Interview by Angela LeBlanc-Ernest. Brighton, MA, 9 December 1991.

Neblett, Renée. Interview by Charles E. Jones. Boston, MA, 10 May 1992.

Nyasha, Kiilu. Interview by Angela LeBlanc-Ernest. San Francisco, CA, 25 January 1992.

Obafemi, Ahmed. Interview by Akinyele Umoja. Birmingham, AL, 20 December 1996.

Pinderhughes, Charles "Cappy." Interview by Judson L. Jeffries. Boston, MA, 12 August 1993.

Seale, Bobby. Interview by Ollie Johnson. Philadelphia, PA, 24 September 1994.

Seale, Bobby. Interview by Ronald Stephens. Philadelphia, PA, 4 May 1989.

Seale, Bobby. Unknown Interviewer. 13 March 1980.

Shakur, Assata. Interview by Tracye Matthews. Cuba. 29 September 1994.

Shakur, Mutulu. Interview by Akinyele Umoja. Atlanta, GA, 19 December 1996.

Spain, Johnny. Interview by Angela LeBlanc-Ernest. Stanford, CA, 9 August 1996.

Tiatt, Diana Lin. Interview by Ollie Johnson. New York, NY, 25 September 1994.

Tyehimba, Watani. Interview by Akinyele Umoja. Atlanta, GA, 24 December 1996.

Wahad, Dhoruba Bin. Interview by Winston Grady-Willis. WKCR-FM. New York City, 16 June 1990.

Wareham, Roger. Interview by Akinyele Umoja. Atlanta, GA, 4 January 1997.

Williams, John. Interview by Charles E. Jones. Detroit, MI, 24 July 1993.

Book Reviews

Abu-Jamal, Mumia. "Another Side of Glory." Review of *This Side of Glory: An Autobiography of David Hilliard and the Story of the Black Panther Party*, by David Hilliard and Lewis Cole. *The Black Panther, Black Community News Service*, Fall/Winter 1993, 7.

Blauner, Bob. "The Outlaw Huey Newton: A Former Admirer Paints an Unromantic Portrait of the Black Panther Leader." Review of *The Shadow of a Panther: Huey Newton and the Price of Black Power in America*, by Hugh Pearson. *The New York Times Book Review*, 10 July 1994, 1, 22.

Cleaver, Kathleen Neal. "Sister Act." Review of *In My Place,* by Charlayne Hunter-Gault, *This Little Light of Mine: The Life of Fannie Lou Hamer*, by Kay Mills, and *A Taste of Power: A Black Woman's Story*, by Elaine Brown. *Transition* 60 (1993): 84–101.

Davis, Angela. "The Making of a Revolutionary." Review of *A Taste of Power: A Black Woman's Story*, by Elaine Brown. *The Women's Review of Books* 10 (1993): 1, 3–4.

Dubois, Ellen. "Sisters and Brothers." Review of *A Taste of Power: A Black Woman's Story*, by Elaine Brown, and *This Side of Glory: An Autobiography of David Hilliard and the Story of the Black Panther Party*, by David Hilliard and Lewis Cole. *The Nation* 235 (September 1993): 251–53.

Lehman-Haupt, Christopher. "Recalling Huey Newton as a Hero and Villain." Review of *The Shadow of a Panther: Huey Newton and the Price of Black Power in America*, by Hugh Pearson. *New York Times*, 30 June 1994, B2.

Major, Reginald. "Lurking in the Shadows: *The Shadow of the Panther* Echoes Now Familiar Attacks on the Life and Times of the Black Panther Party." Review of *The Shadow of a Panther: Huey Newton and the Price of Black Power in America*, by Hugh Pearson. *San Francisco Bay Guardian*, 15 June 1994, 45–46.

——. "Stealth History: A Political Process." Review of *The Shadow of the Panther: Huey Newton and the Price of Black Power in America*, by Hugh Pearson, and *The Rise and Fall of California's Radical Prison Movements* by Eric Cummins. *Black Scholar* 24 (Fall 1994): 39–45.

Robinson, Lori. "A Panther Caged by His Own Demons." Review of *The Shadow of the Panther:Huey Newton and the Prize of Black Power in America*, by Hugh Pearson. *Emerge*, June 1994, 66.

Rohter, Larry. "Black Panther, Long Exiled, Sums Up." Review of *Long Time Gone: A Black Panther's True-Life Story of His Hijacking and Twenty-Five Years in Cuba*, by William Lee Brent. *New York Times*, 9 April 1996, A4.

Turner, Diane D. "In Defense of the Party for Self-Defense." Review of *The Shadow of a Panther: Huey Newton and the Price of Black Power in America*, by Hugh Pearson. *Brown Alumni Monthly Review* 27, November 1994, 27.

Popular Magazines

Acoli, Sundiata. "So What's It Like To Be A Political Prisoner or P.O.W.?" *The Source: The Magazine of Hip-Hop Music, Culture, and Politics*, October 1995, p. 79.

Bernstein, Aaron. "The Global Economy: Who Gets Hurt?" *Business Week*, 16 May 1993, pp. 48–53.

Brown, Elaine. "Tough Love!" *Essence*, December 1988, p.70.

Chandler, Christopher. "The Black Panther Killings." *New Republic*, 161, 10 January 1970, pp. 21–24.

Coleman, Kate, with Paul Avery. "The Party's Over." *New Times: The Feature News Magazine*, 10 July 1978, pp. 23–47.

Edmond, Alfred. "Coming on Strong." *Black Enterprise*, June 1994, pp. 75–84.

Epstein, Jay. "Reporter At Large: Charles R. Garry's List of Panthers Allegedly Killed by a Police with Case Histories." *New Yorker*, 13 February 1971, pp. 45–48, 51–77.

Fuller, Hoyt. "Algiers Journal." *Negro Digest* , October 1969, 72–87.

Hornung, Rick. "The Last Caged Panther." *The Village Voice*, 19 September 1989, pp. 10, 16.

"Is It Too Late for the Panthers to be Pals with You?" *Esquire*, 74, 1970, pp. 141–147.

Isserman, Maurice, and Alexander Cockburn. "Letters: An Exchange." *Nation*, 31 October 1994, 507–8.

Jennings, Regina. "A Panther Remembers." *Essence*, February 1991, p. 122.

Lee, Kendra. "Panther Power." *YSB: The Magazine for Young Sisters and Brothers*, May 1995, pp. 32–50.

Letter. *Right On.* 3 April 1971, p. 8.

McCoy, Frank. "Can Clinton's Urban Politics Really Work?" *Black Enterprise*, June 1994, pp. 178–186.

——. "No Real Recovery for Black Jobs or Income." *Black Enterprise*, June 1994, p. 188.

Major, Reginald W., and Marcia D. Davis. "Prisoner of War: Twenty-Four Years Ago The FBI and LAPD Did Battle with the Black Panthers and Geronimo Pratt Went to Jail. Today, Armed With New Evidence and Support, He May Win His Freedom." *Emerge*, June 1994, pp. 30–35.

Pendleton, Tonya. "The Black Panthers: Party of the People—Part 1." *RapPages*, November 1993, pp. 44–53.

"Power to the People' Sweepstakes." *YSB: The Magazine for Young Sisters and Brothers*, May 1995, p. 40.

Reed, Adolph. "Tokens of the White Left." *Progressive*, 57.12: 18–20.

Robinson, Lori S. "Other Political Prisoners." *Emerge*, June 1994, p. 33.

Santiago, Roberto. "A Dialogue With Kwame Ture." *Emerge*, April 1991, pp. 12–13.

Seventh Pan African Congress Called to Support Political Prisoners and P.O.W.s Held by the U.S." *Crossroads*, September 1994, p. 3, 9.

Tyehimba, CEO. "Panther Mania." *Essence*, February 1995, pp. 108–112.

Willis, Ellen. "Let's Get Radical." *The Village Voice*, 19 December 1994, pp. 33, 66.

Memoranda, Government Documents, Reports

Abron, JoNina. Memorandum to Huey Newton. 1 October 1980.

Brooks, Frederick. Memorandum to Oretha Castle (North Louisiana Director of CORE), Jackson Parish, Jonesboro, Louisiana. Gwendolyn Hall Papers, Box 3, Folder 14, Amistad Research Center, Tulane University.

Congressional Black Caucus. The Quality of Life Alternative Budget. Washington, DC: Congressional Black Caucus, 1990.

Deegan, J.G. FBI Memorandum to W.R. Wannall. 26 August 1974.

Fordus, Jeanne Prial, and Sean McAliden. *Economic Change, Physical Illness and Social Deviance*. Report prepared for the Subcommittee on Economic Goals and Intergovernmental Policy of the Joint Economic Committee, 14 July 1984.

Johnson, Marlon. FBI Memorandum to FBI National Headquarters. SAC Chicago, 30 January 1969.

Jones, Audrea. Memorandum To: Responsible Members. . .Re: Establishment of Birth Control Policy for Party Members, July 22, 1972, Series 2, Box 18, Folder 1, Health Cadre Reports, Newton Foundation Records, Stanford University.

National Advisory Commission on Civil Disorders. *Report of the National Advisory Commission on Civil Disorders*. Washington, D.C.: U.S. Government Printing Office, 1968.

United Nations Development Program. *Human Development Report 1992*. New York: United Nations, 1992.

U.S. Bureau of Census. *Census Bureau Announces Number of Americans in Poverty Up for Fourth Year Although Poverty Rate Unchanged; Household Income and Health Care Coverage Drop*. Press release, Bureau of the Census. Washington, D.C., 6 October 1994.

U.S. Congress. House. Committee on Internal Security. *The Black Panther Party, Its Origin and Development as Reflected in the Official Newspaper, The Black Panther Black Community News Service*. 91st Cong., 2d sess., 1970.

U.S. Congress. House. Committee on Internal Security. *Black Panther Party Part 1: Investigation of Kansas City Chapter; National Organization Data*. 91st Cong., 2d sess., 1970.

U.S. Congress. House. Committee on Internal Security. *Black Panther Party Part 2 Investigation of Seattle Chapter*. 91st Cong., 2d sess., 1970.

U.S. Congress. House. Committee on Internal Security. *Black Panther Party Part 4: National Office Operations and Investigation of Activities in Des Moines, Iowa, and Omaha, Nebraska*. 91st Cong., 2d sess., 1970.

U.S. Congress. House. Committee on Internal Security. *Gun Barrel Politics: The Black Panther Party, 1966–1971*. 92d Cong., 1st sess., 1971.

U.S. Congress. House. Committee on Internal Security. *Staff Study on the Black Panther Black Community News Service*. Washington, DC: U.S. Government Printing Office, 1970.

U.S. Congress. Senate. *Book III, Final Report of the Select Committee To Study Government Operations with Respect to Intelligence Activities*. 94th Cong., 2d sess., S.R. 94–755, 1976.

Weiskrich, Wilbert J. (FBI Special Agent). FBI Memorandum to SAC San Francisco, 28 February 1973.

Television, Film, Theater, and Music

Alexander, Robert. *Servant of the People: The Rise and Fall of Huey P. Newton and the Black Panther Party*. Atlanta: Jomandi Productions, 20 January–12 February 1995. Play.

Bagwell, Orlando, director. *Malcolm X: Make It Plain*. Blackwell, 1994. Documentary.

Court TV. *Lock & Key*. "Geronimo Pratt." 23 November 1994. Television program.

Donahue. "Michael McGee and Black Rage in Milwaukee." New York: Multimedia Entertainment, January 15, 1991. Transcript 3121. Television program.

Eyes on the Prize II: A Nation of Laws 1968–1971. Boston: Blackside, 1991. Documentary.

Gerima, Haile. *Sankofa*. Myphedult Films, Inc., 1994. Film.

Grant, Joanne. *Fundi: The Story of Ella Baker*. New Day Films, 1981. Film.

Greenlee, Sam. *The Spook Who Sat by the Door*. Xenon Entertainment Group, 1973. Film.

Lew-Lee, Lee. *All Power to The People: The Black Panther Party and Beyond*. Electronic News Group, 1996. Film.

Paris. *Devil Made Me Do It*. Tommy Boy Records, 1989/90. Recording.

Pontecorvo, Gilles. *Battle of Algiers*. International Historic Films, Inc., 1967. Film.

Public Enemy. *It Takes Nation of Millions to Hold Us Back*. Columbia Records, 1988. Recording.

———. "Power to the People." *Fear of a Black Planet*. Columbia Records, 1988. Recording.

Pump Ya Fist: Hip Hop Inspired by the Black Panthers. Avatar Records, 1995. Recording.

Puzo, Mario. *Godfather*. Paramount Pictures, 1972. Film.

Shakur, Tupac. "Dear Mama." *Me Against the World*. Interscope Records, 1995. Recording.

Smith, Roger Guenveur. *A Huey P. Newton Story*. Production presented during the 1996 National Black Arts Festival Theater Program in Atlanta, GA. Atlanta: Atlanta Entertainment Media, 28 June–7 July 1996. Play and program notes.

Van Peebles, Mario, and Melvin Van Peebles. *Panther*. Gramercy, 1994. Film.

Van Peebles, Melvin. *Sweet Sweetback's Baadasssss Song*. Magnum Entertainment, Inc., 1971. Film.

Wahad, Dhoruba Bin. *Passing It On: A Story of a Black Panther's Search for Justice*. Directed by John Valadez. New York: First Run Features, 1993. Videocassette.

Conferences and Lecture Papers

Abron, JoNina. "The Black Panther Party." Lecture by Author. English 223, Black American Literature. Western Michigan University. Kalamazoo, MI. 5 December 1994.

Butcher, Belva and Majeeda Roman. "Voices of Panther Women." Video Conference Proceedings at the University of California, Berkeley, CA, 26 October 1990.

Cleaver, Eldridge. "Solidarity of the Peoples Until Victory or Death!" Address of the Black Panther Party USA to the International Conference on the Tasks of Journalists of the Whole World in the Fight Against Racism in Pyongyang, Korea (delivered September 22, 1969).

Jackson, Kai. "Telling Off: Black Feminist Narrative and the Civil Rights Movement in the Oral Narratives of Queen Mother Audley Moore." Paper presented at "In Their Own Right: Women's Solution to Black-White Issues of Race, Class, and Gender, 1895–1985, Spelman College, Atlanta, Georgia, 12–14 November 1995.

Lewis, Tarika. "Voices of Panther Women." Video of Conference Proceedings at the University of California at Berkeley, Berkeley, CA, 26 October 1990.

Pamphlets, Newsletters, Bulletins

Afro-American Liberation Army. *Humanity, Peace and Freedom*. Los Angeles: Revolutionary Peoples Communication Network, 1972. Pamphlet.

Balagoon, Kuwasi. *Trial Statement of New Afrikan Revolutionary Kuwasi Balagoon*. Patterson, NJ: Anarchist Collective, 1994. Pamphlet.

Black Panther Party. *Fallen Comrades of the Black Panther Party*. n.d. Pamphlet.

Carter, Al "Bunchy." "Niggertown." Poem in *Humanity, Peace and Freedom by Afro-American Liberation Army*. Los Angeles: Revolutionary Peoples Communications Network, 1972. Pamphlet.

Cleaver, Kathleen. *On the Vanguard Role of the Black Urban Lumpen Proletariat*. London: Grass Roots Publications, 1975. Pamphlet.

Crossroads Support Network. *Who Are New Afrikan Political Prisoners and Prisoners of War*? Chicago: Spear and Shield Collective, 1990. Pamphlet.

French, Lynn. "The Murder of Fred Hampton." n.d. Photocopy, 21–30.

Horowitz, David. "Black Murder, Inc." *Heterodoxy*, March 1993, 15.

Lumumba, Chokwe. *The Roots of he New Afrikan Independence Movement*. Jackson, MS: New Afrikan Productions, 1993. Pamphlet.

May 19th Communist Organization. *To Free Assata Shakur and African Prisoners of War*. New York: Madame Binh Graphics Collective, 1979. Pamphlet.

Montes, Carlos. "Letter of Solidarity: Brown Berets and the Black Panther Party." Letter read at the 20th anniversary celebration of the Black Panther Party, Oakland, CA, October 11–13, 1996. Personal collection of Charles E. Jones.

National Black Human Rights Coalition. *Free Geronimo Pratt*. Los Angeles: Soulbook, 1979. Pamphlet.

Njeri, Akua (formerly Deborah Johnson). *My Life with the Black Panther Party*. Oakland, CA: Burning Spear Publications, 1991. Pamphlet.

Odinga, Sekou et al. "A Statement in Support of Consolidation from New Afrikan Freedom Fighters in Lewisburg, Toward the Objective of a National Liberation Front." *NALF: New Afrikan Liberation Front*. New York: NALF, 1995.

"Political Prisoners Embrace Nelson Mandela at Rally." *Freedom Now!* Chicago, July–August 1980. Bulletin.

Rice, J. F. *Up on Madison, Down on 75th Street: A History of the Illinois Black Panther Party*. Evanston, IL: J.F. Rice/The Committee, 1983. Pamphlet.

"RICO Test Case for Counter-Insurgency, 1983." *Let Your Motto Be Resistance: Newsletter of Resistance*. 1(April 1983): 1, 24–25. Newsletter.

Shakur, Mutulu. Memorandum to Judge Charles Haight. 26 November 1987.
Sundiata Acoli Freedom Campaign. Letter to Supporters, 15 March 1994.

Questionnaires

Brown, Elaine. Questionnaire Responses to interview questions submitted by Angela
LeBlanc-Ernest. 6 December 1 981.

Index

Additional Works about
The Black Panther Party
available from
Black Classic Press

Seize the Time. Bobby Seale. 1970*, 1991. 429 pp. (Paper $14.95, ISBN 0-933121-30-X). Seale provides a riveting first-person account of the evolution of the Party as a national organization. This is the best book available on the early history of the Party.

Blood in My Eye. George L. Jackson. 1971*, 1990. 195 pp. (Paper $14.95, ISBN 0-933121-23-7). Jackson was an activist, a political theoretician, and a revolutionary. He completed this work only days before he was killed in San Quentin prison during an alleged escape attempt.

This Side of Glory: The Autobiography of David Hilliard and the Story of the Black Panther Party. David Hilliard and Lewis Cole. 1993. 450 pp. (Hardcover $24.95, ISBN 0-316-36415-0). Written with the drive of a novel, Hilliard's riveting story of young militant Blacks reaching toward a vision of justice and radical change is an important historical document and one of the most profoundly telling memoirs of our time.

War Against The Panthers: A Study of Repression in America. Huey P. Newton. 1996. 152 pp. (Hardcover $22.00, 0-86316-246-0). Newton's doctoral dissertation offers an analysis of what happened, and still can happen, when a dissident political organization seeking equal socioeconomic participation challenges government repression.

* indicates first year published

Order from your favorite bookseller or directly from:

Black Classic Press
PO Box 13414
Baltimore, MD 21203

Credit card orders, call (800) 476-8870

Please include $3.00 shipping for the first book ordered, and $1.00 for each additional book.